World Religions

Kathleen Miller

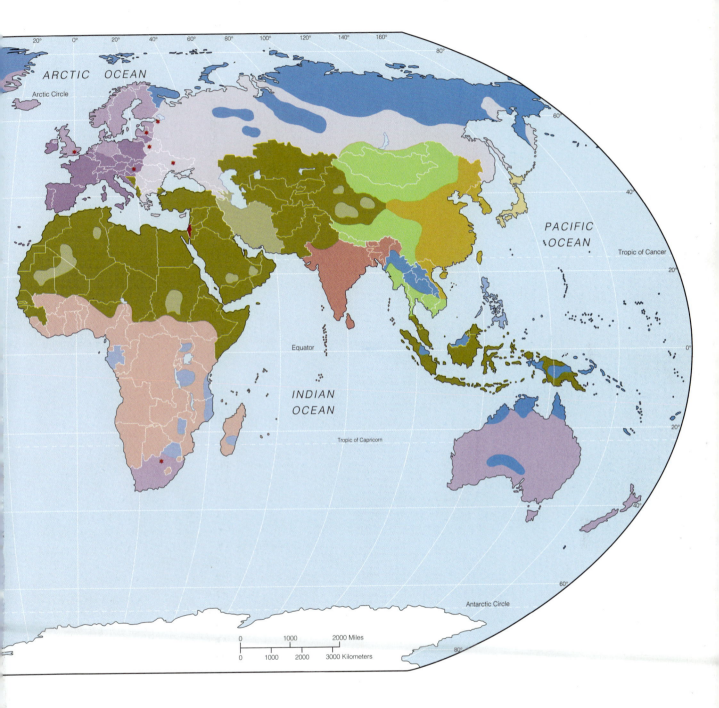

PACIFIC OCEAN

Tropic of Cancer

Equator

INDIAN OCEAN

Tropic of Capricorn

Antarctic Circle

0	1000	2000 Miles
0	1000	2000	3000 Kilometers

World Religions

FIFTH EDITION

WARREN MATTHEWS

Old Dominion University, Emeritus

THOMSON

WADSWORTH

Australia • Brazil • Canada • Mexico • Singapore • Spain
United Kingdom • United States

THOMSON

WADSWORTH

Publisher: *Holly J. Allen*
Acquisitions Editor: *Steve Wainwright*
Assistant Editor: *Lee McCracken*
Editorial Assistant: *Gina Kessler*
Technology Project Manager: *Julie Aguilar*
Marketing Manager: *Worth Hawes*
Marketing Assistant: *Alexandra Tran*
Marketing Communications Manager: *Stacey Purviance*
Project Manager, Editorial Production: *Megan E. Hansen*
Creative Director: *Rob Hugel*
Executive Art Director: *Maria Epes*

Print Buyer: *Rebecca Cross*
Permissions Editor: *Sarah Harkrader*
Production Service: *Nidhi Khanna, Interactive Composition Corporation*
Photo Researcher: *Roberta Spieckerman*
Copy Editor: *AmyLyn Reynolds*
Cover Designer: *Yvo Riezebos*
Cover Image: *William J. Hebert/Getty Images*
Cover Printer: *Coral Graphics*
Compositor: *Interactive Composition Corporation*
Printer: *R.R. Donnelley/Willard*

Printed in the United States of America

3 4 5 6 7 09 08 07

Library of Congress Control Number: 2005936818

Student Edition: ISBN-13: 978-0-495-00709-8
ISBN-10: 0-495-00709-9

Thomson Higher Education
10 Davis Drive
Belmont, CA 94002-3098
USA

For more information about our products, contact us at:
Thomson Learning Academic Resource Center
1-800-423-0563
For permission to use material from this text or product, submit a request online at
http://www.thomsonrights.com.
Any additional questions about permissions can be submitted by e-mail to
thomsonrights@thomson.com.

For My Colleagues and Students

Brief Contents

Contents

II *Religions Arising in India* 63

IV *Religions That Influenced East and West* 209

V *Religions of the Family of Abraham* 231

CHAPTER 8

Judaism 233

Preface

In the absence of first-hand exposure, older people today are likely to have spent most of their lifetime learning about world religions. Perhaps they began by reading *National Geographic* in school. Later they may have met some students from overseas in their college classes. Travel abroad may have come later, in military or business assignments. In retirement they may visit countries with religions and customs quite different from the ones that they have known. For millions of people in the United States, serious discussion of world religions has been primarily academic; few major religions have been present.

Younger people today, however, are more likely to learn about different religions in their home communities. They have classmates and coworkers from other countries and other religions. Learning about other religions may be as natural as learning anything else in the community. The differences may require adjustment and conversations at home, but the diversity generally works out rather well. Academics and people in the larger community sometimes overlook all the everyday opportunities for learning about others.

Civic life requires that members of the community learn about diversity of world religions. The belief that in the United States there is only one historical religion has not entirely vanished, but a large segment of the population concedes that no one religion has exclusive rights at the expense of other religions. People of the various religions in the United States seem to be able to agree that all citizens should honor morality and fairness, respect God, and help fellow humans. Among the diverse religions there is likely to be a shared reservoir of good will that can be tapped for the good of humankind. Many religions have dealt with the same human problems for centuries. Eventually they may cooperate on solutions.

World Religions, Fifth Edition, addresses these opportunities by helping students learn the essential history and beliefs of the peoples of the world. Long discussions have been shortened to essential information. The text concentrates on teaching important concepts and terms. Maps, charts, timelines, pictures, and highlighted blocks of information help students learn more easily. An Overview at the beginning of each chapter points out the themes of the religion. A Consider This box later in the chapter brings together the themes in a more comprehensive view.

The most important changes in the Fifth Edition include:

- An Overview at the beginning of each chapter to preview religions of the chapter.
- New Consider This boxes discussing the themes.

- New religions introduced:
Baha'i
Church of Satan
Druids
Candomblé, Santería, and Vodun
Church of Scientology
Theosophical Society
Family Federation for World Peace and Unification
Wicca

Introduction

Writers comparing world religions have a task beyond satisfying the adherents' views of history. Shall we relate the story of a religion's founder from a natural, humanistic perspective, or shall we include sacred stories of angels, demons, signs, wonders, and miracles as part of its historical development? Either choice requires some reasonable compromise.

At stake is our point of view of all world religions. If we accept all religious stories of faithful followers at face value, we can become lost in vast seas of wonder stories, legends, and beliefs that are rejected even by other followers of the religion. If we insist on objectivity and reject all stories that cannot be easily explained in natural and humanist terms, we discard much that believers in a particular religion find essential to its understanding. Although we want to hear followers' stories about what motivates their faith, we also want to retain enough objectivity not to become lost in one religion at the expense of the others.

To give a balanced view of each religion, *World Religions* tries to present the accounts of faithful followers with understanding and respect while presenting the humanistic and sacred histories of each religion fairly.

This introduction can help learning proceed rapidly and easily. In it readers will find how *World Religions* presents each religion. Some parts of the introduction may need to be reviewed from time to time.

Fortunately, most religions share some common features; this common knowledge simplifies some of the learning. Sacred space, sacred stories, sacred writings, sacred dance, and sacred drama are part of almost every religion of the world.

After the introduction, each chapter will begin with a brief overview of the religions presented in the chapter. In the same overview block, themes selected for emphasis in the chapter will be listed. The themes will be indicated as they are mentioned in the text. The overview topics and themes will be emphasized again in a "Consider This" block which will also sometimes emphasize a current topic in a religion of the chapter.

World Religions employs unique features to help readers learn a whole appreciation of each religion. Historical Development and World View are the two different approaches to the religions. The historical development of each religion is the story of how the religion began and how it grew. Ten topics are employed to help analyze each religion that one encounters. Reviewing the ten topics from time to time will help readers remember the important beliefs and practices of each religion. Some older religions may not have all topics discussed, but the major religions will include all ten.

By the end of Chapter 10, readers will know how to analyze any new religion encountered and how each religion compares with the others.

Common Features of Most Religions

As a guide to unfamiliar landmarks makes a trip easier, so *World Religions* points out what is most important to see. Finding similarities in religions can be as important as finding differences. A common structure for organizing learning helps remember them. *World Religions* organizes some of the most common features of religions.

What Is Sacred?

Religious groups distinguish between what is sacred and what is ordinary. Mircea Eliade, an expert scholar on world religions, explained the **sacred** as that which is set apart for reverence and explained the **profane** as being the ordinary part of life. For example, on the island of Bali (in Indonesia), is a path leading to a gate opening between stone pillars. The gate marks an opening in the perimeter surrounding Hindu altars. Beside the gate is a sign describing conditions for entry; a few visitors are excluded. The pool of deep, spring-fed water is the most sacred area, which is protected by a low wall of stones. At some distance visitors find booths where merchants display souvenirs and other items for sale. This area of commerce is for more ordinary practices of life, the profane, or **secular** (worldly).

Sacred Space

The sacred is set apart, also, by establishing a center in space. A sacred hill, a sacred tree, or a special building may represent the center of sacred space. Whether a Gothic cathedral in Paris or a Hindu temple on a busy corner in Singapore, sacred space is separated from ordinary space. The farther you go from the center, the less holy the space. In Muslim city planning, the mosque is ideally located at the center of the city. In natural spaces, sacred space may be marked by human art or deliberate rearrangement of features.

Sacred Stories

People tell sacred stories to explain who they are. Where did they come from? Where are they going? What do they believe, and how do they act?

sacred [SAY-crid] Set apart for worship of a deity or as worthy of worship.

profane [proh-FANE] Nonreligious. Outside the sphere of religion. Contemptuous of religion.

secular [SEK-u-lur] Wordly. Not spiritual or religious.

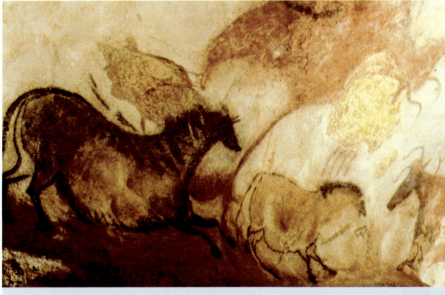

© Francois DuCasse/Photo Researchers, Inc.

Primitive Paintings in Caves of Lascaux, France.

Sacred stories may provide entertainment for a people, as do fairy tales, but they are a more serious explanation of the life of a people. Sacred stories, unlike other stories, belong to the whole community; they are treated with more care and respect.

Most peoples have stories passed on from former generations. From the generation of grandparents, details of the stories are usually clear. Stories that originated with earlier generations are sometimes sketchy. Many cultures have stories about the beginning of heaven and earth, and everything within. Compared to recent hypotheses of astronomers in contemporary societies, these beginning stories from ancient cultures are more believable to traditional cultures. Stories of beginnings often precede the creation or emergence of humans; knowledge comes to them through revelations, visions, or voices. Scholars label stories that represent conversations between humans and supernatural beings as **myths.** Their use of the term *myth* is not meant to convey that the stories are false or without great significance.

Differing from sacred stories and myths, an **epic** is a long narrative poem about the feats of a legendary or traditional hero. Characters in epics represent the values of their creators. In the encounter of protagonist and antagonist, values emerge that reflect a people's fears, hatreds, and joys. Over time, characters and events of epics may attain the status of sacred stories.

Sacred Writings

In the study of world religions, one encounters dozens of sacred books. Each religion believes its sacred writings have divine or spirit-inspired origin. They were either written or spoken by God, written by divinely guided humans, or spoken by teachers of deep spiritual insight. **Scriptures** are sacred writings revered above all other writings. Adherents of a religion regard scriptures as the basis of law, ritual, and ethics; scriptures are the only writings needed for

myth [MITH]
A story dealing with supernatural beings that represents the worldview of a people.

epic [EP-ic]
A narrative poem celebrating the acts of a traditional hero.

scriptures [SKRIP-churs]
Sacred writings. A sacred scroll or book.

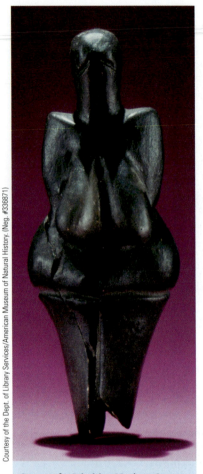

Statue of a Primitive Mother. Some scholars think that statues of this sort were supposed to promote fertility.

faith and practice of their religion. Adherents of a religion regard scriptures of religions that conflict with their own as not being equally true.

Rituals

Rituals are actions that are repetitive, prescribed, and ceremonial. A people may classify actions such as fishing, hunting, gathering, fighting, and dancing as either sacred or secular. Beneficial sacred action must be performed exactly according to a prescribed pattern.

Rituals are performed as social obligations. The **rite of passage,** a ceremonial act marking the transition from one stage of life to another, is common in all religions. Birth, adolescence, marriage, and death are usually accompanied by rituals. The major changes of seasons are often accompanied by prescribed rituals. During a ritual, its history is usually traced to a sacred person, event, or time. As participants repeat the required actions, they identify with the personalities who first performed the observance.

Dance

Although some religions have little dancing, others use dancing to express spirituality. Native American Sioux perform the Sun Dance in summer when participants from a wide area assemble to purify themselves. Dancers may clothe themselves to represent gods, birds, animals, or fish. Painting their faces or wearing masks, dancers conceal their identities and, for a few hours, transform themselves into deities, demons, or creatures of the natural world. Some groups consider the masks divine, animated by the dancers. In dance, participants and observers are transported from ordinary time into the time of ancestors or into the time of the future.

Religious Drama

Religious drama is enjoyed in most parts of the world. Often the whole calendar of a religion is marked by significant actings out of past events, to include each new initiate in their benefits. Favorite themes of dramas are changing seasons, episodes in the lives of founders or organizers, and devotion of their followers. Religious dramas incorporate sacred stories, writings, and performing arts to reflect a particular view of the world. Although some parts of dramas may be open only to the initiated of the religion, most parts are usually open to everyone, including visitors.

rituals [RICH-oo-als] Prescribed religious ceremonies.

rite of passage [riit ov PAS-ij] A prescribed ceremonial act or series of acts. The sign that a person is passing from one stage of life to another.

Distinctive Features of This Textbook

World Religions, Fifth Edition, presents most of the religions discussed in standard courses of colleges and universities. The distinctive approach used here is the combination of the historical development and the worldview of each major

Australian Aborigine Ceremonial Dance. Performed at a Naugalala initiation in Arnhem.

Archaeologists in Israel. To understand beliefs and practices of earlier cultures, archaeologists painstakingly uncover, catalog, and interpret artifacts.

religion. This proven, successful combination facilitates understanding of religious diversity.

Historical Development

As humans have histories, so do religions. Although religions may sometimes appear static, they are always changing. To understand a religion fully, you need to explore its origins, its leaders, and the most significant events in its development. Questions of who, what, when, where, and why can be answered through historical study of each religion.

Beginnings of religions are often associated with a charismatic leader whose personality and teachings attracted enthusiastic followers. Eventually, however—usually after the death of the leader—interpreters split up over beliefs and practices. In a vital, extended religion, at least two major types of divisions appear. First, contemporary practice of a religion can differ from the insights of the founder or organizer; history helps students understand what personalities and events affected the changes. Second, each religion has affected most institutions of its society; the society, in turn, has affected the practice of religion.

Study of the historical development of religions involves contributions from most of the disciplines of a major university. Historians, archaeologists, anthropologists, psychologists, and sociologists regularly research and write about religions. Astronomers, biologists, chemists, engineers, and mathematicians, also, have helped interpret data with more insights and understanding.

Worldview

How do people of a religion today see their world? Understanding a whole religion is quite different from reading about a strange practice, a baffling custom, a belief that strikes one as absurd, or the offering of an animal sacrifice. Observers see pieces of a puzzle that do not seem to fit together. From isolated pieces it may be difficult to guess the whole picture of a religion. When you know how to gather ten essential pieces of information and assemble them, you can construct a more complete picture of beliefs and practices. Moreover, when certain topics have been covered in each religion, religions are much easier to contrast and compare. When you encounter an unfamiliar religion, gathering these pieces of information (we've singled out ten) can help you understand it and how it compares with other religions. The ten topics this book focuses on are the following:

1. *The Absolute.* The Absolute in a religion is the most essential object or concept for the believers. Their lives are interpreted in relationship to a given reality on which all else depends. The Absolute of a religion may be a deity, a male or female god; it may also be Soul, from which all souls derive, a nonpersonal principle, a person, or the absence of any ordering reality. Perhaps surprisingly, you may find that members of a religion do not worship a god or God. Nevertheless, analyzing a religion leads you to what its members consider the most important reality in their view of the world. Remember, *the Absolute need not be a deity.* In each religion, you should know what it considers Absolute.

A Clay Tablet with Cuneiform Writing. Ancient Mesopotamian city-states recorded their history, beliefs, and laws in writing that later scholars learned to translate into modern languages.

Ancient Egyptian Fresco of Deities and Snake. These fresco paintings appear in a tomb of the Valley of the Kings, Luxor, Egypt.

2. *The World.* Each religion has a particular view of the world. Believers may consider the world friendly, unfriendly, or neutral. Should they celebrate the goodness of life in the world, or should they seek to escape its sorrows? Is the physical world the highest reality, or does it only point to a nonphysical reality that is far more important for humans? Does the physical world reflect a creator whose glory is revealed in the study of sciences?

3. *Humans.* Essentially, what are human beings? Are they only a particular kind of animal, or do they have souls, as other animals do not? Are they only one form among living beings, which are all animated by one world soul? Are humans only psychological impressions registered in a brain, no more real than sensations of pleasure and pain? Are humans distinctive in all the universe, created in the image of a divine being? How you think about humans influences how you treat people. Is a human valuable regardless of age, sex, or condition, or is a human valuable only as he or she can increase your economic value? How a religion regards humans may distinguish it in very important ways from other religions.

4. *The Problem for Humans.* Every religion defines a major problem for humans. Something is wrong that needs to be corrected, or that you must be careful to avoid doing because the consequences are quite serious. Although humans experience pleasure, they also experience pain. Religions face not only individual experiences but also the human condition, which every human must encounter and resolve. Whether the problem is defined as sin, ignorance, recurring rebirth of souls, or disharmony with the way of nature or the way of the universe, religion offers a way to overcome the problem.

© Chris Bland/Eye Ubiquitous/Corbis

Lourdes. A chapel in Lourdes, France. An underground spring is recognized to have healing properties for pilgrims.

5. *The Solution for Humans.* What would make human lives ideal? The solution for humans grows out of a religion's description of the problem for humans. In some religions the solution is salvation. In other religions the solution may be harmony with the universe and with other humans. In earlier forms of religion, the solution focused on obtaining more generous agricultural yields, victories over enemies, or preservation of a nation. Later forms of religion have shifted to other views of abundant life.

6. *Community and Ethics.* Most religions advocate that individuals participate in like-minded groups of believers. The religious group reinforces the standards of conduct taught in the religion. Part of the solution for humans is prescribed conduct among humans. This conduct includes prohibited acts, required acts, and neutral acts. The ethical teachings of a religion may have been introduced by a divine being, or by the teachings and examples of one or more leaders who have set moral examples.

7. *An Interpretation of History.* Each religion tells a story from the beginning of a people of faith. Some stories begin before there were humans, others go back only before living people can remember. What happened then may have been related by a bird, an animal, an oracle, a seer, or a god. The story may have been passed down orally or in writing. The story of history helps explain who the people are in the present. The interpretation of history may relate not only the past but also what is in store for members of the religion in the future. In many world religions, a climatic event or a charismatic person may have provided a fixed point for explaining everything that came before it and everything that has happened after it. In different religions some histories may include elements of ordinary, secular history, but usually evaluations of people and events differ considerably from those of historians outside the faith.

8. *Rituals and Symbols.* Sometimes humans are rational, but many of their beliefs and actions are based on intuition and emotions. Religions may use reason in communications, but in their deepest forms they appeal to believers through rituals, prescribed actions, and symbols. Symbols are believed to share in the power of what they represent. Although signs provide information, they do not participate in a greater power; symbols convey the power of what they represent. The flag of a nation or a religion is a symbol; a highway sign is not.

Students at work on a project, Oswego, New York. State University of New York students are similar to those of many colleges and universities in the United States. Interfaith and intercultural differences are often represented.

Rituals are actions repeated according to exact required order. Rituals often have their settings within a religious drama, a story that explains the first performance of the action, what it meant then and what it means for participants now. Rituals and symbols are often used together, helping believers experience more than can be expressed in words. Performing and fine arts are combined to reach individuals or very large crowds of believers. Although insiders of a religion may describe for outsiders what rituals or symbols mean, outsiders are unlikely to experience the deeper understanding of a participant within the religion.

9. *Life after Death.* Most religions answer the question of whether a human will live again after death. Religions describe what forms life after death can take, whether in the same or similar body, a different body, or without a body. Differing on the forms that life after death can take, religions largely agree that people who follow the beliefs and practices of their religion will be rewarded. Those who go against religious requirements, they usually agree, will fare much worse for a while, perhaps for all subsequent time.

10. *Relationship to Other Religions.* People usually support a religion only to the extent that they believe it is the right one to follow. Children are often aware there are religions other than the one in which they are being raised. They, no less than their parents, are curious about how they should relate to peoples of other religions. In democratic societies without a single, established religion, peoples of different religions may freely associate with each other. You are free to follow religion according to your own conscience and to allow all other people to do the same. In many countries people of different religions live and work side by side most of the time with little open conflict.

Most of the chapters of *World Religions* discuss most of these ten topics. Their presentation here will help you know what to look for; while reading later chapters, you may want to look back to this introduction to see what the terms mean and what they do not mean. By the end of the text you should have in mind a

© Noboru Komine/Photo Researchers, Inc.

Students Visit a Temple in Bangkok, Thailand. The Buddhist temples in Thailand are so beautiful and so numerous that a traveler would need many days to visit and appreciate all of them.

proven way for analyzing beliefs and practices of any religion, old or new. *It is not essential to recall the ten topics in a certain order.* Most students, however, seem to recall topics in the order given in the text.

Past editions of *World Religions* have emphasized cooperation among religions more than the potentials for conflict. In response to readers facing different situations, this fifth edition gives increased attention to how diversity may sometimes lead to conflict. I (the author) prefer cooperation rather than conflict in world religions; harmony is much more rewarding for everyone. People of nearly all religions have participated in discussing this text without animosity or conflict. Someone who respects religious diversity is usually welcome in a study of world religions.

The Point of View of the Text

The point of view of this text is that humans live among religious diversity and that learning to appreciate the diversity is better than trying to pretend it does not exist or must be eliminated. It is probably not possible for anyone to be entirely objective in studying something as personal and significant as a religion not one's own. However, inasmuch as one can be open to another person's explanation of his or her religion, there are some wonderful rewards. You can empathize with the religious experience of other people without embracing it as your own. This text avoids judging which religion is best, worst, or better or worse. Readers of whatever view on religion can find rewards by remaining open to the insights of world religions.

VOCABULARY

epic [EP-ic]
myth [MITH]
profane [proh-FANE]

rite of passage [riit ov PAS-ij]
rituals [RICH-oo-als]
sacred [SAY-crid]

scriptures [SCRIP-churs]
secular [SEK-u-lur]

The Americas, North and South, and Africa are home to diverse practices of religion that Europeans have sometimes found mysterious and even frightening. Among groups of two or three indigenous families living near the Arctic Circle, tribes of the southeast United States, and the vast Native American nations of the U.S. Great Plains, city-states of the Inca Andes or ancient Egypt, and rural villages of

names of most peoples presented in Part I have not been widely known. Yet these unknown peoples can draw us to their ways of seeing as we learn how they seek to influence forces of nature and interpret the secret paths of human feelings. Studying peoples such as Naskapi hunters, kachina dancers, and Ifa diviners can offer us deep insights into why ordinary human beings all around the world practice religion.

interpreted the indigenous religions according to their own biases. More recent studies by trained scholars of religions have corrected the impressions recorded by the first visitors. Some of these scholars have come from indigenous peoples who grew up practicing those religions. Many beliefs and practices of these religions continue today alongside practices of religions that arrived much later.

Religions of Tribes and City-States

I

sub-Saharan Africa, people seek to control the hidden forces of the universe with religious practices that may seem remote from well-known rituals of the large world faiths today. Yet however exotic these practices may appear—for example, the sacrifices made by the Incas or divination among the Yoruba—they have parallels in the beliefs of contemporary Western society.

Although the names of Tutankhamen of Egypt and Powhatan of Virginia may be familiar, the

This book, *World Religions*, begins with stories of peoples whose beliefs and practices have been overshadowed by major world religions. Some of their more essential religious experiences have endured, however, and have been incorporated into more recent religions. Unfortunately, as much as we might like to know something about religious life before modern Europeans began to emigrate, most of the historical (written) record comes to us from early European explorers, who often

© Dave G. Houser/Corbis

CHAPTER 1

Religions of the Americas

More than most areas on earth, the Americas have been seed beds for wide varieties of religions. Their seminal forms have arrived on wind and tide from around the globe, germinated, put down roots, and flowered with variegated blossoms. Each has contributed to the beauty and fragrance of religions in the Americas. Christianity grew so quickly that it sometimes threatened the spread of others, tempting some observers to assume that the Americas are Christian. More careful observation reveals that even among the nominal Christians are people who practice rituals and share concepts of the Native Americans. In this chapter we look at some of these non-Christian beliefs and practices.

In exploring traditional Native American beliefs, we enter a world far removed from the Internet and binary languages. We turn to the world of big sky, big seas, big ice, big mountains, and big threats to human life. In this world, human intuition, seasoned by long traditions of each people, actively tests forces of nature, the spirits in animals of earth, sky, and sea; these forces measure resources within the human spirit to survive and endure.

In this encounter between big world and small people, we are rewarded with designs that flow from dreams, totems that represent peoples, wrapped and dried bodies of human leaders, creation myths of the world and humans, and masks of kachina dancers. Not unlike the early conquistadors, we are chilled by Aztec human sacrifices to replenish the life-giving sun and attracted by the hoards of gold reflecting the brilliance of the sun. Curiosity moves us to explore why prior Americans fashioned these particular forms of ordering their lives. We begin to discover not only answers about them but also about our own needs and how religions offer satisfaction for them.

Although we will describe Native American practices before they were significantly changed by

Mexican Feast Costume. In Huachinago, Mexico, this man dressed as a bird celebrates a feast.

encounters with Europeans, remember that many of these American groups are among us today. Since their encounters with those invaders of their lands, they have continued to adjust to and compromise with outside challenges. Native Americans live successfully in their own communities, some still observing many of the traditions of their ancestors. Others are active leaders in other religions. Modern Native Americans are very much part of the business, professional, and political life of the nation. Some may choose to preserve their traditions by gathering with their families and tribe to observe the old ways. Increasingly, too, many non-Native Americans are impressed with the rewards of older traditions of indigenous spiritual living.

Religions of North America

The Naskapi

Less well known than the Inuit (the "people of the deer," or Eskimos) are the Naskapi, who lived in small groups of families on the Atlantic side of Canada. In their struggle to survive near the Arctic Circle, they demonstrated a spiritual view of a world limited in resources.

The following account of the Naskapi Indian religion is based on a study published by anthropologist Frank G. Speck in 1935. Many changes since 1935 have modernized the area where the Naskapi live, so the study helps us understand the lifestyle of a nonliterate hunting people *before* their means of economic support was altered. The strength of Speck's study lies in his having carefully listened to and accurately recorded the information offered by the Naskapi, who were his hosts.[1]

As a hunting people seeking survival in a very cold environment, the Naskapi spent most of their time in isolated groups of two or three families. Only in summer when food was plentiful did families camp together in small communities. Their portable homes were wigwams, wooden poles covered by skins. They moved about their territory in pursuit of wild game. Of special importance to the Naskapi were the caribou, the bear, and the beaver. Of lesser importance were fish and birds.

THE SOUL

For the Naskapi, the whole world is filled with soul, **Mantu.** The physical world is real, but just as real are the souls that animate it. Stars, trees, wind, thunder, fish, birds, animals, and humans are all activated by souls. Knowing how to influence souls in their favor is essential to the survival of individuals and families. Individuals must be on friendly terms with all souls, their own and those of all other beings. Offended souls can withdraw their support, leaving hunters open to weakness, illness, and death. A **shaman,** a person who knows how to control souls, is as important to the Naskapi survival as a chemist or a physicist is for the survival of industrial peoples. All successful Naskapi hunters study ways of influencing souls.

The Naskapi primary contact with soul is through the soul of the individual person, **Mista'peo,** the Great Man.[2] The Great Man is the active, living soul of each person. Located in the heart, it is the essential person. Individuals can meet the

Mantu [MAHN-too]
Among the Naskapi, the soul of nature, animals, and humans. The soul of a person is referred to as the "Great Man."

shaman [SHAH-man]
A Siberian term for people who have been initiated in rituals that enable them to control spirits. Shamanlike men were found among Indians of North America. In Asia, some shamans were women. Today, the term is applied to persons of many cultures.

Mista'peo [mis-TAH-pe-oh]
Among the Naskapi, the Great Man—an individual's soul that lives in the heart; it is a person's essential self. It reveals itself in dreams.

Religions of Ancient City-States.

Selected Native Peoples of the Americas.

Tsaka'bec [tsah-KAH-bec] Among the Naskapi, a hero figure. He was a trickster who altered the natural world. He exhibited a craftiness admired by the Naskapi.

trickster [TRIK-stur] A male character found in stories of Native North Americans as well as most other cultures. Although the trickster was not the creator, he audaciously performed deeds that altered creation. He represents the canniness admired by nonliterate peoples.

reincarnation [REE-in-cahr-NAY-shun] A belief, widely shared among world religions, that a soul that has left a body can, after a period of time, return in the body of a newborn child.

Great Man in their dreams. Besides helping people overcome the souls of hunted animals, the Great Man also helps them become moral and helpful. At times, the Naskapi can smoke, drink, and dance, not to entertain themselves, but to reward the Great Man in themselves.

The Naskapi explain their views of the universe by reciting myths. In their myths, the earth is depicted as a hill floating above water. There is no story of its genesis. A central figure in the myths is **Tsaka'bec,** a human personage endowed with the cleverness and altruistic spiritual powers that the Naskapi valued.[3] He snared the sun and the moon; after getting into it, he became the man in the moon. This type of figure, a **trickster,** also appears in stories of other peoples. The souls of all persons, between the times when they reside in bodies, live among the stars. This concept of **reincarnation,** souls returning to life in another body, is found in many religions, particularly in Hinduism. The four winds, rainbows, the aurora borealis, and the Milky Way are incorporated into the Naskapi mythology of departed ancestors.

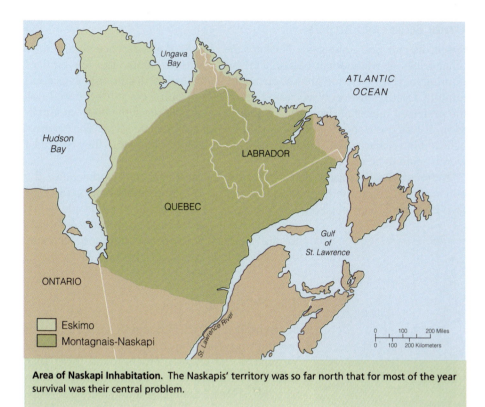

Area of Naskapi Inhabitation. The Naskapis' territory was so far north that for most of the year survival was their central problem.

Recognizing that soul is the absolute of the Naskapi universe leads to an understanding of the essential nature of the universe and humans. Knowing how to live with souls is fundamental to survival, the essential problem for the inhabitants of subarctic regions. Accidents, exposure, illness, and starvation are ever-present reminders that life can end at any moment. Only with help from the environment and its inhabitants can a person survive.

THE HUNT

Naskapi perceive a strong presence of grace in the universe. Animals give themselves to the hunters. In return, hunters must express gratitude to the animals by respecting their carcasses and using them in the most economical way. Hunters and fishers revere their environment, knowing that they will starve if they offend the souls that guard the animals and fish. The technical implements and skills of the hunters and fishers are only minor means of their success; the generous souls of the animals and fish are paramount.

As hunters sleep, animal souls appear in human dreams to show where the animals can be found and how they can be taken. Through dreams, the Naskapi learn the proper designs to work into their art, the kind of drums to make, the required rhythms to use in beating them, and the right way to dance. The traditions of the people are passed along from fathers to sons and daughters, for women also hunt and fish. The general wisdom of the group is supplemented by timely information given by souls of game to hunters who seek and take animals for food, clothing, and shelter. Humans must respect animals, because humans and animals are closely related.

OTHER BELIEFS AND RITUALS

Speck did not find among the Naskapi the rituals of adolescence observed by other tribes of Algonquian (Algonkian) Indians to the south. The few families hunting together were too preoccupied with their survival to initiate boys as adult hunters. Death, however, was treated reverently. Weather permitting, burial was the preferred means of disposal. An alternative was to place the body on a platform. It was positioned a certain way, facing an appropriate scene. The Naskapi believed in reincarnation; good people lived among the stars until they entered a womb again to be reborn.

Although the Naskapi related to other peoples and religions with tolerance, the religion most helpful to the Naskapi economy—hunting and fishing—was their own tradition. Their religion offered survival; moreover, it inspired people to live moral, humane lives. The Naskapi had a reverence for life not usually associated with those who survive only by killing animals.

mamanatowick

[ma-ma-na-TOW-wick] The supreme king or chief of the Algonquian-speaking peoples of eastern Virginia. Powhatan was the first mamanatowick that the English settlers dealt with at Jamestown.

Library of Congress.

The Powhatans of Virginia. The English settlers recorded their impressions of the dress and activities of the Algonquian-speaking peoples of southeastern Virginia.

The Powhatan Peoples

Books by Ben C. McCrary and by Helen C. Rountree inform readers about the Powhatan peoples of Virginia as the English settlers found them after 1607.[4] Eyewitness accounts by John Smith, William Strachey, Henry Spelman, and others are supplemented by that of Rev. Samuel Ames, who in England interviewed Uttamatomakkin, an Indian priest sent to represent Powhatan in 1616–1617. Although none of the observers were trained in writing objective reports, these accounts do describe the Native Americans before they were greatly influenced by Europeans.

The settlers at Jamestown met Algonquian-speaking Indians who were members of tribes dominated by a **mamanatowick,** a "great king" or paramount chief, called Powhatan. He ruled a vast territory of southeastern Virginia through a number of **weroances,** who were commanders, or petty chiefs. Rather than a confederacy, this group of tribes was an empire ruled by Powhatan. He claimed four of every five deer his subjects killed. All copper, iron, and useful metals belonged to him. He used this material and the agricultural products grown by forced laborers in his fields to reward his weroances, to buy services of warriors for battles, and to impress his English guests.

The Powhatans had learned to use what the land offered them. For meat, they hunted deer and turkey, trapped fish in ingeniously crafted pens, and gathered oysters and other shellfish. They gathered berries, nuts, and roots for food and medicine. They also burned and cleared small fields where they planted maize (corn) and beans, which were

Seventeenth- and Eighteenth-Century Territory of the Powhatans. The settlers of the first permanent English colony intruded on the hunting and agricultural society of the Powhatans.

cooked as succotash, a staple dish. They made more than one planting a year to keep their supplies growing through the frost-free months.

RELIGION

The Powhatans classified medicine and religion together. The same men often practiced in both areas.[5] **Wisakon** was the Powhatan word for medicine and bitter substances that tasted like medicine. Native Americans took herbs that helped cure them to their priests, who kept a supply in the temple. Thus the priests became keepers of both lore and medicines. Their knowledge of cures and their rituals of divination secured for the priests a place of superiority in the tribal hierarchy. In addition to using drugs, the priests could perform minor surgery. They also supervised the "sweat house," a kind of sauna, that drove out illness. The user left the sweat house to bathe in a cold stream and then covered his or her body with an oil paint prepared for decoration, which also repelled insects and other pests.

weroances
[WEH-row-ances]
The subchiefs, or commanders, of the Powhatan empire. Female commanders were known as **weroansquas.**

wisakon [WI-sa-kon]
The Powhatan term for medicine and substances tasting like medicine. The priests controlled all medicines of significance.

The Powhatans believed in life after death. Although ordinary Powhatans were buried, weroances were wrapped and dried. Their bones were preserved on platforms in their temples. According to Strachey's account, at death, souls of people of high status journeyed to the west to pleasant fields. Without work they could feast, dance, and live in peace. Eventually they would die there and then enter into a woman's womb on earth to be born again.[6]

Each weroance had a temple, a loaf-shaped building, about twenty by a hundred feet. Some temples had a pole carved with deities at each corner. On a platform at the western end of the interior, the Powhatans kept the bodies of their dead weroances and weroansquas. Under the platform was a carved figure of the god **Okeus.** Although the Powhatans believed in a good god, **Ahone,** who brought forth the sun and fruits from the earth, they paid most attention to a malevolent deity, Okeus, seeking to turn away his wrath. The black figure, sometimes dressed in pearls, wore an angry expression. He was flanked by images of stuffed animals whose traits the Indians wanted to gain. One English writer, Robert Beverley, risked his life to study a temple without the Powhatans' knowledge. He reported that priests could manipulate the image of Okeus in the dark so that in the dim light ordinary Powhatans perceived the god as living.[7]

The Powhatan priests also practiced divination and magic. In addition to the harsh conditions that confronted the Naskapi, the Powhatans had the added problem of attacks from other Native American tribes and the encroachment of English settlers. Wherever they could, the Powhatans used magic to help improve the odds over their enemies. Although the English generally doubted Native American claims of magic, they occasionally witnessed results suggesting the Native Americans were in league with the devil. Native Americans admitted that often their magic did not apply to the English as it did to their enemies among the Native Americans.

Soon after his arrival, the intrepid Captain John Smith was taken prisoner by a Powhatan hunting party. For three days he feared he would be tortured and killed—the way Powhatans disposed of their war prisoners. All the while, several priests practiced divination around Smith to try to learn the English settlers' intentions. The answer they received was that the English would not harm them. Smith was therefore freed and lived to have many more experiences with the Powhatans.

According to Smith, Pocahontas, the twelve-year-old daughter of Powhatan, saved his life by placing her head over his on the killing block when Powhatan was about to bash in his skull with a stone club. During a war between whites and Indians, she was imprisoned on an English ship. On the ship, she fell in love with John Rolfe, a settler. Although at fourteen she had married a Powhatan chief, now Pocahontas converted to Christianity, married Rolfe, and sailed with him to England. They had a son, Thomas. Developing smallpox in England, she died before the return voyage.

We turn now to another Native American people encountered by the colonists as they moved westward in Virginia and North Carolina. Today Cherokees make their homes in North Carolina and Oklahoma.

The Cherokees

In the beautiful ridge of mountains rising from the Piedmont Plateau of the East Coast of the United States, Europeans found the home of the

Okeus [OH-kee-us]
Among the Powhatans, a god, or group of gods, that caused suffering. His counterpart is the beneficent deity, Ahone.

Ahone [A-hone]
The beneficent diety of the Powhatans, whose powers were of less concern than those of the malevolent Okeus.

Library of Congress/Corbis

Commander-in-Chief of the Cherokee Nation. This engraving of 1762 is a portrait of Austenaco, a great warrior, in his native clothing.

Area of Early Cherokee Habitation. The Cherokees attempted to adjust to white culture, but immigrants coveted the rich Cherokee lands.

Cherokees. The tribe was concentrated in the Appalachian Mountains in western North Carolina and Tennessee. Constant encroachment by new white settlers undermined any agreements Indians made with colonists; wars were frequent. No less than the Powhatan group, the Cherokees suffered from smallpox brought by the Europeans.

The Cherokees expressed their animosity toward the white settlers by fighting on the side of the British during the Revolutionary War. After the war, however, the relationship improved for a short period. In 1827, the Cherokees even formed a "nation under God," with a constitution patterned after that of the United States.

When gold was discovered on Cherokee lands, the harmony dissolved. Whites wanted the gold. To get it, they pressured the U.S. government to force the Indians to sell their lands and move. In 1838–1839, government troops organized mounted military escorts and marched the Cherokees, on foot, to the Indian Territories, now the state of Oklahoma. A few Cherokees managed to stay behind; they eventually negotiated a reservation, where many of them live today.[8]

STORIES OF THE CHEROKEES

The Cherokees present a different aspect of Native American life from the Powhatans. Some of their fascinating stories were recorded at the end of the nineteenth century by James Mooney in *Myths of the Cherokee.*[9] Ordinary members of the tribe did not tell stories of creation, and initiates could hear the stories only after participating in a special ceremony. Priests and keepers of the sacred stories met at night in a low log house to recite the stories around a fire. Hearers were admitted, by appointment, for initiation to the **myths.** At daybreak, the party went to a running stream where the hearers stripped and a priest scraped their skin with a bone-tooth comb. While the priest recited prayers, the participants dipped themselves seven times in the water. The creation stories were part of a ritual of remembrance and new beginnings.

In the Cherokee story of the creation of the world, the animals lived above a great stone arch below which lay water. The animals were crowded and wanted a place to live below the arch. But they could find only water. Water Beetle darted over the water without finding a place to rest. It dived down to the soft mud and brought some up. Now, at the bottom of the arch sky, an island—the earth—floats on the water. It is held up at the cardinal points by cords attached to the sky vault. No one remembers who made or tied the cords.

When the animals first came to earth, they were told to keep watch for seven nights. Most animals fell asleep too soon. Only the panther, the owl, and a few others stayed awake, so they now can see to hunt at night. The cedar, pine, spruce, holly, and laurel trees also stayed awake, so they stay green and retain their medicinal qualities all year. All the other trees lose their "hair" each winter. The Cherokees have many stories about how the animals came to be as they are. These tales have lost their sacred character, so now anyone in the tribe can tell them.

myth [MITH]

A story of gods acting in a different time. Creation myths are stories of how the gods acted before humans were created, how they created humans, and how they communicate with humans. The word *myth* in religious studies does not mean untrue.

Dolls. Examples of Native American craftsmanship.

© Chris Marona/Photo Researchers, Inc.

Another Cherokee creation story says that a brother and a sister were the first humans. He struck her with a fish; seven days later she bore a child. A child was born every seven days thereafter until the earth became too crowded. Now a child is born only every year.

Why do Cherokees need to hunt for game and farm the land? Cherokees blame two boys whose curiosity was too much for them. Near Pilot Knob lived a hunter, Kana'ti, and his corn wife, Selu. (Among the Cherokee, the husband hunts and the wife takes care of the corn.) With their son's help, they captured a wild boy to live with them. But Wild Boy led the son of Kana'ti to spy on his father. They saw that when the father wanted meat, he opened a stone door and took from a cave whatever animal he wanted. A few days later, the boys, having made arrows, opened the stone door to try their hand at hunting. Failing to close the door, they let all the game escape and wander the earth. After that incident, hunting became an uncertain venture.

The boys then spied on the mother, Selu, when she went to the storehouse for corn and beans. She produced corn for the basket by rubbing her stomach and beans by rubbing her armpits. Convinced that Selu was a witch, the boys killed her. Before she died, she instructed the boys to drag her body seven times in a circle to clear the ground in front of

© James Chisholm/Anthro-Photo

Navajo Hogan. Navajo peoples of the Southwest sometimes occupy a distinctive type of house. Herding sheep is one means of earning a livelihood that can be done close to home.

the house. But the boys cleared only seven small spots; that is why corn grows in so few places. They dragged her body only twice; that is why Native Americans plant only twice a year.

Theda Perdue, a scholar of Cherokee life, presents Kana'ti as the ideal for men, who hunt animals, and Selu as the ideal for women, who plant corn and beans. She notes, "Theoretically, the sexual division of labor was very rigid, but in reality men and women willingly helped one another." Men who farmed were considered "womanlike," not a positive, but treated with mild humor. Some women fought wars alongside men and won honors as warriors. Descent was reckoned though the mother; house and fields remained with women.[10]

The Hopi

A Pueblo people of the Southwest, the Hopi lived in adobe houses with many rooms. Underground chambers used for religious rituals, **kivas,** were places where **kachinas** danced. These traditional figures still appear in ceremonies today. Kachinas are costumed and masked figures that represent animals, ancestors, or spirits; there are more than five hundred types. Wearing sacred masks, dancers animated them. Uninitiated Hopi are not permitted to see the dancers out of costume; masks are hidden from view when not worn. Until older children are initiated, between ages ten and twelve, adults tell them the kachinas are gods.

Kachinas play a major role in teaching children to obey their parents and to behave according to the preferences of the Pueblo. Wayward children are disciplined not by their parents but by kachinas who visit their homes. Parents side with their children to protect them from the kachinas. Together, parents and kachinas impress on children the importance of following the rules of Pueblo society.

kivas [KEE-vas] Underground chambers that the Hopi used for religious ceremonies.

kachinas [ka-CHI-nas] Among the Hopi, masked, costumed dancers that represent gods, ancestors, or spirits.

Worldview: Common Features of North American Religions

Assessing and summarizing common features of religions of North America has become controversial among scholars. They have challenged not only earlier conclusions but also assumptions that there ever were common features. Scholars from within Native American traditions have disagreed with outsiders. After presenting what have been regarded as common features, the section concludes with some recent objections.

The Absolute

Although many Native American peoples had a chief god, few agreed on one name for that deity. Rather than a god who ruled alone, however, as in **monotheism,** the high god was simply first among many spirits, an arrangement known as **henotheism.** Cottie Burland's summary of Native North American mythology charts some of the Native American gods and spirits. The variety of names, characters, and functions is impressive. Correlating names, spirits, functions, and rankings in hierarchy, however, would be a formidable task. Most animals, forces of nature, natural objects, and heavenly bodies qualify as spirits; different tribes assign the same objects different ranks in their hierarchies. Some of the most impressive spirits combine features of animals and nature. The mythical thunderbird of the Northwest Coast is awe inspiring. The flesh-eating antelope Delgeth appears among peoples of the Southwest.[11] Spirits can be good, like Ahone of the Powhatans, or evil, like his counterpart Okeus. A good creator is sometimes offset by an evil twin or brother who deliberately distorts a good creation. The fluid organization of spirits among most peoples reflects the somewhat open organization of their tribal hierarchies.

The World

Illustrated by the Cherokee myth, which is typical, the earth rises above the waters and separates them from the sky. The world is not a finished creation, fashioned once, long ago; rather, it is a manifestation of active spirits ever involved in its changes. Winds, directions, clouds, seasons, and day and night show that spirits participate in changes of the earth. The emergence of humans and animals from a region beneath the earth is also a common feature of stories of North American peoples.

Humans

In Native American religions, humans and animals are so closely related that kinships abound. Small groups of tribes customarily chose a bird or an animal as their symbol. A buffalo dance of Plains Indians depicts a time when buffalo hunted humans. This theme of role reversal is repeated in stories of various human activities. Although most tribes prize physical strength and endurance, strength of spirit, the highest part of a human, is essential.

The Problem for Humans

Most peoples of North America were well aware the world could have been designed so that humans would suffer less. As illustrated by the Cherokee story of the boys who carelessly released the animals from a cave so they must be hunted,

monotheism
[MAH-nuh-thee-is-um]
A belief that there is only one deity.

henotheism
[HEN-uh-thee-is-um]
A belief that one deity is supreme over other deities.

some problems result from human ignorance or carelessness. The story of infertile soil resulting from boys carelessly dragging the mother on the earth warns about failure to follow directions. Other problems can be traced to the impulsive trickster, whose delinquent behavior amused humans but made their lives more difficult. The California peoples refer to the trickster as Coyote; the Naskapi call him Tsaka'bec. Acting out rebellious impulses, though temporarily enjoyable, introduces disorder into the world.

The Solution for Humans

From the viewpoint of modern urban civilizations, native North American lives may seem to have once been remarkably free and enjoyable. Survival, however, was seldom easy. Societies were highly traditional, governing all lives with customs and regulations. Those who violated prohibitions were severely punished, even to death. Most North American peoples, however, valued both group solidarity and individual insight that contributed to public welfare. The Naskapi hunter's dream was individual, but it contributed to group survival. The widespread practice of the vision quest encouraged adolescents to exercise insight and resourcefulness for the good of the tribe. Isolation of the youth in lonely places, restriction of food and drink, and dedicated search for a vision all emphasized individual responsibility within the context of the tribe. Unlike nighttime dreams, visions reveal a spirit's unique relationship with an individual. Without his own vision, a young man was not ready to contribute to adult society.

Healing has been part of the religion of every indigenous people in North America. Physical illness manifested spiritual disorder. Healing required gaining help from benevolent spirits or appeasing vengeful ones. The old shaman figure of Asia, the person on speaking terms with spirits, also occurred among many peoples in the Americas. Lower in the hierarchy, medicine men and women also depended on visions of spirits. Medicine bundles—wrapped objects that appeared ordinary but possessed great powers—were used in many societies. People valued healing plants and trusted priests and medicine people to master their uses. Through dreams and voices of spirits, practitioners received directions for using drugs and diets. In the Southwest, medicine people made sand paintings on the ground that could elicit powerful healing forces in the person who sat in the middle of the painting. Healing and religion were closely related.

Community and Ethics

Native American individuals and communities shared responsibilities. The tribe enforced its expectations on all members through custom and rigorous training. Nomadic tribes maintained their identities through strong traditions.

From parents and elders, children and youth learned what conduct the tribe expected. Women, no less than men, were indoctrinated in proper behavior. At adolescence, young women learned conduct with men, distinguishing what was prohibited, permitted, or prescribed. Sex outside marriage was usually condemned.

Killing members of one's own tribe was not permitted, but men were expected to kill enemies of their tribe. Chiefs could sometimes hold absolute power; more often, they were influenced by the collective will of their peoples.

An Interpretation of History

Recurring events were a common theme among peoples of North America. Sunrise and sunset recurred daily; the four seasons recurred each year. In the western mountains, medicine wheels—large circles of stones on the ground—marked the changing seasons. The myth of the Morning Star–Evening Star ritual of the Pawnees had a four-year cycle. Recurrence over a period of years was as common as daily and annual cycles. People and animals recurred (by reincarnation) on even longer cycles. For North Americans, time was circular.

Rituals and Symbols

Feathers appear as symbols among all peoples of the Americas. Spirits of birds and humans were similar; perhaps humans envy the ability of birds to soar above the earth. The flights of eagles deeply impressed them. The full headdresses of the Shoshone circled their heads and trailed down their backs. The symbolism was so impressive many other peoples adopted it. One or two feathers worn in the hair was an almost obligatory symbol.

Rites of passage were particularly important. Birth, puberty, marriage, and death required rituals to ensure good lives and tribal success. For example, when a child was born, special care was taken to keep the placenta from animals, and the umbilical cord might be carefully preserved for several months, ensuring the health of the infant.

Puberty was carefully regulated. Because women's blood was considered especially dangerous to men, young women beginning menses were segregated from men. Sometimes they stayed isolated in separate structures for weeks, fed by older women. At the end of this initiation some tribes held a festival or dance to celebrate the new life of an adult woman.

Initiation into puberty for boys could be quite harsh. The vision quest could end in injury or death, although supervision usually prevented permanent damage. Among the Sanpoil of eastern Washington State, young men counted on finding spirit helpers so that they could succeed in society.[12]

Marriage customs and death rites varied by region. Funerals were normal, followed by a period of mourning for weeks or months. Bodies were honored for a few days and then disposed of according to tribal custom. Cremation was not widespread. Burial could be of individuals, or, as among tribes in middle America, in large mounds containing dozens of bodies. A few tribes preserved bodies by drying them. Bones of chiefs and medicine men might be included in medicine bundles.

Life after Death

Belief in reincarnation was widespread; the soul of the departed would be reborn as a child within the tribe. Belief in transmigration of the soul to inhabit an animal body was less common. The cycles of souls were not immediate or automatic, because a soul could enjoy an indefinite stay in a pleasant hunting ground.

Although living and dead were deliberately separated, ancestors were remembered and honored. Often the home of the deceased was disassembled and a new residence was fashioned for the survivors. As far as scholars can tell, the peoples of North America considered death a mystery; few sought to work out in detail exactly what happened to the soul of the departed.

Relationship to Other Religions

Native American peoples had distinctive beliefs and expected other peoples to differ from them. Tribes practiced their own religion; all shared belief in spirits, souls, and the value of rituals. Although many peoples of North America have affiliated with Christian groups, many others preserve their own traditional worship. The Native American Church, which has been granted legal use of peyote cactus in worship, is a notable example of preservation of traditional worship.

Objections to Older Scholarship

Some conclusions of older scholarship regarding native North American religions have been considered distorted or in error. One objection is to the notion that the religions were henotheistic, that is, worshiping a "high god." The terms *good* and *evil* have been criticized as derived from "Christian" interpretations. Women are said to have played a much larger role in government than once believed and may not have been regarded as evil. Women also participated in vision quests. Finally, some say these cultures were not totalitarian, enforcing group will against individual freedom.

With new generations of scholars, particularly among Native Americans, new ways of understanding early traditions are being presented. This exciting progress in scholarship has many rewards for inquiring readers.

Religions of Mesoamerica and South America

The highly developed civilizations in Mesoamerica and South America impressed the Spanish explorers. Whole peoples numbering thousands lived in well-designed cities. Towering pyramids were notable landmarks in these cities. Chiefs and priests communicated with gods and ruled the peoples of the cities. The surrounding countryside was highly developed in agriculture, supporting city inhabitants. The city-state civilizations paralleled the successful organizations of ancient Mesopotamia, Egypt, and Greece. Western explorers were impressed with similarities, and occasionally today people attempt to prove that inhabitants of the Mediterranean area sailed west and settled in the Americas.

The Aztecs

The Aztecs built stone-covered mounds, like the Mesopotamians. In the central plaza of their major city, **Tenochtitlán,** which was built on an island in a lake, pyramids were topped by temples to Aztec gods. The chief deity was **Huitzilopochtli,** god of the sun.

Historical Development

The Spanish explorers who first encountered Aztecs were appalled at Aztec human sacrifices. We should not assume, however, that the Aztecs of that particular period were typical of Mesoamerican peoples or even of Aztecs. Some scholars think large-scale human sacrifice was practiced during only a few decades. For most of their history, the Aztecs were, like their neighbors the Mayans, dedicated farmers of maize, beans, squash, and other vegetables. Animal sacrifices, where practiced, did not include humans.

Precursors of the Aztecs were the Chichimec, who migrated south in the thirteenth century. The Aztecs told a story that they once lived in caves far from their

Tenochtitlán
[TEN-ok-tit-LAN]
The Aztec island city on Lake Texcoco. It was the site of the major temple to the Aztec god Huitzilopochtli.

Huitzilopochtli
[HWEET-zi-low-POK-tli]
The chief god of the Aztecs. He was god of the sun who led his people, the Aztecs, to their home in Tenochtitlán.

city on the lake. They journeyed from the northwest to the site of Tenochtitlán, in the center of today's Mexico City. The Aztecs' ancestors endured a long ordeal of travel, rejection, and oppression by more powerful tribes, and a struggle to make their home in the swampy area around Lake Texcoco. There they built a number of cities, Tenochtitlán being the most famous. Scholars date the settlement of Tenochtitlán at 1325 C.E. Scholars believe that between 1300 C.E. and 1521, all main roads led to the center of this Aztec capital. It had many canals in addition to its roads. Its defenses relied on water and causeways with drawbridges.

Worldview of the Aztecs

From the writings of the early Spanish explorers and missionaries and from the studies of modern scholars, we have developed an understanding of the Aztec religion.

The Absolute

The chief of the several gods of the Aztecs was Huitzilopochtli. Represented as a sacred bundle of potent symbols, he had led the Mexica, a branch of the Chichimec group that became the Aztecs, from Aztlan, their homeland, to the place where they built his shrine at the center of Tenochtitlán. In Aztec accounts, Huitzilopochtli was born miraculously from the goddess Coatlicue on Coatepec (Serpent Mountain), near Tula. Four hundred siblings, enraged at Coatlicue's pregnancy and birthing, attacked her. Huitzilopochtli was born armed with a magic weapon, "a fire serpent," with which he killed the siblings. Some scholars think the story describes the sun conquering the moon and the stars. Huitzilopochtli was the god of war and the sun. He was considered leader of the Aztecs, who viewed themselves as the "chosen people." His symbol was the eagle, king of the birds. As the Spanish learned, the god's symbol was a wooden figure of a man sitting on a blue bench, heaven. His crown was of hummingbird feathers, and he was clothed in feathered garments.[13] He was lord of fertility and agricultural regeneration. In his holy place, a curtain separated him from worshipers. Adjacent to his court was a room for the god **Tlaloc,** who was the original source of waters and vegetation. The rooms of these idols were built at the top of a pyramid, reached by a climb of 120 steps. Around the sacred temple the Mexica built a stone wall resembling serpents. The temple platform was flanked by row upon row of human skulls held in place by a rod running through their temples.

The mother goddesses were sources of abundant powers of earth, women, and fertility. One goddess (Tlazolteotl) governed sexual powers and transgressions. Another goddess (Xochiquetzal), the nubile maiden of love, was goddess of pleasure. A third goddess (Coatlicue), "serpent skirt," both conceived stellar beings and devoured all beings in her repulsive form. Her statue was studded with sacrificial body parts and snake heads.

Rituals and Symbols

The function of the Aztec temple is demonstrated in an event of 1487, when Ahuitzotl celebrated a military victory and dedicated the Great Temple. National leaders were the invited guests; lesser leaders were required to bring sacrificial victims for the service. Thousands of captives (perhaps an exaggeration) lined up along the roadways for sacrifice to the god. Rulers and priests participated in

Tlaloc [TLAH-loc]
The Aztec god of earth and rain.

slashing open the prisoners' chests and ripping out their beating hearts to throw against the god.[14] The Aztecs believed human sacrifices, which furnished ample human blood, were necessary to nourish the sun, personified in **Tonatiuh.**

The Stone of the Sun, a flat stone twelve feet in diameter and weighing nearly twenty-six tons, rested at the top of the temple of Huitzilopochtli.[15] Symbolizing the Aztec cosmos, it was dedicated to Tonatiuh, whose face is in its center. On the side are claws clutching human hearts for the sun god. The disk shows symbols for the twenty-day calendar, the four creations and destructions of the world, and the struggle between **Quetzalcoatl,** the Plumed Serpent, and Tezcatlipoca, the Lord of the Night Sky. The people from the four destructions were transformed into jaguars, monkeys, fish, and birds. The sun of the fifth world is the Aztec sun. The world is not a permanent creation; it must be kept alive through great effort. The gods could be persuaded to keep the fifth sun alive only as long as the Aztecs kept them sufficiently supplied with blood. Aztec life—indeed, all human life—depended on the dutiful conquest and sacrifice of enemies.

During the Flowery Wars of 1450–1519, the Aztecs often attacked their neighbors. Their purpose was to keep their warriors in shape and to provide enough blood to keep strong the source of all life, the sun. Tenochtitlán had eighty ritual temples and skull racks. After their hearts—"precious eagle cactus fruits"—were offered to the deity, victims were prepared for cooking and eating. Facial skin, with beard intact, was often flayed off victims and preserved like glove leather.

In the Toxcotl festival, the most admired warrior captured from the enemy was set apart for a privileged existence in the capital. In the last twenty days of his life, he enjoyed four wives. At the end of that time, he ascended the steps to be sacrificed to **Tezcatlipoca.**

This bloodthirsty period of Aztec history is well attested, but it is inaccurate to think these extreme practices were typical of Mesoamerican peoples, even Aztecs. Their city-state religions focused on forces necessary for agriculture: sun, soil, rain, and seasonal growth. The concept of nourishing the sun with blood drawn from human hearts was an extreme attempt to obtain favor from the sun.

The Aztec religion was not so different from other religions of Mesoamerica in its use of sacrifice to keep the sun shining and civilization blooming. What was different was the extent to which human sacrifice and cannibalism were practiced in preference to sacrifice other animals. In Aztec myth, the gods sacrificed themselves to restore a revolving sun to the world. Mass sacrifice energizes the sun. Humans could do no less than the gods.

Another view is presented by David Carrasco, who saw the city of Tenochtitlán as the idealized battlefield. The eighty pyramids with different temples for special sacrifices to particular deities were an extension of war; it was a place "where

Tonatiuh [TOE-na-TI-uh]
An Aztec sun god.

Quetzalcoatl
[KET-zal-coatl]
The Aztec god known as the Plumed Serpent. He was god of civilization, teacher of the arts and priestcraft.

Tezcatlipoca
[tez-CAT-li-POH-ca]
The Aztec lord of the night sky.

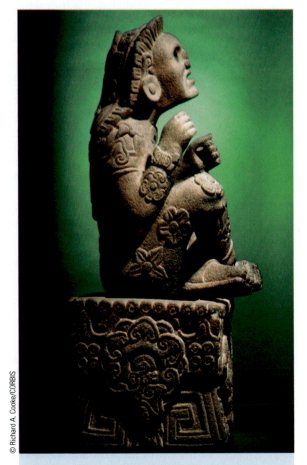

© Richard A. Cooke/CORBIS

Side View of Aztec Statue of Xochipilli, 14th-16th century.

the Jaguars roar" and warriors died a "flowery death." Aztec human sacrifices were debt payment to the gods.[16]

The fall of the Aztec kingdom was caused in part by the religion. In 1519, Montezuma, the Aztec king, welcomed Hernando Cortez (1485–1547), thinking he was the Plumed Serpent from beyond the sea who had returned to his people. The Plumed Serpent, who represented civilization as teacher of the arts and priestly learning, was usually a beneficent deity. When Cortez imprisoned Montezuma, the Aztecs knew Cortez was not their benefactor.

Archaeologists have carefully studied the Aztec religion. For many civilized peoples, however, the Aztecs' human sacrifices cast a shadow over their achievements in cosmology and architecture.

The Incas

The Incas of Peru made a lasting impression on the Spanish explorers who reached them in 1532 C.E. The personal secretary of Francisco Pizarro (1475–1541), Pedro Sancho de la Hoz, described Cuzco, the capital of the Incan empire.[17] Streets were laid out at right angles, and the stonework of buildings was so closely fitted without mortar that a knife blade would not fit between stones.

Pizarro invaded the ancient Inca city of Cajamarca, killed the followers of Atahualpa, the Inca (emperor), and imprisoned him. To ransom Atahualpa, the Incas filled a room in the palace to the height of a man with gold and silver. Pizarro took the treasure but strangled Atahualpa.

Historical Development

The religion of the Incas inspired their building of Cuzco and their expansion of empire. They were their god's people, called to rule the world. Like the ancient Egyptians, the Incas worshiped the sun; the chief Inca was his representative on earth. The stone structures of Cuzco built by each succeeding Inca emperor were their homes in life, their homes and tombs in death, and the places where they would return to life. Two golden pumas guarded the Coricancha, the great Temple of the Sun at Cuzco, and gold and silver plaques covered the walls. Its halls housed statues of cosmic beings and the mummies of earlier kings and queens.

Worldview of the Incas

The Absolute

Inti [IN-ti]
An early god of the Incas, probably symbolized by a hummingbird. Inti was a creator god who was later combined with Viracocha.

Viracocha
[VI-rah-COH-cha]
A creator god of the Incas. He symbolized the sun.

The Inca empire reached its height only shortly before the Spanish arrived. The tribes that initiated it may have begun two thousand years earlier; they told stories of having begun in caves and wandered, with the guidance of their god, to the sacred place where they were directed to build Cuzco among sacred streams of the Andes. Their god at that time, about 1200 C.E., was **Inti,** symbolized by a fetish (perhaps a dried hummingbird) in a closely woven basket. He was carried by priests who interpreted his directions. By the time of Atahualpa's reign, Inti had been superseded by **Viracocha,** the creator and sustainer, a more appropriate symbol for the emperor and lords who ruled the peoples of an empire. The emperor Huascar had a gold image fashioned and named it Viracocha-Inti.[18] In older times, Incas thought each tribe had been created by its patron god. Viracocha, originally a tribal

The Empire of the Incas. The impressive mountains of South America were significant in the religion of the earthly representatives of the sun, the Incas.

god, was thus elevated to a larger office. He was associated with the water and foam of Lake Titicaca. Huari (Viracocha) created all gods and cosmic functions.

Closer manifestations of the holy were the **huacas,** unusual appearances in stones, plants, animals, or people. They were holy in their ability to communicate as well as in appearance, because they spoke to humans who could interpret them. Another example of *huaca* was a stone place of divine appearances and sacrifices. Stars and constellations of the night sky are other examples; the Southern Cross was a llama spirit, and Sirius was a jaguar. Cuzco, the city, was also *huaca,* making holy those selected to live there. Sorcerers practiced magic, and priests had minor roles. Incas thought the only proper person to approach the gods was the emperor.

huacas [WAH-cas]
In Inca religion, natural phenomena that provide unusual manifestations of the holy. Unusual rocks, for example, could symbolize the presence of the holy.

Machu Picchu. City of Incas, fifty miles northwest of Cuzco, Peru. The temple, citadel, and terraced gardens are linked by thousands of steps.

Rituals and Symbols

The generally beneficent Inca deities, who cared for both the living and the dead, could be satisfied with the sacrifice of sacred llamas and food shared by humans. The chief Inca represented the sun. Sometimes human infants were sacrificed to him, but most of the time his needs were met by priests and "virgins of the sun," who made cloth and beer for the cult and served as the Inca's concubines. The sun god and the Inca emperor were much alike, because the first emperor of the Incas was believed to have been the offspring of the sun. The "virgins of the sun," with whom the emperor mated, produced "children of the sun" to serve him. Because there was no metal trade, gold—which like the sun did not tarnish—was used to adorn the gods and royal personages.

Some festivals were religious rituals. The feast of salvation, the Situa, involved heavens, gods, humans, and *huacas* in a great ritual of forgiveness and healing. This Festival of the Queen, the moon goddess, occurred after the planting of seed. The chosen people of the creator expunged any disease or evil from among themselves and participated in renewing heavens. Burr Brundage describes the drama in three acts.[19] The emperor Huascar ordered Cuzco purged of all foreign influences, so that only pure Incas were in the city. Gods were brought to Coricancha: the golden image of Viracocha, the creator; an ugly stone of Huanacauri, the Inca's manhood; and Inti, the sun god. Mother Earth and Mother Moon were present, attended only by women. Eleven ancestors—mummies—attended. At the end of the council, messengers announced to soldiers of the guard the good news of a splendid ceremonial celebration.

The second act of the drama required Inca knights in battle dress to go through the city and bring offenders to the judges, who passed out sentences. Then four groups of soldiers in mock battle went through the city carrying torches, chasing evil. Inhabitants came out and joined the drive to rid the city of any evil spirits. The soldiers proceeded onward outside the city until they had driven all evil from the precincts. Returning, they ceremonially washed their weapons under starlight—now the city was safe from evil for another year.

The third act of the Situa took place the next morning, when inhabitants in their best costumes and cosmetics participated in eating and wearing *yahuar sanco,* a kind of dough made with maize and the blood of a hundred sacred white llamas. The gods received the food, which devotees spread across their mouths. The emperor and his head wife, servants and representatives of the creator, entered wearing feather crowns. The sun god was paraded, and the mummies of prior emperors attended. The emperor prayed to the creator god. The people danced the *huayaya,* using a woolen rope of many colors, decorated with gold, symbolizing a giant anaconda. The celebration and worship to prepare for a successful year occupied four days.

Religions of the Americas in History

12,000 Paintings made in caves of France

2000 ▲
1500 ▲
1000 ▲
500 ▲
B.C.E

0

0
500 ▼
1000 ▼
1500 ▼

C.E

2000 ▼

1200 C.E. Incas build Cuzco in the Andes Mountains

1325 Aztecs settle at Tenochtitlán, Mexico

1487 Ahuizotl dedicates the Great Temple

1492 Columbus sails from Spain

1519 Montezuma welcomes Hernando Cortez

1521 Cortez conquers the Aztecs

1532 Francisco Pizarro finds the Incas

1541 Francisco Vasquez Coronado, Spanish explorer, meets Zuni Indians

1598 Franciscan missionaries bring Christianity to Zuni Indians

1607 English settlers in Virginia encounter Powhatan Indians

17th century English hunters and traders encounter Cherokee Indians in Appalachian Mountains

1776–1781 Revolutionary War; Cherokees join British in fight against colonists

1792 U.S. Congress appropriates funds to teach Indians agriculture and domestic arts

1827 Cherokees call themselves "one nation under God" and adopt constitution based on that of the United States

1838–1839 "Trail of Tears": U.S. government troops force Cherokees to walk to Indian Territories, now Oklahoma

1939–1945 World War II

1861–1865 American Civil War

1914–1918 World War I

1919 Introduction of peyote religion on Wind River Reservation

1935 Frank G. Speck studies Naskapi Indians of the Labrador peninsula

1990 Congress passes Native American Language Act

Inca stone roads, magnificent buildings, and artifacts remain today. With the coming of Christianity, however, most of the beliefs and rituals of the Incas faded away. Those that could be reconciled with the religion of the invaders were retained and incorporated into a new culture.

Worldview: Common Features of Mesoamerican and South American Religions

Although the indigenous cultures of Mesoamerica and South America are all different, the worldviews of the historical city-states share some features.

The Absolute, the World, and Humans

For the Aztecs and the Incas, the Absolute, the world, and humans were active participants in a cosmic drama. The Absolute comprised interactive forces personified as gods and goddesses. Heavenly bodies, phenomena of weather and seasons, and earth and water were deities who played roles in a perpetual drama. These characters struggled, loved, fought, won, lost, and sometimes died. The earth, which produced crops, herds, and marine life to support the city-state civilizations, depended on heaven to sustain it. In its own way, the earth also contributed to the annual cycles of animal and vegetable life. Humans, who received the benefits and shared the hardships of heaven and earth, had to actively help maintain a productive balance between the two. The Absolute, the world, and humans depended on one another to ensure prosperity.

The Problem and the Solution for Humans

This interdependent relationship among the absolute, the world, and humans was the source of both the problem and the solution for humans. The problem was to maintain the balance in order to meet basic needs as well as those for art, effective government, and a strong military. Failure to do so would bring anarchy, famine, slavery, or death. The solution for humans was to keep all the moral and ritual laws of their society. Through public rituals, they guaranteed the annual renewal of sources of life. Through private rituals, they sought assurance of life after death.

Relationship to Other Religions

The city-states had both distinctive and shared symbols and rituals. Each had a patron deity with particular symbols and rituals, and each thought of its religion as distinct from religions of other peoples. Nevertheless, they often borrowed deities, rituals, and symbols from other city-states and integrated them into established beliefs and practices. Deities of hunting-and-gathering peoples were often included among the gods worshiped in advanced agricultural societies. The functions and organization of the gods in these societies also changed to reflect earthly developments such as the division of labor in large city-states and the emergence of kingdoms.

None of the religions discussed in this chapter developed an enduring concept of only one god, monotheism. Instead, the indigenous religions of the Americas conceived of a unified cosmic system of forces that interact in dramatic ways. Religion in the city-states sought to benefit humans by integrating them positively into the perpetual drama of the cosmos. For more examples of religions of tribes and of city-states, we will turn next to religions of Africa in Chapter 2.

What is the difference between living beings, dead beings, inanimate things, and deities? For as long as there have been oral or written traditions of religions, this question has been the source of puzzlement and pronouncements. *Soul* has been defined as that which animates the body. Although postmodern philosophers are critical of the thinking behind this definition, earlier centuries of spiritual leaders were mostly satisfied with it. The soul was not seen directly, but when it was present, the body lived. Other religions identified *spirit* as the source of life; spirit was breath. Often deities, or gods, were identified as spirits. Deities were like humans, but they did not die.

Other peoples have thought of life as blood. Where there is life, blood is present. When blood pours out from a creature, life departs from it. Blood can be seen and is known to be essential. In South America the cycle of the sun, also essential to life, was thought to be ensured with sacrificial blood of animals—and sometimes humans.

As you read the following chapters, consider how each religion thinks of life itself. Does it identify life with soul, spirit, deity, or sacrificial blood?

CONSIDER THIS

Life as Soul, Spirit, Deity, or Blood

VOCABULARY

Ahone [A-hone]
henotheism [HEN-uh-thee-is-um]
huacas [WAH-cas]
Huitzilopochtli [HWEET-zi-low-POK-tli]
Inti [IN-ti]
kachinas [ka-CHI-nas]
kivas [KEE-vas]
mamanatowick [ma-ma-na-TOW-wick]

Mantu [MAHN-too]
Mista'peo [mis-TAH-pe-oh]
monotheism [MAH-nuh-thee-is-um]
myth [MITH]
Okeus [OH-kee-us]
Quetzalcoatl [KET-zal-coatl]
reincarnation [REE-in-cahr-NAY-shun]
shaman [SHAH-man]
Tenochtitlán [TEN-ok-tit-LAN]
Tezcatlipoca [tez-CAT-li-POH-ca]

Tlaloc [TLAH-loc]
Tonatiuh [TOE-na-TI-uh]
trickster [TRIK-stur]
Tsaka'bec [tsah-KAH-bec]
Viracocha [VI-rah-COH-cha]
weroances [WEH-row-ances]
weroansquas [WEH-row-AN-squas]
wisakon [WI-sa-kon]

QUESTIONS FOR REVIEW

1. Describe a Naskapi hunt, using essential religious and sociological terms to show the relationship between humans and animals.
2. How did Cherokees control the content of their sacred stories?
3. Briefly describe the Powhatans' practice of religion.
4. How were Aztecs involved in maintaining the universe?
5. Describe the three acts of the Situa of the Incas.
6. Among the Hopi, how did kachinas function in education of children?
7. How have kachinas supported family discipline?
8. What have indigenous religions of the Americas taught about death?
9. Describe the Absolute of the Incas.
10. What roles have women played in Native American religions?

QUESTIONS FOR DISCUSSION

1. How have various Native American tribes viewed the relationship between religion and healing?
2. How did the Native Americans discussed in this chapter balance individual religious experience with community needs?

3. How does care and disposal of bodies of the dead reveal a people's views of death? Give examples from Native American practices to support your answer.

4. Compare the importance of religious leaders with the importance of chiefs among Native Americans.

5. What are your most favorable impressions of Native American religions? Which beliefs or practices have you most questioned?

NOTES

1. Frank G. Speck, *Naskapi* (Norman: University of Oklahoma Press, 1977).
2. Ibid., p. 33.
3. Ibid., pp. 47–48.
4. Ben C. McCrary, *Indians in Seventeenth Century Virginia* (Williamsburg, VA: Virginia 350th Anniversary Celebration Corporation, 1957); Helen C. Rountree, *The Powhatan Indians of Virginia* (Norman: University of Oklahoma Press, 1989); Helen C. Rountree and E. Randolph Turner III, *Before and after Jamestown: Virginia's Powhatans and Their Predecessors* (Gainesville: University Press of Florida, 2002).
5. McCrary, p. 126.
6. Ibid., p. 139.
7. Ibid., pp. 134–135.
8. John Ehle, *Trail of Tears* (New York: Doubleday-Anchor, 1988).
9. James Mooney, *Myths of the Cherokee* (St. Clair Shores, MI: Scholarly Press, 1970), pp. 239–427.
10. Theda Perdue, *Cherokee Women: Gender and Culture Change 1700–1835* (Lincoln: University of Nebraska Press, 1998).
11. Cottie Burland, *North American Indian Mythology* (New York: Peter Bedrick Books, 1985), pp. 97–98.
12. Harold E. Driver, *Indians of North America* (Chicago: University of Chicago Press, 1961), p. 506.
13. [Fray] Diego Duran, *The Book of Gods and Rites and the Ancient Calendar,* trans. Fernando Horcasitas and Doris Heyden (Norman: University of Okalahoma Press, 1971), p. 73.
14. Nigel Davis, *The Aztecs* (New York: Putnam, 1973), p. 165.
15. Ibid., pp. 143–145.
16. David Carrasco with Scott Sessions, *Daily Life of the Aztecs: People of the Sun and Earth* (Westport, CT: Greenwood Press, 1998), p. 198.
17. Burr Cartwright Brundage, *Lords of Cuzco* (Norman: University of Okalahoma Press, 1967), p. 8.
18. Brundage, p. 143.
19. Brundage, p. 198.

READINGS

North America

Burland, Cottie. *North American Indian Mythology.* New York: Peter Bedrick Books, 1985.

Callaway, Colin G. *New World for All Indians, Europeans, and the Remaking of Early America.* Baltimore: Johns Hopkins University Press, 1997.

Hale, Lorraine. *Native American Education. A Reference Handbook.* Santa Barbara, CA: ABC CLIO, 2002.

Hultkrantz, Åke. *Native Religions of North America.* Hagerstown, MD: Torch, 1988.

Jenkins, Philip. *Dream Catchers.* New York: Oxford, 2004.

Marrott, Alice, and Carol K. Rachlin. *Plains Indian Mythology.* New York: Crowell, 1975.

Minges, Patrick N. *Slavery in the Cherokee Nation, 1855–1867.* New York: Routledge, 2003.

Mooney, James. *Myths of the Cherokee.* St. Clair Shores, MI: Scholarly Press, 1970.

Perdue, Theda. *Cherokee Women: Gender and Culture Change 1700–1835.* Lincoln: University of Nebraska Press, 1998.

Rountree, Helen C. *The Powhatan Indians of Virginia.* Norman: University of Oklahoma Press, 1989.

Rountree, Helen C., and E. Randolph Turner III. *Before and After Jamestown: Virginia's Powhantas and Their Predecessors.* Gainesville, Florida: University Press of Florida, 2002.

MesoAmerica and South America

Austin, Alfredo Lopez. *Tamoanchan: Places of Mist,* trans. Bernard Ortiz and Thelma Ortiz de Montellano. Niwot: University Press of Colorado, 1977.

Carrasco, David, with Scott Sessions. *Daily Life of the Aztecs, People of the Sun and the Earth*. Westport, CT: Greenwood Press, 1998.

Joyce, Rosemary A. *Gender and Power in Prehispanic Mesoamerica*. Austin: University Press, 1992.

Marcus, Joyce. *Mesoamerican Writing Systems*. Princeton, NJ: Princeton University Press, 1992.

Salles-Reese, Veronica. *From Viracocha to the Virgin of Copacabana: Representation of the Sacred at Lake Titicaca*. Austin: University of Texas Press, 1997.

BASIC TENETS OF RELIGIONS OF THE AMERICAS—Significant Beings

NORTH AMERICA			
Naskapi	**Powhatans**	**Cherokees**	**Hopi**
Mantu (soul in living things)	Okeus (wrathful deity)	Kana'ti and Selu	Kachina (gods, ancestors, spirits)
	Ahone (beneficent deity)	Wild Boy	
Mista'peo, or Great Man (individual soul)		Water Beetle (creator)	
Tsaka'bec (trickster)			

MESOAMERICA AND SOUTH AMERICA		
Aztecs		**Incas**
Huitzilopochtli (sun)		Inti-Viracocha (creator and sustainer)
Tezcatlipoca (night sky)		Peaks of the Andes (mother earth)
Tlaloc (earth and rain)		

CHAPTER 2

Religions of Africa

OVERVIEW AND THEMES

"Advance, for we have done away with thy wickedness, and we have put away thy sin, and thy sin committed upon earth, which merited stripes, and we have destroyed all the evil which appertained to thee upon earth. Enter, therefore, into Re-stau, and pass through the secret gates of Amentet. . . ."

Egyptian Book of the Dead, Chapter 126*

THE ANCIENT EGYPTIANS
Body and Soul are unified in this life and in the life to come.
Mummification of the body allows a person to be re-created.

THE BASONGYE OF THE CONGO
Efile Mikulu is the chief god of good and of ancestors.
Kafilefile is the god of evil.

THE ZULU PEOPLES OF SOUTH AFRICA
In the house of the chief is an Umsamo where ancestors commune with their Descendants.

THE YORUBA PEOPLES OF SOUTH AFRICA
Olorun and ancestors affect human lives.

IMPORTANT THEMES
Life beyond death; the body remains behind, but the soul moves on to reward or punishment in a world beyond this one. Ancestors live in another sphere, but their powers can influence the community now.

CONCENTRATION OF RELIGIONS†
Congo: 48% traditional beliefs
Nigeria: 10% traditional beliefs
South Africa: 28.5% traditional beliefs
Togo-Benin: 50% traditional beliefs

*E. A. Wallace Budge, *Osiris* Vol. I (NewHyde Park, NY: University Books, 1961), pp. 338–339.
†John W. Wright, ed., *2005 The New York Times Almanac*, (New York: Penguin Group, 2004).

The continent of Africa has always excited Western imaginations. From ancient times, Mesopotamians, Persians, Greeks, and Romans were fascinated with the peoples, animals, and places of Africa. The pyramids of Egypt and the religion that gave rise to them captivated visitors. Ancient pharaohs represented not only monarchs to be obeyed but also deities to be worshiped.

As ancient Egyptian civilization declined, new groups arrived and spread over the continent. In early days of Christianity, converts multiplied in Egypt and sent missionaries north of the Sahara Desert. In the seventh century, Muslims swept out of Arabia, crossed North Africa, and eventually reached Spain. In the colonial period, British, French, and German interests studied Islam but promoted Christianity.

As the colonial powers moved into sub-Saharan Africa, their religion began to make converts to Christianity. Muslims also began missionary efforts in the southern regions. Through missionary activities many peoples of Africa have become officially either Christian or Muslim. We will study these religions in Chapters 9 and 10. In this chapter we will study some of the distinctively African religions that are still practiced, sometimes by people who are nominally members of either Islam or Christianity.

Powerful figures in African religion arouse both awe and fear. Witches are believed to have influence over forces that can bring either good or evil. Chiefs are not only earthly rulers but also controllers of spiritual forces of life and death. Believers who might seem to be enjoying simple freedoms may feel encompassed by hundreds of prescriptions to avoid powers of evil.

Karnak, Egypt. The site of ancient Thebes is on the right bank of the Nile River. Its remains include the Great Temple of Amon as well as statues of pharaohs.

In this chapter we will examine ancient Egyptian religion and three sub-Saharan religions still practiced today. Many people still regard the civilization of the ancient Egyptians as the finest example of what Africa has produced. The sub-Saharan religions are examples of traditional beliefs that have been subordinated to major world religions that arose in the Middle East. In these religions we will meet dozens of interesting deities and the humans who are believed to have influence over these gods' powers.

The Ancient Egyptians

The pyramid of the Pharaoh Cheops, in Giza, not far from Cairo, was a wonder of the ancient world; it remains so today. Ravages of weather, pollution, and looters have not destroyed the marvelous construction of 2600 B.C.E.[1] Over two million

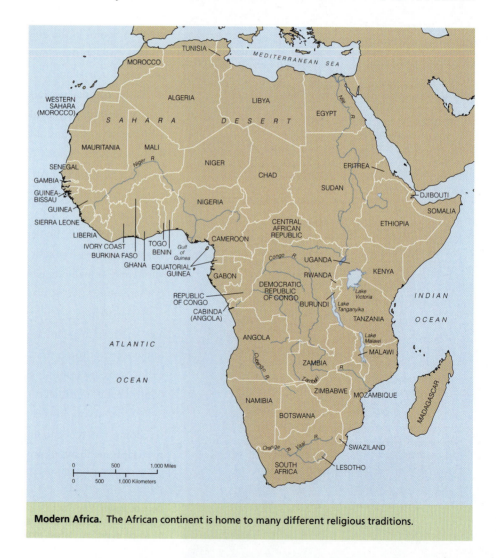

Modern Africa. The African continent is home to many different religious traditions.

blocks weighing an average of 2.5 tons each were assembled to a height of more than 450 feet along the Nile River to provide an inviolable tomb for the body of a pharaoh who believed he would live again in another world.

Historical Development

Written records of Egypt began about 3100 B.C.E. with a king named Menes, who ruled Memphis.[2] Because most of the surrounding land was desert, cities clustered near the Nile River, the main source of fresh water. Some Egyptians were fishers, and others farmed the rich, black soil deposited on the banks of the Nile by annual floods. The Egyptians invented hieroglyphics, a system of writing that used symbols or pictures to represent words or sounds, and recorded their history long before many other civilizations did so. Egyptian written records have provided archaeologists with reliable information about their religion.

From the information on kingdoms and dynasties of Egypt that covers more than 2500 years, we know how the religion developed. More powerful rulers imposed the beliefs and rituals of their own cities on the peoples of cities they conquered. In the process, deities of two or more cities were often combined; deities of the victorious city usually dominated the deities of the conquered cities. Over time, a more national view of Egyptians affected their religious worldview. Royal clans shared deities, rituals, and beliefs over much of the country. In this long history, other peoples, such as the **Nubians** from the south, contributed their cultures as they assumed roles of leadership, even as pharaohs.

The period of the pyramid builders, the Old Kingdom (2700–2200 B.C.E.), was succeeded by the chaotic First Intermediate Period (2200–2050 B.C.E.). Nobles from Thebes reunited Egypt during the Middle Kingdom (2050–1800 B.C.E.).

Nubians [NOO-bee-ans] People of the southern Nile valley; neighbors of the ancient Egyptians. Their leaders formed the twenty-fifth dynasty of Egyptian pharaohs.

© The William MacQuitty International Collection

The Sphinx and the Pyramids of Giza.

During the Second Intermediate Period (1800–1570 B.C.E.), local rulers were replaced by warrior rulers from Asia, the Hyksos. In the Early New Kingdom, (1570–1300 B.C.E.), Egyptians mastered the Hyksos' weapons of war and threw off the yoke of their foreign rulers. Queen Hatshepsut ruled over a peaceful period of building beautiful temples and cities.

In 1370 B.C.E., the Amarna Revolution began with King Amenhotep IV, who worshiped only one god, the sun. He named this one god Aton; he called himself Akhenaton. He moved his court to a new city that he named Akhetaton to avoid the old worship of Amon. Under Tutankhamen, a son-in-law of Akhenaton, Egyptians returned to polytheism. British archaeologists Howard Carter and Lord Carnarvon discovered King Tutankhamen's tomb in 1922; the splendors of his kingdom were dazzling. In the Later New Kingdom (1300–1090 B.C.E.), the Egyptians fought the Hittites and Philistines, recovering much of the territory they had lost in earlier centuries.

With the beginning of the iron age, about 1100 B.C.E., the Egyptians, who had no iron, began to lose territory to invaders armed with iron weapons. From the Period of Invasions to the coming of the Romans in 30 B.C.E., non-Egyptians often ruled the Egyptians. From about 320 B.C.E., the Greek Ptolemies brought about the revival of intellectual, cultural, and commercial activity, and Alexandria, the city founded by Alexander the Great, became a beacon for learning. During the Roman period, Christianity gained a foothold in Egypt. Eventually Egypt became part of the Byzantine empire and later fell to the Muslims in 639 C.E. From that year onward, Islam played an increasing role in Africa.

Worldview of the Ancient Egyptians

The Absolute

By the time Cheops built his tomb, Egyptian religion was well developed. Egyptians considered the sky, earth, river, and sun sources of life. They were visualized as humans, animals, and combined human–animal forms. The symbols of the sun, the highest god, had different names for different times of the day. Isis and Osiris were husband and wife deities who personified the self-renewing vitality in nature. **Horus,** the son of Isis and Osiris, was symbolized by a falcon. As king of the gods, he stood for light and heaven. **Amon-Re,** or Ra, combined the god of Thebes with the god of the noon sun. He was symbolized by a human form wearing a headdress or by an obelisk (the sun's ray). **Aton,** championed by Pharaoh Akhenaton, was the sun, symbolized by a disk. Akhenaton proclaimed that the sun god, Aton, was the only god, as noted earlier.

The gods and goddesses who were patrons of cities had various symbols, but they were often depicted as combined human and animal forms in one figure.[3] The symbol of **Hathor,** the creator of the earth, is a woman's body with the head of a cow. Jackals and crocodiles were combined with human bodies to represent scavengers. A feather at the scene of the final judgment symbolized **Mayet** (Maat), goddess of order and truth.

Cats were especially honored. The goddess Sakhmet, a form of Hathor, was symbolized by the head of a lion atop a woman's body, and the goddess Bast, who represented joy and fertility from the sun, was symbolized by the head of a cat atop a woman's body. Jewelers sometimes put cat figures atop the **ankh,** the circle-topped Egyptian cross that symbolized immortality. The great goddess **Mut** at

---

Horus [HOH-us]
In Egypt, the son of Isis and Osiris who opposed his uncle, Seth. Horus was also the sun, symbolized by a falcon.

Amon-Re [AH-mun-ray]
A sun god of Egypt. His symbol was the obelisk, a ray of the sun. Amon, originally the god of Thebes, became highest god in 2000 B.C.E. when Thebes dominated all Egypt.

Aton [AHT-un]
In Egypt, this god's symbol was a disk, representing the sun. After Akhenaton established his throne in Akhetaton, Aton was the only god worshiped.

Hathor [HAH-thor]
The Egyptian goddess who created the world. Her symbol was a woman's body with the head of a cow.

Mayet [MU-yut]
(Maat) The Egyptian goddess of order and truth, who prompted the deceased at the time of judgment.

ankh [angk]
In Egypt, the circle-topped cross representing life. Some forms incorporate a cat on top of the circle.

Mut [MUT]
In Egypt, a goddess whose symbol was the cat.

Religions of Africa in History

2700–2200 B.C.E. Old Kingdom in Egypt

2700 Pyramid of Cheops built

2500 Document giving Ptahhotep's concept of God

2200–2050 First Intermediate Period in Egypt

2050–1800 Middle Kingdom in Egypt

1800–1570 Second Intermediate Period in Egypt

1570–1300 The Early New Kingdom in Egypt

1370 Akhenaton worships Aton; the Amarna Revolution

1300–1090 Later New Kingdom of Egypt

330 Alexander the Great in Egypt

200 Septuagint, Greek translation of Hebrew Bible, made

31 Octavian, the Roman emperor, conquers Egypt

1st century C.E. Christianity enters Egypt

7th century Islam enters Egypt

12th century Advanced cultures appear in Yoruba area of Nigeria

15th and 16th centuries Portuguese and British slavers appear in Nigeria

17th century Dutch settle in Cape of Good Hope (South Africa)

1806 British seize Cape of Good Hope

1897 Cecil Rhodes and British South Africa Company control Zimbabwe

1899–1902 Anglo-Boer War of South Africa

1923 British take over Southern Rhodesia

1960 Nigeria becomes independent

1963 Nigeria becomes a republic

1969 Belgian Congo becomes independent

1971 Republic of Zaire is proclaimed

1990 Nelson Mandela freed from 27 years in prison, South Africa

1991 President de Klerk announces plans to end apartheid laws in South Africa

1994 South Africa holds first election where all people can vote; Nelson Mandela elected president

1996 Postapartheid constitution becomes law of South Africa

1997 General Laurent Kabila changes name of "Zaire" to "Democratic Republic of Congo"

2000 Northern states in Nigeria impose strict Islamic law

BCE 2000 1500 1000 500 0
CE 0 500 1000 1500 2000

Luxor was said to be fond of cats, which was shown by figures of the animals on cups. Incidentally, Queen Hatshepsut was the first pharaoh said to have been born of Mut and Amun.[4]

The numerous ancient Egyptian representations of the gods express a sophisticated concept of the absolute. Egyptians admired traits of some animals and found these animals suitable symbols of deities. Other symbols of Egyptian deities express qualities, functions, and powers in the annual cycle of life. Egyptians conceived of the universe as a unit. Sky, earth, sun, and river united to bring forth fruits from the earth. These forces cooperated to sustain rewarding lives for humans. Body and soul were unified not only in this life but also in the life to come. As justice required that goodness be rewarded and evil punished in this life, so would righteousness be compensated and immorality penalized in the world of the dead.

The unity of the ancient Egyptian worldview emphasized dependability. The sun rose, sailing as a double-ended boat across the day sky. After sailing under the earth all night, the next day it returned with its light and heat. The shallow Nile River mysteriously increased its flow each year, flooding the lands along its banks. Although at times terrifying, the river brought rich soil in which industrious farmers could produce abundant grain. During its lifetime, the human body grew and then declined to death. With preservation, however, the body could be maintained and restored to life. In Egypt, life was dependable.

Rituals and Symbols

The ancient Egyptian temple of a god (or goddess) represented the mansion of the god, his home on earth. The priests of each temple cared for the statue of the god as if it were alive. As the divine and intermediary of the divine, the pharaoh represented the god to the people and the people to god. High priests made offerings, poured libations, and burned sweet-smelling incense to the gods. The priests also served as judges and supervised the vast temple lands. So important was the office that sometimes, royal princes served as high priests. Other people familiar with the sacred writings—the prophets and the scribes—also had official tasks. And faithful worshipers themselves often performed duties in the temple. From the pharaoh to the lowliest subject, Egyptian society was unified through the service to the patron deity of the city.

As important as the temples to the patron deity were in each city, one story of the gods captured the hearts of many Egyptians. Its theme is the one most often associated with the ancient Egyptian religion—death and life after death. The main characters are **Osiris,** a king who brought a golden age to Egyptians; his devoted wife, **Isis;** and his evil brother, **Seth.** Seth tricks Osiris into lying down in a coffin, seals it, and throws it into the Nile River. It floats to the Mediterranean sea and lands in Byblos, on the coast of Lebanon.[5] Lodged in a tree, it becomes part of a pillar used in building a king's house. The grieving Isis searches for the body of Osiris. Locating it, she persuads the king to give her the body. After taking Osiris's body to a secluded place and employing her magic powers, she embraces it. Osiris revives enough to impregnate her. In secrecy she bears Horus, protecting him from

Egyptian Pharaoh Queen Hapshetsut.
1503–1482 B.C.E. Ruler of Egypt for twenty-one years.

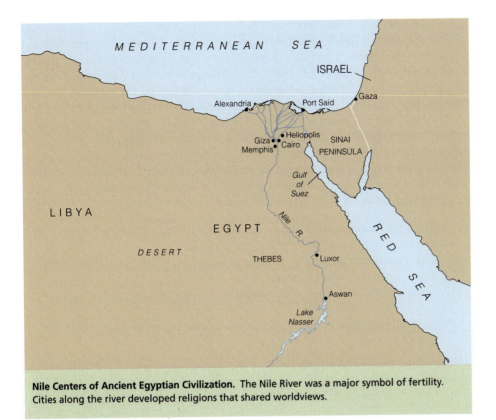

Nile Centers of Ancient Egyptian Civilization. The Nile River was a major symbol of fertility. Cities along the river developed religions that shared worldviews.

his uncle Seth. On reaching manhood, Horus organizes supporters to avenge his father's murder. He defeats Seth, recovering the third eye, a sign of kingship, which Seth had stolen from Osiris. The victorious Horus reigns sovereign over Egypt, and Osiris becomes lord of the underworld, the one who bestows immortality. Osiris symbolizes the perfect king who gives life both on earth and after death, and Isis symbolizes the queen who is a wise, devoted wife.

For the Egyptians the Isis-Osiris myth had meanings tied to the Nile and to birth, death, and life after death. The annual rising and falling of the Nile River was associated with events in the lives of Isis and Osiris. The myth was also associated with the birth and death of pharaohs. The pharaoh was more than a representative of the divine; he *was* divine.

Life after Death

Immortality, at first believed to be restricted to kings, was later extended to common people. For the Egyptians the soul was complex. The **ka** was a spiritual form that mirrored the body. Its physical needs were met after death by food and drink left at the tomb. The **ba** was a spirit that flew as a bird to heaven. An **akh** or **ikhu** was the ghost of a person that went to the land of the blessed. When the ka departed, the body died. Through mummification and funeral rites, a person could be re-created. Mummification bound the ka and the body of the deceased to the world. Because living required eating, funerary meals had to be provided for the dead person. Then the Egyptians embalmed the body and made images of the deceased, servants, and loved ones. British archaeologist Sir Wallis Budge

ka [KA]
In Egypt, divine breath that supported life. Sometimes referred to as the soul.

ba [BAH]
In Egypt, a kind of human consciousness. Sometimes described as the soul.

akh or **ikhu** [AHK]
A part of the soul; the ghost that went to the land of the blessed.

believed the images of servants found in tombs represent servants who were actually buried, alive or dead, with their masters.[6] The servants were not embalmed or found with their masters, so this is difficult to confirm. Egyptians entombed possessions of the deceased, especially boats, to help the person reach the land of paradise. The preserved body, images, possessions, and food served the needs of the soul immediately after death, in the tomb, and in the journey to the land of the blessed.

Egyptians did not consider immortality guaranteed. First each person had to appear for judgment before Mayet (goddess of truth) in the kingdom of Osiris. On entering the Hall of Mayet, the deceased greeted the goddess and sought her clemency. He or she acknowledged the forty-two gods who kept watch over those who had done evil. The deceased then recited a negative confession—the things he or she had *not* done, including these:

1. I have not sinned against men.
2. I have not oppressed (or wronged) [my] kinsfolk.
3. I have not committed evil in the place of truth.
4. I have not known worthless men.
5. I have not committed acts of abomination.

38. I have not repulsed the god in his manifestations. I am pure. I am pure. I am pure. I am pure.[7]

The judge then ordered the heart of the deceased weighed in a balance; the lighter the heart, the better the life. A heart heavy with evil earned for the deceased the condemnation of being devoured by a composite monster that symbolized the most feared creatures in Egypt—the crocodile, the lion, and the hippopotamus. The light-hearted person was sent to a pleasant land that the Egyptians considered ideal.

This organized religion developed along with diversified civilization. The lives of the ancient Egyptians are reflected in the words of the *Book of the Dead*. They found wealth in the Nile River and in the rich farmlands along its banks. The river irrigated their crops and provided fish and game. At the bottom of society, slaves

© Brian Brake/Photo Researchers, Inc.

Tomb of Nektamun, a Sculptor. Anubis, Lord of the Dead, represented by a jackal, presides over Nektamun's mummy.

provided a labor force that supported a class structure of poor and rich, dominated by royalty. Known as the land of two kingdoms, Upper and Lower Egypt, for many centuries Egypt held its own against neighboring countries.

Relationship to Other Religions

Although ancient Egyptian religion is no longer active, it lives on in the history of Western civilization. Greek philosophers marveled at Egyptian wisdom, and historians of Greece and Rome imported Egyptian stories, dramas, and beliefs. Roman soldiers, such as Mark Antony and Julius Caesar, were fascinated with Egypt and its goddess Isis. Egyptians made lasting impressions on Judaism and Christianity. Medieval visitors to Egypt were amazed at the temples and tombs of the pharaohs. Muslims and Jews, such as Maimonides, made their home near the Nile. The Sphinx, located near the pyramid of Cheops, symbolized the mysteries of ancient Egypt. Nineteenth- and twentieth-century archaeologists brought to light the beliefs and practices of a civilization that is still impressive today. Throughout much of the world, ancient Egyptian religion continues to influence religious beliefs of new generations.

The Basongye of the Congo
Historical Development

The Democratic Republic of Congo, formerly called Zaire, has about forty million people. Almost half live in urban areas. The major ethnic group is Bantu, but about two hundred other tribes inhabit the country. Most people are Christians. About 10 percent are Muslims. When Portuguese explorers arrived in the fifteenth century, they found a kingdom of Bantus in this area. From 1876 to 1909, King Leopold of Belgium directed an international group in exploiting the resources of the region around the Congo River. In 1960, the country became independent, under the leadership of Patrice Lumumba, who was assassinated. After a period of warfare, the country changed its name to Zaire in 1971. Shortly thereafter, people with Christian names were required to change them to African names. In a revolution of 1997 the name *Congo* was revived.

Worldview of the Basongye

Alan P. Merriam, in a twentieth-century study of the Congolese Basongye, shows that many perceptions of humans and the universe that antedated the coming of whites remain strong in isolated villages.[8] In the 1960s, Merriam and his family lived in Lupupa Ngye, a village of mud-and-thatch huts. The people were primarily engaged in agriculture and supplemented their crops with fishing and hunting.

The Absolute and the World

Merriam describes the Lupupans' views of the universe as static. They knew a few constellations, the sun and the moon, and the earth. Everything was in the hands of their good deity, **Efile Mukulu.** The earth is a flat circle, resting on water below and covered by water in the sky. The Congo is in the center, and at the edges lie

Efile Mukulu
[ɛ-fu-le mu-ʀoo-loo]
Among the Congolese Basongye, the chief god of good. His counterpart is the evil god, Kafilefile.

the United States, Portugal, and Belgium. Efile Mukulu assigned the masculine sun to dry things; that is good for some purposes but perhaps bad for older people. He assigned the moon, usually feminine, to give light at night and be a mother of all. Mostly good, the moon symbolizes water, which, along with the sun, is needed for growing crops. On the first day of the new moon, the village protector and fertility figure is brought out and made the center of dances. It is the time to promote fertility in crops and women. Stars are friends and advisors of the moon. Shooting stars are symbols of babies to be born.

Inanimate objects and animals do not have spirits. A person may physically abuse animals, whether domestic dogs used in hunting or wild creatures, without fearing evil. Plates and spoons have essences that can accompany human spirits to Efile Mukulu. The villagers have a story, probably from the World War I era, that animals come from a hole in the ground near Lake Tanganyika.

A human consists of body, spirit, shadow, and perhaps a conscience. The essential part of a person is the spirit, which is incarnated up to three times as a human, perhaps a fourth time as a lion or leopard. Each incarnation is determined by Efile Mukulu. Happy ancestors can send a human spirit back to its family as a child. The human spirit, **kikudu,** can return as a child of either sex, carrying on family resemblances. The spirit informs the body through dreams and guides it in responding to most circumstances—the body has no will of its own. Because the spirit knows Efile Mukulu, it always knows more than the body. The body knows only what the spirit already knows. Consciousness, then, extends beyond the short span of a spirit in a body. A spirit can travel abroad from a sleeping body.

kikudu [ki-KOO-doo]
The soul of a human being that may live after the death of the body.

Kafilefile [kah-FI-le-FI-le]
Among the Congolese Basongye, the god of evil. His counterpart is the good god, Efile Mukulu.

mankishi [man-KI-shi]
Among the Congolese Basongye, a small carved figure used to represent a child desired by a couple. The figure can also be used to bring success in fishing and to protect homes and people from bad magic.

Basongye Religion and Magic

Deities spent little time on earth and have largely abandoned it. Opposite to the good god, Efile Mukulu, is the evil god, **Kafilefile.** He has departed, leaving his evil influence. Efile Mukulu rarely extends his beneficence, but in special circumstances he intervenes. Of much greater concern in daily living are four kinds of phenomena.[9] Sorcerers are greatly feared and sometimes fought. They use enormous, witless humanoids to carry out their evil purposes. Witches and *buchi* are persons of evil intent. Ancestral spirits are among the living; most are benevolent, but under some circumstances, a few do harm to humans.

Because ancestors can help or hurt the living and receive or reject a spirit separated from a body by natural death or by magic, they are remembered with gifts and sacrifices. The ancestors are part of Efile Mukulu, who is part of all things. Sacrifices of first fruits honor and please both Efile Mukulu and ancestors.

Humans, not gods, cause death. This concept is intertwined with a very active belief in witches and sorcerers and their magic. In contrast to the small carved **mankishi** figures are human spirits bent on vengeance,

© Irven DeVore/Anthro-Photo

Congolese People. An Efe man bottles honey to trade for food.

mikishi. In contrast to good human spirits, these vengeful spirits cause a special illness unlike the illnesses caused by Efile Mukulu. To some extent, sorcerers control vengeful spirits; a person who wants protection from them can call on a sorcerer for help.

Magic influences every aspect of the Basongyes' daily lives. It is so carefully studied and practiced that some observers classify it as a kind of technology, a body of procedures that can be counted on to produce desired results. Merriam classifies four types of magic, each with subgroups and distinctive functions. One type of magic can be used in protecting crops, another type in producing rain, another for causing death by lightning, and another for destroying an enemy's crops. In addition to concocting potions, members of Basongye cults wear sacred masks to obtain their desires.

The Basongye believe witches are creations of Efile Mukulu but do the work of Kafilefile. They fly away from their houses at night, leaving their legs behind. They seek to cause mischief to humans. People visited by a witch who intends harm see a special light—witch's fire—and are paralyzed. Witches can assume the form of an attacking wild animal when someone is trying to kill them. A chief is often assumed to be a witch. Even a deceased person is not free from witches, because at the cemetery if a witch captures a person's last breath, the soul, the witch can call the body out of the ground. The witch shrinks the body, takes it home, and stores it in a hanging calabash (gourd).

The concept of witch (which is unlike the historical usage in Christian cultures) varies among African traditional religions. For example, anthropologist Paul Stoller reports that for the Songhay of Mali, "Songhay witches were supposed to eat the souls of their victims. They were the most malevolent force in the Songhay cosmos, continuously causing illness and death along their path." In his training as a sorcerer, Stoller reported that he learned to identify and defeat witches.[10]

A person can become a sorcerer only by giving up a family member to be killed. Any kind of magic or power costs human lives. Sorcerers can see evil in others, foretell future events, prevent childhood illnesses in the village, and protect warriors against revenge from spirits of men they have killed in battle. Most important, they can locate and identify the source of a person's death. Because deaths are not natural but are caused by human designs, the sorcerer serves as the chief homicide investigator. In another role, sorcerers can provide magic to cause the death of an enemy.

The Zulu Peoples of South Africa

Zulu religion and Zulu lives are one; for Zulu peoples all life has religious significance. A settled people, they live in kraals (or corrals—thornbush and stick enclosures of houses and stockyards) and keep cattle. Their formal arrangement of simple houses is reflected in their ordering of personalities of religious significance.

Historical Development

South Africa has about forty million people, most of whom live in cities. Christians are most numerous, followed by Hindus and Muslims. Bantus, including **Zulu,** had occupied much of the country before the seventeenth century, when Dutch settlers arrived. The British fought the Dutch and in 1910 formed the Union of South Africa. Apartheid, the separation of races, which had been unofficial, was

mikishi [mi-ĸɪ-shi] Among the Congolese Basongye, human spirits bent on doing harm. Sorcerers can control them.

Zulu [zoo-loo] A member of the Bantu peoples of southeast Africa. Inhabitants of South Africa.

© Ed Kashi/Corbis

Kraal-Zulu Village. Traditional rondoval houses and cattle kraals in the rural village of Dubazane.

official from 1949 to 1991. In 1994 the first election open to all races was held. The first black president, Nelson Mandela, came to office on May 10, 1994.

Worldview of the Zulu Peoples

umnumzane
[oom-nam-ZAH-ni]
The head of the kraal in Zulu society.

umsamo [oom-SAH-mo]
In Zulu religion, the place where people communicate with ancestors.

diviners [di-VII-nur]
Women who are spirit possessed and know how to discover people's destinies.

herbalist [UR-ba-LIST]
(*izinyanga zemithi*)
Men who prescribe medicine for healing.

The chief of the kraal, who is both headman and priest, lives in the **umnumzane,** the chief house. In his house is an **umsamo,** a place for communing with ancestors through objects of ritual significance. Other houses have similar sacred spaces.[11] The chief is responsible for communing with the important ancestors of the kraal, because ancestors know what is happening among their descendants and can help or hinder them.

Ancestors, a source of power, are souls of people who sought to fulfill their moral obligations. Ancestors of the whole kraal are honored by the chief and all families. Ancestors of each family are honored by the head of the family, using rituals at the sacred place within the house.

Ancestors can help heal patients. Below the chief, **diviners,** who are often women, are assisted by ancestors, who communicate by dream or vision. Diviners diagnose what spiritual powers are at work in patients, so healers can do their work. An **Herbalist (*izinyanga zemithi*)** is often a man who prescribes medicine

© Lindsay Hebberd/CORBIS

African Shaman Holding Whisk. The sangoma 'communicates' with the ancestors and acts as an intermediary between the dead and the living.

for healing. As in other cultures, everyone has some general knowledge, or opinions, on diagnosing and prescribing for patients. Medicine is any power that can change situations. Whether specific or abstract, it is respected.

Responsibilities for dealing with transcendent forces of the heavens fall to specialists known as **izinyanga zezulu,** herders of storms. As the Zulus herd cattle, so the sky specialists herd storms. They serve the god of the sky. On uninhabited, sacred hills, these specialists carry out their functions.

Some Zulu peoples, as do the Basongye, believe the spiritual energies of the universe can be used for purposes that are either beneficial or harmful. Sorcerers cultivate the dark side of the forces of healing employed by diviners and herbalists and use neutral forces for evil ends. An **abathakati** (translated "witch") also uses powers for evil purposes. They are believed to exist, but it is only conjecture as to who such persons are. Failure to honor ancestors may give an abathakati power to twist the ancestors' displeasure into forces of death. Witches are "possessed," sometimes without their knowledge.

Rites of Passage

Rites of passage call attention to moments of greatest religious importance in each person's life. The kraal, as well as the individual and the family, has an interest in keeping spiritual forces properly channeled.

izinyanga zezulu
[iz-in-YAN-ga ze-ZOO-loo]
The deity in Zulu religion who herds weather or sky as boys herd cattle.

abathakati
[u-bah-TAH-kah-ti]
In Zulu society, a person who uses spiritual forces for evil ends. A witch or wizard.

A newborn infant must be bathed in the umsamo and treated with traditional medicine. Because boys have responsibilities for handling cattle, a boy's first milk is from a cow. Mothers must observe many ritual precautions and receive medicine.

Puberty is another time of rituals. Bathing, new clothes, and sacrifices of oxen mark this important event in the lives of young men. The custom of young men being inducted into societies of warriors has less significance now, but these organizations traditionally met the need to be part of an exclusive group.

Marriage is a special time not only for the bride and groom but also for their families. Powerful spiritual forces are at work and must be handled carefully, according to traditions. The prospective groom transfers cattle from his kraal to that of his prospective bride. After receiving permission from the bride's family, the two kraals negotiate the terms of marriage. The groom's father sacrifices an ox to the ancestors, and both families feast. The bride shares gifts with her new family and symbolically leaves the kraal of her ancestors. The bride represents powers of different ancestors, so she must be especially respectful of the ancestors of the new kraal. At first she must cover her face when moving about the new kraal.

Death is also threatening for the kraal community. Ancestors are "brought home" with the **ukubuyisa idlozi rite,** which returns the ancestor's spirit to its rightful place in the kraal. During mourning, all rituals must be carefully observed so the ancestor or other forces do not turn against the kraal community. The death of a chief subjects the whole community to potential harm. The chief's body is honored and buried within the kraal. People must use medicine to protect themselves from harmful forces. The **ihlambo** ceremony involves "washing the spears" by using them in a hunt, and women's hoes are "washed" by digging with them in earth. By killing and eating an ox, the kraal closes the long period of mourning for a chief.

Deities of the Zulu Peoples

The first being was **u mueling angi,** who sent a chameleon to humans with a message that they would live forever. He also sent a lizard with a message that all people would die. Because the lizard arrived first, humans die. The creator god, who once was close to earth, is now so remote that he is not worshiped directly.

The sky "above" is sharply delineated from the earth "below." The Lord of the Sky (**Inkosi Yezulu**) personifies heaven that sends thunder and lightning. Feminine forces of the universe are represented by the Princess of Heaven (**Inkosazana**). The sender of rains for growing crops, she protects women and girls who hoe the crops. Inkosazana also protects them from the dangerous energies associated with human procreation. Contact with birth or death weakens a person with darkness or heaviness (**umnayama**), so women are particularly vulnerable to sorcery and malicious beings.

Humans communicate their desires and respect to deities and ancestors with rituals. Deities, spirits, and ancestors communicate with humans through dreams and visions. Ancestors employ deep sleep (**ubuthongo**). A person can become possessed by a spirit, requiring the services of a diviner (**isangoma**) who can intercede with the spirit world.

The Zulu peoples have well-thought-out patterns of individual, family, and kraal life. They also have a reasoned system explaining how the powers of the universe impinge on their lives. As there is a hierarchy of heaven, so there is a hierarchy on earth. As there are rules for dealing with human powers, so there are rules for dealing with spiritual powers. Traditional rituals and customs maintain

---

ukubuyisa idlozi rite
[oo-KOO-boo-YI-sa id-LOH-si]
The Zulu ritual of bringing home the ancestor after a period of mourning.

ihlambo [ih-LAHM-boh]
The ceremony of washing spears after mourning the death of a Zulu chief.

u mueling angi
[oo-MWE-ling AHN-gi]
In the creation story of Zulus, the first "comer out," followed by humans, animals, and nature.

Inkosi Yezulu
[in-KOH-si ye-ZOO-loo]
In Zulu religion, one name for the god of the sky.

Inkosazana
[in-KOH-sa-ZAH-na]
The Zulu Princess of Heaven, who assists women and girls.

umnayama
[oom-nay-YAH-ma]
Zulu term for a weakened state that makes a person vulnerable to environmental influences.

ubuthongo
[oo-boo-THON-go]
Zulu term for deep sleep in which ancestors can appear.

isangoma [I-san-GO-ma]
A Zulu woman diviner.

the vital balance among the living and their relationships with their ancestors and their deities.

The Yoruba Peoples of Nigeria
Historical Development

Nigeria has about ninety million people. The Hausa, Yoruba, and Ibo groups comprise over half the population. Half the people are Muslims, followed closely by Christians. We know of cultures in the area from 700 B.C.E. In the fifteenth century C.E. Portuguese and British slave traders exploited the area. In 1861 a campaign against slavery began. In 1960, Nigeria gained independence, and in 1963 it formed a republic. Since then the population has been divided by civil war between competing governments.

Primarily in southern Nigeria, the Yoruba peoples have developed an impressive civilization. Their central city, **Ife,** functioned as a city-state. Although their farms provided much of their food, they entered into trade with other peoples. Their trade with the Europeans who came for slave trade and colonization made them vulnerable to harsh treatment.

Worldview of the Yoruba Peoples

The basic unit of Yoruba religion is the household, dominated by the male head of family (*olori ebi*) who is the priest at the family shrine. The village, the town, and major cities are the next levels. The chief (**oba**) conducts sacred rites for the community.

The Yoruba peoples believe the god **Olorun** gave them their fates at creation. Unfortunately, humans have forgotten their fates; through divination they can be learned again. An alter ego of Olorun, **Esu,** functions as both trickster and mediator for humans.

The Yoruba of Ife considered their city particularly sacred, because there the god **Orisha-nla** began creation.[12] On all important matters, a diviner (**aworo**) communicates with Orunmila, the deity of Ife. Like the Zulu, the Yoruba believe other deities, ancestors, and spirits play active roles in the universe and in human lives.

Ancestors are believed to be active in Yoruba lives. Mediation enables the living to receive powerful blessings from ancestors. Prescribed rituals assist in the mediation. At the heart of ritual is a sacrifice, which may be only a prayer or a kola nut (a caffeine-containing nut used as a medium of exchange). A slaughtered animal is a more precious sacrifice, which can serve as food for the gods.

The Yoruba people employ specialists for dealing with deities, orisha, and ancestors. A medium (*elegun*) is anyone possessed by divine powers. A specialist in medicine (*oloogun*) diagnoses and prescribes in curing illnesses. The masked dancers (*egungun*) represent ancestors for all festival and ritual occasions. Mediation between spirits and humans is a regular part of life among the Yoruba.

Community and Individual Responsibilities

Festivals involve the whole community in mediation with deities and ancestors. The Gelede festival celebrates the arrival of spring rains and cools the power of

Ife [IF-fe]
The most sacred city of the Yoruba peoples of Nigeria.

oba [OH-ba]
A chief or king of the Yoruba.

Olorun [OH-lu-roon]
Supreme deity of the sky in Yoruba religion.

Esu [E's-zoo]
A Yoruba god who is amoral; he is a trickster deity and a messenger.

Orisha-nla
[oh-REE-sha-nla]
A Yoruba creation god.

aworo [a-WOH-roh]
A priest of the Yoruba.

Yoruba Head Mask with Crown.

© Davis Factor/CORBIS

female witches. It honors the mothers (**awon iya wa**), who are a collective form of divine energy (**ase**). The deity (**orisha**) Agemo is represented by a chameleon in a festival of kings and priests. Sixteen chief-priests approach the city of Ijebu-Ode, where they are invited by the *oba* Awajale. They mutually acknowledge the powers of kings and priests.

In the town of Oshogbo, thousands of people annually honor the goddess **Oshun.** She is the Great Mother, who helps women have healthy children and brings prosperity. As "my Mother," she controls "our mothers," the *aje,* who are powerful, assertive women (sometimes translated as "witches"). Oshun is the paramount deity of feminine power.[13]

Individuals have particular duties toward various orisha who have claim on them. In each person's head a personal orisha (*oriinun*) represents an ancestral guardian of the soul. In heaven, each person has an *ori* who serves as surety for his or her destiny, its possibilities and limitations.

Deities of the Yoruba Peoples

The hierarchy of deities of the Yoruba is somewhat complicated. Olorun is the primary power of **Orun,** the sky. He is also known as **Olodumare.** His lofty status prevents direct approach, but people can approach him through the orisha. Ancestors, who occupy a somewhat lower level, are also subjects of veneration. According to African scholar Bolaji Idowu, each person has a double or guardian spirit.[14]

The earth is *Aiye,* the home of humans, animals, and *omoraiye,* "the children of the world," who are responsible for sorcery and witchcraft. Communications between earth and heaven are facilitated by orisha, such as **Obatala.** He created earth and brought to it sixteen people already created by Olorun. Among the Yoruba, physically unfortunate people are sacred. At Ile-Ife, **Odudwa** is the deity credited with correcting Olorun's errors. Orisha-nla is head of the "white gods," (named not for their skin color but for their white clothes). He prohibits drinking palm wine and associating with dogs.

The Yoruba have a hierarchy of gods, spirits, and ancestors, and theirs is a unified universe permeated by divine energy (*ase*). Religion is their way of channeling the energy for beneficial rather than dreadful results.

Worldview: Common Features of Religions in Sub-Saharan Africa

We have briefly examined four examples of sub-Saharan religion. Each illustrates how a group of people organize their lives around careful handling of energies in the universe. Powers of ancestors and of spirits above them in the hierarchy have

awon iya wa
[u-WON I-YAH wa]
Yoruba term for "the mothers."

ase [AH-se]
Spiritual forces of the Yoruba; divine energy.

orisha [oh-REE-sha]
Various Yoruba spirits.

Oshun [OH-shun]
Yoruba mother goddess.

Orun [OH-roon]
In Yoruba religion, the supreme king; the sky. Also known as Olodumare.

Olodumare
[oh-LOH-du-MA-ree]
In Yoruba religion, supreme deity of the sky. Also called Olorun.

to be channeled into good or evil purposes. All life is ritualized to maintain beneficial relationships between people "below" and the divine "above."

The Absolute

Sub-Saharan peoples are not animists, thinking that all things contain spirits, or polytheists, believing that many gods administer the world in a disorganized, unpredictable fashion. Some peoples, such as the Yoruba, honor and fear one creator god; others honor one god who rules over a hierarchy of gods.

Although they respect a transcendent creator god, many peoples are more concerned with deities who actively affect their survival (such as the supreme gods of the sky, Olorun of the Yoruba and Inkosi Yezulu of the Zulu). The female principle of the universe and women's reproductive role may also be honored with deities such as Inkosazana, the Zulu's Princess of Heaven. These central deities reign over lesser spiritual beings that are responsible for the smooth functioning of heaven and societies. The 401 orisha of the Yoruba living on the road to heaven are examples of these demigods. In addition, ancestors guard and guide their descendants.

The World

The beginning of the world or of humans is an important story in every African religion. Other stories teach how to use the energies "above" or "below." The world of sub-Saharan peoples is filled with energies that people can use for beneficial or destructive purposes. Life can be good or bad; resources can be bountiful or scarce. Although life is not so good that people would choose to live forever, it is not so bad that they would shorten their lives in order to become ancestors. Eventually, ancestors can be reincarnated.

Humans

For the sub-Saharan peoples, the soul or spirit is the essential part of a person, but the body is also good and useful. After death, the person disassociates from the body. Some cultures also consider a person's shadow or their conscience a separate entity. People with unusual physical characteristics, such as twins or albinos, are thought by some to have unusual powers.

The Problem for Humans

The Zulu and Yoruba peoples believe each human being is assigned a personal destiny. The gods know the destiny, but the person has forgotten it and can only rediscover it with the help of divination. Priests and sorcerers can help alter destinies somewhat in order to ensure a more acceptable outcome. The powers of ancestors can affect the living. Neglected or offended ancestors can cause suffering or death, but ancestors can also be an important source of assistance.

The Solution for Humans

Communications between heaven and earth are essential to proper functioning of societies. In some sub-Saharan cultures, kings, priests, diviners, or sorcerers are mediators between the energies "above" and "below," and rituals of mediation

Obatala [OH-bah-TUH-lu] Creator of earth, according to the Yoruba, who brought to it sixteen people created by Olorun.

Odudwa [oh-DOO-doo-wah] A Yoruba creation god associated with the city of Ife.

can ensure harmony between heaven and earth. In the absence of a dream or vision, an individual may consult one of these mediators. Through divination, people can recover memory of their destiny, and through sacrifice, they can alter some aspect of that destiny. Victims of misdirected powers can employ a sorcerer for defense.

Rituals and Symbols

Sub-Saharan people have many rituals and symbols because mediation with spiritual powers is essential. All activities of life are filled with prescribed steps to cultivate favor and avoid the wrath of spirits. Among African peoples, rites of passage are of major importance.

Masks are symbols of deities, spirits, and ancestors. Except for creator gods, personalities of the upper world manifest themselves on earth through masks and other dedicated symbols.

Life after Death

Africans generally believe the soul or spirit lives on after death. The Basongye believe that a sorcerer can capture a person's soul even after death and use it badly. A particularly good person may become an honored ancestor or a minor deity.

Relationship with Other Religions

Christianity, Islam, and Judaism each have many adherents in Africa, especially in large cities. In many regions, however, rites of traditional African religions have influenced the rites of Christianity and Islam, and the traditional religions have also absorbed some influences from Christianity and Islam.

The diverse peoples of Africa celebrate different religions, but, in general, they experience their universe as a meeting place of humans and spiritual powers. At the beginning of the twenty-first century, people outside Africa are beginning to appreciate the sophistication of the indigenous religions. Alone or in conjunction with other religions, traditional African religions have made rich contributions to the perpetual drama of world religions.

The ancient Egyptians believed that although the body was entombed, the soul traveled to another world for judgment and either reward or punishment. Deities presided over each stage of travel and over the destination of the soul.

According to many traditional sub-Saharan religions, ancestors hover near the village where they lived in their bodies, and they can be influenced to reward or punish people in the community of the living. Diviners or other individuals with secret knowledge can cause ancestors to bless or harm their descendants in the community. Ancestors send diviners communications through dreams or visions.

Every religion has something to teach about life after death. As you read this text, consider how each religion agrees with or differs from the beliefs of the African religions. Where are their teachings in agreement and where do they differ? As a personal project, rather than an academic one, you might make some tentative attempts to describe what happens after the death of the body.

CONSIDER THIS

Life after Death

Having studied religions of the Americas and of Africa, we turn now to the subcontinent of India. In this area of South Asia, we find religions that developed more than three thousand years ago. Most still influence the lives of millions in India and in other Asian countries. Our first consideration will be the family of religions that has given India a reputation as the mother of religions. The next chapter focuses on one of those religions, Hinduism.

VOCABULARY

abathakati [u-bah-TAH-kah-ti]
akh or ikhu [AHK]
Amon-Re [AH-mun-ray]
ankh [angk]
ase [AH-se]
Aton [AHT-un]
awon iya wa [a-WON I-YAH wa]
aworo [a-WOH-roh]
ba [BAH]
diviners [di-VII-nurs]
Efile Mukulu [E-fu-le mu-KOO-loo]
Esu [E's-zoo]
Hathor [HAH-thor]
Herbalist [UR-ba-LIST]
Horus [HOH-us]
Ife [IF-fe]
ihlambo [ih-LAHM-boh]

Inkosazana [in-KOH-sa-ZAH-na]
Inkosi Yezulu [in-KOH-si ye-zoo-loo]
isangoma [I-san-GO-ma]
Isis [II-sis]
izinyanga zezulu
[iz-in-YAN-ga ze-zoo-loo]
ka [KA]
Kafilefile [kah-FI-le-FI-le]
kikudu [ki-KOO-doo]
mankishi [man-KI-shi]
Mayet [MU-yut]
mikishi [mi-KI-shi]
Mut [MUT]
Nubians [NOO-bee-ans]
oba [OH-ba]
Obatala [OH-bah-TUH-lu]
Odudwa [oh-DOO-doo-wah]

Olodumare [oh-LOH-du-MA-ree]
Olorun [OH-lu-roon]
orisha [oh-REE-sha]
Orisha-nla [oh-REE-sha-nla]
Orun [OH-roon]
Oshun [OH-shun]
Osiris [oh-SI-ris]
Seth [seth]
ubuthongo [oo-boo-THON-go]
ukubuyisa idlozi rite
[oo-KOO-boo-YI-sa id-LOH-si]
u mueling angi
[oo-MWE-ling-AHN-gi]
umnayama [oom-nay-YAH-ma]
umnumzane [oom-nam-ZAH-ni]
umsamo [oom-SAH-mo]
Zulu [zoo-loo]

QUESTIONS FOR REVIEW

1. How did Egyptian religion describe judgment after death?
2. In African religions, what is the most effective force against evil?
3. How do Zulu beliefs about death differ from those of the ancient Egyptians?
4. Name and identify some of the most important indigenous gods of the Yoruba.
5. Describe how African women participate in indigenous African religions.
6. Describe some traditional rites of passage of the Zulu peoples.
7. How does each indigenous African religion we have discussed define and deal with evil forces?
8. How does each African religion discussed here deal with means of salvation?
9. Why might Zulu peoples see death differently from ancient Egyptians?
10. How does divining work? Is it a positive activity for society? (Explain.)

QUESTIONS FOR DISCUSSION

1. How can African religions affect world beliefs and practices through Christianity and Islam?
2. What differences do you find between the religions of Africa and the religions of the Americas. Are there any similarities?
3. Why do you think so many people have been interested in learning about the Yoruba religion?
4. Why did the ancient Egyptians not have more influence on sub-Saharan Africa?
5. Discuss similarities and differences between the Powhatans (see Chapter 1) and the Basongye.

NOTES

1. For geologic history of Africa, see John Reader, *Africa: A Biography of the Continent* (New York: Knopf, 1998), p. 193.
2. Roland Oliver, *The African Experience* (Boulder, CO: Westview Press, 2000).
3. H. Frankfort, *Ancient Egyptian Religion* (New York: Harper & Row, 1948), pp. 8–14.
4. Barbara S. Lesco, *The Great Goddesses of Egypt* (Norman: University of Oklahoma Press, 1999), p. 136; Ian Shaw, ed., *The Oxford History of Ancient Egypt* (Oxford, UK: Oxford University Press, 2000), pp. 239–240; Nigel Strudwick and Helen Strudwick, *Thebes in Egypt* (Ithaca, NY: Cornell University Press, 1999), p. 45.
5. David Kinsley, *The Goddesses' Mirror* (Albany: State University of New York Press, 1989), p. 166.
6. E. A. Wallis Budge, *Osiris*, vol. 1 (New Hyde Park, NY: University Books, 1961), p. 216.
7. Ibid., pp. 338–339.
8. Alan P. Merriam, *An African World: The Basongye Village of Lupupa Ngye* (Bloomington: Indiana University Press, 1974).
9. Ibid., p. 111.
10. Benjamin C. Ray, *African Religions: Symbol, Ritual, and Ceremony* (Upper Saddle River, NJ: Prentice Hall, 2000), p. 58.
11. E. Thomas Lawson, *Religions of Africa* (Hagerstown, MD: Torch, 1985), p. 19; For background information on ancestors, rites of passage, and so on, see John S. Mbiti, *African Religions and Philosophy*, 2nd ed. (Oxford, UK: Heinemann International, 1990), chaps. 9–14.
12. Lawson, p. 54; For background in Nigerian religions, particularly that of the Yoruba, see also William Bascomb, *The Yoruba of Southwestern Nigeria* (New York: Holt and Winston, 1969); R. E. Dennett, *Nigerian Studies* (London: Cass, 1968); J. S. Eades, *The Yoruba Today* (Cambridge, UK: Cambridge University Press, 1980), chap. 6.
13. Ray, *African Religions*, p. 35.
14. E. Bolaji Idowu, *African Traditional Religion, A Definition* (London: S.C.M. Press, 1973), p. 5.

READINGS

Adekson, Mary Olufunmilayo. *The Yoruba, Traditional Healers of Nigeria.* New York: Routledge, 2003.

Bascomb, William. *Ifa Divination: Communication between Gods and Men in West Africa.* Bloomington: Indiana University Press, 1969.

_____. *The Yoruba of Southwestern Nigeria.* New York: Holt, Rinehart and Winston, 1969.

Budge, E. A. Wallis. *Egyptian Religion.* New Hyde Park, NY: University Books, 1959.

Fage, J. D., with William Tordoff. *A History of Africa.* London: Routledge, 2002.

Hare, Tom. *Remembering Osiris.* Stanford, CA: Stanford University Press, 1999.

Idowu, E. Bolaji. *African Traditional Religion: A Definition.* London: S.C.M. Press, 1973.

Lawson, E. Thomas. *Religions of Africa.* Hagerstown, MD: Torch, 1985.

Lesco, Barbara S. *The Great Goddesses of Egypt.* Norman: University of Oklahoma Press, 1999.

MacGaffey, Wyatt. *Religion and Society in Central Africa: The Ba Kongo of Lower Zaire.* Chicago: University of Chicago Press, 1986.

Mbiti, John S. *African Religions and Philosophy,* 2nd ed. Oxford, UK: Heinemann International, 1990.

Oliver, Roland. *The African Experience.* Boulder, CO: Westview Press, 2000.

Oliver, Roland, and Anthony Atmore. *Medieval Africa, 1500–1800.* Cambridge, UK: Cambridge University Press, 2001.

Parrinder, Geoffrey. *African Traditional Religion.* Westport, CT: Greenwood Press, 1970.

Ray, Benjamin C. *African Religions: Symbol, Ritual, and Ceremony.* Upper Saddle River, NJ: Prentice Hall, 2000.

_____. *Myth, Ritual, and Kingship in Buganda.* New York: Oxford University Press, 1991.

Strudwick, Nigel, and Helen Strudwick. *Thebes in Egypt.* Ithaca, NY: Cornell University Press, 1999.

Shaw, Ian, ed. *The Oxford History of Ancient Egypt.* Oxford, England: Oxford University Press, 2000.

Turner, Harold W. *Religious Innovation in Africa: Collected Essays on New Religious Movements.* Boston: Hall, 1979.

Vasunia, Phiroze. *The Gift of the Nile: Hellenizing Egypt from Aeschylus to Alexander.* Berkeley: University of California Press, 2001.

Whisson, Michael G., and Martin West, eds. *Religion and Social Change in Southern Africa.* Cape Town, South Africa: David Philip, and London: Rex Collings, 1975.

Wilkinson, Richard H. *The Complete Gods and Goddesses of Ancient Egypt.* New York: Thames and Hudson, 2003.

Zahan, Dominique. *The Religion, Spirituality and Thought of Traditional Africa.* Chicago: University of Chicago Press, 1979.

BASIC TENETS OF RELIGIONS OF AFRICA—Significant Beings

Religions of Africa			
Ancient Egyptians			
Devourer	Sun Amon-Re, Aton		Hathor
Seth	Isis	Osiris	Horus
Basongye of the Congo			
Kafilefile (evil deity)		Efile Mukulu (beneficent deity)	
Zulu of South Africa			
Inkosi Yezulu (god of the sky)			
Inkosazana (princess of heaven)			
Izinyanga Zezulu (weather deity)			
Yoruba of Nigeria			
Obatala (creator of earth)			
Olorun (supreme deity of the sky)			
Orunmila (god of Ifa divination)			

Except for Egyptian religion, most of our knowledge of the religions of Africa and the religions of the Americas comes from the Common Era (C.E.). The foundations of the religions of India, except for Sikhism, precede the Common Era. We have little knowledge of the third millennium B.C.E. of India, the period of the early pyramids of Egypt, we have some knowledge of the second millennium, the time of Abraham and Moses of the Jewish Bible, and a lot of information about the first millennium, the influence our future lives, bringing reward or punishment.

A third concept, caste, has also helped shape the religions of India. One is born according to one's karma in prior lives. Hindus and Jains regard caste as a fact of life. Buddhists and Sikhs ignored caste distinctions among their followers, but they did not seek to abolish the caste system of India. Now, in official India, distinctions of caste have been weakened to the point that even the lowest castes participate in government leadership.

Mohandas K. Gandhi, Sri Aurobindo Ghose, Rabindranath Tagore, and Jawaharlal Nehru stimulated fresh expressions of Hinduism in independent India.

From India, some of the greatest religious insights of humans have arisen, and some of the richest traditions have endured. We turn now to the four great religions that have sprouted, taken root, and grown to maturity in the fertile soil of India.

Religions Arising in India II

time since David, Solomon, and the great prophets of Judaism. Early in the first millennium B.C.E. in India, two powerful concepts took permanent root: karma and reincarnation. We have already encountered in religions of the Americas the concept of a permanent soul reborn in a new body after the death of the old body, so we know this concept was not confined to India. In India reincarnation has been a powerful belief of three religions and a stimulus for development of a fourth religion, Buddhism. Hinduism, Jainism, and Sikhism retain the belief in full form. Buddhism, however, retains the concept of karma that underlies the religions of Hinduism, Jainism, and Sikhism: All thoughts and deeds

In religions arising in India, these powerful concepts have guided some personalities who have inspired respect and awe. Peoples far beyond the borders of India still imitate and worship Siddhartha Gautama, the Buddha. Three million Jains of India regard Mahavira, as their role model for release from the Wheel of Rebirth. Sikhs praise Nanak for his faith that intended to transcend the separation of Hindus and Muslims. Although later literature supersedes the early personalities in Hinduism, millions of Hindus honor multiple gods of the Veda, such as Indra and Agni, and later gods of popular Hinduism, such as Shiva and Vishnu. In the twentieth century, personalities such as

CHAPTER 3

Hinduism

*Barbara Stoller Miller. *Bhagavad-Gita*. New York: Columbia
University Press, 1986. 8:3–6, pp. 77–78.

**Unless otherwise noted, information in the Areas of
Concentration in the Overview of each chapter is from
Encyclopedia Britannica Book of the Year for 2004
(Chicago: Encyclopedia Britannica, Inc., 2004).

In the second millennium B.C.E., along the banks
of the Indus River, Hinduism began with the
dynamic encounter of two very different peoples.
The darker-skinned inhabitants of well-developed
cities of the Indus were overwhelmed by the
lighter-skinned Aryans who were nomads from the
area of Persia, and areas to the west. A priestly
caste developed to tend the sacrificial fires that sent
pleasant aromas to the heavens. Worshipers sang
hymns, performed rituals, and established
distinctions between sacred and profane. Over
time, after the sacred sounds and actions had
become engrained in society, inspired people gave
them written form and permanent status as the
Veda, the required guide of every Hindu.

Vital religion, however, ferments and expands,
its popular elixir overflowing the boundaries of one
caste or one set of rituals. Hinduism inspired gurus
such as Yajnavalkya and Uddalaka Aruni, men who
were revered by their wives, sons, and pupils as
revealers of the Great Soul. The Mahabharata,
including the beloved Bhagavad Gita, filled with
stories of deities and their teachings, inspired
ordinary men and women. Manu guided younger
people into the more established rules for good
Hindus. Meanwhile, masses of people paid homage
to male and female deities whose images they
could see, touch, bathe, and feed. Ascetics and
pilgrims immersed themselves in the great rivers of
India, such as the Ganges, and walked the river
banks back to their sources in the lofty Himalayas.
In the twentieth century, devotion to faith
sometimes meant breaking the yoke of the British
stronghold on India. It also included separating
from the people along the Indus who had
embraced a more recent faith from Arabia: Islam.
Hindu leaders against the British government, such

A Hindu Temple. Sri Mhamariamma Temple, Malaysia, Kuala
Lumpur.

as M. K. Gandhi and J. Nehru, having served their time in British jails in India, in 1947 became leaders of a new India where Hinduism is still the dominant religion. The Sikhs have continued to press their case for a separate state, but some Jains, Muslims, Christians, and Zoroastrians have been contented to remain as minorities among Hindus. Although Hinduism is no longer found in strength along the Indus River, now part of the Muslim state of Pakistan, it predominates in India and extends to those countries where its emigrants have established new homes.

Of the one billion people of India, 81 percent are Hindus. For comparison, the next largest group, Muslims, are 12 percent. Outside India, Hindus are established citizens in many countries, including the United Kingdom and the United States.

Hinduism began in the Indus Valley (now in Pakistan) about 3000 B.C.E. and continues to flourish today. What began in a Neolithic agricultural society has stayed alive and is now even integrated into Internet technology. Hinduism, then, is a very old religion that has continued to change with new opportunities.

Because Hinduism has over 830 million adherents, we can expect to find many different ways of understanding it. Over three thousand years, even scholars and teachers of the Hindu way of life have differed on the most essential points of their faith. Anyone who wants to understand Hinduism, then, must evaluate whose views of Hinduism will receive priority. We begin with a look at its historical development.

Although Hindu scholars and teachers do not always agree on their interpretations of Hinduism, they do agree that foreigners cannot grasp the depths of their language and culture. Hindus may be comfortable pointing out similarities between their traditions and those of outsiders, but they are seldom comfortable with outsiders making quick and easy comparisons with Western religions and philosophies. Hindus have particularly rejected accounts of "orientalists," scholars from the United Kingdom and Europe who studied languages of India and offered interpretations from a "scientific" point of view, largely ignoring Hindu evaluations of their own faith and practice.

Both Hindu and non-Hindu writers would agree, however, that presenting the vast riches of Hindu tradition in the limited space of a world religions text is a formidable task. Even the best Hindu scholars would be challenged in deciding what to introduce and what to omit. The non-Hindu approaching from the view of comparative world religions may have a slight advantage. If we ask the questions we ask of all religions and listen to Hindu answers, perhaps we can overcome some of the limitations of orientalists and reap some of the rewards of Hinduism. In recent years in colleges and universities of North America, a kind of agreement has emerged on how to present Hinduism. We will honor that informal agreement of pattern, trusting that in some way it will compensate for not offering the selectivity of individual Hindu teachers. Our goal, of course, is to introduce readers to Hinduism, hoping that they will continue to study, over their lifetimes, its richer varieties.

Historical Development: The Origins of Hinduism

Hinduism formed before anyone kept written records. Oral traditions later preserved in the **Vedas** and artifacts studied by archaeologists provide sources for reconstructing the initial stages of the Hindu religion. Along the banks of the Indus River, in Pakistan, a **Dravidian** people lived in cities. Twentieth-century archaeological excavations in Mohenjo-Daro reveal a large city with houses, underground plumbing, and other refinements of a developed urban population. Some figurines indicate a concern with human fertility and other forces of nature. Also discovered was a tank, or large pool, similar to ones now used in Hindu temples. We do not know the full nature of their religion.

About 1000 B.C.E., **Aryans** migrated into India. Of Indo-European background, they traveled through what is now Iran, bringing with them the language and

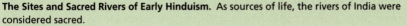

The Sites and Sacred Rivers of Early Hinduism. As sources of life, the rivers of India were considered sacred.

Vedas [VAY-daz] Knowledge or wisdom. Scriptures of the Hindus.

Dravidians [drah-VID-e-uns] Dark-skinned inhabitants of India. They differed from the light-skinned Aryans who entered from the Northwest.

Aryans [AHR-yuns] Indo-Europeans who entered the Indus Valley prior to 1000 B.C.E. They expressed their evolving religion in the hymns of the Rig-Veda.

religious concepts of Persia and Western lands. The Aryans (noble people) were herders, nomads who drove their animals ahead of them. Their deities were the natural powers of heaven and earth. The Aryans honored their gods by sacrificing animals and sharing the flesh with them. The god's portion was sent through smoke rising from the sacrificial fire; worshipers ate their portions during the service. The gods, or *devas*, were shining ones who represented things that are good for humans. *Asuras* were evil powers, representing things harmful to humans. Religion had an ethical concern to keep things on the right path, for good to be ascendant over evil.

As these Aryans mixed with the native peoples, they shared customs, traditions, rites, symbols, and myths. Each contributed and each received. The earliest hymns of Hinduism reveal a worship that retained many Aryan practices. Later worship of Shiva reflects traditions of the Dravidians. Although scholars cannot say exactly when Hinduism began, they believe it developed in an early period of interaction between Aryans and Dravidians.

During this period, groups and strata of Hindu society began to form. One theory is that the organization of Hindu society began as a result of **varna,** color. The invaded peoples were dark; the invading Aryans were light. Because the conquerors were lighter, light color was superior to dark. Some Hindus, however, see it differently. They think stratification developed because of psychological preferences. The Aryans were militant, active, ruling types, and the invaded peoples were settled urbanites who preferred artisan and merchant activities. It is difficult for scholars to determine which is right, for in the early centuries stratification was neither rigid nor universally recognized. The firm **caste** system of India emerged later.

Shruti and Smriti: Revelation and Scriptures

Because *revelation* is that which has been "heard," and the *scriptures* are writings that record what has been heard, we take a moment here to describe how various forms of **shruti,** Hindu sacred writings, are related.[1] The Vedas, the oldest part of shruti, have four collections of scriptures: the Rig-Veda, the Sama-Veda, the Yajur-Veda, and the Atharva-Veda.

The second part of the shruti includes the **Brahmanas,** or "explanations of sacrifices," and the **Aranyakas,** or "forest treatises," which are the later parts of the Brahmanas. The **Upanishads,** "sitting near teachers," are considered **Vedanta,** the "end of the Vedas." Later Upanishads are considered **Agamas,** as ancient and as authoritative as the Vedas.

Shruti is distinguished from **smriti,** or "that which has been remembered."[2] Among the smriti writings are the laws of **Manu** and the **Itihasa-Purana,** which includes the epics of the **Mahabharata** and the **Ramayana.** We will look at these examples of Hindu literature later in the chapter.

The Four Collections of the Vedas

The Rig-Veda is the best known of the Vedas. With it, three other collections, *samhitas,* comprise the Vedas. The Yajur-Veda is a collection of litanies, prayers, and prose dedications used in devotions. The Sama-Veda repeats some of the hymns of the Rig-Veda in its collections of chants to be used by priests in the soma sacrifices. It helps purify the listeners and prepare them for receiving the spirit soma. The Artharva-Veda reflects the concerns of people who have to wrestle day

---

varna [VAR-na]
Color once associated with caste.

caste [CAST]
In Hinduism, the permanent social group into which a person is born and which determines one's social and religious obligations.

shruti [SHROO-ti]
Hindu sacred writings, such as the Vedas, based on "heard," or revealed, knowledge.

Brahmanas [BRAH-muh-nuhs]
Commentaries and manuals instructing priests in rites associated with Vedas.

Aranyakas [ah-RAN-yu-kuz]
Shruti interpreting ritual of the Vedas for ascetics living in the forest.

Upanishads [oo-PA-ne-shads]
"Sitting near teachers"; the last of the Vedas.

Vedanta [ve-DAHN-da]
The "end of the Vedas." Schools of philosophy founded on teachings of Upanishads.

Agamas [AH-ga-mas]
Scriptures from tradition that divide according to deity.

smriti [SMRI-ti]
Writings based on what human authors "remembered" of revelations to Hindus; less authoritative than revealed scriptures.

Manu [MAH-noo]
In Hinduism, the first man.

by day with the emotions of jealousy, lust, hatred, and fear. Charms and spells are written for ordinary people to use to improve their chances for decent life in a hostile environment.

By preserving the Vedas, the Hindus have retained something for everyone, a vital ingredient for literature that is to remain alive for each new generation. The Laws of Manu, 2.6, state that the root of religion is the entire Vedas.

Gods of the Rig-Veda

The Vedas offer varying explanations of beginnings of reality. Many of the passages speak of different gods active in the functioning of the universe. The gods of the Rig-Veda inspired worship through sacrifices. Devotees had a priest, a **Brahmin,** perform exact rites that may have seemed simple but were profound in their influence. Three pits of fire, representing earth, air, and sky were dug; another pit was dug for utensils and offerings. Valuable items, such as vegetables, flesh, and clarified butter (ghee) were offered to deities on behalf of worshipers. Skilled priests influenced the universe to favor worshipers.

AGNI

The *Purusha Sukta* describes **Purusha** as the All from which, through sacrifice, parts of the universe are formed. Gods also arise from Purusha. One of the gods arising from Purusha is **Agni,** the fire used in sacrifice. Here are verses from a hymn to Agni in the Rig-Veda:

> Book I. Hymn 1.
> 1. Agni I call on, who is placed at the fore, the divine ministrant of the sacrifice, the invoker, who bestows the most gifts.
> 2. Agni is worthy of being called on by former seers and present: may he bring hither the gods!
> 3. Through Agni may he obtain wealth, prosperity, every day, splendid and abounding in heroic sons!
> 4. O Agni, the sacrifice and work of the sacrifice, which you encircle on every side—that alone goes unto the gods.
> 5. May Agni, the invoker who has the powers of a sage, true and most brilliant in glory, come hither, as god with the gods![3]

INDRA

A quarter of the verses of the Rig-Veda are dedicated to the praise of **Indra,** who is considered the most important deity of the hymns. He slays demons, such as Vritra, and hateful forces, but he preserves humans and gods. He is a warrior who fights for the Aryans against the aboriginal Dasas. He quenches his thirst with Soma, an invigorating drink.

> Book I. Hymn 32.
> 5. With the thunderbolt, his great weapon, Indra slew Vṛtra, the arch-Vṛtra, the shoulderless: like a tree-trunk split asunder with an axe, the serpent lay flat on the ground.
> 6. For infatuated, like one who has not fought before, he challenged the great hero, distresser of the mighty, the onrusher. He did not survive the impact of his weapons: faceless from the clash, he whose enemy was Indra was completely crushed.

Itihasa-Purana
[iti-HAHT-sah poo-RAH-na]
Ancient mythological texts, including Mahabharata, Ramayana, and 18 *puranas* honoring Brahma, Shiva, and Vishnu.

Mahabharata
[ma-HAH-BAH-ra-ta]
Epic poem featuring activities of the god Krishna.

Ramayana
[rah-MAH-ya-na]
An epic of the ideal man, Rama, and Sita, the ideal woman.

Brahmin [BRAH-men]
In Hinduism, the name of the highest, priestly caste. After the Aryans were settled in India, the priests became more important than the warriors of the Kshatriya caste.

Purusha [PU-roo-sha]
Primal spirit, or soul of an individual.

Agni [AG-ni]
Fire used in sacrifice. The Vedic god of fire.

Indra [IN-dra]
A god of the Rig-Veda. The creator and ruler of the universe.

11. The waters whose master was a Dāsa, whose guardian was the serpent, had been penned up, as were the cows by Pani. Having slain Vṛtra, Indra opened up the orifice of the waters which had been closed.

15. Indra is king of what moves and what has gone to rest, and of the tamed and the horned—he who has the thunderbolt in his arm. He indeed rules as king of the peoples: as a felly the spokes, he encompasses them.[4]

SOMA

After Indra and Agni, **Soma,** the deified plant, is the most important god in the Rig-Veda. Its background can be found among the Haoma of the ancient Persians; perhaps its use came with European immigrants to India.

Book VIII. Hymn 48.
1. I, of good understanding, have partaken of the sweet potion, the well-minded, the best finder of bliss, which all the gods and mortals, calling it "honey," seek.
2. When you have proceeded within, you shall become Aditi, the appeaser of divine wrath. Enjoying the companionship of Indra, O Indu, as an obedient span of horses the wagon-pole, may you promote us to wealth hereafter.
3. We have drunk the Soma. We have become immortal. We have gone to the light. We have found the gods. What shall hostility do to us now? What, O immortal, shall the malice of mortal do?[5]

VARUNA

Varuna, the god of the sky, is another of the more important deities of the Rig-Veda. The protector of Truth, the principal force of the universe, is **Rita,** which orders all things, preventing Chaos. The principle of order arose from chaos, the celestial waters, every drop of which contained Varuna.

Book VII. Hymn 87.
1. Varuṇa traced the paths of the sun. Forth went the floods of the rivers to the sea, as does a charger unpenned to the mares. Conforming to the Ṛta, he has made the mighty courses for the days.
2. Your breath, the wind, roared and roared throughout the atmosphere, like a wild beast in search of fodder in the pasture. Within these two mighty, lofty worlds of your manifestations, Varuṇa, are dear.

5. The three heavens are deposited within him, the three earths below, forming an arrangement of six. The wise king Varuṇa has made this golden swing in the sky for himself, in order to shine.
6. Like the day, Varuṇa has settled down to the sea—like the bright drop, a powerful beast. He, for whom there is profound praise, the traverser of the atmosphere, who has dominion over the sea—he is king of that which is.
7. May we be free of wrong toward Varuṇa, who will have mercy upon him who has done any wrong—we prospering in Aditi's ordinances! Protect us always with well-being![6]

MITRA

Mitra—closely allied with Varuṇa—personifies an agreement or contract. Individuals invoked his name as they entered binding agreements. Perhaps his name appeared later in Mithra worship, devotion to promise-keeping.

Soma [sow-ma]
The Hindu deity of a plant that is intoxicating. In the Vedas, soma was used in worship.

Varuna [va-roo-na]
The Rig-Veda god of the high-arched sky.

Rita [ri-ta]
The Hindu god of order and principles.

Mitra [mi-tra]
A deity of the Vedas. A god of faithfulness and promise-keeping.

Book III. Hymn 59.

1. Mitra, being called, brings about agreements among people. Mitra sustains earth and heaven. Mitra watches with eye unwinking over the tillers. To Mitra pour an oblation rich in ghee![7]

The Brahmanas and Aranyakas

Those who want to understand the meaning of the Vedas for early Hindus without reading into them experiences of later centuries and cultures must turn to the Brahmanas for their interpretations. These commentaries, which began to appear about 800 B.C.E., to guide priests in their sacrifices, helped worshipers appreciate the deeper meanings and traditions of the rituals. Priests, however, began to encourage the belief that correct sacrifice, rather than the whim of deities, brought desired results. The Brahmanas not only provide access to the theology of the Vedic period but also understanding of how priests gained increased status in society.

Careful attention to details made the rituals of the priests effective. The Satapatha Brahmana instructs priests how to set up the Vedic sacrifices by building three fires, whose essence is Agni. Besides gathering combustibles, the priest also pours water on the lines of the fireplaces. The text teaches that water is the female element that joins with the male element, Agni, in procreation of food for the world.

The Aranyakas are the last part of the Brahmanas. These forest treatises sometimes teach practices that require special tutoring from a guru, for they are too esoteric for individual seekers. Some of the Aranyakas are referred to as Upanishads.

The Upanishads

Some Hindus branched out from the tradition of the Brahmins and the Vedas. They never denied these traditions, but they did go beyond them. They explored other paths of speculation about the universe, and they concentrated their investigations on the place of humans in it. Humanity is a gateway to the cosmos. As **Brahman** is behind the changes of the universe, so **Atman** is behind changes in the individual. Atman, which is essentially Brahman, can be found sustaining the core of the individual.

The experience of Atman and Brahman as different is based on **Maya,** illusion. The two may be differentiated in speaking, for that is their appearance. In reality, they are essentially one. The Vedas teach that sacrifices of meat and vegetables bring harmony between gods and humans; the Upanishads seek a sacrifice of many psychological aspects to unite the Atman in humans with Brahman, the absolute of the universe.

Many Hindus look on the Upanishads as natural developments of thoughts already suggested in the Vedas. According to their theory, no social upheavals were necessary to bring about an evolution of religious thought. Outsiders suggest that the Upanishads developed as a result of some castes rebelling against the rigid Brahmin control of all life. In the Upanishads, there is considerable speculation about the nature of the universe without agreement among various gurus. On the whole, the Upanishads have a common spirit of inquiry. Their answers are not all the same, but they tend to be similar.

Another theory is that the Upanishads began in response to an increasing belief that humans die not only at the end of this life but also at the end of the next

Brahman [bram-MUN]
In Hinduism, the name of the highest deity, the Absolute.

Atman [AHT-man]
The essence of Brahman that is present in individuals. The universal self.

Maya [MAH-ya]
Appearance or illusion; power of creation.

life. Wendy O'Flaherty states that "the theory of rebirth does not appear in the Vedas; but the theory of re-*death* appears at a very early stage indeed."[8] The pleasant prospects of living another life, an idea that brought comfort in the sadness of death, was balanced with the dismal thought of having to die another death. How many cycles of birth and death would an individual have to face? What caused the cycle of births and deaths? Was there a way to break free from these animal existences? As the strengths of these fears increased during the period of the Upanishads, so did the solutions offered by spiritual teachers.

The Upanishads began as oral tradition. In the period between 800 and 300 B.C.E., several Upanishads were saved in writing. As a body of literature, they offer ways that religion can supplement other practices of the Vedas.

The Gurus

The **guru,** or teacher of the Upanishads, is more seer than prophet or priest. Gurus are not fortune tellers nor do they warn of wrath from the gods that will certainly befall the unfaithful. Neither do they officiate at rituals, bringing together gods and humans. They are thinkers whose insights and reasoning lead others to believe that they have been illumined by the gods. The gurus present thinking that is neither cold logic nor warmed-over principles; their insights and explanations are warmed by a personality illumined by divine light. A guru's student finds the teacher more than human; the student, at least, sees in the teacher the very presence of the divine. The guru's words, then, are akin to the words of the divine—truth through personality. Their offering made to the gods is not external or material—it is the offering of the very soul and mind.

Some gurus of the Upanishads were married. Some of them were depicted as teaching their sons or wives. Many of them lived ascetic lives, having no more use of riches than did Socrates; indeed, they went beyond him in renouncing rich food and intoxicating drinks. Wealth for gurus is knowledge—the certainty of the soul's relationship with God.

One famous guru of the Upanishads is Yajnavalkya. In one scene, he discusses death with his wife, Maitreyi. As he prepares to go away and dwell in the forest, he proposes to leave her with property. But she does not want property; she wants knowledge of immortality. Yajnavalkya patiently lists many things that humans hold dear and then explains that each is dear only because it has the Self in it. The being behind all these changes is pure knowledge. Knowing oneself is to know this being. Wisdom is knowing that oneself and the Being of the universe are the same.

Uddalaka is another guru of the Upanishads. His conversation with his son Svetaketu, who has completed his Vedic studies with a different teacher, reveals that Svetaketu has missed some important lessons. Uddalaka tells him that by a thorough study of the basic elements of the universe a person can understand the whole. All separate forms have their ground in the same Brahman. Uddalaka's advice to his son, "That art thou" (*tat tvam asi*), emphasizes the divine nature of the human soul.

Monism or Dualism?

The move toward unity in the Upanishads does not reach an absolute monism—the belief that there is only one fundamental reality—nor does it deny some dualism—that there are two irreducible realities. The Shvetasvatara Upanishad speaks of a dualism consisting of physical nature, **prakriti,** and soul or spirit,

guru
[GU-RU] OR [GOO-ROO]
A Hindu teacher of religious duties. For a student, the guru represents the divine in human form.

prakriti [pra-KRI-ti]
In Hinduism, matter, as opposed to *purusha*, spirit.

Atman. In contrast, the Chandogya Upanishad emphasizes the unity of human and divine. The most common name for ultimate reality used in the Upanishads is Brahman. Brahman is the ground of being behind all things. The individual soul of humans is Atman. Although distinctions can be made between Brahman and Atman, they are, if not the same in essence, very similar. The Atman of the self is essentially like the Atman of all living creatures. This is a foreshadowing of the doctrine of Maya, for what appears to humans as ultimately different is ultimately the same. In the Upanishads, such speculation is not idle curiosity but a dedicated search for ways to unite the Atman in individuals with Brahman. Klaus K. Klostermaier has written,

> A person must learn to distinguish the self from what is not the self, reality from appearance, and must be strong enough to reject all that is nonessential and non-real. Through this, the students gain access to new depth and to new horizons that enable them to understand the true meaning of the words used to express the higher knowledge. Self-realization can be neither gained nor taught vicariously; everyone has to gain it personally. The guru points the way, supervises the training, clarifies doubts.[9]

How can the Atman become one with God? The Upanishads teach that insight into the nature of gods and humans is a first step toward overcoming the separation between Atman and Brahman. A person who recognizes that the nature of Atman in living things is very similar to Brahman, the ground of all existence, has an insight into his or her own identity. Humans are not *prakriti,* essentially physical and radically different from the divine. Their true nature is not physical but spiritual. They are Atman rather than body. Their closest kin is not physical matter but the Atman of all living things. The Atman of living things is rooted and grounded in Brahman. Atman striving to be at one with God is not seeking an object strange and different; it is, rather, seeking to be one with itself. Atman returning to God is overcoming a separation, an alienation, that does not need to become permanent. The doctrine of Brahman–Atman recognizes that self and God are ultimately a unity. The release of Atman from the body so that it can join Brahman is **moksha.**

What is the experience of the Atman joining Brahman? Brahman can be considered personal, a God among gods. In this mode, Brahman is **saguna Brahman,** God with attributes. In the role of ultimate reality, Brahman is **nirguna Brahman,** Brahman impersonal, without attributes. The analogy sometimes employed to explain Atman joining Brahman is falling asleep. As there are levels of sleep, so there are levels of experience in joining Brahman. The purest form of the Atman joining Brahman is the obliteration of distinction between them—Atman and Brahman become one.

When can devotees experience this joining? They can approach it closely by living well in this life so as to attain release, *moksha.* Some Hindus believe that the universe comes into being, evolves for a period, and then dissolves, releasing all souls into suspended being. Then another **kalpa,** or age of creation, begins, bringing souls back among the living in the universe. In the Upanishads, there is no absolute end for either humankind or the universe. Their conceptions of the universe's age come close to those of geologists and astronomers today.

Prior to its final release to join Brahman, the Atman survives as an individual. The Upanishads mention the soul's **reincarnation** in different bodies until it is worthy to join Brahman. They also mention the **law of karma,** the law that every act, either in thought or deed, has a consequence for future reincarnations.

moksha [MOWK-sha]
In Hinduism, the release of the soul from a cycle of rebirths; one of the four goals of life for Hindus.

saguna Brahman
[SA-goo-na]
In Hinduism, Brahman as he is known with his attributes; this form has personlike qualities.

nirguna Brahman
[NIR-goo-na]
In Hinduism, Brahman as he is in himself, beyond attributes.

kalpa [KAL-pa]
In Hinduism, a long period of the created world. When one period ends, a new one begins with another creation.

reincarnation
[REE-in-cahr-NAY-shun]
The soul leaves one body at death and is reborn in a new body. Although bodies are replaced, the soul remains essentially the same.

law of karma [KAHR-ma]
The principle in Hinduism that a person's thoughts and deeds are followed eventually by deserved pleasure or pain.

Instead of replacing the Vedas, the Upanishads offer an additional way for Hindus to reach God. Together with the Vedas and the Brahmanas, the Upanishads are shruti, revealed, rather than smriti, the product of human authors remembering revelation. For a thoughtful approach to religion, the Upanishads are one of the richest sources available. They have given rise to several different schools of philosophy in Hinduism, some emphasizing monism and others rejecting it for dualism; we will look at these systems later in the chapter.

Karma, Samsara, and Castes

After the Upanishads were completed, the doctrines of karma and **samsara** played a more important role in Hindu thinking. The Vedas and the Upanishads project a positive view of the universe. The world can be a good place for those who seek to please the gods or God. But before the beginning of the Common Era, the Hindu doctrines of karma and samsara had combined with the doctrines of caste to form a view of the world that displeased many Hindus. The smriti tradition of Manu assumes that humans are divided between those who are twice-born and those who are not. Among the twice-born are the Brahmins (priests), those of the **Kshatriya** caste (rulers and warriors), and those of the **Vaishya** caste (commoners). The Kshatriya was originally the highest caste but was later subordinated to the Brahmins. Those not twice-born are **Shudras.**

The law of karma states the principle that people reap what they sow. This principle of justice requires that every thought or deed—good or bad—counts in determining how a person will be born in his or her next life on earth. A person with bad karma could be reborn many times into lower castes of humans, or even lower animals, and then not be released until he or she has been reborn in the Brahmin, or priestly, caste. The doctrine of samsara is that the soul is reborn on earth many times, each time in a different body appropriate to a person's karma. The permanent soul changes bodies just as a person changes worn-out clothes.

The Shudras, the castes of laborers, were not permitted to practice the religion of the Vedas or even to hear the books being read. The Vaishyas and the Kshatriyas, the merchant and military castes, were able to listen to the Vedas and practice the Vedic religion, but they, too, lost enthusiasm for an endless wheel of rebirths. Some Hindu thinkers gave highest priority to discovering ways of gaining release from rebirth.

The Bhagavad Gita

The classic Bhagavad Gita, consisting of 700 verses which are part of the longer Mahabharata, presents a variety of options for those who would find release from rebirth. Although the Mahabharata is part of Itihasa-Purana, combining what is remembered and what is heard, this more popular literature is often attributed to the same source as the Vedas.[10] The "Song of the Blessed Lord" is regarded by Hindu philosophers and those of the masses of other people as a book of profound spiritual insight that can revitalize spiritual life. In its earliest form, the Gita probably dates from the fourth century B.C.E. The setting for the dialogue is a field of battle in which Arjuna and his chariot driver (really the god **Krishna** in human disguise) are drawn up in formation against Arjuna's cousins. Arjuna protests to his driver that he would rather be killed or live as a beggar than be guilty of taking the lives of his kinsmen. Lord Krishna reminds Arjuna that as a member of the Kshatriya

samsara [sam-SAH-ra]
The Hindu concept of the wheel of rebirth that turns forever. Souls are reborn until they reach perfection.

Kshatriya [KSHA-tri-ya]
Hindu caste of warriors and administrators.

Vaishya [VAI-shya]
The third Hindu caste, that of merchants and artisans.

Shudras [SHOO-dras]
In Hinduism, the fourth caste, the caste of laborers.

Krishna [KRISH-na]
An incarnation of Vishnu, who is also the chariot driver of the warrior Arjuna of the Bhagavad Gita.

caste, it is his duty to fight in order to bring good out of a bad situation. Kshatriyas must protect the right by fighting if necessary. Arjuna would be rejecting the duty of his caste if he were to lay down his arms.

The Path of Work

Krishna opens the way to other possibilities for deliverance. Humans can find release through doing their caste duties. **Karma yoga,** the yoke of work, is an acceptable way of approaching God. Useful knowledge is that which is inward and not merely academic. The motivation for work should be duty, not an attachment to results, to maintain its saving effect. The measure of a person's deed is at the point of intention rather than in the results. According to the Bhagavad Gita, a person should renounce any attachment to the deed itself or to its results. An individual who can approach his or her caste duties in a spirit of detachment is closer to release than an ascetic who renounces all action:

> No one exists for even an instant without performing action; however unwilling, every being is forced to act by the qualities of nature. (5) When his senses are controlled but he keeps recalling sense objects with his mind, he is a self-deluded hypocrite. (6) When he controls his senses with his mind and engages in the discipline of action with his faculties of action, detachment sets him apart. (7) Perform necessary action; it is more powerful than inaction; without action you even fail to sustain your own body. (8) Action imprisons the world unless it is done as sacrifice; freed from attachment, Arjuna, perform action as sacrifice! (9)[11]

The Path of Knowledge

Krishna declares that **jnana yoga** is also helpful for obtaining release. The yoga of knowledge does not demand original thought; a person has only to internalize the lessons taught by the ancient masters. Rediscovering the truths of earlier masters is enough to lead a person to salvation. There is no joy in doubt. A person who has knowledge finds pleasure in this world and even knows how to enjoy sense objects so as to make a pleasurable experience a sacrifice to God. The very essence of sacrifice is restraint, so restraint in enjoying the senses is considered a sacrifice. The avatar of Vishnu, Krishna, is perfection who has assumed imperfection in order to inaugurate a new world; he begins by imparting to Arjuna a knowledge that can save him:

> Though myself unborn, undying, the lord of creatures, I fashion nature, which is mine, and I come into being through my own magic. (6) Whenever sacred duty decays and chaos prevails, then, I create myself, Arjuna. (7) To protect men of virtue and destroy men who do evil, to set the standard of sacred duty, I appear in age after age. (8) He who really knows my divine birth and my action, escapes rebirth when he abandons the body—and he comes to me, Arjuna. (9)[12]

The most important thing to learn is renunciation, which leads to release from the wheel of rebirth so an individual can come to God. Renunciation need not mean leaving home or caste duties or turning from knowledge of the world. Whether

karma yoga
Doing one's caste duties without expecting a reward; selfless action.

jnana yoga [JYNAH-na]
Jnana means knowledge or wisdom. Jnana yoga, the Hindu path of release based on intellectual knowledge, appeals to people who emphasize rational understanding of religious beliefs.

Krishna and his brother Balarama. They are in the forest with cowherds. Bhagavata Purana.

a person chooses karma yoga or jnana yoga, the results can be the same if his or her attitude is one of renunciation.

> Learned men see with an equal eye: a scholarly and dignified priest, a cow, an elephant, a dog, and even an outcaste scavenger. (18)[13]

The Path of Physical and Mental Discipline

Raja yoga, the yoga of disciplining the body and the mind through correct postures and breathing, is also presented by Krishna as an acceptable way of release. It requires *brahmacharya,* which means celibacy.

The Path of Love

To the other three ways of release, Krishna adds **bhakti yoga,** devoted love for God. For individuals attaining union with the god whom he or she loves is the very highest goal of living.

> He who sees me everywhere and sees everything in me will not be lost to me, and I will not be lost to him. (30)[14]

Krishna reveals that God is not dependent on the universe, for he lives even when the universe ceases. The true self is not the doer; it is only the witness. It is a spectator rather than an actor. Nothing in the subject world is true reality. Suffering is the process through which humans fight for their true nature. The great Brahman is the father of all beings, giving rise to everything that exists. As is any other creature, man is dependent on God. Although any person has the freedom to refuse the grace of God, surrender to him is the easiest way of release. The Blessed Lord said,

> *Lord Krishna[:]* Eternal and supreme is the infinite spirit; its inner self is called inherent being; its creative force, known as action, is the source of creatures' existence. (3) Its inner being is perishable existence; its inner divinity is man's spirit; I am the inner sacrifice here in your body, O Best of Mortals. (4) A man who dies remembering me at the time of death enters my being when he is freed from his body; of this there is no doubt. (5) Whatever being he remembers when he abandons the body at death, he enters, Arjuna, always existing in that being. (6)[15]

The Laws of Manu

The **Laws of Manu** appeared between 200 B.C.E. and 200 C.E. among the new literary forms that developed full discussions around a thread of precepts, or *sutra.* The Brahmins designed moral codes that set the standards of conduct for every Hindu, including the caste system and duties at each stage of life. Hindus had great freedom in what they believed; they had little freedom in what they could do. Attributed to Manu, the Laws of Manu describe an ideal code of behavior for Hindus. Here readers find described the Brahmin ideals for each caste and for each member of society. For example, before giving details on women in society, the Laws of Manu sketch a general attitude that men should take toward women:

chapter 9.1–5

[1] I will tell the eternal duties of a man and wife who stay on the path of duty both in union and in separation. [2] Men must make their women dependent day and night, and keep under their own control those who are attached to sensory

raja yoga [RAH-jah] Path to salvation by disciplining the mind and body.

bhakti yoga [BAKH-ti] Personal devotion to deity. In Hinduism, a path that leads to salvation.

Laws of Manu [MAH-noo] A Hindu code of conduct compiled from about 200 B.C.E to 200 C.E.

objects. [3] Her father guards her in childhood, her husband guards her in youth, and her sons guard her in old age. A woman is not fit for independence.[16]

These directions are balanced by another section (3.55–59):

[55] Fathers, brothers, husbands, and brothers-in-law who wish for great good fortune should revere these women and adorn them. [56] The deities delight in places where women are revered, but where women are not revered all rites are fruitless. [57] Where the women of the family are miserable, the family is soon destroyed, but it always thrives where the women are not miserable.[17]

Hindu conduct today is not determined by Manu, but the Laws still have some influence. For faithful Hindus, this code is still a standard to be considered.

Duties of the Four Stages of Life

Hinduism has different duties for a person according to his or her stage in life. The first stage is student. A young man between ages eight and twelve, but no later than age twenty-four, is introduced to study of the Vedas. A sacred cord is placed over his shoulder, signifying that as a member of one of the three highest castes, he has been reborn as a spiritual person. Studies with his guru may last through his twenty-fourth year.

When the former student marries and becomes a householder at age twenty-five, he lives as closely to the ideals of wisdom as he can. He tries to observe the rituals required of householders and, at the same time, tries to avoid unnecessary injury to living things. Above all, he tries to observe caste duties in marriage, in his occupation, and in raising children. He follows the model of a spiritual man who has the duties of earning a living, raising children, supporting parents, and maintaining a household. He is also expected to meet the obligations of entertaining guests and supporting holy men. Only when he has a son to whom he can turn over responsibilities can he cease being a householder and move to the next stage of life.

The Laws of Manu describe the next stage:

chapter 6.1–5
[1] After he has lived in the householder's stage of life in accordance with the rules in this way, a twice-born Vedic graduate should live in the forest, properly restrained and with his sensory powers conquered. [2] But when a householder sees that he is wrinkled and grey, and (when he sees) the children of his children, then he should take himself to the wilderness. [3] Renouncing all food cultivated in the village and all possessions, he should hand his wife over to his sons and go to the forest—or take her along. [4] Taking with him his sacrificial fire and the fire-implements for the domestic (sacrifice), he should go out from the village to the wilderness and live (there) with his sensory powers restrained.
[5] He should offer the five great sacrifices with various sorts of the pure food of hermits, or with vegetables, roots, and fruit, ritually prepared.[18]

This period of life enables the aging householder to reflect on earlier studies and duties without having to engage in them. The essential orientation is away from home, family, human endeavors, and worldly concerns and toward Brahman, with whom he hopes to unite. Although the percentage of men who take this drastic step is small, many other men use this stage of life to retire from day-to-day responsibilities. They devote their time to the study of sacred writing and meditate on uniting their souls with God.

The goal of the optional fourth stage is **samadhi,** the release of the soul from the body so that it can unite with Brahman. Raja yoga, disciplines based on a special psychology developed by Hindus, trains the body to be subservient to the soul. In the later stages of life, this exercise can assist in meditation and liberation of the soul from the body. Ultimate success is uniting the Atman with Brahman.

Women observe three stages of life. As a student, a woman is instructed in religious duties. As a householder, she has a separate set of duties that complement those of her husband. She may join him as a forest dweller in the third stage. In India, a woman is not expected to become a **sannyasin,** a wandering ascetic, though some indeed do.

Two groups of women have departed from the old ideal of a woman being subject to her father, then her husband, and then her son. They have chosen to be free from supervision of a man of their own family. One group has trained as gurus, studying under a male guru before being ordained to teach. Gauri Ma, Jayashin Ma, Meera Ma, and Gurumayi are examples of female gurus who participate in the classical guru tradition.[19] Other women, such as Anasuya Devi, take instruction or initiation from an older female guru or are self-initiated. A rather extreme choice is to become a sannyasin by study, ordination, and participation in rites of her own death. She is free from marriage and family and cannot inherit any goods or property from her family. She has sacrificed all worldly pleasures to pursue spiritual liberation (moksha).[20]

samadhi [sa-MAH-di] Concentration that unifies; absorption.

sannyasin [san-NYAH-sin] One in the last stage of renunciation or detachment.

Four Goals for Hindus Today

A Hindu is not required to seek the highest goals of release in this lifetime. In its breadth and tolerance, Hinduism permits four major goals in living: *kama, artha, dharma,* and *moksha.* A person can choose a life in search of pleasures, kama. Those

United Nations/neg. #125261/J. Issac

A Hindu Wedding. These Hindus of a high caste participate in traditional rites. Parents usually arrange marriages for their children.

who seek the pleasure of the literary arts can turn to the Natyashastras for guidance. The more fleshly pleasure of making love can be guided by the Kamasutra. Pursuing politics or the materialism of commercial competition is the goal of artha. All Hindus are expected to choose the goal of dharma and live according to the duties of their caste. Moksha, release, is the goal of those who have grown tired of the other pursuits in previous lifetimes and who now seek release from the wheel of rebirth.

Popular Hinduism: Four Ways of Salvation

Hinduism has welcomed all the ways of salvation set forth in the Bhagavad Gita. The ways suggested by the Bhagavad Gita have developed into well-established paths that many Hindus walk today. The **puranas** and **tantras** add further information on deities and ways to serve them. Popular Hinduism's understanding of the four ways offers more varieties than those outlined in the Bhagavad Gita.

Karma Yoga

Karma yoga, the Way of Works, is valued, in part, because it is praised by Krishna in the Bhagavad Gita. Those who perform the proper rituals every day and at the turning points in their passage of life can fulfill all of their religious obligations. Although not the highest road to salvation, it nevertheless leads to the goal of release. The Vedas guide in the proper hymns and sacrifices to be used in greeting the rising sun or in marking birth, marriage, and death. The Vedic sacrifices are the heart of the path of works.

For men and women, there are different duties. A man has special duties as priest in the home, remembering daily offerings of food to the gods. But his most essential duties come in the *shraddha* rites to ancestors. Besides keeping the rites of the funeral pyre, a male descendant is required to make additional offerings to nourish the souls of ancestors and keep them from the wheel of rebirth. Women cannot perform these rites, so the birth of a son is a particular blessing to Hindu families. However, women also have their duties to perform. They prepare the food that is used in sacrifices or offerings to the gods in daily remembrance and on the special yearly religious festivals. Beyond that, the Laws of Manu prescribe many duties for women. In contemporary Hinduism, the laws that require a woman to be under the control of some man and to be almost worshipful toward her husband have been relaxed. Higher education for women and employment outside the home in business and government have made the old ways seem repressive.

Jnana Yoga

The Way of Knowledge, jnana yoga, is based on a method developed in the Upanishads and refined through the centuries. The Sankhya system of Hindu philosophy, in its dualism, emphasizes freeing Atman from *prakriti*. There is perhaps a stronger emphasis on the nondualism of Brahman–Atman. Although these two aspects of ultimate reality can be experienced separately, they are one. A human's alienation from God rests on ignorance—not knowing (*avidya*) or not seeing that the human soul (Atman) is ultimately of the same essence as Brahman.

The ignorant soul, not knowing its nature, thinks that the self is identified with the world rather than with the universal soul. The misconception involves the

puranas [pu-RAHN-as] "Ancient Lore" treatises or the deities of popular Hinduism.

tantras [TUN-trus] Religious treatises for developing latent powers in persons. Dialogues between Shiva and Shakti.

individual soul in a long series of rebirths, in which it experiences not only the sufferings of human existence but also estrangement from its true nature. In this state of ignorance, humans' identity can never be complete—they are always separated from themselves. The Way of Knowledge in the Upanishads indicates that knowledge can overcome ignorance. The truth that liberates is that Atman and Brahman are as similar as river and sea or as the ocean wave and the spray that the wind blows from it.

Salvation lies in a person's recognizing that his or her identity is grounded not in the world but in Brahman–Atman. In this realization lies homecoming for the soul, the release from rebirth. The home of the soul is an unchanging realm of being, Nirvana. Insight is of utmost importance, but training and guidance can help a person move more quickly toward release.

Bhakti Yoga

The Way of Devotion provides a third means for helping overcome the vicissitudes of human existence and gaining release from them. *Bhakti yoga,* the Way of Devotion, is strongly emphasized in the Bhagavad Gita. Those who serve God through *bhakti* passionately embrace him, in love. The grace of God is far more effective in salvation than is any law or ritual. A person need only trust and love God in order to be preserved in eternity. A person who trusts the ultimate deity cannot perish.

The roots of this path of loving God can be found in the hymns of the Rig-Veda. The later Upanishads offer treatises on bhakti, and the puranas and the Ramayana are popular sources of its inspiration. Bhakti was widespread among the masses of Hindus during the reign of the Gupta emperors, 300–500 C.E. The eighteen puranas explain beliefs in *trimurti,* the triad of Gods: Brahma, Vishnu, and Shiva.

Those who want to follow the Way of Devotion can commit themselves to one of several Hindu gods. Brahman is regarded as the one God, who may appear in popular Hinduism as many gods. One of three gods is **Brahma,** the creator. His responsibilities are shared with **Vishnu,** the preserver, and **Shiva,** the destroyer. Vishnu is worshiped in his incarnation as Krishna as the personification of divine love. Although Shiva destroys life in order to make room for new creations, he can be generous to his devotees. In popular Hinduism, most people usually choose to serve either Shiva or Vishnu.

Those who choose to serve Shiva in the Way of Devotion may also worship one of his consorts. Shiva, the one who brings death and destruction, is also powerful in creating new life. By joining with his consorts, he can generate life-giving forces. Parvati is his kind and gentle consort; Kali is a terrifying figure who can spread disease and death. Durga is pictured as requiring sacrifices—even human sacrifices. She is a warrior superior to male gods, for after they failed, she subdued the demon Mahisha. Nevertheless, these personalities of wrath have attracted their devotees. To a non-Hindu, Kali, who wields a sword and wears a necklace of skulls, while her mouth drips blood, may seem altogether frightening, but thousands of women look upon her as the deity who can be kind and helpful to them. According to Lynn Foulston, the Sanskrit goddesses are more Brahmanic, more pure, and less accepting of animal sacrifice. The non-Sanskrit goddesses are considered less pure and often accept animal sacrifice. Kali and Durga are considered fierce goddesses.[21]

In various contexts, Kali and Shiva are partners in dance. In Kapalakundala's hymn in Bhavabhuti's Malatimadhava, they "appear as mad partners in a cosmic dance that is destined to destroy the worlds."[22] Devoted men have called her the

Brahma [bram-HAH]
Ultimate reality; the creator.

Vishnu [VISH-noo]
The Supreme Lord; the preserver.

Shiva [SHEE-va]
The Auspicious; Ultimate Lord; the destroyer.

Divine Mother. Ganesh, the son of Shiva and Parvati, is the elephant-headed god who can work like an elephant to lift heavy burdens and clear the road of life. Nandi, the bull, guards Shiva's temples and protects four-footed beasts. A person may practice bhakti with Shiva or with one of his consorts. Only a minority of Shaivites have worshiped Shiva through tantrism, a religious practice that includes sexual intercourse as a ritual to generate the power of the spirit.

Vaishnavites choose to serve Vishnu or one of his avatars, or incarnations. As the preserver, Vishnu is kind and compassionate. Lakshmi, his beloved consort, exhibits loyalty and love for him. Vishnu is divine love that redeems the world from evil. In times of human troubles, he has assumed human forms in order to come to the aid of his people. Among his better-known incarnations is Lord Krishna, the one who reveals himself in the Bhagavad Gita. Krishna is the Divine Child, the embodiment of Beauty of Grace who plays his flute to attract women in divine love, particularly his beloved Radha.[23] Rama, the hero of the Ramayana, is also an incarnation of Vishnu, and Rama's wife, Sita, is an incarnation of Lakshmi. Rama is the perfect ruler and husband, and Sita is the perfect wife. Their love story, which ends tragically when, after renewing their love, Rama, due to public suspicion, sends Sita away, draws masses of Hindus in devotion to the divine pair. Judged before the gods, Sita is praised for her innocence in a miracle:

Kali, a Consort of Shiva. Her fierce appearance indicates that she can destroy forces of evil that attack her devotees.

> From the earth rose a marvelous celestial throne supported on the heads of Nagas of immeasurable power, their bodies adorned with divine gems. The Goddess Dharani, bidding her welcome, took Maithili in her arms, causing her to be seated on that celestial seat and, while she occupied the throne, a shower of blossoms fell without ceasing from the sky. Then the Gods burst into loud acclamations, crying "Excellent! Excellent! O Sita, thy virtue is supreme!"[24]

Raja Yoga

The Way of Physical Discipline, *raja yoga*, is often identified with the Yoga Sutra, attributed to Patanjali about the second century C.E. The goal of raja yoga is training the physical body so that the soul can be free. Samadhi comes after restraint of all physical and mental activity. The system set forth by Patanjali is not one that can give desired results to those who approach it lightly while doing routine work in the world. As the Bhagavad Gita teaches, the first step is to embrace an ethic that emphasizes detachment from the world. A person who is serious about approaching God must concentrate on cleanliness and strong control over bodily desires. The third step concentrates on forming the body into the correct posture—learning to sit in the lotus position until the body is no longer of any concern. The fourth step teaches controlling breathing in order to attain serenity of mind. The fifth step is withdrawal from all stimulation of the senses. In the sixth step, a person concentrates on only one object until it fills his or her whole mind. The seventh step requires withdrawing the object that has filled the mind until the person is no longer conscious of it. The eighth step extinguishes all consciousness of the world.

Orthodox Hindu Systems of Philosophy

Hindu philosophy is a way of perceiving the universe. The Hindu philosopher is one who intuits reality, who knows the basis of the universe and the purpose of human life. From intuitions, the philosopher reasons a systematic understanding of the universe and humanity. Philosophers are concerned with both metaphysics, the general understanding of reality, and ethics, the principles that direct human conduct. However, as we have seen, Hindus can vary in their interpretation of the universe; there are six major systems of philosophy.

Sankhya

The *Sankhya* system of philosophy is attributed to Kapila, who lived at the beginning of the period of the Upanishads. However, the earliest written statement of the six systems that we have may come from the second or third century C.E. The Sankhya system is dualistic and explains the universe without employing gods; it argues that there are two irreducible realities in the universe. Prakriti is matter; it is real and not an illusion. Purusha is the stuff of souls or spirits. Purusha is composed of individual souls rather than one undifferentiated soul. These souls attract prakriti to themselves. The souls are in a foreign environment, imprisoned by their attachment to matter. Only by enlightening souls so that prakriti dissolves can they be released. Living in ways that do not involve the soul with matter leads to release. The purpose of Sankhya philosophy is to free souls from bondage to matter.

Advaita Vedanta

Advaita Vedanta, probably the best-known part of the Vedanta system, refers to itself not as a monism but as a nondualism, *advaita.* Set forth by Shankara (788–829 C.E.) in a commentary on the Vedanda Sutra, the system rests on Brahman. The phenomenal world is not as we experience it. What we experience is Maya; things, though real, are not what they seem to be. Appearances are not ultimate reality. It is ignorance, **avidya** (not seeing), that keeps individuals from the reality of Brahman. Believing in the independent human soul is also avidya. Belief in the various gods of Hinduism demonstrates an ignorance of Brahman–Atman, the one reality. The world can be overcome through rituals and worship as well as ascetic living. The key to release is recognition that Atman and Brahman are not ultimately separate.

Other Philosophic Systems

The other four systems of Hindu philosophy are also concerned with knowing how humans can best attain spiritual maturity. *Yoga,* which was discussed in this chapter as raja yoga, is dualistic. The classical explanation of this philosophy was given by Patanjali in the second century C.E. Yoga, often allied with the Sankhya system, is the choice of people who experiment in liberating the soul from the body. *Nyaya* focuses on intellectual analysis and logic in understanding obligations for humans. It is attributed to a person named Gautama, who emphasized that all knowledge must be empirically tested, for most suffering in life comes through false notions. *Vaisheshika* philosophy studies the external world and understands it in terms of atoms. Kanada, its founder, believed that atoms and soul are both eternal. The entire process of souls entering and leaving the world is governed by the power of Advishta, an unseen force or deity. *Purva-Mimamsa* emphasizes the literal truth of the Vedas, which sets forth the *dharma,* or duty, of humans. Founded by Jaimini, the system maintains the Vedas are uncreated and eternal. They are the ground of Being itself. The Purva-Mimamsa system is closer to the priestly interests of the Brahmanas than to the speculations of philosophers.

avidya [a-VID-ya]
In Hinduism, the term means "ignorance," or not seeing things as they are.

These four systems, as well as Sankhya and Advaita Vedanda, focus on the ways humans can best realize their spiritual potentialities. All of the six orthodox systems of Hindu philosophy aim to release humans from the suffering involved at the animal level of life.

Hindu Responses to Western Influence

In India, Hindus responded to British influence, which was nominally Christian, in a variety of ways. Ram Mohan Roy (1772–1833), an early reformer, found in Hinduism many ideas similar to those of the Christian Protestant denomination of Unitarianism. In contrast, Dayananda Sarasvati (1824–1883) rejected all Western influence and all Hindu writing after the Vedas. He was the champion of the Vedas as true Hinduism. Rabindranath Tagore (1861–1941) emphasized an intuitive experience of God, a view that drew admiration from Hindus and from members of some Western religions. Sarvapalli Radhakrishnan (1888–1975) wrote on Hinduism and Western philosophy, appealing to intellectuals in Britain and India. Although these writers are still read and admired, some others from India have become better known in the West. Ramakrishna (1836–1886), Mohandas K. Gandhi (1869–1948), and Sri Aurobindo (1872–1950) have sustained influence past the twentieth century.

Ramakrishna

Ramakrishna (1836–1886) is the holy title for Gadadhar Chatterji, who lived most of his Brahmin life in a temple of Kali near Calcutta. Neither an organizer nor an ardent social reformer, he was, nevertheless, a model for a different approach to harmony among religions and cultures. His absolute devotion to Kali led him to repeated experiences of samadhi. In a direct vision of the goddess, he came to understand that all divinities experienced by humans are manifestations of the one God. Through experiments, he found God in the worship not only of Krishna, Sita, and Rama but also of Allah and Christ.

> Different creeds are but different paths to reach the Almighty. Various and different are the ways that lead to the temple of Mother Kali at Kalighat (Calcutta). Similarly, various are the ways that lead to the house of the Lord. Every religion is nothing but one of such paths that lead to God.[25]

Ramakrishna's views were spread in India by people who came to visit him and by disciples who gathered about him in his later years. Swami Vivekananda, a young law student, organized a Ramakrishna movement that had centers throughout the world.

Mohandas K. Gandhi

In contrast to the earlier Hindu reformers, Mohandas K. Gandhi (1869–1948) studied in Britain and practiced law in South Africa. He was keenly aware of the social injustices imposed by the British; he became aware of the injustices imposed by Hindus, especially against **untouchables.** Untouchables were Hindus, often of the Shudras, who are considered by higher caste people too defiling to contact physically. He referred to them as Harijans, "Children of God." In life he worked for their welfare, and in death he inspired continuing care for them.

untouchable
In Hinduism, a person, often a Shudra, who is considered by upper castes to be too impure to allow physical contact. Untouchability has been abolished.

© Bettmann Corbis

Mohandas K. Gandhi. He is the Hindu pacifist leader who demonstrated against British rule in India.

Gandhi neither embraced Western culture nor rejected it. He sought to use its resources to help India. At the same time, he tried to kindle by example the light of truth available in the simple virtues of Hinduism.

The outside world saw a small, ascetic man who kept the British rulers in India in turmoil by organizing mass demonstrations against injustices. That his followers were nonviolent resisters was sometimes ignored in the British show of force and arrests of demonstrators. His fasting in prison until others did his bidding was a new weapon in the arsenal of social reform. The British lion was not amused at being bearded in public; the masses of Hindus loved Gandhi for it. What many observers overlooked was that he had a sound spiritual foundation for his program of reform.

Gandhi was influenced by the Isha Upanishad. Two doctrines shaped his personal commitments and public actions. *Satyagraha* can be translated "truth force." For Gandhi, God is truth. A person's whole life should be a commitment to seek and fulfill truth. The other doctrine is *ahimsa,* which is usually translated "noninjury" or "nonviolence," but it can also mean "love." To love God is also to love the beings in whom God dwells. From these doctrines it follows that there is no room for hatred and violence among any humans. Before anyone can correct the impurities and injustices of the world, they must first purify themselves. Gandhi is, perhaps, the best-known example in the twentieth century of using spiritual force to effect political change.

> He said that having rejected the sword, he had nothing to offer his opposition but love. He lived in expectation that in some future life he would be able to hug all humanity as friends.[26]

Gandhi's spiritual approach was influential in moving the British government to grant independence to India in 1947.

Sri Aurobindo

Aurobindo Ghose, now referred to as Sri Aurobindo (1872–1950), received his education in Cambridge, England. His studies of European languages did not sever his ties with Hindu friends. Once back in India, he soon joined Bal Gangadhar Tilak (1856–1920) in political action for nationalism. Between 1906 and 1950, he led a group that published the *Bande Mataram* ("Hail to the Mother"), espousing noncooperation, passive resistance, boycott, and national education. Although Sri Aurobindo did not participate in active guerrilla warfare, he endorsed and inspired it. Eventually, he was arrested by the British and served time in prison. While there, he had a mystical experience that changed his life. He abandoned his Western ways and spent the last years of his life in Pondicherry practicing yoga exercises and writing his philosophy in English. Not abandoning the struggle against imperialism, he intended to find the source of spiritual power that would defeat India's enemies.

Sri Aurobindo thought of the universe as essentially spiritual. There are gradations of spirituality from the insentient up the scale of conscious being until the highest levels *sat-chit-ananda,* or being-consciousness-bliss. Through yogin practices a person can become conscious of the universal spirit that resides within. Being conscious of God's dwelling within opens up possibilities for freedom and the full realization of bliss. Through spiritual discipline, a person comes to experience the life divine:

> The Divine that we adore is not only a remote extracosmic Reality, but a half-veiled Manifestation present and near to us here in the universe. Life is the field of a divine

manifestation not yet complete: here, in life, on earth, in the body . . . we have to un-veil the God-head.[27]

The spiritual world has a firm order, the Rita of the Vedas. As the soul comes to know itself, it becomes aware of universal principles that govern conduct leading to life divine. Thus, the moral law is not a foreign regimen to be suffered but a re-alization of principles deep within the self. By practicing spiritual discipline, a person discovers the freedom and bliss of life divine.

World reform comes through spiritual development of the self.

> If there is, as there must be in the nature of things, an ascending series in the scale of substance from matter to spirit, it must be marked by a progressive diminution of those capacities most characteristic of physical principle and a progressive increase of the opposite characteristics which will lead us to the formula of pure spiritual self-extension. . . . Drawing away from durability of form, we draw towards eternity of essence; drawing away from our poise in the persistent separation and resistance of physical matter, we draw near to the highest divine poise in the infinity, unity and indivisibility of spirit.[28]

Sri Aurobindo has had a profound effect on many current Hindu philosophers and religious leaders. His influence continues through his voluminous writings and his ideal community at Pondicherry.

Historical Development: Independent India

In 1947, India gained independence from Britain. For the first time in a thousand years, its peoples were free to develop their own government, laws, economy, and educational systems. Independent India has guaranteed freedom of religion for all the faiths in its borders. Hindus and Muslims are large groups, and Jains and Sikhs are important native religions. Although they came from other countries, Parsis and Christians have been in India for many centuries. All these religions have a place of respect in India.

At the same time, the insights of the reformers have been retained in modern India. India's constitution guarantees freedom of religion, life, liberty, and due process of law. It makes illegal practices of untouchability, forced labor, and dis-crimination due to caste, race, sex, belief, and place of birth.[29] As in other coun-tries, laws are not always observed. Humanitarian and educational concerns have changed practices from the old ideals of the Laws of Manu. As experience helps evaluate old answers, India changes, revises, and redesigns programs.

Since the independence of India, traditional roles for Hindu women have been greatly expanded. The Constitution made women equal in matters of social, political, and economic acts. Health and education became matters of state and central governments, which sought to improve the status of women. Mar-riage, divorce, and inheritance fell to the Hindu Code Bill.[30] Indira Gandhi's service as leader of India proved a role model for women. Many women, how-ever, stay home, performing traditional roles of householders. Some women study the traditional subjects in universities. A few women are active in the sciences and professions.

The independence of India has permitted religious rivals to express themselves more freely. The first clashes were between Hindus and Muslims when Pakistan was set aside for a Muslim state. More recently, in 1980, Sikhs have demonstrated,

Hinduism in History

BCE				
1500 Aryans move into India	**1200** Vedas recorded			
800 Upanishads begun; Kapila, Sankhya philosophy	**599** Birth of Mahavira	**563** Birth of Buddha/ Bhagavad Gita written		
326 Alexander the Great invades India	**300** Upanishads completed	**200** Laws of Manu begun	**200** Laws of Manu completed	

CE				
711 Muslims reach Dabul (Pakistan)	**788** Birth of Shankara, Advaita Vedanda			
1440 Birth of Kabir	**1469** Birth of Nanak			
1526 Baber establishes Mogul Empire	**1757** British East India Company gains control of Bengal			
1772 Birth of Ram Mohan Roy, Brahmo Samaj	**1824** Birth of Dayananda Sarasvati, Arya Samaj	**1858** British control government of India	**1861** Birth of Rabindranath Tagore	**1863** Birth of Ramakrishna of Calcutta
1869 Birth of Mohandas K. Gandhi	**1885** Indian National Congress formed	**1888** Birth of Sarvepalli Radhakrishnan	**1920** M. K. Gandhi leads Indian National Congress	**1940** Moslem League demands that a Muslim country, Pakistan, be carved out of India
1947 India independent of Britain; Pakistan formed for Muslims	**1948** M. K. Gandhi assassinated	**1950** India becomes a republic	**1962** Chinese Communist forces invade India, then withdraw	**1966** Indira Gandhi, daughter of Jawarhalal Nehru, becomes prime minister of India
1984 Golden Temple of Sikhs invaded by Indian Army; Indira Gandhi assassinated	**1992** Hindus and Muslims clash over sacred site in Ayodhya	**1995** Shiv Sena leader Bal Thackera changes "Bombay" name to Mumbai; opposes secular constitution	**1998** Atal Bihari Vajpayee, prime minister	

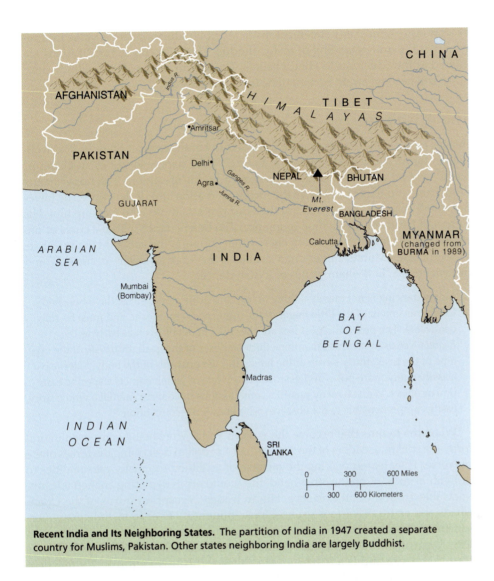

Recent India and Its Neighboring States. The partition of India in 1947 created a separate country for Muslims, Pakistan. Other states neighboring India are largely Buddhist.

sometimes violently, for a separate state in the Punjab. The Bharatiya Janata party in the 1990s has pushed hard for Hindu rights as representing the majority of the population. In Ayodhya, Hindus destroyed a Muslim mosque to erect a temple to Lord Rama, claiming that Muslims had earlier destroyed a Hindu temple on that spot. The incidents prolong a dispute over who shall have ascendancy in India. The conflict has continued in the twenty-first century.

Worldview

Since its earliest centuries, Hinduism has encouraged a variety of beliefs and practices. Hindus start with guidance from the Vedas; from that scriptural basis is freedom to develop manifold expressions of faith and action. As we have seen, describing what Hindus believe and practice is difficult, for there are many Hindus, many sources, and many types of belief and practice. Although there can be exceptions to almost any statement made about Hinduism, there is value in summarizing the understanding of many Hindus. The following generalizations are offered as introductions to Hindu beliefs. Those who read widely in Hindu literature will become aware of variations from these views.

The Absolute

Images of the Hindu gods are not intended to be understood literally. The well-known figure of Nataraja, or Shiva, as lord of the dance, serves as an example. Shiva has four arms and hands extending from his shoulders. The upper hands with drum and flame symbolize the forces of creation and destruction. The lower hands tell observers not to fear, for the Lord protects those who worship him. His right foot treads on the demon ignorance. The Lord's dance within a circle of fire represents the incessant dancing energy that supports the action of the universe. The universe exhibits rather than exhausts the Lord's power of creation and destruction. A. L. Basham writes of Indian dance,

> Indian dancing is not merely a thing of legs and arms alone, but of the whole body. Every movement of the little finger or the eyebrow is significant, and must be fully controlled. The poses and gestures are classified in detail, even as early as the *Bharata Natyasastra*, which mentions thirteen poses of the head, thirty-six of the eyes, nine of the neck, thirty-seven of the hand, and ten postures of the body. Later texts classify many more poses and gestures, every one of which depicts a specific emotion or object. With so many possible combinations the dancer can tell a whole story, easily comprehensible to the observer who knows the convention.[31]

When the hymns that became the written Vedas were being composed in oral form, the spiritual leaders of the Aryans had a problem describing the forces of the universe. They feared making the mistake of ascribing too many personalities to individual gods or, on the other hand, they could err in depicting an ineffable, unknowable ground of all existence. Hindu leaders, except for gurus of the Upanishads and saints of various groups, have thought it better to include many personalities. It is better to have people choose among images of many gods than to leave them unable to feel any devotion for an abstract principle. Hinduism, in contrast to Judaism and Islam, has not seen image worship as a threat. If a few people worship images as literal depictions of the gods, they are still better off than not worshiping at all. In time, if they have the capacity, they will come to know that the divine transcends the image. Able worshipers will realize that images are symbols of the various powers at work in the universe. Some sophisticated Hindus prefer one image or god to another—for example, either Shiva or Vishnu. Many more Hindus prefer one of the more personal deities, such as Kali or Krishna. Few images of Brahma are found. Intellectually, it can be understood that Brahman is the ground of all gods. How can Brahman be worshiped? Answering the question of how many gods there are, Yajnavalkya gave all sorts of figures, from 3 to 3,300. In the end, there is only one divine; all the others are but manifestations of powers. Ramakrishna began by finding the divine through Kali; before he died, he could find the divine through either Hindu gods or the God of Christians or Muslims. He told a story of Shiva, who denounced one of his devotees because he refused to worship Vishnu. The devotee did not realize that all the gods are only powers of the one Brahman.

In studying Hinduism, traditional labels of polytheism, monotheism, or atheism are inappropriate. They are not helpful in understanding Hindu attitudes toward the divine. Perhaps the term *henotheism* is better, for it emphasizes one superior god in the presence of lesser gods. The traditional terms, however, are inadequate to Hindu attitudes toward the divine.

A distinctive attitude of Hinduism is that there is more to the universe than meets the eye. There is a reality that embraces all we experience; to understand the universe and ourselves, its presence is necessary. Behind all the phenomena of life, a source of energy makes it possible. This unit can be experienced, however, in a great variety of ways. No one way in itself is complete.

The World

The Hindu world, or the universe, is more complicated than in religions from the Middle East. The ancient Hindu writings speak of time and space in terms that stagger the imagination of all but modern astronomers and physicists. Other Hindu scriptures speak of cycles of expansion and collapse in the universe that are consistent with the big bang theory, except following the bang is another expansion phase followed by collapse and another bang. Hinduism has no problem with island universes or black holes. These theories support rather than threaten Hindu views of the divine and the universe.

Hinduism finds polarities of energy everywhere. Creation is balanced by destruction. Shiva is symbolized in both the phallus of creation and the trident of destruction. Kali wears a necklace of skulls, a symbol of death; she is also the divine mother who is gentle and kind to those who seek her help. The world is both good and bad. Life is followed by death, and out of decay comes life. Seasons repeat in cycles. Water from the sea goes to the sun and descends as rain that runs through the rivers of the sea—a process that never ends. In a balance of forces is peace; in the gods is a balance of forces.

Hindus are less prone than Westerners to judge the world in moral terms. It is hardly meaningful to speak of the world as good or bad. It is both and neither. Some things seem helpful to humans, and others seem destructive. These immediate human impressions and assessments made in the short term, however, may not be correct in the long term. In assessing processes over very long periods, it is difficult to judge whether a result is good or bad.

Hindus can speak of the universe as not being divine. Most Hindus do not think that the divine is physical the way the universe is. Yet the physical universe exists because it is influenced by the divine. The universe may be atoms and space, but spirit is also a reality.

Humans

Hinduism teaches a lengthy existence for humans. The physical body is not the whole story of

Nelson-Atkins Museum of Art, Kansas City Mo. (Purchase: Nelson Trust) 50-20: Robert Newcombe

Shiva as Nataraja, Lord of the Dance. This figure is in bronze, from Tanjore, twelfth or thirteenth century.

a human. The body that we see is only one chapter in a volume of a whole set of books on the life of a soul, or Atman. Our appearance now only hints of what we have been or will become. A human is a soul who wears, in succession, many different costumes. Each is appropriate to a human's current condition. When a soul reaches its destiny, it has no need of costumes. Should the released soul return sometime in the distant future to a cycle of births and deaths, it will not be exactly the same soul with the same self-consciousness.

The law of karma is the most important doctrine of Hinduism. More than any other religion, Hinduism emphasizes that people get exactly what they deserve. Humans cannot change the fact that they are exactly what they are supposed to be in life. In this life, however, people can change what they will become in future lives.

The Problem for Humans

The problem for humans, as Hindus understand it, is an immortal soul that continues to inhabit one body after another until it is freed from the wheel of rebirth. The soul is bound to the revolving wheel through karma, its own choices of thoughts and deeds. Karma does not end with a body's death, so its influence may extend through many incarnations of the soul, where other karma is generated. *Varna*, or caste, is a lifetime status in a body. Be it superior or inferior in the social order, one's caste is exactly the appropriate condition according to the karma that one has accumulated. A person is responsible for his or her own condition in this life, for though a person cannot change the effects of past decisions, he or she is free to change thoughts and actions now so as to alter lives in the future. Soul, karma, wheel of rebirth, and individual choice are the ingredients of the problem of humans; they are also the ingredients of its solution.

The Solution for Humans

For Hindus, the human solution is harmony with the Absolute; harmony is overcoming life's polar tensions. Purusha is liberated from prakriti; Atman is liberated from Maya. In raja yoga, the soul is liberated from the body; in jnana yoga, the mind is liberated from avidya, not seeing the truth of the universe. In bhakti yoga, the devotee is detached from the world and attached to God. Instead of being pulled apart by divided loyalties, reconciled people have a single base of identity. They return to themselves undivided, focused, and serene.

Paths of harmony are available for each type of personality. People differ, and their approaches to God differ. Some people need the emotional ties of personal relationships; bhakti yoga is their road. Some people are intellectuals, preferring mind over body and emotions; jnana yoga fulfills their desires. Some people need to be involved in activities with their family and community; karma yoga is the most rewarding path for them. In Hinduism, all these ways are of equal value.

Harmony is according to the law of karma. Bad actions produce disharmony; good actions produce harmony. The four paths to reconciliation are four ways of good action that bring rewards according to the law of karma. There are no shortcuts, for only meritorious acts bring release and harmony. Meritorious acts are fueled by devotion to spiritual values.

For masses of Hindus, solution of their problem depends on assistance from a deity. For Shaivites, Shiva and his consorts are sources of help. For Vaishnavites, Vishnu and his avatars respond to human petitions. Of course, the great devas of the Vedas can still be approached through ancient sacrifices. The goal of the universe is the full realization of humans.

Community and Ethics

Hindus usually enter the religious community by birth. Males of the three higher castes participate in the *upanayana* rite, which invests them with the sacred thread that symbolizes their being born a second time, of the spirit. Females have traditionally been dependent on males for their spiritual guidance, but they have their own responsibilities in worship, rites, fasts, and moral obligations. Hinduism allows great variety in paths of harmony. It has had strong control, however, over individual acts.

Hinduism has a rigid moral code, although it is not always the same as a Western moral code. In the Vedas, Rita is the principle of right order in the universe; all things conform to its control. For the individual, the principle of right action is dharma. Dharma is Rita incorporated into the life of individuals. Sri Aurobindo pointed out that correct moral action for individuals is not foreign to them—something imposed by society. Freedom comes through living according to the universal principle within humans. Being true to themselves, their own highest principles of the self, brings freedom to individuals.

In Hinduism, the family is sacred. Husbands and wives should be loyal to each other. They should be responsible in generating children, providing for their physical needs, and educating them in spiritual as well as secular disciplines. Younger people should care for older generations.

Hindus have obligations to the community. They are to do no harm to other people or their property. They are responsible to help holy people who have forsaken the world to seek the divine. Expressing compassion to all humans and animals, especially cows, is of special merit. The cow, which gives milk and manure that serves as fuel, disinfectant, and building material, is a symbol of the value of all living things. Some Hindus act according to very strong humanitarian principles. For other Hindus, humanitarian activities are secular rather than religious obligations.

An Interpretation of History

History for Hindus differs from history in Western religions. Western religions think of a definite beginning of history, progress through centuries in which God intervenes in human lives, and a final judgment separating good from evil. Hindus honor the Vedas, ancient beliefs and practices, and acknowledge appearances of deities in specific times and places. The big difference is that Hindu literature implies that the whole process can end and begin again for successive repetitions. What is true for the universe is also true for humans.

Rituals and Symbols

The most important rituals of Hindus are the **Samskaras,** the sacraments or rites by which a Hindu is fully integrated into the community.[32] The birth of a child and his or her name giving is assigned great importance.

The **upanayana** sacrament initiates a boy as a twice-born person, one who is responsible for his actions in religious regulations. It is the beginning of the student stage, or ashram. He is invested with a sacred thread, **janëu,** which he must wear

Samskaras
[sam-SKAHR-as]
The sacraments or rites by which a Hindu is fully integrated into the community.

upanayana
[oo-PA-na-YAH-na]
The initiation rite indicating that a boy is a twice-born person.

janëu [JAN-eu]
The sacred thread worn by the three upper castes.

The Sacred Cow. Hindu women pet a sacred cow on Teej, a women's day festival in Kathmandu, Nepal.

at all times if he would remain in his caste. He must respect the janëu and his guru at all times.

Marriage, **vivaha,** symbolizes entry into the second stage, or ashram, that of householder. Monogamy is the most common form of marriage today. India now recognizes civil marriage and the right of divorce, which can be initiated by either man or woman. The marriage ceremony proper is usually culminated with a generous feast. The purpose of marriage, according to the Vedas, was to allow a man to produce a son who would continue the sacrifices. Today, various motives in marriage are acknowledged.

Funerals, **antyesti,** are the last rites observed by almost all Hindus. Although a few Hindus are buried, most are cremated in a **shraddha,** the last rites. The eldest son of the deceased is usually the one who performs the rites. The ideal wood used in the funeral pyre is sandalwood, which is pleasantly fragrant. These sacraments, at birth, second birth, marriage, and death, complete the obligations of a Hindu.

Between times of these major sacraments, Hindus practice many rituals and use many symbols.

Hindu worship in temples can be either individual or congregational. Worship may be assisted by a priest. Worshipers may recite Vedic hymns, light candles or other sacred flame, offer pure food to the gods, offer money to be used for religious purposes, and comment on a guru's insights regarding religious duties. The pool, or tank, found at some temples is used for ritual bathing. There may be only one god image or images of several different gods. Different acts of worship may be occurring at the same time in different parts of the temple.

Puja is a form of worship that an individual addresses to the image of a deity or a pair of deities. This devotion of a person to an image, then, becomes an

vivaha [vi-VA-ha] Marriage. The rite of entry into the second stage or ashram, that of householder.

antyesti [un-TYES-ti] Funerals. Last rites.

shraddha [SHRAD-dha] Last rites. The prescribed rituals for the deceased.

puja [POO-ja] Hindu worship of deities. Brahmins often perform rituals desired by householders. The ritual worship of India.

important person in the residence, cared for with personal attention as one would care for a member of the family.

Other religious obligations may also be either individual or communal. It is quite common for different members of the same family to choose separate paths of duty for themselves. They may worship at different temples at different times, keep separate fast days, and meet different humanitarian obligations. Some festivals bring local communities together; other observances bring together all the followers of a particular guru or saint; and there are some national holy days. Festivals integrate society in several ways; the lives of the deities in Hindu myths "serve as guides for individual daily behavior." Especially for women, whose status can change overnight with widowhood, the festivals are important. Stanley and Ruth Freed describe the varied functions of festivals in India:

> Festivals treat the emotional and social needs of individuals. Fear of disease and death, the maintenance of important relationships, the enhancement of character and karma through pious acts, and the desire to break daily routine, eat special food and have a little fun, all play a role in the yearly round of festivals.[33]

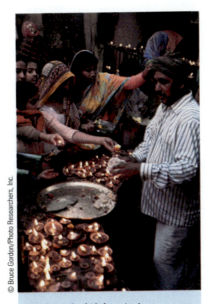

© Bruce Gordon/Photo Researchers, Inc.

Divālī Festival Lights. In Agra, a man sells ghee lamps.

Some of the nationwide festivals are described here as they appear in Dr. I. C. Sharma's *Ethical Philosophies of India*.[34] During Raksabandhana, Indians tie a thread around their wrists to symbolize the individual's obligation to sacrifice personal, family, and community interests to the welfare of the nation and all humanity. Everyone who has this concern for humanity is a Brahmin at heart. Vijayadasami celebrates the victory of Rama over Ravana. The celebrant rejoices in the victory of good over evil and assumes responsibility for being a keeper of righteousness. Divālī is a festival of lights, awakening aesthetic appreciation. All castes recognize that the aesthetic gifts of the Vaisyas reside, in some measure, in them. During Holi, all castes become as Shudras. Through costume and actions, the roles of participants are temporarily reversed. Castes are a temporary condition; ultimately everyone has the same spiritual unity. Some Brahmins think that in mass celebrations the ideals of the festivals are often lost.

Life after Death

> He who thinks this self a killer and he who thinks it killed, both fail to understand; it does not kill, nor is it killed. (19) It is not born, it does not die; having been, it will never not be; unborn, enduring, constant, and primordial, it is not killed when the body is killed. (20) Arjuna, when a man knows the self to be indestructible, enduring, unborn, unchanging, how does he kill or cause anyone to kill? (21)[35]

In this passage of the Bhagavad Gita, the Lord Krishna assures the young warrior Arjuna he can neither kill his family in warfare nor be killed by them. Each soul is indestructible. Inevitably it will endure the death of the present body and be reborn in another body. The soul changes bodies as a person changes worn-out clothes. Among the dozens of doctrines of Hinduism that have fascinated peoples all over the world, none is more interesting than the concept of reincarnation, or its Hindu term, *samsara*.

In Hinduism, reincarnation is expressed as samsara, a course or succession of states of existence. One author has translated samsara as "what turns round forever."

Hinduism has analyzed humans into many more parts than body and soul. Essentially, the Bhagavad Gita asserts that the self is unchanging, for it is of the essence of the great self. The embodied self, however, is subject to the changing conditions of life. Although the self is inviolable, the distinctive personality is involved in karma and the conditions of rebirth. Many Hindus found pleasures in life, but they realized that at some point they would desire release from the wheel of rebirth. As a person can tire of seeing a motion picture film too many times, so he or she can tire of birth, life, death, and rebirth. The Hindu sages differ in their opinions whether a person can find final liberation in an embodied state.

The last rites complete the sacraments required to prepare a Hindu for the next life. One who has followed the approved paths and completed the required sacraments can anticipate blessing one's family. The most holy can anticipate release from rebirth.

Hinduism and Other Religions

Hinduism's response to other religions has varied according to the religions and the circumstances of history. In general, Hinduism has gone its own way, independent of the religions of other peoples. Most often it has been tolerant of other religions in India. It has resisted religions that have tried to prove Hinduism is wrong or insisted Hindus should convert. Many Hindu religious leaders have pointed out the similarities between the teachings and practices of other religions and Hinduism. They are glad to have peoples of other religions gain insights from the sacred writings of the Hindus. Upper-caste Hindus, however, have been harsh to peers who abandon the faith of their birth. Hinduism has had centuries of experience in religious diversity. More than any other religion, it has produced saints and teachers who have taught ways for peoples of many religions to find a common spiritual ground.

In practice, however, relationships among Hindus, Muslims, and Sikhs have erupted into violence. A decade after the partition of India and Pakistan, a young Akbar Adil said to Jan Myrdal, "Don't tell me about Hindus! They got hold of my aunt and hacked her to pieces. Before burying her we had to put the corpse together again from sixteen pieces. And still there were parts missing."[36] Myrdal shows that terrible murders were perpetuated by both Muslims and Hindus. The Sikhs, he reported, participated as well. Some Sikhs revolted against President's Rule in the state of Punjab. On June 6, 1984, Indian Army troops invaded the Sikh Golden Temple at Amritsar to remove revolutionary followers of Sant Jarnail Singh Bhindranwale. On October 31, 1984, Sikh members of Indira Gandhi's bodyguard assassinated her.[37] Many Hindus responded by murdering Sikhs. These reports were deeply shocking; they were even more shocking because Hinduism has a history of living peacefully alongside many different religious minorities.

Hinduism has inspired other religious expressions that incorporate its teachings and practices but whose devotees are not accepted by most Brahmins as real Hindus. Two forms that appeared in the Western world, as well as in India, are of particular interest. They are Theosophy and the International Society for Krishna Consciousness (ISKCON) movements.

In Madras, India, residents are cognizant of the Theosophical Society, a group organized by Helena Petrovna Blavatsky (1831–1891) in the United States in 1875. Theosophy, which means "divine wisdom," played a role in promoting independent India by supporting Swami Dayananda Sarisvati in his Arya Samaj.

© Katrina Thomas/City Lore

A Hindu Temple in Flushing, New York. Hindus living in this metropolitan area express their faith in traditional Hindu yogas of release.

Blavatsky's teachings appeared in *The Secret Doctrine* (1888) and *The Voice of Silence* (1889). The ancient masters of religion, she wrote, knew and taught a single, universal wisdom. In each person there is something eternal and divine that can be brought together with that wisdom, liberating the soul from endless deaths and births. Not limited to Hindu culture, Blavatsky claimed knowledge from Tibet and cooperated with Colonel Olcot in winning social reforms for Buddhists in Sri Lanka who felt discriminated against by their British rulers. After Blavatsky's death, the movement continued to grow and prosper, particularly in the United States and Great Britain.

Annie Besant promoted Theosophy in India by identifying its messiah with a young Brahmin, Krishnamurti (1885–1986). In 1929 he had a religious experience that caused him to reject that role and travel alone in the world. According to Arvind Sharma, Krishnamurti's goal was "to set men free from all the cages which divide man from man, such as race, religion, class, and tradition, and thus bring about a transformation of the human psyche."[38]

The ISKON began in the United States in 1966. Abhay Charyan De worked among the young men and women of the counterculture, involving them in the bhakti movement. He taught them kirtana, chanting the name of Lord Krishna. Dressed as Hindus, men and women lived separately until they married. Couples were taught to engage in sex only for procreation. Their activities are public chanting, offering food, distributing literature, collecting contributions, and talking with potential converts. Members of the society may practice puja and are sometimes seen in Hindu temples. Their most conspicuous temple is New Vrindavran in Wheeling, West Virginia.

Historical Development: Hinduism and the United States

After Indian independence, the United States changed its immigration laws to permit more people from India to enter the country. The immigration laws of 1968 gave preference to large groups of Indian professionals. The status of all Indians in the United States was improved by the independence of India.

American corporations have strengthened ties with India, and there is growing respect for Indian attainments in sciences, technologies, and businesses. Indians' success in operating customer-service phone centers for American businesses has disturbed some American workers, however. Internet technology is another area of competition: three of the top ten global firms are in India. Not only are Bangalore and the nearby Electronics City developing rapidly, but also many other centers are expanding similarly.[39] Indian engineering and technology graduates are in demand in the United States and in many other countries. The United States receives three times as many imports from India as from European Union countries or Japan. The strengthening ties between the people of India and the United States have developed so quickly that they are sometimes difficult for both peoples to grasp.

Having introduced Hinduism, the largest religion in India, we now turn to Buddhism, a distinctive faith that had its roots in Hinduism. Buddhism retained many Hindu concepts, but it added fresh insights and practices. In turn, Buddhism helped influence later Hinduism. Through efforts of missionaries, however, Buddhism spread its influence across Asia and now touches all parts of the world.

CONSIDER THIS
Samsara and Moksha

Since caste has been officially abolished in India, it is not fair to keep discussing it as if it were an unassailable part of Hinduism. In the past it was usually discussed as a part of the teachings karma, samsara, and moksha. Karma is an essential part of Hinduism; caste is not.

In the past, one was thought to be born in a caste in which one remained for a lifetime. Karma held one to the wheel of rebirth and re-death, samsara. The solution was to choose the proper discipline, or yoga, that would help one gain release from samsara. The effects of one's thoughts and actions in previous lives could, perhaps, be softened or shortened in the turning wheel of life. The goal was rising through the castes over many lifetimes until one obtained release. Practicing the proper yogas helped move one toward release.

Was there any way to obtain release in only one lifetime? The answer for masses of Hindus seemed to be negative. Siddhartha Gautama, a Kshatriya, found that answer too pessimistic. He later announced that he had found the way of release in one lifetime: The Buddha and Buddhism offered a more hopeful alternative to Hindu tradition.

VOCABULARY

Agamas [AH-ga-mas]
Agni [AG-ni]
antyesti [un-TYES-ti]
Aranyakas [ah-RAN-yu-kuz]
Aryans [AHR-yuns]

Atman [AHT-man]
avidya [a-VID-ya]
bhakti yoga [BAHK-ti]
Brahma [bram-HAH]
Brahman [bram-MUN]

Brahmanas [BRAH-muh-nus]
Brahmins [BRAH-mens]
caste [CAST]
Dravidians [drah-VID-e-uns]
guru [GU-RU] or [GOO-ROO]

Indra [IN-dra]
Itihasa-Purana [iti-HAHT-sah poo-RAH-na]
janëu [JAN-eu]
jnana yoga [JYNAH-na]
kalpa [KAL-pa]
karma yoga [KAHR-ma]
Krishna [KRISH-na]
Kshatriya [KSHA-tri-ya]
law of karma [KAHR-ma]
Laws of Manu [MAH-noo]
Mahabharata [ma-HAH-BAH-ra-ta]
Manu [MAH-noo]
Maya [MAH-ya]
Mitra [MI-tra]
moksha [MOWK-sha]

nirguna Brahman [NIR-goo-na]
prakriti [pra-KRI-ti]
puja [POO-ja]
puranas [pu-RAHN-as]
Purusha [PU-roo-sha]
raja yoga [RAH-jah]
Ramayana [rah-MAH-ya-na]
reincarnation [REE-in-cahr-NAY-shun]
Rita [RI-ta]
saguna Brahman [SA-goo-na]
samadhi [sa-MAH-di]
samsara [sam-SAH-ra]
Samskaras [sam-SKAHR-as]
sannyasin [san-NYAH-sin]
Shiva [SHEE-va]
shraddha [SHRAD-dha]

shruti [SHROO-ti]
Shudras [SHOO-dras]
Soma [sow-ma]
smriti [SMRI-ti]
tantras [TUN-trus]
untouchables
upanayana [oo-PA-na-YAH-na]
Upanishads [oo-PA-ne-shads]
Vaishya [VAI-shya]
varna [VAR-na]
Varuna [VA-r̊oo-na]
Vedanta [ve-DAHN-ta]
Vedas [VAY-daz]
Vishnu [VISH-noo]
vivaha [vi-VA-ha]

QUESTIONS FOR REVIEW

1. What divisions of society in India indicate that integration of Aryan and Dravidian culture was not entirely peaceful?
2. What is the condition of caste and outcaste in India today?
3. Name the four castes and describe how they differ.
4. Describe the four yogas. Which personality type does each accommodate?
5. Tell the story of the Ramayana.
6. What is the ideal relationship between Brahman and Atman?
7. How is karma related to samsara and caste?
8. Tell the life story of Mohandas K. Gandhi.
9. Describe some deities of popular Hinduism.
10. How do Hindus worship the divine?

QUESTIONS FOR DISCUSSION

1. What concepts are most important in understanding Hinduism?
2. Can a non-Hindu ever become a Hindu?
3. Can a Hindu woman be active in India's new business economy and uphold the ideals of the Laws of Manu?
4. Compare Hindu gurus with other teachers.
5. What challenges do Hindu women face in the twenty-first century?

NOTES

1. Klaus K. Klostermaier, *A Survey of Hinduism* (Albany: State University of New York Press, 1989), p. 63.
2. Ibid., p. 67.
3. Walter H. Maurer, *Pinnacles of India's Past: Selections from the Ṛgveda* (Philadelphia: John Benjamins, 1986), p. 12.
4. Ibid., pp. 42–43.
5. Ibid., pp. 76–77.
6. Ibid., p. 99.
7. Ibid., p. 108.
8. Wendy Doniger O'Flaherty, ed., *Karma and Rebirth in Classical Indian Traditions* (Berkeley: University of California Press, 1980), p. 3.
9. Klostermaier, p. 193.
10. Ibid., pp. 68, 94.
11. *Bhagavad-Gita*, trans. Barbara Stoller Miller (New York: Columbia University Press, 1986), 6:5–9, pp. 41, 42. Copyright © 1986 by Columbia University Press.
12. Ibid., 4:6–9, p. 50.
13. Ibid., 5:18, p. 59.

14. Ibid., 6:30, p. 67.
15. Ibid., 8:3–6, pp. 77–78.
16. Wendy Doniger and Brian K. Smith, *The Laws of Manu* (London: Penguin Books, 1991), p. 197. Copyright © 1991 by Wendy Doniger and Brian K. Smith. Reproduced by permission of Penguin UK Ltd.
17. Ibid., pp. 48–49.
18. Ibid. p. 117.
19. Karen Pechilis (ed.), *The Graceful Guru: Hindu Female Gurus in India and the United States* (New York: Oxford University Press, 2004), p. 5.
20. Meena Khandelwal, *Women in Ochre Robes: Gendering Hindu Renunciation* (Albany, NY: State University of New York Press, 2004), p. 1.
21. David R. Kinsley, *The Sword and the Flute* (Berkeley: University of California Press, 1975), pp. 104–105.
22. Lynn Foulston, *At the Feet of the Goddess: The Divine Feminine in Local Hindu Religion* (Brighton, UK: Sussex Academic Press, 2002), p. 99.
23. Ibid., pp. 41–43.
24. Hari Prasad Shastri, trans., *The Ramayana of Valmiki,* vol. 3 (London: Santi Sadan, 1959), p. 617.
25. Swami Abhedananda, ed., *The Sayings of Sri Ramakrishna* (New York: Vedanda Society, 1903).
26. Louis Fischer, ed., *The Essential Gandhi* (New York: Random House, 1962), p. 309.
27. June O'Connor, *The Quest for Political and Spiritual Liberation* (Rutherford, NJ: Fairleigh Dickinson University Press, 1977), p. 95.
28. Sri Aurobindo, *The Life Divine* (New York: Greystone Press, 1949), p. 233; Radhakrishnan and C. A. Moore, *A Source Book in Indian Philosophy* (Princeton, NJ: Princeton University Press, 1957), p. 599.
29. Richard F. Nyrop, *India: A Country Study* (Washington, DC: U.S. Government Printing Office as represented by the Secretary of the Army, 1985), p. 72.
30. Katherine K. Young, "Hinduism," in *Women in World Religions,* ed. Arvind Sharma (Albany: State University of New York Press, 1987), p. 97.
31. A. L. Basham, *The Wonder That Was India* (New York: Grove Press, 1959), p. 385.
32. Klostermaier, p. 175.
33. Stanley A. Freed and Ruth S. Freed, *Hindu Festivals in a North India Village.* American Museum of Natural History Anthropological Paper No. 81 (Seattle: University of Washington Press, 1998), p. 294.
34. I. C. Sharma, *The Ethical Philosophies of India* (Lincoln, NB: Johnsen, 1965), pp. 83–85.
35. Miller, 2:19–22, p. 32.
36. Jan Myrdal, *India Waits,* trans, Alan Bernstein (Chicago: Lake View Press, 1986), p. 25.
37. Nyrop, p. 377.
38. Arvind Sharma, *Modern Hindu Thought, The Essential Texts* (New Delhi: Oxford University Press, 2002), p. 345.
39. "The Bangalore Paradox," *The Economist,* April 23, 2005, pp. 67–69.

READINGS

Doniger, Wendy, and Brian K. Smith. *The Laws of Manu.* London: Penguin Books, 1991.

Fischer, Louis, ed. *The Essential Gandhi.* New York: Random House, 1962.

Foulston, Lynn. *At the Feet of the Goddess: The Divine Feminine in Local Hindu Religion.* Brighton, UK: Sussex Academic Press, 2002.

Freed, Stanley A., and Ruth S. Freed. *Hindu Festivals in a North India Village.* American Museum of Natural History Anthropological Paper No. 81. Seattle: University of Washington Press, 1998.

Isherwood, Christopher. *Ramakrishna and His Disciples.* New York: Simon & Schuster, 1965.

Khandelwal, Meena. *Women in Ochre Robes: Gendering Hindu Renunciation.* Albany, NY: State University of New York Press, 2004.

Kinsley, David. *Hinduism: A Cultural Perspective.* Englewood Cliffs, NJ: Prentice Hall, 1982.

Klostermaier, Klaus K. *A Survey of Hinduism.* Albany: State University of New York Press, 1989.

Koller, John M. *The Indian Way.* New York: Macmillan, 1982.

Maurer, Walter H. *Pinnacles of India's Past: Selections from the Ṛgveda.* Philadelphia: John Benjamins, 1986.

O'Flaherty, Wendy Doniger. *The Rig Veda.* London: Penguin Books, 1981.

Orr, Leslie C. *Donors, Devotees, and Daughters of God: Temple Women in Medieval Tamilnadu.* New York: Oxford University Press, 2000.

Pechilis, Karen, ed. *The Graceful Guru: Hindu Female Gurus in India and the United States.* New York: Oxford University Press, 2004.

Radhakrishnan, S. ed. and trans. *The Bhagavadgita.* New York: Harper Colophon Books, 1973.

Sharma, Arvind. *Modern Hindu Thought, The Essential Texts.* New Delhi: Oxford University Press, 2002.

Sharma, I. C. *Ethical Philosophies of India.* Lincoln, NB: Johnsen, 1965.

Younger, Paul. *Playing Host to Deity: Festival Religion in the South Indian Tradition.* New York: Oxford University Press, 2002.

BASIC TENETS OF HINDUISM—Significant Beings

GODS OF THE RIG-VEDA	
Indra (storms, monsoons)	
Mitra (faith-keeping, loyalty)	
Rudra (mountain storms, plants)	
Savitar, Surya (sun)	
Varuṇa (the high-arched sky)	
GODS OF THE SACRIFICE	
Agni (god of fire)	Soma (drink of communion)
PRINCIPLE OF ORDER	
Rita [Ṛta]	
GODS OF POPULAR HINDUISM	
Brahma (creator)	
Shiva (destroyer)	Vishnu (preserver) (Lakshmi)
Devi or Shakti	**Avatars of Vishnu**
Durga (avenger)	Krishna [Radha]
Kali (wrathful goddess)	
Parvati (young lover)	Rama [Sita]
Umma (protecting mother)	
Sons	
Ganesha	
Kumara or Karttikeya	
Adherents	**Adherents**
Shaivites	Vaishnavites

CHAPTER 4

Buddhism

OVERVIEW AND THEMES

"Now this, monks, is the Ariyan truth about the arising of Ill.

"It is the craving that leads back to birth, along with the lure and the lust that lingers longingly now here, now there: namely, the craving for sensual pleasure, the craving to be born again, the craving for existence to end. Such, monks, is the Ariyan truth about the arising of Ill.

"And this monks, is the Ariyan truth about the ceasing of Ill:

It is the utterly passionless cessation of, the giving up, the forsaking, the release from, the absence of longing for this craving."

—*Sanyutta Nikaya, Part V**

IMPORTANT TEACHINGS OF BUDDHISM

Siddhartha Gautama is the Buddha, the Enlightened One. Through him release is possible in this lifetime.

There are Four Noble Truths.

Follow the Eightfold Path to gain Nirvana.

AREAS OF BUDDHIST CONCENTRATION

Asia: 366,790,000

Europe: 1,594,000

United States: 2,450,000

Major Divisions: Mahayana (larger group) and Theravedin (smaller group)

*Rhys Davids and F. L. Woodward, trans., *The Book of the Kindred Sayings* (Oxford, London: Pali Text Society, 1979), pp. 356–357; copyright 1979 by the Pali Text Society.

About the time that some of the Upanishads were being written, a handsome young prince appeared among the Shakyas of northern India. His proud parents, King Suddhodanna and Queen Maya, named him Siddhartha Gautama. Hidden and protected from the harshness of the world, he grew up surrounded by luxury and sensual pleasures. Later, when he did make his brief excursions outside his palace, into the environment of common people, he became so disturbed by their suffering that he wanted to devote his life to relieving them of their pain. Beginning his search in his late twenties, he found his answers in his mid-thirties. Having discovered how to accomplish release of humans from suffering, he became known as the Buddha, the enlightened one. During the remainder of his eighty years he was revered as Shakyamuni, the sage of the Shakyas, and as the compassionate Buddha.

In India, about two centuries later, the Four Noble Truths of the Buddha's message reached the remorseful heart of the powerful monarch Ashoka Maurya. As penance for his wanton destruction of the kingdom of Kalinga some years earlier, he reformed his own court, making it more compassionate for living creatures, and taught his people the Buddha's message that emphasized family and community values. He was so devoted a follower that he enlisted his family in carrying the Buddha's teachings to the neighboring island of Ceylon (Sri Lanka).

The monks and nuns who had left their homes to follow the Buddha took his teachings also to the isolated heights of Tibet. In that mountainous region they initiated a form of Buddhism that eventually produced a twenty-first century celebrity, the Dalai Lama. When monks took their message to China, Chinese peoples learned that sons who became monks could help both ancestors and living relatives. Buddhism joined Confucianism

Buddhist Monk. Head of Sherpa Monastery, Nepal, Everest Region.

and Daoism as vital religions in China. From China, missionaries influenced the Koreans, who, in turn, introduced the Buddha's dharma in Japan. From China and Japan emmigrants took their Buddhism to Canada and the United States, where it continues to grow from its Asian roots.

Buddhism has rewarded both its ordinary and its exceptional followers. On the surface, there are no religious teachings easier to appreciate than the Four Noble Truths of the Buddha. In depth, there are no religious teachings more profound. For gifted followers who have patience and persistence, Buddhism has offered some of the most challenging doctrines found in religions. What could be more challenging than to understand the meaning of a "selfless mind"? From its simplest rites to its greatest philosophies, Buddhism has offered a faith to motivate millions of followers around the world.

Unlike Hinduism, whose Vedas rise from the dim mists of prehistoric times, Buddhism began with a founder. The personality of the Buddha in history is absolutely essential to understanding the character of Buddhism. The appearance of a central person with whom believers can identify introduces fresh possibilities for varieties of interpretation. The task is complicated because believers themselves are divided about interpretation.[1]

Historical Development: The Life of the Buddha

Within Buddhism, believers in two major points of view contend to tell the "correct" story of the Buddha. The more conservative view, the Theravadin, emphasizes the down-to-earth, practical example of an exceptional man, Siddhartha Gautama, the Buddha. The more creative view, the Mahayana, emphasizes the divine character of the Buddha, who revealed to his precocious followers profound insights of human minds, heavens, and hells. Both these views, which will be discussed later, are represented in the dynamic tradition of a powerful, living faith. From widely differing points of view, devoted Buddhists interpret the same facts in the history of the Buddha.

The Birth of the Buddha

Some facts about the adored Buddha are generally accepted. He began life on earth as Siddhartha Gautama about 563 B.C.E. (some scholars say 560) in northern India at Lumbini Grove, about a hundred miles from Benares. As pictured in Buddhist art, his mother, Queen **Maya**, stood holding with her right hand the branch of an ashoka tree as she gave birth to the future Buddha.[2] Being from the Shakya clan, he was later known, particularly to the Chinese, as **Shakyamuni** (sage of the Shakyas). His father, **Suddhodana,** was a powerful lord, a Kshatriya, in the feudal system.

Maya (queen) [MAH-ya] The mother of Siddhartha Gautama, the Buddha.

Shakyamuni [SHAH-kya-MOO-nee] The sage of the Shakya clan, Siddhartha Gautama, the Buddha. The term is widely used in China and Japan.

Suddhodana [SUD-DHOH-da-na] The king who was father of Siddhartha Gautama. He is said to have tried to keep Siddhartha ignorant of human suffering.

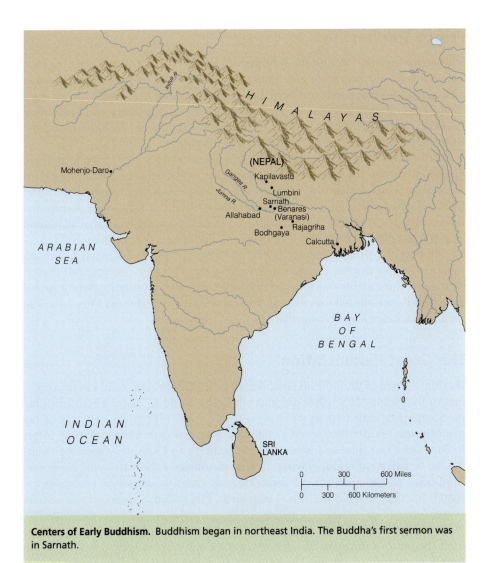

Centers of Early Buddhism. Buddhism began in northeast India. The Buddha's first sermon was in Sarnath.

Beyond these facts, there are many different interpretations.[3] Queen Maya dreamed, the night before conceiving the Buddha, that she lay on a heavenly couch in a golden mansion in the Himalayas. The Buddha became a beautiful white elephant, bearing in his trunk a white lotus flower. He seemed to touch her right side and enter her womb. From this dream, some Buddhists believe that is how the Buddha was incarnate into Queen Maya. At the time of her deliverance, she was traveling from Kapilavastu to Devadaha. In a Sal grove along the way, she stood as she delivered the child. Angels received the new baby in a golden net. The child stood, walked, and cried, "I am supreme in the world. This is my last birth: henceforth there shall be no more birth for me!"[4] There are also accounts of consternation among demons who attempted to destroy such a power for good in the world. To provide a contrast to Buddha's later monastic life, his family's riches are described in detail. Another story tells about Suddhodana's being informed that if Siddhartha could be prevented from becoming a monk, he would become a powerful king.

Prince Siddhartha

Siddhartha moved through the Brahmanic (Hindu) steps as a student and then as a householder, marrying a neighboring princess, **Yashodhara,** when he was nineteen. From that union was born a son, Rahula. Siddhartha had done his duty according to Brahmanic custom. He had all the riches of a prince and everything he needed to fulfill the expectations of an orthodox member of the Kshatriya caste. Restless, he wanted to see the world beyond his palace.

Siddhartha's father, thinking of his son's potential as a ruler, tried to prevent him from seeing any painful human experiences; instead, he surrounded him with every kind of pleasure. His plan was thwarted when Siddhartha went out into the community and, on separate occasions, saw four sights that deeply disturbed him. He saw an old man and learned from his chariot driver that all human beings must grow old. He saw a sick person and learned that sickness and suffering are part of human existence. Siddhartha saw a corpse and learned that death is an experience that befalls every human. His deep concern and anguish caused by the first three sights was relieved only when he saw a wandering ascetic; to his mind this figure offered the only way to deal with the sufferings of humanity. The seed of his future identity was planted.

The Great Renunciation

Having learned of the suffering entailed in birth, Siddhartha could not find comfort in the palace. His father did everything he could to distract him from his preoccupation with human suffering—to no avail. Within the confines of his princely life, Siddhartha could not find a way out of human suffering. After looking for a last time on his beloved Yashodhara and Rahula, who were sleeping, he departed at night. Having gone some distance, he sent home his horse, Kanthaka, and his servant, Channa. He was twenty-nine when he began his search for release from the wheel of rebirth. His arduous quest was to last six years.

Shaving his head, Siddhartha put on the clothes of a wandering ascetic. Eventually he reached Rajagaha, a royal city, and went in succession to the caves of two Brahmin yogins, whom he chose in turn as gurus. Alara Kalama and Uddaka Ramaputta attempted to teach him through intellectual order and discussions the way to the realms of nothingness. Siddhartha gave each of them an opportunity to help him, but he did not think he was making progress.

Artists and writers devoted to the Buddha have depicted him in the grove of Uruvela as emaciated from six years of fasting. As long as a person is enjoying the pleasures of the flesh, Siddhartha reasoned, he or she cannot find the light of truth or release from rebirth. The anecdotes of his devotion are truly impressive. He held his breath until his head roared, ate little food—and what he did eat was sickening—endured painful body positions for lengthy periods, became encrusted with filth, and lost weight until his bones protruded and he could feel his spine by pressing on his abdomen. The five ascetics who were his friends during this ordeal thought he would die from his privations.

He did lose consciousness. One tradition claims his life was saved by a village maid, Sujata, who gave him a little food. As he gained the strength necessary to return to life, he concluded he had followed the extreme path of asceticism as far as he could go, and it had brought no release for him.

Yashodhara
[ya-SHOW-dha-ra]
The wife of Siddhartha Gautama and mother of Rahula. She is said to have been a neighboring princess chosen for Prince Siddhartha.

The Enlightenment

He moved on to a grove (now **Bodhgaya**), where he found a pipal tree under which he could sit in isolation. The paths suggested by others had not worked for him. Abandoning the path of rigid asceticism, he practiced a form of meditation that did not cause such bodily pain. It was in that state of meditation that he became enlightened, the Buddha. Under the Bo tree, the tree of enlightenment, he saw why he had not attained release.

In one account of his meditation, Buddhist tradition describes the steps of his awakening.[5] His mind cleansed and concentrated, Siddhartha remembered his former existences—his names, roles in life, and sufferings. Early in the night he found knowledge dispelling ignorance. Concentrating his powerful vision on the order of beings coming into existence and passing away, he interpreted the process in terms of their karma. In a third exploration, during the third watch, he concentrated on destruction of binding influences of desire that caused suffering. He realized that destroying desire would eliminate suffering, leaving him free, awake, and enlightened.

According to Buddhist tradition, the incident is full of godly and demonic characters who enter Buddha's struggle to aid or mislead him from his goal. **Mara** tempted him to return to the Kshatriya duties of the Shakyas. When he had withstood the temptations, the Buddha experienced the blessings of the gods. Tradition says he stayed under the tree for seven weeks.

Bodhgaya Stupa. Site of the tree where the Buddha was enlightened.

The enlightened one knew he had overcome the ignorance that leads to suffering with the knowledge that brings release. He could now experience a glimpse of what it would be like to escape rebirth. He was ecstatic, enlightened, and released. Filled with joy and compassion, the Buddha wanted to share his good news with the five ascetics who had endured the ordeal that had ended in fortune for him. Tradition says he waited seven weeks before he began to teach.

The First Sermon at Benares

Siddhartha's enlightened state changed his outward appearance to the extent that the five reluctant ascetics accepted him again, curious to learn what had happened to him. In the Deer Park of Sarnath, outside Benares (now called Varanasi), the Buddha, the enlightened one, delivered his first sermon. Essentially he presented the Middle Path between the two extremes of self-indulgence and self-mortification. He went on to list the four truths of his enlightenment.

> Monks, these two extremes should not be followed by one who has gone forth as a wanderer. What two?

Bodhgaya [bowd-GAH-ya] A temple that commemorates the grove where the Buddha found enlightenment.

Mara [MAH-rah] The evil one who tempted the Buddha at Bodhgaya.

Devotion to pleasures of sense, a low practice of villagers, a practice unworthy, unprofitable, the way of the world (on the one hand); and (on the other) devotion to self-mortification, which is painful, unworthy and unprofitable.

By avoiding these two extremes the Thatāgata has gained knowledge of that middle path which giveth vision, which giveth knowledge, which causeth calm, special knowledge, enlightenment, Nibbāna.

And what monks, is that middle path which giveth vision . . . Nibbāna?

Verily it is this Ariyan eightfold way, to wit: Right view, right aim, right speech, right action, right living, right effort, right mindfulness, right concentration. This, monks, is that middle path which giveth vision, which giveth knowledge, which causeth calm, special knowledge, enlightenment, Nibbāna.

Now this, monks, is the Ariyan truth about Ill:

Birth is Ill, decay is Ill, sickness is Ill, death is Ill: likewise sorrow and grief, woe, lamentation and despair. To be conjoined with things which we dislike: to be separated from things which we like—that also is Ill. Not to get what one wants—that also is Ill. In a word, this body, this fivefold mass which is based on grasping—that is Ill.

Now this, monks, is the Ariyan truth about the arising of Ill: In a word, this body, this fivefold mass which is based on grasping, that is Ill.

Now this, monks, is the Ariyan truth about the arising of Ill:

It is the craving that leads back to birth, along with the lure and the lust that lingers longingly now here, now there: namely, the craving for sensual pleasure, the craving to be born again, the craving for existence to end. Such, monks, is the Ariyan truth about the arising of Ill.

And this, monks, is the Ariyan truth about the ceasing of Ill:

Verily it is the utter passionless cessation of, the giving up, the forsaking, the release from, the absence of longing for this craving.[6]

The First Disciples

Convinced of his doctrine, the five ascetics became his disciples. Their identification with Gautama's experience was the beginning of Buddhist religion. The **Sangha,** the Buddhist religious order that included ascetics and, eventually, laypeople, was the first organization.

After the five ascetics joined the Buddha, fifty-five men of good families joined the order. All became **arhats,** instructed in the **dharma,** teachings, and attained enlightenment. They would not be reborn. These men became the vanguard of monks wandering the countryside, villages, and towns, teaching the dharma. Brahmins, also, such as Sariputra, a chief disciple, joined the order. Caste was not abolished, but in the sangha it was accepted without distinction.

At a grove in Uruvela, the Buddha met three Brahmin monks who worshiped the sacred flame. He received them and their disciples into his order. The most important of the three was Uruvela Kashyapa. To these fire worshipers the Buddha delivered his famous sermon on fire. Everything is on fire, or burning, he said. Everything burns with desire and suffering. The true monk despises sensations, desires, and suffering. He is freed from sensations, desires, and suffering. Kashyapa (Mahakashyapa) understood and became one of the Buddha's leading disciples. He appeared at the great turning points of Buddhism, when his leadership was most needed.

Sangha [SANG-ha]
The Buddhist monastic order. Buddhism accepted both monks and nuns. The term can also include laity.

arhat [UR-hut]
An enlightened, holy person.

dharma [DAR-ma]
In Buddhism, law. It can be the law of the universe or the law or tradition taught by the Buddha.

On his early missions, the Buddha traveled through the powerful kingdoms of Koshala and Magadha, along the river Ganges. Recognizing Siddhartha Gautama as a prince, the lords generously welcomed him and provided for his needs. His charisma attracted men and women of all castes. When he returned to his father's home in Kapilavastu, he was honored in his own country.

Members of the Buddha's family, who had missed his presence, now responded warmly to his spiritual leadership. Suddhodana, his father, embraced his teachings. Rahula, his son, entered monastic life. His cousin Ananda joined the order and became his faithful companion. Although his cousin Devadatta, brother of Yashodhara, joined, he was often portrayed as acting from resentment toward his brother-in-law. Perhaps the most influential person on the future of Buddhism, however, was Mahajapati, a wife of Suddhodana and sister of Queen Maya, who had died shortly after the birth of the Buddha.

Seeing that most of her family had entered the order, Mahajapati earnestly requested she be allowed to join. The Buddha denied her request. Again and again she implored him to admit her to an order for women. A story relates that rather than accept as final his decision, she organized a group of women who dressed as ascetics and traveled a far distance in bare feet to entreat the Buddha. When he saw their suffering, he was impressed with their earnestness and relented. Buddhism accepted into the monastic order men, and separately, women. The Buddha was reluctant to upset family life; he was already criticized for it.

The Buddha attracted social classes as different as that of a barber and a wealthy courtesan. The great success of the order, however, flowed from devotion of householders who wanted to support the monks, nuns, and the Buddha. Householders could observe the first five of the Ten Precepts, and in lieu of observing the second five, could support the monks who observed all ten.

The Buddha Addressing Monks at Sarnath. The newly enlightened Siddhartha Gautama delivers his sermon to ascetics.

1. Not taking life
2. Not stealing
3. Being chaste
4. Not lying
5. Not drinking intoxicants
6. Eating moderately and not after noon
7. Avoiding spectacles such as singing or dramas
8. Not using flowers, perfumes, or jewelry
9. Using simple beds
10. Accepting no gold or silver

Monks in the Sangha practiced the lives of wandering ascetics or of Hindu forest dwellers. Although a distinction arose between monks who lived near villages and those who avoided villages, they all observed the Ten Precepts. All received their daily food from nature or from offerings of laypeople. In return, monks taught the dharma, offered chants, and practiced simple forms of medicine. Each day a monk spent time in meditation. The plain, yellow robes of the monks also were donated by the laity.

The Buddha was an example for his monks; he lived as simply as they did. For forty-five years the winsome person comforted and taught wayfarers he met, entered conversations, and offered lectures to people of high or low social standing. He never lost sight of his mission: to overcome suffering and to help all who would receive the Noble Truths find Nirvana. Annually he renewed the serious commitment of monks in the Sangha.

In the rainy season, the Buddha and the monks gathered to renew the Sangha. New monks were presented and initiated. Rules of the order were recited. Dialogues on the dharma and its implications were held frequently. Daily meditation was practiced, keeping the holy ones free from undesirable traits. Monks gained further insights into the Three Jewels of Buddhism, reciting, "I take refuge in the Buddha, I take refuge in the Dharma, and I take refuge in the Sangha."

The Buddha's Ministry

For forty-five years, the Buddha moved from kingdom to kingdom, leader to leader, and people to people in northern India. He appointed monks to care for territories. The scriptures present his dialogues with kings, princes, military leaders, ordinary people, and monks. Firm in discipline, the Buddha set high standards for conduct. Compassionate, he understood human suffering and the difficulty encountered in converting to his teachings. He was a winsome person, eagerly sought and eagerly followed.

From his early ministry, the Buddha's loyal companion had been his cousin Ananda. But his most renowned disciple was Mahakashyapa. The teacher's doctrines remained with his pupils; they had learned their lessons well. In the classification of Buddha's principal disciples, there are lists of disciples who became Bhikkus (monks), women who became mendicant sisters, laymen, and laywomen.[7] The Buddha continued to travel and teach until his eightieth year. Some food, perhaps spoiled, brought on a short illness and his death in 483 B.C.E. (or 480). Among his last words to Ananda were:

> 2.25. Ānanda, I am now old, worn out, venerable, one who has traversed life's path, I have reached the term of life, which is eighty. Just as an old cart is made to go by being held together with straps, so the Tathagata's body is kept going by being strapped up. It is only when the **Tathagata** withdraws his attention from outward signs, and by the cessation of certain feelings, enters into the signless concentration of mind, that his body knows comfort.
>
> 2.26. Therefore, Ānanda, you should live as islands unto yourselves, being your own refuge, with no one else as your refuge, with the Dhamma as an island, with the Dhamma as your refuge, with no other refuge. And how does a monk live as an island unto himself, . . . with no other refuge? Here, Ānanda, a monk abides contemplating the body as body, earnestly, clearly aware, mindful and having put away all hankering and fretting for the world, and likewise with regard to feelings, mind and mind-objects. That, Ānanda, is how a monk lives as an island unto himself, . . . with no other refuge. And those who now in my time or afterwards live thus, they will become the highest, if they are desirous of learning.[8]

Tathagata [ta-TAH-ga-ta] A title of the Buddha, meaning one who has thus gone.

Their serenity overcome with grief, the Buddha's disciples openly wept at his death. For six days they kept his body in the grove where he died. The monks honored it with music, hymns, dance, and flowers. On the seventh day, they carried the body out the eastern gate of the city to the shrine of the aristocratic Mallas, where it was cremated.

Buddhists relate that the fire did not catch until Mahakashyapa arrived with five hundred monks to salute the Buddha. When flesh and fluids of the body were consumed, rain extinguished the flames. Bones of the Buddha's body were honored in the council hall of the Mallas for another seven days. Then the remains were divided into eight parts and distributed to representatives from different territories. They took the remains away and built monuments to enshrine them. A great mound was erected over the ashes of the funeral pyre. Eight monuments, stupas, in different places witnessed to the life of the Buddha.

In Buddhism, relics of the body are most important, but objects of use or objects of commemoration are also valued. Nagasena is quoted saying, "Venerate the relic of him who is to be venerated: by doing so you will go to heaven."[9]

The Four Noble Truths

The foundations of the Buddha's teaching are found in the Four Noble Truths. First, all of life is suffering, **dukkha.** Second, the cause of suffering is craving, **tanha.** Third, the end of suffering is getting rid of craving and grasping. Fourth, the method to use in overcoming suffering is the **Eightfold Path:**

1. *Right view.* The disciple gains proper knowledge about illness—how he or she becomes ill, endures illness, and is released from illness.
2. *Right aim.* The disciple must be prepared to renounce attachment to the world and give benevolence and kindness.
3. *Right speech.* The disciple must not lie, slander, or use abusive or idle talk.
4. *Right action.* The disciple must abstain from taking life, from taking what is not given, and from carnal indulgence.
5. *Right living.* The disciple must put away wrong livelihood, acts that are condemned in the fourth step, and seek to support him- or herself by right livelihood.
6. *Right effort.* The disciple applies the force of his or her mind to preventing potential evil from arising in him- or herself, to getting rid of evil that has arisen in him- or herself, and to awakening and sustaining good potentials within him- or herself.
7. *Right mindfulness.* The disciple looks on the body so as to remain ardent, self-possessed, and mindful. The disciple has overcome the craving and dejection common in the world. The disciple also looks on each idea, avoiding craving and dejection common in the world.
8. *Right concentration.* Aloof from sensuous appetites and evil desires, the disciple enters the first **jhana** (meditative state), where there is cognition and deliberation born of solitude, joy, and ease. The disciple moves a step toward the fourth jhana—purity of mind and equanimity where neither ease nor ill is felt.

The Buddha developed his basic teachings similarly to the way a physician diagnoses an illness. What are the symptoms? What causes the suffering? Can anything be done about the patient's distress? What is the treatment that can

dukkha [DUK-kah]
The Buddhist term for the suffering of humans and other sentient beings.

tanha [TAN-ha]
In Buddhism, the thirst or craving that leads to suffering. In the second Noble Truth, it is identified as the cause of suffering.

Eightfold Path
The fourth Noble Truth, the path of deliverance in Buddhism.

jhana [JHAH-na]
Buddhist meditation, or the states reached in Buddhist meditation.

bring relief or a cure? The Buddha was more a physician than a priest, prophet, or metaphysician.

The dharma, which is used in Buddhism as religious teaching of the Buddha, focuses on two terms and a path. Because suffering is the problem, understanding what suffering is requires much attention.

Dukkha

By suffering (*dukkha*), Buddha meant more than having pain in body or mind. Dukkha pervades all human existence.[10] It is having to endure physical and mental phenomena that are unpleasant, that humans want to avoid, and it is losing those things humans want to keep, such as parents, loved ones, and possessions. These sufferings are balanced by pleasures found in other people and possessions. But the one who enjoys people and possessions is just as impermanent as they are. There is no permanence either in the world that is experienced or in the one who experiences it. The search for permanence in any experience leads to dukkha.

There is no permanent self to experience anything. Instead, the appearance of a self is generated by five basic groups, or **skandhas,** of experience. There are activities in humans' physical bodies and sense organs. There is the process of feeling. The mind that receives the sensations is part of the perceiving activity. There are responses to sensations in the form of impulses toward action. Accompanying these sensations and responses is consciousness. None of the skandhas, including consciousness, exists alone.

skandhas [SKAN-dhas]
Five strands, similar to strands in a skein of yarn, that constitute the self.

The Buddha differed sharply with Hindu belief in an eternal self that continues on through a series of bodies. Consciousness is not identical with self. A person is an aggregation of psychological activities, all temporary. In death, the aggregation comes apart. These five skandhas make up what we refer to as a person. Those who seek permanence of the self suffer, for no self exists.

In Buddhism, no self exists over and beyond the five skandhas, nor can a self be identified in any skandha or group of skandhas. Even consciousness cannot be identified with the self, for consciousness arises out of groups of factors. Without matter, sensations, perceptions, and mental activities, consciousness cannot arise.

Buddhist Monk in Laos Receives Alms. Laypeople gain merit by supporting monks in their ascetic lives.

Tanha

"Grasping," "craving," and "coveting" are better translations of *tanha* than is "desire." Simple desires of the body are not, in themselves, causes of suffering. A deep craving or grasping to make permanent what is impermanent is the cause of suffering. Assuming a permanent ego when there are only psychological processes produces suffering. Trying to keep objects, persons, and processes, which are impermanent, produces suffering. A craving to make a permanent ego that can grasp and hold all things produces suffering, for there is no ego to grasp the impermanent psychological processes.

Our thinking that over and above processes of body and mind we are permanent selves increases our suffering. For thinking that we are permanent selves we seek to attach the world of experience to ourselves. What we cannot befriend, we fear. We are caught between grasping and aversion. Changes fuel our attempts to rearrange and enlarge what we grasp or avoid. The more we seek permanence, the more we suffer.

The whole existence of humans is becoming. Birth depends on death. All the psychological processes that make a person depend on birth. Cravings, grasping, and the desires to continue existence depend on psychological processes. Old age leads to death, which leads to rebirth, which initiates a repetition of the process. Early in his ministry, Buddha carried on a careful analysis of dependent origination, **pratitya-samutpada,** with his disciple Ananda:

> Ananda, if it be asked, "Do old age and death depend on anything?" the reply should be, "Old age and death depend on birth."
>
> Ananda, if it be asked, "Does birth depend on anything?" the reply should be, "Birth depends on existence."
>
> Ananda, if it be asked, "Does existence depend on anything?" the reply should be, "Existence depends on attachment."
>
> Ananda, if it be asked, "Does attachment depend on anything?" the reply should be, "Attachment depends on desire."
>
> Ananda, if it be asked, "Does desire depend on anything?" the reply should be, "Desire depends on sensation."
>
> Ananda, if it be asked, "Does sensation depend on anything?" the reply should be, "Sensation depends on contact."
>
> Ananda, if it be asked, "Does contact depend on anything?" the reply should be, "Contact depends on the mental and physical phenomena."
>
> Ananda, if it be asked, "Do the mental and physical phenomena depend on anything?" the reply should be, "The mental and physical phenomena depend on consciousness."
>
> Ananda, if it be asked, "Does consciousness depend on anything?" the reply should be, "Consciousness depends on the mental and physical phenomena."
>
> Thus, Ananda, on the mental and physical phenomena depends consciousness;
> On consciousness depends the mental and physical phenomena;
> On mental and physical phenomena depends contact;
> On contact depends sensation;
> On sensation depends desire;
> On desire depends attachment;
> On attachment depends existence;
> On existence depends birth;
> On birth depend old age and death, sorrow, lamentation, misery, grief, and despair. Thus does this entire aggregation of misery arise.[11]

This wheel of becoming fuels our suffering as long as we ignorantly assume we are selves independent of the processes. Our clinging to the processes, either to grasp or to avoid them, extends our suffering.

The End of Suffering

Knowledge or enlightenment puts an end to suffering. Seeing clearly the nature of a person—that there is no permanent self—helps bring an end to craving. Realizing that everything is only part of impermanent psychological processes makes grasping foolish. There is nothing to have and nothing to be had. Individuals can simply let go. Destiny is each person's decision. Letting go is the end of suffering.

pratitya-samutpada
[pra-TEET-ya sam-ut-PAH-da]
The Buddhist doctrine of dependent origination. It explains the experienced universe without resorting either to chance or a first cause.

Letting go, however, does not mean obliteration of our lives. The purpose of overcoming suffering is liberation for living, not eradication of the processes of living. The processes of living do not cause suffering; the cause of suffering is unwarranted attachment to the processes. Through recognition that there is no permanent self, one can eventually overcome unreasonable attachment, craving, and desire. We can replace attachment with detachment.

The Eightfold Path

The Eightfold Path, the Middle Path of the Buddha, was the path he discovered between two extremes. The Brahmins who practiced Vedic rituals in temples and homes appeared too much identified with worldly endeavors. The wandering ascetics with whom he had lived were too dedicated to denying their bodies. The path that leads to Nirvana, the cessation of suffering, avoids these two extremes. It allows a person to experience life free from the suffering that ensues from attachment to extreme practices.

The Middle Path is marked by observing all the precepts at the same time. As psychological creatures, humans require more than insight to free themselves from dukkha. The first two requirements are right understanding and intention, a kind of wisdom. Unless humans understand the nature of suffering and release and that they can do something about it, they will not make an effort. Understanding does not require being an expert in metaphysics; humans need concentrate only on the goal of ending suffering. Unless humans intend to stop grasping, there can be no end to suffering. Intention must include proper conduct. Those who seek an end to suffering are careful in speaking and avoid lying, slander, abusive language, and gossip. Injury to any living being must be avoided. Dishonesty, stealing, drinking intoxicating beverages, and illicit sex lead to suffering. Earning a living in any way that injures or exploits other people is prohibited. Prostitution, trading weapons or intoxicants, or killing animals cannot be engaged in by anyone who is dedicated to ending suffering. Correct meditation or contemplation comprises effort, mindfulness, and concentration. The mind is the center of suffering and release; those who would escape suffering must learn to control all thoughts. When humans are fully aware of all psychological processes and bodily functions, they can be released to a sense of joy and contentment. The goal of contemplation is direct insight, an equanimity above all suffering.

The Buddha on Samsara and Karma

karma [KAHR-ma]
The law that a person's thoughts and deeds are followed eventually by deserved pleasure or pain. In Hinduism, it is an explanation for caste. In Buddhism, karma is primarily psychological; in Jainism, it is understood in primarily physical terms.

The Buddha agreed with the Brahmin idea of samsara, in that he believed that birth follows death. Like the Brahmins, he saw the cycle of rebirths as a prison to be escaped. He differed with them in that he believed a righteous person, regardless of caste, could escape in his or her present lifetime from suffering rebirth. Moreover, it was not necessary to follow the Vedas, the Brahmin priests, or the rigors of Jain asceticism. By concentrating on the Four Noble Truths, a man or a woman could attain release from suffering in this life.

Karma, in Buddha's understanding, is psychological instead of physical. Grasping, desires, and intentions bind the psychological processes. Humans become what they intend. In grasping for the impermanent world, the psychological processes become attached. At death, something carries over to influence another psychological aggregation. The psychological processes that are detached from this world and its people have nothing to carry over to another aggregation. The lighted candle is extinguished. Where does it go? Nothing passes over to another candle, and nothing remains. When grasping ceases, humans pass beyond suffering to the state of **Nirvana.**

The Buddha and Metaphysics

The Buddha's teachings concentrated on the pragmatic means of relieving human suffering. Metaphysical questions that intrigued the Brahmin gurus, such as whether the world is infinite and eternal and whether a person continues to exist after death, did not seem to hold any speculative attraction for the Buddha. Human psychology that leads to pain and suffering, on the other hand, attracted his careful analysis and exposition. He did not need to quote gurus, saints, or scriptures; he had been there, and he spoke from the authority of firsthand experience. He did not find the traditional religious devotion of prayer and ritual sacrifices worth practicing or advocating.

He explained these points to a monk, Malunkyaputta, who had tried to engage him in a discussion of metaphysics. The Buddha compared metaphysical queries to someone who, wounded by an arrow, wanted to know all the details of being wounded. The physician focused only on removing the arrow and healing the suffering person. The Buddha declared that he concentrated on suffering, its nature, cause, and cure:

> And what, Malunkyaputta, have I elucidated? Misery, Malunkyaputta, have I elucidated; the origin of misery have I elucidated; the cessation of misery have I elucidated; and the path leading to the cessation of misery have I elucidated. And why, Malunkyaputta, have I elucidated this? Because Malunkyaputta, this does profit, has to do with the fundamentals of religion, and tends to aversion, absence of passion, cessation, quiescence, knowledge, supreme wisdom, and Nirvana; therefore have I elucidated it. Accordingly Malunkyaputta, bear always in mind what it is that I have not elucidated, and what it is that I have elucidated.[12]

Buddhists tell the story of Kisagotami, a woman who carried her dead baby to the Buddha that he might heal it. The Buddha told her that he could heal the infant if she could find some mustard seed that came from a home where there had never been a death. Householders gladly offered the young mother mustard seed, but every family had experienced death. Kisagotami learned what the Buddha was trying to teach—death comes to everyone. She placed her dead baby in a forest and returned to learn more from the Buddha.

Historical Development: Buddhism after the Buddha

Through all the story of the Buddha radiates the light of a gifted, winsome leader. Rich and powerful people wanted to be near him; they offered him gifts that would support his ministry of compassion. Ordinary people, too, found their

Nirvana [ner-VAH-na] In Buddhism, the state of being free of egocentrism and the suffering that it causes. Positively, it is joy and peace.

fulfillment in his service. A son of a humble family could honor his parents in following the Buddha. The courtesan Ambipali and the simple mother Kisagotami are exalted in stories not by their status in society but through their devotion to the ideals of the compassionate Buddha.

Artists and raconteurs sought to convey the importance of the one who offered release from the wheel of suffering. While he lived, no statues of his youth, ascetic struggle, or contented old age were required. Early symbols were footprints of the Buddha. Whether in the path he walked and taught or the paths he traveled for forty-five years through kingdoms of India, the Buddha's footsteps were revered. Stories of his birth include an account that a holy man, with keen spiritual insight, recognized on the soles of infant Siddhartha's feet the thousand-spoked wheel, the sign of a great man.

The Buddhist Scriptures

Like Hinduism, Buddhism has a manifold collection of sacred writings. Unlike Hindus, Buddhists are not bound to the Vedas, or to the entire collection of Buddhist writings. Tables listing Buddhist scriptures help us understand the impossibility of large numbers of people mastering all the scriptures. In the Pali collection, of the language the Buddha preferred, there are three groups, totaling fifteen collections. The Chinese collection has sixty-one volumes. The Tibetan collection comprises a hundred or more volumes in the *Kanjur* and two hundred and twenty-five in the *Tanjur*. Buddhists have been extraordinarily diligent and creative in collecting, preserving, and interpreting everything about the Buddha, the dharma, and the Sangha. In practice, Buddhist groups focus their attention on a few volumes, sometimes basing their central doctrines on one *sutra (sutta)*.

The first stories of the life of the Buddha and his teachings were preserved in the memory of his early disciples. In time, these oral accounts were compiled into written treatises that could be used to guide the faithful. The **Tripitaka** (threefold basket), the collected Buddhist scriptures, was named in the early days when sayings were written in the Pali language on palm leaves and gathered into separate baskets (*pitakas*). The first basket, called the "Discipline Basket" ("Vinaya Pitaka"), contains the obligatory 227 rules for monks. Explanations are given in extensive detail so that laity and monks would have little doubt about how to conduct themselves. The teachings of the Buddha on various subjects are set forth in discourses and dialogues preserved in the "Discourse Basket" ("Sutta Pitaka"). One of the five sections contains stories of the Buddha's previous lives and devotees' poetry and songs to the Buddha. The third basket, "Further Teaching" ("Abhidhamma Pitaka") is an expansion and elaboration of the basic teachings in other places. In it are the fine points of advanced, nondiscursive analysis of the Buddha's teachings and an indication of differences of interpretation between Pali and Sanskrit scriptures.

Tripitaka [TREE-PI-ta-ka] The "three baskets" collection of Buddhist scriptures. It is comprised of the "Vinaya Pitaka" (monastic rules), the "Sutta Pitaka" (discourses), and the "Abhidhamma Pitaka" (supplement to the doctrines).

The First Buddhist Councils

Historians of religion do not usually accept as accurate the tradition reported in the "Vinaya" that soon after the Buddha's death, five hundred monks gathered at Rajagaha to recite the Tripitaka as it was remembered by Ananda and Upali.

They think the Buddhist scriptures continued to develop over several centuries. Although scholars using sources external to the "Vinaya" question the traditional account of the first council, they do generally agree on some of its results. Three results were the affirmation of the authority of the religious community, the purity of the monks, and the establishment of essential, official scriptures.

A second council met a hundred years later at Vaisali to settle disagreements over the strictness of the Buddhist discipline. The council addressed the tensions between essentially conservative, rigorous views and traditions, and progressive, relaxed views and practices. Whether emphasis should be placed on monasticism or the life of the laity was debated. The monks also considered the sacred community as opposed to the secular community. A breach between two opposing tendencies was, for a time, healed.

Other councils followed, many of them held in India. Under King Mahapadma, less than fifty years after the second council, a third, noncanonical, council was held at Pataliputra to debate orthodoxy. The larger party, the Mahasamghikas, withdrew. The minor party, the Sthaviras, or Elders, went its own way. Each party began to develop its own collection of scriptures and its own community. The third canonical council was held at Pataliputra in 247 B.C.E. under the reign of King Ashoka. The king chose a respected Buddhist monk to help restore orthodoxy by condemning those viewpoints that had introduced heretical views into the Buddhist doctrine. Influenced by the example of King Ashoka, King Kanishka (ca. 100 C.E.) sponsored a council that compiled a new "Vinaya" and a commentary, the *Mahavibhasa*.

Over the centuries, Buddhism continued its dynamic generation of alternative views and practices. Councils were held in various countries to reach agreement in faith and practice. A sixth Theravadin council was held in Rangoon, Burma, in 1954.

Two Ways of Experiencing the Buddha

The councils had confronted the deep feelings of monks and laity as they applied their creative questions and imaginations to living by the dharma in their particular circumstances. The oldest continuous group became that of the elders, Sthaviras, who followed the path of the monks. They were the **Theravadins.** This group elevated the monk who, following the example of the Buddha, lived a strictly monastic life directed intently toward the experience of Nirvana, release from craving. Other people who revered the Three Jewels envisioned a larger order that included monks and laypeople. They became known as the **Mahayanists.** Which was more like the Buddha, the person who sought only his own release or the person whose compassion led him into the world to help release other beings from suffering? The Theravadins and the Mahayanists divided on the answer.

Theravadin Buddhism

The two major divisions of Buddhist religion, the Theravadin and the Mahayana, differ according to where emphasis is placed in the life of the Buddha. Buddhism, as do most other religions, has a conservative branch (Theravadin) and a liberal

Theravadins
[ter-a-VAH-dins]
The elders, monks who imitated the Buddha's ascetic life to attain enlightenment.

Mahayanists
[ma-HAH-YAH-nists]
Those of the great vehicle, who emphasized universal Buddhist enlightenment.

branch (Mahayana). Theravadin devotees focus on the life of the monk Buddha. Thus they favor imitating the Buddha in monasticism or asceticism. They follow the one who worked out his own salvation through right aspiration and meditation. A monk who attains supreme enlightenment is an *arhat*. In the societies of southern Asia, this form of Buddhism glorifies the example of the monk, with many laypeople spending at least some period of life in monastic discipline. Monks can count on receiving gifts of food for their one meal a day from faithful Buddhist believers who admire their lifestyle even though they cannot always practice it themselves.

Theravadins were always conservative, but through the centuries, they did change. They emphasized that the Buddha was a man and remembered him with symbols of a footprint, an empty throne, or a stupa for relics. Eventually they accepted images of the Buddha and allowed placing flowers or fruit before them. They permitted temples to house the images. They included **Jatakas,** stories of the Buddha's previous lives. They spoke of Maitreya, the Buddha who awaits in Tusita heaven to descend to the earth in the future. But always they have emphasized that the monk's lifestyle is the ideal to follow, for the monk imitates the way of the Buddha. Salvation is through dedicated self-effort rather than through intervention of heavenly beings.

Mahayana Buddhism

Mahayana, the large vehicle, offers a variety of ways to release from suffering; it appeals to laypeople and monks of widely differing personalities and cultural orientations.

It applies the derogatory term *hinayana*, lowly vehicle, to the Theravadin Buddhists. The Mahayanists find the Theravadins too fundamentally tied to the simple, basic acts of this world, a group of literalists compulsively bound to imitating one aspect of the Buddha's life. The Mahayana Buddhists think of themselves as having risen above such pedestrian concepts to the finer and higher teaching revealed or alluded to by the Buddha. They claim Siddhartha Gautama pointed them toward far more beautiful truths than he ever discussed in detail for his first disciples. Mahayanists identify with the advanced insights of the Buddha, which he communicated to those disciples who were capable of receiving this higher knowledge.[13] Typically, Mahayana groups believe in heavenly beings who can assist human beings in escape from suffering here to beautiful lives beyond the grave. **Bodhisattvas** are beings who, although qualified for Nirvana, remain outside to assist humans in need. Although the Buddha may not have been interested in speculation about the universe and its spiritual inhabitants, these subjects attracted many of his followers in India. The development grew as Buddhism moved later into China, Korea, and Japan. Writings were introduced showing that the Buddha had taught a higher philosophy for those who were ready to move beyond the elementary experiences of the world of senses.

Soon after the death of Siddhartha Gautama, the Buddha grew in the eyes of many of his followers to be more than a human monk. The Mahayanists came to believe there were many other Buddhas. They held that salvation is not simply a matter of escape through working off karma at the end of this life. Individuals are not dependent solely on their own resources or those of the Sangha; on the contrary, the heavens are populated with all sorts of enlightened beings, or Buddhas,

Jatakas [JAH-ta-kas] Stories of the previous lives of the Buddha, which were collected and used in the teachings of Theravadin monks.

bodhisattvas [bow-dhee-SAT-tvas] In Buddhism, people who have qualified to enter Nirvana, but who, out of compassion for others, remain available to help others.

who can help each generation as Gautama helped his. One example is a bodhisattva of mercy, a male, Avalokiteshvara (the Lord Who Looks Down), in India; and a female, Guanyin (Kwan Yin) in China. Moreover, everyone is a potential Buddha.

A Comparison of Theravadin and Mahayana Buddhism

Although Theravadin and Mahayana Buddhism developed a multitude of doctrines and practices over the centuries, from the early years people viewed differently how individuals related to the Sangha. We have emphasized their early differences over whether laypeople should be valued in the Sangha. Mahayanists favored wide participation; Theravadins preferred only those who observed the monastic ideal. Theravadin monks believed that in imitating the practices of the Buddha, they alone, as individuals, could work out their own experiences of enlightenment, Nirvana. If they followed his path in every respect, they also would experience release from suffering. Early Mahayanists, whose householder obligations altered the ways they could participate in the Buddha's teachings, found merit in deeds that householders could offer the Buddha. Acts of giving food, clothing, shelter, and medicines were surely of merit that would bring reward. Their obligations to families concentrated their sense of being individual selves. Detachment from obligations could not be so extreme as to allow their very selves to disperse. The Buddha's body had been burned and his bones distributed for memorials. Even the elders thought the relics retained Buddha power. Mahayanists thought the Buddha continued beyond death; surely the compassionate one would respond to their suffering. Help, thought the Mahayanists, is available from the Buddha, who knows and cares about each suffering creature.

The Mahayanists' value of the Buddha's compassion extended to other people who demonstrated compassion. Mahayanists did not value the wise monk seeking to become an *arhat* as highly as a compassionate person who qualified for Nirvana, but who remained available to hear the prayers of suffering humans. As offering of food, clothing, and shelter had aided the Buddha on earth, so ritual offerings and supplications could reach him and his compassionate associates in heaven. The Mahayanists sought explanations of how earth and heaven could communicate and cooperate. The Theravadins who looked within themselves in meditation could renounce metaphysics; the Mahayanists who looked heavenward needed metaphysical teachings. Let the Theravadin slavishly imitate the earthly Buddha; the Mahayanists preferred to communicate with the Buddha who is now liberated from the confines of a body. Mahayanists were sure the Buddha had taught many more exciting doctrines to those who were open to spiritual insights.

Inspired by the Buddha, Theravadins and Mahayanists were all Buddhists. They sought to board rafts of the dharma that would take them to the farther shore. They differed on the size and accommodations of the preferable raft. As Buddhists reached out in compassion to share their good news with other peoples of India and other countries, passengers chose one of the two rafts. We could simplify the picture, for clarity of concept, by saying that the Theravadin raft sailed south and east in India, Sri Lanka, Burma, Thailand, and Indonesia. The Mahayana raft sailed first north, then east and west. It gathered passengers in the central Asian regions such as Uzbekistan; it loaded millions of Buddhists in

CHART OF COMPARISON: 10-POINT WORLDVIEW OF MAHAYANA AND THERAVADIN BUDDHISM

Worldview	Mahayana	Theravadin
Absolute	The Buddha is a savior	The Buddha is not a god but the very highest human
World	Experience is only appearance	Renounces householder's world
	Enlightenment shows true world	The *arhat* is preferable
	Enjoys metaphysics	Avoids metaphysics
Humans	Anatta—no soul	Anatta—no soul
	Nothing permanent	Nothing permanent
Problem for Humans	Suffering, ignorance	Suffering, ignorance
Solution for Humans	Help from bodhisattvas	The Buddha's Eightfold Path requires a disciplined life
Community and Ethics	Extend compassion Karuna—empathy	Search for wisdom
Interpretation of History	Lacks strong agreement on end of history	Lacks strong agreement on end of history
Rituals and Symbols	Image of the Buddha	Image of the Buddha
	Prayers for self and others	Meditation
Life after Death	Personal identity retained after death	Nirvana
Buddhism and Other Religions	Somewhat open to innovation	Prefers imitation of the ascetic life of the Buddha
	Often coexists with other religions	Usually tolerant of other religions

China, Korea, and Japan. In Tibet, it attracted a distinctive group of passengers. That is how the two different visions of Buddhism were enacted in history.

In the development of these two ways of following the Buddha, two schools of Mahayanist philosophy contributed their insights. Before turning to Buddhist missionary outreach, we should consider how the insight of philosophers contributed to Mahayanist interpretations of dharma.

The Madhyamika School

Nagarjuna
[NAH-GAHR-ju-NAH]
The Buddhist philosopher of the second century C.E. who established the Madhyamika school of philosophy.

Madhyamika
[ma-DYAM-ee-ka]
The Buddhist philosophy that the phenomenal objects one experiences are not ultimately real. Nagarjuna founded the Madhyamika school.

Nagarjuna, of the second century C.E., is associated with the **Madhyamika** school of philosophy. The Buddha had taught that there is no ego, no soul; there is only a temporary gathering of skandhas. Nagarjuna's ideas were based on the Middle Way, a path between asceticism and hedonism and between teachings of absolute reality and nonreality. To teach the impermanence and interrelatedness of all existing things, he eliminated ties to ideas, even those of revered Buddhist doctrine. He asserted that all existing things are empty of absolute reality. Nagarjuna is most remembered for his teaching on emptiness, which he identified with interdependent origination, *pratitya-samutpada*.

To understand the theory behind Buddhist practices of meditation, pratitya-samutpada, the doctrine of dependent origination, must be understood. *Samutpada* means "co-arising" or "arising in combination." *Pratitya* means "moving toward." The combined term means "dependence" or "dependent arising." The

Buddha's understanding of human existence avoided many traditional metaphysical questions, but his theory explained human experiences without relying on an ultimate, first cause. His accounting for the continuity of human experience on the one hand allows nothing to be permanent, but on the other hand, there is not complete discontinuity. The doctrine is so important that some Buddhists consider understanding it tantamount to enlightenment.

The discussion of dependence addresses both the process of human bondage and freedom. As devotees understand dependent origination they pacify their dispositional tendencies and understand their own personality and the experienced world. The impermanence of the experienced world, when seen for what it is, makes foolish any craving for an attachment to it. As devotees abandon craving and attachment, suffering diminishes and they are freed to lead a happy life. Through meditation, devotees replace avidya with jnana, or compassion, and freedom.

The Yogacara School

Asanga, of the fourth century C.E., is associated with the **Yogacara** school, which goes farther than the Madhyamika position. Even the individual mind and mental constructs of the phenomenal world are not real. There is a great single consciousness that holds all experiences and ideas. These ideas rise to the surface of consciousness and give the impressions humans have of the phenomenal world. However, even this consciousness is not ultimate reality. Ultimate reality is a void that the human mind cannot comprehend. Those who would identify with ultimate reality must abandon phenomena and ideas and become released into the Void. Differing with many scholars, David Kalupahana, an authority on Buddhism, does not find these ideas in the works of Vasubandhu.

In later development, adepts practicing yoga conjured up visions that seemed as real as their subjective experiences of the world. They realized that when they imagined themselves a mighty god leading lesser gods against Mara, the Evil One, god of desire and death, their visions were just as real as their perceptions of the external world. Both exist only in consciousness, which is also only apparent in what is really a void.

Buddhism in Asia

From a consideration of the various early Buddhist schools, we turn now to explore the development of Buddhism in other countries. We first discuss the missionary activities in Asia. Then we trace Buddhism's development in China, Japan, Tibet, and the West through recent times.

Buddhist monks had begun their missionary activities under supervision of the Buddha. After his death, monks wandered ever farther from the Ganges Valley, carrying the dharma to larger India. As the Theravadins and the Mahayanists diligently pursued implications of their views of the dharma, new groups formed to emphasize their particular interpretations. Buddhist enthusiasm steadily increased. The young faith attracted thousands of believers and stimulated reexamination of Hinduism and Jainism, India's other ancient religion.

An emperor, however, enjoyed the highest visibility in promoting Buddhist missions. **Ashoka** Maurya came to the throne in Magadha in 273 B.C.E. and was formally crowned four years later. As grandson of Chandragupta, who defeated

Asanga [a-SANG-a]
Made famous in the fourth century C.E., the Yogacara school of Buddhist philosophy that was founded by Maitreyanatha.

Yogacara
[YOH-ga-CHAH-ra]
The Buddhist school of philosophy that teaches that neither the phenomenal world nor the mind is real. Founded by Maitreyanatha in the third century C.E., it was made famous in the fourth by Asanga.

Ashoka [a-SHOW-ka]
This king, who reigned in India 273–232 B.C.E., sponsored Buddhist missionary activities.

the garrisons left in India by Alexander the Great, Ashoka had strength to expand his empire through conquest. His violent attack on the kingdom of Kalinga brought him that prize of the east coast. Ashoka controlled most of India except the extreme south. His military success, however, left him discontented. With passing time, his remorse over the suffering his conquest caused soldiers and captives deepened. To remove his guilt, he initiated a program of contrition. First, he publicly proclaimed, by carving in stones erected in highly visible places, his guilt for causing suffering in so many peoples. He would henceforth pursue a course of peace. Second, he severely limited, and then altogether eliminated, killing animals for sport or for food on his own table. He instituted a program that would preserve the lives of many species of creatures. Third, Ashoka had stones carved so that rules to direct his people's values and morality would be easily observed. He emphasized ideals of family, school, and community; respect and gentleness should be extended to persons and animals. These rules did not quote Buddhist dharma and mentioned other religions too, so one could argue that they were not particularly Buddhist. Their ideal, however, was the spirit of Buddhist life. Fourth, Ashoka required civil servants to teach laypeople the dharma and supervise their conduct. Fifth, he promoted Buddhism as an international religion, sending representatives as far west as Egypt and members of his own family to the island of Sri Lanka (Ceylon).

The *Chronicles of Ceylon* support tradition that Ashoka's family brought Buddhism to the island. The mixture of legend and history has not been definitely determined, but the story reflects the high esteem Buddhists had for Ashoka. He sent his son Mahendra to teach Buddhism in Ceylon. The king of Ceylon and thousands of his subjects embraced Buddhism. At the request of the Ceylonese leader, Ashoka sent his daughter Sanghamitta bearing a slip of the sacred Bodhi tree to be planted in Ceylon. Sanghamitta ordained princess Anula, who became an *arhat*. These persons formed the nucleus of a cell that grew into a major branch of Theravadin Buddhism; it overshadowed all religions on the island except that of the Tamils, who established a kingdom in the northern part around the tenth century C.E.[14]

Theravadin Buddhism won the allegiance of peoples in southeast India, Sri Lanka, Burma, Thailand, and Indonesia, but its venture into China was less successful. In northern and eastern Asia, the Mahayanists enrolled the converts to Buddhism.

Buddhism in China

Buddhism in China did not have a promising beginning; Chinese peoples of the first century found Theravadin Buddhism unattractive. In the year 65 C.E., the emperor Ming Ti (58–75) permitted a statue of the Buddha to be erected. The Theravadin emphasis on the monk was not accepted by the Chinese people, who wanted their sons to marry and raise families. Ancestor worship in China made essential the continuation of male heirs. When invaders from Mongolia introduced a Mahayanist form of Buddhism, the Chinese people responded favorably. The Mahayanists described many heavenly beings and features that supplemented ancestor worship. Sons who became Buddhists could help their ancestors.

Soon Mahayana Buddhism flourished in China. Pagodas dotted the landscape; images of Gautama and other Buddhas were housed in numerous temples; and monasteries became part of country, village, and city life. Many new schools of thought were formed to teach particular approaches to salvation.

Despite the Chinese people's rejection of Theravadin Buddhism, the Mahayana forms continued to grow in China. Under the Southern Dynasties (420–589 C.E.), dialogues carried on between representatives of Chinese thought and representatives of the Buddhist doctrine. *The Disputation of Error* (Li-huo lun) provides an example of these debates. In them, Mou Tzu responds to questions such as why Buddhism is not mentioned in the Chinese classics, why Buddhist monks injure their bodies (by shaving their heads), and why monks do not marry.[15]

Buddhism in China reflected some philosophies and schools found elsewhere, but it developed into a number of schools of thought that excited for centuries and were later transported to Japan. Among the most important schools are the Lotus, the Flower Garland, Pure Land, and Meditation.

TIAN TAI (TYIAN-TAI)

Tian Tai (Tyian-Tai) is based on the Lotus Sutra as interpreted by the Chinese monk **Zhiyi** (538–597), who taught on the Tian Tai (Heavenly Terrace) Mountain in Chekiang province. Zhiyi (Chi Kai) interpreted the Lotus, a guide to salvation. He combined a philosophical content with meditative practice. Wm. Theodore de Bary summarizes the teaching on the Lotus:

> In short, this is a philosophy of One-in-All and All-in-One, which is crystallized in the celebrated saying that "Every color or fragrance is none other than the Middle Path." Every dharma is thus an embodiment of the real essence of the Ultimate emptiness, or True Suchness. It follows that all beings have the Buddha-nature in them and can be saved. This is the great message of the Lotus.[16]

HUA-YEN

The scriptural basis was the Avatamsaka Sutra, which means "wreath" or "garland." The Tian Tai (Tyian-Tai) had identified absolute Buddha nature with each phenomenon. The **Hua-Yen** emphasized that all phenomena interpenetrate each other. Fa Zang (Fa Tsang), a teacher who used mundane examples to explain the most difficult doctrines, delighted the Empress Wu with a Buddha image and eight mirrors. In an octagonal pattern around the image he placed the mirrors so that the Buddha image appeared in each mirror and each mirror reflected the other seven. Ultimate reality and particular phenomena are interrelated at every moment! Through meditation one realizes the great truth.

JINGTU (CHING-T'U)

The complex philosophical schools attracted some students, but the masses of people needed more easily understood, attractive interpretations of Buddhism. A heaven ruled by a loving god who welcomed all who called his name attracted millions of suffering people.

Pure Land Buddhism, or **Jingtu (Ching-t'u)**, in India known as Sukhavati, is based on a belief that in the present age there is a sphere, Sukhavati, ruled over by Buddha **Amitabha.** After each Buddha is incarnated and has attained Nirvana, his dharma gradually declines until the hope of salvation lies only in faith. Based on the Sukhavativyuha Sutra, the teaching is that a person can be saved by faith in Amitabha.

The Pure Land believers find little merit in a life devoted to deeds of holiness. They emphasize that one is saved by faith rather than by works. A person can be saved by calling on Amitabha Buddha, A-mi-t'o-fo. This is the easy path to the Pure Land, ruled by Amitabha, who sits on a lotus throne accompanied by **Guanyin (Kwan-yin),** the bodhisattva of Mercy.[17]

Tian Tai [TYIAN-TAI] The Mahayana Buddhist sect of China (and Japan) that is based on the Lotus Sutra. All beings can actualize their Buddha nature and become Buddhas.

Zhiyi (Chi-kai or Chi-i) [ZHIR-YEE] The monk who founded the Tian Tai sect of Buddhism in China.

Hua-Yen [HWAH-YEN] The Chinese Buddhist sect whose primary Buddha is Vairocana. The school had a holistic view of Buddha nature and the universe.

Jingtu (Ching-t'u) [JING-too] Pure Land, or Western Paradise, Buddhism. It believes in Sukhavati, which is ruled by Amitabha Buddha. [In Japan the sect is Jodo.]

Amitabha (Amida) [a-mee-TAH-ba] The Buddha who presides over Western Paradise. Hozo Bosatsu is the Japanese name for a legendary monk who long ago took a vow to become a Buddha if his merits could be used to help others. After fulfilling 48 vows, he became Amitabha.

Guanyin (Kwan-yin) [GUAHN-YIN] Guanyin, bodhisattva of mercy, is also known as Avalokiteshvara. In Pure Land Buddhism, she is placed beside Amitabha as his attendant.

CHAN (CH'AN)

One of Buddha's sermons consisted only of his holding a flower.[18] Because Kashyapa smiled, indicating that he understood, he was given the True Law. It was brought to China in 520 C.E. by **Bodhidharma.** Although his teachings were based on the Lankavatara Sutra, he emphasized that meditation is more important than expounding scriptures. The **Chan (Ch'an)** school emphasized that through meditation alone can a person come to Truth. By discovering his or her own nature, a person becomes a Buddha. Although all Buddhist groups value meditation, its practice in Chan is unique. In Japan, as we shall see, the school became known as Zen Buddhism.

Buddhism in Japan

The date usually given for Buddhism's entering Japan is 552 C.E., during the reign of the Emperor Kimmei. Popular stories focus on the Soga clan, of which the prime minister was a member, who were entrusted with caring for the image of the Buddha. Although powerful clans had opposed Buddhism, the Soga clan prospered to the extent that other Japanese accepted Buddhism. Some Japanese peoples received the Buddha as a *kami* (supernatural being) belonging to a foreign people.[19]

After a civil war, the Soga clan seized the emperor's throne in 592 C.E. The Empress Suiko, placed on the throne by the Sogas, was a devout Buddhist. Her regent was Prince Shotoku, under whose brilliant rule Japanese culture matured, the state consolidated, and Buddhism was made the national religion.[20] Prince Shotoku founded the first major national Buddhist temple, Horuji Temple, outside Nara, in 607.

Several of the Mahayana sects of China found their ways into Korea and then into Japan by the seventh century C.E. There they established a place among the practices of Shinto, the native Japanese religion of patriotic belief structure. Along with Buddhism came other aspects of Chinese culture such as writing, literature, and art. Buddhism brought substantial advancement to the whole Japanese civilization. In turn, Japan provided an environment for some of the most creative ideas in the ongoing drama of Buddhism. There Chinese sects took hold and were transformed. In Japan, new groups formed around charismatic personalities who gave Buddhism the rich varieties of expression so visible in the twentieth century. Some of these schools will be briefly described to show the many implications of the Buddha's teachings for some of his followers.

TENDAI

In Japan, the Tendai school of Buddhism expanded from Indian Buddhism into a Buddhist drama for all people who would participate in it. A. K. Reischauer dates Tendai from the ninth century C.E., when it was introduced by **Saicho. (Dengyo Daishi** was his posthumous name.)[21] In China, the sect was known as Tian Tai (Tyian-Tai).

Saicho brought from China what he considered the very best elements of all the Buddhist schools. The Tendai sect still claims to harmonize the truths from all the Buddhist sects; yet even in Tendai temples there are variations, and certain Buddhas are singled out for honor. Amida (the Japanese form of Amitabha Buddha) is a common figure of honor in all temples of Tendai. Japanese people could choose to identify according to their personality types, and they could still hold to Shinto, the native, patriotic religion of Japan, while being Buddhists.

Bodhidharma
[BOW-dee-DAHR-ma]
The monk who brought meditative Buddhism to China. His example inspired Chan (Zen) Buddhism.

Chan (Ch'an) [CHAHN]
The Chinese Buddhist school of meditation founded by Bodhidharma.

Saicho (Dengyo Daishi)
[SAI-CHOH]
The monk who introduced Tendai (T'ien-T'ai) Buddhism in Japan. He helped the emperor Kwammu establish a new capital at Kyoto, diminishing the power of Buddhists at Nara.

SHINGON

Also entering Japan in the ninth century C.E. was the Shingon sect, established by **Kukai (Kobo Daishi),** a contemporary of Saicho. These two men shared insights in the beginning of their careers but later parted on bitter terms. Kukai brought the insights of the Chinese Chen Yen School, which became in Japanese the **Shingon,** or True Word, sect. Besides meditating on pure intellectual concepts, Kukai is sometimes credited with establishing schools for public education and the industry of silk worm cultivation. In Buddhist doctrine, the sect emphasizes mystery and magic, the Secret Teachings, which are in essence the truth that a person can attain Buddha-hood in this life because he or she and the eternal Buddha are essentially one. Whereas Saicho had five steps to salvation, Kukai had ten steps on an intellectual ladder or ten steps on a moral ladder. At the pinnacle joining the real world of ideas and its phenomenal counterpart is the All, Buddha **Vairocana,** also known as Dainichi or Great Sun. Matter and other Buddhas emanate from Vairocana.

Kukai made another move that helped Shingon gain a wide acceptance quickly in Japan. He identified Vairocana with the Japanese Shinto goddess of the Sun, Amaterasu. In Ryobo Shinto (double aspect), Buddhism and Shinto are only two different sides of the same reality. Human beings and gods and goddesses are all only aspects of one central reality, Vairocana. Amitabha was also admitted along with other figures and symbolized by the sun.

The most important mystery of Shingon, the True Word, is transmitted by speech, a word or phrase, which in religious terms is called a **mantra.** Body positions, **mudras,** are a second way to truth, and a third way is meditation on a sacred picture, a **mandala.** Fire and water ceremonies are also used to help devotees reach Buddhahood.

JODO

Amida worship in Japan seems to have been inspired by **Ryonin** (1072–1132). Although he studied Tendai and Shingon, he began to seek his own path by reading and reciting the phrase of adoration of Amida Butsu, the Buddha of eternal light. He eventually had a vision of Amida, who asked him to teach others to say the "Namu Amida Butsu" and thus enter paradise. Through the power of another person, individuals can enter paradise.

The **Jodo** sect began with **Genku (Honen Shonin).** He was first a student of the Tendai sect. He discovered that salvation depends not on a person's own efforts but on the grace of Amida. The way of working out salvation through virtue and wisdom was replaced with the way of faith in Amida.[22] Jodo is also known as the Pure Land or Paradise sect. Another interesting feature of this sect is the belief that salvation comes through the vicarious suffering of **Hozo Bosatsu,** a supremely good man, who became Amida Buddha.

SHINRAN

Whereas Jodo was revolutionary in concentrating on salvation by grace through faith rather than through works of individual wisdom or virtue, **Shinran,** a disciple of Genku, introduced even more radical practices through the Shinran sect. His vision at about age thirty was of Kwannon, the bodhisattva of mercy (the guanyin of Buddhism). Through the influence of his vision, he took the drastic step of marrying a princess. He also broke Buddhist tradition by eating meat. Through him, Buddhism established a separate branch of tradition, with temple

Kukai (Kobo Daishi)
[KOO-KAI]
The ninth-century C.E. founder of the Japanese Buddhist Shingon sect. All Buddhas are emanations of the great sun, Vairocana or, in Japan, Dainichi.

Shingon [SHIN-GOHN]
Japanese for the Chinese Chen Yen school of Buddhism. It taught that matter and other Buddhas emanate from Vairocana.

Vairocana
[vai-ROH-cha-na]
In Japanese Buddhism, the Sun, who is also the Buddha, also known as Dainichi and Amaterasu.

mantra [MAN-tra]
A special formula of words recited in worship.

mudras [MUD-ras]
Special positions of hands used in worship.

mandala [MAN-da-la]
A geometric pattern used in worship.

Ryonin [RYO-neen]
In the early twelfth century C.E., founder of Amida worship in Japan.

Jodo [JO-DO]
The Japanese sect of the Pure Land. Founded in the twelfth century C.E. by Genku. Salvation comes by grace, through faith.

Genku (Honen Shonin)
[GEN-koo]
Twelfth-century C.E. founder of the Jodo Buddhist sect in Japan who was trained at Tendai monasteries on Mt. Hiei.

Hozo Bosatsu
[ho-zo bo-SAHT-soo]
In Shinran Buddhism, a meritorious person who became Amida Buddha.

Shinran [SHIN-RAN]
Genku's disciple, who established the Jodo-Shin sect of Buddhism in Japan.

priests serving as heads of families, living much closer to the practices of laypeople. For his troubles, he was exiled to Hitachi. Twenty-eight years later, he returned to Kyoto, having made many converts and established many temples after his six-year ban was lifted. Shinran did not offer alternative methods of salvation; he said that in recent times, the golden age being over, human beings could no longer save themselves. Only by faith in Amida could a person be saved. Through Hozo Bosatsu, people could receive the merit needed for their own salvation.

ZEN

The sect that has most captured the attention of Westerners is **Zen.** It has its roots in the meditative practices of India, where this particular form of Buddhism was called the **Dhyana.** The personality often connected with its spread abroad is Bodhidharma (probably from the fifth century), who shocked the Chinese emperor Wu Ti by claiming that studying sacred Buddhist scriptures and building monasteries are worthless acts, and good works performed for fellow humans do not provide merit for salvation. Only comprehending our real nature is of value. The way of salvation for Bodhidharma was demonstrated when he retired to Shao Lin Monastery and sat in meditation facing a wall for nine years. The whole purpose of meditation is self-knowledge and an inward vision.

In China, the meditative sects went by the name of Ch'an. They eventually focused on two basic approaches. The Lin Chi used rigorous methods and abrupt tactics to produce enlightenment, whereas the Ts'ao-tung took a longer, more gradual path through instruction and practices of meditation to reach enlightenment. Zen entered Japan when the Buddhist monk Dosho (628–670) brought it from China. He had studied in China in 653, learning Yogacara philosophy from his Chinese teacher, Hsuan-tsang.[23]

The Japanese pronounced *Ch'an* as *Zen.* Lin Chi became Renzai and Ts'ao-tung became Soto. The enlightenment experience in Japan is called **satori.** Problems used in meditation, designed to destroy ordinary logical ways of thinking, are known in Japan as **koans.** The word *kung-an* in Chinese referred to a public law case, so it is likely that the problems were first argued in public.[24] A few examples of koans illustrate that focusing the mind on a problem can destroy usual forms of logic and, perhaps, bring a flash of insight into the nature of self and world. Consider these cited by Christmas Humphries: "If all things are reducible to the One, to what is the One reduced?" "A man hangs over a precipice by his teeth, which are clenched in the branch of a tree. His hands are full and his feet cannot reach the face of the precipice. A friend leans over and asks him, 'What is Zen?' What answer would you make?"[25] By destroying paths of customary logic, Zen seeks to proceed beyond them. What is a koan? There is no answer—not even one word.[26]

The rigorous Zen form of Buddhism is practiced by only a dedicated minority of Buddhists. However, its principles of rigid control of body and strength of mind have appealed to Japanese athletes and warriors. There is Zen influence in the beautiful art forms of *hai-ku,* the seventeen-syllable Japanese poem, and in flower arranging. The Japanese tea ceremony is also expressive of the controlled spirit of Zen.

NICHIREN

Nichiren Buddhism began as a vigorous reform movement. **Nichiren** was a prophet of the thirteenth century in Japan who attempted to restore the pure Buddhism taught by Dengyo. He thought this could be done by reciting the sacred title of the scripture, the Lotus. He announced the formula on the morning he

Zen [ZEN]
The Japanese Buddhist meditation sect (in China, Chan) that was based on the practices of the Indian Buddhist, Bodhidharma.

Dhyana [DYAH-na]
In Buddhism, mental concentration. It is the term for Buddhist meditation.

satori [SAH-TOH-ree]
The Japanese term for the Zen Buddhist experience of enlightenment.

koan [KO-an]
A problem used by Zen Buddhists to reduce dependence on ordinary ways of thinking about self and the universe.

Nichiren [NEE-chee-REN]
A monk in Japan who established a school based on the Lotus Sutra.

© Fujifotos/The Image Works

Japanese Flower Arrangement. Behind it is a paper window in Nikko, Japan.

launched his reform movement, using the sun as his witness—"Namu Myohorenge-kyo," adoration be to the scripture of the Lotus of the perfect truth.[27] As he explained later in the day to protesting monks at his monastery on Kyozumi, those who recite this scripture are in possession of the Buddha's golden body. The divine beings in the scriptures are more than helpers to believers; they provide examples of behavior believers are to practice in their own lives.

Nichiren's old comrades rejected his ideas. The local lord sought to take his life for such radical doctrines but did not succeed.

In Japan, Buddhism flowered into a religion that appealed to every personality type. To the Theravadin appeal, which had attracted Southeast Asians, the Chinese and Japanese added the myriad opportunities of Mahayana. Monasticism was available for those who sought it in several sects, but Shinran opened the door for family life. Several sects attracted mystics, and Zen appealed to those who were rigorous about meditation. The moralist, the ritualist, and the world reformer all had models in the various Japanese schools. Each group had its intellectuals who developed theory and explanations. There were no exclusions based on sex, class, nationality, or even membership in other religions. Buddhism was available for all who found it helpful.

Buddhism in Tibet

Srong Tsan Gampo, a ruler of Lhasa who had two Buddhist wives, sent an invitation to Buddhists in India in 630 C.E. to introduce Buddhism into his realm. The Tibetans, however, found the new religion difficult to understand and remained with their native religion, **Bon** (pronounced *pain*). The word *Bon* meant "murmuring spells."[28] Bon was a kind of animism, a worship of spirits in nature. It took another century before exciting teachers from Bengal arrived with a brand of

Bon [PAIN]
The ancient animistic religion of Tibet.

Tenzin Gyatso, 14th Dalai Lama. At home in Dharamsala, India.

Buddhism that captured the attention of the Tibetans. In the eighth century, Shantarakshita, a wandering yogin, taught Tantric Buddhism. Tantrism invites human males and females to experience, through disciplined sexual energy, cosmic forces present in the individual. About the same time, Padma-Sambhava urged the Tibetans to build monasteries.

In the works of Stephan Beyer is a myth about the origins of the Tibetan peoples that may show their preparation for receiving Indian tantrism.[29] According to the *Red Annals* of the fourteenth century C.E., Tibetans descended from the monkey bodhisattva, Avalokiteshvara incarnated, and the rock ogress, an incarnation of **Tara.** Her Tibetan adherents call Tara "mother." Her worship spread along with Buddhist law; she became a folk figure worshiped beyond any particular Buddhist sect. The two wives of King Srong Tsan Gampo were canonized as incarnations of Tara, the savioress, or goddess of mercy.

The drama of Tibetan Buddhism combined features of Hinduism in Hatha Yoga and tantrism with Buddhist deities of Mahayana. Tibetan Buddhism teaches three vows: the monastic vows of the Vinaya, the progressive path of the bodhisattva, and the esoteric precept of the tantras.[30] Tantric books emphasize the masculine and feminine aspects of gods, goddesses, and the universe. Creation is through pairs of deities, male and female, who generate the whole process of the universe through their sexual intercourse. Human beings also reflect the universe and can participate in its forces. The **Kalachakra** (time and space) doctrine is that the whole universe moves in a cycle and that there is "a correspondence between the flow of the vital currents in the body and the flow of time in the universe."[31] It postulated that the experience of time is only the functioning of the vital currents.

Humans have a pure consciousness or transcendent self in a reservoir at the base of the spine, and through special postures, they can pass beyond the limits of the physical body to experience the pure consciousness. Exercises of controlled sexual energy are believed to purify the nervous system so that humans can experience pure consciousness. Monks require nuns or consorts to aid them in this form of worship. Special words are spoken in formulas, or mantras; and dramas of the gods take place in abstract geometric constructions, or mandalas; in special positions formed by the hands, or mudras; and in the act of worship, puja. But the culmination of the lengthy worship in tantrism, which some books regard as primarily figurative rather than literal, is the copulation of a man and a woman as an act of worship, to generate power and perhaps a spiritual enlightenment.[32] The heightening of all energies is the goal rather than relaxation or expending energies. Indeed, some Indian tantrists believe that yogins can recover any energy lost during tantric exercises. The older tantric form of Tibetan Buddhism, the **Nyingmapa,** was known as the Red Buddhism because the monks wore red garments instead of the usual yellow. A later reform movement opposed some of the practices of Red Buddhism. The **Gelugpa** monks wore yellow hats and belts to signify their differences from the monks of the old order and practices, who continued to wear red.

Both the Gelugpa and the Nyingmapa form of Buddhism contain some tantric elements. However, the Gelugpa form was initiated as a protest against the sexual abuses and lax practices of the Nyingmapa, who ate meat and consumed much alcohol. The Gelugpa advocated celibacy, vegetarianism, and restricted use of alcohol. It is at this point that a second striking feature in the Tibetan drama of Buddhism occurs.

How could the Gelugpa find replacements for their order if they did not have sons to take their places? The answer went beyond mere recruitment to promotion

Tara [TAH-rah]
The popular mother goddess of Tibet, associated with Avalokiteshvara, the Lord Who Looks Down.

Kalachakra
[kah-lah-CHAK-ra]
The space–time doctrine in Tibet. The whole universe is related in its flow to the vital currents of the human body.

Nyingmapa
[ning-MAH-pa]
The Red Hat Buddhists of Tibet. Their Buddhism retained an element of pre-Buddhist beliefs and practices.

Gelugpa [ge-LUG-pa]
The Buddhists of Tibet known as Yellow Hats. They reformed the practices of the Nyingmapa, or Red Hat Buddhists.

Buddhism

563 Siddhartha Gautama born

483 The Buddha dies

327–325 Alexander the Great in northwest India

273 Ashoka begins reign

247 Third Buddhist Council at Paliputra

140–15 King Milinda (Menander), a Greek, reigns

200 Mahayana Buddhism begins

65 Ming Ti of China permits Buddha statue to be erected

2nd Century Nagarjuna begins Madhyamika philosophy

399 Buddhism introduced to Korea

5th Century Buddhaghosa

520 Bodhidharma brings Chan (Zen) meditation to China

538 Zhiyi, founder of Tian Tai (T'ien-T'ai) Buddhism in China

Buddhism introduced to Japan by Korea

552 Buddhism enters Japan under reign of Emperor Kimmei

630 Srong Tsan Gam Po invites Buddhist missionaries to Tibet

740 King Khri-strong establishes Mahayana Buddhism in Tibet

845 Wu Tsang of China persecutes Buddhists

9th century Dengyo Daishi (Saicho) introduces Tendai in Japan

Kobo Daishi (Kukai) establishes Shingon in Japan

1200 Muslims destroy Buddhist centers in north India

1212 Honen, founder of Jodo in Japan, dies

1262 Shinran, founder of Jodo Shin in Japan, dies

1282 Nichiren, founder of Nichiren Sect in Japan, dies

1898 Jodo Shinshu sect comes to America with Japanese immigrants

1931 Zen Buddhist society formed in New York

1937 Makiguchi Tsunesaburo founds Soka Gakkai in Japan

1945 Hiroshima, Japan, destroyed by atomic bomb

1949 Mao Zedong controls People's Republic of China

1950 North Korea invades South Korea

1960 Nichiren Shoshu chapter founded in California

1964 Thich Tri Quang leads United Buddhist Association in Vietnam

1995 Dalai Lama recognizes 6-year-old boy as reincarnated Panchen Lama

BCE	CE
▲ 2000	0
▲ 1500	500 ▼
▲ 1000	1000 ▼
▲ 500	1500 ▼
0	2000 ▼

from within their ranks. They held that the head **lama** would be reborn shortly after death. Thus they conducted an elaborate drama to search out a newborn male child who would bear on his body markings of the deceased lama and also show familiarity with a few of his personal belongings. The child, when found, would become the next lama, a living Buddha.

Historical Development: Buddhism and the West

lama [LAH-mah]
The term means "supreme being," comparable to the term *guru* in Indian Buddhism. A priest in Tibetan Buddhism.

In the global community, Buddhism has followed Asians to Europe and North and South America. It entered Hawaii in 1889 with a Jodo Shinshu priest, Soryu Kaghi. At that time Hawaii was neither an American possession nor one of the states. In the mid-nineteenth century, Buddhism reached the West Coast of the mainland United States with the Chinese who settled in San Francisco. The first temples provided Buddhist worship, but their Buddhism was not a pure, exclusive form. The World Parliament of Religions in Chicago, 1893, focused attention on world religions. Renzai Zen Buddhism was promoted in America by Soyen Shaku. Arriving in San Francisco in 1898, two priests brought Pure Land Buddhism from Kyoto. Its first movement was the Buddhist Mission of North America; in 1942, it became known as the Buddhist Churches of America. The Jodo Shinshu Group is the largest Buddhist group in America. Aside from this group, the history of Buddhism in America is largely the story of Zen Buddhism.

Among newly arrived forms of Buddhism are schools from Japan, Tibet, and China. Nichiren Shoshu Sokagakkai came to South America and California through

© Gary Conner/PhotoEdit

Thai Woman Prays in Buddhist Temple in New York. Celebration of Songkran (Thai New Year)

the efforts of Daisaku Ikeda. Its program was similar to that in Japan; it promised better living for its adherents, who had only to chant "Namu Myoho Renge Kyo" ("Hail to the holy law of the Lotus Sutra"). Two Tibetan centers have expanded rapidly since their beginnings about 1970. The Tibetan Nyingma Meditation Center in California and Karme-Choling of Barnet, Vermont, have attracted many followers. Chinese Buddhism has been especially active in making American monks and nuns; the Sino-American Buddhist Association of San Francisco has been quite successful.

At the beginning of the twenty-first century, American Buddhism has many adherents; the membership of its organization is growing. The scholars who assess Buddhism in America, such as those who presented papers at the First Buddhism in America Conference (Boston, 1997), represent a variety of views of past, present, and future.[33] Richard Hughes Seager describes three broadly defined groups in American Buddhism. The first is native-born Americans who have embraced teachings of the Buddha; Seager calls them convert Buddhists. The second is new immigrant and refugee Buddhists from a range of Asian nations. The third group is Asian Americans from China and Japan who have practiced Buddhism in this country for four or five generations. Each of these groups of Buddhists has a unique perspective, and together they shape the expression of Buddhism in America.[34]

Charles Prebesh thinks that American Buddhists "might look beyond North American borders and learn from other Western Buddhists." Some factors that will influence the future of Buddhism in America are (1) the definition of *sangha,* (2) democratization within the entire tradition, (3) ethnicity, (4) gender equality, (5) level of orthodoxy, and (6) social engagement and sectarian issues that challenge the future.[35]

Buddhism in America is pulled between imitating the ideals of monks in Asia and relating to concepts and practices compatible with more established Christianity of the West.[36] Richard M. Jaffe has found a particular example in American Zen Buddhists who are not defined as they are in Japan. Shunryu Suzuki has said that American students are neither priests nor laity. Despite their marriages and the imperative to find a successor abbott, most non-Jodo Shin Japanese Buddhist clerics continue to view ascetic monasticism as the desired, if unattainable, way of life.[37]

Theravadin Buddhism was introduced institutionally and permanently established in 1966 with the Washington, D.C., Buddhist Virha Society.[38] To serve the 600,000 people in the United States who are Burmese, Cambodian, Laotian, Sri Lankan, or Thai, hundreds of temples and Theravadin meditation centers have been established. Although some of the temples and centers are served by local leaders and lecturers, one near Philadelphia has Theravadin monks, who, like all monks; live by the *vinaya.* Monks are prohibited from trade, use of money, driving, preparing their own meals, storing food, eating solid food afternoon or before dawn, or having relations with women. Laypeople prepare and serve the meals and drive the monks when they need transportation.

Worldview

The Absolute

In learning that Buddha did not worship a god, many people have concluded he was an atheist. His doctrine that there are no permanent entities in the universe (**anicca**) removed any ground for traditional beliefs in gods. A more careful reading of his conversations with his monks indicates he had not had an experience

anicca [a-NICH-cha] Impermanence. The Buddhist doctrine that there are no permanent entities. All phenomena continuously change.

with any god he found worth describing. He also asked whether the Brahmins who taught so much about gods and sacrifices knew from experience what they were teaching or were only repeating hearsay and tradition. He did not denounce belief in gods; he taught that belief in gods was not essential to his mission of finding release from suffering. A *sutta* (Buddhist form for *sutra*) reports this comment from the Buddha:

> 14. "Then you say, Vasettha, that none of the Brahmanas, or their teachers, or of their pupils, even up to the seventh generation, has ever seen Brahma face to face. . . . So that the Brahman versed in the three Vedas have forsooth said thus: What we know not, what we have not seen, to a state of union with that we can show the way, and can say: 'This is the straight path, this is the direct way which makes for salvation, and leads him, who acts according to it, into a state of union with Brahma!'"
>
> "Now what think you, Vasettha? Does it not follow, this being so, that the talk of the Brahmans, versed though they be in the Three Vedas, is foolish talk?"[39]

Buddha's followers, however, were less careful to avoid discussing deities. Theravadins still deny that the Buddha is a god—he is a man, but such a man! Westerners visiting a Theravadin temple, if uninstructed, would conclude that the devotees are worshiping the Buddha. Theravadins' beliefs include spiritual beings who can influence human lives and be influenced by humans. Mahayanists speak of three bodies of Buddha (**Trikaya**). One is the body of Siddhartha Gautama, which is the Transformation Body (Nirmanakaya). Another is the spiritual reality in all things; it is the Body of Essence (Dharmakaya). Some philosophical schools identified it with Nirvana, or the World Soul—Brahman of the Upanishads. The third is the combined body of Siddhartha and spiritual reality; he is the incarnation of spiritual reality. It is the body of Bliss (Sambhogakaya).[40]

Mahayanists opened the door for all sorts of spiritual beings. Bodhisattvas are saints qualified for Nirvana who remain in contact with the world to help the suffering. Devotees can pray to them and offer adoration. There are figures such as Avalokiteshvara and Guanyin (Kwan Yin), Vairocana, and Amitabha. There are countless Buddhas and Buddha fields. There is a "Suchness" in which all Buddhas participate. All humans who now live can become Buddhas. Although Buddhism did not emphasize salvation through gods of the Vedas, its spirit deified persons and ideals. Mahayana Buddhism appeals to masses who prefer to personify aspects of the Absolute.

The World

Buddhists shared with Hindus many aspects of interpreting the world. The Brahmin emphasis on sacrifices according to the Vedas seemed to the Buddha too worldly; the sannyasin emphasis on denying the world, and especially the human body, seemed too harsh. The Middle Path led him to accommodation with the world, its creatures, and its householders. The world can be accepted, appreciated, and valued. The cause of suffering is not the world but individuals' attachment to it.

Theravadins and Mahayanists differed in their interpretation of detachment from the world. Theravadins emphasized the ideal of the *arhat* who turned away from the householders' involvement in creative processes of life. Mahayanists emphasized that the world of experience is only appearances; the real world is one revealed in the enlightenment experience. According to Zen Buddhism, one can

Trikaya [tre-KAH-ya] According to Buddhist doctrine, the three bodies of Buddha. The first body was indescribable, the second body is the almost divine body in which the Buddha appeared to the Mahayana faithful, and the third body was his appearance as a human being.

experience this insight into the nature of reality in this lifetime; for other Mahayana groups, the insight comes after death.

Humans

The Hindu division of a human into body and soul, a view shared by many world religions, was too simplistic for the Buddha. These two entities suggested more permanence to humans than he could find in his enlightenment experience. He agreed with Hindus that the human body is not permanent. He differed with them by denying that there is any permanent soul, or purusha. His doctrine is labeled **anatta,** no soul. The soul and the body of the Hindus could best be analyzed as psychological experiences. The skandhas of psychological activities arise and fall without any permanence. Even mind or consciousness is dependent rather than absolute.

The Buddha acknowledged that karma influences each life; one must live with results of cravings of the past. Choice, however, can change the future. One can choose how to see oneself and the world and how to interpret experiences. The *Anguttara-nikāya* V, 147 says,

> By getting rid of three mental states: passion, aversion and confusion, one is able to get rid of birth, ageing and dying. By getting rid of three mental states: false view as to "own body," doubt and dependence on rite and custom, one is able to get rid of passion, aversion and confusion. By getting rid of three mental states: unwise reflection, treading the wrong way and mental laziness, one is able to get rid of false view as to "own body," doubt and dependence on rite and custom.[41]

The Problem for Humans

The problem for humans is suffering. Suffering is primarily produced by humans' ignorance of the impermanence of the world, people, and even their own psychological processes. Assuming that the world and its contents are permanent, humans crave and grasp in order to possess and control. Because psychological experiences and things experienced are impermanent, efforts to make permanent and to control are futile. Suffering is the symptom of alienation caused by ignorance.

The problem is also ignorance that something can be done about suffering. Suffering people often assume they can overcome suffering by increasing their possessions or by introducing permanence into their living conditions. Proceeding along these lines leads humans to greater suffering and intensifies the vicious circle. Humans may conclude, wrongly, that there is no way out of suffering, and may become resigned to it. In the *Samyutta-nikāya* II, the Buddha offers this teaching:

> Whoso says, "He who does (a deed) is he who experiences (its result)," is thereby saying that from the being's beginning suffering was wrought by (the being) himself—this amounts to the Eternity-view. Whoso says, "One does (a deed), another experiences (the result)," is thereby saying that when a being is smitten by feeling the suffering was wrought by another—this amounts to the Annihilation-view.
>
> Avoiding both these dead-ends, Kassapa, the Tathagata teaches Dhamma by the mean: conditioned by ignorance are the karma-formations . . . *and so on*. This is the origin of this whole mass of suffering. By the utter stopping of that very ignorance is

anatta [a-NAT-ta] The Pali word for "no soul," or Sanskrit for "no Atman."

the stopping of the karma-formations . . . *and so on.* Thus is the stopping of this whole mass of suffering.[42]

The Solution for Humans

The solution for humans is found in knowledge. They learn the cause of suffering and know that something can be done about it. The Buddha taught the Middle Path that leads to release from suffering. Theravadins emphasize that humans must work out their own salvation. The Buddha is a model to follow, but his Eightfold Path requires a disciplined life.

Buddhists believe that meditation is the primary solution to the problem for humans. Mahayanists regard the Theravadin form of meditation as elementary instruction for unimaginative followers. The Buddha taught many lessons over a forty-five-year period. To those capable of receiving a higher knowledge, he revealed better ways of release. The essence of the higher knowledge is that there are savior beings who will help those who call on them. These wonderful beings have looked over the wall of the garden of Nirvana, and, although they had every right to enter, turned back to help others find the way. Humans in distress can call on one of these bodhisattvas to come to their assistance. Release comes not so much from ceasing to be as from ceasing to grasp. Freed from attachment that produces suffering, humans can experience joys of life, joys figuratively described in terms of physical heavens. The *Pañcaviṃśatisāhasrikā* says,

> *The Lord:* But such are the intentions of a Boddhisattva. A glowworm, or some other luminous animal, does not think that its light could illuminate the Continent of Jambudvipa, or radiate over it. Just so the Disciples and Pratyekabuddhas do not think that they should, after winning full enlightenment, lead all beings to Nirvana. But the sun, when it has risen, radiates its light over the whole of Jambudvipa. Just so a Bodhisattva, after he has accomplished the practices which lead to the full enlightenment of Buddhahood, leads countless beings to Nirvana.[43]

Although Nirvana is spoken of in religions of India, Buddhism's use of the term has acquired specific usage. In general, Nirvana is the state the Buddha achieved, the end of the spiritual path all Buddhists seek. In various times, places, and groups, Nirvana acquired distinctive features. Perhaps in the beginning it meant enlightenment, the bodhi experience, an awakening beyond the powers of speech to describe.

In Theravadin Buddhism, the connotations of Nirvana are both negative and positive. Negatively, Nirvana means the extinction of samsara, what can be reborn. Positively, it means direct insight into truth, bypassing language distinctions between Nirvana and samsara. The *arhat,* who has achieved Nirvana, can experience it but not express it in language. Nirvana is the dying out of the three fires: greed, anger, and illusion. It is best described as *not* this or *not* that.[44]

Mahayana schools and philosophies seek a common ground for samsara and Nirvana. Yogacara Buddhism asserts that the mind is the common ground, a core of Buddhahood in each person. Chinese Mahayanist schools of Tian Tai (T'ien T'ai) and Hua-Yen make the difference apparent. Tian Tai seeks immersion into the pure mind; Hua-Yen teaches that there is no underlying mind. Fa Zang (Fa-tsang) argues that all phenomena reflect all other phenomena (as his demonstration of the Buddha image and the eight mirrors illustrates).

Mahayanists emphasize an ideal that combines enlightenment and compassion, a life exemplified by a bodhisattva. Enlightenment is open to everyone in this lifetime. Its experience is lived out in one's harmony with the universe.

Other Buddhist schools emphasize slightly different dimensions of Nirvana. Chan, or Zen, seeks to pass the Buddha's enlightenment experience from master to disciple in an unbroken chain. The newest experience of enlightenment, then, is the end of a series of experiences that begin with the Buddha. Pure Land Buddhism thinks that humans are incapable of achieving Nirvana by their own power; relying on Amida's compassion enables them to experience it.

In Tantric Buddhism, the enlightenment, Nirvana, experience is participation in the Buddha's reality. Shingon Buddhism emphasizes experiencing the Buddha's enlightened activity through his body. Participating in the world, one exemplifies the Buddha's enlightened action.

Nirvana's two aspects run through the course of Buddhist history. Negatively, Nirvana is the burning out of the craving that brings suffering from lifetime to lifetime.[45] Positively, Nirvana is the enlightenment that inspires compassion for all living beings and a sense of harmony with the universe.

> Some philosophers conceive Nirvana to be . . . a state where there is no recollection of the past or present, just as when a lamp is extinguished, or when a seed is burnt, or when a fire goes out. . . . But this is not Nirvana, because Nirvana does not consist in simple annihilation and vacuity. . . .
>
> Nirvana is where the manifestation of Noble Wisdom expresses itself in Perfect Love for all; it is where the manifestation of Perfect Love that is Tathagatahood expresses itself in Noble Wisdom for the enlightenment of all;—there, indeed, is Nirvana![46]

Community and Ethics

Buddhism maintains an interesting balance between adherent and society. The Sangha was a close organization of monks, but it involved laypeople in monastery activities. Where Buddhism flourished over the centuries, it developed a strong social organization built on cooperation between laity and monks. At the same time, Buddhism has emphasized individual responsibility in community living.

The law of karma is recognized by Buddhists; there is a consequence for every thought or deed. All thoughts and deeds make impacts on the universe. Impacts of deeds carry over from one lifetime to another. There is no self to be reborn, but impulses from an individual's life carry over into another life. Individuals have a responsibility to the future to live an exemplary life now. In the Buddhist teaching of *karuna*, or compassion, there is a strong social concern. Buddhism has taught compassion for all living creatures, animal life as well as human. Those who have compassion are not attached or moved toward a given creature. They have an impersonal goodwill toward all living beings. Expressed in terms of counseling, Buddhist compassion is more empathy than sympathy. Out of respect for living things, most Buddhist monks avoid eating meat or fish—they are vegetarians. Many Buddhist laypeople follow their examples.

Buddhist morality avoids theft, drunkenness, careless speech, and injury to others. With the exception of tantric rituals, Buddhists require celibacy for monks and nuns and loyalty in marriage for laypeople. Fornication and adultery are usually condemned.

The Buddha did not fight to eliminate the caste system or the inferior status of women. He did set an example in his own order for all the world to see; he made no caste distinctions, and he recognized that women can be as holy as men.

Buddhist Nun.
Syracuse, New York.

Women in Buddhism

Chapter 3 describes the restricted role of women in India when the Buddha was born. When Mahajapati, his stepmother and aunt, asked to become one of his disciples and lead a monastic life, he was at first reluctant. But eventually he established an order of *bhikkunis,* the female counterpart of *bhikkus* (monks). However, the rules he set for the bhikkunis made them subordinate to the monks. As Buddhism moved eastward from India, the tradition of bhikkunis disappeared, although Buddhist women continued to serve as nuns. According to Diana Y. Paul's study of women in Mahayana Buddhism, nuns were considered second in order to the elite males, the monks.[47]

In recent decades, the role of women in Buddhism has come under discussion. "Buddhism is paradoxically neither as sexist nor as egalitarian as is usually thought," observes Bernard Faure. "Women played an important role in Buddhism, not only as nuns and female mystics, but also as mothers (and wives) of the monks."[48] But, asks Karma Lekshe Tsome,

> If Buddhist education and full ordination are valuable for men's achievement, are they not equally valuable for women? . . . "The most eye-opening element of Buddhism for women is its liberation psychology. Enlightened mind, being totally pure and perfected, is not limited by gender or anything else . . . . Why should access to teachings and practice be limited by gender?[49]

Although Western Buddhists may be more open to leadership from women, Asian Buddhist women are becoming more active and visible. Most notably, in 1991 Aung San Suu Kyi of Burma won the Nobel Peace Prize for her nonviolent campaign against Burma's military dictatorship. More recently, a Buddhist nun named The Venerable Zhengyan has won recognition and praise as the head of the Taiwan-based Compassion Relief Diaspora, "the first modern Buddhist organization in any Chinese society to carry out humanitarian missions on a large international scale that include delivery and relief on every continent."[50]

An Interpretation of History

Buddhism has no overpowering vision of the end of history, so an interpretation of history as found in Western religions is absent. As in Hinduism, Buddhism emphasizes progress of a person toward release rather than fulfillment of some purpose in history. Popular Buddhist thought, however, anticipates future developments.

Marjorie Topley describes the beliefs in Buddhist folk religion among the Kueiken (Return to the Root) sect of twentieth-century Singapore:

> The third major cycle, that of **Maitreya,** has already begun and [its] own present patriarch is Maitreya incarnate. . . . [To avoid the end of the world in a great catastrophe] the patriarch must be given the opportunity for reaching the masses to teach them the Truth. This can be achieved only if there is a return to the dynastic system and the patriarch sits on the Dragon Throne as emperor. . . .
>
> Truth cannot reach the people, moreover, if the head of the state does not hold Heaven's Mandate to rule. Ideally, Maitreya himself should head the earthly state as the Buddhas did in Tibet. Then he could easily reach all the people.[51]

Maitreya [mi-TRAY-ya]
In the tradition of East Asia, the next Buddha to appear on earth.

Despite its universal missionary outreach, Buddhism has been more concerned with the progress of the individual toward release than with the progress of society or the world toward some final judgment or disposition. In theory, as the individual overcomes attachment to becoming, so the universe can overcome the generation of opposites. In either case, there is peace and stability, the end of becoming.

Rituals and Symbols

Buddhism's extension into many nations and cultures makes it difficult to describe its rituals. Almost everywhere, the central figure of devotion is an image of Buddha. Placed in open air, housed in a great temple hall, or seated in a small temple room, the figure of the meditating Buddha is approached by devotees who bring candles, fruit, flowers, or even a gold leaf. At times, large congregations kneel before an image; most times individuals or families approach for a few moments of bowing or kneeling. At times, a monk assists in worship; at other times, no assistance is given to the devotee. Although the figure is usually inspired by Siddhartha Gautama, it may be one of the other Buddhas or bodhisattvas.

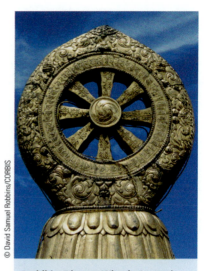

Buddhist Dharma Wheel. A metal emblem near Baudhanath Stupa in Kathmandu, Nepal.

Another symbol is the wheel of the law, or the dharma. It is not so much an object of worship as a reminder of the perfect way of release offered by the Buddha. Although the term *dharma* has both general and technical meanings in Buddhism, the wheel stands for the Buddha's teaching. It includes his exposition of the general order of nature and his proclamation of the path toward deliverance. The shortest dharma was the Buddha's first sermon, in which he set in motion the wheel, or lore, of dharma.

Devotees enter the Buddhist faith by repeating the three refuges. They take refuge in the Buddha, in the Dharma, and in the Sangha. In the Theravadin countries of Southeast Asia, small boys may go through the ritual of becoming a monk— their heads are shaved and they put on the saffron-colored robes of monks. Older males may spend several weeks as monks who listen to the law and go out with bowls to receive their food from laypeople. Initiation into the monastic life of most Buddhist orders is very rigorous and extensive. In China and Japan, short-term stays and temporary status as a monk are discouraged. Monastic life has several rituals associated with the laws of entrance and conduct. The "Vinaya" governs the monastic practice of dharma.

In Mahayana countries, there are other interesting observances in life and death. In life, Buddhist monks offer the faithful several ways of discovering the wish of the Buddha for their lives at the moment. To an unsympathetic outsider, the process may appear to be commercial fortune telling offered in a temple. To the devout, the systems offer very practical ways of learning what the Buddha would have individuals do about personal problems or opportunities. In death, families are assured that the deceased has experienced a satisfactory process to a good resting place in heaven and to a comfortable life once he or she has arrived. Buddhism teaches that karma can be removed by a religious professional chanting verses for the deceased.

Life after Death

In theory, there is nothing to carry over from one life to another. Yet the Buddha believed in samsara. Unless humans cease all grasping in this life, something carries over. A consciousness of former existence or a personal identity is not what carries over; what carries over is an individual's moral impact in personal and social life.

Mahayana Buddhism had great success in China, Korea, and Japan because it was concerned with the life of the person after death. The body might be buried or cremated, but the person may retain identity as an ancestor in a spiritual realm. Many Buddhists would explain that the symbols of heavens and beautiful lands of paradise are not to be taken literally. They stand for the ancestor's psychological and spiritual states. It seems that for the typical adherent of Mahayana Buddhism, however, joys after death are found in heavens similar to ideal physical places on earth.

A short quotation from the *Sukhāvativyūha* gives a view of Pure Land Buddhists:

> 21. . . . And the beings who are touched by the winds, which are pervaded with various perfumes, are filled with a happiness as great as that of a monk who has achieved the cessation of suffering.
>
> 22. And in this Buddha-field one has no conception at all of fire, sun, moon, planets, constellations, stars or blinding darkness, and no conception even of day and night, except (where they are mentioned) in the sayings of the Tathagata. There is nowhere a notion of monks possessing private parks for retreats.
>
> 24. And all the beings who have been born, who are born, who will be born in this Buddha-field, they all are fixed on the right method of salvation, until they have won Nirvana. And why? Because there is here no place for and no conception of the two other groups, i.e., of those who are not fixed at all, and those who are fixed on wrong ways. For this reason also that world-system is called the 'Happy Land.' . . .[52]

Buddhism and Other Religions

From its inception, Buddhism has had to live among other religions. As a missionary religion, it has reached out peacefully to win converts through meeting their needs and desires rather than through force. It has been more ready to cooperate than to condemn. When it has not agreed with another position, it has quietly gone its own way. Hinduism absorbed or emphasized many Buddhist ideals. Chinese ancestor worship found it supportive. For a time, Taoists and Buddhists cooperated. For most of Buddhism's history in Japan, Shinto and Buddhism have lived together peacefully, even sharing the same temple compound. Christians have been instrumental in helping translate Buddhist scriptures for other cultures and in promoting dialogues between Buddhists and Christians.

Buddhists believe that the Buddha was enlightened in order to escape the wheel of suffering in one lifetime. Followers of the Buddha have experienced two primary ways of finding that release for themselves. One group, the Theravadins, follow the way of imitation, much as the monks did during the lifetime of the Buddha. The other group, the Mahayana, has developed a variety of ways of experiencing the compassion of the Buddha, which assures release from suffering but does not imitate the Buddha's monastic life exactly.

Buddhism is not the only religion in which there is a division of opinion about which is the right way to health and wholeness in this lifetime and after this life. In later chapters of this text, try to identify which movements believe that the best way is imitation of the founder and which ones believe that only by the compassion of the founder or the deity can one be released from suffering.

CONSIDER THIS

Release from Suffering: Imitation or Compassion?

Having considered Buddhism, the great religion that arose in response to Hinduism, we turn now to two other religions of India. The older, Jainism, claims its beginnings can be traced to the Vedic period. The younger, Sikhism, arose centuries later, after Islam and Hinduism had shared allegiance of India's peoples for a number of centuries. Through encounters with explorers, traders, and emigrants, these vital religions have made an impact on Western civilization.

VOCABULARY

Amitabha [a-mee-TAH-ba]
anatta [a-NAT-ta]
anicca [a-NICH-cha]
arhat [UR-hut]
Asanga [a-SANG-a]
Ashoka [a-SHOW-ka]
Bodhgaya [bowd-GAH-ya]
Bodhidharma [BOW-dee-DAHR-ma]
bodhisattvas [bow-dhee-SAT-tvas]
Bon [PAIN]
Chan [CHAHN]
dharma [DAR-ma]
Dhyana [DYAH-na]
dukkha [DUK-kah]
Eightfold Path
Gelugpa [ge-LUG-pa]
Genku [GEN-koo]
Guanyin [GUAHN-yin]
Hozo Bosatsu [ho-zo bo-SAHT-soo]
Hua-Yen [HWAH-YEN]
Jatakas [JAH-ta-kas]
jhana [JHAH-na]

Jingtu [JING-too]
Jodo [JO-DO]
Kalachakra [kah-lah-CHAK-ra]
karma [KAHR-ma]
koan [KO-an]
Kukai [KOO-KAI]
lama [LAH-mah]
Madhyamika [ma-DYAM-ee-ka]
Mahayanists [ma-HAH-YAH-nists]
Maitreya [mi-TRAY-ya]
mandala [MAN-da-la]
mantra [MAN-tra]
Mara [MAH-rah]
Maya [MAH-ya]
mudras [MUD-ras]
Nagarjuna [NA-GAHR-ju-na]
Nichiren [NEE-chee-REN]
Nirvana [ner-VAH-na]
Nyingmapa [ning-MAH-pa]
pratitya-samutpada [pra-TEET-ya sam-ut-PAH-da]

Ryonin [RYO-neen]
Saicho [SAI-CHOH]
Sangha [SANG-ha]
satori [SAH-TOW-ree]
Shakyamuni [SHAH-kya-MOO-nee]
Shingon [SHIN-GOHN]
Shinran [SHIN-RAN]
skandhas [SKAND-has]
Suddhodana [SUD-DHOH-da-na]
tanha [TAN-ha]
Tara [TAH-rah]
Tathagata [ta-TAH-ga-ta]
Theravadins [ter-a-VAH-din]
Tian Tai [TYIAN-TAI]
Trikaya [tre-KAH-ya]
Tripitaka [TREE-PI-ta-ka]
Vairocana [vai-ROH-cha-na]
Yashodhara [ya-SHOW-dha-ra]
Yogacara [YOH-ga-CHAH-ra]
Zen [ZEN]
Zhiyi [ZHIR-YEE]

QUESTIONS FOR REVIEW

1. Tell the story of the young prince Siddhartha Gautama.
2. Tell the story of the Great Renunciation and search.
3. Why did the ascetics at Sarnath think that Siddhartha Gautama was the Enlightened One?
4. How did the Buddha's return of Kapilavastu affect Buddhism?
5. How did rules for Buddhist monks differ from those of Buddhist householders?
6. State the Four Noble Truths and the Eightfold Path.
7. Outline the events of the Buddha's ministry.
8. Distinguish between Theravadin and Mahayana Buddhism.
9. Give examples to support the claim that Buddhism is a missionary religion.
10. What distinctive features of Tibetan Buddhism may not be covered in an introductory speech by the Dalai Lama?

QUESTIONS FOR DISCUSSION

1. What beliefs and practices of Buddhism are most important to Buddhists? Which are attractive to non-Buddhists?
2. Does the Buddha's teaching understand the full nature of suffering and deliverance? Explain.
3. Where did Buddhism go after India? Why is Buddhism not stronger in India today?
4. What considerations beyond the Buddha's personality and teachings may have contributed to the success of Buddhism, and why?
5. Why did Mahayana Buddhism become widely established in the United States before Theravadin Buddhism was started in Washington in 1966?

NOTES

1. Richard F. Nyrop, *India: A Country Study* (Washington, DC: U.S. Government Printing Office as represented by the Secretary of the Army, 1985), p. 156.
2. René Grousset, *In the Footsteps of the Buddha*, trans. J. A. Underwood (New York: Grossman, 1971), p. 140.
3. Robert O. Ballou, *The Portable World Bible* (New York: Penguin Books, 1967), p. 90.
4. Ananda Coomaraswamy, *Buddha and the Gospel of Buddhism* (New Hyde Park, NY: University Books, 1969), p. 14.
5. Robert C. Lester, *Buddhism* (San Francisco: Harper & Row, 1987), p. 23; Majjhima Nikaya, 1. 247–249.
6. F. L. Woodward, trans. *The Book of the Kindred Sayings* (*Sanyutta-Nikaya*. Part V: Maha-Vagga) (London: Pali Text Society; distributed by Routledge & Kegan Paul Ltd. London, Henley and Boston, 1979), pp. 356–357. Copyright © 1979 by The Pali Text Society. Reprinted with permission.
7. J. G. Jennings, *The Vedantic Buddhism of the Buddha* (London: Oxford University Press, 1948), pp. 158–164.
8. Maurice Walshe, trans., *Thus Have I Heard: The Long Discourses of the Buddha, Digha Nikāya* (London: Wisdom Publications, 1987), p. 245.
9. Brian D. Ruppert, *Jewel in the Ashes: Buddha Relics and Power in Early Medieval Japan*, The Harvard University Asia Center (Cambridge, MA: Harvard University Press, 2000), p. 6.
10. John M. Koller, *The Indian Way* (New York: Macmillan, 1982), pp. 148–161.
11. "Maha-Nidana-Sutta," Digha-Nikaya, *Buddhism in Translations*, ed. Henry Clarke Warren (Cambridge, MA: Harvard University Press, 1915).
12. Majjhima Nikaya, *Buddhism in Translations*, ed. Henry Clarke Warren (Cambridge, MA: Harvard University Press, 1915), Sutta 63.
13. John Blofeld, *The Jewel in the Lotus* (Westport, CT: Hyperion Press, 1948), chap. 3.
14. Coomaraswamy, pp. 180–186.
15. Wm. Theodore de Bary, ed. *The Buddhist Tradition in India, China, and Japan* (New York: The Modern Library, 1969), pp. 131–138.
16. Ibid., p. 157.
17. Ibid., pp. 198–199; see also Hajime Nakamura, *Indian Buddhism* (Delhi: Motilal Banarsidass, 1987), p. 180.
18. A. V. Grimstone, ed., *Two Zen Classics*, trans. Katsuki Sekida (New York: John Weatherhill, 1977).
19. Yoshiro Tamura, *Japanese Buddhism: A Cultural History*, trans. Jeffrey Hundu (Tokyo: Kosei Publishing, 2000), p. 26.
20. Robert Ellwood and Richard Pilgrim, *Japanese Religion: A Cultural Perspective* (Englewood Cliffs, NJ: Prentice Hall, 1985), pp. 23–24.
21. A. K. Reischauer, *Studies in Japanese Buddhism* (New York: AMS Press, 1970), p. 91.
22. Ibid., pp. 106–107.
23. Heinrich Dumoulin, *Zen Buddhism: A History*, vol. 2, trans. James W. Heisig and Paul Knitter (New York: Macmillan, 1988), p. 5.
24. de Bary, pp. 208–209.
25. Sakya Pandita Kunga Gyaltshen, *A Clear Differentiation of the Three Codes: Essential Distinction among Individual Liberation, Great Vehicle, and Tantric Systems*, Trans. Jarad Douglas Rhoton (Albany: State University of New York Press, 2002), p. ix.
26. Christmas Humphries, *Buddhism* (Baltimore: Penguin Books, 1951), p. 184. Copyright © 1951 by Christmas Humphries. Reproduced by permission of Penguin UK Ltd.
27. Masaharu Anesake, *Nichiren, The Buddhist Prophet* (Gloucester, MA: Peter Smith, 1966), p. 16.
28. S. K. Ramachandra Rao, *Tibetan Tantrik Tradition* (Atlantic Highlands, NJ: Humanities Press, 1978), p. 1.

29. Stephan Beyer, *The Cult of Tara* (Berkeley: University of California Press, 1973), pp. 4–5.

30. L. Austine Waddell, *Tibetan Buddhism* (New York: Dover Publications, 1972), p. 22.

31. Rao, p. 57.

32. Ibid., p. 100.

33. Brian D. Hotchkiss, ed., Al Rapaport, organizer, *Buddhism in America: Proceedings of the First Buddhism in America Conference Boston January, 1997* (Rutland, VT: Charles E. Tuttle, 1997).

34. Richard Hughes Seager, *Buddhism in America* (New York: Columbia University Press, 1999), p. 248.

35. Charles S. Prebish, *Luminous Passage: The Practice and Study of Buddhism in America* (Berkeley: University of California Press, 1999), pp. 267–268.

36. Joseph B. Tamney, *American Society in the Buddhist Mirror* (New York: Garland Publishing, 1992), p. 79.

37. Richard M. Jaffe, *Neither Monk nor Layman* (Princeton, NJ: Princeton University Press, 2001).

38. Wendy Cadge, *Heartwood: The First Generation of Theravada Buddhism in America* (Chicago, IL: University of Chicago Press, 2005).

39. *Buddhist Suttas*, trans. T. W. Rhys Davids (New York: Dover Publications, 1969), pp. 171–173; Republication of *The Sacred Books of the East*, vol. 11 (Oxford, England: Clarendon Press, 1881).

40. de Bary, p. 76.

41. Conze, p. 81.

42. Conze, pp. 68–69.

43. Conze, p. 119.

44. Humphries, p. 156.

45. Coomaraswamy, p. 117.

46. Lewis Browne, *The World's Great Scriptures* (New York: Macmillan, 1961), pp. 198, 200; the Lankavatara Sutra [Mahayana text] reprinted from a translation by Suzuki and Dwight Goddard in *A Buddhist Bible*, ed. Dwight Goddard (Thetford, VT: 1938), pp. 352, 356).

47. Diana Y. Paul, *Women in Buddhism* (Berkeley, CA: Asian Humanities Press, 1979).

48. Bernard Faure, *The Power of Denial: Buddhism, Purity, and Gender* (Princeton, NJ: Princeton University Press, 2003), p. 1.

49. Karma Lekshe Tsomo, ed., *Innovative Buddhist Women: Swimming against the Storm* (Richmond, Surrey: Curzon Press, 2000), p. 327.

50. Julia Huang, "The Compassion Relief Diaspora," in Linda Learman ed., *Buddhist Missionaries in the Era of Globalization* (Honolulu, HI: University of Hawaii Press, 2005), p. 185.

51. Marjorie Topley, "Great Way," in *Folk Buddhist Religion*, by Daniel L. Overmyer (Cambridge, MA: Harvard University Press, 1976), p. 159.

52. Conze, pp. 205–206.

READINGS

Bertholomeusz, Tessa J., and Chandra de Silva, eds. *Buddhist Fundamentalism and Minority Identities in Sri Lanka.* Albany: State University of New York Press, 1998.

Burtt, E. A., ed. *The Teachings of the Compassionate Buddha.* New York: New American Library, 1955.

Cadge, Wendy. *The First Generation of Theravada Buddhism in America.* Chicago, IL: University of Chicago Press, 2005.

Conze, Edward. *Buddhist Meditation.* New York: Allen and Unwin, 1956.

Coomaraswamy, Ananda. *Buddha and the Gospel of Buddhism.* New Hyde Park, NY: University Books, 1969.

De Bary, W. Theodore, ed. *The Buddhist Tradition in China, India, and Japan.* New York: Modern Library, 1969.

Ellwood, Robert S., Jr., and Richard Pilgrim. *Japanese Religion: A Cultural Perspective.* Englewood Cliffs, NJ: Prentice Hall, 1985.

Faure, Bernard. *The Power of Denial: Buddhism, Purity, and Gender.* Princeton, NJ: Princeton University Press, 2003.

Gyaltshen, Sakya Pandita Kunga. *A Clear Differentiation of the Three Codes.* Albany: State University of New York Press, 2002.

Gyatso, Tenzin (fourteenth Dalai Lama). *The Buddhism of Tibet and the Key to the Middle Way*, trans. Jeffrey Hopkins and Lati Rimpoche. New York: Harper & Row, 1975.

Harvey, Peter. *The Selfless Mind.* Richmond, Surrey, England: Curzon Press, 1995.

———. *An Introduction to Buddhism.* Cambridge, England: Cambridge University Press, 1990.

Hotchkiss, Brian D., ed., Al Rapaport, organizer. *Buddhism in America. Proceedings of the First Buddhism in America Conference Boston January, 1997.* Rutland, VT: Charles E. Tuttle, 1997.

Jayatillike, K. N. *The Message of the Buddha*, ed. Ninian Smart. New York: Free Press, 1975.

Jones, Charles Brewer Jones. *Buddhism in Taiwan.* Honolulu: University of Hawaii Press, 1999.

Learman, Linda, ed. *Buddhist Missionaries in the Era of Globalization.* Honolulu, HI: University of Hawaii Press, 2005.

Lester, Robert C. *Buddhism.* Hagerstown, MD: Torch, 1987.

Monius, Anne E. *Imagining a Place for Buddhism.* New York: Oxford University Press, 2001.

Prebish, Charles S. *Luminous Passage: The Practice and Study of Buddhism in America.* Berkeley: University of California Press, 1999.

Prebish, Charles S., and Kenneth K. Tanaka, eds. *The Faces of Buddhism in America.* Berkeley, CA: University of California Press, 1998.

Robinson, Richard H., and Willard L. Johnson. *The Buddhist Religion.* Belmont, CA: Wadsworth, 1982.

Ruppert, Brian D. *Jewel in the Ashes: Buddha Relics and Power in Early Medieval Japan.* Harvard University Asia Center. Cambridge, MA: Harvard University Press, 2000.

Seager, Richard Hughes. *Buddhism in America.* New York: Columbia University Press, 1999.

Suzuki, D. T. *Manual of Zen Buddhism.* New York: Grove Press, 1960.

Tamney, Joseph B. *American Society in the Buddhist Mirror.* New York: Garland Publishing, 1992.

Tamura, Yoshiro. *Japanese Buddhism: A Cultural History,* trans. Jeffrey Hondu. Tokyo: Kosei Publishing, 2000.

Tsome, Karma Lekshe, ed. *Innovative Buddhist Women: Swimming against the Storm.* Richmond, Surrey: Curzon Press, 2000.

Wallace, Vesna A. *The Inner Kalacakratantra: A Buddhist Tantric View of the Individual.* Oxford, England: Oxford University Press, 2001.

Welch, Holmes. *The Practice of Chinese Buddhism 1900–1950.* Cambridge, MA: Harvard University Press, 1967.

SCHOOLS OF BUDDHISM

Theravadin	Mahayana	Tibetan
China	Japan	Gelugpa
Tian Tai	Tendai	Kegyupa
Hua-Yen	Kegon	Nyingyapa
Chan	Zen	Sakya
Jingtu	Shingon	
Chen Yen	Jodo Shinshu	
	Nichiren	

CHAPTER 5

Jainism and Sikhism

OVERVIEW AND THEMES

But just by chanced a drop of honey fell on his head,
  Rolled down his brow, and somehow reached his lips,
  And gave him a moment's sweetness. He longed for other drops,
  And he thought nothing of the python, the snakes, the elephant, the mice, the well, or the bees,
  *In his excited craving for yet more drops of honey.**

IMPORTANT JAIN TEACHINGS

Soul and non-soul comprise all things.

Soul should not be destroyed.

Follow Mahavira so that the soul can be released from rebirth.

AREAS OF JAIN CONCENTRATION

Asia: 4,270,000

North America: 7,000

SIKHISM

"How shall we know the Truth?

How shall we rend the veils of untruth away?

Abide thou by His Will, and make thine own,

His will, O Nanak, that is written in thy heart"

—*Selections from the Sacred Writings of the Sikhs***

IMPORTANT TEACHINGS

There is one God, who is found in the heart.
Only the ten gurus and the Adi Granth are to govern life.
Human hair is not to be cut.

AREAS OF SIKH CONCENTRATION

Asia: 23,410,000
Europe: 243,000
United States: 234,000

*W. Theodore de Bary, ed. *Sources of Indian Tradition* (New York: Columbia University Press, 1958), pp. 56–58. Copyright Columbia University Press, New York.

**Selections from Sacred Writings of the Sikhs.* Translated by Dr. Trilochan Singh et al. (London: Allen & Unwin, 1973), p. 29.

After the Rig-Veda was committed to writing and gurus were teaching the union of Brahman–Atman, a Jain spiritual leader appeared who offered his followers a way to "cross the stream." Parshva, who is less well known than the Buddha he preceded in India, receives honor from Jains as their first Tirthankara, or "ford finder." Although deities had little role in salvation of Jains, karma and reincarnation were important concepts. The best way to avoid bad karma and increase good karma was to revere all soul present in living things, human or not. Despite its lack of deities, Jainism influenced Hinduism through its high priority of reverence for all life.

About the time that Christopher Columbus sought to add Asia to the possessions of Queen Isabella and King Ferdinand of Spain, Nanak, a young Hindu of the Punjab, saw God. He astonished his friends, when he rejoined them after his walk in a forest, by announcing that there is no Hindu and no Muslim. Instead of salvation without gods or with many gods, he taught salvation through only one God. As did Hindus, he believed in reincarnation; unlike Jains, his followers employed swords in preserving their faith. As he traveled with his friend Mardana, a professional singer, he helped stir the hearts of converts with songs of love for God. In the twenty-first century, Sikhism is a vital religion of India.

Golden Temple. *Amritsar.* The chief gurdwara, or house of worship of Sikhs in Amritsar, Punjab.

Jainism

Jainism, although a minority religion of India, is considered so much a part of the religious scene that some people regard it as a subcaste of Hinduism. However, since its views on the Vedas and deities differ from those of Hindus, it must be considered a separate religion. Its views on karma and samsara, however, are evidence of its origins in the fertile climate of India's religions.

In Jain temples, twenty-four role models, **Tirthankaras,** are often represented by statues. The first, Parshva, is believed to have lived from the early days of the written Vedas; the last, Mahavira, was born about 599 B.C.E. The focal point of Jain beliefs and practices today is Mahavira.

Two groups of Jain monks disagree sharply about the life of their Tirthankara. Their points of view reflect their own choices of how to practice their faith. The more numerous, liberal monks and nuns, **Shvetambaras,** wear white garments. The more conservative monks, the **Digambaras,** are "sky clad," or "without clothing." Each group is sure Mahavira set the example for their particular practices.

Clothing is a symbol that expresses the different beliefs of the Digambaras and the Shvetambaras. Digambaras believe wearing clothes demonstrates a person's attachment to the physical world. Because salvation is achieved through renouncing the physical world and karma, which has physical attributes, Digambara monks symbolize their renunciation by being only "sky clad." The Digambaras, disagreeing with the Shvetambaras, argue that although the absence of clothing does not necessarily signify a true monk, the presence of clothing on a monk indicates residual shame, a character flaw not found in a true monk. All the previous Tirthankaras were nude, say the Digambaras. They believe only Digambaras can attain *moksha*, release from bondage to the world.

Tirthankara
[ter-TAN-ka-ra]
In Jainism, a spiritual leader who has found the crossing, or ford, to the farther shore.

Shvetambaras
[SHVAY-TAHM-ba-ras]
The Jains who follow the tradition that allows monks to wear clothes. They believe women can obtain release from life without being reborn as men.

Digambaras
[di-GAHM-ba-ras]
The Jains who believe that a true monk is "sky clad." These monks think women cannot become liberated until they are reborn as men.

A Jain Temple. Located near Jaiselmere, Rajasthan, India.

© Mary Altier

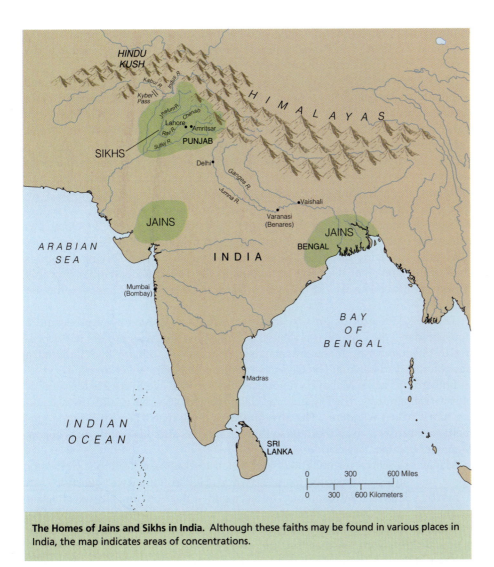

The Homes of Jains and Sikhs in India. Although these faiths may be found in various places in India, the map indicates areas of concentrations.

India accepts nudity for its holy men, but not holy women, so the Digambara practice prevents women from becoming nuns in their order. Digambaras deny that women can, from this lifetime, become Tirthankaras. Only by being reborn as a man can a woman become a Tirthankara. The Shvetambaras disagree, believing that wearing clothes is irrelevant to a person's commitment to freeing soul from body. Accepting nuns in their practices, Shvetambaras believe women can, in this lifetime, become liberated. These attitudes are manifested in the traditions and stories of each group.

The Life of Mahavira

The difference between Digambaras and Shvetambaras extends into their beliefs about their twenty-fourth Tirthankara. Both agree there were twenty-three Tirthankaras prior to the twenty-fourth, Mahavira. They also agree he was born as Jnatrputra Vardhamana about 599 B.C.E. However, they are divided over his life in the womb of his mother, Trishala, and over the role of his father, Siddhartha, a Kshatriya chieftain of the Jnatr clan, in his birth. Before his birth Trishala had a series of dreams predicting the greatness of her son.

The symbols in her dreams indicate to the faithful that Mahavira was destined to be either a monarch or a saint. This story demonstrates the importance of dreams in prophecy, Jain symbols of a Tirthankara, and the elevation of Jnatrputra Vardhamana to that rank. It is interesting to compare this account with the stories surrounding the birth of the Buddha or the Christ.

The Shvetambaras tell an astonishing story of an embryo transfer. Mahavira was conceived through the union of a Brahmin couple, Rshabhadatta and Devananda. Shakra, king of the gods, intervened and exchanged the embryo with that in the Kshatriya woman Trishala. Thus the Brahmins were rejected in favor of Kshatriyas, who could become either spiritual or temporal monarchs. Shvetambaras believe the embryo transplant was an auspicious moment in the life of Mahavira. The value that Jains place on **ahimsa,** or nonviolence toward living things, is shown in a story that the baby in the womb did not kick his mother but only stirred gently, so she would not worry. He was born in the Bihar region, near Vaishali.[1]

The two Jain groups are divided over whether Mahavira ever became a householder—the Digambaras deny it, and the Shvetambaras profess it. According to Shvetambaras, Mahavira married Princess Yashodhara and fathered a daughter, Priyadarshana. The Digambaras insist Mahavira never married.

Both groups agree Mahavira renounced the world at age thirty. He tore out his hair in five handfuls. The Digambaras claim the gods took his clothes away, making him a naked wanderer. The Shvetambaras think that when his tattered garment was torn away by a thorn bush thirteen months after his wanderings began, Mahavira became "sky clad."

Mahavira's search for enlightenment lasted twelve years. Without clothes or home, he wandered, detached from the world. He did not answer questions put to him by villagers; they responded by siccing their dogs on him. He was attacked by animals and by humans, who drove nails into his body to test the depths of his meditation. Eventually he experienced Nirvana. He was then known as a **Jina,** or conquerer. The word *Jain* means a "follower of a Jina."

Once Mahavira attained enlightenment, he escaped from the cycles of human biological and psychological needs and weaknesses, say the Digambaras. Sitting in a lotus posture, he maintained an omniscient trance, sending forth only a divine sound. Above his head was a white umbrella, a symbol that nothing can be higher or holier than he. The Jain community around him, attracted by his Tirthankara nature, consisted of monks, nuns, and laypeople and was formed by efforts of his closest disciples. A Brahmin, Indrabhuti Gautama, came to him seeking an interpretation of a revelation of Jain teachings sent by the king of gods, Indra. In the presence of Mahavira, all the teachings became clear.

The Shvetambara account is somewhat different, although in it, also, Mahavira astonished Brahmins with his holiness. Eleven converted to become his followers. However, according to this sect, Mahavira continued to eat sparingly and to preach sermons on not harming life. He continued teaching for thirty years. His omniscient cognition was not disturbed in this activity.

Both groups recognize that after his renunciation of the world, Mahavira attracted a very large congregation of devotees. According to the Shvetambaras, there were some 14,000 monks; 36,000 nuns; 159,000 laymen; and 318,000 laywomen.[2]

ahimsa [U-HIM-su]
The Sanskrit word that is translated "nonviolence." In Jainism, it is a reverence for all living things.

Jina [JI-na]
In Jainism, a person who has conquered rebirth. Mahavira was a Jina.

His ranks of followers were deeply impressed with his holiness. At his death in 527 B.C.E. (other authorities date his life from 540 to 468 B.C.E.), a number of kings decided to celebrate a festival of lights to mark the passing of his internal light, which had gone to Nirvana.[3] They also celebrated the enlightenment of Indrabhuti Gautama to supreme knowledge. Jains believe that Mahavira is now in the blissful state of **ishatpragbhara,** beyond life and death.

Jain Scriptures

When Mahavira entered Nirvana, forever free from embodiment, his earthly impact was left in the care of his inner circle of eleven disciples, who were all Brahmins. In some way the "heavenly sounds" of Mahavira are translated by them into holy scriptures to enlighten followers in future generations. Collectively, the canon is known as the **Agamas,** written in Ardhamagadi, an ancient Magadhan language. It is subdivided into three categories: *Purva, Anga,* and *Angabahya.* Jains claim to have existed before their twenty-fourth Tirthankara, Mahavira, and they logically carry their scriptures back to the time of Parshva, the first Tirthankara. However, these *Purvas,* or ancient texts, no longer exist, and the contents of these fourteen books are known only by references in later writings, such as the *Angas,* which originated with Mahavira.

The *Angas,* or limbs, consisted of twelve books, eleven of which still exist. Under critical analysis, they seem to have been written over a long period and to contain material from different authors. Among this material are some of the basic teachings of Mahavira. The *Acaranga* contains the life of Mahavira and rules of conduct for monks and nuns. Other *Angas* give warnings against heretical doctrines, questions on systematic philosophy, tales of edification for laypeople, and an explanation of the rigorous law of karma.

The *Acaranga* states that anyone who does not refrain from injuring animals and who does not teach others not to harm animals continues to s   A sage is one who knows that injuring animals is a sin.[4]

Worldview: Jainism

Jainism offers several beliefs that impress many outsiders. The most important is the sacredness of life, whether human or not. Causing pain or death snares humans in a net of suffering. Another idea is that the physical world is always subordinate to the soul and should not be embraced. A third idea is that humans can have only relative knowledge—no absolute proof of God exists. Humans best find release for the soul in following the example of a person who has already shown the way. Wise people accept full responsibility for their actions and destiny.

The Absolute

The Jains think the universe is without beginning, so they do not believe in a creator god. They do believe their doctrines originate from an omniscient and omnipotent being. Their Jinas collectively are "the Jina," an Absolute. Thus they do not require or seek any verification of doctrines from any other source. Consider

ishatpragbhara
[ee-shut-PRAHG-bu-ru]
The Jain state beyond life and death.

Agamas [AH-ga-mas]
Collection of Jain scriptures whose three parts are *Purva, Anga,* and *Angabahya.*

the selection from the *Great Legend* (Mahapurana) of the Digambara teacher Jinasena of the ninth century C.E.:

> Some foolish men declare that Creator made the world
> The doctrine that the world was created is ill-advised, and should be rejected.
>
> If God created the world, where was he before creation?
> If you say he was transcendent then, and needed no support, where is he now?
>
> No single being had the skill to make this world—
> For how can an immaterial god create that which is material?[5]

Jains do not deny some truth in the doctrines of other philosophies; however, other philosophers who claim any sort of absolute truth are going to extremes. To Jains, statements depend on time, place, and circumstances for the truth they contain. And for each statement of fact, an almost opposite statement can also be true. After all, times change, and places and circumstances change so that more than one statement of fact becomes possible.

Several authors claim the story of the blind men and the elephant is a Jain story told to illustrate exactly this point: A king had five blind men examine an elephant and tell him what they had encountered. One, feeling the trunk, identified it as a huge snake. The second, feeling the tail, thought it was a rope. The third, feeling a leg, called it a tree trunk. The fourth, examining an ear, called it a winnowing fan. The fifth, feeling the side, called it a wall.[6] The point of the story is that human knowledge, limited and relative, is likely to be misleading.

The World

The **loka** is the emptiness of the vast but finite universe in which entities interact. The **triloka** is the triple world, seen by the omniscient ones. Humans live in the Middle World. Below are hells; above is Ishatpragbhara, where liberated souls live.

Five fundamental entities permeate the loka, providing the essentials of life. The most important is the **jiva,** which can be translated soul, or perhaps, "life monad."[7] Non-soul is divided into four entities: motion, rest, atoms, and space. Jiva acts through the mechanism of the four entities. Jiva is characterized as eternal, consciousness, and will, in purity without form. Because jiva is identical with knowledge, it can be immediately known.

In a world of experience, jiva is enmeshed with **ajiva,** or nonjiva. Karma, a sticky substance, binds jiva to nonjiva. The goal of jiva is to act so as to wear away non-soul, including karma.

The world comprises individual souls. Some souls inflict suffering on other souls. There are many individual souls, not one undivided soul.[8]

Humans

An example of how miserable and fruitless human life in the world can be is given in *The Story of Samaraditya* by Haribhadra, of the seventh century C.E. A man left home to seek another country. Becoming lost, he was hungry and thirsty. A mad elephant charged at him. A demoness with a sharp sword appeared before him. He sought to reach refuge in a distant banyan tree. Unable to climb the tree, he dove into a well:

> A clump of reeds grew from its deep wall, and to this he clung,
> While below him he saw terrible snakes, enraged at the sound of his falling;

loka [LOW-ka]
The universe where categories of sentient beings are reborn.

triloka [tri-LOW-ka]
The areas of the universe considered together: upper, middle, and lower.

jiva [JEE-va]
In Jainism, the soul. The opposite is *ajiva,* body.

ajiva or nonjiva
[AH-JEE-va]
Category of existence that is insentient; lacking soul.

And at the very bottom, known from the hiss of its breath, was a black and mighty
   python
With mouth agape, its body thick as the trunk of a heavenly elephant, with terrible
   red eyes.
He thought, "My life will only last as long as these reeds hold fast,
And he raised his head; and there, on the clump of reeds, he saw two large mice,
One white, one black, their sharp teeth ever gnawing at the roots of the reed-clump.
Then up came the wild elephant, and enraged the more at not catching him,
Charged time and again at the trunk of the banyan tree.
At the shock of his charge a honeycomb on a large branch
Which hung over the old well, shook loose and fell.
The man's whole body was stung by a swarm of angry bees,
But just by chance, a drop of honey fell on his head,
Rolled down his brow, and somehow reached his lips,
And gave him a moment's sweetness. He longed for other drops,
And he thought nothing of the python, the snakes, the elephant, the mice, the well,
   or the bees,
In his excited craving for yet more drops of honey.[9]

After Haribhadra translates for a prince the story of the evils of the world, he concludes by saying that the drops of honey are the trivial pleasures for which humans
cling to life despite its hardships.

The Problem for Humans

Jains share with Hindus and Buddhists the doctrine of an absolute law of karma.
The other side of the doctrine for Jains is the absolute nature of soul (jiva), for even
in the very lowest form of life, the soul is present, no matter how oppressed with
the weight of karma. Moreover, as the soul can fall through accumulation of
karma, so it can rise by release from karma. The soul accumulates karma through
a creature's selfish desires; it loses karma by unselfish desires. Karma is the glue
that binds humans to the cycle of rebirth—it is the operative element in samsara,
the recurring rebirth of the soul. Of Hinduism, Buddhism, and Jainism, the Jains
have the most physical analogies to the nature of karma.

   Although Jains think that souls journey through infinite reincarnations in lower
forms as well as human, they think that the human incarnation is the most important. Only from human form can a person obtain release, and only from human
form can a person choose and carry out those thoughts and actions that can bring
escape from eons of drudgery. Indeed, a person must thoroughly know the nature
of karma to deal with it effectively. Jains have arrived at eight major types of karma.

   A person who seeks glory and honor is kept from happiness and wisdom. A
person who causes pain on earth or who permits others to harm earth is deprived
of happiness and wisdom.[10]

The Solution for Humans

Salvation comes through the soul's active desire and labor for its own release.
From the depths of delusion, the soul begins a climb up fourteen steps of a ladder
until at the top it achieves knowledge and freedom. Salvation is through a person's
own effort; the only reward promised in worship is focusing the mind on release.
A priest is not required; humans can worship alone or with other laypersons.

Some exception is found in the form of Digambaras in the south of India who have Jaina-Brahmins residing at temples to take care of rituals. Even here their roles are not comparable to the role of Brahmins among the Hindus, and their existence does not replace the freedom of laymen to worship.

The earliest forms of *pratima,* or stages for a layperson's fasting and contemplation, declined in number from the medieval period. Now there are only two: *upsaka,* one who attends a service of worship, and *shravaka,* one who performs the service. "However," notes Paul Dundas, "the original sense of *upsaka* is preserved by many Jain writers in a popular etymology of *shravaka* which would explain it as meaning 'someone who attains (*shri*) faith in the Jain doctrine, sows (*va*) wealth unceasingly upon appropriate objects and makes (*ka*) merit by serving good monks."[11]

One who follows Mahavira in good works without deceit will eventually attain final liberation. Dedication and hard work in following the right path will bring reward.

All the wise men have taught an unchanging law, teaches The Book of Good Conduct. No living things should be injured or slain.

Ahimsa, the doctrine of nonviolence, is often associated with Mohandas K. Gandhi, who attributed his practice to Jain influence. The Jains practiced it centuries before Gandhi appeared in history to exemplify it for the rest of the world. *Ahimsa* is a Sanskrit word that is appropriately translated "nonviolence."[12] The doctrine appeared in the Upanishads; about 500 B.C.E. in India many people among the Brahmins, the Buddhists, and the Jains emphasized reverence for all life instead of the sacrifices of animals. Contemplative values superseded ritual values. Ahimsa, also, became ritualistic. It included self-control that arose from self-purification. Jains practiced chastity, renunciation of possessions, and identification with all living beings.

© Ann and Bury Peerless. Slide Resources/Picture Library

Jain Nuns. They cover their mouths to avoid taking lives of small creatures through breathing.

Some scholars point to a Vedic belief in an "inverted" order in the "world to come," a situation in which a person would have to endure any pain he or she had inflicted on other beings. It seemed to many holy men that in the light of such belief, a person should abstain as far as possible from injuring other beings. The doctrine of Brahman–Atman illustrated fellow-feeling with all living creatures. The law of karma taught that a person could not escape the consequences of any act. Compassion became a virtue of those who sought liberation from rebirth. Ascetics of the three major religions of India agreed that "life should not be destroyed, whether in mind, in words, or in deeds."

The Jains, laypeople as well as ascetics, hold that all forms of violence, including passions, keep the soul from attaining perfection. Violence turns against those who do not refrain from it. However, observes Dundas, the Jain laity does not generally apply the doctrine of nonviolence to government policy, international politics, or capital punishment.[13]

The extreme examples in Jainism are holy men who believe that care should be exercised to avoid taking life from any living thing. Water is strained to removed any creatures in it. Masks are worn to prevent breathing in insects. Paths are swept before taking a step, to avoid killing an insect.[14] The only acceptable food is that which does not cost a life. To avoid eating all living creatures and cutting any vegetable, the most holy men survive only on fruits that have fallen naturally from trees.

Although the pain and suffering of earth bodies is not seen, it is real. A sage avoids sinning against earth.

Respect for all living beings distinguishes Jain emphasis on the importance of soul. "Deliverance, if never denied as the theoretical aim of existence, is very much a far-off goal," says Dundas.[15] The Buddha had escaped the problem of re-death by declaring there is no permanent soul. Hindus focused on the re-death of souls of humans. Jains emphasized respect for life itself in all living things. Sikhs emphasize the soul's relationship to God.

Community and Ethics

Jain ethics begin with principles of reverence for soul and detachment from physical things. Every Jain is expected to revere life, for beneath the karma that distinguishes individual creatures, all life, human or animal, is the same. Proper speech is a second requirement. Truthfulness (*satya*) is required, lest one injure another person and the community. Complete honesty in all relationships is so ingrained in the Jain community that its business and professional leaders are highly regarded by all people of India. The requirement not to steal (*asteya*) includes not taking anything that belongs to another. Sexual purity (*brahmacharya*) is a requirement for monks and laity. For monks and nuns, it means no sex at all; for laity it means no sex except in marriage. The requirement of nonattachment (*aparigraph*) is to avoid actions that lead to attachments to the physical world. The extreme form of nonattachment is a holy death (**sallekhana**), which is death by fasting. These requirements are accepted by people who take vows in becoming Jains. The vows help Jains make progress toward release from karma; they help the Indian community respect the moral principles of the Jain faith. Among Jain women, fasting is a pious ideal that confirms the seriousness of their commitment. If their fasting is rigorous, it may be conducted in a community hall.[16]

A wise person concentrates on liberation from rebirth. Avoiding attachment, a sage subdues the body, using only plainest food. This person will be liberated from rebirth.

sallekhana
[sal-lek-HAN-na]
In Jainism, a holy death achieved by fasting.

Rituals and Symbols

On a green plain northwest of Delhi, a temple of white stone reflects the rays of the dazzling sun. The dome impresses on visitors the sacredness of the building. Monks greet visitors and receive their offerings. Outside the walls, visitors remove their shoes and wash their hands and feet in water flowing from taps. The shadowy interior is cool, and the terrazzo floor comforts bare feet. Between the walls and the roof is an open space that admits light and fresh air; birds fly in and out, celebrating with song. Under the dome is a life-size statue of a nude man. Jains and their guests walk slowly around the statue a number of times. A solitary devotee stands in one place at the pedestal of the statue, reading from a book and looking up to the dome. Although Jainism has no creator god, it does have temples for worshipers and meditating on the lives of its Tirthankaras (pathfinders or ford builders) to release their followers from the pain of rebirth.

What, then, is the point of worship if humans do not pray to a god for help and the twenty-four Tirthankaras are beyond reach? The images in the temple, sometimes twenty-four or only one, remind humans to approach as if in the presence of a living Jina, who is omniscient and sends forth a heavenly sound of inspiration and guidance to those who seek their own moksha. The images focus the human's physical eyes so that the mind can visualize the image of the kind of being he or she seeks to become. In the seventeenth century C.E., a third group of Jains, the **Sthanakvasis,** broke from the Shvetambaras, protesting against idolatry and temple worship.

What other actions can Jains take to illustrate their devotion to the example of Mahavira? Erecting a Jina image and caring for it by bathing it is one acceptable demonstration. Walking around an image of a Tirthankara in a Jain temple, bathing it, or waving a lighted lamp before it are also rituals of devotion. Celebrating the birthday of Mahavira in the spring and his liberation in the fall are customary. Or a Jain may recall in late spring Prince Shreyamsa's giving food to the mendicant Rshabha, establishing a model for laypeople to give food to wandering monks. Devotees may go on pilgrimages to sacred places and worship there, participating in an annual rite of confession, fasting, and giving alms.

Jainism and Other Religions

Jainism and Buddhism appeared side by side with Hinduism and have often been confused with each other. Jains, however, claim that Mahavira and Buddha may have lived in the same century but that many Tirthankaras preceded Mahavira. Jainism is a much older religion, according to Jain claims, than Buddhism. Texts show, they argue, a separate Jain religion at the time Buddhism began. Buddhism and Jainism are two additional religions besides Hinduism with distinctive ways of dealing with karma and release. Although some Jains have claimed to be part of Hinduism, most scholars place them outside orthodox Hinduism. Jains do not, they argue, have Vedas for their scriptures.

Although Jains have coexisted in peace with Hindus and Buddhists for most of their history, one seventh-century C.E. king, who was a Jain convert to Shiva worship, attempted to convert Jains in southern India to the worship of Shiva. When they refused, he impaled thousands of martyrs.[17]

In spite of the absence of a creator deity in Jainism, it shares some beliefs with Hinduism. The law of karma; the existence of the soul, which is reincarnated; and

Sthanakvasis
[STAHN-AK-va-sees]
A group of Jains that separated from the Shvetambaras over use of idols in worship.

the cycle of rebirths until moksha is earned are similar to Hinduism. The extremes of depriving the body of clothing and food are closer to Hinduism than to the Middle Path chosen by Buddha. Like Buddha, however, the Jains can obtain release without deities. The focus is on humans and human models for them to follow. Jainism, too, has a logic that takes into account the relative truths and knowledge of humans. What we experience and reason as humans is more relative than absolute. Jainism requires of humans a commitment in faith long before they can know whether they will obtain release.

Jains are widely respected in India, and their deep reverence for all forms of life has made a deep impression on Hindus and Buddhists. Very much a part of the modern world, Jains take advantage early of Western education. In general, they are prosperous urban dwellers. In a twentieth-century revival, Jains adapted their older beliefs to current events. Through education of their priests, restoration of their numerous temples, and publication of periodicals, they have widely disseminated their renewed views of the world.[18]

Sikhism

Approximately two thousand years after Jainism was firmly established in India and about the time India became a Mogul (Muslim) empire, Nanak appeared as the first guru of the Sikhs. After receiving a revelation from God, he challenged the numerous gods and castes of Hinduism, the reverence for life in Jainism, and denial of the world in Buddhism. He denied also the Qu'ran, the revelation of Allah to Muhammad. The initial response to Nanak's audacity was confusion and puzzlement. His success in establishing a rival faith, however, brought animosity from most other faiths, particularly from the Mogul (Muslim) leaders. Some of them attacked particular successors of Guru Nanak.

Two views of the historical development of Sikhism circulate today. Older scholarship describes Sikhism as Nanak's attempt to develop a religion that would incorporate the best spiritual insights of both Hinduism and Islam. More recent scholarship represents Sikh views of their own history; it emphasizes that Sikh religion is not a syncretism of two prior religions but a response to a new revelation to Nanak. Sikhism begins, according to more recent scholarship, with God's revelation to Guru Nanak.

Although Nanak's vision once seemed to offer a meeting ground for polytheistic Hindus and monotheistic Muslims, it eventually brought rejection from both. Only single-minded devotion to the Sikh faith preserved later gurus. Their determination to bear arms to preserve their religion was successful in their times and inspires many of their followers today.

The Life of Guru Nanak

Nanak (1469–1539 C.E.) was born a Hindu in the town of Talwandi in the Lahore district of the Punjab. His father, Kalu, was an accountant, and his mother, Tripta, was a very religious woman.

As other religions, Sikhism has a pious biographical tradition of its founder. In the *Janamsakhi* is a reconstruction that scholars do not classify as reliable history. Stories, however, help us understand the spirit of many people who have embraced the faith. Sikh tradition reports that the astrologer who visited the infant soon after birth worshiped him, saying he would grow up to sit under the umbrella,

© Christine Osborne/CORBIS

Sikh Homage to Guru Nanak. In Lahore, Pakistan, these Sikhs pay homage to the founder of Sikhism.

the symbol of prophetic dignity.[19] The astrologer also regretted he would not live to see the great accomplishment that Nanak would bring about—the common worship of both Hindus and Muslims.

The next incident of some importance occurred when Nanak's father invited Hardial, the family priest and a Brahmin, to initiate the boy into Hinduism. This ceremony was attempted when Nanak was nine years old and consisted of having him invested with the sacrificial thread placed on his neck. Nanak rejected the thread, or *janëu,* even though the priest explained it was a part of Vedic ritual required of all Hindus. Nanak was more interested in pure conduct than in traditional symbols made of materials that decayed and never did anything to keep a person morally upright.

Nanak's parents arranged a marriage for him when he was twelve. Sulakhani was the bride selected, from Batala, a distant town. She came to live with him when he was nineteen. Nanak's duties then were those of a herdsman. He was not involved in great responsibility looking after buffaloes, but even in that occupation he is said to have shown miraculous powers. On one occasion, the shadow in which he was sleeping during the day did not move with the passing of time, and on another occasion a large cobra protected him by shading him with its hood. Two sons were born to this marriage.

Invited by his married sister, Nanak left his home and journeyed to Sultanpur, where he entered the service of the governor, Daulat Khan. He here carried out the duties appropriate to his profession as an accountant.[20] The governor not only praised his work but also hired friends of Nanak who came to live and worship with him. When Nanak was thirty years old, he reached his spiritual crisis. Even his pious life was too closely identified with the business of the world.

One morning, after his ritual bathing in a river, he disappeared in a forest and there had a direct vision of God. Receiving a cup of nectar, he was given a promise of God's blessing for those who took his name and remained uncontaminated by the world. Nanak responded with these words of the **Japji,** the meditation:

Proem
There is one God,
Eternal Truth is His Name;
Maker of all things,
Fearing nothing and at enmity with nothing,
Timeless is His Image;
Not begotten, being of His own Being:
By the grace of the Guru, known to men.

Jap: The Meditation
AS HE WAS IN THE BEGINNING: THE TRUTH,
SO THROUGHOUT THE AGES,
HE EVER HAS BEEN: THE TRUTH,
SO EVEN NOW HE IS TRUTH IMMANENT,
SO FOR EVER AND EVER HE SHALL BE TRUTH ETERNAL.[21]

In response, God appointed Nanak his Supreme **Guru.**

Nanak withdrew from his duties and wandered in the forest. His acquaintances called a Muslim *mulla* in hopes of exorcising the demon they believed was in Nanak. After a time, many concluded Nanak was insane. He rejected any claims of the Khan. Moreover, he uttered the shocking and puzzling statement, "There is no Hindu and no [Muslim]." He cut all geographic ties and became a wanderer.

After his renunciation of the world, Nanak entered the most productive phase of his life. Sikh scholars believe he had, during his three days in the forest, a genuine encounter with God and was called to evangelize India in the one True Name. He began to do so, accompanied by his constant companion, Mardana, a member of the Dums, or hereditary minstrels. The northern part of India was gradually covered as he went from town to town singing and reciting in marketplaces, street intersections, and places of Hindu or Muslim pilgrimage. Usually he made a few disciples, or Sikhs, before he had to move on either because of hostility from local religious leaders or of his mission to reach many places. According to the *Janamsakhi,* his clothing was distinctive: he wore the lower garments of a Hindu and painted a saffron Hindu mark on his forehead, but on his torso and head he wore Muslim garments. He was a walking symbol of a religion that could receive both Hindus and Muslims. However, it was a symbol that could confuse and anger as well as impress and attract. He seems to have accepted caste as a civil custom and made no religious effort to combat it. His methods did, nevertheless, inevitably offend the Brahmins when he did not keep their priesthood or ceremonies or base his teachings and actions on the Vedas.[22]

However, Nanak did believe in the Hindu ideas of karma and samsara. He taught that karma from previous lives is worked out in the present life, and present deeds can modify the rewards and penalties for former lives. In these respects, Nanak agreed with Hindus, but he did not regard the Vedas as binding on his

Japji [JAP-ji]
A Sikh hymn recited in devotions every morning. A guide for Sikh conduct.

Guru
[GU-ru] OR [GOO-ROO]
In Sikhism, one of ten early spiritual leaders. God is the one, true Guru.

Jainism and Sikhism in History

BCE				
799–700 (8th Century) Parshva				
	563–483 The Buddha	**599–527** Mahavira (Shvetambara dates)	**510** Mahavira (Digambara date)	

CE				
1469–1539 Nanak, first Sikh Guru	**1479–1574** Amar Das, third Sikh Guru			
1504–1552 Angad, second Sikh Guru	**1526** Babur founds Muslim empire in India	**1534–1581** Ram Das, fourth Sikh Guru	**1563–1606** Arjan, fifth Sikh Guru	**1595–1644** Har Gobind, sixth Sikh Guru
1605–1627 Emperor Jahangir persecutes Sikhs	**1630–1661** Har Rai, seventh Sikh Guru	**1656–1664** Har Kishan, eighth Sikh Guru	**1621–1675** Tegh Bahadur, ninth Sikh Guru	**1666–1708** Gobind Rai, tenth Sikh Guru
1687 Bombay becomes seat of English rule in India	**1858** British take over government of India	**1920** Mohandas K. Gandhi leads Indian National Congress	**1939–1945** World War II	**1947** Partition of Pakistan and India
1757–1769 Ahmad Shad Abdsali of Afghanistan repeatedly invades the Punjab in a "holy war" against Sikhs	**1984** Indian Army invades Golden Temple in Amritsar. Indira Gandhi assassinated; police accuse two of her Sikh bodyguards. In India many Hindus not against Sikhs			

beliefs and practices. He found the Vedas and the Qu'ran both false. Nanak emphasized liberation through divine grace.

In one intriguing account, Nanak and Mardana made a journey to Arabia and actually went to Mecca. According to the story, he ran afoul of Muslim customs and went to sleep with his feet directed at the sacred Ka'bah. Muslims awakened him and said he should not point his feet toward God. He told them to try to point his feet where God is not, because God is everywhere.

Old age, illness, and death caught up with the wanderers, and they settled in Kartarpur. Mardana died first, seated by a river. Nanak took the responsibility for appointing his own successor so there should be no dissension after his death. His choice was Angad, chosen above Nanak's sons, whom he considered unworthy.[23] When Nanak died at the age of 70 in 1539, it was said that his body disappeared and the flowers from Muslims and Hindus that surrounded it remained fresh. The Sikhs erected a shrine to him and the Muslims made a tomb; both memorials have since been destroyed by the river.

The Teachings of Guru Nanak

The most important teaching of Nanak was on the nature of God. God is one (Ek Oankar), preceding all divisions. God is known directly by experience through encounter within the believer. God has the character of Nirguna Brahman, except that he wills to be Saguna Brahman, making himself known to individuals in a relationship of love. His unity includes the world, which manifests his glory. God is too great to be identical with the world; the world is in him, but he exceeds its greatness. God is one reality. Apart from him there is no happiness or immortality.

> He cannot be installed like an idol,
> Nor can man shape His likeness.
> He made Himself and maintains Himself
> On His heights unstained for ever;
> Honored are they in His shrine
> Who meditate upon Him.[24]

Humans are essentially souls in bodies. The soul has functions of Atman, mind, and emotions. The soul is made for communion with God; when separated from God, it suffers. For a soul that loves God, being in the body does not cause suffering. However, for a self-centered soul, loving only itself, body and world can intensify suffering. The world can be a place of beauty for the soul who loves God properly; it is a place of suffering for a soul that loves self more than God. Through their love, humans are either drawn to God or separated from him. By their wills, humans control their lives.

How do humans know God? The Word of God is his sound vibrating in creation. The Word is both the means of knowing God and a path leading to him. Focusing on the Word, which is present in everything, leads to personal experience of God. God's name is his personal being and the means by which he is known. God is the essential Guru, the one who brings truth that leads to salvation. The earthly guru, Nanak, imparts what he has experienced directly from the original Guru. God also expresses his truth through the divine law, Hakum. It regulates all order of the universe, and those who learn it are led to God. God seeks to make himself known by all these ways, so humans learn of him. He does not abandon humans to their own efforts; God's grace comes to assist them on their path.

The focus of Sikhism is God, who exists in the human heart. Humans turn inward to their own hearts, to find God. By meditating on God's name and listening to the original Guru, humans begin to know God and love him. The grace of God then helps humans love God more and the world less. Sin is weakened and goodness is strengthened. Sikhism is so internal that Nanak cared little for the external ceremonies of the Hindus or Muslims. He replaced their rituals with hymns—singing praises to God.

Guru Nanak thought there are five stages in a person's progress toward union with God. The first stage is a piety that honors God and his law and seeks to help others. The second stage increases knowledge. Sikhs learn that the world is beyond comprehension and that other people have experienced God in their hearts. This knowledge leads Sikhs beyond self-centeredness to a greater love of God. The third stage is effort or humility, which focuses on knowing God within the heart. Sikhs listen to God's Word in creation. The fourth stage is being filled with the power of the spirit. Sikhs realize God in their heart, experience peace and fulfillment, and know that beyond death they can join God. The fifth stage is an experience of Truth. Sikhs enter into union with God.

> How then shall we know the Truth?
> How shall we rend the veils of untruth away?
> Abide thou by His Will, and make thine own,
> His will, O Nanak, that is written in thy heart.[25]

The Nine Gurus after Nanak

One identity of a Sikh is as a disciple of the ten gurus. After Nanak were the gurus Angad (1504–1552), Amar Das (1479–1574), Ram Das (1534–1581), and Arjan (1563–1606), who began construction of the Golden Temple at Amritsar. Arjan died a martyr's death, prompting his son, the sixth guru, Har Gobind (1595–1644), to wear two swords. One sword represented spiritual power and the other represented temporal power. He successfully defended Sikhism from Hindu and Muslim attacks. Har Rai (1630–1661) and Har Kishan (1656–1664) continued those battles. The ninth guru, Teg Behadur (1621–1665), was tortured and beheaded by Emperor Aurangzeb, a Muslim. The tenth and last human guru was Gobind Rai (1666–1708), better known as Gobind Singh (Lion).

In 1699, Guru Gobind emphasized the fierce struggle with the world the Sikhs had to face and the need for sacrifice. He invited every man willing to sacrifice his life to the sword to come to his tent. After the first man entered the tent, Gobind emerged with a bloody sword. Another man entered and again Gobind came out with a bloody sword. Five men entered the tent, all expecting death. Then Guru Gobind brought them out alive, for the blood of an animal had been on his sword.

The five men were baptized first as **Singhs.** Gobind Singh baptized the five men ready to die for their faith in water mixed with spices in an iron pot and stirred by a double-edge sword. The water was sprinkled five times into their eyes and on their hair. The five men in turn baptized Gobind. They repeated the war cry of the Sikhs, "The Khalsa are of God, and the victory is to God." They were members of the Khalsa Singhs, or Lions. They wore the five *K*s, which are:

1. Kesh—long, uncut hair on head and chin
2. Kangha—comb

Singh [sing]
A "lion" of the Sikhs. The term was initiated by Guru Gobind, the tenth guru, in 1699 C.E.

3. Kach—short pants
4. Kara—steel bracelet
5. Kirpan—sword

Further disciplines of the Singhs included a requirement to worship only the one God, to revere the Granth, to bathe in cold water at dawn and pray, and to renounce alcohol and tobacco. In turn, they were allowed to eat the meat of animals slain by a single stroke of the sword. They were not to molest any Muslim women. It was a rigorous order of fighting men, but it welcomed all castes who could accept the discipline.

Gobind Singh declared himself the last Sikh guru—after his death Sikhs were to honor only the **Adi Granth** as their guru. He also abolished all caste distinctions among Sikhs and directed them to avoid other Hindu practices of worship. A Muslim assassin stabbed him, and despite efforts by the emperor's surgeons to save him, he died several days later. Since the death of the tenth guru, Sikh worship has centered around the Adi Granth, the perpetual guru. It is ritually honored and read on a daily schedule.

According to Gurinder Mann, "The Sikhs consider the Adi Granth as the highest authority within the community, and it plays a central role in Sikh devotional and ritual life." Its authority is based on two fundamental assumptions: "that its text is revealed and hence immutable and unchangeable, and that answers to all religious and moral questions are available in it."[26]

Sikh customs today are largely community-reinforced in Punjab, but there are many Sikhs residing in other countries. Anyone can become a Sikh by believing in the one God, the teachings of the ten gurus, and the Adi Granth. Beyond that, Sikhs are to live a life of prayer and meditation, recite or read hymns each day, and

Recitation of the Guru Granth Sahib. The text is ritually honored and read on a daily schedule.

Adi Granth
[AH-di-grunth]
The scripture of the Sikhs. Hymns by the Sikh gurus are recorded in the Adi Granth.

generally support the community of the faithful. Their guide to this life is the *Rahat Maryada,* the Sikh Way of Life, approved by Sikh authorities in Amritsar in 1931.

Worldview: Sikhism

The first guru of Sikhism, Nanak, emphasized that God is within the heart. One does not need the Vedas or the Qu'ran to find God. Regardless of one's caste or gender, God is within, Truth immanent. To symbolize a religion open to both Hindus and Muslims, Nanak wore Hindu-style clothing on his lower body and Muslim-style apparel on his torso and head. A century later, the sixth guru, Har Gobind, wore two swords, one representing spiritual power and the other temporal power, to signify defense of the Sikh religion against Muslim and Hindu armies. In 1699 the tenth and last human guru, Gobind Singh, created an initiation ceremony for the Khalsa (the "Pure") that required showing willingness to die for their faith and to take the life of anyone who attempted to persecute its members.

The Absolute

The Sikh understanding of God is based on direct experience of a personal God in the human heart. God is as close to a person as his or her heart but is a unity unlimited in time and space. The Hindu deities and the Muslim deity are human experiences of God but are more limited than God. God cares for humans and approaches them through his Word. Through his Word he is known and the way to him is made clear.

God is both Impersonal (Nirguna) and Personal (Saguna). Impersonal and formless, God is beyond reach. Relating to his creation, he is personal. Although no finite form, even the guru, can be worshiped as God, all forms come from the formless source. Formless, God became NAM, the divine name, and created nature.

The World and Humans

The world and humans are not essentially opposed to God. God is immanent in the world, but he also transcends it. God is available in the human heart but is also beyond complete human comprehension. According to a person's soul, the world can be experienced as good or evil. A person making progress toward unity with God finds the world a beautiful place that witnesses to God's glory. A person absorbed in self-love finds the world an enemy. The human soul has potential to live in peace and harmony with God; unfortunately, most humans love physical possessions rather than God.

The Problem and the Solution for Humans

Karma affects the lives of all people, but God can forgive even the worst sinners. One who turns toward God can be forgiven. The unaided individual cannot succeed. Seeing or hearing the guru is insufficient. One must become committed to God in one's heart. Salvation is available only through baptism.

The human soul can choose to love itself rather than God. Absorbed in self-centeredness, the soul is alienated from God. This alienation is exhibited in sin, immorality, and refusal to help others. By seeking to turn outward to God and to others, the soul overcomes the self-centeredness that alienates it from God. In turning to God and seeking to experience him in the heart, humans find that God graciously makes himself known as guru. He sheds an illumination that leads humans, in stages, along a path of salvation. The ultimate goal for a Sikh is to experience union with Truth, or God. Peace, joy, and unity endure for eternity for humans who have found union with God.

Community and Ethics

Sikhs have an affirmative attitude toward creation. The world is good and to be enjoyed. Although they can eat meat as well as vegetables, they do not use tobacco, which many other peoples also regard as harmful to the body. The human body is good and to be strengthened. Aggressive behavior is not prohibited by any doctrine of ahimsa—force can be used where needed in warfare and in civil life. Besides guarding the **gurdwaras,** the **nihangs** attend fairs and stage mock battles, skills of horsemanship, and other martial arts. Belief in God and in the teachings of the gurus and the Adi Granth can give strength for victory over enemies. Sikh attitudes toward the world are more likely to conquer it than to befriend it.

Sikhs admit people of various castes and economic circumstances, for these distinctions are made by humans, not God. The first Sikhs baptized into the Khalsa represented different castes. In the Khalsa, members acknowledge ethical and religious duties for all humans.

Women in the Sikh religion have experienced both high and low status, depending on customs in India. Because women are not considered unclean or impediments to salvation, association with them or marriage to them does not make a man lower or higher. The householder is superior to the ascetic. Women, who give birth to men, including kings, cannot be considered obstructions to salvation. Early Sikhs avoided older Hindu practices of committing infanticide, burning widows on their husband's funeral pyre, and making women wear veils. Widows were allowed to remarry. Women's relationship to sons and husbands influences their status in the community.

Rituals and Symbols

The Golden Temple at Amritsar houses the object of veneration of all Sikhs, the Adi Granth, the scripture. Worshipers approach the golden-domed building by crossing a bridge over a pool (tank) of water. The building, open on all sides, welcomes all people. Before entering the shrine, worshipers are expected to remove their shoes, wash their feet, and cover their heads. Inside, people assemble to listen to the reading of scriptures, the combined insights of the ten gurus, beginning with Nanak.

Sikhs learned from Guru Nanak that salvation, overcoming separation from God, is achieved through meditation, charity, and hard work. A spiritual union takes place; it does not depend on external rituals. Nanak rejected both Islam and Hinduism for emphasis on rituals. The Sikhs who attend their places of worship and listen to the Adi Granth, however, have established patterns of correct behavior.

Worship at the gurdwaras, symbolic homes of the guru, the Adi Granth, is recommended often. The gurdwara is also used in rites of passage from birth to death.[27] These centers of worship are marked by the yellow flag of Sikhism

gurdwara [GUR-dwah-ra] A place of Sikh worship, fellowship, and hospitality. It is a temple, the dwelling of the guru.

nihangs [NI-hangs] The Sikhs with military skills who are always ready to fight for the community.

regardless of the style of architecture. The center of worship inside the building is the Adi Granth, placed on a dais in the center of a room on cushions and usually under a canopy. The faithful remove their shoes on entering the building, as is the custom in the East. Out of respect, men and women cover their heads in the presence of the Adi Granth and do not turn their backs on it. Worship in a congregation can be at any time, and the hymns of the gurus are important in worship. As from their earliest days, Sikhs enjoy singing with accompaniment by musical instruments.

Eating is a symbolic act emphasized in the activities in the gurdwara. Sikhs can bring sweets into the regular service and give them to one of the **bhais,** or brothers, who puts them in the common collection. The worshiper is then given other sweets from the collection. Eating together from a common source removes any caste distinctions among worshipers. At the end of the service, sweets cooked beforehand from wheat flour, ghee, water, and brown sugar are distributed. The mixture is kept near the Adi Granth during the service. At the conclusion of the service, it is stirred with a *kirpan* (sword) and served to worshipers, symbolizing the sustenance drawn from the guru.[28] A free kitchen prepares and serves meals outside the area of the Adi Granth to all who come. Gurdwara kitchens serve only vegetarian food. Eggs and meat are prohibited.[29]

Bhais, wearing white, attend the temple. As the bhais represent the spiritual side of Sikhism, the nihangs represent the military side. Murray J. Leaf writes,

> As one important practical application of religious ideas, the relation of *nihang* to *bhai* and of the weapons to the book in the gurdwara has a symbolic parallel in the current practice of seeing the Sikh community as a single, "national," political entity.[30]

In addition to routine worship, there are special occasions when religion is an essential part of the drama of life. Rites of passage include the celebration of births as joyous occasions. Funerals, held the day after death end usually in cremation of the body. The birthdays of Guru Nanak and Guru Gobind are days of rejoicing, and a memorial day is set aside to mark the martyrdom of Guru Arjan. On the days of remembering the gurus, the Adi Granth may be read through in its entirety.

Life after Death

Although Nanak believed in reincarnation, he also believed a person can, in this lifetime, find a way of release. The body is not needed for personal identity after death; cremation in the Hindu fashion is commonly practiced. Sikhism seeks a mystical union of the soul with God; that is the only reward worth seeking. Being separated from God is as severe a punishment as can be endured.

> There can be no peace for man
> So long as he thinketh that of himself he can do anything;
> He shall wander from womb to womb in the cycle of births;
> So long as he deemeth one man a friend and another an enemy,
> So long shall he have no rest for his mind;
> So long as man is in love with the illusory goods of the world
> So long shall Dharmraj, the Justiciar King, continue to punish him.
> It is by God's Grace that many can be freed from bondage;
> And by the Guru's grace, saith Nanak, pride and self-will are removed.[31]

bhais [BA-iz]
The brothers of a Sikh gurdwara who assist in worship. It is also the title used for a Sikh priest.

Sikhism and Other Religions

Sikh temples are open to all who observe respect for the holy place and the Adi Granth. The gurdwaras in rural areas provide food and lodging for travelers. Sikhism welcomes men and women from any economic or social class—caste does not matter. Gurus shared beliefs of Hinduism and Islam, but Nanak's position that both the Vedas and the Qu'ran are wrong angered Hindus and Muslims. That fact makes it difficult to maintain that he sought a harmony of Hinduism and Islam. His mysticism shares experiences of Muslim sufis and Hindu yogins, but the hymns of the Adi Granth reveal that the experiences of God reported by the Sikh guru were original.

Sikhs have had their bloody conflicts with both Hindus and Muslims. Their military stature developed as a defense for survival rather than a desire to overcome other religions. Nothing in Sikhism requires force to convert peoples of other religions.

Sikhs have sought to have the Punjab area declared an independent state, for they have felt oppressed by India and Pakistan. In 1984 about 70,000 Indian troops occupied the Punjab and assaulted the Sikh Golden Temple in Amritsar. Hostility between Sikhs and Hindus has been smoldering since then. In 2004, however, Manmohan Singh, a Sikh, became Prime Minister of India. Hindu nationalists objected to the candidate even though he had won the most votes. The consequences for Sikh-Hindu relations remain to be seen.

Considering Jainism and Sikhism along with Hinduism and Buddhism helps us realize what a fertile country India has been for religious life. Hinduism, Buddhism, Jainism, and Sikhism are pearls on a single strand; they are concerned with the soul, karma, re-death, and rebirth. Of the four, only Buddhism has denied a permanent soul. It has retained the idea of karma and influence of each life on subsequent lives. All four religions believe that suffering in the world can be overcome by renouncing attachment to changing phenomena that have the illusions of permanence.

The next family of religions, the Chinese and Japanese, have seen the human problem in different terms. Their goal is not escape but harmony.

To people outside a religion, reverence for life may seem a more praiseworthy goal than defending life. Jain commitment to avoid taking any life inspires respect for the religion; Sikh commitment to defending its adherents is more controversial. Both religions, however, seek to preserve valuable life.

New, rapidly growing religions may seek peace with everyone on hopes of enlisting more believers. In a region of established religions, however, a new religion may be seen as a threat, to be eliminated by persecution. If the strongest power in the region adopts and protects the new religion, their peaceful, reverence-for-life doctrines may remain "pure." Otherwise, the new religion must choose between persecution, flight, or defense of its believers.

Reverence for insect or rodent life allows one to abstain from killing. Reverence for the life of one's fellow believers may require a defense at the risk of taking other human lives. Which life, then, is to be more revered?

CONSIDER THIS

Reverence for Life or Self-Defense

VOCABULARY

Adi Granth [AH-di-grunth]
Agamas [AH-ga-mas]
ahimsa [u-HIM-su]
ajiva [AH-JEE-va]
bhais [BA-iz]
Digambaras [di-GAHM-ba-ras]
gurdwara [GUR-dwah-ra]
guru [GU-ru] or [GOO-ROO]

ishatpragbhara
[ee-shut-PRAHG-bu-ru]
Japji [JAP-ji]
Jina [JI-na]
jiva [JEE-va]
loka [LOW-ka]
nihangs [NI-hangs]

sallekhana [sal-lek-HAN-na]
Shvetambaras
[SHVAY-TAHM-ba-ras]
Singh [sing]
Sthanakvasis [STAHN-AK-va-sees]
Tirthankara [ter-TAN-ka-ra]
triloka [tri-LOW-ka]

QUESTIONS FOR REVIEW

1. Describe Mahavira (a) from the viewpoint of Digambaras and (b) from the viewpoint of the Shvetambaras.
2. What is the difference between jiva and ajiva?
3. Describe the Jain scriptures.
4. Tell the story of Samaraditza by Haribhadra.
5. Give a full explanation of *ahimsa*.
6. What religions conflicted with the Sikh religion?
7. Tell the story of Nanak (1469–1539 C.E.).
8. Tell the story of Gobind Rai (1666–1708 C.E.) and the Khalsa.
9. Describe the Delhi Gurdwara Act of 1971, in regard to characteristics of Sikhs.
10. Distinguish functions of bhais and nihangs in Sikh gurdwaras.

QUESTIONS FOR DISCUSSION

1. Why are Jains not a Hindu caste?
2. Can a rock be considered jiva?
3. What separates Hindus and Sikhs in beliefs and practices?
4. How do Sikhs differ from Muslims?
5. Why do Sikhs want a separate state for themselves?

NOTES

1. W. Theodore de Bary, ed., *Sources of Indian Tradition* (New York: Columbia University Press, 1958), pp. 45–46. Copyright © Columbia University Press, New York.
2. Padmanabh S. Jaini, *The Jaina Path of Purification* (Berkeley: University of California Press, 1979), p. 37; for further comparisons of the groups, see S. Gopalan, *Outlines of Jainism* (New York: Halsted Press, 1973).
3. W. H. Moreland and A. C. Chatterjee, *A Short History of India* (New York: David McKay, 1957), p. 40.
4. Hermann Jacobi, trans., "*Jaina Sutrās*," in *Sacred Books of the East*, vol. 22, ed. Max Muller (Delhi: Motilal Banarsidass, 1968), pp. 12–13.
5. Quoted in de Bary, pp. 79–80.
6. John M. Koller, *The Indian Way* (New York: Macmillan, 1982), p. 123.
7. Paul Dundas, *The Jains* (London: Routledge, 1992), pp. 77–83.
8. Hermann Jacobi, trans., *Jaina Sutrās*, Part I (Delhi: Motilal Banarsidass, 1964), *Âkârânga Sûtra*, Bk. 1,

lect. 1, lesson: verse 2:3. (First published Oxford University Press, 1884.)
9. Quoted in de Bary, pp. 56–58.
10. Jacobi, p. 4.
11. Dundas, p. 162.
12. Quoted in de Bary, pp. 61–62.
13. Dundas, p. 165.
14. Jacobi, pp. 4–5.
15. Dundas, p. 162.
16. Ibid., p. 172; also, Jacobi, Bk. 1, lect. 5, lesson: 4:46–47.
17. Moreland and Chatterjee, p. 109.
18. Richard F. Nyrop, *India: A Country Study* (Washington, DC: U.S. Government Printing Office, Secretary of the Army, 1985), pp. 159–160.
19. Max Arthur Macauliffe, *The Sikh Religion*, vol. 1 (London: Oxford University Press, 1909), p. 1.
20. A. Barth, *The Religions of India*, trans. J. Wood (Delhi: S. Chand, 1969), p. 243.

21. *Selections from the Sacred Writings of the Sikhs,* trans. Dr. Trilochan Singh et al. (London: Allen & Unwin, 1973), p. 28.
22. Singh, vol. 1, p. 43.
23. Macauliffe, vol. 2, p. 11, reports an interesting anecdote on this subject.
24. *Selections from the Sacred Writings of the Sikhs,* pp. 31–32.
25. Ibid., p. 29.
26. Gurinder Mann. *The Making of Sikh Scriptures* (Oxford, England: Oxford University Press, 2001), p. 198.
27. Ibid., p. 131.
28. W. H. McLeod, *Sikhism* (London: Penguin Books, 1997), p. 215.
29. Murray J. Leaf, *Information and Behavior in a Sikh Village* (Berkeley: University of California Press, 1972), p. 157.
30. Ibid., p. 160.
31. *Selections from the Sacred Writings of the Sikhs,* vol. 168, no. 36.

READINGS

Axel, Brian Keith. *The Nation's Tortured Body.* Durham, NC: Duke University Press, 2001.

Cole, W. Owen, and Piara Singh Sambhi. *The Sikhs: Their Religious Beliefs and Practices.* New York: St. Martin's Press, l993.

Dundas, Paul. *The Jains.* London: Routledge, 1992.

Folkert, Kendall W. *Scripture and Community: Collected Essays on the Jains,* ed. John Cort. Atlanta, GA: Scholar's Press, 1993.

Fox, Richard G. *Lions of the Punjab.* Berkeley: University of California Press, 1985.

Grewal, J. S. *Contesting Interpretation of the Sikh Tradition.* New Delhi: Mansha Publishers, 1998.

Jaini, Jagmanderal. *Outlines of Jainism.* Cambridge, England: Cambridge University Press, 1916.

Jaini, Padmanabh S. *The Jaina Path of Purification.* Berkeley: University of California Press, 1979.

Mann, Gurinder. *The Making of Sikh Scriptures.* Oxford, England: Oxford University Press, 2001.

McLeod, W. H. *Sikhism.* London: Penguin Books, 1997.

Purewal, Shinder. *Sikh Ethnonationalism and the Political Economy of Punjab.* New Delhi: Oxford University Press, 2000.

Singh, Harbans. *The Heritage of the Sikhs.* New Delhi: Mansha Publishers, 1995.

Singh, Kushwant. *A History of the Sikhs.* 2 vols. Princeton, NJ: Princeton University Press, 1966.

Tatla, Darshan Singh. *The Sikh Diaspora.* Seattle, WA: University of Washington Press, 1999.

Woolpert, Stanley. *A New History of India* (7th ed.). Oxford: Oxford University Press, 2004.

BASIC GROUPS OF JAINISM AND GURUS OF SIKHISM

JAINS		
	Main Groups	
Digambaras		Shvetambaras
	Tirthankaras	
Parshva (first)		Mahavira (twenty-fourth)
SIKH GURUS		
	Nanak	
	Angad	
	Amar Das	
	Ram Das	
	Arjan	
	Har Gobind	
	Har Rai	
	Har Kishan	
	Teg Behadur	
	Gobind Rai (Singh)	

In the religions of China and Japan, we meet two Chinese teachers whose own distinctive views have been added to the insights of the Buddha, who lived almost at the same time. Laozi is as remote and mysterious as some of his followers who preferred solitude in the mountains over social relations in villages or cities. Confucius, ever seeking the centers of political power, impresses us as a wise man of the world. Laozi preferred nature, and Confucius preferred society. Both renewed ancient traditions of

as being a home for good spirits, nature itself is good. Rewards of living can be enjoyed here and now.

Among religions of India, harmony is to be found beyond this life, after one escapes from samsara. In religions of China and Japan, harmony with nature, families, neighbors, and ancestors can be realized in this life, on earth. India supported a relaxed, longterm view of finding oneself; China and Japan support an urgency brought on by termination of opportunities at one's

You may find some exceptions to these generalizations about religions in China and Japan, but you are more likely to find examples that support them. You can find similarities between religions of India and religions of China and Japan; however, if you are like most people, you will sense a shift of interpretation of human life in the world as you move from one to the other area.

Religions of China and Japan

III

China, which, as we will see, had a different spirit from those in India.

As religions of India emphasize karma and reincarnation, so religions of China emphasize reverence for lands and ancestors. Instead of numerous deities, as Hindus honor, Chinese and Japanese religions honor millions of ancestors with vital relationships to their descendants on earth.

Peoples of India tended to find life in the world primarily suffering; peoples in China and Japan found it primarily good. As well

death. One has only this lifetime in which to find the way, to follow it, and to take one's place in the larger scheme of things.

In India, salvation is primarily for the individual, for karma is in the sheath of the soul or in the skandhas that affect future lives. In China and Japan, salvation of persons involves families, communities, and a state or nation. The concept of an isolated, individual person is more common in the West than in China and Japan.

CHAPTER 6
China and Japan

CHAPTER 6

China and Japan

When Buddhist missionaries from India arrived in China and Japan, people there were of course already practicing their own traditional religions. In China, traditional concepts of heaven, ancestors, and forces of nature long preceded the religions of Daoism and Confucianism. In Japan, villagers worshiped kamis and paid homage to the goddess of the sun. When Buddhism joined these nature religions, each tradition affected the others. Because accommodation was mutually beneficial, China retained three indigenous Asian religions, and Japan four, having added Daoism and Confucianism to Buddhism and Shinto. We discussed Buddhism in China and Japan in Chapter 4; in this chapter, we focus on religions that began in those countries.

OVERVIEW AND THEMES

TAOISM

"Few in the world can understand teachings without words and the advantage of taking no action."

—*Dao De Jing**

IMPORTANT TAOIST TEACHINGS
The unseen Dao influences everything.
Harmony with the Dao is the best way to live.
Embracing society or organizing it leads to suffering.

AREAS OF TAOIST CONCENTRATION
Asia: 2,684,000
United States: 11,100

CONFUCIANISM

"The Gentleman understands what is moral. The small man understands what is profitable."

—*The Analects***

IMPORTANT CONFUCIAN TEACHINGS
Confucius set an example for role models in society.
Confucius should be revered as the number one ancestor of his people.
Society should be ordered; rejecting society to follow nature is a mistake.

AREAS OF CONFUCIAN CONCENTRATION
Asia: 6,330,000
United States: 0 (There may be some individuals.)

SHINTO

"So the two deities . . . stirred the brine . . . and drew the spear up, the brine that dripped down from the end of the spear was piled up and became an island."

—*The Kojiki*†

IMPORTANT SHINTO TEACHINGS
Amatarasu is goddess of the Sun, the most important deity.
Japan, its land, and its people, are special creations of the deities.
Ancestors are to be worshiped, and ancestors who have led the nation are to receive special honors.
Fruits of nature are to be offered to the spirits or deities of nature.

AREAS OF CONCENTRATION
Asia: 2,615,000
United States: 56,200

*Tao Te Ching, *A Source Book in Chinese Philosophy,* Wing-Tsit Chban, trans. (Princeton, NJ: Princeton University Press, 1963), pp. 137–138.

**Confucius, *The Analects,* trans. D. C. Lau (New York: Penguin Books, 1979).

†*The Kojiki,* trans. Basil Hall Chamberlain (Rutland, VT: Tuttle, 1981), p. 19.

Torii Gate.

China honors two "sages," or very wise ancestors, as founders of its religions. The more mysterious sage, Laozi, is reflected in the lines of the cryptic classic the *Dao De Jing (Tao Te Ching)*. He is believed to have written about the time of the gurus of the Upanishads, perhaps preceding the enlightenment of Siddhartha Gautama. Confucius, the more widely known sage, is thought to have been a contemporary of the Buddha, although it is unlikely that they met each other. Confucius's emphasis on good education for government eventually placed his teachings at the core of education and government in China. His successful disciples assured him a prominent role in the life of China until the beginning of the twentieth century. Toward the end of that century, Chinese peoples again embraced many of his values. In this chapter we discuss the background of Chinese traditions that influenced both sages and their particular interpretations that established separate traditions for their students.

Beliefs in China before the Sages

The Chinese had developed religious beliefs, rites, and literature long before the births of the founders of Daoism and Confucianism. Alongside the religion taught by scholars, priests, and official religious institutions there exists in most cultures a religion understood and practiced by the general population. For ordinary people, the distinction between folk religion and the "official" versions of religions is often difficult to detect.

The Chinese peoples have a long tradition of myths and folktales. Creation and founding myths have been circulated along with stories about saviors, destroyers, goddesses, immortality, and the Yellow Emperor. Annie Birrell's collection of these myths in *Chinese Mythology* helps us understand much of the spirit of life in traditional Chinese communities.

Folk religion also includes methods of communication with ancestors and deities. Satisfying the needs of departed humans is a constant concern in Chinese folk religion. Ancestors deserve attention and care, but "hungry ghosts," uncared-for humans, can be a persistent problem if their needs are not met. Chinese peoples can simply burn money as a way of sending it to the departed who need it, or they may send clothes and other material things in "care packages" assigned to the flames. Often, in conjunction with other celebrations, tables of food are prepared for hungry ghosts so that they will not consume the food prepared for ancestors or gods.

What beliefs did the early Chinese peoples hold? First, in Chinese thought heaven is not radically separated from earth. Heaven is **Yang** and earth is **Yin**—both exist in balance, seeking harmony. Humans may be male, predominantly Yang, or female, predominantly Yin, but as philosopher–psychologist C. G. Jung noted, there are always some feminine characteristics in males and some masculine characteristics in females. In Chinese thought, there must be harmony in Yang and Yin, male and female, if there is to be peace in the family. Heaven, which is Yang, contains living ancestors who are both Yang and Yin. Earth, Yin, is inhabited by males (Yang) and females (Yin) who will one day become ancestors in heaven, Yang. All these dynamic manifestations in balance, harmony, and peace flow in **Dao (Tao),** the way of the universe. Is this concept philosophy or religion? It is both. It is the canopy on which, to borrow an image from sociologist Peter Berger, the religions and philosophies of China project their interpretations of individuals and social groups.

Yang [YAHNG]
In China, the male side of the Dao. It is exemplified in bright, warm, and dry conditions. Its opposite is Yin, the female side of the Dao.

Yin [YIN]
In China, the female side of the Dao. It is exemplified in dark, cool, and moist conditions. Its opposite is Yang, the male side of the Dao.

Dao (Tao) [DOW]
In China or in Daoism (Taoism), the path, course, or way of the universe. Although its influence is in nature, the eternal Dao is believed to be hidden from empirical experience.

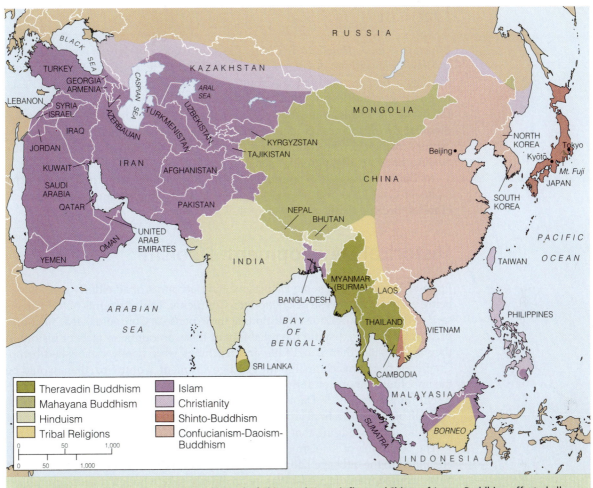

Asian Religions. Confucianism and Daoism (Taoism) of China and Korea influenced Shinto of Japan. Buddhism affected all these religions. Islam of Arabia touched the lives of Jains, Zoroastrians, Sikhs, and Hindus.

The **Yijing (I Ching)** is so much a part of Chinese culture that in its earliest forms it predates even the earliest sages who are assigned names. Its present form may date from the third century B.C.E. It attempts to relate the day-by-day life of the individual to the ways of the universe. How does the Yijing function? Around the symbol of Yin-Yang are sixty-four (2^6) hexagrams. Each hexagram comprises six lines. The patterns include all possible mixtures of long lines and divided lines. For example, at one extreme is a hexagram of six long lines; at the other is a hexagram of six divided lines. Using either a coin or yarrow stalks, an interpreter is guided to the appropriate figure of lines. In the hands of a skillful interpreter, the Yijing can offer guidance in the choices available to an individual so that he or she can obtain the support of heaven and nature, or at least avoid offending them. The Yijing was an established guide for Chinese life when Daoism and Confucianism were in their formative stages.

Yijing (I Ching) [YEE-jing] An ancient book of China that assists people in deciding how to plan their lives in accord with the forces of the universe. The *Yijing* influenced both Daoism and Confucianism.

Daoism

Daoism's **Dao De Jing (Tao Te Ching)** has stimulated a variety of responses in its readers. Philosophers of China have emphasized its teachings about going with the flow of nature rather than resisting it in artificial structures of culture. Priests, responding to challenges from Buddhism, built temples for a religion based on Daoist ideals. Healers and herbalists engaged in experiments with folk remedies that gave Daoism a reputation for magic. Before the advent of mid-twentieth-century medicine, who could afford to ignore remedies that might affect health, healing, and long life, perhaps even immortality?

As Daoism's teachers expounded their own doctrines, they criticized the principles of Confucius and his disciples. Along with Mohists and Fajias, **Daoists (Taoists)** became rivals to the way of the Confucians.

Historical Development: Daoism

From early writings of some Daoists we have accounts of an elderly sage, Laozi, being visited by an awestruck neophyte, Confucius. Their accounts of the conversations flatter Laozi's Daoist traditions at the expense of Confucius's teachings and practices. Scholars dispute the reliability of these accounts on facts of history. If they are reliable, then Laozi's life and teachings were firmly established before Confucius began his campaign for good government. Confucius, then, would be the impetuous innovator. If the Daoist accounts are not reliable, perhaps they represent only attempts of Daoists to hold their own against Confucian disciples. Without attempting a final judgment, we will present something of a consensus of scholars, acknowledging that the earliest days of Daoism are open to conjecture.

The beginning of Daoism as a philosophy in the sixth century B.C.E. has been attributed to the old sage **Laozi (Lao Tzu),** or Lao Tan. Speculations about his life have inspired many legends. Was he an elderly sage who left a deep impression on the young Confucius? Did the two masters ever meet, or are their dialogues the dreams of devoted disciples imagining what their teachers might have said? Scholars do not agree on an answer. According to Moss Roberts, a scholar of Chinese philosophy, the works of Laozi and Confucius, who wrote *the Analects,* represent the Yin and the Yang of Chinese culture: "The Dao De Jing is primarily reflective in nature, while the Analects is more activist."[1]

Although some scholars favor the sixth-century B.C.E. date, others prefer a later date, in the fourth, third, or even later centuries B.C.E. Another possibility is that the *Dao De Jing (Tao Te Ching)* contains the teachings of Laozi but was compiled later by more than one person.[2] However, tradition does attribute to Laozi authorship of the classic *Dao De Jing (The Way and Its Power).* The circumstances of the writing were that Laozi, tired of living in society, journeyed to the West on a water buffalo. Before Laozi's departure, the gatekeeper persuaded him to write down and leave behind his most important ideas. The book has been passed down for centuries in Chinese civilization, and its author, believed to have been Laozi, has been deeply revered.

Dao De Jing

The *Dao De Jing* focuses on the harmony of opposites within the peaceful flow of the Dao. Beneath phenomenal changes of the natural order, there is a relentless

---

Dao De Jing (Tao Te Ching) [dow-du-JING] *The Way and Its Power.* A book attributed to Laozi, founder of Daoism.

Daoists (Taoists) [DOW-ists] Followers of a philosophy or religion expressed in the *Dao De Jing,* attributed to Laozi, a sage of ancient China.

Laozi (Lao Tzu) [LAHOW-dzi] The sage of China believed to have been the author of the *Dao De Jing (Tao Te Ching).* He is regarded as the founder of Daoism.

flow, or way, which is neither entirely visible nor open to full knowledge. Nevertheless, it influences the process of the changes that can be observed. The way of the Dao includes a peaceful harmony of opposites.

To these ideas, which were a part of Chinese beliefs before Laozi lived, the *Dao De Jing* adds the concept of the individual's relationship to society and nature. Although it may be too extreme to label Daoists anarchists, they do emphasize values of the solitary individual rather than organized society.[3] Daoist philosophy renounces many of society's expectations. In summary, the *Dao De Jing* argues that the natural course of things is the best; left undisturbed, the natural course leads to harmony and perfection. Artificial structures among persons or in societies eventually bring discord.

What can be said about the Dao? Although no one can define exactly the full dimension of the way of the universe, the Dao is the mysterious cosmic power present in all human experiences. The Dao is not only the actuality of experiences but also the potential activity of the universe unfolding itself; it is the nonbeing that gives rise to phenomenal reality. Hidden, the Dao nevertheless manifests itself to those who patiently observe and reflect. Enough can be known of the Dao that a person can choose to live in harmony with it.

> The Tao (Way) that can be told is not the unchanging Tao;
> The name that can be named is not the unchanging name.
> The Nameless is the origin of Heaven and Earth;
> The Named is the mother of all things.
> Therefore let there always be non-being so we may see their subtlety, and let there always be being so we may see their outcome.
> The two are the same.[4]

Daoists believe that societies suffer when they disregard the Dao. History shows that societies often base standards on principles at odds with the Dao. Eventually, human efforts are destroyed and human purposes are thwarted, bringing misery on entire societies. Humans can gradually intuit the Dao's strength and undeterred direction. If they develop wisdom in the face of the Dao's inevitability, they learn to abandon their petty desires and designs and resign themselves to the flow of the Dao. Those who insist on their own way or who force society into their own plan may seem to succeed for a while, but inevitably the pendulum will swing the other way.

The sage, or the wise person, comes to realize that in the long run, humans cannot conquer nature. They can do much better by planning their lives so as to use the natural cosmic force and direction. The individual who harmonizes his or her purposes with the way of the Dao can reach the highest possible achievement. There is a learning process for humans that involves their realizing that life cannot always be as they would have it. For the sage, there is a certain amount of learning to accept frustrated desires and purposes, of bending to the inevitable course of events.

Although Daoism is more than a philosophy, an intellectual exercise, it lacks some of the features often associated with a religion. No formal worship or prayer is necessary, for communication is limited between a human and an impersonal force (or perhaps a force that far transcends the limits of persons). Laozi sometimes refers to the Dao as the "Mother" of all living things. Daoism requires the response of a whole person. Contemplation and meditation in a quiet way of life are most helpful in intuiting the way of the Dao.

A central concept of Daoism is **wuwei.** Humans can learn to practice wuwei, a lifestyle that emphasizes quietism and avoids aggression. Sages act without

Reunion des Musees Nationaux/Art Resource, NY

The Jingting Mountains and Waterfall in Autumn. Tai-chi (1630–1717). Ink on paper.

wuwei (wu wei) [WOO-WAY] The Daoist principle of accomplishing tasks without assertion. Individuals in harmony with the flow of the Dao can accomplish more than individuals who assert themselves.

acting, accomplishing without motion, influencing without seeming to exert themselves. Humans need not run about the world to know the way of the Dao. Sages do not seek to polish their personality for society in order to gain status, but seek to discover the natural, undistorted self. In all things, the sage seeks to be good, even returning good for evil. Many people in society may consider sages fools, but sages know that although water may seem the most pliable or unresisting element of the world, over time it can wear down even mountains of the most solid rock. The *Dao De Jing* explains,

> The softest things in the world overcome the hardest things in the world.
> Non-being penetrates that in which there is no space.
> Through this I know the advantage of taking no action.
> Few in the world can understand teaching without words and the advantage of taking no action.[5]

A further explanation reads,

> There is nothing softer and weaker than water,
> And yet there is nothing better for attacking hard and strong things.
> For this reason there is no substitute for it.
> All the world knows that the weak overcomes the strong and the soft overcomes the hard.
>
> But none can practice it.

Disciples of Daoist sages argue that humans can develop mysterious powers to the extent that wild animals will not attack. However, these sages would never engage in offensive warfare; they know the wisdom of pacifism.

Daoism scorned social institutions. Education corrupts the natural goodness of humans:

> Abandon sageliness and discard wisdom;
> Then the people will benefit a hundredfold.
> Abandon humanity and discard righteousness;
> Then the people will return to filial piety and deep love.
> Abandon skill and discard profit;
> Then there will be no thieves or robbers.
> However, these three things are ornament (*wen*) and not adequate.
> Therefore let people hold on to these:
>> Manifest plainness,
>> Embrace simplicity,
>> Reduce selfishness,
>> Have few desires.[6]

Social conventions and governments are artificial, at odds with the natural flow of people in the universe. The ideal society is a small village where each family tends to its own affairs. People in the village know other villages exist, for they hear roosters crowing and dogs barking there. They do not exchange visits. That government is best that governs least, so the best situation is not to have any government. If there must be government, rulers should remember that "ruling a big country is like cooking a small fish."[7] They should be careful not to overdo it.

Zhuangzi (Chuang Tzu)

Zhuangzi (Chuang Tzu, c. 369–286 B.C.E.), a champion of the Daoists, expanded on the teachings of the *Dao De Jing*. He, too, exalted nature above culture, the

Zhuangzi (Chuang Tzu)
[JYAHNG-dzi]
A later Daoist. Zhuangzi wrote, in part, to distinguish Daoism from Confucianism.

individual above society, and freedom to flow above rigid social forms. He accepted changes brought by the Dao; indeed, he may be said to have enjoyed them, seeking to ride the crests of the waves of change. Even the simple task of making a rack to hold a suspended bell can involve Daoism. By concentrating on their own nature—the nature of self—on the nature of a tree, and on the nature of heaven that brings them together in harmony, humans turn a practical task into a Daoist experience. The government can be handled in a similar way. Zhuangzi is reported to have turned down a civil service post in order to remain free from the constraints of society, even those that carried veneration.

> Once Chuang Tzu was fishing the P'u River when the King of Ch'u sent two of his ministers to announce that he wished to entrust to Chuang Tzu the care of his entire domain.
>
> Chuang Tzu held his fishing pole and, without turning his head, said: "I have heard that Ch'u possesses a sacred tortoise which has been dead for three thousand years and which the king keeps wrapped up in a box and stored in his ancestral temple. Is this tortoise better off dead and with its bones venerated, or would it be better off alive with its tail dragging in the mud?"
>
> "It would be better off alive and dragging its tail in the mud," the two ministers replied.
>
> "Then go away!" said Chuang Tzu, "and I will drag my tail in the mud!"[8]

Zhuangzi is also known for the philosophical questions he raises regarding the experience of dreaming. Beneath the apparently simple questions lie some profound questions about what is real and how to know what is real.

> Once upon a time, Chuang Chou [Chuang Tzu] dreamed that he was a butterfly, a butterfly fluttering about, enjoying itself. It did not know that it was Chuang Chou. Suddenly he awoke with a start and he was Chuang Chou again. But he did not know whether he was Chuang Chou who had dreamed that he was a butterfly, or whether he was a butterfly dreaming that he was Chuang Chou. Between Chuang Chou and the butterfly there must be some distinction. This is what is called the transformation of things.[9]

Religious, Sectarian Daoism

Historically, Daoism developed forms that included common people as well as philosophers. Some Daoists sought special ways to healing and health, some sought magical and political power, and others sought immortality through alchemy.

Zhang Daoling, of about the first century C.E., founded a secret society that promoted faith healing, health, and long lives. His male descendants organized many groups that exorcised illnesses. They used confession of sins to remove the cause of illnesses. Then they gave believers consecrated water and ashes of burned writings to drink. So numerous were their followers that they developed significant political power. Zhang Daoling was deified as "Celestial Master" and praised for having found the secret formula for immortality.

One promoter of magical Daoism is Ge Hong (Ko Hung), of the fourth century C.E., who spent many years as a soldier and civilian gathering herbs and experimenting with formulas to help humans fly to heaven as a genie or attain immortality. His *Baopuzi (Pao P'u-tzu)* is an example of the folk beliefs that led to experiments with herbs obtained from mountains, such as Dragon-Tiger or Lofu Mountain. In developing elixirs of immortality, the alchemists preferred using gold.

Shang Di [shang-DI]
In China, the lord of
heaven. Ancestors are
believed to be obedient to
Shang Di as living persons
are to the emperor.

Jade Emperor
A mythical emperor of
ancient China. In 1012 C.E.,
the emperor (Chen Tsung)
claimed to have received
revelation from Huang
Di (Yu Huang), the Jade
Emperor.

Zaoshen (Tsao Shen)
[zow-SHEN]
In Daoism, the god of
the stove. The stove was
essential in family life
and in work of the
Daoist alchemists.

The theory was that because gold does not tarnish or decay, ingesting it can lead to immortality. Often unable to obtain gold, the alchemists used mercury to turn base metals into gold. Ingesting mercury, however, led to the deaths of many researchers. Those who know the Dao can change the bodies of animals, ride on a phoenix or a crane, and caress crocodiles and whales. Charms can prevent all sorts of evils, such as assaults from weapons and wild animals.[10] This form of Daoism still survives in Chinese cultures but is rejected by many Chinese intellectuals.

Daoism had a sect that emphasized worship in its own temples. During the Han dynasties (206 B.C.E to 220 C.E.) Laozi was elevated to the status of a god, Taishang Laojun, "Lord Lao on High." During the Song dynasty, shortly after 1000 C.E., Daoists, claiming a recent revelation, identified the **Shang Di,** ruler of heaven, with Huang Di, the **Jade Emperor.** The popular revival of Daoism was also enhanced with the addition of teachings of heaven and hell. Ling Bao, leader of supernatural beings, was added to Laozi and the Jade Emperor to form the Three Purities of Daoism. Daoist priests led worship of the Eight Immortals. Folk religion elevated the god of the stove, **Zaoshen (Tsao Shen),** so high that he received recognition from the emperor. Nevertheless, Buddhism eventually eclipsed Daoism. According to Robert Hymes, "Two models informed how the Chinese saw gods, and whether they were bureaucrats or personal protectors depended on and still depends on who worships them or who tells about them, and in what context, and to what purpose."[11]

Humans are part of nature, and to be all that we can be, we should emphasize our harmony with nature. Worrying about society, neighbors, traditions, and governments leads us away from what is most important. Unseen, but influencing everything, is the Dao; aligning ourselves with the way of the universe brings a harmony between humans, nature, and the universe. Health, power, and longevity come to those who allow the Dao to work its way in their lives. Artificial structures cannot withstand the way of the Dao. Go with the flow of the Dao; bend, don't break.

CONSIDER THIS
Humans Are Best as Part of Nature

Worldview: Daoism

The Absolute

The Dao is impersonal, an invisible way that the universe follows, a harmony of tensions between opposites. This powerful force is indifferent to human desires and artificial structures. It is not influenced by prayer, hymns, or rituals. Humans can only seek to discern it, because it does not reveal itself.

The **Three Purities** of sectarian Daoism, although incongruous with the *Dao De Jing*, were not foreign to Chinese tradition. Humans who died became ancestors who were worshiped as gods. If families worshiped departed grandfathers, why should the country not worship illustrious emperors and rulers of spirits? These personal deities satisfied the masses and fulfilled their need for folk heroes. The development resembled that in Mahayana Buddhism as it departed from the way of the elders.

Three Purities
In China, three deities of
Daoism: Ling Bao, the Jade
Emperor, and Laozi.

The World

The Daoists were enthusiastic about the universe. Daoists feel it is hardly proper to think of the universe as either good or evil. It is beyond good and evil—it just is. It provides all that humans and animals need. By living close to nature and studying its ways, humans can learn to remain healthy and wise. Trying to conquer nature or to improve on it is futile.

No design of "ought to be" rules the world, according to scholar David Hall's view of Daoism: "In the Daoist world everything is local." His associate, Roger Ames, has outlined six principles of Daoist ecology: change, situation, myth, contingent harmony of existing ingredients, uniqueness of participants in unpredictable consequences, and priority of a dynamic radial center over boundaries. We could add that one may experience what is local, but one cannot experience the way of the Dao itself.[12]

Humans

The best human is the natural human. Humans are essentially good and can enjoy a good life in the world. They should seek to live as long as possible, for old age is a sign of wisdom in fulfilling the proper human role. People should not be forced into education, rituals, social organizations, and etiquette. Humans are best when they remain as they were born—weak and simple.

The Problem for Humans

The problem for humans is their disharmony with the universe. The more humans depart from the simple, natural way of the universe, the more they are alienated from the Dao and from each other. Suffering comes from trying to conquer nature, altering the way of the universe, and establishing artificial human organizations. Artificial needs develop, and values foreign to natural order entice humans away from the source of their peace and harmony. Civilization is an enemy of the contented human.

The Solution for Humans

Humans solve their problem by returning to a simple life. Living in harmony with nature, either in a forest or in a small village, is the best way for a person to resolve tensions and experience peace of body and soul. A good, long life is the reward of those who learn to go with the flow of the Dao. Apart from the philosophies of Laozi and Zhuangzi, Daoist religion developed techniques of meditation.

> The breathing of the Sage, we read in many passages, must be like that of an infant. Later Taoist writers go a step further, saying that it must be like that of a child in the womb.[13]

> Embryonic respiration and *nei tan* are essentially mental operations, since it is thought processes that make the breath circulate through the body and that manipulate the internal alchemical symbols. One particular technique of concentration makes it possible to "gaze inward." While the breath circulates through the body, the eyes fix on it and follow its movement. Since the pupils of the eyes—small concretions of pure Yang—have illuminating power, they put darkness to flight and cause the triumph of the Yang, the principle of light and life.[14]

Daoists use techniques in contemplation that are similar to some of those used by Hindus. The most interesting, perhaps, is described as embryonic breathing, **taixi (t'ai-hsi),** that is, becoming like an infant who breathes through the umbilical cord in its mother's womb. Essentially, it is a technique that Daoists use to hold their breath for extended periods. Accompanying breathing is inward vision, which enables Daoists to experience light and the divinities of the human organs. Other techniques include engaging in sex without ejaculation and practicing alchemy, the marriage of elements of the universe.

In Daoist religion, contemplation of nature is a technically developed art. Daoists do more than simply sit at some vantage point and gaze at the landscape. Daoists guide the practice of **shouyi (shou-i),** which means "to preserve meditating on the One."[15] Preserving the One means to return to the origin, to unite with the Dao. Having arisen from the Dao, the One is both emptiness and nonbeing. The One is also the cosmos, mother, matrix, primordial breath, and origin of all things. The One divided into the Three, and the Three divided into the Ten Thousand Things. Thus, multiplicity is accounted for as well as the unity of all things.

Contemplation recognizes the relationship of the human to the cosmos. In contemplation, the One is thought of in human terms. The person who contemplates visualizes the light of the One and concentrates on the three primordial breaths, the Sanyi (San I), three ones. Although the three primordial breaths exist apart from humans, the breaths can also dwell in them in the Three Cinnabar Fields. Visualizing them during contemplation causes them to descend into the body of the meditator. According to the Mao Shan sect, if a person does not practice contemplation the divinities that inhabit the bodies of individuals return to heaven. Their departure brings about illness or death. Daoists may also contemplate the Nine Palaces or the Nine Divinities from the Nine Heavens, which represent the One in totality.

The Daoist theory of contemplation of nature asserts that each organ of the human body is energized by a divinity. Those who recite sacred texts can stimulate this hierarchy of divinities. Another beneficial visualization is contemplation of heavenly bodies, and planets. As meditators visualize the light of heavenly bodies, their own body increases in luminescence, becoming like the heavenly bodies.

The goal of Daoist meditation is the harmony of the human, the divine, and the cosmos. In contemplating nature, the Daoist seeks to internalize the energies of the universe to promote health and a long, rewarding life.

Community and Ethics

Nothing is so bad that action will not make it worse. Inaction is the secret of good life, not only for the Daoist but also for any neighbors. (Daoists preferred to ignore or avoid neighbors.) Trying to do good leads only to trouble. Live and let live is the best guide to conduct. By doing nothing, humans have a positive influence on society, according to the *Dao De Jing.*

> Here are my three treasures. Keep them and cherish them. The first is mercy, the second is frugality; the third is never to take the lead over the whole world. Being merciful, one has courage; being frugal, one has abundance; refusing to take the lead, one becomes the chief of all vessels. If one abandons mercy in favor of courage, frugality in favor of abundance, and humility in favor of prominence, he will perish.
>
> Mercy will be victorious in attack and invulnerable in defense. Heaven will come to the rescue of the merciful one and with mercy will protect him.[16]

taixi (t'ai-hsi) [tai-SHEE] In Daoism, the art of embryonic breathing, a method of holding one's breath in contemplation.

shouyi (shou-i) [shoo-yi] In Daoism, to preserve the One or to meditate on the One. It includes methods of meditation on the One.

Rituals and Symbols

Rituals are not needed, except in magical and sectarian Daoism. The alchemist's stove was once a symbol of Daoism. Charms, formulas, and drugs continue to be a part of folk Daoism. But philosophical Daoism had no rituals, for they were considered useless. The symbol of the Dao, the Yin and Yang in harmony, is sufficient for many Daoists. Artists' paintings of humans absorbed in nature are also acceptable.

Philosophic Daoists think the "gods" of the people are only ghosts, dead mortals wrongly deified. However, "disease and its cure are a paramount focus in the earliest accounts of Taoism," writes Michel Strickmann; "All healing pivots on a vital axis of ritual." The exorcisms of the Indians and the Chinese involve interrogation, a ritual style that may have helped merge Buddhist and Daoist rituals.[17]

Daoist priests in Taiwan learn esoteric rituals that are carefully hidden from all except initiates. Studying with a master, disciples learn singing, dancing, ceremonial texts, and other matters of standard ritual. Students excel in priesthood when they learn cures for illness, exorcism of evil spirits, and magic. The most powerful priests learn to contact at least one of the other ancient spirits listed as deities; the more spirits contacted, the higher the rank of the priest.[18]

Confucianism

Although Daoism has been a part of the philosophies of China, and later Japan, for many centuries, the most influential philosophy of China has been Confucianism. Wherever Chinese peoples have lived, they have been influenced by their greatest teacher, **Confucius** (**Kongfuzi**) (551–479 B.C.E.). (This text will use the conventional Western names for *Confucius* and *Confucianism*.)

Confucians disagree with some of the claims of philosophical Daoism. Granted, some individuals find the social world overpowering. Is government necessarily bad? Are social organizations disruptive of harmony in the universe? Is it necessary to abandon conventional social rituals in order to find peace? Are social contracts self-defeating? Although there are many examples that support what the Daoists say, can there also be some exceptions to their principles?

Despite numerous attacks over their long history, Confucian ideals have withstood the tests of time. Chinese peoples, in both the People's Republic of China and beyond the mainland, have maintained their respect for the basic values Confucius taught. Like Daoism, Confucianism has been seen sometimes as more a philosophy than a religion. Other readers have thought it a political science or a system of education. It has been all these things and more, because the *Four Books*, including the *Analects*, present Confucius as a leader who was larger than life. His brilliance still inspires awe and reverence. In the minds of Chinese peoples, Confucius is at least as great as Siddhartha Gautama, Jesus, or Muhammad, some of the most influential leaders in history.

Historical Development: Confucianism

Chinese peoples believe that three dynasties preceded the birth of Confucius. The legendary Xia (Hsia) kingdom is considered to date from about 2000 B.C.E. The emperor Yu claimed to be the sky god, and his successors considered themselves

Confucius (Kongfuzi)
[kun-FYOO-shus]
Kongfuzi, the Chinese founder of Confucianism. Primarily a teacher, he sought to develop good government through a responsible ruler and ethical people.

"sons of heaven."[19] The Shang dynasty, 1500 to 1027 B.C.E., was located in the valley of the Yellow River. Ancestor worship was clearly important to that historical family. The famous Zhou (Chou [in the Pinyin system of romanization, spelled *Zhou*]) dynasty ruled from 1027 to 256 B.C.E. The founders of the Zhou family exerted such strong leadership that Confucius looked back to it as an example of how society should be governed.

In the long history of China, Confucianism has interacted with many different philosophies, religions, and political systems. For Confucius, the Zhou dynasty was the golden age of China, that had degenerated into warring states during his lifetime. After him came a time of good government, the product of an educated and dedicated civil service. Princes appeared who were obedient to Heaven and worthy of imitation by their subjects. Children grew up in homes with honor for father and mother. If Confucius had doubts about his success, today he could count himself as one of the most successful teachers of all time.

The Life of Confucius

Although we seem to know so much more about Confucius than about Laozi, some scholars of Confucius, such as D. C. Lau, challenge our assumptions. They would classify much of our information about the biography of Confucius as legend or tradition rather than fact. The supposed conversations of Laozi and Confucius are only minor problems compared with some of the stories of Confucius's success in his various appointed positions. Did crime really disappear when he was "chief of police"? Is it only conjecture that he would have had two wives, to demonstrate his skill at maintaining harmony in his own home? These stories and others like them support the status of a great man of history, but what is the strength of the evidence for them? Historians today are not so tolerant of tales and legends. If we follow our pattern of describing the lives of other religious leaders, however, we can see Confucius through the eyes of his devoted followers. To be consistent, we should include some of the stories recounted by Confucians. From time to time, however, we will present the opposing views of his critics. In activities of rival philosophies, we find evidence of Confucius's effectiveness.

Master Kong, Kongfuzi, or Confucius, is definitely a historical figure, but the process of time has won him a place among legendary heroes. Dates given for his birth vary somewhat, but 551 B.C.E. seems likely to many scholars. The "official biography" set forth in the Historical Records (Shiji) by Sima Quin, about 100 C.E., supplies information on the family of Confucius. Today, critical historians doubt the reliability of the records.

The son of a tall, old soldier, Confucius was born to a young woman in the state of Lu, or Shantung province. He was only a child when his father died, leaving the young widow of a genteel but poor family to raise her son in the tradition of gentlemen. Confucius became a lover of literature, art, music, archery, traditional ceremonies, and life at the courts of nobles. Carl Crow wrote, "At the age of seventeen he secured his first employment, the task of keeping the granary accounts of the Chi family, one of the three great baronial houses in the ducal state of Lu."[20] Although the job was of limited status, the experience it provided opened his eyes wide to the injustices of systems that burdened peasants with heavy taxes to support leisure and luxury for the extremely small ruling class.

Confucius married and had a son to carry on the family name. He also had a daughter. After mourning the death of his mother for twenty-seven months, (counted as three years in China), Confucius spent his days as a teacher for young

Confucius. 17th century Chinese scroll painting from Bibliotheque National, Paris, France.

men from some of the finest families in Lu. Teaching was always his best-received activity; nevertheless, he believed that his greatest impact on social change could be made in government posts. From age fifty to fifty-five, he served under the Duke of Lu in several posts. Tradition says that he was disappointed with the Duke's neglect of government in favor of pleasant living with women. Leaving office in Lu, Confucius traveled to various districts in search of other positions. At times he was rejected. Once he was chased, and once he was imprisoned. The powerful official Huan Tui even attempted to have him assassinated. But usually the traveling scholar, who brought his students with him, was received with courtesy and even honor. Nevertheless, through pride or fear on the part of their civil servants, nobles in other provinces did not give him a position. In 484 B.C.E., Duke Ai of Lu invited him to come home and act as his adviser. He returned home, but he spent his closing years as a scholar editing the classics. In 479 B.C.E. he died.

The Teachings of Confucius

Confucians think that Confucius had a fundamental belief—humans are by nature good. Observing the society known to him, he had to have a strong faith in humans to make such an assumption. He was surrounded all his life by cruel wars, unjust societies, numerous forms of humans' inhumanity to each other, discord in families, and neglect of scholarship, writing, and the fine and performing arts. What had gone wrong?

Beginning with his foundational principle of human goodness, Confucius added a second principle. Humans, who are naturally good, learn best through example. The great need in every society is a model human being—a person who will set an example for others to follow. Confucius called his model person a **junzi (chun-tzu).** Translators use words such as *gentleman* or *superior man* to convey the idea. These words may be poor choices now, for they also carry other meanings. The junzi is opposite to the narrow-minded person, the selfish, petty, or aggressive person. The two are contrasted in the following passages from the *Analects* (Lun Yu).

> The Master said, "The gentleman understands what is moral. The small man understands what is profitable."[21]
>
> 23. The Master said, "The gentleman agrees with others without being an echo. The small man echoes without being in agreement." . . .
>
> 25. The Master said, "The gentleman is easy to serve but difficult to please. He will not be pleased unless you try to please him by following the Way, but when it comes to employing the services of others, he does so within the limits of their capacity. The small man is difficult to serve but easy to please. He will be pleased even though you try to please him by not following the Way, but when it comes to employing the services of others, he demands all-round perfection."
>
> 26. The Master said, "The gentleman is at ease without being arrogant; the small man is arrogant without being at ease."[22]

Confucius tried to be the kind of model he wanted his students to become.

> The Master said, "At fifteen I set my heart on learning; at forty I came to be free from doubts; at fifty I understood the Decree of Heaven; at sixty my ear was attuned; at seventy I followed my heart's desire without overstepping the line."[23]

When Confucius became a role model as well as a reciter of wisdom, he exhibited some characteristics of a reformer inspired with a religious zeal. Confucius's goal

junzi (chun-tzu) [JUN-dzi] In Confucianism, the gentleman or superior man. He was a role model for the conduct of the Chinese people.

was not only to inform but also to form and reform. He taught principles of conduct that could be measured in human social interaction. His goal was to reform corrupt societies through princes, nobles, and civil servants who based their lives on the example of the junzi.

PRINCIPLES OF THE JUNZI

In *Li Ji (Li Chi)*, Confucians present **li** as the principle of harmony that should rule the home, the society, and the empire. Li has to do with ritual, the correct formal way to behave in religious rites or in court ceremonies. Words associated with it are *propriety, appropriateness,* and *conformity* (to prevailing customs). It is the opposite of confusion. Confucius recommended li for every area of life—as in **The Five Relationships** between superior and inferior persons. They are ruler–subject, husband–wife, elder brother–younger brother, elder friend–junior friend, and father–son. Although the persons are unequal, each has a formal responsibility to carry out toward the other. The husband has responsibility for li toward his wife as she has an obligation for li toward him. The family is formally structured among males. Friendships outside the family are ritually governed. Relationships between ruler and subject entail obligations on each side. The junzi always acts from the internalized principle of li and is never at a loss on how to behave in any situation. Younger people learn from their elders, and the elders learn from observing the junzi. Li applied to the naturally good human being yields **yi,** which is the personalization of li.

Yi is internalized li. When humans internalize the rites, selfishness is overcome and benevolence takes its place. The personal self becomes orderly, and humans regulate themselves appropriately in society. They act on what is appropriate to themselves and to their position in society. They attain the mean that gives harmony.

Confucius taught that li is learned in studying rites and music, which included poetry. "Music was a required study, as its performance accompanied all ceremonies, whether religious sacrifice, court assembly, or family entertainment."[24] Harmony in music reflects harmony in society and the universe.

The junzi also exhibits **ren (jen).** Essentially, ren is humaneness, the quality of being a genuine human being to other human beings. This quality of human kindness is in balance with li and yi to keep formalism from destroying the highest and best possibilities of human personalities. Ren seeks the good of others as well as the self. Compassion for others is the mark of a good person.

> Fan Ch'ih asked about benevolence. The Master said, "Love your fellow men."
>
>   The Master said, "One who is not benevolent cannot remain long in straitened circumstances, nor can he remain long in easy circumstances.
>
>   "The benevolent man is attracted to benevolence because he feels at home in it. The wise man is attracted to benevolence because he finds it to his advantage."[25]

Confucius is known for his emphasis on reciprocity.

> Tsu-kung asked, "Is there a single word which can be a guide to conduct throughout one's life?" The Master said, "It is perhaps the word **shu.** Do not impose on others what you yourself do not desire."[26]

In summary, there are five distinctive qualities or virtues in the junzi. First, humans exert their own uprightness regardless of outward circumstances. Second, humans are magnanimous, expressing forgiveness toward others. Humans are not to be ruled by laws but follow an internal principle. Third, humans are sincere

Li Ji (Li Chi) [LEE-jee]
The Chinese classic on rites supposedly edited by Confucius. Although it is one of five Confucian classics, it is now regarded as coming from a period later than Confucius.

li [LEE]
The Confucian principle of righteousness or propriety. Li can refer to ritual and correct conduct in society.

The Five Relationships
In Confucianism, ruler–subject, husband–wife, father–son, older brother–younger brother, and elder friend–younger friend.

yi [YEE]
In Confucianism, internalized li, or righteousness; li as it has become a part of an individual's conduct.

ren (jen) [RUN]
In Confucianism, the humane principle, based on fellow-feeling. Deep empathy or compassion for other humans.

shu [SHOO]
In Confucianism, reciprocity; individuals treating others as they would like to be treated. They do not do to others what they would not want done to themselves.

in speech and action and are not a mouthpiece for hire; their word is their bond. Fourth, humans are earnest. They want to be rather than seem to be. Genuine good work replaces the mere appearance of it. Fifth, humans are benevolent, always generous in their relationships with people.

CONFUCIUS AND RELIGION

Confucius was clearly a teacher of political philosophy and ethics. Is it appropriate for us to think of his work as religion as well as philosophy? In the teachings, Confucius did not speculate much about heaven. In the *Analects,* Confucius says, "When you have offended against Heaven, there is nowhere you can turn to in your prayers."[27] That statement shows reverence for heaven. His actions, his love for the Chinese classics, and his participation in traditional rituals indicate a reverence for worship. Ancestor worship was a duty of every person in China— whether peasant or prince. Much as Confucius mourned at the grave of his mother for three years, his disciples, when he was gone, spent many months at his grave honoring him. Confucius enjoyed participating in religious ceremonies— for him they were an essential part of life, the basis for an orderly society. He insisted they be performed correctly and in the old traditions. Confucius could assume religion in his life; to teach its importance he needed only to participate in it. His ethics were for humans engaged in practical life; his ethical principles, however, were derived from a tradition that transcended present time and the confines of earth. In his own life he knew, at age fifty, the mandate (*ming*) of heaven.[28] As a man who felt a sense of mission, Confucius thought the mandate of heaven was especially important. He sensed that heaven had given him the mission to restore morality to China, to help everyone achieve the virtues of ren and li.

Other Teachings in the Time of Confucius

Some philosophies challenged Confucius's point of view. These philosophies had differing views about human nature and about the role, and even the desirability, of government.

THE MOHISTS

The **Mohists,** followers of **Mozi (Mo Tzu),** who lived sometime between 479 and 381 B.C.E., taught that if everyone would love each other, society would be transformed.[29] Little is known about Mozi aside from his writings. He probably was born before Confucius died and died before Mencius was born. Perhaps he was at one time a follower of Confucianism. He had about three hundred disciples. He was a native of either Song or Lu and was once the chief officer of Song. Yi-Pao Mei summarizes his attempts to serve as an adviser to princes:

> But for all his efforts he succeeded in holding a state office only once. That was in Sung and apparently for a short time; it was put to an end when the Lord listened to Tse Han and imprisoned Motse.[30]

Mozi's teachings are centered on the requirement for humans to love one another. Through love, the evils of the world could be abolished. Of universal love (*jainai*) Mozi said,

> It is the business of the benevolent man to try to promote what is beneficial to the world and to eliminate what is harmful. Now at the present time, what brings the

Mohists [MOW-hists] Followers of Mozi (Mo Tzu). They advocated curing the ills of society by practicing mutual love among people. Confucians objected to Mohist universal love because it did not allow for special feelings for kin.

Mozi (Mo Tzu) [MOW-dzi] Founder of the Mohist philosophy, which advocated brotherly love. Brotherhood meant sharing equally the essentials of food, clothing, and shelter.

greatest harm to the world? Great states attacking small ones, great families overthrowing small ones, the strong oppressing the weak, the many harrying the few, the cunning deceiving the stupid, the eminent lording it over the humble— these are harmful to the world. So too are rulers who are not generous, ministers who are not loyal, fathers who are without kindness, and sons who are unfilial, as well as those mean men who, with weapons, knives, poison, fire, and water, seek to injure and undo each other.

When we inquire into the cause of the various harms, what do we find has produced them? Do they come about from loving others and trying to benefit them? Surely not! They come rather from hating others and trying to injure them. And when we set out to classify and describe those men who hate and injure others, shall we say that their actions are motivated by universality or partiality? Surely we must answer by partiality, and it is this partiality in their dealings with one another that gives rise to all the great harms in the world. Therefore we know that partiality is wrong.[31]

As did Confucius, Mozi looked to an ancient society for an example, but he preferred the Hsia to the Zhou dynasty. Life should be lived on a basic level of share and share alike. Mozi believed in the firm discipline of society to achieve this sharing of life's goods. Although he permitted defensive wars, he condemned warfare as state policy. He was thoroughly utilitarian; the good must be practical. What is good brings pleasure to society and what is evil brings pain.

How can people learn to love each other? Confucius did not believe people should do good to their enemies, for what would they then be able to do for their friends? Do not do unto others what you would not have done to you was principle enough in those situations. Parallels to Confucius's position on the Golden Rule can be found in the Bible. Confucius believed that in relationships relatives are superior to others and that they deserve more than others. Love did not necessarily mean share and share alike, thought Confucius.

The Fajia (Legalists)

The **Fajia (Legalists)** school of philosophy argued that human nature respects only strong laws and rigorous enforcement. Formal statement of this position dates from the third century B.C.E., but some scholars think that the philosophy predated Confucius. Burton Watson thinks that the Legalist philosophy dated from the statesman Guan Zhong (Kuan Chung) (d. 645 B.C.E.).[32] A prince should rule by causing fear in his subjects. He must control laws, methods, and all powers of state. The individual exists for the state, not the state for the individual. Confucians did not agree with the Legalists' assessment of human nature. Nevertheless, prior to the Han dynasty (206 B.C.E. to 220 C.E.), princes preferred caution and usually agreed with Legalist philosophy rather than with the faith of Confucius.

Because he stuttered, **Han Feizi (Han Fei Tzu)** (d. 233 B.C.E.) preferred to write. Being from a noble family of the state of Han, he was jailed by the king of Qin. The king admired Han Feizi's work but had him imprisoned as a threat; the Qin had designs on Han territory. Unable to plead his innocence to the Qin ruler, Han Feizi drank poison provided for him by the man who had led the Qin ruler to have him imprisoned.[33] The writings he left show how his philosophy competed with that of Confucius as he sought a position of leadership with a prince.

Han Feizi believed humans were not to be trusted. The king had to rule by a firm system of rewards and punishment. As did the Italian political theorist

Fajia (Fa-Chia or **Legalists)** [fah-JEE-a]
In China, the Legalist school of philosophy that taught governance by reward and punishment. An example of a Fajia philosopher is Han Feizi.

Han Feizi (Han Fei Tzu)
A representative of the Fajia, or Legalist, school of philosophy in China. He taught that people were governed best by a ruler who harshly enforced rigid laws.

Niccolo Machiavelli (1469–1527 C.E.) in *The Prince,* Han Feizi urged rulers to support fully law and order.

> The enlightened ruler in bestowing rewards is as benign as the seasonable rain; the dew of his bounty profits all men. But in doling out punishment he is as terrible as the thunder; even the holy sages cannot assuage him. The enlightened ruler is never overliberal in his rewards, never overlenient in his punishments. If his rewards are too liberal, then ministers who have won merit in the past will grow lax in their duties, and if his punishments are too lenient, then evil ministers will find it easy to do wrong. Thus if a man has truly won merit, no matter how humble and far removed he may be, he must be rewarded; and if he has truly committed error, no matter how close and dear to the ruler he may be, he must be punished. If those who are humble and far removed can be sure of reward, and those close and dear to the ruler can be sure of punishment, then the former will not stint in their efforts and the latter will not grow proud.[34]

Confucians could not agree with the Fajia understanding of humans. The difference in their advice grew out of their different estimates of human nature. The Fajia thought that by nature all men are evil; Confucians thought that by nature all men are good.

THE DAOISTS

The Daoists and Confucius disagreed about the desirability of government and social conventions. Literature describes visits between Laozi and Confucius. In their conversations, Laozi is very critical of the social conventions advocated by Confucius, and Confucius makes some rather confused responses. Many scholars think the conversations never occurred but that they do reflect the differences between the Daoists and the Confucians. The writings of Zhuangzi, also, report conversations in which Confucius is portrayed as embracing a position, such as being rid of body and mind, that is quite different from the thrust of his teachings.

CONFUCIUS AND THE STATE

Confucius can be contrasted with Daoists, Legalists, and Mohists in his concept of the good ruler. Confucius envisioned a reciprocal, though unequal, relationship between ruler and people. The ruler, a polestar around whom others circulate, must, in his moral behavior, set an example of the superior person. In all things he abides by propriety and ritual. His conduct is so correct that all people, from ministers to peasants, must follow him. He does not permit the anarchy of Daoism or the harsh law-and-order government of the Legalists. He rectifies names, keeping the position and function of persons clear; he does not follow the Mohist principle of equality. He is economical in his expenditures, and he employs people in proper tasks according to the seasons. Above all, he loves his people, for the people's confidence in the ruler is more important to the success of the state than either food or military equipment. The evidence of a happy state, which begins in a good ruler–subject relationship, is that people within the state are happy, and those outside are eager to enter it.[35]

During his lifetime, it was difficult for Confucius to keep his faith in his life and teaching—he had not been appointed to many of the administrative positions that he sought. He probably wondered, would history judge him to have been a complete failure?

Confucianism after Confucius

It is beyond question that the academic work of Confucius was useful. He was a one-man faculty. He collected and revised Chinese classics, composed and performed music, and competed in archery tournaments. In his leisure he liked to hunt or fish with a pole and line. His rewards in life were good friends and good conversations. The long list of accomplishments of generations of students demonstrates that his faith in them was justified. Generations later, **Mengzi (Mencius)** (about 371–289 B.C.E.) added his own examples based on the teachings of Confucius and gave yet another source for seeing wisdom unfold from Master Kong. Tradition has attributed to Confucius the revision of five Chinese classics: the *Shujing,* or *Book of History;* the *Shijing,* or *Book of Poetry;* the *Liji,* or *Book of Rites;* the *Yijing,* or *Book of Changes;* and the *Ch'un Ch'iu,* or *Annals of Spring and Autumn.* The details of Confucius's teaching as they are remembered by his disciples are presented in the Confucian "Four Books." The *Analects (Lun Yu);* the *Great Learning, Daxue (Ta Hsueh);* the *Doctrine of the Mean, Zhongyong (Chung Yung);* and the *Book of Mencius, Mengzi (Meng-tze).*

MENGZI (MENCIUS)

Mengzi surpassed Confucius in emphasizing the internal goodness of the individual. A pupil of Confucius's grandson, according to the legend, Mengzi was more concerned for the individual than for the state. Humans must have security of employment in order to live a moral, productive life and make a contribution to society. They must first be a member of a family, for the family rests on the individual and the state and the empire rests on families. Government has a duty to treat its subjects well; if not, heaven gives a mandate for subjects to remove and replace the ruler. The ruler who abides by the will of heaven governs by virtue.

> Mencius said, "When the Way prevails in the Empire men of small virtue serve men of great virtue, men of small ability serve men of great ability. But when the Way is in disuse, the small serve the big, the weak serve the strong. Both are due to Heaven. Those who are obedient to Heaven are preserved; those who go against Heaven are annihilated."[36]

As A. C. Graham has put it, for Mengzi moral inclinations belong to nature in the same way as the physical growth of the body. They germinate spontaneously and can be fed or starved; they cannot be forced.[37]

Mengzi stated it this way:

> As far as what is genuinely in him is concerned, a man is capable of becoming good. . . . That is what I mean by good. As for his becoming bad, that is not the fault of his native endowment. The heart of compassion is possessed by all men alike; likewise the heart of shame, the heart of respect, and the heart of right and wrong.[38]

XUNZI (HSUN TSU)

Xunzi (Hsun Tsu, 298–230 B.C.E.) differed with Mengzi on the nature of human beings. Xunzi could not agree that all men are by nature good. Burton Watson writes,

> As a philosophical system, Hsun Tzu's thought rests upon the harsh initial thesis that man's nature is basically evil. . . . It flatly contradicts the view of Mencius, who taught that man is naturally inclined to goodness, and in later centuries, when

Mengzi (Mencius)
[MENG-dzi]
A later disciple of Confucius who emphasized an inborn goodness of humans. He differed from Xunzi (Hsun Tzu), who argued that men are born evil.

Xunzi (Hsun Tsu)
[SHUN-dzi]
A Confucian who argued that humans are evil by nature and must be taught good rather than evil. He differed from Mengzi (Mencius), who believed that humans are born good.

Mencius' view came to be regarded as the orthodox one, it led to an unhappy clouding of Hsun Tzu's entire system of thought.[39]

This conclusion is supported by the words of Xunzi:

> Man's nature is evil; goodness is the result of conscious activity. The nature of man is such that he is born with a fondness for profit. If he indulges his fondness, it will lead him into wrangling and strife, and all sense of courtesy and humility will disappear. He is born with flings of envy and hate, and if he indulges these, they will lead him into violence and crime, and all sense of loyalty and good faith will disappear. Man is born with the desires of the eyes and ears, with a fondness for beautiful sights and sounds. If he indulges these, they will lead him into license and wantonness, and all ritual principles and correct forms will be lost. Hence, any man who follows his nature and indulges his emotions will inevitably become involved in wrangling and strife, will violate the forms and rules of society, and will end as a criminal. Therefore, man must first be transformed by the instructions of a teacher and guided by ritual principles, and only then will be able to observe the dictates of courtesy and humility, obey the forms and rules of society, and achieve order. It is obvious from this, then, that man's nature is evil, and that his goodness is the result of conscious activity.[40]

Xunzi taught that all humans are born equal in every respect. Only through training can a person become good. Society has a responsibility for education so that everyone will be trained in desirable morality. A person must be taught to cultivate the proper conduct and aspire to be wise. He did not believe in gods or spirits; heaven is indifferent to the needs of humans. He was, perhaps, too much of a naturalistic philosopher to win the love and devotion of the masses—his work is not considered one of the Confucian classics.

With some exceptions, the reverence that Confucius's students expressed for him both in his life and in his death continued over succeeding generations. Early in the Han dynasty (206 B.C.E. to 220 C.E.), an emperor offered animal sacrifices at the grave of Confucius. Images, and more often, memorial tablets were placed in his honor. Through the centuries, schoolchildren recited his teachings. Until the twentieth century, civil servants in China had to pass a test on his teachings. The revered teacher in heaven became a revered ancestor, and temples were built so that everyone in China could worship him. The teacher who had once seemed such a failure in influencing the politics of a single province later influenced whole dynasties of emperors of China.

NEO-CONFUCIANISM

Neo-Confucianism was a revival of declining Confucianism, which began with Han Yu (768–824 C.E.). He opposed the Buddhist influence on a Tang emperor. Mahayana Buddhism and Daoism had so embraced folk religion that Confucians had only weak public support. Only when the Sung (Song) dynasty was evidently impotent in military resistance did Confucians begin to recover. In reaction to the Yuan (Mongols) and other foreigners, the Chinese peoples returned to their cultural roots.

An outstanding leader of the revival was **Zhuxi (Chu Hsi)** (1130–1200 C.E.). He was a scholar whose personal life epitomized the ideal of Confucius. He examined the writings of Xunzi and concluded that they did not belong among the orthodox Confucian classics. More important, he concluded from the classics that the ancients advocated an objective study of nature and the universe. Everything comes

Zhuxi (Chu Hsi)
[JYOO-SHEE]
The leader of the Neo-Confucian revival in the twelfth century.

into being by natural force, Qi, and natural order, li. Li in cosmic proportions can be called the great ultimate, **Taiji (Tai Chi).** This force stimulates natural matter to exercise the opposites of Yang and Yin and produce the elements of earth, fire, water, wood, and metal. There is only one Great Ultimate, which is also reason, but in all things the One is present. The same principle works in man, making him good. Julia Ching explains that Zhuxi's central teaching, the *Doctrine of the Mean,* was not the midpoint between two extremes, but "the discovery of one's own spiritual *middle,* the profound center of one's existence."[41]

In the Great Ultimate, Zhuxi found an impersonal absolute of the universe. It was more knowable than the hidden Dao of the Daoists. It was more positive than the Void of the Buddhists. Li can be seen at work in all things, and the Great Ultimate never ceases to stimulate matter to create.

> 115. *Question:* The Great Ultimate is not a thing existing in a chaotic state before the formation of heaven and earth, but a general name for the principles of heaven and earth and the myriad things. Is that correct?
>
> *Answer:* The Great Ultimate is merely the principle of heaven and earth and the myriad things. With respect to heaven and earth, there is the Great Ultimate in them. With respect to the myriad things, there is the Great Ultimate in each and every one of them. Before heaven and earth existed, there was assuredly this principle. It is the principle that "through movement generates the yang." It is also this principle that "through tranquility generates the yin."[42]

Zhuxi performed the function for Confucianism that Thomas Aquinas (1225–1274 C.E.) performed for Christianity: He interpreted prior centuries of doctrine for all succeeding generations.

Historical Development: The Rise and Fall of Confucianism

The traditional institution of Confucianism reached its height in 1906 when the Manchu rulers issued an edict to place sacrifices to Confucius on the same level as those to heaven.[43] The edict was both an attempt to extend the highest honor to Confucius and to deify him. The Manchus fell, and so did Confucianism as an institution. A republic was declared under **Sun Yat-sen** (1866–1925), and attempts to have Confucianism recognized as a state religion failed, in part because of objections from Confucians. Under **Chiang K'ai Shek,** leader of the Nationalist party Quomindang (Kuomin-tang), a New Life movement was launched in 1935 that emphasized Confucian virtues. When the Nationalists left the mainland of China for Taiwan (Formosa) in 1949, the government of **Mao Zedong (Mao Tse-tung,** 1893–1976) further weakened Confucian practices.

A valid question is whether reciprocity, mutual support, and the give-and-take of the family can be extended to the larger world of political discourse and government policy. Chinese delegates supported the 1948 Declaration of Human Rights, which seemed fully incompatible with Confucian humanism.[44] Confucianism has oppressed women in the past, but there is room for moral and personal growth, which permits a convergence between Confucian and feminist ethical thinking.[45] Rights are based on interests. The interests of individuals must sometimes compromise with interests of larger society; thus individual rights are relative rather than unlimited and absolute, according to Chinese writers.[46]

Taiji (Tai Chi) [tie-JEE] The Great Ultimate in Zhuxi's (Chu Hsi's) Neo-Confucian philosophy. It is the rational law, or li, that works within everything.

Sun Yat-sen The first leader of the republic in China after the fall of the Manchus. He reasserted Confucian virtues.

Chiang K'ai Shek [CHUNG-kai-SHEK] The leader of Nationalist China who established a government in Taiwan. He was driven from mainland China by Mao Zedong.

Mao Zedong (Mao Tse-tung) [MAOW-tse-DONG] The Marxist leader of China who overthrew the Nationalist government of Chiang K'ai Shek in 1949. He established the People's Republic of China.

Worldview: Confucianism

The Absolute

Confucius participated in sacrifices to heaven, the home of ancestors who functioned as divine beings. That was the tradition in China that Confucius supported. Some scholars think that Confucius, following the Zhou beliefs of about 1000 B.C.E., conceived of heaven as a singular, personal deity; other scholars disagree. The sacrifices offered at the grave of Confucius during the Han dynasty could be construed as treating Confucius as a god. Perhaps it is more accurate, however, to say that he was honored as everybody's moral ancestor. He was revered as an educator.

Confucius said of heaven,

> The Master said, "There is no one who understands me." Tzu-king said, "How is it that there is no one who understands you?" The Master said, "I do not complain against Heaven, nor do I blame Man. In my studies, I start from below and get through to what is up above. If I am understood at all, it is, perhaps, by Heaven."(14/25).[47]

Neo-Confucianists were more likely to think of the Great Ultimate as impersonal, the source of li in nature and humans. Reverence for Confucius was expressed in imitating his example and honoring his teachings by practicing them in society.

Tian (T'ien), or heaven, often functioned as a moral absolute. Kings who prospered considered that they ruled by the mandate of heaven, **tianming (t'ien-ming).**[48] Humans believed that when they followed the mandate of heaven they prospered; when they disobeyed, they suffered. Confucianism supported the concept of heaven (and mandate of heaven) that was among the beliefs of the Zhou dynasty and continued under the Han dynasty. From the early days after Confucius, there was disagreement among his followers whether heaven was impersonal (following its own course regardless of human desires) or of the nature of persons (able to respond to prayers and supplications).

The World

Confucians think the natural world is a good place. When humans work with nature in accordance with the principles of heaven, the earth brings forth most things humans need. Humans need only to know and do the will of heaven. The Neo-Confucians were concerned with studying the natural world to find li in it. The search for order in nature was not properly science, but it was a concept that could be used when the scientific revolution extended to China.

Confucians supported developing technologies to make human life productive and enjoyable. Although their first concerns were ethical, Confucians encouraged the state to support good agriculture, transportation for commerce, and studies of the stars and planets. They favored using the earth for the benefit of humans.

tianming (t'ien-ming)
[TYIAN-MING]
In Confucianism, the mandate of heaven. Zhou and Han emperors claimed to rule successfully because they followed the mandate of heaven.

Humans

The controversy between Mengzi and Xunzi over the nature of humans was important, if sometimes exaggerated. Perhaps Xunzi did not think of humans as being born evil so much as he thought they were born neutral, capable of becoming

© Ewing Galloway

Temple of Heaven, Beijing. As late as the Ming period, thirteenth century, the emperor was thought to stand between heaven and earth.

good or bad. But he agreed with Confucius and Mengzi that humans required education. More than his successors, Confucius thought humans must have role models. They seek role models without being told. Confucius used that search to help humans develop their greatest moral potentials.

> The Master said, "I have no hopes of meeting a sage. I would be content if I met someone who is a gentleman."
>
> The Master said, "I have no hopes of meeting a good man. I would be content if I met someone who has constancy. It is hard for a man to have constancy who claims to have when he is wanting, to be full when he is empty and to be comfortable when he is in straitened circumstances.[49]

The Problem for Humans

The problem for humans is disharmony. Disharmony in Confucianism arises when humans think of their own advantage at the expense of others. Those who are small, mean, and petty think only of themselves. They forget their responsibilities to members of their family, their friends, and their ruler. They forget they are both student and teacher of morals. To live without consideration of others is not only bad for the individual; it also harms society—it sets a bad example.

The Solution for Humans

The solution for humans is harmony. They begin by not doing to others what they do not want done to themselves. Stated positively, reciprocity means taking your own feelings as a guide in how to treat others. Learning the lessons of propriety and setting good examples take most of a lifetime. Learning to fulfill obligations to parents, siblings, friends, and ruler requires constant vigilance. Little is said about the grace of heaven, although common belief holds that ancestors can help the living. Society supports humans in their quest for harmony, but they have to do most of the work themselves.

The individual subject should obey the good ruler. A good ruler embodies the Confucian virtues and loves his people. Because he has the mandate of heaven, the good ruler brings a good life to his subjects.

Confucius thought that harmony requires good government. A. C. Graham states,

> An extremely remarkable feature of Confucius' thought is his conviction that all government can be reduced to ceremony.

> If you guide them by government, hold them even by punishment, the people will elude you and have no shame. If you guide them by Potency, hold them even by ceremony, the people will both have shame and draw near you. (2/3)[50]

Community and Ethics

The word *reciprocity* is a good description for Confucian ethics. People should avoid doing to others what they would not want done to them. They should do those things that they would like done to themselves. People live their lives fulfilling their duty to superiors. Confucianism assumes an authoritarian father and an authoritarian ruler. It also assumes the authority of older persons. However, age does not free people from all responsibilities; they must be kind to those who show deference, and they are always to be aware that they teach by their conduct. The emperor himself is not free from responsibility to heaven and his people.

> The Master said, "The rule of virtue can be compared to the Pole Star which commands the homage of the multitude of stars without leaving its place." (2/1)

> Someone said to Confucius, "Why do you not take part in government?"
> The Master said, "*The Book of History* says, 'Oh! Simply by being a good son and friendly to his brothers a man can exert an influence upon government.' In so doing a man is, in fact, taking part in government. How can there be any question of his having actively to 'take part in government'?" (2/21)[51]

Theresa Kelleher describes reciprocity in relationships of cosmic order and society. The harmonious interaction of the life-giving cosmos should influence society.[52] Humans have received life from their parents, who received it from the cosmos. Children owe their parents marriage and children. Marriage and childbirth are rituals of reverence and gratitude, part of ancestor worship. The monastic ideals of Theravadin Buddhism could not easily adapt to the Confucian society.

Men were seen in the context of family and state; women belonged in the context of family. As in Hinduism, a woman was always subject to a male: her father, her husband, or her son. A wife could not divorce her husband; if he died, she could not remarry, for she had obligations to the ancestral family into which she had married.

Rituals and Symbols

The Chinese calendar was full of festivals, both summer and winter. Season changes were marked in state ceremonies and in homes. Activities associated with farming had to be coordinated with changes in the world. Some celebrations were religious; others were primarily social. The New Year celebrations, which lasted for many days, were very popular with ordinary people. Derk Bodde has written of the Chinese love of New Year festivals:

> The Han Chinese had no fewer than four major days of annual recurrence, plus a fifth of lesser importance, each of which in its own way could be regarded as inaugurating a new yearly cycle and therefore as constituting a New Year's Day. These beginnings, like their counterparts in other civilizations, expressed in varying degrees certain basic human concerns. They were times of religious activity—manifested by the Han Chinese primarily through sacrifices to the ancestors and the immediate household gods. They were also times of feasting, merriment, and relaxation, marking a break in the usual round of toil. And finally, they were times of *renewal,* when the old and bad was cast off and replaced by the new and good, and when omens were carefully studied to determine the good or bad fortune of the coming year. This last factor means that to some extent, at least, they were times of uncertainty and anxiety as well as of enjoyment.[53]

Confucius liked rituals and symbols; he supported those already observed in his society. He was the first full-time teacher in China for students who were not aristocrats, so it is not surprising that he became a symbol of the ideal Chinese gentleman, the junzi. He was also looked on as the ideal ancestor, a moral father of his country. It seems only a natural development that the rituals that were applied to other ancestors should be applied to him. He was a sage, a symbol of one who is more than human, a rare person who stands head and shoulders above centuries of people in his country. The first Han emperor honored Confucius at his grave; other emperors and governments gave him distinctive titles and ceremonies of recognition. According to Thomas A. Wilson, "The imperial courts of the last thousand years worshipped him as the 'supreme sage' of state orthodoxy in temples devoted to him."[54] Reflecting the Confucian doctrine of universal harmony, rites to honor Confucius include hymns of praise consisting of eight lines of four words each and orchestras of eight kinds of instruments.[55] For more than two thousand years, Confucius was a symbol that molded Chinese culture.

Life after Death

Confucius participated in rituals that honored ancestors, particularly parents. He observed mourning for his mother the prescribed time and lamented not having been old enough to mourn properly for his father. His emphasis was on duties of the living rather than speculation about the life of the dead.

> Chi-lu asked how the spirits of the dead and the gods should be served. The Master said, "You are not able even to serve man. How can you serve the spirits?"
> "May I ask about death?"
> "You do not understand even life. How can you understand death?" (11/12)[56]

Having discussed the religions of China, we will turn to Japan to see how Shinto developed as the distinctive religion of the Japanese people.

Shinto

We have no exact measurement of how long inhabitants of the islands of Japan worshiped *kami no michi,* the way of the gods. In the sixth century C.E., when Buddhism came from Korea to Japan, farmers and fishers already had a religion that honored spirits of sacred persons, places, or heaven and earth. Places were marked as sacred by a rope, a gateway (**torii**), or a small structure. To the **kami** of these places, people brought gifts of fruit, vegetables, or wine. Peoples of an area honored both a place and their ancestors who had inhabited it. Stories of local kami and cosmic kami mingled; the Japanese royal family traced their descent from a kami. The islands of the Japanese peoples were a special creation of kami. These vital traditions survived in oral forms until, inspired by Buddhist writings from Korea, leaders in Japan had their beliefs and practices described in writing. **Shinto** took its place among the world's religions that are based on written records.

Historical Development: Shinto

As with many other religions, Shinto's history stretches from prehistory until the twenty-first century. During that long period there have been many different ways of selecting and grouping aspects of Shinto's beliefs and practices. The upheavals of the nineteenth and twentieth centuries were as great as any that preceded them.

Three periods brought changes in perspectives on the history of Shinto. The first change occurred when Shinto and Buddhism encountered and adjusted to each other. Buddhists found advantage in interpreting Shinto as supplementary to Buddhist doctrines of China and Korea. The second change came in the nineteenth century when, in response to Western challenges, the Meiji reinterpreted Shinto, purifying it of many Buddhist influences. The third major change occurred in the mid-twentieth century, after Emperor Hirohito denied his divinity. Historians within Shinto revised their views to reflect both ancient traditions and present political reality. Their changes have preserved the traditions of Shinto and ensured its vital role in contemporary culture of Japan.

Prehistoric Japan

From prehistoric times, Japanese peoples worshiped kami, powers in natural phenomena. Plants and stars, rain and wind, stream and sea, animals and mountains, forests and crops were all manifestations of powers that exceeded those of humans. Dead leaders who dominated and defended village and districts also manifested

© Victoria & Albert Museum; London/Art Resource, NY

Amaterasu, Shinto Goddess of the Sun. Woodblock print. Victoria and Albert Museum.

torii [TOH-RE-EE]
In Shinto, a formal gate to a shrine. It marks the entrance to sacred space.

kami [KAH-mee]
Natural and supernatural persons and powers worshiped in Shinto. Kami are present everywhere, in nature and in people.

Shinto [SHIN-TOOH]
The Japanese religion of *kami no michi,* the way of the gods. Japanese people participate in Shinto, a combination of religion and patriotism.

these powers. The kami were manifestations of absolute power in the phenomenal world. Kami could become humans; humans could become kami. Worship was a formal communication between these distinct but interacting realms. Shamanism played an important role in these early communities, often with a woman serving as a shaman (in Japanese, a *miko*). A shaman is a Charismatic person with priestly and healing powers. A book by Carmen Blacker, *The Catalpa Bow*, describes the practices that have lingered into recent times.[57]

Visitors from Korea

At the beginning of the Common Era, Japan was sparsely settled in numerous villages. There were regional rulers, but no one controlled the largest island. Although there was no national identity, the peoples were somewhat isolated from China and Korea. Later in the Common Era, however, visitors from Korea called on local rulers. Some of their receptions were friendly, and through them Buddhism came to Japan. Koreans also brought writing, books, paintings, and other art forms. Many Japanese leaders and their powerful allies were favorably impressed. The new, foreign culture that influenced Japanese in high places challenged the traditions of the native farmers and villagers. Adherents of the way of the gods, the *kami no michi*, responded by gathering the stories of Shinto.

The Myths of Shinto

Competition from Chinese writings in the eighth century C.E. stimulated the Japanese to record their own religious dramas. The islands of Japan have a special place in the written works of the *Kojiki* (712) and the *Nihongi* (720). The islands were generated from interaction of the male principle, **Izanagi** (He Who Invites), and the female principle, **Izanami** (She Who Invites), who descended from heaven on a bridge shaped like a rainbow.

> So the two Deities, standing upon the Floating Bridge of Heaven, pushed down the jewelled spear and stirred with it, whereupon, they had stirred the brine till it went curdlecurdle, and drew [the spear] up, the brine that dripped down from the end of the spear was piled up and became an island.[58]

The couple, innocent as children, explored the differences in their bodies. Desiring offspring, they decided to attempt cohabitation. Unfortunately the woman spoke first, and their two offspring displeased them. Something was wrong! They had to ascend to the Sky-Kami for counseling.

> Then the Heavenly Gods divined this by the greater divination. Upon which they instructed them, saying—"It was by reason of the woman's having spoken first; ye had best return thither again." Thereupon having divined a time, they went down. The two Deities accordingly went again round the pillar, the male Deity from the left, and the female Deity from the right. When they met, the male Deity spoke first and said. "How pretty! a lovely maiden!" The female Deity next answered and said:—"How pretty! a lovely youth!" Thereafter they dwelt together in the same palace and had children.[59]

Izanagi [ee-zah-NAH-gee] In Shinto, the male-who-invites. Cocreator, with Izanami, of Japan.

Izanami [ee-zah-NAH-mee] In Shinto, the female-who-invites. Cocreator, with Izanagi, of Japan.

After producing the islands, the couple produced many kami. The birth of the fire god killed Izanami, and she went to the land of the dead, Yomi. Seeking her in the corrupt land of the dead, Izanagi polluted himself. Ceremonial cleansing was required for him, and out of his act of cleansing, other deities were created who came to have a superior place of importance in Shinto. They were **Amaterasu,** the sun goddess, who was the highest; **Susanoo,** god of storms; and **Tsukiyomi,** the moon god.

Purification rites have played an important part in Shinto, and they are traced not only to Izanagi but also to the rites of Susanoo, who was, in the eyes of his sister Amaterasu, something of a delinquent. One story tells of her hiding in a cave, withholding her light from the world because she was unhappy with her brother's mischief. Several symbols of Shinto are attached to Susanoo's efforts to lure his sister from the cave. With the invention of music, he aroused her curiosity, and with the brilliance of jewels and a mirror, which became other sacred objects in Shinto, he persuaded her to come out of the cave and shed her light over the world again.

> Hereupon the Heaven-Shining-Great-August-Deity was amazed, and, slightly opening the door of the Heavenly Rock-Dwelling, spoke thus from the inside:

> "Methought that owing to my retirement the Plain of Heaven would be dark, and likewise the Central Land of Reed-Plains would all be dark: how then is it that the Heavenly-Alarming-Female makes merry, and that likewise the eight hundred myriad Deities all laugh?" Then the Heavenly-Alarming-Female spoke saying: "We rejoice and are glad because there is a Deity more illustrious than Thine Augustness." While she was thus speaking, His Augustness Heavenly-Beckoning-Ancestor-Lord and His Augustness Grand-Jewel pushed forward the mirror and respectfully showed it to the Heaven-Shining-Great-August-Deity, whereupon the Heaven-Shining-Great-August-Deity, more and more astonished, gradually came forth from the door and gazed upon it, whereupon the Heavenly-Hand-Strength-Male-Deity, who was standing hidden, took her august hand and drew her out, and then His Augustness Grand-Jewel drew the bottom-tied rope along at her august back, and spoke, saying: "Thou Heaven-Shining-Great-August-Deity had come forth, both the Plain of High Heaven and the Central-Land-of-Reed-Plains of course again became light."[60]

The struggle between Susanoo and Amaterasu continued with their descendants. Okunushi, of Susanoo, and Ninigi, grandson of Amaterasu, had a struggle for power, but Ninigi won, and through his great-grandson, **Jimmu,** began to dominate human affairs in Japan. The first human emperor, Jimmu, began his rule in 660 B.C.E. With the establishment of the Japanese state, the Japanese royal family, believed to be related to Jimmu, took a divine aura. The shrine sacred to Amaterasu at Ise displays a mirror, beads, and a sword that belonged to Jimmu. Because he was a human with kami nature, he could communicate with the sun goddess. Humans and kami are involved together in the ebb and flow of natural phenomena and human dramas of life. "In the Shinto myth, all the stress is on immanence and the continuity between procreators and procreated. Everything is divine, *kami*-like. All things proceed from heavenly divine spirit."[61] Worship is not so much a human attempt to obtain a special gift or blessing as to share, through ritual, fellowship of life with the kami.

During the Nara (710–784 C.E.) and Heian, Kyoto, periods of the emperors' courts, Chinese influence was quite strong in literature, art, and architecture. Shinto, however, was kept as part of the court ceremonies, whereas Buddhism had to settle for other places of worship. Shinto was cared for by a government department with a rank equal to all others.

Buddhist Influence on Shinto

Under Prince **Shotoku** (574–622 C.E.), cooperation among Shinto, Buddhism, and Confucianism was encouraged. He reasoned that Shinto helped Japanese peoples relate to their natural environment and Confucianism helped build solid families.

Amaterasu
[AH-MAH-te-RAH-su]
In Shinto, the goddess of the sun, created by purification of Izanagi. She is sister to Susanoo, the god of storms.

Susanoo [su-SAH-NOOH]
In Shinto, the storm god, who was brother of Amaterasu, the sun goddess.

Tsukiyomi
[tsoo-ki-yoh-mi]
In Shinto, the moon god. He is related to Amaterasu and Susanoo.

Jimmu [jee-moo]
In Shinto, the first human emperor, a descendant of the gods. As part of the Shinto religion, the emperor of Japan has been revered.

Shotoku (Shotoku Taishi)
[SHOOH-TOH-ku]
The Japanese prince who supported the establishment of Buddhism in his country.

Buddhism guided preparation for life after death. Although there was a brief attempt to restrict Buddhism to aristocrats, denying it to peasants, all the religions, including Daoism, became a part of folk practices. Japanese peoples responded well to the Chinese systems of holidays, which the Daoists modified for them.

In the eighth century, the Emperor Shomu greatly expanded Buddhism by establishing *kokubunji,* official Buddhist temples, in every province. These temples were for monks and were used to support the government—they were not for missionary activities among common people. Shinto was still the native religion for the common people. As may be expected, Buddhism continued to strengthen its influence beyond the aristocracy. Common people combined kami and the spiritual beings of Mahayana Buddhism; in an emerging folk religion, Japanese peoples called on both kami and Buddhist deities.

We have discussed the Buddhist groups in Japan that developed third doctrines outside Kyoto on Mt. Hiei. In that remote area, they were beyond strict control of the court of the city. Japanese common people, who already associated kami and mountains in Shinto, could easily associate the Buddhas with the spirits of their native religion.

The Bushido Code of the Samurai

During the Kamakura period (1192–1333), several religions worked together to develop the code of the feudal warrior or knight, **bushido.** This code, which emphasized absolute loyalty of the warrior to his lord, also included gratitude, courage, and justice. So fierce and devoted was the knight, that should he fail in his mission the code required him to commit **hara-kiri,** ritual suicide. This unique code had its roots deep in Shinto, with extreme patriotism for emperor and country, but scholars find in it strong influences from Confucianism with emphasis on the ethics of the junzi. Individual self-discipline and harmony of self and duty bear the strong stamp of Zen Buddhism. Thus these religions influenced bushido, the warrior code; those who lived by it had a religious respect for it. Yamaga-Soko, given credit for establishing bushido, said, "The first and surest means to enter into communion with the Divine is by sincerity. If you pray to a deity with sincerity, you will surely feel the divine presence."[62]

Reactions to Foreign Religions

In the sixteenth century, military leaders sought to reduce the influence of foreign religions and to restore native customs, including the emperor as a symbol of Japanese unity. Lord Nobunaga burned Buddhist buildings on Mt. Hiei and a fortress belonging to a Pure Land sect. His successor, Toyotomi Hideyoshi grew tired of Christian infighting. Jesuit missionaries had come in 1549 to help carry on trade with the West. But other Catholic and Protestant missionaries promoted competitive doctrines that divided Japanese loyalties. In 1587, Hideyoshi prohibited Christians from interfering with Shinto and Buddhists and from proclaiming their own doctrines. A crucifixion of Franciscan missionaries in Nagasaki in 1597 was followed in 1614 by a ban on the practice of Christianity.

But the Tokugawa regime, along with its strict policy of keeping foreigners out of Japan, established Neo-Confucianism and Buddhism as pillars to support the state. Neo-Confucianism was the philosophy of the civil service that required absolute loyalty to family and obedience to the ruler. Three principles governed the ideal sovereign. He should lead his people in conduct according to virtue conferred on them by heaven.[63] He should help them preserve pure heart and mind.

bushido [bu-shi-DOOH]
A code of honor for Japanese warriors. It incorporated both Daoist and Zen Buddhist concepts and governed the samurai, the feudal military class.

hara-kiri
[HAH-RAH-kee-ree]
In Japan, a ritual suicide to preserve or to restore a person's honor. It is considered an act of bravery rather than cowardice.

He should preserve the ideal society that results from these principles. Buddhism, already established in every province, became a means of keeping contact with each family; each was required to belong to a Buddhist temple. Although Shinto priests had to become Buddhists, in the long run the move helped them. Through its ties with the state, Buddhism became perfunctory, but Shinto priests strengthened their ties with folk religion and syncretized popular Buddhist ideas with vital Shinto practices.

State Shinto

One of the most significant changes in the status of Shinto is usually tied to a nonreligious event, the visit of Commodore Matthew C. Perry, who insisted in 1853 that Japan open its ports to the United States. Many scholars interpret this visit as the occasion when Japanese leaders decided to pursue Western technology in order to compete among nations of the West. The **shogun,** or military ruler, resigned in 1867, and the Emperor Meiji became the ruler of Japan in 1868. Immediately he imposed a sharper division between the Shinto and Buddhist priesthoods. From 1872 on, Buddhist priests could not teach that kami were really Buddhas. "State Shinto" was identified with the emperor, the government, and patriotism; citizens were required as a matter of national loyalty to participate. They could also participate in either Buddhism or sectarian Shinto, which did not receive state support. The Imperial Constitution of 1889, the Meiji constitution, stated that within certain bounds of order and loyalty as subjects, Japanese peoples were to enjoy freedom of religion.[64] In the early twentieth century, the Japanese government maintained that State Shinto was not a religion.[65]

The popular form of State Shinto affirmed the connection of the nation with ancestors, the will of the emperor, and the goddess. The individual was not a free being or even primarily a unit of a family or class; the individual belonged to the state. In half a century, this powerful concept of roots and identity, combined with a conscious plan to imitate the Western industrial and military powers to the point where the Japanese could compete successfully with them, resulted in an astounding change in Japan. Shrines at Ise, in the Imperial Palace, and in various parts of the nation numbering a hundred thousand kept State Shinto before the people, promoting reverence for ancestors, patriots, and, above all, the emperor.

State Shinto went into sharp decline, if not collapse, when the Japanese surrendered to the Allies in 1945. The emperor was no longer considered divine, at least officially. Although the Allies insisted on a separation of Shinto and state, the Association of Shinto Shrines has been instrumental in bringing Shinto ceremonies into the construction of government buildings and in obtaining government support for the periodic rebuilding of the shrine at Ise, as tradition requires.

In their introduction to *Shinto in History,* John Breen and Mark Teeuwen note that

> in discussions of contemporary Japanese religiosity, . . . it is vital to distinguish between shrine cults—the reality of those multifarious activities and beliefs that are manifest in shrines both local and central—and "Shinto"—the ideological agenda of the establishment rooted especially though certainly not uniquely, in reverence for, or at least identification with, the imperial institutions.[66]

Of course, Shinto can still be found in Japanese homes in the **kami-dana,** or spirit shelf. The **butsudan,** a center for observing reverence for ancestors and departed members of the family, is not as prominent as it once was.

shogun [SHOW-GUN]
In Japan, a military ruler serving, ostensibly, under the emperor.

kami-dana
[KAH-mee-DAH-NAH]
In Japanese homes, a center of symbols honoring the kami. Sometimes the center is a shelf.

butsudan
[Bu-tsu-DAH-NAH]
A Buddhist altar. Tablets commemorating ancestors are kept on it.

A kami-dana in a Home.

Recent Shinto and New Religions

Traditional Buddhism and many Shinto sects thrive in Japan. Buddhist temples of all schools are everywhere, and it is not unusual to find Shinto shrines even on the premises of some of Japan's most technologically advanced centers of communication. These religions still inspire the people of Japan.

The Agency for Cultural Affairs in Japan classifies sectarian Shinto into three groups, according to their history and distinctive practices.[67] The three classifications are traditional sects, mountain worship sects, and sects based on revelation.

Tenrikyo, a spiritual healing group, is an example of a sect based on revelation. It was formed in the nineteenth century around a peasant woman (1798–1887) named **Miki Nakayama.** Experiencing the presence of the kami of Divine Reason when she reached middle age, she believed that she had been the medium of healing for her son in 1838. Her eldest son, Shuji, suffered such pain in his leg that he was unable to work. A healer led séances to help him. During one session, Miki took the place of the assistant to the healer. In her trance, which lasted three days, she was the medium of a voice that claimed to be the true God, who came down from heaven to save the world.[68] Of course she shared the secrets of her healing with her neighbors, and the Teaching of the Heavenly Reason was soon established. A person who lives reasonably; that is, in line with the Heavenly Reason, will have prosperous and healthy life in the present world. For a time, she was opposed by her husband and her neighbors, who found her desire to give away her property evidence of her being possessed. She persisted, however, in her witness that illness could be overcome through a healthy belief. Her successes in healing mounted over the years, and her examples of virtue won her respect and adherents. Her teachings are passed down in four texts that her adherents consider

Tenrikyo [TEN-ree-KYO]
A religion of Japan based on the teachings of Miki Nakayama. It reveres the kami of Divine Reason.

Miki Nakayama
[MI-ki NAH-KAH-YAH-MAH]
In Japan, founder of the new religion, Tenrikyo. She experienced divine healing through the kami of Divine Reason.

scripture. Tenrikyo continues to thrive today in faith healings and voluntary work for public charity.

Three twentieth-century religions of Japan developed out of one of the Shinto sects based on revelation. P. L. (Perfect Liberty) Kyodan; Miki Tokuchika which emphasizes aesthetic experiences and rites for healing; and Seicho-no-le (House of Growth), which emphasizes American-style positive thinking. Suffering is not real; it is the result of bad attitudes. All beings are perfect children of God. These religions complement new religions of Japan based on Nichiren Buddhism: Soka Gakkai, Rissho Koseikai, and Reiyukai.[69]

Summarizing his views on the new religions of Japan, H. Paul Varley wrote,

> Despite the diversity of the new religions, they share certain general characteristics. For example, they have tended to spring up during times of intense crisis or social unrest, such as the early Meiji and post-World War II periods; their founders have typically been charismatic figures who have served as vehicles for the revelation of religious truth; they are highly syncretic, often partaking freely of Shinto and Buddhism, as well as Christianity; and they are millenarian in that they characteristically promise the advent of a paradise on earth. Also, the new religions have always appealed chiefly to people lower on the social and economic scales: to those who have in some sense been left behind in the march for modern progress.
>
> What makes the new religions most fascinating within the larger context of Japanese cultural history is the degree to which they reflect fundamental religious values and attitudes that have been held since ancient times. This can be seen perhaps most tellingly in the kinds of the charismatic figures who have found new religions, the most interesting of which are the female shamanistic types.[70]

Worldview: Shinto

During its long history, Shinto has meant so many things to different people that it is difficult to describe its worldview. The worldview outline used to explain beliefs of other religions does not apply in every instance to Shinto.

The Absolute

Traditionally, Shinto has focused its worship on the goddess of the sun, Amaterasu-Omikami. The sun has been an object of veneration in many religions, for example, the Egyptian. But the Japanese have looked on Amaterasu-Omikami not so much as a universal deity but as a deity partial to the peoples of Japan. Nature kami are revered without any disrespect for Amaterasu. Emperors can be revered or worshiped at shrines because they have historically carried the title of descendants of the goddess of the sun. Emperor Hirohito, since 1945, denied descent from Amaterasu. In sectarian Shinto, such as Tenrikyo, other kamis or principles such as Heavenly Reason can be approached in reverence. Along with these powers an adherent can, without necessarily being disloyal, worship Confucius, the Dao, various Buddhas and Bodhisattvas, and his or her own ancestors.

Japanese people revere the extraordinary power and order immanent in nature and animals, including humans. Power and order are revered where they impinge on human experience. Although Shinto can be classified as polytheism, it is, perhaps, more accurately described today as a reverence for manifestations of power that have had special value for the Japanese people.

The World

Shinto reveres many natural phenomena. The Japanese islands as a group are regarded as sacred. The Japanese feel that their country is a special creation and gift of Amaterasu. Mt. Fuji, other mountains, streams, rivers, and the sea are all blessings bestowed on the Japanese people. The land belongs to the Japanese; it was made for them. There is still a feeling among some Koreans and other peoples who have lived in Japan for several generations that Japanese people will never accept them as Japanese and grant them a share in the country.

Humans

Shinto is concerned with Japanese peoples rather than with humanity. Humans are potentially kami. They came from acts of kami, and by acting heroically, they can become kami. As do Confucians, Japanese look on humans as servants of family, state, and ancestors. An individual is never isolated; he or she is always part of an extended family and a national people. People are expected to do their best for all these groups. To fail to do their best is disgraceful. There is freedom enough for individuals to have responsibility for their conduct, but they are never free to act with disregard for the welfare of all the constituent groups.

Denise Lardner Carmody has described the role of Japanese women in terms similar to those of Confucian family culture, as bushido woman, as shaman, or as court lady.[71] As a Japanese woman, she was subservient to father, husband, and son. As warrior, she was expected to die to protect her honor. As court lady, she cared for the aesthetic traditions of art, literature, and music. As shaman, she held power over men as well as women. Leaders in new religions, such as Tenrikyo, were honored as mediums of kami, elevating their status beyond that of ordinary humans. Although most Japanese women have attained more freedoms as they have participated in general education and employment, they still have lower status than men in their homes and workplaces.

Traditionally, women of Japan have remained in the background publicly, although they have had immense responsibilities in their homes, especially at the beginning of the twenty-first century. Sacrificing personal ambition for home has sometimes been a means of achieving self-realization as a woman, as has been helping others and changing society.[72] However, some contemporary Japanese women have constructed a new individuality that has broken the old boundaries for women. They have found a sense of worth and enjoyment in their spontaneity.[73] Some have explored the world through language study, study abroad, work abroad, and employment in international organizations or foreign-affiliated firms.[74]

The Problem for Humans

The problem for humans is alienation. Alienation can take several forms. Humans can be ritually unclean, in need of purification. They can be estranged from the kami, in need of communication. They can be alienated from family, ancestors, community, or emperor through loss of face—failure to do what has been expected.

The Solution for Humans

The solution for humans is reconciliation. Purification at a shrine can remove ritual pollution and permit humans to approach the kami. They can be reconciled by offerings and prayers. Reverence for ancestors and prayers to them can remove minor estrangements. Heroic deeds for the state can atone for some alienation from the nation. When all else fails, ritual suicide is considered an honorable way to atone for guilt.

Community and Ethics

Devotion to family and country governs all conduct. A person is part of a family, a school, a business organization, and a nation. Sacrificing impulses to selfishness for the good of these larger groups is a duty. Maintaining the honor of these groups guides conduct. If the existence of these groups does not influence a person's actions, he or she also must consider that ancestors and kami are observing. For those who act unethically, or illegally, law enforcement officials may be the least of their worries.

Rituals and Symbols

Robert Ellwood and Richard Pilgrim have emphasized the importance of pilgrimages in Japanese religion, the need to move from one place to another.[75] One pilgrimage destination was the Grand Shrine of Ise. In the Heian era, only members of the imperial house and officials could worship there. A princess was chosen to be the priestess-shamaness to help lead the services to Amaterasu. In later periods, beginning with the Tokugawa, when common people could worship at Ise, it was important for people to go at least once during their lifetime. Those persons who could not go might help send a delegate to worship and bring back tokens.

Two forms of pilgrimage developed. One was an official pilgrimage undertaken by those with gifts and money. For these pilgrims there was a festival atmosphere in the inns, shops, and houses along the highway they traveled. Later, spontaneous pilgrimages occurred among thousands of poor people. Without permission or provisions, men, women, and children set out for the shrine, depending on the grace of the divine to provide for their safe arrival. Each day they traveled, holding aloft banners and dancing their way to Ise. When the Tokugawa era gave way to imperial rule, these pilgrimages to Ise ended. Today many worshipers observe traditions at Ise; other worshipers prefer to climb sacred mountains.

Shinto believes in the power of spoken words in prayer. The *Norito,* Shinto prayers, consist of words that praise the kami and list the offerings presented, persons reciting the prayer and those to be remembered, and any petitions. There are formal prayers for harvest and for the various shrines.[76]

Many of the other symbols of this religion have already been mentioned: the rising sun, a mirror, beads, a sword, the torii, a rope, and last, but by no means least, the emperor of Japan. All these symbols remind the Japanese of their community ties in their homes, villages, and nation.

Life after Death

The traditional Japanese view is that on death, the body should be cremated. The departed joins his or her ancestors. Ancestors know what the members of their family are doing and can assist them when necessary. They can also receive honors and gifts from devoted members of the family.

Many Japanese families use Buddhist concepts, priests, and rituals to help them in times of bereavement. A popular way to express this eclecticism, which is more inaccurate than accurate, is that Japanese are Shintoists at the birth of a child or at the opening of a business, Christian for a wedding ceremony, and Buddhist at the death of a loved one.

Religions of China and Japan

1500–1027 Shang dynasty of China	**1027–256** Zhou dynasty of China			
660 Jimmu, the first human emperor of Japan	**600–300** Laozi lived sometime during this period	**551–479** Confucius		
479–381 Mozi lived sometime during this period	**369–286** Zhuangzi	**371–289** Mengzi	**298–230** Xunzi	**215** Great Wall of China was begun
206–220 Han dynasty of China	**300s** Ge Hong, the Taoist			
574–622 Prince Shotoku of Japan	**589–618** Sui dynasty of China	**618–907** Tang dynasty of China	**710** Nara period of Japan	**712** *The Kojiki* **720** *The Nihongi* **794** Heian period of Japan
960–1279 Song dynasty of China	**1130–1200** Zhuxi, Neo-Confucian	**1186** Kamakura period of Japan	**1275–1292** Marco Polo visits China	**1279–1369** Kublai Khan, Yuan dynasty of China **1336** Muromachi period of Japan **1368–1644** Ming dynasty of China
1549 Jesuits enter Japan	**1600** Tokugawa period of Japan	**1610–1695** Huang Zongzi, Neo-Confucian	**1622–1685** Yamaga-Soko; Bushido	**1644–1912** Manchus rule China
1798–1887 Miki Nakayama: Tenri-Kyo	**1842** Hong Kong transferred to British	**1853** Admiral Perry in Japan	**1868** Meiji period of Japan	**1900** Boxer Rebellion in China
1912 Republic of China established	**1931** Japan invades China's northern provinces	**1941** Japanese bomb Pearl Harbor	**1945** United States drops atomic bombs on Japan; Emperor of Japan no longer divine	**1946** Civil war in China; Communists against Nationalists
1947 Japan puts into effect democratic constitution	**1950** Chinese troops assist North Korea in fighting UN forces in South Korea	**1962** Chinese troops invade India, pull back	**1972** U.S. President Richard M. Nixon visits China, new relations established	**1976** Mao Zedong, People's Republic of China dies
1989 Emperor Hirohito of Japan dies	**1993** Jiang Zemin president of People's Republic of China	**February 1997** Deng Xiaoping dies	**July 1, 1997** Hong Kong returns to People's Republic of China	

A common belief, according to Robert J. Smith in *Ancestor Worship in Contemporary Japan,* is that at death each person becomes a "buddha." Some years pass before one is regarded as an ancestor. When no one in the family is alive who can remember the ancestor, that person is regarded as a kami of the community. The change of status proceeds with passing time.

Shintoism and Other Religions

Shinto has received rich blessings throughout its history from association with other religions. Traditionally it has cooperated, except for very brief periods, with Buddhism. Most Japanese can participate in Shinto and Buddhism without feelings of conflict. But Shinto is for Japanese people. It seeks no converts, but it is, today, generally tolerant of other religions. Christianity in Japan has only about 1 percent of the population. World religions, other than the early Chinese have not made widespread converts in Japan.

With Shinto, we close our discussion of the religions of eastern Asia. We have studied only the best-known religions in that part of the world. Every country in Asia has its own history of religion that includes not only the major world religions but also lesser-known religions that preceded them. As you go beyond an introductory study of world religions, you may find it rewarding to explore religious developments in each country of eastern Asia.

We turn next to the religions of Mesopotamia: Babylonian religion and Zoroastrianism. Many scholars of world religion have found in them convenient bridge to study world religions that began in Central and West Asia (as some Asians call it), or, as it is known in Europe and the Western Hemisphere, the Middle East. Although Mesopotamian religions help prepare us for study of Judaism, Christianity, and Islam, Zoroastrianism is also a living world religion, worthy of study for its influence in the modern world.

Humans achieve their highest potentials when they revere their ancestors and their land. Honoring outstanding role models brings honor to one and to one's family. However, mutual official support between government and religion leads to problems. Establishing a religion in the name of the state can detract from both the religion and the state. People can be loyal to their state and support a variety of religious expressions. Patriotism may not always mean agreeing with a particular government policy or belonging to a particular type of religious organization. Love of one's country and one's ancestors is much broader than particular beliefs or practices of a government or a religion.

CONSIDER THIS

Humans Are Best as Part of a Nation

VOCABULARY

Amaterasu [AH-MAH-te-RAH-SU]
bushido [bu-SHI-DOOH]
butsudan [bu-tsu-DAH-NAH]
Chiang K'ai-shek [CHUNG-kai-SHEK]
Confucius [kun-FYOO-shus]
Dao [DOW]
Dao De Jing [dow-du-JING]

Daoists [DOW-ists]
Fajia [fah-JEE-a]
Five Relationships
Han Feizi (Han Fei Tzu)
hara-kiri
[HAH-RAH-kee-ree]
Izanagi [ee-zah-NAH-gee]

Izanami [ee-zah-NAH-mee]
Jade Emperor
Jimmu [JEE-moo]
junzi [JUN-dzi]
kami [KAH-mee]
kami-dana
[KAH-mee-DAH-NAH]

Laozi [LAHOW-dzi]
li [LEE]
Li Ji [LEE-jee]
Mao Zedong [MAOW-tse-DONG]
Mengzi [MENG-dzi]
Miki Nakayama
[mi-ki NAH-KAH-YAH-MAH]
Mohists [MOW-hists]
Mozi [MOW-dzi]
ren [RUN]
Shang Di [shang-DI]
Shinto [SHIN-TOOH]

shogun [SHOW-GUN]
Shotoku [SHOOH-TOH-ku]
shouyi [shoo-yi]
shu [SHOO]
Sun Yat-sen
Susanoo [su-SAH-NOOH]
Taiji [tie-JEE]
taixi [tai-SHEE]
Tenrikyo [TEN-ree-kyo]
Three Purities
tianming [TYIAN-MING]

torii [TOH-RE-EE]
Tsukiyomi [tsoo-ki-yoh-mi]
wuwei [WOO-WAY]
Xunzi [SHUN-dzi]
Yang [YAHNG]
yi [YEE]
Yijing [YEE-jing]
Yin [YIN]
Zaoshen [ZOW-SHEN]
Zhuangzi [JYAHNG-dzi]
Zhuxi [JYOO-SHEE]

QUESTIONS FOR REVIEW

1. Describe the *Dao De Jing*.
2. What was the relationship between Zhuangzi and Confucius?
3. Tell the story of Confucius.
4. What are the characteristics of the Junzi?
5. Describe teachings in China that competed with those of Confucius.
6. Was Confucius religious? What reasons can you give for your position?
7. Tell some of the early stories of Japanese deities.
8. In Japan, what forms of religion supplement State Shinto?
9. In Japan, how do Shinto and Buddhism relate to each other?
10. What roles do women and men each have in Japanese religions?

QUESTIONS FOR DISCUSSION

1. Are Asian religions very different from others that you know? Give examples.
2. How would you describe and rate the strengths and weaknesses of Daoism?
3. Was Confucius right about the responsibility of role models? Explain.
4. Which features of religions of Japan do you find most impressive? Why?
5. How are the religions of China and Japan described in this chapter influential today? Do they have any influence on global politics or the world economy? Explain.

NOTES

1. Laozi, *Dao De Jing: The Book of the Way,* trans. and comment. Moss Roberts (Berkeley: University of California Press, 2001), p. 8.
2. Wing-Tsit Chan, trans., *A Source Book in Chinese Philosophy* (Princeton, NJ: Princeton University Press, 1963), pp. 137–138.
3. Roger Ames, *The Art of Rulership* (Honolulu: University of Hawaii Press, 1983), p. 7.
4. Chan, p. 139.
5. *Tao Te Ching,* 43, as quoted in Chan, p. 161.
6. Ibid., 19; p. 149.
7. Ibid., 60, 1.1; p. 168.
8. *Chuang Tzu,* chapter 17, as quoted in Li-tai ming-hua chi, 6:5b–6b, in *Sources of Chinese Tradition,*
ed. Wm. Theodore de Bary (New York: Columbia University Press, 1960), p. 79.
9. Ibid., chapter 2, p. 75.
10. N. J. Girardot, *Myth and Meaning in Early Taoism* (Berkeley: University of California Press, 1983), p. 291; James R. Ware, *Alchemy, Medicine and Religion in the China of A.D. 320* (Cambridge, MA: MIT Press, 1966).
11. Robert Hymes, *Way and Byway: Taoism, Local Religion, and Models of Divinity in Sung and Modern China* (Berkeley: University of California Press, 2002), p. 1.
12. *Daoism and Ecology,* ed. N. J. Girardot, James Miller, and Liu Xiaogan, Center for the Study of World Religions, Harvard Divinity School (Cambridge,

MA: Harvard University Press, 2001); David L. Hall, "From Reference to Deference: Daoism and the Natural World," pp. 245–249. ff; Roger T. Ames, "The Local and the Focal in Realizing the Daoist World," pp. 250–278.

13. Arthur Waley, *The Way and its Power* (London: Allen & Unwin, 1968).

14. Max Kaltenmark, *Lao Tzu and Taoism* (Stanford, CA: Stanford University Press, 1969), p. 136.

15. Barzeen Baldvian, "Taoism, An Overview," in *The Encyclopedia of Religion*, vol. 14, ed. Mircea Eliade (New York: Macmillan, 1987), pp. 288–306.

16. Ed. de Bary, pp. 62–63.

17. Michel Strickmann, *Chinese Magical Medicine,* ed. Bernard Fauré (Stanford, CA: Stanford University Press, 2002), pp. 1, 280–281.

18. Michael Saso, "Orthodoxy and Heterodoxy in Taoist Ritual," in *Religion and Ritual in Chinese Society,* ed. Arthur P. Wolf (Stanford, CA: Stanford University Press, 1974), pp. 325–336.

19. James K. Feibleman, *Understanding Oriental Philosophy* (New York: New American Library, 1976), p. 79.

20. Carl Crow, *Master Kung* (New York: Harper, 1938), p. 62.

21. Confucius, *The Analects,* trans. D. C. Lau (New York: Penguin Books, 1979), p. 74. Copyright © 1979 by D. C. Lau. Reproduced by permission of Penguin UK Ltd.

22. Ibid., pp. 122–123.

23. Ibid., p. 63.

24. *The Sacred Books of Confucius and Other Confucian Classics,* trans. and ed. Ch'u Chai and Winberg Chai (New Hyde Park, NY: University Books, 1965). There is more information on music in the "Yoki" section of the *Li Chi.*

25. Confucius, p. 72.

26. Ibid., p. 135.

27. Ibid., p. 69.

28. Benjamin I. Schwartz, *The World of Thought in Ancient China* (Cambridge, MA: Belknap Press of Harvard University, 1985), pp. 117–126.

29. Yu-Lan Fung, *A History of Chinese Philosophy,* vol. 1, trans. Derk Bodde (Princeton, NJ: Princeton University Press, 1952), pp. 76–77.

30. Mei Yi-Pao, *Motse: The Neglected Rival of Confucius* (Westport, CT: Hyperion Press, 1973), p. 45.

31. *Basic Writings of Mo Tzu, Hsun Tzu, and Han Fei Tzu,* trans. Burton Watson (New York: Columbia University Press, 1967), p. 4.

32. Ibid.

33. Ibid., p. 3.

34. Ibid., p. 20.

35. Wing-Tsit Chan, "Confucian Thought: Foundations of Tradition," in *The Encyclopedia of Religion,* vol. 4, ed. Mircea Eliade (New York: Macmillan, 1987), pp. 15–24.

36. *Mencius,* trans. D. C. Lau (Baltimore: Penguin Books, 1979), p. 120. Copyright © 1979 by D. C. Lau. Reproduced by permission of Penguin UK Ltd.

37. A. C. Graham, *Disputers of the TAO* (La Salle, IL: Open Court, 1989), pp. 125–126.

38. *Mencius,* book IV, part A, 163.

39. *Basic Writings of Mo Tzu, Hsun Tzu, and Han Fei Tzu,* pp. 4–5.

40. Ibid., p. 157.

41. Julia Ching, *The Religious Thought of Chu Hsi* (Oxford, UK: Oxford University Press, 2000), p. viii.

42. Chan, *A Source Book in Chinese Philosophy,* p. 638.

43. Wing-Tsit Chan, *Religious Trends in Modern China* (New York: Octagon Books, 1969), pp. 4–20.

44. *Confucianism and Human Rights,* ed. Wm. Theodore de Bary and Tu Weiming (New York: Columbia University Press, 1998), pp. xvi, 24.

45. *The Sage and the Second Sex: Confucianism, Ethics, and Gender,* ed. Chenyang Li (Chicago: Open Court, 2000), pp. 18–19.

46. Stephen C. Angle, *Human Rights and Chinese Thought* (Cambridge, UK: Cambridge University Press, 2002), pp. 214–216.

47. Confucius, p. 129.

48. *Sources of Chinese Tradition,* ed. Wm. Theodore de Bary, 1960. Columbia University Press, New York.

49. Confucius, p. 89.

50. Graham, pp. 13, 14.

51. Confucius, pp. 63, 66.

52. Theresa Kelleher, "Confucianism," in *Women in World Religions,* ed. Arvind Sharma (Albany: State University of New York, 1987), pp. 137–143.

53. Derk Bodde, *Festivals in Classical China* (Princeton, NJ: Princeton University Press, 1975), p. 45.

54. Thomas A. Wilson, "Ritualizing Confucius/Kongzi: The Family and State Cults of the Sage of Culture in Imperial China," in *On Sacred Grounds,* ed. Thomas A. Wilson (Cambridge, MA: Harvard University Press, 2002), p. 43.

55. Isabel Wong, "Music and Religion in China, Korea, and Tibet," in *The Encyclopedia of Religion*, vol. 10, ed. Mircea Eliade (New York: Macmillan, 1987), pp. 195–202.

56. Confucius, p. 107.

57. Carmen Blacker, *The Catalpa Bow* (London: Allen & Unwin, 1975).

58. *The Kojiki,* trans. Basil Hall Chamberlain (Rutland, VT: Tuttle, 1981), p. 19.

59. *Nihongi,* trans. W. G. Aston (Rutland, VT: Tuttle, 1972), pp. 15–16.

60. *The Kojiki,* p. 65.

61. Floyd Hiatt Ross, *Shinto: The Way of Japan* (Boston: Beacon Press, 1965), p. 19.

62. Ibid., p. 122.

63. *Japanese Religion, A Survey by the Agency for Cultural Affairs* (Tokyo and Palo Alto: Kodansha, 1972), p. 108.

64. Ibid., p. 26.
65. D. C. Holthom, *The National Faith of Japan* (New York: Paragon, 1965), chap. 19.
66. John Breen and Mark Teeuwen, eds. *Shinto in History.* (Honolulu: University of Hawaii Press, 2000), p. 3.
67. *Japanese Religion*, pp. 174–190.
68. Robert Ellwood and Richard Pilgrim, *Japanese Religion in a Cultural Perspective* (Englewood Cliffs, NJ: Prentice Hall, 1985), p. 81.
69. Ibid., pp. 150–151.
70. H. Paul Varley, *Japanese Culture* (Honolulu: University of Hawaii Press, 1984), p. 297.
71. Denise Lardner Carmody, *Women and World Religion* (Englewood Cliffs, NJ: Prentice Hall, 1989), pp. 115–120.
72. Joanna Liddle and Sachico Nakajima, *Rising Suns, Rising Daughters* (London: Zed Books, 2000), p. 301.
73. Nancy Rosenberger, *Gambling with Virtue: Japanese Women and the Search for Self in a Changing Nation* (Honolulu: University of Hawaii Press, 2001), p. 157.
74. Karen Kelsky, *Women on the Verge: Japanese Women, Western Dreams* (Durham, NC: Duke University Press, 2001), p. 2.
75. Ellwood and Pilgrim, pp. 56–60.
76. Joseph M. Kitagawa, *On Understanding Japanese Religion* (Princeton, NJ: Princeton University Press, 1987), p. 154.

READINGS

China

Angle, Stephen C. *Human Rights in Chinese Thought.* Cambridge, UK: Cambridge University Press, 2002.

Bell, Daniel A., and Hahn Chaibong, eds. *The Contemporary Relevance of Confucianism.* Cambridge, U.K.: Cambridge University Press, 2003.

Bokenkamp, Stephen R. *Early Daoist Scriptures.* Berkeley: University of California Press, 1997.

Ching, Julia. *The Religious Thought of Chu Hsi.* Oxford, UK: Oxford University Press, 2000.

Clarke, J. J. *The Tao of the West: Western Transformation of Taoist Thought.* London: Routledge, 2000.

Confucius. *The Analects,* trans. D. C. Lau. New York: Penguin Books, 1979.

Daoism and Ecology, ed. N. J. Girardot, James Miller, and Liu Xiaogan. Center for the Study of World Religions, Harvard Divinity School. Cambridge, MA: Harvard University Press, 2001.

de Bary, Wm. Theodore, and Weiming, Tu, eds. *Confucianism and Human Rights.* New York: Columbia University Press, 1998.

Eskildsen, Stephen. *Asceticism in Early Taoist Religion.* Albany: State University of New York Press, 1998.

_____. *The Teachings and Practices of the Early Quanshen Taoist Masters.* Albany, NY: State University of New York Press, 2004.

Graham, A. C. *Disputers of the TAO.* La Salle, IL: Open Court, 1989.

Hymes, Robert. *Way and Byway: Taoism, Local Religion, and Models of Divinity in Sung and Modern China.* Berkeley: University of California Press, 2002.

Kirkland, Russell. *Taoism: The Enduring Tradition.* New York: Routledge, 2004.

Laozi. *Dao De Jing; The Book of the Way,* trans. Moss Roberts. Berkeley: University of California Press, 2001.

Mencius, trans. D. C. Lau. Baltimore: Penguin Books, 1970.

Schwartz, Benjamin I. *The World of Thought in Ancient China.* Cambridge, MA: Belknap Press of Harvard University Press, 1985.

Shun, Kwong-loi, and David B. Wong, eds. *Confucian Ethics.* Cambridge, UK, 2004.

Strickmann, Michel. *Chinese Magical Medicine,* ed. Bernard Fauré. Stanford. CA: Stanford University Press, 2002.

The Sage and the Second Sex: Confucianism, Ethics, and Gender, ed. Chenyang Li. Chicago: Open Court, 2000.

Thompson, Laurence G. *Chinese Religion.* Belmont, CA: Wadsworth, 1989.

Watson, Burton, trans. *Mozi: Basic Writings.* New York: Cambridge University Press, 2003.

Wilson, Thomas A., ed. *On Sacred Grounds.* Cambridge, MA: Harvard University Press, 2002.

Japan

Anasake, Masaharu. *History of Japanese Religion.* Rutland, VT: Tuttle, 1963.

Breen, John, and Mark Teeuwen, eds. *Shinto in History, Ways of the Kami.* Honolulu, HI: University of Hawaii Press, 2000.

Kelsky, Karen. *Women on the Verge: Japanese Women, Western Dreams.* Durham, NC: Duke University Press, 2001.

Liddle, Joanna, and Sachico Nakijima. *Rising Suns, Rising Daughters.* London: Zed Books, 2000.

Rosenberger, Nancy. *Gambling with Virtue: Japanese Women and the Search for Self in a Changing Nation.* Honolulu: University of Hawaii Press, 2001.

DEITIES AND PERSONAGES OF RELIGIONS OF CHINA AND JAPAN

CHINA			
Daoism	**Confucianism**	**Mohism**	**Fajia**
Laozi	Confucius	Mozi	Han Feizi
Zhuangzi	Mengzi		
Neo-Confucianism			
Zhuxi			
JAPAN			
Izanagi (male principle)		**Izanami (female principle)**	
Amaterasu (sun)	Susanoo (storms)	Tsukiyomi (moon)	
Ninigi			
Jimmu (first emperor)			

For peoples in other lands, ancient Iraq and Iran were symbols of advanced civilizations. Their cities, agricultural systems, religions, and laws fascinated all who visited them. To such a rich area, immigrants brought their own ideals and values, and from it traders and adventurers carried away a wealth of ideas and produce.

The heart of Iraq is the land between the Tigris and the Euphrates rivers. These rivers brought the water and the silt that made possible fertile agriculture.

sciences. The Babylonians were especially famous for mathematics and astronomy.

Until recently, peoples of the West often referred to peoples of Iran as Persians. The land to the east of Iraq is distinguished by regions of mountains and plateaus. Its climate ranges from the extreme heat on the Persian Gulf to the extreme cold near Azerbaijan. People who settled in different regions have distinctive backgrounds and cultures. Today, about half the people speak Farsi. About a fourth speak forms of

Salamis, Zoroastrianism might have had greater influence in the West.

In the first millennium C.E., important religious changes influenced peoples of Iraq and Iran. Jews of Babylon developed the Babylonian Talmud, the guidebook of rabbinic Judaism. Christians, especially the Nestorians, organized churches as they made converts ever farther east. In the seventh century, Islam expanded from Arabia, converting peoples of the Middle East and Central Asia. Seeking a more

Religions That Influenced East and West IV

Through use of irrigation, the land could support large populations concentrated in city-states. Wood was scarce, but clay was abundant and it distinguished the architecture of the country.

Through the centuries, Mesopotamia has been home for many different peoples. Because it lacked sharply defined borders, migrating peoples could arrive from all directions. Arabia and Egypt were sources of many immigrants. As city-states formed in Mesopotamia, their rulers organized hierarchies of deities that indigenous and immigrant peoples worshiped. These religions reflected the organization of city-states and inspired collections of literature, laws, and

Indo-European languages, a gift from the Aryans who came and went in the second millennium B.C.E.

In the first millennium B.C.E., the Assyrians expanded their empire to encroach on peoples of Iran. The Medes and the Persians of Iran asserted their influence toward Mesopotamia. Cyrus the Great, the Persian king, defeated the Medes in 550 and overthrew the Mesopotamian city-state of Babylon in 538. His influence on Judaism is recorded in the Bible. The successors of Cyrus the Great developed Zoroastrianism, a distinctive religion of the Persians. Had the Greeks not defeated the Persians in battles such as those at Marathon and

hospitable environment for their faith, many Zoroastrians moved into what is now Pakistan. Eventually, Zoroastrians formed large communities in India, where they are known as Parsees (from the Persian word for "persian").

Although their religions could have exerted greater influences on the West and on the East, Iraq and Iran have helped shape beliefs of peoples in both areas. In Zoroastrianism, Iran has contributed an ancient religion that continues to serve thousands of believers.

CHAPTER 7

Ancient Religions of Iraq and Iran

CHAPTER 7

Ancient Religions of Iraq and Iran

OVERVIEW AND THEMES

"Inanna took Dumuzi by the hand and said:
    'You will go to the underworld
    Half the year.
    Your sister, since she has asked, will go the other half.'"*

IMPORTANT TEACHINGS
    Dumuzi and Inanna, queen of heaven, married and
        increased the vital forces of nature.
    Inanna, visiting her sister in Hades, was not allowed to
        return to earth until she found a replacement. Dumuzi
        replaced her half of each year. When Inanna returned
        to earth, vegetation, which had died in her absence,
        recovered.

ZOROASTRIANISM

"I made answer to him: 'I am Zarathustra, first,
    A true enemy to the wicked with all my might
    But a powerful support for the righteous,
    So that I may attain the future blessings of the absolute
Dominion
    By praising and singing thee, O Wise One!'"

                                    —The Hymns of Zarathustra**

IMPORTANT TEACHINGS
    Ahura Mazda is represented by a sacred flame tended
        by priests.
    Angra Mainyu is an evil one who struggles against
        Ahura Mazda.
    Believers who choose to serve Ahura Mazda faithfully
        are rewarded in a final judgment.

AREAS OF CONCENTRATION
    Africa: 1,000
    Asia: 2,553,000
    Europe: 91,000
    North America: 83,000 (Of which 52,700 reside in the
        United States.)

*Diane Walkstein and Samuel Noah Kramer, *Inanna* (New York:
Harper and Row, 1983), p. 89.

**Jacques Duchesne-Guillemin, ed. *The Hymns of Zarathustra*, Trans,
Mara Henning (London: Murray, 1952), p. 135.

As we move westward from southern and eastern Asia, we encounter the fascinating cultures of south-central Asia. Today we refer to these lands as Iraq and Iran. In Mesopotamia, the land between the Tigris and Euphrates rivers, we learn of deities such as Dumuzi, Inanna, and Ishtar, the mother goddess of Babylonia. We meet Gilgamesh, the wandering king of Uruk, who met with Utnapishtim, the immortal who made an ark to preserve pairs of all animals from a great flood. In Iraq, we learn of Zarathustra, the Persian who, after he healed a favorite horse of Vishtaspa, his king, was released from prison to lead a new religion.

On the Mesopotamian plain and the Persian plateau, we discover persons and religious beliefs that Jewish exiles of the sixth century B.C.E. may have encountered. In Babylon, Jews probably learned about the law code of Hammurabi. They probably saw sacred hills made by humans, ziggurats, that were crowned by temples to Babylonian gods. As Persians defeated Babylonians and freed exiled peoples, Jews may have learned of the sacred flame of the Zoroastrians, probably honored by Cyrus, the monarch honored in the Bible.

Our journey through south-central Asia helps us make the transition from religions of India, China, and Japan to religions of the Middle East, Judaism, Christianity, and Islam. From your studies of religions in earlier chapters, some of the religious concepts and practices of ancient Iraq and Iran will be familiar. Other concepts will be new, or perhaps different; some of them will appear again in religions of Palestine and Arabia.

The Ishtar Gate, Babylon. Built in 575 B.C.E., it was the eighth fortified gate in the city. The Processional Way ran through it; brick lions decorated the sides of the street.

Mesopotamian Religion

Mesopotamia, the area along the banks of the Tigris and the Euphrates rivers in Iraq, was once the site of pyramid-like structures called **ziggurats.** The earth mounds, covered outside with baked bricks or with stones, were symbols of primal mountains; small temples crowned their summits. The impressive brickwork of Babylon can be seen in museums of Great Britain and Germany. In Iraq are ruins of city-states. The Mesopotamians developed sophisticated underground irrigation systems and designed cities that could accommodate thousands of people within fortress walls. With their advanced political structures, Mesopotamians developed integrated orders of gods and goddesses.

Historical Development: Mesopotamian Civilizations

Aside from the literature and carvings that have survived from ancient Mesopotamia, we receive most of its history through interpretations of outsiders. For example, the Hebrew Bible presents some history of Mesopotamia in the accounts of patriarchs in Genesis, in accounts of Babylon's overthrow of Egyptian rule in Palestine, and in accounts of the destruction of the Temple in Jerusalem. In the Hebrew prophets we have a view of Babylon through the eyes of Jews who were exiled there. The Persian defeat of Babylon is reflected in later books of the Bible. The Jewish scriptures stimulated interests of nineteenth- and twentieth-century orientalists, particularly British scholars. In the last half of the twentieth century, history by outsiders has been balanced by views of scholars within Iraq. In recent years, Muslim interests have overshadowed appreciation of earlier religions of the area.

Until the mid-nineteenth century, the glory of the ancient Mesopotamians was lost. Then archaeological work by Sir Austin Henry Layard and Sir Max (Edgar Lucian) Mallowan at Nineveh brought to light the thoughts of these ancient peoples. The discovery of the library of Ashurbanipal yielded thousands of cuneiform tablets for study. Cuneiform writing was done with a wedge-shaped stylus on clay tablets. On one set of tablets, George Smith of the British Museum recognized the story of Gilgamesh,[1] which included the Babylonian story of the flood.

In contrast to the predictable, recurring events of Egypt, events in Mesopotamia, a more accessible area, were unpredictable and often tragic. Floods could not be forecast as well as in Egypt. Borders were not clearly defined or easily defended. Mesopotamians sought a good life on earth, for little in their experience led them to expect permanent existence after death.

A long succession of different peoples fiercely contested rights to control the water, land, and cities of Mesopotamia. Around 4000 B.C.E., the Sumerians moved north from Arabia. Although the northern region, along the fertile plateau, receives some rain, the southern region could support agriculture only when the Sumerians built irrigation systems. From cuneiform records, historians can reconstruct a picture of their culture. An Akkadian-speaking group of Semites gained control by 2300 B.C.E., built cities, and consolidated in sequence, the Akkadian, the Assyrian, the Babylonian, and the Chaldean empires.

Babylon had many claims to greatness. Hammurabi (eighteenth century B.C.E.), its early builder, issued a famous code of laws, which were supposed to have come

ziggurats [ZIG-gu-rats] In Mesopotamia, pyramid-like structures used in worship. The brick- or stone-covered mounds were topped by a house that represented the court of the deity.

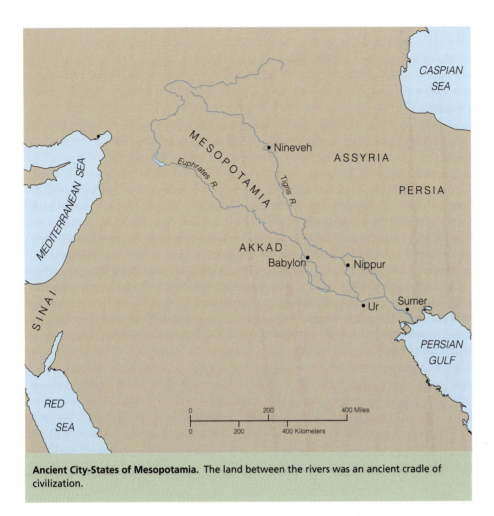

Ancient City-States of Mesopotamia. The land between the rivers was an ancient cradle of civilization.

from the sun god, Shamash.[2] In his code, Hammurabi invited oppressed people to come before him to receive justice according to the inscribed law. Centuries later, Nebuchadnezzar rebuilt the city and made it a home for, among others, exiles from Jerusalem. Many Jews considered it a good place, for they maintained a creative community there well into the fifth century of the Common Era. The famous Babylonian Talmud, the book that governed Jewish life in medieval times, was produced by Jewish scholars in Babylon.

The Semitic domination ended in 538 B.C.E when Cyrus, a Persian, seized power. The next-to-last ruler of ancient times was Alexander the Great, who defeated the Persians in 331 B.C.E. After the Romans defeated the Greeks, the new rulers controlled the territory well into the Common Era.

Myths of Mesopotamia

According to Babylonian myths, **Tiamat,** salt water, married Apsu, fresh water, and produced many divine descendants. Apsu, angry with their noisy play, tried to kill them. He was killed by Enki. The hero of the Enuma Elish myth of Babylon is **Marduk,** to whom all the gods delegated their authority. Tiamat went on a rampage of revenge until Marduk, the only god strong enough, subdued her. He split

Tiamat [TYU-mut]
The Babylonian goddess of chaos. She was defeated by the god Marduk, who created the world.

Marduk [MAHR-dook]
The Babylonian god of creation. To create the world, he defeated the goddess of chaos, Tiamat.

Tiamat in half, as if he were opening an oyster shell, the top forming heaven and the bottom earth. **Ea** helped him create humans from the blood of Kingsu, a husband of Tiamat. Marduk continued cosmic creation until he had completed the city of Babylon. The Enuma Elish creation myth was recited in the festival of the New Year as the king, priests, and people participated in the re-creation of the world.

An old story of the fertility god, **Dumuzi,** and **Inanna,** queen of heaven, became in later Babylonian accounts the story of **Tammuz** and **Ishtar.** The various versions of the story agree that Dumuzi and Inanna, after a passionate courtship, consummated marriage. Through their marriage the vital forces of nature increased. Inanna, desiring to visit her sister, Ereshkigal, the ruler of the underworld, descended into the underworld of Hades. In her descent, she had to pass through seven guarded gates. At each gate she had to remove a piece of clothing. She arrived completely naked before the royal powers, bowing to submit to their judgment. Held hostage and subjected to indignities, Inanna was not released and resurrected until her father, Enki, sent gifts. During her absence underground, all vegetation on earth died. Inanna was permitted to return to earth for a few months each year, provided she could find another hostage to take her place during her absence. Angry that Dumuzi had not rescued her, she had him sent underground as her replacement. Moved by the weeping of Dumuzi's mother and sister, Inanna took pity on him:

> Inanna and Geshtinanna went to the edges of the steppe.
> They found Dumuzi weeping.
> Inanna took Dumuzi by the hand and said:
> > "You will go to the underworld
> > Half the year.
> > Your sister, since she has asked,
> > Will go the other half.
> > On the day you are called,
> > That day you will be taken.
> > On that day Geshtinanna is called,
> > That day you will be set free."
> Inanna placed Dumuzi in the hands of the eternal.[3]

Annually, during the New Year festival, Babylonians recounted this explanation of the changing seasons.

The story of Inanna, however, affected the beliefs of Babylonians and Akkadians about the nature of the underworld. The land of Kigal, the subterranean realm, was entered where the sun sets. It could also be entered from the grave, for all graves led underground. The dead were ferried to the Great City of Ereshkigal. Ereshkigal's attendants included a plague god and seven judges called the Anunnaki. Demons spread pestilence and suffering among humanity, ensuring that there would always be new subjects for Ereshkigal.

Gilgamesh

Another story, the Epic of Gilgamesh, reveals a Mesopotamian concept of human destiny. **Gilgamesh,** king of Uruk, was opposed by a wild man of the wilderness, **Enkidu.** Enkidu, a wild, hairy, naked creature from the wilderness, challenged Gilgamesh, who dwelled in urban luxury. Gilgamesh was an urban leader whose warrior skills had deteriorated somewhat in city life. Gilgamesh

Ea [eah]
A water god. He was sometimes known as Enlil.

Dumuzi [DUM-u-zi]
(Tammuz) The Mesopotamian god of fertility, who gave life to vegetation and children to women.

Inanna [in-AHN-nu]
In Mesopotamia, the goddess who was wife of Dumuzi (Tammuz). She descended into the underworld to seek her husband's release.

Tammuz [TAM-muz]
The Babylonian version of Dumuzi, the Mesopotamian god of springtime. He was a god of fertility.

Ishtar [ISH-tar]
In Babylonia, a mother goddess who descended into the underworld. She was also known as Inanna.

Gilgamesh [GIL-gu-mesh]
A Mesopotamian king of Uruk about 2600 B.C.E. He searched for immortality, found the plant that was its source, and lost it to a serpent.

Enkidu [IN-ki-du]
In Mesopotamian tradition, a wild man befriended by Gilgamesh. He was killed by Enlil for slaying the monster Huwawa.

and Enkidu fought as enemies until they began to respect each other's strengths. They became good friends. Gilgamesh, realizing he needed a physical challenge, invited Enkidu to join him in an expedition to slay the monster Huwawa in his cedar forest to the west. Death separated the friends soon after Enkidu killed Huwawa, who was part of the security force of Enlil. Enlil killed Enkidu. Gilgamesh mourned his friend and, grieving over his loss, began a journey to find immortality.

An interlude in the story of the journey recounts the tale of **Utnapishtim.** Because he was a religious man, the gods warned him that Enlil was about to destroy the earth and its creatures in a great flood. Utnapishtim made an ark for his wife and a pair of all animals. They survived the flood, which wiped out all other living things. To make amends, Enlil conferred on Utnapishtim and his wife the gift of immortality.[4]

Utnapishtim, being unselfish, told Gilgamesh how to find the plant of immortality, which grew at the bottom of the sea. Gilgamesh reached the place and recovered the precious plant. While he was resting from his exertions, a serpent ate the plant. Thus the serpent, shedding his old skin, became immortal, and Gilgamesh returned to Uruk without a means of restoring his dead friend. The advice Ishtar gave Gilgamesh had merit:

> O Gilgamesh, whither wilt thou go?
> The life thou seekest thou shalt not find.
> When the gods created mankind,
> Death they prepared for man,
> But life they retained in their hands.
> Fill thou, O Gilgamesh, thy belly.
> Be merry day and night.
> Everyday prepare joyfulness.
> Day and night dance and make music.
> Let thy garments be made clean.
> Let thy head be washed, and be thou bathed in water.
> Give heed to the little one that takes hold of thy hand.
> Let a wife rejoice in thy bosom.
> For this is the mission of man.[5]

The Mesopotamian stories that have been recovered emphasize human joys of this life rather than existence after death.

By 2400 B.C.E., Gilgamesh was named among the gods.[6] The stories made him king of the underworld, identifying him with Dumuzi (Tammuz) or Nirgal. His statue was present at burial rites, in which his blessing was invoked. The point of the didactic Gilgamesh epic is that even the strongest humans are limited in what they can accomplish. Extending the good life of earth after death is beyond the capabilities of kings.

Worldview: Mesopotamia

The Absolute

The earliest Mesopotamians had symbolized the diversity of their universe in naming not one god, but many gods. Over thousands of years, the concepts of gods changed along with the fortunes of the peoples who worshiped them. One of

Utnapishtim
[OOT-nu-PISH-tim]
In Mesopotamia, a religious man whom the gods saved from the world flood and to whom they gave immortality. He informed Gilgamesh where he could find the plant of immortality.

the most systematic accounts of these changes is provided in the work of Thorkild Jacobsen.[7]

According to Jacobsen, the earliest gods of the agricultural peoples, in the fourth millennium, were names of forces of nature. The interaction of these forces was related in stories of courtship and marriage, such as that of Dumuzi, god of grain, and Inanna, goddess of the storehouse. In the third millennium, as Mesopotamian government changed, the gods were perceived as rulers, extending power not only over large city-states but also over the cosmos. In that period, the Mesopotamians developed concepts of individual divine figures. For example, An, god of the sky, was the force of authority and the power that gave being to all nature and gods. Enlil, an energy force of crop-growing weather, was god of the moist winds of springtime. Ninhursaga was the female deity manifest in the stony ground at the eastern and western boundaries of Mesopotamia. As giver of births, Ninhursaga governed wildlife and gave birth to kings. The cunning Enki, a rival of Ninhursaga, was the divine power of the sweet waters of rain, rivers, and marshes. There were other deities in the third millennium, but the triad of An, Enlil, and Ninhursaga, plus Enki, were the most important.

Gods of autonomous cities preceded those of the larger states. When the large city-states formed, these deities were sometimes combined into families. A political union of the city-states Sumer and Akkad brought about a unity of their gods. A triad of heavenly bodies appeared as Sin, the moon god; Shamash, the sun god; and Ishtar, the morning (and evening) star, Venus. The best-known and most-loved deity was Ishtar, goddess of fertility, whose popularity won her worship under other names in other cultures.

Jacobsen describes the second millennium as a time when the gods were given roles as parents. Personal gods served as objects of devotion in the religion of individuals. This was the period of the Enuma Elish myth of creation and the Gilgamesh epic. With the rise of Babylon, the deities of the earlier cities, such as Ur and Akkad, were combined in new stories that emphasized the superiority of Babylon.

Rituals and Symbols

Although the Mesopotamian religion did not satisfy the deep human longing for immortality, it did offer benefits in this life. The hierarchy of priests in state temples controlled large areas of land. Within the temple compounds, buildings and a ziggurat symbolized a meeting place for gods and humans. The room at the top of the ziggurat was the god's court. A wall with a door separated the courtroom from the god's private abode. Wood carvings in human form represented the gods. Priests provided food for the gods, who opened their eyes and mouths and took the nourishment offered to them. The priests taught that the deities were alive, so they were cared for as if they were living people. Worshipers praised and petitioned the gods, offering them libations and sacrificial animals in many temples.

Public festivals, involving the whole community, centered around dramas. In the drama of the sacred marriage, the ruler of Uruk became the god of the date palm, Amaushumgalana, and his wife became Inanna, goddess of the storehouse. Their marriage guaranteed powers that produced and stored dates. The battle drama was the account of Marduk versus Tiamat, and the journey drama told the story of Emerkur, the founder of Uruk, who journeyed to Eridu to reconfirm his office as lord and provider.

The god ruled the community from his palace atop the ziggurat. The deities communicated through signs in stars, dreams, or signs on the entrails of animals offered in sacrifice. Humans communicated with gods through gifts, greetings, libations, and formal prayers, to which could be added private petitions. In the family home, parents could become habitations of the gods.

The king represented the god, but the king was also subservient to the god. In one ritual that took place during the Babylonian New Year festival, the king took off his crown, scepter, ring, and ceremonial weapon so that they could be placed before Bel-Marduk. The priest struck the king's cheek and pulled his ears. Stripped of power, the king knelt before the god; there he recited:

> I have not sinned, lord of countries; I have not despised thy divinity;
> I have not destroyed Babel; I have not caused it to be scattered;
> I have not shaken Esagila; I have not forgotten its rituals;
> I have not smitten suppliants on the cheek;
> I have not humiliated them;
> I care for Babel: I have not broken down its walls.[8]

The priest then pronounced assurance of the god's blessing on the king. People were under the law of the king, and the king was under the law of the god. The king was responsible to the god for conduct in his kingdom.

Humans

The Mesopotamian concepts of deities changed over many centuries. Eventually Mesopotamians came to believe life on the land was made possible when salt waters were divided from fresh waters. The sun of heaven and warm, moist breezes activated the forces of fertility in animals, plants, and humans. The process of growth was followed inexorably by death and the decay of all things on earth. The forces of life disappeared as if swallowed up by the earth. In nature, life would return annually; in humans, the periods of renewal, after a span of years, would end. Rivkah Harris remarks that "although the view that human life is made up of a series of periodizations is common in many cultures, there was little reflection of this in ancient Iraq." No evidence of rituals, such as rites of passage, marking the transitions from one way to another has been found.[9]

Instead, one of the most enduring contributions of the Mesopotamians was the concept that human life must be lived justly under the laws of the gods. The Mesopotamians believed, as did the later Hebrews, that all humans, including the king, must answer for their conduct toward fellow humans.

Relationship to Other Religions

The Mesopotamian religion, unlike the Egyptian religion, did not retain its hold on human imagination. It lacked the promise of immortality offered in Egyptian religion. But in the ancient world it carried considerable influence with the Mesopotamians, with the peoples they conquered, and with the peoples who later conquered them: the Persians and the Greeks. Philosophers in other countries viewed Babylon as a center of learning and wisdom. Persians and Greeks were particularly attracted to Mesopotamian astronomy and astrology. The ancient Babylonian religion has passed away, but the civilization it shaped has influenced modern times.

The Tigris and Euphrates rivers were dominant features of Mesopotamia. In early days myths told about the struggle between fresh (river) water and salt (gulf) water. The river towns grew, and some became city-states with international influence. The important deities were Marduk and Tiamat, whose struggle created heaven and earth, and Dumuzi and Inanna, whose drama explained the annual change from winter to summer.

Gods were more than characters in stories or dramas. They lived, attended by priests who represented them to the king, on top of human-built mountains called *ziggurats*. The gods were believed to reside among the people they ruled, although the gods were on a higher plane, at least as high as the sacred hill. The idea of a sacred hill topped by a temple appealed to the Mesopotamians, as it did later to the Aztecs.

CONSIDER THIS
Sacred Hills

Iranian Religion

The religions of the peoples of Iran, or Persia, are probably reflected to an extent in the religions of India. The Aryans who arrived in India had lived for a time in Persia, the region of Iran. Aryan deities in the Vedas may reflect some of the beliefs and practices there, where people worshiped *Ahuras*, or lords, and *Devas*, shining ones of the heavens.

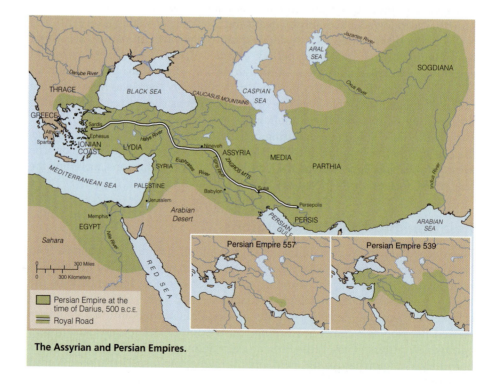

The Assyrian and Persian Empires.

Ancient Religions of Iraq and Iran in History

c. 2000 Abraham lived in the city-state of Ur	**c. 1700** Hammurabi establishs a law code for Babylon			
c. 628–551 Zarathustra lived in Iran	**586** Jews exiled from Jerusalem to Babylon	**550** Cyrus the Great defeats the Medes	**538** Cyrus the Great defeats the Babylonians	**522–486** Reign of Darius I of Persia
		331 Alexander the Great defeats the Persians		
200s Magi assert influence on Zoroastrianism in Persia	**200s** Manes, a Persian, teaches Manichean faith	**200s** Priest Kartir establishes Zoroastrianism as Persian religion	**224–651** Sasanians rule Persia	**300s** Christianity gains strength in areas of Persia
331 Parthians rule Persia	**431** Nestorian Christians flee to Mesopotamia-Persia	**480** Jewish scholars complete Babylonian Talmud	**632** Muhammed dies, successors launch expansion of Islam	

▲ 2000 ▲ 1500 ▲ 1000 ▲ 500 0   BCE

0 500 ▼ 1000 ▼ 1500 ▼ 2000 ▼   CE

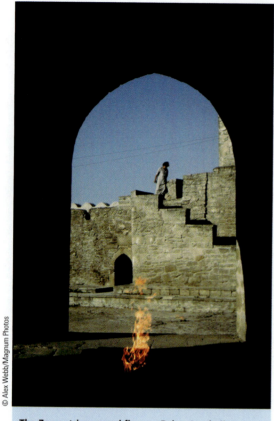

The Zoroastrian sacred flame—Baku, Azerbaijan.

Historical Development: Zoroastrianism

The best accounts of the history of Zoroastrian religion have emerged from Zoroastrians or from recent scholars sympathetic to that often-persecuted faith. Most Iranians today favor Shi'ite Islam, so they have little incentive to pursue studies of pre-Islamic beliefs and practices.

The Life of Zarathustra

Zarathustra, known in the West by his Latin name, Zoroaster, was born in the seventh century B.C.E, as early as 660 or as late as 628—scholars disagree. R. C. Zaehner dates the life of the prophet from 628 to 551 B.C.E. More recent scholarship dates him from the end of the second millennium B.C.E.[10] According to Sir Rustom Masani, whose opinions are generally respected by Zoroastrians, his home was ancient Iran.[11] Of the warrior clan Spitama, his father was Pourushaspa and his mother was Dughdhova, of a noble family. Zarathustra grew up in the religion that shared some deities and concepts with the Aryans, who produced the hymns of the Rig-Veda. At fifteen he received the sacred thread of initiation and lived an exemplary life, except that at age twenty he left his parents and the wife they had chosen for him. His religious upheaval began at age thirty.

Our legendary information on Zarathustra comes not from his hymns, the *Gathas,* preserved in the liturgy of the *Yasnas,* but from later sources. He had a vision, or revelation, of Good Thought, **Vohu Manah,** who appeared to him as a figure nine times human size. Leaving his body, Zarathustra responded to a command to come to the court of heaven. **Ahura Mazda,** Wise Lord, revealed the fact that immortality would be given to the followers of Zarathustra. Worshiped by the cattle owners and farm peoples, Ahura Mazda was opposed by **Angra Mainyu,** the spirit of evil, worshiped by rustlers. Zarathustra's first vision was followed by six others containing angels, messengers of Ahura Mazda. The struggle between Ahura Mazda and Angra Mainyu could be aided by humans deciding to live moral lives. At the end of time, each would be judged according to his or her deeds and rewarded in the pleasant courts of Ahura Mazda or the pits of Angra Mainyu.

The visions continued over a period of ten years, during which Zarathustra began to preach the message of the angels. Until he was about forty, he had only limited success. Then he converted King Vishtaspa. Although scholars think that the king was a historical figure, they differ on whether he was the father of Cyrus the Great, ca. 585–529 B.C.E. Converting King Vishtaspa was not easy, for the monarch was surrounded by wicked ministers who had Zarathustra thrown into prison. When he healed the favorite horse of King Vishtaspa, he was released. Zarathustra won his convert. The king brought his household into the new religion, and his subjects soon embraced it.

Vohu Manah
[VOH-hoo-MAH-nu]
In Zoroastrianism, Good Thought, one of the Amesha Spentas.

Ahura Mazda
[u-HOOR-u MAZ-du]
The Zoroastrian god of light; the Wise Lord who is the highest deity.

Angra Mainyu
[ANG-gra MIN-yu]
In Zoroastrianism, the evil spirit who opposes Ahura Mazda.

Zarathustra continued to teach and serve at the altar of the fire temple until he was seventy-seven. The kingdom was at war twice with Turanians; Zarathustra died in the second war, either serving at the altar or defending it from its enemies.

Teachings of Zarathustra

The scriptures of Zoroastrianism were written over several centuries. The Avesta, or book of the law, has the Gathas, or hymns, of Zarathustra in its oldest part, the Yasna. In addition are the Visperad, used to honor the ahuras, or lords; the Yashts, or hymns of praise; and the Vindevdat, or rituals against demons. The Avesta available to scholars is only the Videvdat, the one surviving book of what were originally twenty-one books.

In the Gathas of the Avesta, Zarathustra declares that he has been dedicated to a divine mission of reform. In Yasna 43:7–8, he says,

> (7) As the holy one I recognized thee, O Wise Lord,
> When he came to me as Good Mind and asked me:
> "Who art thou, whose art thou? Shall I appoint by a sign
> The days when inquiry shall be made about thy living possessions and thyself?"

> (8) I made answer to him: "I am Zarathustra, first,
> A true enemy to the wicked with all my might,
> But a powerful support for the righteous,
> So that I may attain the future blessings of the absolute Dominion
> By praising and singing thee, O Wise One!"[12]

A firm monotheist (one who worships only one god), Zarathustra taught his converts to worship only Ahura Mazda. He is served by six **Amesha Spentas,** who are Vohu Manah, Asha Vahista, Khshatra Vairya, Spenta Armaiti, Hourvatat, and Ameretat. These messengers bridge the gap between the holiness of God and human beings. Amesha Spentas are moral beings who set examples for human morality. They fight against Angra Mainyu and his daevas, or evil forces. R. C. Zaehner refers to them as "aspects of god, but aspects in which man too can share."[13]

Humans have a choice between the way of the lie associated with Angra Mainyu and the way of good activity exemplified by the Amesha Spentas. What was the source of Angra Mainyu? For Masani, the evil one was not created by Ahura Mazda nor did he fall from grace. He was present from the beginning. This explanation does not satisfy Cyrus Pangborn that Zarathustra believed in monotheism rather than a dualism.[14] He thinks Zoroastrian priests and scholars are not interested in settling a very real dispute for objective students of Zoroastrianism.[15]

At death, every person is judged according to his or her morality and commitment and is assigned either to Angra Mainyu or to Ahura Mazda. The soul of the person must cross the **Chinvat Bridge,** which is an instrument of judgment. The followers of good are rewarded with life in paradise, and the followers of evil are rewarded with a life of punishment.

Zoroastrianism after Zarathustra

Later Persian monarchs who embraced Zoroastrianism assisted its international influence.[16] Cyrus, who ruled from 558 to 530 B.C.E and was hailed by the Jewish prophet Isaiah as the Lord's anointed one, may have been a Zoroastrian. Darius, who claimed to be king by will of Ahura Mazda, and Xerxes were strong supporters of the kind of justice advocated by Zoroastrianism.[17] Some Biblical scholars think that belief in angels, heaven and hell, and the resurrection of the dead

© Charles & Josette Lenars/Corbis

Ahura Mazda. This relief sculpture stands on the Apadana at the ruins of Persepolis, residence of Persian kings beginning with Darius.

Amesha Spentas
[u-MEE-shu SPIN-tas]
In Zoroastrianism, the higher spirits directly under Ahura Mazda. They are modes of divine being that bear names of ethical virtues, such as "Good Thought."

Chinvat Bridge
[CHIN-vaht]
In Zoroastrianism, the bridge of judgment that a soul must walk over after death.

came to Judaism from Persian influence. A particular priestly group, the **Magi,** came to identify themselves with Zoroastrianism. They are known through their role in the Gospel of Matthew at the birth of the Christ.

The Magi made a very important contribution to the historical development of Zoroastrianism. Through their efforts, the faith was extended throughout the world that was under the influence of Iranian thought. They permitted older Zoroastrianism to be mixed with both Iranian and foreign religious concepts and practices. They emphasized dualism both in cosmic principles and in the conflicts of each human life. The Sassanians, who ruled Persia from the third to the seventh century C.E., were Zoroastrians who changed the faith to incorporate more of the elements rejected by Zarathustra and the Persian kings of the Achaemenid dynasty that began with Cyrus. Their essential refoundation of Zoroastrianism consisted of a revival of the concept of royalty that well served the monarch, the warrior aristocracy, and the priesthood. An Iranian nationalism was supported in a reorganization and canonization of tradition.[18]

Zarathustra's monotheism was replaced with dualism, a fight between two equally powerful forces. Manichaeism developed from the teachings of **Mani** in the third century C.E. Mani's dualism was between flesh, which was evil, and spirit, which was good. He advocated denying flesh in order to free the spirits imprisoned in it. Manichaean dualism left a deep mark on the Roman Catholic saint Aurelius Augustine, who became bishop of Hippo at the end of the fourth century. Zurvanism attempted to overcome the dualism in Zoroastrianism. The theory was that **Zurvan** was boundless time or space transcending both Ahura Mazda and Angra Mainyu.[19] Zurvanism was rejected later by orthodox Zoroastrians.

Later Zoroastrianism added more deities. Zoroastrians regarded Zarathustra as a god who became a man. Evil forces struggled with the good forces to control the infant Zarathustra. The heavens and hells were filled with good and evil beings struggling over his supernatural deeds. A mother deity, **Anahita,** was added to receive fertility rites. **Haoma,** the recipient of animal sacrifices, and **Mithra,** the god of light, became part of ongoing Zoroastrianism. The final judgment was described in great detail, and a kind of universal salvation replaced the sharp eternal division of good and evil.

At first, Muslims did not grant Zoroastrians the status reserved for Jews and Christians—people of the Book. Shortly after the death of Muhammad, Zoroastrians were extended protected status and allowed free practice of their religion.

According to Mary Boyce, events in the late twentieth century led Zoroastrians to Tehran and abroad. Now they are city dwellers, secular, and more open to outside influences.[20] Either for trade or for religious freedom, Zoroastrians migrated to Gujarat in India. Most are now concentrated in Mumbai (Bombay), where they are a small minority among the other religions of India.

Worldview: Zoroastrianism

The Absolute

The deity worshiped by Zoroastrians is Ahura Mazda. The evil force that opposes God is Angra Mainyu. Whether these two forces are of equal strength is a question that has provided considerable variation in the concept of God throughout the history of Zoroastrianism. If God is ultimately the most powerful, then Angra Mainyu is not an equal force. However, if Angra Mainyu is of

---

Magi [MAY-jii]
Among the ancient Persians, priests. Their doctrine reduced Ahura Mazda from a transcendent principle to a good spirit, opposed by an evil spirit.

Mani [MAH-nee]
A Persian teacher of religious dualism; he considered himself the Holy Spirit.

Zurvan [ZUR-van]
Among a minority of Zoroastrians, boundless time. It embraces both Ahura Mazda and Angra Mainyu.

Anahita [anna-HEE-tu]
In later Zoroastrianism, a mother goddess who was worshiped with fertility rites.

Haoma [HOE-mu]
In late Zoroastrianism, the divinity of the sacred elixir prepared during Zoroastrian ritual.

Mithra [MITH-ra]
The god of light in Zoroastrianism.

equal strength and the struggle is undetermined, then it seems that Zoroastrianism has two gods.

The World

Yasna 44 includes Zarathustra's question-assertions about the creation of the universe:

> 3. This I ask thee, O Lord, answer me truly:
> Who was the first father of Righteousness at the birth?
> Who appointed their path to sun and stars?
> Who but thou is it through whom the moon waxes and wanes?
> This I would know, O Wise One, and other things too!
>
> 4. This I ask thee, O Lord, answer me truly:
> Who set the Earth in its place below, and the sky of the clouds, that it shall not fall?
> Who the waters and the plants?
> Who yoked the two steeds to wind and clouds?
> Who, O Wise One, is the creator of the Good Mind?
>
> 5. This I ask thee, O Lord, answer me truly:
> What artificer made light and darkness?
> What artificer sleep and waking?
> Who made morning, noon, and night,
> To remind the wise man of his task?
>
> 6. This I ask thee, O Lord, answer me truly:
> Whether things are such as I would make them known?
> Shall Devotion by her deeds support the Right?
> Is it as Good Mind that thou hast founded thy Dominion?
> For what men has thou fashioned the mother-cow, the source of good fortune?
>
> 7. This I ask thee, O Lord, answer me truly:
> Who created Devotion, sacred with the Dominion?
> Who made the son reverential in his soul towards his father:
> Thus I strive to recognize in thee, O Wise One,
> As Holy Spirit, the creator of all things.[21]

The world is clean and good. Zoroastrians will not permit a human corpse to contaminate earth, air, fire, or water. Ahura Mazda creates all things for the pleasure of humans. Unlike Mani, Zarathustra did not despise the body or its functions. He advocated responsible use of the world and its creatures, particularly cattle.

Humans

Humans are both soul and body. Personality involved the body as well as the mind. The body should remain under the control of the mind, which makes moral choices. Humans have choices in their actions; they are responsible to God for making moral decisions. Their choices can affect the outcome of the struggle between good and evil. The doctrine of the resurrection of the body emphasizes the importance of the body in personal identity. A living body can be clean and good; when governed by temperance, it is a means for doing good deeds, which are more pleasing to God than sacrifice.

The status of women in Zoroastrianism has been slow to improve. In the time of Zarathustra, women served men and gave religious instruction in the home. In the fire temples, men are the center of attention. However, because of Western influence in education, women may now become scholars and educators. Defending themselves, Zoroastrian men point out that childbearing is a religious service open only to women; it helps defeat the evil one.[22]

The Problem for Humans

Humans are alienated from God when they choose to violate his law and follow the behavior of Angra Mainyu. There is no karma to build up and hold a soul to a body. Creation of the world and the fall of human beings are not identical. Humans are created by Ahura Mazda to abide by his laws. They can rebel against those laws and serve Angra Mainyu. In this life and in the world to come, there are penalties for those who persist in rebellion against Ahura Mazda.

Mary Boyce describes the problem for humans this way:

> The present struggle is a hard one, with each man's wise choice and actions being needed to sway it; but the issue to Zoroaster's mind was plainly not in doubt. Angra Mainyu and his legions are formidable and inflict harm generally, for even the man who is good by choice cannot escape cruelty and suffering at the hands of others, or afflictions such as famine, disease, bereavement and death. Yet in the end, the prophet was convinced, this dreadful power would be broken, defeated by the unity and positive force of the world of good. Zoroaster's radical dualism, of two separate principles from the beginning, thus ends with the destruction of the evil one, so that Ahura Mazda will finally reign supreme, his sway at last undisputed.[23]

Peter Clark writes, "Zoroastrian eschatology [doctrine of "last things"] posits the fullness of creation, which will be realized at the *frashokeriti* [event that urges creation into renewal] will be on the physical planes. This is certainly a vision original to the Iranian prophet himself and one which is maintained in the Pahlavi writings." Ahura Mazda cannot descend to the physical realm (where evil can be defeated), so he relies on his attributes personified in the Amesha Spentas. Men and women may choose to be agents to defeat or obey the influence of Ahura Mazda.[24]

The Solution for Humans

Reconciliation is effected through the worship of Ahura Mazda and keeping his commandments. Humans choose constantly between the way of good and the way of evil. Choosing good actions brings reconciliation with Ahura Mazda. Throughout life a person must continue to struggle, for final reconciliation is achieved only after a judgment that the individual is worthy of a place in paradise. According to Masani, the Zoroastrian code of ethics requires that humans cultivate civic virtues, **asha,** or spiritual truth, justice, chastity, self-help, planting corn, caring for cattle, compassion for the weak, charity for the poor, promotion of education, and good deeds.

asha [ASH-u]
In Zoroastrianism, spiritual truth. Some scholars equate Asha with the Hindu Rita.

> "Be Like God!" These are the three words in which the entire philosophy of life may be summed up. Likeness to God is the only way of communion with the Heavenly Father. There is no other path of Heaven.[25]

Rituals and Symbols

Hereditary priests are responsible for tending the holy fire in the temple and preparing the haoma every day. Today, Zoroastrians offer daily sacrifices of bread, milk, and sandalwood. New Year's day is a particularly important day for sacrifices. Dressed in their finest clothes, Zoroastrians bring to the fire temple their offerings for the fire, which is not an object of worship but the symbol of Ahura Mazda. During the sacrifice, the priest reads or recites from the Avesta. The priest, his face covered with a mask like a surgeon's, receives the offerings and places them on the fire. Small spoons of ashes are gathered and offered to the worshipers to rub on their foreheads. The priest offers a benediction, and the worshiper is free to depart.

Zoroastrians have a system of rituals for adherents at important points of passage. Adherents enter the religion by birth. Because Zoroastrians emphasize a strong family, they welcome children. After delivering a child, the mother must refrain from touching fire or water and from contacting the materials used in worship. In the seventh year, children participate in **Naozot,** in which they are vested with a sacred shirt called a **sudreh,** and a sacred thread, or **kusti.** From that time on, the child is expected to offer prayers and fulfill other obligations of the religion. Asceticism is not advocated by Zoroastrians; the normal lifestyle for adults is marriage and family. Faithfulness in marriage is expected by both men and women.

In Iran, lay Parsees attend seven obligatory festivals or feasts. These *gahambars* are listed in the Saddar Bundahes and the creation each celebrates. The first gahambar is celebrated to give health and strength to body and mind. Endowments are given for the donor's soul or for relatives' souls. The seventh feast of obligation

© Jehangir Gazdar Woodfin Camp & Associates

The Naozot Ceremony. The number of holy participants emphasizes the importance of this Zoroastrian initiation.

Naozot [NAY-ow-zot]
Zoroastrian vesting of a child with a sacred shirt.

sudreh [SHOOD-reh]
The sacred shirt used in vesting a Zoroastrian child.

kusti [KOOS-ti]
A sacred thread worn to indicate initiation into a religion. Hindus and Zoroastrians use the symbol.

Parsee Haoma Ritual, India. Only the highest priests can perform this sacramental ritual with the sacred elixir.

is the *No Roz,* a most important ritual cleansing. The Festival of the New Day is for living people—giving of presents and gifts to the poor.[26]

To outsiders first encountering the study of Zoroastrianism, customs surrounding earth compel intense interest. Upon a person's death, the body is washed and placed on hard material, such as stone. The area is marked by a circle drawn with an iron bar or nail, segregating the corpse from the living. A dog with a black spot above each eye is brought to examine whether life in the body is extinct. A vase of fire burns fragrant wood as sacred texts of the Avesta are recited. During daylight hours, two or four corpse-bearers take the iron bier bearing the body to the Tower of Silence (**dakhma**). To avoid contaminating the soil, fire, air, or water with a corpse, Zoroastrians construct permanent circular towers about twenty feet high. Entering a door with the corpse, the bearers place it in one of three areas, according to whether it is a man, woman, or child. The bearers open the clothes of the corpse and leave. Within a few hours, vultures descend and strip the bones clean. When the bones are clean and dry, they are placed in a central pit of the tower where they crumble into harmless residue. Back at the home, priests pray to Sraosha, the guardian of souls after death. On the third afternoon, there is an Uthamna ceremony in which charity contributions are announced in memory of the deceased. On the dawn after the third night, the soul is prepared to cross the Chinvat Bridge.[27]

dakhma [DAHK-ma]
A Zoroastrian Tower of Silence used for disposal of corpses of the faithful. It is believed to be necessary because a corpse cannot be allowed to contaminate either soil or fire.

Life after Death

Zoroastrians believe humans are born and die only one time. There is no concept of reincarnation. On the fourth day after death, humans must cross the Chinvat

Bridge, the bridge of judgment. For the souls of good thought, the bridge is an easy path to heaven. To souls of evil thought, it is as narrow as the edge of a knife, causing them to fall to perdition. Souls can continue to make progress after death; those who make enough progress will participate in life on a renewed earth. "There is no end to life; there are different stages in existence," says Farhang Mehr. "The goal is *Ushta* (happiness) and *Vahishta Ahu* (the best existence)."[28] At the last judgment all forces of evil will be defeated, and souls cleansed by punishment will dwell together in a transformed world.

Relationship to Other Religions

J. Hinnells has described the persecution that Zoroastrians have experienced in their long history. They eagerly embraced English education in India and welcomed Christians who studied their religion and culture. In some cases, their tolerance for others has been limited. In particular, they have been severe with heretics and have opposed any conver-

A Zoroastrian Dakhma. This Tower of Silence is atop a hill in Yard, Iran. According to Zoroastrians, this method of disposal of bodies preserves purity of fire and soil.

sions to their religion. In March 1983, an American, Joseph Peterson, was initiated at the Zoroastrian center in New York. The action was widely opposed in Zoroastrian circles, particularly in Bombay. General Zoroastrian sentiment is against any conversion of others to their religion. Hennels wrote,

> But, if there is one common theme in Zoroastrian attitudes to religious pluralism, it is perhaps a general tolerance to outsiders (though not to others within the walls considered heretics). Throughout recorded history Zoroastrians have balanced a pride in their own religion with an acceptance of religious differences between races.[29]

In modern times, Zoroastrians from both India and Iran have had meetings in Tehran and Bombay. The interest in each other has provided some support and stimulation of faith. However, because Parsees participate in a hereditary tradition and seek no converts, political and sociological adversities have led to dwindling numbers of adherents. The faith that once was so vigorous at the eastern end of the Mediterranean Sea has made its contribution to the Western religions of Judaism, Christianity, and Islam.

Our discussion of the ancient religions of Iraq and Iran has brought us to a discussion of Western religions, those from the Middle East. Although they are distinctive, the ancient religions of Iraq and Iran share some beliefs with religions of India and of the Middle East. Having studied the various religions of India and of China and Japan, we turn to three great religions of the West: Judaism, Christianity, and Islam. These three religions belong to one family, whose father, Abraham, descended from an inhabitant of Ur, in Mesopotamia.

When Ahura Mazda called Zarathustra to worship him, Zarathustra required his followers to reject the ways of thieves and liars. A cosmic struggle was in progress between Ahura Mazda and Angra Mainyu. Amesha Spentas, the intermediaries between humans and Ahura Mazda, were available to help those who chose to serve the Wise Lord against evil. After death, each soul would be judged on the basis of how well it had favored good over evil.

Abraham, from Ur of the Chaldeans (Mesopotamia), is often considered the father of three great world faiths: Judaism, Christianity, and Islam. Some scholars think that Zoroaster's religion influenced concepts of God, angels, Satan, and final judgment in other religions of the Middle East. As you read chapters on Judaism, Christianity, and Islam, consider arguments for and against Zoroastrian influence.

CONSIDER THIS

Humans Are the Battleground between Good and Evil

VOCABULARY

Ahura Mazda [u-HOOR-u MAZ-du]
Amesha Spentas
[u-MEE-shu SPIN-tas]
Anahita [anna-HEE-tu]
Angra Mainyu [ANG-gra MIN-yu]
asha [ASH-u]
Chinvat Bridge [CHIN-vaht]
dakhma [DAHK-ma]
Dumuzi [Du-mu-zi]
Ea [eah]

Enkidu [IN-ki-du]
Gilgamesh [GIL-gu-mesh]
Haoma [HOE-mu]
Inanna [in-AHN-nu]
Ishtar [ISH-tar]
kusti [KOOS-ti]
Magi [MAY-jii]
Mani [MAH-nee]
Marduk [MAHR-dook]
Mithra [MITH-ra]

Naozot [NAY-ow-zot]
sudreh [SHOOD-reh]
Tammuz [TAM-muz]
Tiamat [TYU-mut]
Utnapishtim [OOT-nu-PISH-tim]
Vohu Manah [VOH-hoo-MAH-nu]
ziggurats [ZIG-gu-rats]
Zurvan [ZUR-van]

QUESTIONS FOR REVIEW

1. What stories surround Dumuzi and Inanna?
2. Who was the Babylonian mother goddess, the morning (and evening) "star," known to us as the planet Venus? Who were the other stars of the triad?
3. What was the role of Shamash in Babylon?
4. Describe the myth recited at New Year festivals in Babylon.
5. Tell the Mesopotamian story of the great flood and of immortality given and lost.
6. What common background may have been shared by Zarathustra and Aryans of India?
7. Describe the consequences of Zarathustra's vision of a figure nine times human size.
8. In Zoroastrianism, what are the relationships among Ahura Mazda, Angra Mainyu, and the Amesha Spentas?
9. How is the Chinvat Bridge related to human choice?
10. Who were the Magi? Why are they widely known?

QUESTIONS FOR DISCUSSION

1. How were the ancient gods and goddesses of Mesopotamia related to its city-states?
2. In what ways are Zoroastrian funeral practices unusual?
3. How was the religion of Zoroaster related to royalty in Persia?
4. If one believes in an all-powerful, all-good god, what problem arises if one also believes in a second being who is very powerful and evil?
5. Historically, how have Zoroastrians related to other religions?

NOTES

1. S. H. Hooke, *Babylonian and Assyrian Religion* (Norman: University of Oklahoma Press, 1963), p. xi.
2. James B. Pritchard, *Archaeology and the Old Testament* (Princeton, NJ: Princeton University Press, 1958), chap. 6.
3. Diane Wolkstein and Samuel Noah Kramer, *Inanna* (New York: Harper & Row, 1983), p. 89.
4. Alexander Heidel, *The Gilgamesh Epic and Old Testament Parallels* (Chicago: University of Chicago Press, 1949), chap. 4.
5. Jack Finegan, *Light from the Ancient Past* (Princeton, NJ: Princeton University Press, 1946), p. 28.
6. William L. Moran, "Gilgamesh," in *The Encyclopedia of Religion,* vol. 5, ed. Mircea Eliade (New York: Macmillan, 1987), pp. 557–560.
7. Thorkild Jacobsen, *The Treasures of Darkness* (New Haven, CT: Yale University Press, 1976).
8. Hooke, p. 110.
9. Rivkah Harris, *Gender and Aging in Mesopotamia* (Norman: University of Oklahoma Press, 2000), p. ix.
10. R. C. Zaehner, *The Dawn and Twilight of Zoroastrianism* (New York: Putnam, 1961), p. 33.
11. Sir Rustom Masani, *The Religion of the Good Life* (London: Allen & Unwin, 1954), p. 25; Cyrus R. Pangborn, *Zoroastrianism: A Beleaguered Faith* (New Delhi: Vikas, 1982).
12. Jacques Duchesne-Guillemin, ed., *The Hymns of Zarathustra,* trans. Mara Henning (London: Murray, 1952), p. 135.
13. Zaehner, *Dawn,* p. 46.
14. Cyrus R. Pangborn, *Zoroastrianism, A Beleaguered Faith* (New Delhi: Vikas, 1982), p. 38.
15. Ibid., p. 48.
16. Jacques Duchesne-Guillemin, Introduction, in *Symbols and Values in Zoroastrianism* (New York: Harper & Row, 1970).
17. Zaehner, *Dawn,* p. 155.
18. Gherardo Gnoli, "Zoroastrianism," in *Religions of Antiquity,* ed. Robert M. Seltzer, trans. U. F. Lubin (New York: Macmillan, 1989), p. 143.
19. R. C. Zaehner, *Zurvan* (New York: Biblo and Tannen, 1972), chap. 3.
20. Mary Boyce, *Zoroastrianism: Its Antiquity and Constant Vigor* (Costa Mesa, CA: Mazda Publishers in association with Bibliotheca Persica, 1992), p. 184.
21. Duchesne-Guillemin, *Hymns,* pp. 65–66.
22. Peter Clark, *Zoroastrianism: An Introduction to an Ancient Faith* (Portland, OR: Sussex Academic Press, 1998), pp. 145, 148.
23. Mary Boyce, *A History of Zoroastrianism,* vol. 1 (Leiden and New York: Brill, 1989), p. 233.
24. Clark, *Zoroastrianism,* p. 77.
25. Masani, chap. 13, p. 89.
26. Boyce, *Zoroastrianism,* pp. 179–180.
27. Masani, pp. 99–105.
28. Farhang Mehr, *The Zoroastrian Tradition* (Costa Mesa, CA: Mazda Publishers, 2003), p. 148.
29. J. Hennels, "Parsi Attitudes to Religious Pluralism," in *Modern Indian Responses to Religious Pluralism,* ed. Harold G. Coward (Albany: State University of New York Press, 1987), pp. 195–233, 224–225.

READINGS

Mesopotamian Religions

Gilgamesh: Translated from the Sin-leqi-unninni Version. Trans. John Gardner and John Maier, with Richard A. Henshaw. New York: Knopf, 1984.

Harris, Rivkah. *Gender and Aging in Mesopotamia.* Norman: University of Oklahoma Press, 2000.

McCall, Henrietta. *Mesopotamian Myths.* London: Published for the Trustees of the British Museum by British Museum Publications, 1990.

Myths from Mesopotamia: Creation, the Flood, Gilgamesh, and Others, trans., with introduction and notes by Stephanie Dalley. New York: Oxford University Press, 1989.

Zoroastrianism

Boyce, Mary. *A History of Zoroastrianism.* 2 vols. New York: Brill, 1989.

———. *Zoroastrianism: Its Antiquity and Constant Vigor.* Costa Mesa, CA: Mazda Publishers in Association with Bibliotheca Persica, 1992.

Clark, Peter. *Zoroastrianism: An Introduction to an Ancient Faith.* Portland, OR: Sussex Academic Press, 1998.

Mehr, Farhang. *The Zoroastrian Tradition.* Costa Mesa, CA: Mazda Publishers, 2003.

BASIC TENETS OF ANCIENT RELIGIONS OF IRAQ AND IRAN—
Significant Beings

IRAQ		
Ancient Religion of Babylon		
Erishkegal		Gilgamesh
Tiamat-Marduk		
Inanna		Dumuzi
IRAN		
Zoroastrianism		
Angra Mainyu (evil spirit)	Amesha Spentas Vohu Manu (good thought) Asha Vahista Khshatra Vairya Spenta Armaiti Hourvatat Ameretat	Ahura Mazda (god of light)

About the beginning of the second millennium B.C.E., in ancient Mesopotamia, land of the Tigris and Euphrates rivers, Terah, father of Abraham, set out for Haran, a city on the way to Canaan. At the age of seventy-five, Abraham responded to God's revelation that he should journey to Canaan and there become a great nation, a blessing to all peoples of the earth.

Abraham's two sons, Ishmael through Sarah's servant Hagar, and Isaac through Sarah, became patriarchs of nations. God blessed

That singleness of faith among descendants of Ishmael and Isaac emerged only after centuries of struggle with polytheism. Contrasted with other families of faith in this text, the family of Abraham was the earliest to emphasize that there is only one God who has no equals, partners, or rivals.

Missionary outreach was present in the faith of Abraham from its earliest days. Members of this family of faith believed that God wanted them to bring other peoples to worship him and

Religions of the Family of Abraham

V

Ishmael as ancestor of the peoples of Arabia; God blessed Isaac as ancestor of the people of Israel. Through centuries of inspired leaders, the ancient faith of Israel developed into Judaism, and after the appearance of the Prophet Muhammad in Mecca in the sixth century C.E., Islam developed in Arabia. Beginning with a descendant of Israel, Jesus, and evolving through the efforts of Paul, Christianity emphasized that the faith of Abraham was a model for Christians to follow.

follow his teachings. To this day Christianity and Islam fervently seek converts; Judaism has been more subdued in its invitations but equally genuine in its welcomes. All three religions openly advocate, however, that all humans should live by the teachings of God, which are intended for all peoples of the world.

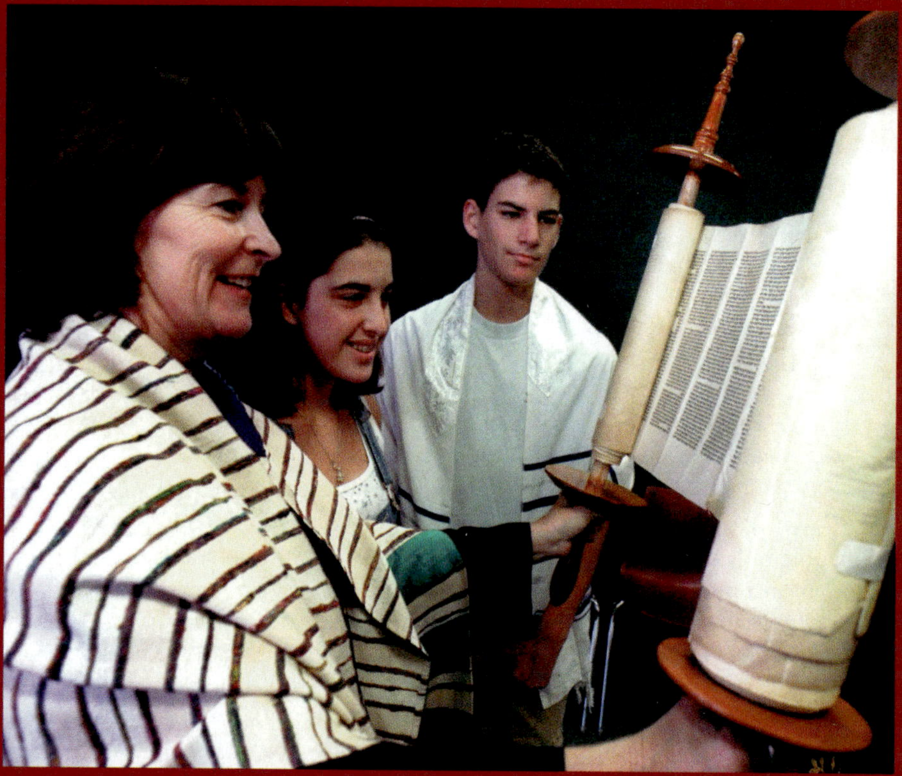
AP Photo/Arizona Daily Star/Benjie Sanders

CHAPTER 8

Judaism

OVERVIEW AND THEMES
"Hear O Israel! The Lord is our God, the Lord alone. You shall love the lord your God with all your heart and with all your soul and with all your might."

—Deuteronomy 6:4, 5*

IMPORTANT JEWISH TEACHINGS
The Torah is the word of God revealed to Moses who wrote it.

The Talmud is the accepted opinion of rabbis applying Torah to daily life.

Jews are the covenant people of God who have accepted his offer of that relationship.

AREAS OF JEWISH CONCENTRATION
Worldwide: 14,551,000
United States: 5,621,000
Africa: 220,000
Asia: 4,465,000
Europe: 2,427,000
Latin America: 1,152,000

DIVISIONS OF OBSERVANCE
Orthodox, the largest group
Conservative, the next largest group
Reform, the smallest group

*The Tanakh, The New JPS Translation according to the Hebrew Text, (Philadelphia: Jewish Publication Society, 1985); copyright 1985 by the Jewish Publication Society.

Before the Rig-Veda was written, the Buddha received enlightenment, Mahavira taught *ahimsa*, or Confucius revised and edited the Chinese classics, Judaism arose when God appeared to its ancestors, challenging them to follow his commands. Although the written story of Judaism as we know it appeared some centuries later, the first ancestors received God's revelations in Mesopotamia about 1800 B.C.E.

Judaism sparkles with personalities who have dazzled generations of peoples in Europe and the Americas. Abraham, the father of faith, raised sons Ishmael, who became father of the Arab peoples, and Isaac, who became the father of Israel. Joseph, son of Israel, sold as a slave, became second only to the pharaoh of Egypt, saving a whole region from starvation through his shrewd agricultural policies. After a period of decline and suffering of Hebrews in Egypt, Moses, under God's direction, led his people from slavery to the threshold of abundant life in God's promised land to Israel, later known as Palestine. Joshua used strategy, tactics, and God's strength to overpower many walled cities of the Canaanites, such as Jericho. David, the king, established Jerusalem as his center and incorporated the mighty Philistines into a peaceful coalition. His son, Solomon, negotiated with foreign leaders who brought religious, economic, and diplomatic forces to an apex unequaled before or since in Judaism. Great prophets such as Isaiah, Jeremiah, and Ezekiel inspired not only return to God's covenant in Torah, but also fresh visions of individual freedoms and responsibilities for the future. Psalms and songs from David and Solomon inspired poets, musicians, and religious leaders. All these men were supported, and sometimes led, by remarkable women such as Sarah, Rebekah, Deborah, Bathsheba, and Esther.

Rabbi Stephanie Aaron, on the left, is working with Scott Handler, 13, right, and his twin sister Jordan Handler, 13, center, as they are rehearsing for their B'nai Mitzvah at the Jewish Community Center in Tucson, Arizona.

Because Judaism did not end with the closure of the text of the Bible, about 200 C.E., dozens of other outstanding personalities have also molded its faith and influenced larger civilizations. Yohannan ben Zakkai escaped Roman destruction of Jerusalem to organize rabbis in compelling discussions of Torah that culminated in the remarkable Babylonian Talmud. Maimonides wrote in both Hebrew and Arabic as he explained Judaism for medieval scholars, all the while supporting himself as the trusted physician to the Muslim emperor Saladin. Golda Meir was an influential prime minister of the young state of Israel. These names are only a sampling of the widely acclaimed persons who have influenced Judaism in its ancient and modern forms.

Fewer than twenty million Jews inhabit the earth. Their influence, and that of their ancestors, however, has been so immense, that Judaism is traditionally counted as one of the major world religions. Important in its own right, the study of Judaism is also needed to explain the development of both Christianity and Islam, which also worship the God of Abraham.

The Jewish Bible

The Jewish Bible (**Tanakh**) is the sacred book that interprets history as Jews have experienced it. Although it is proper to think of the Bible as a single book of scriptures, it is more accurate to describe it as a library of books assembled under three major headings. Most important is the **Torah,** which means divine instruction and guidance. Its books are Genesis, Exodus, Leviticus, Numbers, and Deuteronomy. The Prophets (Nevi'im) are divided into the former prophets: Joshua, Judges, First and Second Samuel, and First and Second Kings; and the latter prophets: Isaiah, Jeremiah, Ezekiel, and the twelve, who are Hosea, Joel, Amos, Obadiah, Jonah, Micah, Nahum, Habakkuk, Zephaniah, Haggai, Zechariah, and Malachi. The Writings (Kethuvim) are Psalms, Proverbs, Job, and the Festal Scrolls: Song of Songs, Ruth, Lamentations, Ecclesiastes, and Esther. Daniel, Ezra, Nehemiah, and First and Second Chronicles complete the list.[1] This is the canon (official collection) prepared by the rabbis in Yavneh about 90 C.E.

The Bible is the foundation on which a Jewish life is built. It traces God's activities in beginning the world, in calling a family from Mesopotamia who would respond to the progressive revelation of his will, and in establishing a nation of Jewish families responsible above all other peoples to demonstrate God's requirements and blessings for all peoples of the earth. It is the story of the education of a people who have a special mission to be:

A covenant people, a light of nations—
Rescuing prisoners from confinement,
From the dungeon those who sit in darkness. (Isaiah 42:6, 7)

In the Bible, maturity emerges through suffering, and leadership in faith is earned in schools of rigorous experience. In the rapidly vanishing moments of human lives, eternal truths are revealed.

Tanakh [ta-NAK]
The complete Jewish Bible, comprising three parts: Torah, the five books of Moses; Nevi'im, the prophets; and Kethuvim, the writings. The first letters of the three terms yield Tanakh.

Torah [TOR-ah]
Teachings that comprise the first five books of the Bible: Genesis, Exodus, Leviticus, Numbers, and Deuteronomy.

Interpreting the Bible

The Bible has been understood in two very different ways. For most of history, and by most people today, it has been regarded as a document from God that is without error. Because it is not the product of humans, it is a reliable guide of God's requirements and promises. It is a factual account of history. This understanding of the Bible may be labeled "conservative" or "traditional."

The second way of understanding the Tanakh assigns a greater human role in its origin. The Bible, in this interpretation, is a record of human encounters with God. Their revelatory experiences and their responses to them form the traditions of the Bible. Although in this tradition the words of the Bible are not literal words of God, they are words expressing human understanding of God's revelation. Because it assigns to humans a more prominent role in producing the Bible, this approach has sometimes been labeled "liberal" or "critical." Many books, of which R. E. Friedman's *Who Wrote the Bible?* (1987) is only one example, have been produced over the last century and a half to explain this different interpretation. This interpretation will be described in more detail later.

Although people may differ on interpretation of the Bible, they begin with its accounts of events. Only when we know the accounts can we begin to interpret. In all the religions of the Near East, I emphasize the account in the scriptures. All readers can recall that there are both conservative and liberal interpretations for every account. In Judaism, too, I report the scriptural accounts at face value, allowing readers to decide how to interpret them.

The Tanakh orders accounts according to historical development. The worldview of Judaism grows out of the historical development. The worldview of Abraham was not the full-blown worldview of modern Judaism. The worldview of Judaism that began in the Bible has continued to develop for another two thousand years. To understand the worldview of Judaism, we study its historical development. In the Bible, however, we do not have history as historians today write it. German scholars have a word for biblical accounts—*Heilsgeschichte,* salvation history. The Bible, they think, is an interpretation of the events of history in light of their religious significance for Jews.

Historical Development: Studying Judaism

Although Judaism's history is celebrated by both Jews and Christians, its interpretation has been divisive and controversial. One question is, When did Judaism begin? With creation of the world more than five thousand years ago, or with the exodus from Egypt? Did Judaism proper begin in Jerusalem after leaders returned from exile in Babylon, or only after the destruction of the Temple in 70 C.E.? All Jews agree that present-day Judaism is not confined to beliefs and practices that Christians read in their "Old Testament." Whether Orthodox in Israel or Reform in the United States, Judaism today is different from much of the religion reported in the Bible. Our challenge is to examine not only the biblical accounts but also the historical developments since the Tanakh was closed to new books.

Two approaches dominate the historical studies of Judaism. One approach, which is more widely known and practiced, is traditional salvation history. God does all good things, and after the earliest days of creation, acts with and through individual humans to accomplish his purposes. Thus all events of history are influenced by God and cannot be understood apart from his will. In this view, the Bible itself, particularly Torah, is the word of God. Records of all events, including the creation of heaven and earth, are reliably provided by God. The other approach considers Judaism's development from the point of view of humanistic studies that include other peoples of the Middle East, Europe, and the Americas.

The more humanistic accounts of Jewish history emphasize a variety of oral traditions, periodic collecting, editing, and selecting for preservation. The achievements, failures, and sufferings of Jews are analyzed as humanists explain events in other cultures and histories. Although the humanist approach recognizes Judaism as a remarkable and impressive religion, it is hardly without parallels in development. These two different approaches to the history of Judaism also influence interpretation of its most important source, the Bible. This text is based on Jewish scriptures rather than on independent historical sources.

Abraham

The dramatic history of Judaism, which gives it a unique identity, focuses on encounter, a searching God confronting human beings in the progressing stream of time. In the second millennium B.C.E., God appeared in Haran and encountered Abraham, the son of Terah, a man who came there from Ur of the Chaldeans. God challenged Abraham to immigrate to the land surrounding the Sea of Galilee and the Dead Sea.

1. The Lord said to Abram, "Go forth from your native land and from your father's house to a land that I will show you.
2. I will make of you a great nation,
    And I will bless you;
    I will make your name great,
    And you shall be a blessing.
3. I will bless those who bless you
    And curse him that curses you;
    And all the families of the earth
    Shall bless themselves by you." (Genesis 12:1–3)

Having faith in God, Abraham, his wife Sarah, and Haran's son Lot began a migration to the land of promise located at the lower eastern end of the Mediterranean Sea. There he settled into a nomadic life among the local inhabitants, differing from them not only in his heritage but also in his covenant relationship with his God. If Abraham would be faithful to his God, God promised, his descendants would inherit the land in which he was grazing his flocks. The covenant, a contract without a date of expiration, was sealed by the slaying of valuable animals, drawing their blood, and exposing their flesh to flames.

Sacrifice was the act of worship used by Abraham and his descendants. Something of value—sheep, goats, or cattle—the very means of survival for nomads, was killed, and its blood (life) was poured out to demonstrate the worshiper's bond to God, who gives life. The animal flesh was then placed on hot coals, so the flames and smoke (essence) rose toward the sky. Sacrifice removed doubt, impediments, and any alienation between worshipers and God. It sealed a **covenant** in which each participant had duties to perform and rewards to receive. Only after the destruction of the Jerusalem temple by Romans in 70 C.E. did Judaism omit animal sacrifice as a central act of worship.

covenant [CUV-u-nunt] The binding agreement between God and his chosen people. The covenant was repeatedly renewed. Unlike a contract, the covenant had no date of expiration.

Abraham's covenant with God continued through his son with Sarah, Isaac. God enabled Sarah, who had been barren, to bear Isaac.

The son of Hagar and Abraham, Ishmael, departed to another land, where he would become a respected leader of the Arabs. Isaac's son Jacob had twelve sons, and eventually he was also known as Israel. The covenant was preserved through the twelve sons of Israel, each of whom became head of a tribe of the children of Israel. Joseph, a favorite son of Israel, became viceroy of Egypt. During a famine, the pharaoh invited Joseph's father, his brothers, and their families to settle in Egypt. But after the death of Joseph, the new Egyptian pharoah enslaved the Israelites.

Locations of Biblical and First-Century C.E. Judaism. Although Jews settled primarily in the land around the Sea of Galilee, the Dead Sea, and the Jordan River, they also settled for periods of time in Egypt and in Mesopotamia.

Historical Development: Life under the Egyptians

The children of Abraham and of Israel lived often among the Egyptians. During the lifetime of Joseph they were honored residents who followed their own culture and religion. The Hebrews knew, from the days of Abraham, that Egyptians worshiped gods and goddesses that represented sun, earth, water, and changing seasons, the forces essential in agriculture. City-states along the Nile depended on the seasonal overflow of the river and the sun to sustain the lives of humans and domestic animals. Joseph, who married an Egyptian, may have used these Egyptian beliefs to build reserves of grain against years of drought, but there is no evidence that he abandoned his own God in favor of Egyptian deities. Hebrews explained the workings of the world in terms of the God of Abraham, Isaac, and Jacob; they did not require Egyptian explanations.

The center of attention of Egyptian religion presented in the Bible is the pharaoh. Egyptians considered any pharaoh both a god and a representative of the gods. The image of the pharaoh in the Bible is negative. The pharaonic dynasty that elevated Joseph was overthrown; a new dynasty instituted a policy of repressing Hebrews. Although the Bible describes Hebrew suffering in some detail, it fails to give enough evidence for modern scholars to identify with certainty the name and dynasty of the pharaoh who first turned against the Hebrews. Through the pathos of the biblical account it is clear that the pharaoh was so powerful that only God could prevail against him. Many scholars have identified the pharaoh of the exodus as Ramses II, of the Nineteenth Dynasty, who lived about 1290–1224 B.C.E.

Moses

The laws that are part of the Torah were brought to the Hebrews by God's chosen leader, Moses. Moses was an exemplary man of God. As leader of the Hebrews, he not only received the Torah but also established a system to institute it among God's people. Born to Hebrew slaves and hidden in the bulrushes by his mother to escape annihilation, just as the Egyptian goddess Isis had hidden her child,

Horus, from his hateful uncle, Moses grew up in the pharaoh's court, supervised by the pharaoh's daughter. Outlawed by the pharaoh for killing an Egyptian who harassed a Hebrew, Moses escaped to Midian, where he lived with a priest and his daughters. God came to Moses as he kept the flocks of Reuel, his father-in-law.

3:2. An angel of the Lord appeared to him in a blazing fire out of a bush. He gazed, and there was a bush all aflame, yet the bush was not consumed. 3. Moses said, "I must turn aside to look at this marvelous sight; why doesn't the bush burn up?" 4. When the Lord saw that he had turned aside to look, God called to him out of the bush: "Moses! Moses!" He answered, "Here I am." 5. And He said, "Do not come closer. Remove the sandals from your feet, for the place on which you stand is holy ground. 6. I am," He said, "the God of your father, the God of Abraham, the God of Isaac, and the God of Jacob." And Moses hid his face, for he was afraid to look at God.

7. And the Lord continued, "I have marked well the plight of My people in Egypt and have heeded their outcry because of their taskmasters; yes, I am mindful of their sufferings. 8. I have come down to rescue them from the Egyptians and to bring them out of that land to a good and spacious land, a land flowing with milk and honey, the region of the Canaanites, the Hittites, the Amorites, the Perizzites, the Hivites, and the Jebusites. 9. Now the cry of the Israelites has reached Me; moreover, I have seen how the Egyptians oppress them. 10. Come, therefore, I will send you to Pharaoh, and you shall free My people, the Israelites, from Egypt." (Exodus 3:2–10)

God revealed himself to Moses as Ehyeh-Asher-Ehyeh (Exodus 3:14). The Hebrew meaning is uncertain; it is variously translated "I Am That I Am"; "I Am Who I Am"; "I Will Be What I Will Be."[2] He called Moses to become leader of God's chosen people, to deliver them from the pharaoh. Moses became a successful instrument of theocracy, God's rule of a people through a human leader. Moses knew God as few men have known him, and God used him as few men have been used (Deuteronomy 34:10).

God chose Moses to deliver the Hebrews from slavery in Egypt and gave him divine assistance at crucial points. A series of ten plagues convinced the pharaoh he should let the Hebrews go. The last plague, in which the angel of death killed all Egyptian firstborn sons but passed over the homes of Hebrews without harming them, is still recalled in the Jewish holiday **Passover.** By a mighty act of God, the Hebrews crossed the Red Sea on dry ground, but the waters returned in time to drown the pharaoh's army. The Hebrews were guided by a pillar of cloud by day and a pillar of fire by night as they crossed the Sinai Peninsula. They were fed by manna and quail on an almost daily schedule, and water was also provided miraculously. The Hebrews were not only chosen by God, according to Jewish sacred history, but also miraculously supported by him against enemies, both human and natural.

The events of the first Passover occurred in Egypt about 1300–1200 B.C.E. The Passover meal, based on the one in Exodus 12, is celebrated in the spring. Unleavened bread, called **matzah,** is baked to symbolize the bread prepared and eaten in haste before the Hebrew slaves escaped from Egypt. Other dishes of food in the meal symbolize the slaves' work with bricks and their tears shed because of the harsh treatment they received from slave masters. During each meal, the story of Hebrew deliverance from Egypt is recited and explained so that each new generation is incorporated into the covenant people whom God delivered through a power far superior to that of Egypt's pharaoh or nature.

Passover [PASS-o-ver]
A Jewish holiday in the spring. It celebrates God's deliverance of the Hebrews from slavery in Egypt during the time of Moses.

matzah [MUT-za]
(pl. *matzot*) Unleavened bread eaten by Jews during Passover. During Passover, no leaven should be present in a Jewish home.

The summit of experience for the Hebrews under Moses was the receiving of the commandments of God, given by God to Moses on the top of Mt. Sinai. Essentially, the covenant between God and his people was renewed. If the Hebrews would serve God exclusively, he would give them a promised land and make them a great nation. If they accepted the promise, they had obligations to fulfill that were moral, ceremonial, and cultural. All life was to be lived under the command of God, a theocracy. God appointed human leaders through whom he was represented to the people. His mighty acts in history, however, are apparent to all humans. The symbol of his presence was the **Ark of the Covenant,** a wooden chest containing the stones bearing the Ten Commandments; in processions, the Ark was carried by priests. These commandments in Exodus were distinctive in the government of the Hebrews.

1. God spoke all these words, saying:
2. I the Lord am your God, who brought you out of the land of Egypt, the house of bondage:
3. You shall have no other gods besides Me.
4. You shall not make for yourself a sculptured image, or any likeness of what is in the heavens above, or on the earth below, or in the waters under the earth.
5. You shall not bow down to them or serve them. For I the Lord your God am an impassioned God, visiting the guilt of the parents upon the children, upon the third and upon the fourth generations of those who reject Me,
6. But showing kindness to the thousandth generation of those who love Me and keep My commandments.
7. You shall not swear falsely by the name of the Lord your God; for the Lord will not clear one who swears falsely by His name.
8. Remember the sabbath day and keep it holy.
9. Six days you shall labor and do all your work,
10. But the seventh day is a sabbath to the Lord your God: you shall not do any work—you, your son, or daughter, your male or female slave, or your cattle, or the stranger who is within your settlements.
11. For in six days the Lord made heaven and earth and sea, and all that is in them, and He rested on the seventh day; therefore the Lord blessed the sabbath day and hallowed it.
12. Honor your father and your mother, that you may long endure on the land that the Lord your God is assigning to you.
13. You shall not murder.
    You shall not commit adultery.
    You shall not steal.
    You shall not bear false witness against your neighbor.
14. You shall not covet your neighbor's house; you shall not covet your neighbor's wife, or his male or female slave, or his ox or his ass, or anything that is your neighbor's. (Exodus 20:1–14)

There were penalties for failing to keep the law that extended to several generations, just as there were rewards for keeping the law that extended to future generations.

The Ten Commandments and their interpretations are part of a larger discussion of moral, ceremonial, and cultural laws contained in four books of the Torah: Exodus, Leviticus, Numbers, and Deuteronomy. These books, together with Genesis, the book that describes the beginning of creation, humans, and the ancestors

Ark of the Covenant
A box containing the Ten Commandments. Priests carried it in processions and then housed it in the tabernacle.

of the Jewish people, constitute the sacred books that Jews still read in their services of worship and study in their homes and schools.

A passage in the Torah known as the **Shema,** the commandment in Deuteronomy 6:4–9 that begins "Hear," directs adherents of Judaism:

4. Hear O Israel! The Lord is our God, the Lord alone.
5. You shall love the Lord your God with all your heart and with all your soul and with all your might.
6. Take to heart these instructions with which I charge you this day.
7. Impress them upon your children. Recite them when you stay at home and when you are away, when you lie down and when you get up.
8. Bind them as a sign upon your hand and let them serve as a symbol on your forehead;
9. Inscribe them on the doorposts of your house and on your gates.

Historical Development: Settlement in Canaan

The religion developed in the Sinai Peninsula was an ideal form that was severely tested under practical conditions in Canaan. For the descendants of the former slaves in Egypt, their entry was a return of the children of Israel to join their people who remained in Canaan. The initial entry of the Hebrews into Canaan was announced by a series of battles against the Canaanites.

Under Joshua's leadership, the battles were won with assistance from God. However, few fortified cities were conquered immediately, and the nomadic Hebrews settled in open country, competing with the agricultural developments of the natives. Hebrew life was organized around twelve tribal leaders, descendants of the children of Israel.

This loose federation was occasionally strengthened by the timely appearances of folk heroes, the judges, who championed the Hebrew cause against local oppressors. The real threat to Hebrew survival, which was centered in the worship of their God, came through the fertility rites that the **Canaanites** practiced in order to influence their deities **Baal** and **Asherah** to produce crops. Canaanite worship included bowing to idols. Because making statues and worshiping idols were activities clearly in violation of the Ten Commandments, the Hebrew religious leaders constantly denounced Hebrew participation in Canaanite worship.

For a very few centuries in Jewish history, human kings were chosen to give greater visibility to the nation among other nations, who were not always impressed by a theocracy led by a prophet or seer, such as Samuel. (A seer is one who foretells the future through oracles.)[3] In succession, Saul, David, and Solomon built an expanded earthly kingdom by subduing ancient Hebrew enemies and forming alliances and trade agreements with many foreign powers.

David is a major figure in Judaism, a hero to his own age and a model of any deliverer of Israel. He defeated the Philistines, who had plagued the Israelites and killed King Saul and his son Jonathan. He won Jerusalem and established it as the center of religion and government. He brought the Ark of the Covenant to the city and projected building the first temple to replace the sacred tent or tabernacle. In the collection of Psalms, the hymns of worship of Israel, many are labeled "A Psalm of David." He is credited not only with composing words and music but also with playing the harp and organizing musical groups who helped lead the worship of God.

Shema [SHEE-ma]
Hear. The beginning word of Deuteronomy 6:4, "Hear, O Israel!" A declaration of God's unity, it is recited twice daily.

Canaanites
[kay-nu-NIGHTS]
The people among whom the Israelites settled on their return from slavery in Egypt. Canaan comprised the area bordered by the Sea of Galilee, the Jordan River, and the Dead Sea.

Baal [BAA-ul]
A god or gods of Canaan. Baals were landlords or keepers of the land. Canaanites worshipped them to make crops grow.

Asherah [ash-u-RAH]
A goddess of Canaan and a counterpart to the male god, Baal. She was another example of the Mediterranean mother goddess.

Solomon, son of David and Bathsheba, built on his father's successes. In times of peace he reached out to neighboring countries to form alliances and trading partnerships. Wealth poured into his palace in Jerusalem. Judaism honors him for building the first temple in Jerusalem. He generously consecrated it by having priests and Levites sacrifice a staggering number of animals. Under Solomon, the Hebrews reached their height of political and economic power. To support beautiful architecture and a handsome lifestyle, Solomon instituted forced labor and heavy taxes. Rehoboam's continuation of Solomon's heavy tax program led to a revolt by the ten northern tribes, who established a rival capital for religion and state in Samaria. In the forsaking of a unified worship of God and a unified kingdom, many religious leaders foresaw disaster for the Hebrews.

The Hebrew Prophets

Hebrew **prophets** established a pattern for a different kind of holy man in Hebrew life. The words they spoke were not their own; they were prefaced "Thus said the Lord." (Prophets are those men who feel called to speak for God.) In Judaism, their message was that the only way to avert national and personal disaster was through exclusive devotion to the God of Abraham, Isaac, Jacob, and Moses that was required in the Torah. Part of that devotion, emphasized by priests, entailed keeping the regulations of worship in the temple and on hygiene and diet in the home. Another part, emphasized by prophets, required a scrupulous application of laws on individual rights and social responsibilities.

The earliest prophets were men found in groups who stimulated ecstatic experiences. Later individuals stood apart from the groups and, in the name of God, criticized the immoral acts of monarchs. The prophet Elijah, by defeating Baal prophets and condemning King Ahab's murderous seizing of a vineyard belonging to his neighbor Naboth, stirred Queen Jezebel to seek revenge against him. Elijah performed dramatic public acts, such as a contest with Baal prophets on Mt. Carmel to demonstrate whose deity would send down fire from heaven to consume a prepared sacrifice. Baal failed to light a fire; God answered Elijah's prayers and consumed not only the sacrifice but also the stones on which it rested. Later, the voice of God came to Elijah not in earthquake, wind, or fire, but in the stillness of a mountain cave.

After King David had conspired to have Uriah the Hittite killed to cover up David's adultery with Uriah's wife, Bathsheba, the prophet Nathan confronted his king. Nathan told a simple story of a rich man who slew a neighbor's pet lamb to feed his guest. In a rage, King David said to Nathan, "As the Lord lives, the man who did this deserves to die!" Nathan answered, "That man is you." Nathan proceeded to tell David the word of God: "The sword shall never depart from your House" (II Samuel 12:1–12). The prophets believed that God's law was above prophets, priests, and yes, kings.

In the eighth century B.C.E., about 750, four prophets appeared with messages that left permanent imprints on Judaism. Amos, a prophet from the Southern Kingdom, prophesied in Bethel, of the Northern Kingdom, denouncing extreme inequalities among the economic classes of Hebrews. A nation could not survive such injustices among its people. Unless the people voluntarily restored justice in their relationships, God would use other nations as a scourge to discipline their rebellion against his law. Amos is remembered for his ringing challenge:

> But let justice well up like water,
> Righteousness like an unfailing stream. (Amos 5:24)

prophet [PROF-it]
A person inspired by God to speak in his name. In Hebrew history, prophets in groups gave way to the messages of individual prophets such as Isaiah, Jeremiah, and Ezekiel.

Hosea used his unfaithful wife as an illustration of Israel's unfaithfulness to God. As Hosea sought to restore his marriage by rehabilitating Gomer, so God, in strong love, sought to renew his marriage with Israel.

Isaiah, in response to an awesome experience of God in the Jerusalem temple, challenged King Ahaz to avoid alliances with infidel kingdoms and meet an invasion threat with trust in the Lord. God told Isaiah not to follow the people but to trust only in God:

> None but the Lord of Hosts
> Shall you account holy;
> Give reverence to Him alone,
> Hold Him alone in awe. (Isaiah 8:13)

The nature of God and his relationship with Israel requires more than exact ceremonial observances, wrote the prophet Micah:

> He has told you, O man, what is good;
> And what the Lord requires of you:
> Only to do justice
> And to love goodness,
> And to walk modestly with your God;
> Then will your name achieve wisdom. (Micah 6:8–9)

People listened to the prophets; some took their messages to heart. But many messages of the prophets remained unheeded at the time they were delivered. Some prophets were denounced by their contemporary leaders, only to be honored by most people in later generations. The destruction of the Northern Kingdom, followed a few decades later by the exile of leaders of the Southern Kingdom, caused the Jews who survived exile to have new respect for the old messages of the prophets.

Historical Development: Destroyed Kingdoms, Exiled Leaders

The destructions that came on the divided kingdoms left an enduring imprint on later Judaism. The ten northern tribes were conquered in 721 B.C.E. by the Assyrians from Mesopotamia and carried away to be dispersed and replaced by immigrants of other peoples sent by the Assyrians. Only the Southern Kingdom survived. A few years later, in 701, they were besieged in Jerusalem. They were delivered when supernatural powers came to their aid.

> That night an angel of the Lord went out and struck down one hundred and eighty-five thousand in the Assyrian camp. . . . So King Sennacherib of Assyria broke camp and retreated, and stayed in Nineveh. (II Kings 19:35–36)

Jews interpret this deliverance of their pivotal city as God's fulfillment of his promise to King David.

However, the period of safety lasted only for 115 years, and then another Mesopotamian power, the Babylonians, conquered Judah and took Hebrew leaders and upper classes to settle in Babylon in two stages, 597 and 586 B.C.E. The Hebrew temple was destroyed. Only a puppet state survived.

Editing the Scriptures

With the temple destroyed, the priests favored the Torah. According to most scholars, the priests not only studied the scriptures but also revised them. There are some Bible scholars who believe that God dictated directly to Moses the Torah as it is today. But there is a strong scholarly movement, perhaps the mainstream of biblical scholarship, that takes a different view.

In their efforts to understand the Bible as deeply as possible, scholars have disputed not only the proper meaning of words and passages but also the nature of the literature itself. In the nineteenth century C.E., some scholars in Germany asked questions that led to a revolution in the interpretation of the Torah. How reliable is the Torah as a history of the Jewish people? Were the patriarchs, such as Abraham, real people, or were they fictional characters representing the ideals of later generations of Jews?

Wellhausen, a German scholar, saw the Genesis stories as unreliable history, reflecting the ideals of a period long after Moses. The effect of the Wellhausen approach to the Torah was to undermine its value as a reliable account of the persons and events of Jewish history.

A reaction against this doubting of the Torah led to an opposite position—that the Torah is *in every sense* a reliable historical document. This position is represented by Yehezkel Kaufmann. Other scholars turned to archaeological evidence patiently gathered from sites in Mesopotamia, Egypt, the Sinai Peninsula, and the ancient land of Canaan. After considering both the text and archaeological evidence, Abraham Malamat writes,

© Christel Gerstenberg/CORBIS

Hebrew Book of Abraham. This first page was printed by Eliesser Toledano, in Lisbon, in 1489.

> In examining the historical authenticity of the patriarchal traditions, one is instantly struck by their twofold nature, alluded to in our opening remarks on Israel's proto-history. On the one hand, they contain early, authentic material and, on the other, late, anachronistic conceptions.[4]

Torah materials, archaeology, and the study of epigrams enable scholars to construct a reliable history of the Jews. Archaeological excavations of sites have yielded evidence that supports many of the accounts in the Torah and other books of the Bible.

Although these scholars have differences of emphasis and interpretation, they agree that to form the Torah, priestly editors combined at least three documents. One is the *J* account or document, so labeled because the author refers to God as *Yahweh* (early German scholars used a *j* instead of a *y*). A second account used the term *Elohim* for God—it is labeled *E*. The third document, *D*, is Deuteronomy, found in the temple in the seventh century B.C.E. A fourth source of information is labeled *P*, for *priestly*, because it contains so much priestly legislation. The Torah is the edited account based on the three major documents. The accounts do not exist separately now; finding two accounts of the same event in the Bible gives some insight into the documents and the editing. In Babylon, much of the Torah was available to be used in instruction and in a new form of worship. A few scholars think that Ezra, who arrived in Jerusalem in 458 B.C.E., completed the Torah.

Creating Congregations

In Babylon, the seeds were planted for the surviving tree of Judaism, which would last until the present day. An alternative to temple worship was instituted so that

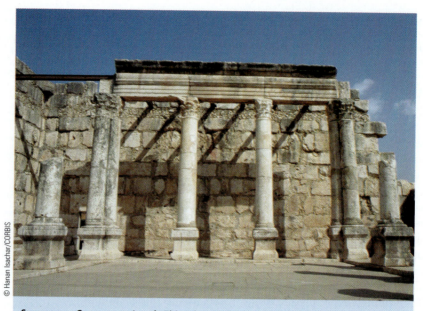

Synagogue, Capernaum, Israel. This 4th century C.E. ruin in Galilee still stands today.

the exiles could worship in a strange land. The new institution took the form of a congregation. In later centuries congregations were housed in buildings that were known by the Greek term *synagogue.* Any group of ten Jewish men could form a congregation to worship God without the use of a priest or animal sacrifice. A layman could read the Torah and comment on it. A person who studied the Torah and commented on it was revered as a teacher, or **rabbi.** Prayers and hymns accompanied the reading and interpretation of the Torah, and Judaism emerged as a religion that could be practiced either with animal sacrifices in the Jerusalem temple or in congregations that met almost anywhere. The mode of worship was not an issue between rabbis and priests; their main concern was to find ways to unify the people.

Congregational worship was led not by priests but by laymen. Ritual focused not on a burning altar but on truth in a book. The Torah scrolls, God's words for Israel, were the visible and audible center of attention. Worshipers offered hymns and prayers to God; he spoke through the Torah as it was read by laymen and commented on by scholars of the scriptures. Those who worshiped were introduced to an experience similar to Isaiah's in the temple (Isaiah 6:1–13), praising God's holiness and being challenged to live as if on a mission from God.

Postexilic Judaism

Although exiles succeeded in worshiping God without the temple, they had serious questions about their loss of homes and temple. Preserving the Jewish faith required leaders to issue a **theodicy,** a rational explanation why in spite of their suffering Jews should still worship God. Some reasonable meaning for the national tragedy had to be given, or traditional faith in God would fade before the proven strength of Marduk, god of Babylon. Isaiah, Jeremiah, and Ezekiel were

rabbi [RAB-eye]
In Judaism, a teacher. After 70 C.E., rabbis were ordained interpreters and leaders of Judaism.

theodicy [THEE-od-i-se]
A justification, in the presence of evil, of God's goodness, justice, and knowledge. How can an all-good, all-powerful, and all-knowing God allow evil?

the names of prophets attached to scrolls that interpreted the sufferings of Judah. These prophets pictured God as being in charge of the vast international rise and fall of powers. He had not been overpowered by Marduk, but he used the Babylonians to discipline and purify his people, the Hebrews. He chastised the unreliable shepherds of Israel (their leaders) and would revive a people from the dead bones of the old nation (Ezekiel 37:3). Each person would answer to God for his or her own deeds, and the law would be internalized in human hearts rather than housed in vast social institutions:

> But such is the covenant I will make with the House of Israel after these days—declares the Lord: I will put my teaching into their inmost being and inscribe it upon their hearts. Then I will be their God, and they shall be My people. (Jeremiah 31:33)

When Cyrus of Persia defeated the Babylonians and permitted the Jews to return to Judea, the prophet Isaiah hailed him as the anointed of the Lord (Isaiah 45:1). Bearing the same name as the eighth-century prophet, this prophet of the sixth century is sometimes called the second Isaiah. Many scholars designate chapters 40 through 66 of Isaiah as Second Isaiah. In beautiful poetry, Isaiah challenges the exiles to prepare for return to their homeland:

> Comfort, oh comfort My people,
> Says your God.
> Speak tenderly to Jerusalem,
> And declare to her
> That her term of service is over,
> That her iniquity is expiated;
> For she has received at the hand of the Lord
> Double for all her sins. (Isaiah 40:1–2)

The theological view that God was in charge of history made the Jews more cosmopolitan in their understanding of international affairs and at the same time more determined than ever to maintain their distinctive heritage.

Ezra, a **scribe** (one who is a scholar of the Torah), and Nehemiah, a governor appointed by Artaxerxes of Persia, cooperated to reestablish Jerusalem and renew the covenant with God. Nehemiah succeeded in organizing Jews in Judah to rebuild the walls of Jerusalem. He selected people to move into the city, organized defenses against jealous non-Jews, and persuaded Jews of substance to offer interest-free loans to their Jewish neighbors in need. In 444 B.C.E., in the courtyard of the second temple, finished in 515 B.C.E., Ezra read the Torah to the congregation. The people agreed to keep all the commandments, ordinances, and statutes of the Lord. Through the renewal of the covenant between the Jews and God, the bitter years of Babylonian exile were replaced with a fresh hope for a better future in the homeland of the Jews.

The Greeks

Purity was almost impossible to maintain among people living in a corridor through which kings periodically marched to and from war. It was only a matter of time until the Greeks replaced the Persians as rulers of the area. In 332 B.C.E. Greek influence under Alexander the Great took the form of broad cultural changes identified as Hellenism. There was great attractiveness in the Greek way of doing things, and some permanent imprints were left. For example, a Greek translation of the Hebrew scriptures, the Septuagint, was made in Egypt and well

scribe [SCRIIB]
From the centuries after the Babylonian captivity of the Jews, a scribe was a trained scholar, particularly in Torah studies.

served the Jews living outside the homeland, most of whom did not easily read Hebrew.

Wisdom Literature

Wisdom literature, scriptures that praise wisdom and learning, parallel Greek writings that elevate philosophy (love of wisdom), the use of reason to discover truth. Both Greek philosophy and Jewish wisdom literature break with traditional myths. The symbol of wisdom as a desirable woman to be pursued and loved, however, is present in both Jewish and Greek literature. Jewish wisdom literature generally maintains a strong faith in God, a feature present in some Greek literature. The writings of the Greek philosopher Aristotle on belief in God, when rediscovered in the medieval period, influenced not only Judaism but also Christianity and Islam.

Proverbs and Ecclesiastes, ascribed to King Solomon, are examples of wisdom literature. In Proverbs, the writer speaks as a father to a son, giving advice from experience:

> The beginning of wisdom is—acquire wisdom:
> With all your acquisitions, acquire discernment.
> Hug her to you and she will exalt you;
> She will bring you honor if you embrace her.
> She will adorn your head with a graceful wreath;
> Crown you with a glorious diadem. (Proverbs 4:7–9)

In Ecclesiastes, the writer also seeks wisdom, but he experiences disappointment in the supposed pleasures of life. His most famous lines are the following:

> Utter futility!—said Koheleth—
> Utter futility! All is futile!
> What real value is there for a man
> In all the gains he makes beneath the sun? (Ecclesiastes 1:2–3)

The pleasures of the body that had been a sign of God's blessings in Judaism were discovered to be meaningless. The dead were more fortunate than the living, and one not born was more fortunate than either (4:2–3). However, wisdom is more valuable than weapons of war (9:18). The book concludes,

> The sum of the matter, when all is said and done: Revere God and observe His commandments! For this applies to all mankind: that God will call every creature to account for everything unknown, be it good or bad. (12:13–14)

The Maccabean Revolt

In the hands of the Seleucids of Syria, Hellenism was a threat, for Antiochus IV (175–163 B.C.E.) prohibited possession of the Torah, observation of the Sabbath, and the practice of circumcision; he also desecrated the rebuilt temple of Jerusalem in 167 B.C.E. and rededicated it to the Greek god Zeus. The Maccabean revolt was the Jewish response that led to the defeat of the Syrians and to the rededication of the temple in 164 B.C.E., an event celebrated in the Jewish festival of Hanukkah.

The revolt against Antiochus IV had begun in the city of Jerusalem; the popular leaders of a prolonged resistance movement began their work in a village northeast of Jerusalem, Modi'in. Jews were tired of being forced to eat pork, a food forbidden by the Torah, and being threatened with death for practicing their faith. When Syrian officers came to Modi'in, assembled the people, and attempted to force Jews, using threats of death, to desecrate their altar to God, the Jews faced an immediate crisis. Mattathias, a priest, refused to sacrifice an unclean animal on the altar. When a Jew came forward to obey the command of the king's officers, Mattathias, killed him. In the fight, Syrians were killed. Mattathias and his sons escaped to the hills.

Supported by pious Jewish people, the Maccabees waged war on the Syrians to good effect. Simon and Judas, the Maccabee (probably from the Hebrew word for hammer), became popular leaders. Judas, son of Mattathias, succeeded in controlling the temple area of Jerusalem so that devout priests could cleanse the corrupted temple and hold an eight-day festival to rededicate it to the worship of God. Rabbis today explain that the Jewish holiday **Hanukkah** is not so much a celebration of Judas's victory over the Syrians as it is a celebration of the miracle that a container of consecrated oil, which was enough to light the lamps for only one day, lasted eight days.

The Romans

The Romans, expanding their empire, eventually overcame the Jews as well. Pompey and the Romans came in 63 B.C.E. to settle a dispute between rivals for the post of high priest in Jerusalem; they stayed for centuries. Generally, the Romans were administrators who ignored Jewish peculiarities so long as the Jews paid their taxes and kept the peace. Jews had to work hard to meet Roman demands and at the same time maintain the purity of their culture and worship. Under the challenge, some Jews sought accommodation, some sought peace, and still others could not rest until they had driven the Romans from the land.

During the first and second centuries C.E., a variety of Jewish leaders and groups proposed their own ways to deal with Rome. The conservative **Sadducees,** who rejected prophetic writings and embraced only the first five books of the Bible (the Torah), found ways to cooperate with the Romans. At the other extreme were the **Zealots,** who sought a forceful overthrow of the Roman government in Palestine. In between were groups that had a variety of responses. The **Essenes,** for example, were intent on living purified lives apart from the troubles of the present world until God's final judgment should appear. Recent scholarly study of the Qumran community, near the Dead Sea, has given us a better understanding of these pious people who withdrew from society. The **Pharisees** believed that the Torah, both written and oral, should be applied to every aspect of daily life. They regarded as scriptural many books besides the Torah. Josephus, a Jewish historian, stated in his *The Antiquities of the Jews* (13.10.6), that Sadducees thought Pharisees required many observances not written in the Law of Moses (the **Mosaic Law**).

A great many common people believed that the time for a deliverer—some sort of anointed one of God—to appear had drawn near. There was, however, much dispute about the qualifications and platform for any deliverer of the Jews. The expected deliverer was often referred to as the **Messiah.** The word, meaning "anointed," is used only twice in the Bible, both times in the book of Daniel (9:25 and 26). There are many references to the anointing of Hebrew kings, and one foreign king, Cyrus of Persia, was referred to as the Lord's anointed (Isaiah 45:1). In Daniel, however, "Messiah" is spoken of in Daniel's vision of Gabriel, who reveals the future. Scholars differ over whether the term applies only to a figure who will appear in the last days before judgment or may apply also to any kings or priests chosen by God.

The appearance of Judas the Galilean in 6 C.E. initiated the struggles of the first century, which ended with the execution of Judas and perhaps two thousand other Zealots on crosses, the Roman instrument for capital punishment. John the Baptist, who worked beyond the Jordan River announcing that the kingdom of God was at hand and that everyone should repent, be baptized, and bear fruits of repentance, attracted large crowds and a group of devoted disciples. King Herod jailed and eventually beheaded him. Jesus of Nazareth, a cousin of John, announced the imminence of the kingdom of God, attracted large crowds, and had twelve apostles as well as numerous disciples. Despite a large, popular following, he angered many scribes and Pharisees of the Jews and eventually disrupted the operation of their temple to the extent that he was arrested, tried before members of the **Sanhedrin,** the highest court, found guilty of blasphemy by the high priest, and then turned over to Pilate, the Roman prefect, who allowed him to be crucified by Roman soldiers. Disciples of both John the Baptist and Jesus of Nazareth continued the works of their masters and stirred people to the extent that they were of concern to the Sanhedrin. Their story will be told in the next chapter.

Rabbinic Judaism

The Judaism that had been expressed in both temple and synagogues was about to end. From the time of their return to Jerusalem under Persian rule, Jews had maintained synagogue worship, and when the building was completed, temple worship. Then, in 66 C.E., the temple's survival was threatened by a Jewish revolt in Jerusalem.

Many Jews, especially the Zealots, who had always opposed Roman rule of Palestine, found Roman administration unbearable. Romans controlled the temple and the high priest. They placed the burden of heavy taxes and duties on the population. In disputes between Jews and the Greco-Syrian population of Palestine, the Romans took the side of the foreigners. Roman administration had deteriorated to the point that the Romans could no longer guarantee peace and security.[5]

Already in turmoil because a Roman court decided in favor of foreigners against Jews in Caesarea, the crowds in Jerusalem were furious when Florus, the Roman procurator, took money from the temple. Jews in Jerusalem revolted, attacking Roman soldiers. In their battle with the Romans, the Jews gained control of the Temple Mount. In this opening revolt, Romans retained control of the Antonia fortress, but later lost control to the Jews. The Jews exterminated the Roman garrison. Jews in other cities, hearing news of the courageous fight of the Jerusalem Jews, attacked the Romans occupying their cities. The Jews disrupted the law and order so prized by Rome and challenged the authority of the strongest military power in the world.

It was a rebellion that the Romans could not ignore or settle by negotiation. Mobilizing sixty thousand troops, the Roman general Vespasian marched into Galilee and proceeded to conquer much of the country. When Vespasian returned to Rome to become emperor, his son Titus took charge of the siege of Jerusalem in 70 C.E. In the five-month siege, the Romans broke down the third wall and then the second wall until they reached the defenders in the Antonia fortress. Destroying

Sanhedrin [san-HEED-rin] In times of the temple, the supreme judicial body of the Jews.

The Western Wall, Jerusalem Israel. An ultra-Orthodox Jew approaches Judaism's Holiest site, before the start of Yom Kippur.

the fortress, the Romans turned to the Temple Mount. Flavius Josephus, a historian of the period, described the destruction of the temple.

> While the holy house was on fire, everything was plundered that came to hand, and ten thousand of those that were caught were slain, nor was there a commiseration of any age or any reverence of gravity; but children and old men, and profane persons, and priests, were all slain in the same manner.[6]

To this day, the temple has not been rebuilt. Only the **Western Wall** of the platform survives. The Romans overcame the last resisting group in the Upper City. Only Machaerus and Masada, on the eastern and western banks of the Dead Sea, continued resistance.

Resisting from the top of Masada, a mountain stronghold, a group of Jewish patriots and their families stood off the Roman army for three more years. The historian Josephus praised the defenders, who braved repeated attacks from superior numbers. Under Flavius Silva, the Roman tenth legion built an earthwork against the side of the cliff and breached the walls of the fortress. They found no army to imprison or families to enslave because the 960 defenders had destroyed themselves by their own hands; the Romans gained only smoldering ruins and corpses.[7]

During the struggle for Jerusalem, a rabbi, Yohanan ben Zakkai, a student of rabbi **Hillel,** managed to obtain permission from the Romans for the Sanhedrin to move to the town of Yavneh. There, they established Jewish scriptures, prepared commentaries on the Torah, and developed a calendar of Jewish festivals so that all Jews, wherever they happened to be, could celebrate at the same time. The work of ben Zakkai and his fellows helped Jews preserve their identity in widely dispersed communities. Again, as in Babylon, the congregations came to be the

Western Wall
In Jerusalem; the platform of the former Temple, destroyed by the Romans in 70 C.E.

Hillel [hil-EL]
A prominent Jewish teacher and founder of the Hillel school of rabbis in the first century. He was considered more liberal in his views than the conservative Shammai.

© David Silverman/Getty Image

main institution of Judaism other than the home. However, the rabbis replaced the old priesthood as the leaders of religious life.

As important as the Bible is for Jews as a guide to living, it is the first word rather than the last of their developing faith. For Judaism did not stop changing and growing when the last official book of the Bible was certified by rabbis. The records of their adapting faith are contained in other books, such as the **Mishnah** and the **Talmud.** Although Judaism has changed significantly in the last two centuries, these two books and the Bible continue to guide Jews in their daily lives and in their aspirations for the future.

By about 90 C.E., the canon of the Jewish Bible had been assembled. It included the Torah, which had been accepted as scripture at least since the Babylonian captivity, the writings of the major and the minor prophets as well as the preliterary prophets, and miscellaneous writings of the ancestors, such as Solomon. Other books were rejected as being instructive and helpful but not scriptures, for example, First and Second Maccabees, which describe the restoration of the temple in 164 B.C.E. after Syrian desecration. In the early centuries of Christianity some of these books, which were included in the Septuagint (Jewish scriptures in Greek), Christians accepted as part of their Old Testament, or Old Covenant. Scattered Jewish communities wanted further unity of their teachings. The interpretations of the rabbis needed to be gathered and preserved so that no matter where rabbis might be teaching, they would have continuity of opinion with the great rabbis, such as Hillel. There was a large body of unwritten Torah, and traditional commentaries by rabbis, **Midrash.** Rabbi Akiba had demonstrated that under six headings all these unwritten subjects could be gathered and grouped. It remained only for them to be written; the old fear that their written form might rival the Torah was no longer a primary concern.

The Jewish community in Babylon, continuous since the sixth century B.C.E., thought it desirable to expand the Mishnah. Scholars gathered **Aggadah,** traditions of the rabbis, and **Halakhah,** juristic tradition, into the **Gemarah.** Then they combined the Gemarah and the Mishnah into the exhaustive Babylonian Talmud, which was completed by 485 C.E. Although a smaller Talmud, the Palestinian, had been completed earlier, the Babylonian Talmud became the enduring standard for Judaism. Almost anything a Jew needed to know about keeping the faith under any circumstances could be found therein.

By the time the Western empire of Rome fell to the northern tribes of Europe, Judaism was prepared to maintain a continuity of distinctive existence, even though Jews lived in a great variety of cultures, the **diaspora.** Some societies honored Jews, others tolerated them, and still others persecuted them severely. Dress, food, marriage, family, death, holidays, Sabbath observance, subjects of study, prayers, and offerings—all distinguished the Jews as a particular community, giving them a common identity among cultures that varied according to time and geographic location. Ritual and legal observance, as well as Torah study, helped Jews preserve their identity and their pride as a separate people called by God. Rabbinic Judaism became the nucleus of modern Judaism. In the absence of a temple, the rabbis' interpretation of Torah became the only living Judaism.

Medieval Judaism

Medieval Judaism was Talmudic Judaism existing in cultures dominated by either Christian or **Muslim** faith. Although both these religions acknowledged God's revelation to the Jews, both had quarrels with Jews. Jews had not accepted a later

Mishnah [MISH-na] Teachings of the rabbis compiled about 200 C.E. The Mishnah records discussions of rabbis on how best to live according to the Torah.

Talmud [TAL-mud] The collection of rabbinic teachings. It had deep influence over the lives of Jews from the beginning of the medieval period. The Mishnah and the Gemara were incorporated in the Talmud.

Midrash [MID-rash] (pl. *Midrashim*) Rabbinic exposition explaining the meaning of the scriptures. The root meaning is "to search out."

Aggadah [ug-GAHD-u] The nonlegal, story aspect of rabbinic literature. It is distinguished from Halakhah, the legal side of Judaism.

Halakhah [ha-la-KAH] The legal part of Jewish religion that was developed in rabbinic writings.

Gemarah [ge-MAHR-u] The "learning" of the rabbis. It was combined with the Mishnah to form the Talmud.

diaspora [di-AHS-pe-ra] A Greek word for the dispersion of Jews. These were the Jews who lived outside the Holy Land.

Muslim [MUS-lim] One who surrenders to God. A follower of the prophet Muhammad.

revelation by God either through Jesus as the Christ or through Muhammad as the reciter of the Quran. Except under threats of certain death, most Jews did not convert to another religion. Many Jews died rather than compromise their faith. Under generally good circumstances, Jews were permitted to live as second-class citizens among people of the dominant faith. A few Jews reached positions of great respect and reward as scholars, physicians, bankers, and merchants.

In any given place, conditions were only temporarily good for Jews. They had to seek the protection of holders of political power. From the thirteenth century on, they were labeled "king's serfs."[8] A king could charge them for the privilege of living in his territory or drive them out, confiscating their properties, whenever conditions in his territory supported drastic persecutions. Jews were severely restricted in occupations and property. They had to abide by the laws of the land as well as by the Talmud. Although they did not want to share in the social lives of Christians or Muslims—Jewish teachings restricted these relationships—they did desire equal protection and treatment under law. Every Jew had to remember that any offense he or she gave to a Christian or Muslim could invite wholesale persecution, even slaughter, of the entire Jewish community. Christian extermination of Jewish communities in medieval times was far too extensive to describe in this brief summary of Jewish history.

Two major traditions of Judaism predominated in the medieval period. The Babylonian tradition continued in the **Sephardic** tradition in southern Spain, and the **Ashkenazic** tradition, which developed from Latin roots, influenced northern Spain, France, and Germany. Although the two traditions competed in northern Spain, they were generally separated in geography.

Major Centers of Judaism in Europe. Jews settled around the Mediterranean by the first century C.E. and soon became inhabitants of many of the cities in Europe.

Sephardim [se-fahr-DIM] Jews who lived in medieval Spain until expelled in 1492. Those who refused to become Christians moved to North Africa, Italy, and especially Turkey, where Sultan Bayzid II admitted them gladly.

Ashkenazim [ahsh-ku-NAH-zim] A Yiddish-speaking group of Jews who settled in central and northern Europe. The term in Hebrew referred to Germany.

Maimonides

In Cordoba, Spain, the young Jew Moses ben Maimon (1135–1204) began a comfortable life enjoying the library of his father, a rabbi. But with the arrival of the Almohads from North Africa, Muslim persecution of Jews affected his life. He migrated with his family to Morocco, then to Palestine, and then to Egypt. He eventually settled in Fostat, a suburb of Cairo. His reputation for Torah study and mastery of Aristotle brought him the title "Nagid," or leader of Jewry in Egypt. Judaism was his love, but he supported his studies with a humanitarian trade, medicine. He made a dedicated study of pharmacy and methods of physicians. His reputation in that field led to his appointment as court physician to the emperor Saladin.[9] Maimonides, as he came to be known, declined an invitation from King Richard II to come to England.

Rambam, as he was respectfully known, gave first place in life to Jewish scholarship—in particular, reconciling the newer interpretations of Aristotle with his studies of the Torah. Although he liked Aristotle's proof for the existence of God, he preferred the creator in Plato's *Timaeus* to explain God's relationship to the world. His monumental works were the *Mishneh Torah,* a companion to the Torah written in Hebrew, and a *Guide for the Perplexed,* written in Arabic.

In the Torah commentary, he expressed the essential beliefs of Judaism in thirteen articles, including the existence, unity, spirituality, eternity, and omniscience of God; that God alone should be worshiped; that God bestowed the gift of prophecy; that Moses was the greatest prophet; that God gave the Torah and will never alter it; that he is omniscient; that he rewards the righteous and punishes the wicked; that he will send the Messiah; and that he will resurrect the dead. These articles were soon being repeated as a creed for Jews. Despite objections by later scholars such as Hasdai Crescas (1405) and Moses Mendelssohn (eighteenth century), Jewish masses wanted these articles repeated as part of their expression of faith. From the fourteenth century, they were included in Jewish worship. The Yigdal, which expresses the articles in poetry, is part of the Siddur (Prayer Book) and is recited in the daily service. The following is a translation of the Yigdal (the Thirteen Articles of Jewish Faith) in metric form:

> We praise the living God,
> For ever praise His name,
> Who was and is and is to be
> For e'er the same;
> The One eternal God
> Before our world appears,
> And there can be no end of time
> Beyond His years.
>
> Without a form is He,
> Nor can we comprehend
> The measure of His love for us—
> Without an end.
> For He is Lord of all,
> Creation speaks His praise.
> The human race and all that grows
> His will obeys.
>
> He knows our every thought,
> Our birth and death ordains;

He understands our fervent dreams,
Our hopes and our pains.
Eternal life has He
Implanted in our soul.
We dedicate our life to Him—
His way, our goal![10]

As had Philo centuries earlier, Maimonides interpreted the Genesis stories allegorically. He believed revelation is reasonable, even when revelation gives truth that could not have been reached by unaided reason. He believed also that God can best be described in terms of what he is not, for denying limits to God indicates what God is. For his genius in combining reason and scholarship in philosophy with deep devotion and analysis of the Torah, Maimonides is recognized as the greatest Jewish philosopher.

The Kabbalah

Revelation and rationalism in religions have been balanced by the esoteric. Hidden knowledge is not generally available to the masses but is available to a select few who are initiated into its mysteries. Behind the phenomena of the physical world are mysterious, irrational forces generated in a more powerful, unseen world. Those who have discovered special, secret knowledge can have access to codes that decipher information from the higher realm of being. **Kabbalah** is a Jewish form of the hidden knowledge that appeared in the medieval period and continued into the modern.

The best-known text of the Kabbalah is the *Zohar,* a text that scholars believe was written by Moses de Leon (1250–1305).[11] Through the practice of assigning numerical values to letters of the Hebrew alphabet, Kabbalists could exercise what appeared to be a more scientific deciphering of mystical truths in scriptures. The phenomenal world, that experienced by the five senses, is a corrupted product of the spiritual world, which can be encountered only mystically. Similar to Gnostic systems of earlier centuries, the Kabbalah has the absolute, named En Soph, at the top of a hierarchy of male and female pairs of emanations named Divine Will, Wisdom, Knowledge, Grace, and Power. Thus the purity of God is safely removed from the corruption of the phenomenal world. Man—male and female—is a symbol that directly corresponds to the universe. Through proper knowledge, formulas, and rituals, humans can influence the forces of the universe.

The hidden powers are also in the human organism. Through a study of the physiology and psychology of humans and a proper application of that knowledge, humans can release the energies stored in body and mind. Some find similarities with the theories of Hindu yoga, in which energy centers are located along the spine. When activated, the centers produce a higher level of consciousness. Symbols, rather than arguments, are characteristic of Kabbalah. Kabbalists' belief that the Messiah could be recognized by a certain symbol led to a few incidents of Jews accepting messiahs who later proved false.

Isaac Luria (1534–1572), of Spain, focused on Adam, the ideal human symbol. Adam embraced the universe; in his fall, he shattered into sparks of divine nature, illuminating souls. The goal of time is to unite these fragments into the ideal Adam. Reincarnation of the souls in plants, animals, and humans is part of the process of purification that enables souls to reach dimensions of higher union.

Kabbalah [COB-u-lah]
A form of rabbinic teaching giving "hidden" or "secret" meaning to Hebrew scriptures.

Luria advocated ascetic living and recitation of formulas to help his followers experience direct union with highest reality. The goal of the hidden powers in Kabbalah is mystical union with God.

Judaism, Christianity, and Islam in Spain

Most societies have placed restrictions on Jews that made them permanent second-class citizens or subjects. Because they were forbidden to own land, Jews were seldom farmers. Excluded from Gentile institutions of learning, they could not enter most trades and professions. Segregated into ghettos, they turned inward to family, community, and study of the Torah. Forced to live by their wits, many Jews became astute in business. Because Muslims and Christians would not lend money for interest to members of their own religion, Jews discovered a service they could render to kings, nobles, and merchants of other religions. Jewish money lenders became an indispensable part of later medieval society. Their services rewarded them well, but their success brought them envy and resentment from Gentiles. Powerful people who had difficulty paying debts were tempted to fan the ever-present sparks of prejudice among Christians. They stirred violent mobs to torture, kill, and seize the property of Jews. No debts remained to be paid. Destruction was justified by pious rationalizations based on general Christian contempt for Jews. Some of those claims were that Jews had murdered Christ, that Jews used the blood of Christian children in their rituals, and that Jews poisoned the wells of Christians.[12]

In 1492, any pleasant life for Jews in Spain ended. King Ferdinand and Queen Isabella, devoted Christian rulers, brought to a close the exemplary cooperation of Jews, Christians, and Muslims in Spain. Desiring their realm to be inhabited only by Christians, the monarchs gave Jews and Muslims a choice of converting to Christianity or leaving Spain. Devout Jews had no choice; they abandoned their properties and migrated to other countries. The Jews of Spain suffered a displacement similar to that of the Jews of France, who had been expelled earlier. Many of the displaced Jews, especially those of Spain (the Safed) settled in the Jewish homeland (Israel), reviving it as a center of Jewish life.

Jews who converted to Christianity were under constant examination by the Inquisition. The Grand Inquisitor, Tomas de Torquemada, was especially devoted to rooting out heretical ideas. Both those Jews who left Spain and those who converted to Christianity suffered for their faith.

Judaism in the Modern Age

Judaism in the Middle Ages was excluded from full participation in Gentile society. In the modern age, some Jews found ways to escape from the ghettos and to participate in the intellectual and political life of their nations.

Islam [is-LAHM] Like other religions of the family of Abraham, it emphasizes worship of one God. It believes that Muhammad is the last and most important of the prophets of God.

The Enlightenment, with its emphasis on human reason and scientific knowledge, deeply challenged the traditions of Judaism, Christianity, and **Islam.** Christian philosophers such as John Locke (1632–1704) of England and René Descartes (1596–1650) of France held the mind to be the measure of all things. Priority was assigned to reason over revelation and to science over tradition. God was relegated to a position of creator of the universe and establisher of its laws. The job of human beings was to discover the laws and to plan their lives to use them for their benefit. The philosopher replaced the theologian, the scientist the priest. Young men at the universities accepted views of the Enlightenment as proper for leaders.

Emphasis on reason over revelation is called **modernism.** In Judaism and Christianity, the emphasis on secular knowledge above traditional, revealed knowledge began to affect young people of the seventeenth century. In our time, it has also affected Islam. In response to these challenges, some religious groups changed their beliefs to accommodate new knowledge; others held more firmly to the teachings of their ancient traditions.

Jews who examined the traditions found different treasures. In the nineteenth century, Jews in Europe and the United States found new opportunities to express different interpretations of the traditional faith. In the United States, Jews enjoyed the rights of citizens. The first president, George Washington, wrote to Jews in Newport, Rhode Island, affirming religious freedom of citizens.

> The citizens of the United States of America have a right to applaud themselves for having given to mankind examples of an enlarged and liberal policy—a policy worthy of imitation. All possess alike liberty of conscience and immunities of citizenship.
>
> It is now no more that toleration is spoken of as if it were the indulgence of one class of people that another enjoyed the exercise of their inherent natural rights, for, happily, the Government of the United States, which gives to bigotry no factions [sanctions], to persecution no assistance, requires only that they who live under its protection should demean themselves as good citizens in giving it on all occasions their effectual support.[13]

France, Great Britain, and Germany granted Jews rights as citizens to practice their religion without discrimination. Free to leave the ghettos and participate in civil and intellectual life of their countries, many Jews reexamined what Judaism meant to them. Forms of interpretation began to separate into movements or traditions, especially in Germany and then in the United States. Most traditional Jews, especially in eastern Europe, wanted to keep all possible provisions of the Torah and Talmud. A few Jewish thinkers thought ethical teachings were more important than ritual. Other Jewish scholars sought to compromise ancient and medieval customs with opportunities for life in a larger community.

Reform Judaism

In the United States, Reform Judaism was inspired by David Einhorn (1809–1879) and Isaac Mayer Wise (1819–1900). In its Pittsburgh Platform of 1885, the group of rabbis stated that the Torah is binding only in its moral teachings and that rabbinic teachings on diet, ceremonial purity, and dress are no longer binding in the new age. Orthodox and Conservative Judaism required Jews to abstain from all unclean foods, such as pork and shellfish, and to avoid eating meat and milk dishes at the same meal. Reform Judaism abandoned these kosher food laws. The Columbus Platform of 1937 gave stronger emphasis to the Torah and for the first time expressed the need for a Jewish homeland. In 1976, the Central Conference of American Rabbis emphasized religious practice, Sabbath observance, and keeping holy days, as well as a Jewish home. In Reform synagogues, most of the service is in English, and males are not required to wear hats. As in Conservative Judaism, Reform Judaism permits males and females to sit together. Women can be ordained rabbis.

modernism
[mod-ur-NIZ-um]
In religion, emphasis on reason in philosophy and science instead of traditional beliefs.

Conservative Judaism

Influenced by Frankel, Solomon Schechter (1850–1915) became the leader of Conservative Judaism. The Torah and Talmud must be followed. **Zionism,** a movement to establish a Jewish homeland, is important. **Mitzvoth,** responses to God, must be followed as interpreted by congregations. They can vary in their practices, following a democratic spirit in America on such matters as whether to use organ music in their worship services. In Conservative synagogues, most parts of worship services are in Hebrew, males wear head coverings (*kippot* or *yarmulkes*), and members are encouraged to observe **kashruth,** or **kosher,** food laws, Shabbat, and holidays. Women fill roles of leadership in the congregation; qualified women can be ordained rabbis.

Reconstructionism

In the twentieth century, a new, scientifically oriented view of Judaism appeared. Reconstructionism was a school of thought that has grown into a denomination.[14] In 1955, Mordecai Kaplan (1881–1983) established a Federation of Reconstructionist Congregations. Kaplan's concern was to revitalize Judaism for modern, scientifically oriented Jews. A naturalist, Kaplan rejected supernatural elements in Judaism. He emphasized the ethical values of Judaism and the importance of realizing these ethical values in the contemporary world. Rituals and holidays of the Jewish community should be observed, because if God is only an intellectual idea people will not have the motives and strengths to live ethical lives. Kaplan's denial that Israel is a chosen people brought sharp criticism from Orthodox Judaism.

Orthodox Judaism

Orthodox Judaism retains as much as possible from the Torah and Talmud. Women and men do not sit together in worship. Men wear hats and prayer shawls. The service is in Hebrew. Members are expected to keep kashruth. Since 1948, a Jewish homeland has been generally supported. Orthodox Jews are free to participate as citizens in the modern world, but they are never to compromise their Jewish faith. In Israel, Orthodox Judaism is standard, and the American varieties of Reform Judaism and Conservative Judaism are not recognized as fully legitimate. For example, Orthodox rabbis in Israel do not accept Reform and Conservative rabbis as their equals in authority.

When speaking of Judaism outside Israel, it is desirable to indicate which group of congregations is being discussed, for groups vary considerably in their beliefs and practices, especially in the United States.[15] Ways of dress, observances of dietary restrictions, practices during synagogue worship, ways of keeping holidays, and attitudes toward the Torah and Talmud are areas where Jews can differ considerably and still be Jews. The differences occur in observances rather than in beliefs about God.

Hasidism

The Hasidim, or "pious ones," of the modern world are devoted to the Torah and to pure lives. They are actively engaged in their societies, but, as a group, they maintain Judaism in the most ancient form possible. Purity can be kept with joy, even ecstasy.

Zionism [ZII-e-NIS-em] A movement led by Jews to provide a home country for themselves. Theodor Herzl was a leader at the end of the nineteenth century.

Mitzvoth [MITZ-VOTH] (sing. mitz-va) In Judaism, responses to obedience to God according to the covenant. How to live in covenant relationship; with God is a central teaching of Judaism.

kashruth [KASH-root] Jewish dietary regulations.

kosher [KO-sher] In Judaism, meat that has been properly prepared for eating. One requirement is that most of the blood be removed from the meat.

In this tradition, a Zaddik, or holy man, can become a channel for God's saving power. He is a power in himself and can inspire enlightenment in others. The Hasidim prize humility and cultivate a love for every human that epitomizes the teachings of Judaism. Martin Buber (1878–1965), a Jewish philosopher, devoted his life to the study and interpretation of Hasidism. He emphasized that the world is waiting to be "hallowed" by devoted humans.[16] In his work *I and Thou,* he held that God is the eternal Thou.[17] Only in relationship with him can persons become fully human. In relationships with others, humans must relate to another "thou," a person, rather than to an "it," an object. In "I-and-Thou" relationships to God and others, people become fully human. In these relationships, the world, which has the potential for more goodness than in material relationships, is hallowed.

Zionism

Zionism was a Jewish movement of the late nineteenth century that intended to establish a Jewish homeland. Since 135 C.E., Jews had lost control of life in Jerusalem. Jews living in many different countries had no land of their own, a particular disadvantage in times of persecution. For example, although France had given Jews citizenship in the nineteenth century, behavior in the trial and sentencing of Capt. Alfred Dreyfus showed strong anti-Semitism. In 1896, Theodor Herzl published *The Jewish State,* which stimulated a determined migration of Jews to Palestine. The Balfour Declaration of 1917, obtained by efforts of Chaim Weizmann, a British chemist, lent support of the British government to migration. When Hitler came to power in Germany in 1933, approximately 220,000 Jews lived in Palestine. At the height of the **Holocaust,** the Nazis' systematic extermination of the Jewish population of Europe, Arab protests led the British to place a quota on Jewish immigrants to Palestine. In response to Nazi atrocities, Reform and Conservative congregations favored a permanent homeland for Jews in Palestine. Virtually all Jews now insist on Israel as a homeland for Jews.

Holocaust [HOL-u-cost] An offering brought to a deity and completely burnt. The term now refers to the Nazi extermination of Jews in occupied countries during World War II.

The Holocaust

Jews listened to the news of the Nazi invasion of Poland with the same shock as the rest of Europe and America. In the next few weeks, they were bombed, invaded, and occupied along with other citizens in European countries. In later months, as they were singled out with special registrations, passports, and clothing, they experienced a continuation of the persecutions that had increased in Germany since the rise of Hitler in 1933. They agonized over their families' being separated by force, some going to slave labor and others to "resettlement." Some Jews, such as those in Warsaw, were forced into a new ghetto. From ghettos and camps in Europe, Jews were selected for

© AP Photos

Death Camp at Belsen. This man barely survived the hardships that Nazis inflicted on Jews in Europe. Six million Jews were put to death.

further "resettlement." Only when imprisoned in the death camps did most comprehend their horrible future.

In the Holocaust, 1933–1945, the Nazis exterminated six million Jews in Europe. Theodor Herzl had been right about the rising tide of anti-Semitism. In camps such as Auschwitz, they were gassed, and their clothes, possessions, and even their body parts were salvaged for the Nazi war effort. Bodies were burned in crematoriums. The Allied forces that liberated the camps produced photographs and eyewitness accounts that were, even in a time calloused to war atrocities, almost incredible. Records of the Nuremberg trials show widespread cooperation of the population of Europe with the scheme of Nazi officers for a "final solution" to the Jewish "problem." Despite heroic efforts by individual Gentiles to save Jewish friends, almost no help came from the Christian church or from Allied governments.[18] Today, the extent of anti-Semitism shocks most people. The Holocaust has had an indescribable impact on every Jew. For Gentiles, it counteracts any claim that with increased education humanity is becoming more humane. For many Jews and Christians it challenges traditional beliefs in the existence of a moral, knowing, and caring God.

Older and younger Jews emphasize different aspects of the Holocaust. Jews born before the Holocaust, such as Elie Wiesel and Emil Fackenheim, emphasize the suffering Hitler imposed on Jews. Jews must remain faithful to Judaism lest they themselves accomplish the work Hitler began.[19] Jews born after the Holocaust, such as Marc Ellis, emphasize the implications of the Holocaust for Christians as well as Jews. Christians, too, are now bound historically to the tragedy of the Holocaust.

Israel

In 1948, despite determined Arab opposition, the state of Israel was carved out of the British Mandate. Initially, guerrilla bands fought each other constantly for control of city blocks, acres of farmland, and the water required for life in cities or on farms. In the twentieth century, Jewish immigrants established farms where families worked together to defend their land and produce crops. These cooperative farms, which people could enter or leave as they pleased, became known as *kibbutzim* (the singular form is *kibbutz*). Immigrants planted forests on hills and orchards in valleys. In cities, they built factories. Military service was made compulsory for both men and women. Not only guerrilla attacks have been made but also international wars have been waged to dislodge the Jews from Palestine. Only a minority of Arabs agree that Israel should exist. A majority of Jews are willing to sacrifice to make sure Israel remains strong.

Through leaders such as David Ben Gurion and Golda Meir, Israel has gained and retained the support of the United Nations. Nevertheless,

© David Rubinger/CORBIS

David Ben Gurion. Planting trees was both symbolic and useful in the young nation of Israel.

rocked by protests of Arabs within its borders and Palestinians seeking a nation for themselves, Israel must also face forces in other nations that are devoted to its destruction. Israel is now an established, recognized nation. It is, however, a very young nation still defining the course of its future.

The Roots of the Arab–Israeli Conflict

The tangled roots of the Arab–Israeli conflict cannot be summarized easily. Each side chooses which information to select, group, and explain. Historians who are neither Jews, Muslims, nor Palestinians, trace Muslim control of Palestine in the seventh century through the Ottoman Empire, which ended in the first quarter of the twentieth century. British rule ended in 1948, leaving American influence dominant after World War II.

Golda Meir. An emigrant from Poland to Wisconsin at age eight, Meir helped found Israel and served as prime minister of Israel.

Palestinians argue that their people tended the land under family ownership that endured for centuries. They believe Israelis unfairly used military power, discriminatory laws, and U.S. influence to evict Palestinians from their land and force them into refugee camps.

Israelis argue that their occupation of the land goes back to Abraham. More recently, however, they bought land from Ottoman investors to whom Palestinians had defaulted on loans. Israelis cite, also, that when Arabs made war on them they repulsed the aggressors, acquiring in victory the territory of the West Bank, the Golan Heights, and the Gaza Strip.

Who is a Jew? The Halakhic definition is that a child born of Jewish parents or a convert to Judaism is considered a Jew, possessing the sanctity of the Jewish people and the obligation to observe the commandments.[20] From the Mishnah and the Talmud, in a mixed marriage the child's status is determined by that of the mother. The child of a Jewish mother is a Jew; the child of a non-Jewish mother is required to undergo ritual conversion even though the father is a Jew.

This straightforward answer has been particularly controversial in modern Israel. Converts to Judaism agree to follow 613 commandments, which most born Jews do not do (since the second Temple was destroyed, fewer than 613 commandments can be observed). Many people exterminated by the Nazis as Jews did not meet the Halakhic standard for a Jew. Were these people who gave their lives for their Jewish identity not really Jews? The Rabbinate of Israel has opposed any secular definition of Jew. In the early days of the modern state of Israel, most Jews supported the rabbinical definition.

Since 1970, the national identity of a Jew may differ from the rabbinical definition. Conversions to Judaism under non-Orthodox rabbis and congregations can meet the standards of the Law of Return and automatic Israeli citizenship. However, a person born a Jew and who has converted to another religion cannot be accepted as a Jew. As one Reform rabbi expressed it, "There are no 'Jews for Jesus'; these *former* Jews are Christians." Non-Jews who marry Jews are not Jews by marriage alone; to become a Jew they must undergo a ceremony of conversion.

Despite almost daily threats and weekly terrorist attacks, Israel is committed to survival as a nation and to security for its people. Whether or not reprisals in Palestinian territories deter future attacks, they do demonstrate Israel's determination to endure. Steven T. Katz has written that "Zionism is the momentous Jewish response to modernity." It is not enough to be free in thought, he says; one must also be free in will. Real freedom entails the freedom to be different.[21]

In 2008–2009 Judaism celebrates year 5769 since the creation of the world. Jews recall many mountaintop experiences and milestones in those millennia. Over three thousand years ago, they began to settle in the "Promised Land," the land God gave them as the home of the "twelve tribes" of Israel. In later centuries Jews began to settle in other lands all over the world. At the Western Wall of the Temple platform in Jerusalem, visitors can see men and women from all those lands praying in the traditions of their fathers and mothers.

The first relationship with God is described in Torah, the first five books of the Bible. The sacrificial system that was eventually established in the Temple of Jerusalem lasted until the Romans burned the Temple during the war of 70 C.E.

The second relationship with God included the Torah, but the sacrificial system of the priesthood was replaced by the rabbis, who eventually wrote the Talmud, commenting on the Torah. That period continues today.

The third relationship includes Torah, Talmud, and freedom of observance in the age of civil rights for Jews. Basic Judaism has not changed, but how it is observed depends on how congregations of Jews balance tradition with the practices of the cultures in which they live. Thus, in the United States, Jews may be Orthodox, Conservative, Reconstructionist, or Reform. Living in the United States, they have a strong urge to support the nation of Israel as their homeland.

What will distinguish a fourth stage of Judaism? Some Christians have speculated that the earlier promises of God to the Jews will be realized, including the "Promised Land." There are Jews and non-Jews who anticipate a different stage, but many Jews look forward to the time when God intervenes to reestablish the Temple in Jerusalem and gather his people to himself. Judaism is a religion of tradition, but it looks toward a future that is better than the past.

CONSIDER THIS
Timeless Judaism

Worldview: Judaism

The worldview of Judaism today reflects about four millennia of God's interaction with the children of Abraham, Isaac, and Jacob. The worldview presented in the Bible has been foundational rather than final. Interactive experiences in rabbinic, medieval, and modern Judaism have produced other interpretations. Modern Judaism, then, comprises many living traditions that change as they interact with each other, with other religions, and with historical developments.

The Absolute

The creed of Judaism (the Shema) is brief: "Hear, O Israel! The Lord is our God, the Lord alone" (Deuteronomy 6:4). This is what every religious Jew believes. The next part of the creed is what a Jew does. "You shall love the Lord your God with all your heart and with all your soul and with all your might" (Deuteronomy 6:5). As part of the Torah, the creed comes from the most sacred part of the Bible.

Judaism has usually expressed the nature of the Lord, Adonai, in the analogy of a person. Where Greek philosophers preferred to conceive of God as unchanging and remote from the created world, the Bible is a record of God's involvement in changing seasons, the rise and fall of nations, and the activities of the families of his chosen people. Dialogues between the Lord and successive generations of

Judaism in History

3760 First year of the Jewish calendar

2000 Abraham

1600 Amoses frees Egyptians from Hyksos rule

1300 Moses leads Hebrews to Promised Land

1004–965 King David reigns

965–928 King Solomon reigns

721 Assyria conquers Israel

597 Babylonians exile Jews

586 Nebuchadnezzar of Babylon destroys Jerusalem

538 Cyrus releases Jews from Babylon

515 Jews build second temple in Jerusalem

490 Greeks defeat Persians at Marathon

444 Ezra renews the covenant

332 Alexander the Great arrives

264–241 Punic Wars: Rome defeats Carthage

29 Christianity begins

70 Romans destroy Jerusalem temple

73 Romans capture Masada

90 Jewish scriptures formed into canon

135 Romans expel Jews from Jerusalem

220 Rabbis complete the Mishnah

480 Rabbis complete the Talmud in Babylon

167 Antiochus IV provokes Jewish revolt

164 The temple rededicated

63 Pompey establishes Roman rule

1000 Year 4760 of the Jewish calendar

1135 Maimonides born

1250 Moses de Leon born

1492 Spain expels Jews; Columbus sails for New World

1800 Napoleon becomes first consul in France

1842 Herman Cohen born

1896 Theodore Herzl launches Zionism

1917 Balfour Declaration

1933 Nazis begin persecution of Jews

1939–45 World War II fought; Jews suffer Holocaust

1948 Israel becomes a state; in India, Mohandas K. Gandhi assassinated

1956 Suez war between Israel and Egypt, Israel takes Gaza Strip

1962 Lt. Col. John Glenn Jr. first man to orbit Earth Adolph Eichman hanged in Israel for his role in the Nazi persecution of the Jews

1990 Jews and Muslims clash at Temple Mount, Jerusalem

1967 Six-Day War, Israel defeats enemies and expands its territory, holding Golan Heights, West Bank, Old City of Jerusalem, and Sinai

1993 Israel and Palestinians negotiate a peace treaty

1979 Israel and Egypt, in cooperation with President Jimmy Carter, sign a final peace treaty

1994 Israel and Jordan negotiate a peace treaty

1982 Israelis assault PLO forces inside Lebanon

1995 Rabbi Bea Wiler becomes Germany's first female rabbi since the Holocaust

1987 Israeli occupied territories torn by civil disobedience

2001 Ariel Sharon becomes prime minister of Israel

BCE

CE

2000 1500 1000 500 0 500 1000 1500 2000

humans are reported in detail. Yet as knowledge of the universe has increased, the concept of God developed to assimilate new knowledge.

In the early stories of the Torah, the Jewish concept of God emerges. The whole world is his. He enters the lives of good people and makes covenants with them. He hears their cries when they need him and responds to deliver them. He guides and directs his people. He makes impotent toys of the greatest kings of the nations. He is compassionate to the fatherless, the barren woman, slaves, and prisoners. He is a warrior fighting for his people.

For the prophets, the Lord is clearly God of all Hebrews and an effective contender with gods of other nations. Other gods, such as the Baals of the Canaanites, are not reliable or powerful when compared to the God of Elijah. For the eighth-century B.C.E. prophets, God controls the kingdoms of Israel and Judah. The Lord is the standard of justice, like a plumb line used by masons to test the perpendicular tolerance of walls. God is the source of forgiving, redeeming love, like a husband who forgives an unfaithful wife. The Lord is holy, set apart, high and lifted up. Above the petty ambitions of upstart kings, he preserves those who trust in him. The Lord is one who chose his servant while he was in his mother's womb. The Lord is ineffable, great beyond the power of words. He is one who saves remnants of his chosen people. He establishes peace on earth. David describes the Lord as a faithful shepherd.

> *A Psalm of David*
> The Lord is my shepherd;
>   I lack nothing.
> He makes me lie down in green pastures;
>   He leads me to water in places of repose;
>   He renews my life;
>   As befits His name.
> Though I walk through a valley of deepest darkness,
>   I fear no harm, for You are with me;
>   Your rod and Your staff—they comfort me.
> You spread a table for me in full view of my enemies;
>   You anoint my head with oil;
>   my drink is abundant.
> Only goodness and steadfast love shall pursue me
>   all the days of my life,
>   and I shall dwell in the house of the Lord
>   for many long years. (Psalm 23:1–6)

The World

The Genesis account of creation establishes the theme of the relationship of God and the world that is retained in the history of Judaism.

> When God began to create heaven and earth—the earth being unformed and void, with darkness over the surface of the deep and a wind from God sweeping over the water—God said, "Let there be light"; and there was light. God saw that the light was good, and God separated the light from the darkness. God called the light Day, and the darkness He called Night. And there was evening and there was morning, a first day. (Genesis 1:1–5)

The universe is subordinate to God and dependent on him; it is always less than God and other than God. Established in a thoughtful, systematic process, all its parts are good, and everything together is very good (Genesis 1:31). The phenomenal universe is not God, but it is evidence for God's creative power and love. Frightening oceans are balanced by fertile lands; unpleasant animals are balanced by tasty meats. The seasons change predictably; humans can plan their lives according to them.

Judaism celebrates the universe. The Psalms praise many features of the sky and the earth (Psalm 19:24).

> The heavens declare the glory of God,
> > the sky proclaims His handiwork.
> Day to day makes utterance,
> > night to night speaks out.
> There is no utterance,
> > there are no words,
> > whose sound goes unheard.
> Their voice carries throughout the earth,
> > their words to the end of the world.
> He placed in them a tent for the sun,
> > who is like a groom coming forth from the chamber,
> > like a hero, eager to run his course.
> His rising-place is at one end of heaven,
> > and his circuit reaches the other;
> > nothing escapes his heat. (Psalm 19:2–7)

Sun and rain cause the earth to yield food. The moon marks the seasons for thanksgiving and celebrating harvests. Increasing herds and crops are signs of God's blessings. In Judaism, the universe is made for humans; it is to be enjoyed with gratitude during a long life. Human suffering is not attributed to the created nature of the universe. Judaism rejects any worldview that sees nature as evil, a place to be escaped. The phenomenal world is God's world; he is present in the heavens, in the earth, and in the place of shadows (Sheol) under the earth. The world is other than God, but it is not opposed to God. In celebrating the nature of the universe, Jews praise the activity of God. Judaism's approach to ecology has always been based on the concept of humans as stewards of God's creation.

> The earth is the Lord's and the fullness thereof, the world and those who dwell therein. (Psalm 24:1)

As the story of Genesis explains, God created the world and everything in it; he entrusted Adam and Eve with its care. Only when humans act responsibly to God can they enjoy the bounty of the earth.

Humans

Genesis describes humans as God's highest creatures:

> And God created man in His image, in the image of God He created him; male and female He created them. God blessed them and God said to them, "Be fertile and increase, fill the earth and master it; and rule the fish of the sea, the birds of the sky, and all the living things that creep on the earth." (Genesis 1:27–28)

Male and female humans are created in the image of God. Each is a soul and body united. Each is created for fellowship with God. Humans should rule over all the earth, which has been given to them for food and pleasure. They are little less than gods (or angels); God has crowned them with glory and honor. How small and weak humans are in comparison to the vastness and power of the heavens and earth! Yet humans, rather than the impersonal universe, are the purpose of God's creation. God made humans good; in harmony with his plan for the universe, they are very good.

Humans are responsible. They are answerable to God for their conduct (Genesis 3:9–24). Unlike animals, which are governed solely by instincts, humans can evaluate situations and make choices. They can obey or disobey God, serve or reject God, live in harmony or in enmity with other humans, have nature for or against them. Humans can live any way they choose; they have only to bear the consequences.

Jews are part of the covenant people of God, having additional responsibilities in life. The covenant relationship between God and Israel was mediated by Moses. In the general obligation between two unequal parties, God and the children of Israel, God offers blessings to Israel on condition of its keeping his commandments. The covenant was sealed by a sacred meal and sacrifices.[22]

The Problem and the Solution for Humans

Torah history describes the creation of Adam and Eve and their subsequent rebellion against God. Their exclusion from the Garden of Eden accounts for the miseries and frustrations humans must endure. God chose Noah and his family, righteous people, to survive a worldwide flood, forming a remnant of humans to repopulate the earth. The most righteous humans were soon involved in sinful acts; their children were no better than they. The biblical history of the Hebrews and their descendants, the Jews, relates God's ongoing endeavors to restore, for brief periods of time, a covenant relationship of loving-kindness and faithfulness.

Jews understand the teachings of Moses from Exodus through Deuteronomy as explanations of beliefs and practices that invite compliance with the covenant and permit restoration after human lapses. God, powerful and just, extends compassion to all generations.

> Have mercy upon me, O God,
>   as befits Your faithfulness;
>   in keeping with Your abundant compassion,
>   blot out my transgressions. (Psalm 51:3)

At various times, Jewish groups sought help from individuals other than priests. One group expected a descendant of King David to restore Judaism. Others expected someone in the prophetic tradition, such as the prophet Elijah, to help renew the covenant. Groups have identified one of their contemporaries as the Messiah, who would usher in a new age. Most Jews agree that although the Messiah is expected, he has not come. In this belief, Jews do not agree with Christians that Jesus is the Messiah.

Community and Ethics

Religious Jews consider themselves members of a family and of a larger community in covenant with God. The Passover observance reminds them of their membership in a community God redeemed from bondage in Egypt and led to a land of promise. The community has often been severely persecuted, but God has always saved a remnant to fulfill his purposes. Jews may be of almost any nationality or race. There have been Ethiopian Jews since biblical times. Into modern times, these "falashas" continued to practice sacrifices in their temples. Israelis recognized them publicly as Jews by airlifting many of them to Israel. Those who claim to be Jews and who are accepted by the Jewish community are Jews.

In the age of universalism, or emphasis on a global community, the traditional Jewish idea of a chosen people strikes some non-Jews as an archaic concept. In the Bible, however, particularly in the writings of the Deuteronomist, God rules universally, but he has chosen Israel as the people of God. God's election of Israel is based on its response to the covenant he has offered. Accepting the blessings of the covenant requires, in return, accepting its responsibilities. Israel is obligated to keep its law and statutes. Although God does not always approve of Israel's actions—he sometimes condemns the actions—he does not utterly reject Israel. In all history, he seeks to restore the covenant relationship with his people.

Beyond the age when the scriptures were written, rabbis have emphasized that God's choosing Israel is based on its accepting the Torah at Sinai. No other peoples on earth, except those who have become Jews, have accepted the conditions laid down in the Torah. In medieval Judaism, Judah Halevi advanced the idea that from the time of Adam, Jewish people were endowed with a special religious faculty. In modern Judaism, Moses Mendelssohn argued that Judaism is identical with a "religion of reason."[23] Since the Holocaust, Jews have wrestled with developing a revised, up-to-date understanding of what it means to be a chosen people. Being chosen and set apart from other peoples brings suffering as well as the blessings of pleasant living.

Judaism thinks in terms of a community chosen to be responsible to God. Membership in a community of chosen people, however, requires commitment to universal values. Judaism promotes care for humans, animals, and the environment among all peoples. Ethical behavior is directed not only to Jews but to all peoples. It attends to both its particular origin and its universal vision.

Jews look to the ethical laws of the Torah to guide their relationships. The law requires them to love their neighbors as themselves. The Ten Commandments state the minimum requirements; the remainder of the Torah explains responsibilities in daily circumstances, especially in those where commandments have been violated. Widows, orphans, the poor, strangers, the homeless, and stray animals have always been given special compassion and aid.

The goal in ethics is to imitate the behavior of God. A person must love the Lord and walk in his ways, holding fast to him (Deuteronomy 11:22). "As the Holy One, blessed be He, is called righteous, be you also righteous; as He is called loving (Psalm 145:17), be you also loving" (Sifra Deuteronomy 49:85a). A. Cohen concludes,

> No finer summary of the Rabbinic teaching on the subject of brotherly love could be suggested than the pithy epigram: "Who is mighty? He who turns an enemy into his friend."[24]

Ethics for Jews are based on the entire halakhah. Although Orthodox Judaism considers halakhah absolutely binding, Reform Judaism rejects its absolute binding force.

In the 1960s, some women in Reform and Conservative Judaism began, in the words of Susannah Heschel, "struggling to become full members of [the community . . . and] to seek changes within *halakhah* to end discrimination in areas from divorce laws to synagogue separation; for inclusion in secular leadership; [and] for concrete changes in the structure of the community to accommodate changing lifestyles of women."[25] In the decades since, many of those goals have been realized, including women serving as rabbis. Another milestone occurred in 1998 when a group of Jewish women approached the women's section of the Western Wall with a Torah scroll intending to pray and read from it. The administrator of the Wall announced that they were not violating halakhah. They had claimed holy ground.[26]

On issues of marriage and family in the twenty-first century, Jews already have their answers.[27] Women may practice family planning, and should their health be compromised seriously by pregnancy, an abortion may be performed to protect them. By indirect inference, practicing lesbians are unworthy in Judaism, as are men who practice sodomy (homosexual acts).[28] Some non-Orthodox Jews may choose to differ, but Judaism supports relationships for men and women who give each other pleasure and seek to create children.

Rituals and Symbols

Other than belief in one God and in the thirteen points of Maimonides, Judaism emphasizes deeds rather than beliefs. To be a practicing Jew is to participate in a lifetime of rituals using unique symbols. A Jew participates with hands and heart as well as with ear and mind. Each Jew is to keep mitzvot (plural of *mitzvah*), or religious duties. Traditionally, there are 248 positive and 365 negative mitzvot, a total of 613. Jewish boys are responsible for keeping them at age thirteen plus one day, and girls are responsible at age twelve plus one day. Mitzvot are performed as commanded by God; no reward follows immediately, but those who are obedient have confidence in the hereafter.[29] Rituals that mark the seasons and stages in each life work their way into the very fibers of practicing Jews' lives. Only a practicing Jew can grasp the full meaning of the rituals and symbols that have been a part of Judaism since the giving of the Torah.

Observances that mark important experiences for Jews are celebrated by both the community and individuals. The Sabbath is observed each week, beginning with sundown on Friday. Holidays are observed annually. The Jewish calendar is based on a lunar month, which means that each year holidays fall on different days of the solar calendar. Regulations in the Jewish calendar, however, keep the festivals in the same season. The new year begins in the fall.

In the month of Elul, a ram's horn (*shofar*) is sounded, calling the faithful to *teshubah,* openly confessing their sins against their neighbors. Prepared for the new year, Jews celebrate Rosh Hashanah, New Year's Day.[30]

Celebrating God's creation of the world, **Rosh Hashanah** is observed on Tishri 1 and 2. It is the beginning of the **Days of Awe,** ten days when Jews concentrate on prayer, contemplation, and self-searching.[31] A period of repentance ensues and ends with twenty-four hours of atonement and fasting, **Yom Kippur,** the holiest day of the Jewish calendar. Jews spend much of their time standing or kneeling in the congregation.

Hanukkah comes near the end of the solar year and celebrates the rededication of the Jerusalem temple in 164 B.C.E. The sacred oil that was enough for only one day miraculously lasted for eight days of celebration. The menorah of nine branches marks this special Feast of Lights. Hanukkah is a minor festival, as is Purim. A happy holiday observed as the days of winter lengthen, it recalls Queen

Rosh Hashanah
[ROSH hah-SHA-nah]
In Judaism, the first of the Days of Awe, Tishri 1 and 2. Celebrates God's creation of the world. Fall of the year period of prayer and self-examination.

Days of Awe
In Judaism, ten days in the fall of the year when Jews observe their new year and a period of prayer and self-examination, ending with Yom Kippur. Also known as the High Holy Days.

Yom Kippur
[yom-kip-PUR]
The tenth day of the Days of Awe. A twenty-four-hour period of fasting when Jews stand or kneel in prayer much of the time in the synagogue.

Hanukkah [KHAN-nu-ka]
A celebration near the end of the solar year. It commemorates the lights in the rededicated Temple, 164 B.C.E. after Syrians had desecrated it during the Maccabean revolt.

Esther, who helped her people escape a sinister plot of genocide in Persia; the holiday of Purim celebrates the deliverance of Jews from their enemies.

In the spring, Jews celebrate two holidays. The most important holiday in the Jewish year is Passover, which marks God's deliverance of the Hebrews from slavery in Egypt through the leadership of Moses. The other holiday, **Shavuot** marks an early harvest and calls attention to the giving (revelation) of the Ten Commandments.

During Passover, Jews eat a sacred meal, the **Seder.** The order of the meal is based on **Haggadah,** the Story. The words recited differ somewhat, according to the tradition of the family.[32] By custom, a child asks four questions about why the meal is different from all other meals.

"Why is matzah eaten instead of bread?"
"It is the symbol of enslavement."

"Why are bitter herbs eaten?"
"They are symbols of enslavement."

"Why do we dip our bread (vegetables) in condiments?"
"They are symbols of freedom."

"Why do we sit in cushioned chairs (recline)?"
"It is a symbol of freedom."

One way that Jews have kept their separate identity is through food laws, kashruth. Arthur Hertzberg explains their purpose this way:

> Essentially the traditional writings have produced two basic reasons for kashruth: that these laws represent a curbing of man's animal appetites and that they are ordained as a way of setting the Jews apart in their day to day life, so that they might be conscious of their responsibility as members of a priest-people. Ultimately, the laws of kashruth cannot be rationalized. The believer accepts them as part of a total system, the Jewish way to holiness, ordained by God. The nonbeliever may cling to kashruth out of sentiment or attachment to a cultural past, but this clinging has demonstrably seldom outlasted one generation of disbelief.[33]

The dietary laws of Judaism are directly related to the concept of a chosen people. The laws of kashruth, food that is fit or proper for preparation or consumption, are binding on Jews. In the Torah, all fruits and vegetables are permitted. Other laws describe which animals, birds, and fish may be eaten, how they may be prepared, and how they cannot be eaten with milk or dairy products.[34]

In the Pentateuch, ten clean animals are listed: ox, sheep, goat, hart, gazelle, roebuck, wild goat, ibex, antelope, and mountain sheep (Deuteronomy 14:4–5). Camels and pigs are forbidden. The Bible lists twenty-four unclean birds, especially birds of prey; it does not list any clean birds. Among Jews, pheasants and turkeys are disputed birds; goose and duck may be eaten. Although four kinds of locusts can be eaten, insects are forbidden; honey can be eaten. Fish must have at least one fin and one scale. Sturgeon and swordfish are disputed among Jews.

Shavuot [sha-voo-OT] In Judaism, marks the early harvest and commemorates God's giving of the Ten Commandments.

Seder [SAY-der] The meal of unleavened bread eaten after sundown at the beginning of Passover.

Haggadah [hah-gah-DAH] The story used at the Seder during the Jewish holiday of Passover. This term is distinguished from *aggadah,* nonlegal stories of rabbinic Judaism.

© Richard Nowitz/CORBIS

A Torah Scroll. The Scroll is removed from the ark in the temple (synagogue) and read to the congregation. Writings of Moses contain the central teachings of Judaism.

Slaughtering must be according to rules of **Shehitah** and carried out by a licensed **shohet.** An animal that died a natural death or one that was torn by a wild beast cannot be eaten. After the slaughter, the shohet must examine the meat for any signs of disease. If certain signs are present, the meat is forbidden. Neither the sciatic nerve nor fat attached to the intestines and the stomach can be eaten.

Because Jews are not permitted to eat blood, meat must be prepared so as to remove veinal blood. After proper slaughtering, which removes most of the blood, the remaining blood can be removed either by placing it in salt or by roasting the meat over an open flame. The proper preparation of meat is called *koshering.*

In the book of Exodus, Jews are forbidden to seethe a kid in its mother's milk (Exodus 23:19; Deuteronomy 14:21). Jews have interpreted this law to mean that milk and meat shall not be eaten in the same meal. The prohibition extends to cooking, eating, or deriving benefit from such a mixture. Prohibition on milk extends to all dairy products. To protect themselves from violation, Jews keep everything connected with preparation, serving, and eating meat separated from everything connected with preparation, serving, and eating milk and dairy products. In Orthodox Jewish homes there are complete, separate utensils for meat and milk preparation and consumption. Although fish, vegetables, and fruit are neutral, rabbis have prohibited eating meat and fish together. As only meat prepared by a Jew can be used, so also only milk production supervised by a Jew may be used.

Although Reform Judaism does not insist on observance of kashruth, other congregations emphasize compliance as highly desirable. Orthodox Jews insist on compliance.

Rituals also mark the most significant points of development in individual lives. Male infants are circumcised on the eighth day after birth; the ritual brings them into the covenant established with the patriarchs of Judaism. At age thirteen a boy is considered responsible for his religious acts. He becomes, on his birthday, a **Bar Mitzvah,** a son of the commandment. In recent times, a service in the synagogue celebrates the occasion. During the service, the boy reads from the Torah in Hebrew. Some congregations also hold **Bat Mitzvah** services, celebrating a girl's becoming responsible for her religious duties.

A betrothal precedes the marriage service, which is held under a canopy, the *huppah.* The groom gives the bride a ring; she may also give him a ring. The bride and groom share a cup of wine. Although sharing the wine completes the marriage service, custom has added the breaking of a glass, symbolic of the fragile nature of supreme happiness.

At death, the corpse is washed, simply clothed, and placed in a plain coffin. Family, members of the congregation, and friends express their grief and their faith in God. Judaism meets this important passage, as all others in a person's life, with distinctive ritual that reinforces identity with the community of believers. The identity is not only with the present community but also with past communities of Jews. Samuel C. Heilman has recorded what was done and why when his father died. In his descriptions of the dozens of small acts, one begins to understand not so much what should be done, but what Jewish communities down through the centuries have built as tradition in times of death.[35]

The custom of sitting **Shivah** encompasses a period of seven days devoted to mourning the deceased. Mourning ends after thirty days, except for father or mother. Remembered for a year, parents are honored morning and evening by the sons who say **Kaddish** in the synagogue, for eleven months. Parents are recalled on the anniversary of their deaths, **Yahrzeit,** and children visit their graves if

Shehitah [she-HEE-tah]
The Jewish method of slaughtering permitted animals or birds for food. The method is to kill the living thing as swiftly and as painlessly as possible with one swift cut across the throat.

shohet [SHOW-het]
A Jewish slaughterer of animals, who kills according to ritually correct methods.

Bar Mitzvah [bar-MITS-vu]
The ceremony that recognizes a thirteen-year-old Jewish boy as a son of the commandment. He is considered an adult responsible for religious duties.

Bat Mitzvah [bat-MITS-vu]
In Reform and Conservative Judaism, the ceremony that recognizes a daughter of the commandment, a Jewish female between twelve and fourteen years of age. She is considered an adult responsible for her religious duties.

Shivah [SHI-vah]
In Judaism, the seven days of mourning that Jews observe for loss of members of their family.

Kaddish [KAY-dish]
In Judaism, a prayer. Recited also by mourners, it begins with words of Ezekiel and asks that God's name be blessed forever.

Yahrzeit [YAHR-zeit]
Based on German for year-time, it is an anniversary of the death of a parent. Children leave a stone at the grave to recall the custom of adding a stone to maintain a grave.

possible. The leaving of a small stone recalls the ancient custom of adding a stone to the grave to maintain it, explains Rabbi Leo Trepp.

Life after Death

Judaism has emphasized a good life on earth more than the joys of heaven. In early Judaism, there was a belief that souls of the departed slept in Sheol, but most people did not find the prospect attractive. The Pharisees in the first century believed the body is resurrected; the Sadducees denied it. Judaism today avoids embalming bodies and uses plain wooden boxes that will decay after burial. There are references in the Psalms to heaven and hell, concepts that some scholars believe were influenced by Zoroastrians. Jewish services lack specific descriptions of life beyond death. There is life with God in the age to come, and the joy of fellowship with God is more important than real estate, property, status, and activities. Isaac Luria taught that souls are reincarnated. But rabbis taught as a matter of faith that there is resurrection from the dead; to deny it is sinful. "Since a person repudiated belief in the Resurrection of the dead, he will have no share in the Resurrection" (Sanhedrin 90a).[36]

Judaism and Other Religions

Although Jews think of themselves as God's chosen people; that is, selected from among all others to live by the Torah, they believe other peoples can worship God, overcome sin, and live according to his universal moral laws. From biblical times, converts have been welcomed to Judaism. Nevertheless, peoples can serve God in their own religions.

How do Jews view Christianity? Rabbi Leo Baeck (1873–1956), a brilliant scholar in Germany, survived the Gestapo's assault on his books and person. In his book of essays *Judaism and Christianity,* Rabbi Baeck describes Christianity as one of several postbiblical movements in Judaism.[37] The early followers of Jesus were Jews who drew heavily on the traditions of the fathers, especially in their expectations of a Messiah. After the destruction of the temple in 70 C.E., they formed the views presented in the gospels of the New Testament. They developed a romantic view of the world. By this term Rabbi Baeck meant they abandoned the discipline of living ethical lives, preferring instead to give primacy to miracles and doctrines of a supernatural end of time. In a recent dialogue with a Christian, Pinchas Lapide advanced these theses for response: (1) Jesus did not present himself to his people as Messiah; (2) the people of Israel did not reject Jesus; and (3) Jesus never repudiated his people.[38]

The distinctive worldview of Judaism has developed from Jews' concept of themselves as a people in covenant with God. The events of history have helped them shape their particular identity. Although Jewish interpretation differs from that of all other peoples, it has influenced all culture of the West and, through Christianity and Islam, all peoples.

In the next chapter we will study Christianity. We will see how the Jewish worldview helped shape the response of people to Jesus of Nazareth as the Messiah. As a religion of the family of Abraham, Christianity shares many of the events of historical development and worldview with Judaism. Although acknowledging Judaism as preparation, Christians emphasize that Christianity is a separate, more acceptable religion. We will see how Christians have interpreted history and worldview to establish a different "chosen people."

VOCABULARY

Aggadah [ug-GAHD-u]
Ark of the Covenant
Asherah [ash-u-RAH]
Ashkenazim [ahsh-ku-NAH-zim]
Baal [BAA-ul]
Bar Mitzvah [bar-MITS-vu]
Bat Mitzvah [bat-MITS-vu]
Canaanites [kay-nu-NIGHTS]
covenant [CUV-u-nunt]
Days of Awe
diaspora [di-AHS-pe-ra]
Essenes [ES-eens]
Gemarah [ge-MAHR-u]
Haggadah [hah-gah-DAH]
Halakhah [ha-la-KAH]
Hanukkah [khan-nu-ka]
Hillel [hil-EL]
Holocaust [HOL-u-cost]
Islam [is-LAHM]

Kabbalah [COB-u-lah]
Kaddish [KAY-dish]
kashruth [KASH-root]
kosher [KO-sher]
matzah [MUT-za]
Messiah [mi-SIGH-u]
Midrash [MID-rash]
Mishnah [MISH-na]
Mitzvoth [MITZ-VOTH](sing. mitz-va)
modernism [mod-ur-NIZ-um]
Mosaic Law
Muslim [MUS-lim]
Passover [PASS-o-ver]
Pharisees [PHAR-i-sees]
prophet [PROF-it]
rabbi [RAB-eye]
Rosh Hashanah [ROSH-hah-SHA-nah]
Sadducees [SAD-u-sees]
Sanhedrin [san-HEED-rin]

scribe [SCRIIB]
Seder [SAY-der]
Sephardim [se-fahr-DIM]
Shavout [sha-voo-OT]
Shehitah [she-HEE-tah]
Shema [SHEE-ma]
Shivah [SHI-vah]
shohet [SHOW-het]
Tanakh [ta-nak]
Talmud [TAL-mud]
theodicy [THEE-od-i-se]
Torah [TOR-ah]
Western Wall
Yahrzeit [YAHR-zeit]
Yom Kippur [yom kip-PUR]
Zealots [ZEL-uts]
Zionism [ZII-e-NIS-em]

QUESTIONS FOR REVIEW

1. Tell the story of Abraham.
2. Tell the story of Moses.
3. Why do Jews honor King David and King Solomon?
4. Who were the Hebrew prophets? What did they do?
5. Who were the early rabbis? How did they influence Judaism?
6. What outside countries helped shape biblical Judaism?
7. How did Jews in the Middle Ages relate to Christians? To Muslims?
8. What forms of observance did Judaism take in nineteenth- and twentieth-century America?
9. How important is Israel in the life of Judaism worldwide?
10. How has establishment of civil rights affected Jews and Judaism?

QUESTIONS FOR DISCUSSION

1. What practices of Jews constantly remind them of their faith and identity?
2. If Jews have a concept of universal salvation under one God, how are other religions included?
3. Describe in general the dynamics of relations among Jews, Christians, and Muslims.
4. Why are memorials and museums of the Holocaust so important to Jews?
5. What do Jews and Christians consider the "Promised Land"? How is it related to the state of Israel?

NOTES

1. From *The Tanakh, The New JPS Translation According to the Traditional Hebrew Text* (Philadelphia: Jewish Society, 1985). Copyright © 1985 by the Jewish Publication Society. Used by permission. Unless otherwise indicated, all biblical references come from this text.

2. Ibid., p. 88.

3. Hayim Tadmore, "The Period of the First Temple, the Babylonian Exile and the Restoration," in *A History of the Jewish People,* ed. H. H. Ben-Sasson (Cambridge, MA: Harvard University Press, 1976), p. 91.

4. A. Malamat, "Origins and the Formative Period," in *A History of the Jewish People,* ed. H. H. Ben-Sasson (Cambridge, MA: Harvard University Press, 1976), p. 33. Dates in this chapter are taken from this source.

5. M. Stern, "The Period of the Second Temple," in *A History of the Jewish People,* ed. H. H. Ben-Sasson (Cambridge, MA: Harvard University Press, 1976), pp. 296–299.

6. Flavius Josephus, "The Wars of the Jews," in *The Works of Josephus,* trans. William Whiston (Peabody, MA: Hendrickson, 1987), p. 741.

7. *The Interpreter's Dictionary of the Bible,* vol. 3 (Nashville, TN: Abingdon Press, 1962), p. 294.

8. Jacob Katz, *Exclusiveness and Tolerance* (New York: Oxford University Press, 1961), p. 5.

9. Jacob S. Minkin, *The World of Moses Maimonides* (New York: Thomas Yosaloff, 1977).

10. *Gates of Prayer, The New Union Prayerbook* (New York: Central Conference of American Rabbis, 1975), pp. 732–733; for a translation that makes clearer the points of Maimonides, see Bernard Martin, *Prayers in Judaism* (New York: Basic Books, 1968), pp. 84–85.

11. Daniel Chanan Matt, *Zohar* (New York: Paulist Press, 1983).

12. Katz.

13. William W. Hallo, David B. Ruderman, and Michael Stanislawski, *Heritage, Civilization and the Jews: Source Reader* (New York: Praeger, 1984), p. 245.

14. Leo Trepp, *A History of the Jewish Experience* (New York: Birmon House, 1973), p. 397.

15. Bernard Martin, *Movements and Issues in American Judaism* (Westport, CT: Greenwood Press, 1978).

16. Martin Buber, *The Origin and Meaning of Hasidism,* trans. Maurice Friedman (New York: Harper & Row, 1960).

17. Martin Buber, *I and Thou* (New York: Scribner's, 1958).

18. S. Ettinger, "The Modern Period," in *A History of the Jewish People,* ed. H. H. Ben-Sasson (Cambridge, MA: Harvard University Press, 1976), p. 1035.

19. Emil Fackenheim, *Quest for Past and Future* (Bloomington: Indiana University Press), 1968.

20. See "Jew" in *Encyclopedia Judaica,* vol. 10, ed. Cecil Roth and Geoffrey Wigoder (Jerusalem: Keter, 1971), pp. 23–25.

21. Steven T. Katz, *Historicism, the Holocaust, and Zionism* (New York: New York University Press, 1997), pp. 291, 329.

22. See "Covenant," in *Encyclopedia Judaica,* vol. 5, ed. Cecil Roth and Geoffrey Wigoder (Jerusalem: Keter, 1971), pp. 1012–1022.

23. See "Chosen People," *Encyclopedia Judaica,* vol. 5, ed. Cecil Roth and Geoffrey Wigoder (Jerusalem: Keter, 1971), pp. 498–502.

24. A. Cohen, *Everyman's Talmud* (New York: Schocken Books, 1978), pp. 211, 216.

25. Susannah Heschel, ed. *On Being a Jewish Feminist* (New York: Schocken Boos, 1983), p. xv.

26. Phyllis Chesler and Rivka Haut, eds., *Women at the Wall* (Woodstock, VT: Jewish Lights, 2003), pp. xix–xx.

27. Daniel Maguire, *Sacred Rights* (Oxford: Oxford University Press, 2003), p. 21.

28. Rabbi Steven Greenberg, *Wrestling with God and Man* (Madison: University of Wisconsin Press), 2004.

29. See "Mitzvah," in *Encyclopedia Judaica,* vol. 12, ed. Cecil Roth and Geoffrey Wigoder (Jerusalem: Keter, 1971), pp. 162–163.

30. Trepp.

31. Philip Goodman, *The Rosh Hashanah Anthology* (Philadelphia: Jewish Publication Society, 1970).

32. Ruth Gruber Fredman, *The Passover Seder* (Philadelphia: University of Pennsylvania Press, 1981).

33. Arthur Hertzberg, *Judaism* (New York: Brazillier, 1962), p. 100; copyright © 1961 by Arthur Hertzberg; reprinted by permission of Simon & Schuster, Inc.

34. See "Kashruth," in *Encyclopedia Judaica,* vol. 6, ed. Cecil Roth and Geoffrey Wigoder (Jerusalem: Keter, 1971), pp. 26–45.

35. Samuel C. Heilman, *When a Jew Dies* (Berkeley: University of California Press, 2001).

36. Cohen, p. 357.

37. Leo Baeck, *Judaism and Christianity,* trans. Walter Kaufmann (New York: Atheneum, 1970).

38. Pinchas Lapide and Ulrich Luz, *Jesus in Two Perspectives,* trans. Lawrence W. Denef (Minneapolis: Augsburg, 1979).

READINGS

Bandstra, Barry L., *Reading the Old Testament*. Belmont, CA: Wadsworth, 1999.

Ben-Sasson, H. H. *A History of the Jewish People*. Cambridge, MA: Harvard University Press, 1976.

Chesler, Phyllis, and Rivka Haut, eds. *Women at the Wall*. Woodstock, VT: Jewish Light Publishing, 2003.

Clapp, Nicholas. *Sheba*. Boston, MA: Houghton Mifflin, 2001.

Cohen, A. *Everyman's Talmud*. New York: Schocken, 1978.

Fishbane, Michael. *Judaism*. Hagerstown, MD: Torch, 1987.

Greenberg, Irving. *The Jewish Way: Living the Holidays*. New York: Summit Books, 1988.

Greenberg, Rabbi Steven. *Wrestling with God and Men*. Madison: University of Wisconsin Press, 2004.

Halo, William, Davie Ruderman, and Michael Stanislawski, eds. *Heritage: Civilization and the Jews*. New York: Praeger, 1984.

Heilman, Samuel C. *When a Jew Dies*. Berkeley: University of California Press, 2001.

Holtz, Barry, ed. *Back to the Sources: Reading the Classical Jewish Texts*. New York: Summit Books, 1984.

Katz, Steven T. *Historicism, the Holocaust, and Zionism*. New York: New York University Press, 1997.

Maguire, Daniel C. "Each One an Entire World: A Jewish Perspective on Family Planning," *Sacred Rights*. Oxford: University Press, 2003.

Neusner, Jacob. *Judaism's Theological Voice: The Melody of the Talmud*. Chicago: University of Chicago Press, 1995.

Plaskow, Judith. *Standing Again at Sinai: Judaism from a Feminist Perspective*. San Francisco: Harper, 1991.

Trepp, Leo. *Judaism*. Belmont, CA: Wadsworth, 1982.

BASIC TENETS OF JUDAISM

FORMS OF JUDAISM		
Reform	**Conservative**	**Orthodox**
Abraham Geiger (1810–1874) Germany	Zacharias Frankel (1801–1875) Germany	Samson Raphael Hirsch (1808–1888) Germany
Isaac Mayer Wise (1819–1900) United States	Soloman Schechter (1850–1915)	
Reconstructionism	**Hasidism**	
Mordecai Kaplan (b. 1881)	Israel Baal Shem (1700–1760)	
THE TANAKH (JEWISH BIBLE)		
Torah: The Five Books of Moses	**The Twelve Minor Prophets**	**Kethuvim: The Writings**
Genesis	Hosea	Psalms
Exodus	Joel	Proverbs
Leviticus	Amos	Job
Numbers	Obadiah	The Song of Songs
Deuteronomy	Jonah	Ruth
	Micah	Lamentations
Nevi'im: The Prophets	Habakkuk	Esther
Joshua	Zephaniah	Daniel
Judges	Haggai	Ezra
I Samuel	Zechariah	Nehemiah
II Samuel	Malachi	I Chronicles
I Kings		II Chronicles
II Kings		
Isaiah		
Jeremiah		
Ezekiel		

CHAPTER 9

Christianity

OVERVIEW AND THEMES

"For God so loved the world he gave his only begotten son that whoever believes in him shall have eternal life."

—*John 3:16***

IMPORTANT CHRISTIAN TEACHINGS

There is one God, the creator of all that exists.

Jesus is the "Son of God" and the mediator of salvation.

Christians respond to God's love through good works.

AREAS OF CHRISTIAN CONCENTRATION

Worldwide: 2,069,883,000

North America: 269,399,000

South America: 501,319,000

Europe: 554,234,000

Asia: 325,034,000

Africa: 394,640,000

MAJOR DIVISIONS OF OBSERVANCE

Roman Catholic: 1,092,853,000

Eastern Orthodox: 217,030,000

Protestant: 364,530,000

Anglicans: 79,988,000

*Thanks to Lee McCracken for his contributions to the overview.

**Revised Standard Version of the Bible* (New York: Thomas Nelson New Testament Section, 1946).

Under Roman rule in Palestine, which began in 63 B.C.E., the house of Herod gained favor by helping keep peace and collect taxes. After the death of Herod the Great in 4 B.C.E., however, Jews were divided in their religious and political loyalties. Sadducees remained loyal to Torah, temple, and Rome; Pharisees advocated innovations in Torah interpretation; Essenes sought greater purity in religion; and Zealots stirred open revolt against Rome. Romans crucified followers of Judas the Galilean in 6 C.E., casting a shadow over subsequent advocates of religious and political change.

To ordinary people of Palestine, these revolutionaries may have seemed innocent, but they awakened in Jewish leaders a keen sense of impending collapse. Strong personalities stirred the simmering pot. John the Baptist, the son of a Jewish priest, baptized people for their sins in preparation for the imminent arrival of the Kingdom of God. His cousin, Jesus, was accused of blasphemy for forgiving people's sins and driving money changers from the Temple. Peter, James, and John, the fishermen from the Sea of Galilee who left their work to follow Jesus, helped organize and announce a new way of life in Jerusalem. Mary, the mother of Jesus, would be honored as the mother of God. These troublemakers were exceeded only by another Jew, who changed his name from Saul to Paul and brought Gentiles (outsiders) into the Way without requiring circumcision or observance of Torah.

Early Christians, nevertheless, played little part in the war that Vespasian and his son Titus waged to destroy the Temple in Jerusalem in 70 C.E. Earlier, many Christian leaders had been executed; their revolution in the Roman Empire

Baptism of Christ. A Byzantine mosaic in S. Marco, Venice, Italy.

was more protracted, not reaching a truce until the time of Constantine or victory until the reign of Theodosius. From these humble beginnings and an endorsement from a powerful Roman government, missionary-minded Christians tried faithfully to follow the Great Commission that Jesus gave his followers, "Go therefore and make disciples of all nations" (Matthew 28:19).[1] In this chapter we will see how Jesus and his followers launched their teachings to all the world.

As we examine the story of Christianity, we will see how these personalities within the Jewish religion so changed their views and emphases that they gave rise to a religion distinct from Judaism and all other religions. The term *Judeo-Christian religion,* sometimes used in the United States, emphasizes the common roots, beliefs, and practices of Judaism and Christianity. Nevertheless, both Jewish and Christian scholars know that in the twenty-first century Judaism and Christianity are two distinct faiths; they may cooperate, but they do not coalesce. As we emphasize the chronological development of Christianity, we will explain the unique view of Christian historiography.

Historical Development: Jesus of Nazareth

Most Christians think of their history as a special plan of God that reached its apex in the birth, life, death, and resurrection of Jesus as **Christ.** All prior world events were but preparation for his coming; all events after him are but realization of God's plan that was clearly revealed. Early in their separate religion, Christians added to the Jewish concept of their history. Jews were God's chosen people, richly blessed by God until their leaders rejected Jesus as their Messiah. After that rejection, the old covenant was replaced by a new covenant for the new people of God, those who accepted Jesus as the Messiah, or Christ. These elements contribute to the particular "salvation history" of Christians. With these ideas in mind, we will outline the chronological development of contemporary Christianity. The central person of Christian history is, of course, Jesus of Nazareth, who is worshiped as the Christ, the Son of God.

Our knowledge of Jesus is based on accounts in the Christian sacred writings, the New Testament. Except for the birth stories, which many scholars believe were the last sections of the gospels composed, we know little of Jesus' youth. The Gospel of Luke reports that he was related to John, who was known as "the Baptist." Although John was the son of a Jewish priest, Zechariah, he chose to preach outside the establishment, as had former Hebrew prophets. John announced that the kingdom of God was at hand. He challenged hearers to repent and believe the good news. Then he used water as a symbol of washing away the sins of those who repented and accepted the message. When Jesus was about thirty years old, he participated in one of the gatherings and received baptism from John. The Holy Spirit descended on Jesus as he came from the water, and a voice came from heaven saying, "Thou art my beloved Son, with thee I am well pleased" (Mark 1:11).

Jesus did not appear in public immediately but spent a period of time in fasting and prayer. The gospels report that he engaged in a dialogue with Satan before

Christ [KRIIST]
The Greek word meaning "the anointed one." The Hebrew word for the concept was *messiah.* Christians believe that Jesus was the long-awaited Messiah.

returning to everyday life. When King Herod imprisoned John the Baptist, Jesus appeared in public announcing, "The time is fulfilled, and the kingdom of God is at hand; repent, and believe in the gospel" (Mark 1:15). Jesus chose disciples who would learn his teachings and help him in his work. Besides teaching, Jesus sometimes announced that a person's sin had been forgiven, or he sometimes performed a mighty work (**miracle**) healing individuals or influencing natural phenomena. Luke emphasized that Jesus was concerned to help the poor, the ill, and "sinners" who did not measure up to rabbinical standards of piety. On occasion he raised people from the dead. Such stories inspired wonder and awe among the common Jewish people; because Jesus seemed to perform these deeds in his own name, they raised deep concern and resentment among priests, scribes, and rabbis.

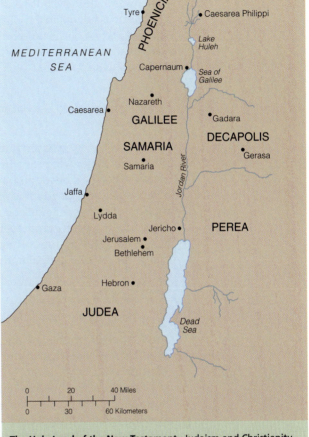

The Teachings of Jesus

The general theme of Jesus' teachings was the kingdom of God. He announced standards of human conduct that would prevail in the lives of people who lived according to the will of God. Jesus established God's perfection as the only standard by which personal conduct could be measured. The generous mercy of God set the pattern for the kind of generosity with which people were to treat each other. The kingdom could begin with a few like-minded people at any one time and place, and increase as others freely chose to participate.

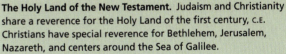

The Holy Land of the New Testament. Judaism and Christianity share a reverence for the Holy Land of the first century, C.E. Christians have special reverence for Bethlehem, Jerusalem, Nazareth, and centers around the Sea of Galilee.

The final, fullest participation in the kingdom under the direct rule of God could not be predicted in terms of time; it is a mystery known to God rather than to humans. Jesus taught that the kingdom of God had come and is coming when God chooses. Jesus emphasized the personal side of religion, referring to God as "our Father." He challenged men and women to fulfill their roles as children of the Most High. He welcomed children who came to him, saying the kingdom of God was composed of people having childlike faith. He was content to eat with tax collectors, to talk with a prostitute in the home of a host, to defend a woman whom a crowd accused of adultery, to talk with a Samaritan woman at a public well, and to dismiss criticisms from the Pharisees with the words:

> Those who are well have no need of a physician, but those who are sick; I came not to call the righteous, but sinners. (Mark 2:17)

Although Jesus defended the letter of Mosaic Law in the Sermon on the Mount (Matthew 5:1–7:29), he argued that a righteous person would go beyond the letter

miracle [MIR-a-kul]
An event judged to be brought about by divine intervention in the ordinary events of history.

of the law and fulfill the spirit as well. He supported Mosaic Law, which says humans must not kill another human being, but he went beyond it, saying humans must not even be angry with their brothers. He agreed with the Mosaic Law that denounced adultery, but he disagreed with easy divorce, which in his eyes contributed to adultery. In the Gospel of Mark 10:9, he said God joins man and woman in marriage; no one should break them apart. He denounced lust, which is a prelude to adultery. Mosaic Law teaches "eye for eye and tooth for tooth" (Exodus 21:24). Jesus said,

> Do not resist one who is evil. But if any one strikes you on the right cheek, turn to him the other also . . . and if any one forces you to go one mile, go with him two miles. (Matthew 5:39, 41)

For Jesus, piety was an inner spirit that motivated good deeds, not a series of rituals that might win praise from religious people but disguise a mean spirit. God knows a person's heart, and a simple prayer for forgiveness of sins and for the coming of God's kingdom is more valued than elaborate prayers offered to gain praise from other religious people. If people cannot forgive their neighbors, they should not expect forgiveness from God. They must first be righteous before God before undertaking the correction of humanity and in the end, only God is the final judge of who is right and wrong. Jesus encouraged people to pray to God.

> Ask, and it will be given you; seek and you will find; knock, and it will be opened to you: For every one who asks receives, and he who seeks finds, and to him who knocks it will be opened. (Matthew 7:7–8)

Jesus summed up the law and the prophets with the words "So, whatever you wish that men would do to you, do so to them; for this is the law and the prophets" (Matthew 7:12).

The people who followed Jesus thought he showed them the proper way of relating to God. Early Christians were known as members of the Way; John's gospel reported Jesus saying, "I am the Way" (John 14:16). Using a Jewish concept of the Way in the Old Testament, Jesus and his followers emphasized it as God's preferred path for human conduct.

Jesus's teachings were memorable. Ordinary people called him rabbi, "teacher." It was a title of respect, but Jesus had no formal rabbinic training. His hearers were aware no one else spoke the way he did; he taught without giving references and quotations from Hillel or Shammai, leaders of rabbinic schools, or their disciples. Instead he told **parables,** or stories, that helped ordinary people consider profound religious questions. In the parable of the Good Samaritan, a Samaritan rescues the victim of highway robbery who had been passed by pious Jews who refused to help. The Samaritan, though despised by Jews, is a good neighbor (Luke 10:36). The Prodigal Son is a parable of universal appeal. A wayward son rebels against his father and leaves home to seek a more exciting, worldly life. Later, penniless and friendless, he comes to himself and returns to seek his father's forgiveness. The father, who sees him coming, runs to meet him, embraces him, and prepares a feast to celebrate his return, saying, "For this my son was dead, and is alive again; he was lost and is found" (Luke 15:24). Jesus used a very familiar situation to convey his concepts of God and human alienation and reconciliation. Sometimes he used paradoxes to drive home a point: "Why do you see the speck that is in your brother's eye, but do not notice the log that is in your own eye?" (Matthew 7:3). Or, "Woe to you, scribes and Pharisees, hypocrites! . . . You blind guides, straining out a gnat and swallowing a camel!" (Matthew 23:23, 24).

parable [PARE-u-bul]
A simple story told to illustrate a religious truth or lesson.

Jesus's Authority and the Gospel of John

The question about the source of Jesus's authority was of utmost importance to Jewish officials in his day. How did he claim to know the truth of what he taught? He was not given to quoting authoritative rabbis or even to proving every point by citing scriptures. Had he been appointed by any Jewish officials? Was his forgiving sins blasphemous of God, an act inviting capital punishment under Jewish law? His measuring human conduct by God's perfection criticized Jewish religious leaders for falling short of the kingdom of God.

The disciples who accompanied Jesus, both men and women, recognized his authority as of God. He trained twelve of these disciples to convey his teachings and healings to villages he could not immediately visit. Women from families of his disciples helped support his work among the multitudes who followed him.

Trying to analyze Jesus' true identity stirred speculation among his hearers. The people of Nazareth, his hometown, saw him only as a son of Mary and Joseph, with brothers and sisters who lived in their midst. In Capernaum, he shocked people by his healing sick people on the Sabbath. His disciples, when he asked them at Caesarea Philippi, reported that people regarded him as Elijah returned, or one of the prophets, or as John the Baptist raised from the dead (Herod had beheaded John). Simon, son of Jonas of Capernaum and later known as Peter, which means "rock," said that Jesus was the Messiah—the anointed one the Jews had expected to be sent from God. Jesus told Simon not to tell anyone because he, Jesus, would be put to death (Matthew 16:21–23).

Although Christians have selected four gospels to present their official views of Jesus as the Christ, John, the fourth gospel, offers a perspective that is somewhat different from the first three gospels. The Gospel of John presents the teachings and authority of Jesus in impressive accounts, such as those that feature the "I am" sayings, or teachings, of Jesus. The person Jesus is presented as the believer's way to God: "I am the way, the truth, and the life" (John 14:6). These pronouncements are usually connected with a memorable event, such as John's account of Jesus' raising from the dead his friend Lazarus. Jesus arrived four days after Lazarus' entombment. Directing that the tomb be opened, Jesus, after praying to God, called, "Lazarus, come out!" The dead man came out wrapped in his burial clothes. Jesus told bystanders to unbind him and let him go. Thus Jesus demonstrated the truth of his promise to Martha, "Your brother will rise again." He also stated why Lazarus would live again: "I am the resurrection and the life; he who believes in me, though he die, yet shall he live, and whoever lives and believes in me shall never die" (John 11:25, 26). Other favorite sayings in John are "I am the bread of life" (6:35), "I am the light of the world" (8:12), "I am the door" (10:7), "I am the good shepherd" (10:11), and "I am the true vine" (15:1).

The Last Week of Jesus's Life

The gospel accounts focus on the week before Jesus' death. The celebration of Palm Sunday recalls Jesus' entry into Jerusalem for the feast of the Passover. When he rode into the city on a small donkey, the crowds recognized the symbolism from Isaiah 62:11 and Zachariah 9:9:

> Tell the daughter of Zion,
> Behold, your king is coming to you,
> humble, and mounted on an ass,
> and on a colt, the foal of an ass.
>   (Matthew 21:5)

© Chris Hellier/CORBIS

The Last Supper. This engraving by Gustave Doré recalls the event that is commemorated by Christians in the Eucharist.

Those who had known Jesus in Galilee waved palm branches in the air, spread their garments on the road before him, and shouted, "Hosanna to the Son of David! Blessed be he who comes in the name of the Lord! Hosanna in the highest!" (Matthew 21:9). Although his reception could have caused concern among religious leaders in Jerusalem, the next act of Jesus sealed his doom. The next morning he went into the temple and drove out the buyers and sellers and the money changers, saying,

> It is written, "My house shall be called the house of prayer";
> but you make it a den of robbers. (Isaiah 56:7; Jeremiah 7:11; Matthew 21:13)

The last supper for Jesus and his disciples together has a special meaning for Christians. During the meal, Jesus took a piece of bread, and blessed and broke it, saying, "Take, eat; this is my body" (Matthew 26:26). Then he took a cup of wine and, having blessed it, said, "Drink of it, all of you; for this is my blood of the covenant, which is poured out for many for the forgiveness of sins" (Matthew 26:27–28). These acts are recalled by most Christians in the sacrament of Holy Communion, the Lord's Supper, one of the most sacred occasions of worship for Christians. Jesus and his disciples ended the evening in the upper room by singing a hymn.

Jesus and eleven of his disciples then went to the garden of Gethsemane; they were to watch for him while he prayed. Later, a group carrying swords and clubs came from the priests and scribes to arrest him. Judas, the twelfth disciple, identified Jesus for them, an act making him the betrayer of Christ. The group arrested Jesus and took him to the high priest's house, where he was given a hearing before members of the council.

The high priest, Caiaphas, said,

> "I adjure you by the living God, tell us if you are the Christ, the Son of God." Jesus said to him, "You have said so. But I tell you, hereafter you will see the Son of man seated at the right hand of Power, and coming on the clouds of heaven." Then the high priest tore his robes, and said, "He has uttered blasphemy. Why do we still need witnesses? You have now heard his blasphemy. What is your judgment?" They answered, "He deserves death." (Matthew 26:63–66)

The next morning, the high priest delivered Jesus to Pilate, the Roman prefect who governed Jerusalem at that time. The high priest charged Jesus with claiming to be king of the Jews, which caught the attention of Pilate because insurrection, led by Zealots, had long been a threat to peace. Zealot Jews had used force in an attempt to overthrow Roman rule in Palestine. Again, Jesus made no defense. Pilate asked the crowd what prisoner they would like to have released. They chose

Barabbas, "a man who had been thrown into prison for an insurrection started in the city, and for murder" (Luke 23:19). Pilate said to them,

> "Then what shall I do then with Jesus who is called Christ?" They all said, "Let him be crucified." And he said, "Why, what evil has he done?" But they shouted all the more, "Let him be crucified." (Matthew 27:23, 24)

After torturing and scourging Jesus, the Romans led him outside the city to a place called Golgotha and fastened him to a cross, where he remained until he died at about three in the afternoon. The male disciples having forsaken Jesus, only the female disciples kept watch at the cross. An earthquake shook the region. It is reported that it tore the curtain from the Holy of Holies in the temple and that shortly afterward, many bodies of the saints were seen, resurrected from the dead. The centurion said, "Truly this was the Son of God!" (Matthew 27:54). A Roman speared Jesus in the side (John 19:34). Joseph of Arimathea, a disciple of Jesus, wrapped the body in a linen shroud and placed it in his own, new tomb (Matthew 27:60).

Easter, the day God raised Jesus from the dead, is the most important day of the Christian calender. Belief in Jesus' **resurrection** is based partly on stories of the tomb's being empty when female disciples returned the morning after the Sabbath to finish preparing Jesus' body for burial. It is also based on stories that individuals and groups saw and visited with the resurrected Jesus. Sometimes he was readily identifiable; sometimes people took more time to make sure they had encountered Jesus. At times he was clearly in a physical body; at other times he was a recognizable spirit—one who could enter through barred doors. Certain accounts mention that some of his followers doubted the resurrection, but most who remained in the fellowship believed. According to the accounts in the Acts of the Apostles, Jesus appeared on earth for forty days and then ascended into heaven on a cloud. Angels told his disciples he would return in the same way he had left them. For Christians, Jesus is not a dead prophet, but the living Son of God.

For Christians, Jesus of Nazareth is a person who is both human and divine. Considered in his human aspect, he was a carpenter, a Jewish layman who knew the scriptures and worshiped in synagogues and the temple. He attracted hundreds of ordinary people wherever he went; they wanted to hear him teach and watch him heal sick people. He was concerned for the last, the least, and the lost. He was critical of people who had set themselves up as models of Jewish piety, such as the scribes and the Pharisees. He spoke of a kingdom of God that was coming; indeed, it had already arrived. He taught the most profound lessons in terms easy to understand and remember. But in this ordinary person many people saw the presence of God. He had the power of God to heal broken bodies and sick minds—he could cast out demons. He could calm the waves of a stormy sea, walk on water, feed thousands of his followers with a few fish and loaves of bread, and appear, before the eyes of his closest apostles, in the presence of Moses and Elijah. He was surely the anointed one for whom the Jews waited to establish the rule of God on earth.

The high priest and his friends did not see a divine aspect to Jesus. He was a threat to the power they had received from Rome—it could be withdrawn if they

© National Gallery Collection/Corbis

The Crucifixion of Jesus. This detail by Messina shows the women who watched as Romans crucified Jesus.

resurrection
[RES-u-REC-shun]
A belief that a person who has been dead will be restored as a whole, living person.

Christianity in History

31 Caesar Augustus begins reign
6 Jesus born

14 Caesar Augustus dies
29 Romans execute Jesus; Pentecost
34 Paul converted to Christianity

64 Peter and Paul executed in Rome
94 Domitian persecutes Christians; Revelation recorded

200 Canon of scriptures formed
213 Clement of Alexandria dies
253 Origen of Alexandria dies

325 Constantine presides over Council of Nicaea
354 St. Augustine of Hippo born

407 St. John Chrysostom dies
430 St. Augustine of Hippo dies

543 St. Benedict dies

596 Pope Gregory I sends Augustine to Kent, England

1054 Roman Catholic and Eastern Orthodox Churches separate
1099 Crusaders take Jerusalem from Muslims

1157–1199 Richard the Lion-Hearted, crusader
1170 Thomas à Becket, Archbishop of Canterbury, martyred
1182 St. Francis of Assisi born

1204 Roman Catholic troops sack Constantinople
1215 King John of England signs Magna Carta
1221 St. Dominic dies
1225 St. Thomas Aquinas born

1468 Johannes Gutenberg, inventor of movable type, dies
1484 Huldrych Zwingli born

1491 St. Ignatius Loyola born
1492 Columbus sails from Spain for the New World

1506 Francis Xavier born

1515 Teresa of Avila born

1517 Martin Luther posts 95 Theses in Wittenberg

Christianity in History

1542 John of the Cross born

1543 Copernicus's theory of heliocentric universe

1547 Henry VII, King of England, dies

1554–1618 Sir Walter Raleigh, colonizer of North Carolina

1555 Peace of Augsburg

1559 Calvin completes last version of *Institutes*

1566 Pius VI is pope

1588 Spanish Armada destroyed before reaching England

1642 Galileo Galilei, astronomer and physicist, dies

1647 George Fox preaches in England

1734 Jonathan Edwards leads revival in Northhampton, Massachusetts

1775 Bunker Hill, first major battle of American Revolution

1786 Greek Orthodox Church in Florida

1831 Joseph Smith organizes Church of Jesus Christ, Latter-day Saints

1848 Marx and Engels publish *Communist Manifesto*

1865 Lee surrenders to Grant at Appomattox, Virginia, ending Civil War

1869 Vatican Council I

1946 Nag Hammadi codices discovered

1954 Rev. Sun Myung Moon organizes Unification Church in Korea

1965 Second Vatican Council ends

1969 Martin Luther King Jr. assassinated; first humans walk on moon

1989 Mikhail Gorbachev visits Pope John Paul II in Rome

1992 Religious liberties extended to religious in former Soviet Union

1993 Pope John Paul II visits Lithuania

1994 Anglican Church ordains women priests in England

1995 Pope Paul II and Patriarch Bartholomew celebrate mass together in St. Peter's Basilica

2000 Golden Jubilee of Queen Elizabeth II, head of Church of England

2005 Joseph Ratzinger becomes Pope Benedict XVI

BCE
▲ 2000
▲ 1500
▲ 1000
▲ 500
0

CE
0
500 ▼
1000 ▼
1500 ▼
2000 ▼

failed to keep the peace. For these powerful Jews, Jesus was a rebel, a false prophet who had to be destroyed. Other Jews named in the New Testament regarded Jesus as a true prophet.

The Apostles and the Growth of the Church

Jewish pilgrims had crowded the streets to celebrate the Feast of Weeks, which Greeks called **Pentecost.** On that morning, a few days after Jesus' ascension into heaven, the Holy Spirit descended on the disciples. While **apostles** and disciples met in an upper room in Jerusalem, the Spirit descended on them in tongues of fire. The followers began speaking ecstatically in a spiritual language and went into the streets of Jerusalem to proclaim to Jewish pilgrims that Jesus was indeed the Christ, the long-awaited deliverer of God's people. This proclamation, or **kerygma,** of the **church** concluded,

> Let all the house of Israel therefore know assuredly that God has made him both Lord and Christ, this Jesus whom you crucified. (Acts 2:36)

About three thousand people joined the church. The movement the chief priest had sought to eliminate now expanded rapidly.

The early church regarded speaking in tongues as a sign of the gift of God's Spirit. Wherever Christians gathered, this experience was part of worship. A few years later, a Christian leader, Paul, attempted to limit the practice by having only one or two people speak and by having interpreters translate for hearers. Nevertheless, through the centuries recurrent movements have sought to restore the practice of speaking in tongues.

Persecution accelerated the expansion of "the Way," as the organized followers of the Christ became known. Angry Jews, carrying out their penalty for blasphemy, dragged Stephen, a deacon of the Greek-speaking congregation in Jerusalem, into the street and stoned him to death. The stoning of Stephen became a signal for a general persecution of members of the Way. Those who could not flee were cast into prison, but many of those who could leave Jerusalem went to Galilee and even to Damascus. It was only a question of how seriously Jewish leaders wanted to take the threat to Judaism and how vigorously they wanted to prosecute members of the Way.

Saul of Tarsus

During this persecution, Christianity gained a convert who would transform it into a world faith. Saul of Tarsus, who had been present when Stephen was stoned in Jerusalem, volunteered to take writs to Damascus to find members of the Way, arrest them, and return them in chains to Jerusalem where they would be tried. He was completely dedicated to eliminating the Christian influence within Judaism. However, as he approached Damascus, he was struck blind. Seeing a great light and falling to the ground, Saul heard a voice speaking to him.

> "Saul, Saul, why do you persecute me?"
> And he said, "Who are you, Lord?"
> And he said, "I am Jesus, whom you are persecuting; but rise and enter the city, and you will be told what you are to do." (Acts 9:5, 6)

Pentecost [PEN-ti-cost]
A festival coming fifty days after Easter. The time when the Holy Spirit descended on the early Christian church. A Christian name for Feast of Weeks in Judaism.

apostle [a-POS-ul]
A person who was a disciple of Jesus sent out to proclaim the coming of the kingdom of God. Traditionally, Jesus chose twelve apostles.

kerygma [ke-RIG-ma]
The message or proclamation of the early Christians. Peter gave a proclamation on the day of the Pentecost.

church [CHURCH]
A congregation of Christians. All Christians considered together as the mystical body of Christ.

© Erich Lessing/Art Resource, NY

The Conversion of St. Paul. Museo del Prado, Madrid, Spain.

Saul remained blind and had to be led into Damascus. Eventually a member of the Way, his former enemies, contacted him and helped him escape from the Jews, who sought his life because he had betrayed their cause. Saul recovered his sight and changed his Jewish name to the Greek form, Paul, to mark his change of commitment. For a time before becoming a missionary, he participated in the Jerusalem church.

Paul was never completely at home with the Jewish Christians, who remembered his part in their persecution. Some Jews harassed him all his remaining life for rejecting their cause. Paul found it easier to work from Antioch, where members of the Way were first called Christians, as a missionary sent under sponsorship to win converts. His first efforts were in cooperation with Joseph Barnabas, who accompanied him on visits to synagogues in other regions to proclaim Jesus as the Christ. His success was usually interrupted by other Jews, who arrived to denounce him and to explain how the Jerusalem Jews had rejected his positions. But Paul usually established a church separate from the synagogue. That church, under local leadership, continued to grow, while Paul traveled abroad to establish other churches.

Paul's visit to Macedonia and Greece changed forever the religion of Greece and shaped the message of Christianity. Attracting non-Jews as well as Jews, Paul couched his message so all could grasp the significance of Jesus as the Christ. Paying little attention to the gods and goddesses of the Olympian **pantheon,** Paul drew deeply on the reservoir of belief among Greek **mystery religions.** He presented the Christ as a dying and rising God who offered salvation and life after death to all who lived by faith in him. Paul's letters to Greek churches, such as those in Thessalonica and Corinth, are examples of his message.

pantheon [PAN-the-on] All the gods or a temple dedicated to them.

mystery religions Greek religions that practiced secret rites guaranteeing initiates immortality.

Especially attractive was the teaching that salvation comes through faith in God's gracious forgiveness and that because Christ lives, believers in him shall also overcome death. Paul rejoiced that Gentiles sought to become Christians. Their presence in the church created, however, a Gentile question. The question was, Did Gentiles convert to Judaism to become Christians? In deciding the series of events, scholars debate over how to reconcile the account in Acts with the account in Galatians.[2] Most scholars conclude, on the basis of Acts 15:19–21, that through negotiation with leaders in the Jerusalem church, Paul obtained permission to initiate Gentile members by baptism alone—circumcision was no longer required for male Christians. Kosher diets were not mandatory, nor were Jewish liturgical laws. Christians were only to avoid eating meat offered to idols, meat that had been strangled, and blood. They were also to avoid the gross sexual excesses of some Gentiles. Indeed, Paul had to outline new, Christian ethics for those not raised under Torah. Christianity under Paul became a religion for all nations and peoples, one that included Jews but did not require a convert to become a Jew or to keep the Jewish law. Recommending that Christians live according to the Spirit rather than according to the law, Paul wrote to the church in Rome:

1. There is therefore now no condemnation for those who are in Christ Jesus.
2. For the law of the Spirit of life in Christ Jesus has set me free from the law of sin and death.
3. For God has done what the law, weakened by flesh, could not do: sending his own Son in the likeness of sinful flesh and for sin, he condemned sin in the flesh,
4. in order that the just requirement of the law might be fulfilled in us, who walk not according to the flesh but according to the Spirit.
5. For those who live according to the flesh set their minds on the things of the flesh, but those who live according to the Spirit set their minds on the things of the Spirit.
6. To set the mind on the flesh is death, but to set the mind on the Spirit is life and peace.
7. For the mind that is set on the flesh is hostile to God; it does not submit to God's law, indeed it cannot;
8. and those who are in the flesh cannot please God. (Romans 8:1–8)

Judaizers, Jewish Christians who insisted that Christians first become Jews, openly denounced Paul's activities.

Paul's ethics emphasized purity of body and mind. Based on Judaism, he particularly denounced homosexual acts, fornication, incest, and adultery. He abhorred prostitution. Differing from Judaism, his ideal for men and women was virginity. Marriage was a concession for those who burned with passion. Once married, however, a person was to stay married, forgoing sex only when the spouse agreed. He condemned drunkenness and thievery. On the positive side, he challenged Christians to have the mind of Christ, to consider themselves part of the body of Christ. Above all he challenged Christians to live by *agape,* self-giving love. He composed a beautiful hymn to love, recommending it to Christians as "a still more excellent way."

1. If I speak in the tongues of men and angels, but have not love, I am a noisy gong or a clanging cymbal.
2. And if I have prophetic powers, and understand all mysteries and all knowledge, and if I have all faith, so as to remove mountains, but have not love, I am nothing.

Judaizers [JOO-day-iiz-ers] Persons who advocated the practice of Jewish observances for all Christians. They opposed Paul's emphasis on freedom from the law.

3. If I give away all I have, and if I deliver my body to be burned, but have not love, I gain nothing.

4. Love is patient and kind; love is not jealous or boastful;

5. It is not arrogant or rude. Love does not insist on its own way; it is not irritable or resentful;

6. It does not rejoice at wrong, but rejoices in the right.

7. Love bears all things, believes all things, hopes all things, endures all things.

8. Love never ends; as for prophecy, it will pass away; as for tongues, they will cease, as for knowledge, it will pass away.

9. For our knowledge is imperfect and our prophecy is imperfect;

10. but when the perfect comes, the imperfect will pass away.

11. When I was a child, I spoke like a child, I thought like a child, I reasoned like a child; when I became a man, I gave up childish ways.

12. For now we see in a mirror dimly, but then face to face. Now I know in part; then I shall understand fully, even as I have been fully understood.

13. So faith, hope, love abide, these three; but the greatest of these is love.
(I Corinthians 13:1–13)

The apostles of Jesus also preached in other countries. Christian tradition describes the apostles as men who spread the good news, or gospel, to countries such as Ethiopia, Egypt, Italy, and India. Roman Catholics cherish the tradition that Peter became Rome's first bishop. As the Acts of the Apostles indicate, Christians were already active in Rome when Paul arrived for the first time, as a prisoner who was awaiting action on an appeal to the Roman emperor. Paul had been taken into custody in Jerusalem when a mob of Jews attempted to kill him. Traditions also indicate violent deaths awaited many of the apostles; by tradition, Peter and Paul died during Nero's persecution of Christians after the great fire in Rome in 64 C.E.

Christians, drawing on precedents in Jewish literature, developed their own interpretation of religious persecution. The Book of Daniel established models for servants of God remaining true to their beliefs in times of severe persecution. In that story, divine intervention saved Daniel from a den of lions and three Hebrew youths from burning in a fiery furnace. A theme of Jewish and Christian literature is that God will deliver safely those who are faithful to him. The New Testament employs a similar theme in gospels and letters.

Roman Persecution and Acceptance

Judaism was a recognized, legal religion in the Roman Empire. Jews informed the Romans that Christianity was not Judaism and not legally included within Judaism. After Rome burned in 64 C.E., Nero accused Christians of starting the fire and labeled them enemies of the state. Romans thus began a history of persecuting Christians that lasted until Constantine came to power. Stories of Christian martyrs abound, but few are more moving than that of Vibia Perpetua and her slave Felicitas. Not yielding to the pleas of her father to renounce Christ, Perpetua, a twenty-two-year-old mother of a nursing infant, was condemned to die in an arena in North Africa. Felicitas, her servant, who had recently given birth to a baby girl, joined her mistress. Refusing to wear clothes of pagan deities to the arena, the women were stripped naked to stand against a mad heifer.

Even the crowd was horrified when they saw that one was a delicate young girl, and the other a woman fresh from childbirth, with milk still dripping from her breasts. And so they were brought back again and dressed in loose tunics.[3]

Major Centers of Christianity in Europe. Having begun in the Holy Land, Christianity quickly spread to cities about the Mediterranean Sea. Soon missionaries carried Christianity to all major centers of Europe.

These women, though outwardly frail, were inwardly heroines seeking victory. Challenging their tormentors, they won victory for Christ.

Perpetua was, however, executed anyway. She is reported to have helped her own executioner. Perpetua, Felicitas, Saturus, Saturninus, and Revocatus died in front of Romans who saw no point in the new religion. But these martyrs and witnesses helped convert other people to the Christian faith.

Christians accepted persecution for a period of time as an inevitable testing. Because Jesus had been tortured and crucified, how could they, who were but servants, expect to escape the martyrdom of their master? They did not interpret persecutions to mean they were wrong, their cause was lost, or God had abandoned them. They believed that God was always in charge of history and that after a period of testing them, he would deliver them. They had no doubt God would eventually destroy the wicked people of the world. They believed Christ would at some point return from the heavens to which they had seen him ascend, and would usher in his kingdom. The righteous dead would be raised. Each person would stand before God to be judged according to his or her deeds, and more important, the contents of his or her heart.

> Then the King will say to those at his right hand, "Come, O blessed of my Father, inherit the kingdom prepared for you from the foundation of the world; for I was hungry and you gave me food, I was thirsty and you gave me drink, I was a stranger and you welcomed me, I was naked and you clothed me, I was sick and you visited me, I was in prison and you came to me." Then the righteous will answer him,

> "Lord, when did we see thee hungry and feed thee, or thirsty and give thee drink? And when did we see thee a stranger and welcome thee, or naked and clothe thee? And when did we see thee sick and in prison and visit thee?" And the King will answer them, "Truly, I say to you as you did it to one of the least of these my brethren, you did it to me." (Matthew 25:34–40)

The wicked would be cast into fire, and the righteous would be gathered into the presence of God the Father. God would end all the persecutions, tears, and conflicts; resolve all differences; and finally establish his will among humans, all creatures, and all creation.

The last book in the New Testament is an **apocalypse** that includes this vision:

> Then one of the elders addressed me saying, "Who are these, clothed in white robes, and whence have they come?" I said to him, "Sir, you know." And he said to me, "These are they who have come out of the great tribulation; they have washed their robes and made them white in the blood of the Lamb.
>
> Therefore are they before the throne of God
> and serve him day and night within his temple;
> and he who sits upon the throne will shelter them with his presence.
>
> They shall hunger no more, neither thirst any more;
> the sun shall not strike them, nor any scorching heat.
>
> For the Lamb in the midst of the throne will be their shepherd,
> and he will guide them to springs of living water;
> and God will wipe away every tear from their eyes." (Revelation 7:13–17)

Emperor Constantine, who ruled from 306 to 337 C.E., ended Roman persecution of Christians. Under his leadership, Christianity became a legal religion, although not the only one. Constantine eventually became a **catechumen,** a student of Christianity, and helped it gain a measure of unity in the first ecumenical council held in Nicaea in 325. His policy was a dramatic shift from the practices of Nero, Diocletian, Domitian, and others who had had Christians killed for refusing to worship the Roman emperor as divine. Christianity increased in acceptability and respectability until it had, by the end of the fourth century, gained a place as the official religion of the Roman Empire.

Formation of the New Testament

During those centuries, the churches in countries near the Mediterranean Sea developed a **Christian canon** of writings known as the New Testament, which they understood as a new covenant to amend the old covenant God made with Moses. These were the scriptures of a new people of God, called by him to believe in his Son, whom he had sent to save the world.

The four **gospels,** or accounts of the life of Jesus, overlap and supplement each other so as to give a composite picture of the various churches' views of Jesus. Most New Testament scholars believe the Gospel of Mark was written first. Matthew and Luke used much of Mark in their gospels. Matthew added special material, emphasizing that Jesus fulfilled Jewish prophecies. Luke added accounts that showed Jesus among the common people. In some passages, Matthew and Luke agree word for word on information not found in Mark. Scholars

apocalypse [u-POCK-u-lips]
A revelation. A prophetic vision of the destruction of evil and salvation of righteous people.

catechumen
[KAT-i-KYOO-mun]
A convert to Christianity who received instruction in preparation for baptism.

Christian canon [CAN-on]
The list of books accepted as scriptures by Christians.

gospels [GOS-puls]
Messages of good news. The four stories of the life of Christ found in the New Testament.

suggest they copied from a common source, *Q,* which stands for the German word *Quelle,* or "source." John is an independent account of the life of Jesus—it does not rely on the other three gospels. For example, instead of reporting Jesus' giving his disciples bread and wine at a supper, John reports Jesus' wrapping himself with a towel and washing his disciples' feet. He asked,

> Do you know what I have done to you? You call me Teacher and Lord; and you are right, for so I am. If I then, your Lord and Teacher, have washed your feet, you also ought to wash one another's feet. For I have given you an example, that you also should do as I have done to you. Truly, truly, I say to you, a servant is not greater than his master; nor is he who is sent greater than he who sent him. If you know these things, blessed are you if you do them. (John 13:12–17)

Most scholars date the composition of the gospels after 70 C.E. Raymond Brown, a noted scholar of the Gospel of John, dates its completion about 90 C.E.[4]

The letters of Paul, called the **epistles,** are the oldest literature in the New Testament. Prior to 65, these letters of Paul were in circulation: Thessalonians, Corinthians, Galatians, Romans, Philippians, Philemon, and Colossians. After 65, other letters in a style similar to Paul's were written: Ephesians, Timothy, and Titus.[5]

The New Testament includes other kinds of literature. The Acts of the Apostles, a book written by Luke, describes the expansion of the church after the ascension of Jesus. Besides Paul's letters, there are the letters of Peter, James, John, and Jude. One book is Hebrews. The Revelation of John is an example of **apocalyptic literature,** a book that describes the end of time. It was probably composed during the persecution of Christians during the reign of Emperor Domitian, about 95.

The New Testament became the special, later word of God for Christians, although they continued to read and receive guidance from the Old Testament. The Old Testament spoke of God's covenant people, the suffering servant, and the anointed one. The liturgical and dietary laws of Judaism were no longer binding for Christians, but the moral law continued to have influence. Many other gospels and letters not chosen for the official canon influenced limited groups of Christians. These noncanonical writings played an important role in influencing not only Christians but also religious groups outside the church. Recently, scholars have studied other gospels found in 1947 near Nag Hammadi, Egypt. The Gospel of Thomas, for example, reported other sayings of Jesus that may supplement the four canonical gospels.

Age of the Church Fathers

Christian teachings continued to develop beyond the canon of the New Testament through the works of church leaders and councils. Bishops were spiritual leaders and administrators in each city who supervised other leaders in the churches. Elders and presbyters are other church leaders.

Christian worship was patterned after synagogue worship. Singing psalms or hymns to God, offering prayers, reading scriptures and interpreting them, exhorting believers to live according to the teachings of the apostles, and receiving offerings for the needy were common activities. Baptizing converts and sharing the Lord's Supper commemorating Jesus's last supper with his apostles were **sacraments** in which Christians sought especially to identify with their Christ.

epistles [i-PIS-els] Letters particularly those, that have become part of the New Testament scriptures. Many epistles of the New Testament were attributed to Paul and to the apostles who walked with Jesus.

apocalyptic literature [u-POCK-u-LIP-tic] Writings describing the last days, or the end of time. This literature inspires the faithful to stand firm in spite of the severe hardships of their time.

sacraments [SAK-ra-mints] Rites instituted by Jesus as recorded in the New Testament to bestow a grace of God.

Essentially two major traditions were at work within the Roman Empire. The churches at the eastern end of the Mediterranean Sea were basically Greek speaking. They developed liturgies and practices that tended to emphasize the theological or mystical union of believers with God. Churches at the western end of the Mediterranean Sea adopted Latin as the official language. They developed legal and administrative practices that reflected the Roman hierarchy. Greek and Roman traditions were different-colored strands that knit together Christianity's main testimony. Intellectual, traditional, ethnic, and political concerns were always present as the churches negotiated agreements on orthodox doctrine and to expel **heretics** who insisted on teaching what the main body of Christians officially rejected.

Ethnic diversity among Christians was reflected in the major traditions of the Greek and Roman churches. From the first century, however, other ethnic traditions of Christianity were also present. For example, the Coptic church, of Egypt, has had a distinguished record into the twentieth century. The Armenians have retained their traditions despite attempts by their conquerors to exterminate them. Arab Christians have persisted among Jews and Muslims as a faithful minority. They are active in many cities of Israel. Nestorian and Ethiopian Christians formed smaller churches, which were no less courageous in faithful service of their Lord.

Christian Platonists of Alexandria

Although Christians developed their own worldview, they lived among peoples whose worldviews were shaped by Greek philosophy and religions. Dialogues between these groups were essential if converts were to be won for Christ.

From its inception, Christianity was influenced by Greek thought. Hellenistic influence in Judaism dated from the time of Alexander the Great. Once Paul and other Christians launched their missionary journeys into Greece and adjacent territories, their messages incorporated Greek ideas. Many Jewish concepts were recast in forms Greeks could understand. Paul's sermon in the Areopagus of Athens is one example (Acts 17:22–31). In Alexandria, Egypt, a stronghold for Greek thought among Jews, Christian leaders relied on Greek philosophy for ideas that would lead able thinkers to respect and, perhaps, embrace Christianity.

In Alexandria, two outstanding Christian thinkers, Clement and Origen, presented Christian teachings as compatible with those of the Platonists, Plato and his followers.[6] They used the allegorical method to find spiritual and philosophic truths in the Old Testament and the teachings of Christ. In Alexandria, philosophy was the "handmaiden" of Christianity.

Clement and Origen inspired later thinkers, such as Ambrose, bishop of Milan, and Augustine, bishop of Hippo, to examine how Christian beliefs are related to Greek philosophy. Although councils rejected some of their conclusions, they did not eliminate the quest to reconcile Christianity with secular philosophy. Ambrose employed the allegorical method of interpreting scriptures to reconcile them with the teachings of Plato and his followers, such as Plotinus. St. Augustine, in his early writings, employed many Platonist ideas in interpreting doctrines of the church. Centuries later, St. Thomas Aquinas studied Aristotle, a pupil of Plato. Using Aristotle's logic, St. Thomas helped develop an expression of Christian beliefs that used many of Aristotle's philosophical ideas. Christian thinkers were loyal first to scriptures and the church, but they found Greek philosophy helped them express their beliefs to intellectual leaders of their times.

heretics [HER-i-tiks] People who have been judged by the church to teach doctrine dangerously contrary to the teachings of the church.

Ecumenical Councils

Christians were free to study, believe, and teach until someone taught a doctrine that aroused serious objection from bishops of the church. The teachings of Arius, who argued that Christ is the highest creature made by God, aroused opposition from the bishop of Alexandria. Bishop Alexander argued that Christ, the Son, or Logos, is of the *same* divine nature as the Father, in Greek, *homoousia.*

Constantine, the Roman emperor, seeking unity of empire through unity of religion, called an **ecumenical** (whole household of faith) council in Nicaea and paid the expenses of attending Catholic bishops, both Greek and Latin. Meeting in 325, they rejected the view of Arius and declared the Son was begotten of the Father, not made by him. The Son of God was the same essence as God. For the remainder of the fourth century, the Arians appealed their defeat, but eventually supporters of the Arian position were driven out of the Roman Empire. The second ecumenical council, in 381, issued the Niceno-Constantinopolitan Creed, which states the Catholic position against the Arians:

> We believe in one God the Father All-sovereign, maker of heaven and earth, and of all things visible and invisible;
>
> And in one Lord Jesus Christ, the only-begotten Son of God, Begotten of the Father before all the ages, Light of Light, true God of true God, begotten not made, of one substance with the Father, through whom all things were made; who for us men and for our salvation came down from the heavens, and was made flesh of the Holy Spirit and the Virgin Mary, and became man, and was crucified for us under Pontius Pilate, and suffered and was buried, and rose again on the third day according to the Scriptures, and ascended into the heavens, and sitteth on the right hand of the Father, and cometh again with glory to judge living and dead, of whose kingdom there shall be no end:
>
> And in the holy Spirit, the Lord and the Life-giver, that proceedeth from the Father, who with Father and Son is worshiped together and glorified together, who spake through the prophets:
>
> In one Holy Catholic and Apostolic Church:
>
> We acknowledge one baptism unto remission of sins. We look for a resurrection of the dead, and the life of the age to come.[7]

The Council of Nicaea defined Catholic beliefs about Christ. It also established precedent of bishops and monarchs working together in defining and enforcing doctrine. Christian emphasis on creeds is a departure from Judaism, which emphasizes observance over belief.

Other **heresies** developed concerning the person of Christ. Was he man or God? How were the divine and the human combined? An **adoptionist** was someone who claimed Christ was essentially human; at Jesus' baptism, God had adopted him as his son. A **monophysite** was someone who claimed Jesus was essentially divine. Others thought he had a human body and a divine mind. The Council of Chalcedon in 451 settled the question with a compromise statement. Christ had to be God in order to have power to save sinful humans; he had to be man for his deeds to be effective for humans. The church's position is that he is fully God and fully man in one person.

How is Christ related to the Father and to the Spirit? The Bible speaks of God the Father; it says those who have seen the Son have seen the Father. The Holy Spirit is also the Spirit of God; Jesus said he would send the Spirit. How are these three related? How does a Christian who recognizes the reality of Father, Son, and Holy Spirit avoid polytheism?

---

ecumenical
[ek-yu-MEN-i-kul]
Refers to the whole household of faith. It is in contrast to matters of local or special interest.

heresies [HER-i-sies]
Beliefs contrary to the accepted teachings of the religious organization.

adoptionists
[a-DOPT-shun-ists]
Persons who believed that at the baptism of the man Jesus, God adopted him as his Son.

monophysites
[mu-NOF-u-SITES]
Persons who believed that Christ had only one nature—divine.

Some of the greatest teachers in Christianity explored the problem. The solution Christianity accepted was set forth in a doctrine on the **Trinity**. One well received solution was suggested by an early churchman from Carthage: Tertullian. He used the term *persona,* which could mean either a mask through which an actor spoke or a leading character in the state, such as Cicero. Father, Son, and Holy Spirit are three *personae* (persons) but only one essence. Where one is, the other two are fully present. They have their unity in the *economia,* or ruling, of God. The difference that eventually divided Greeks and Latins on the Trinity arose later. The Roman Catholics added a teaching that the Holy Spirit proceeded from the Son (*filoque*) as well as from the Father. The Orthodox Church believed the Spirit proceeded only from the Father. Christians agree that God can be fully present in three ways, but there is never more than one God. Some Hindus, who believe there is only one God, who manifests himself through different persons, have few difficulties with the Christian Trinity; most Jews and Muslims consider it polytheism.

Grace of God for the Sin of Man

St. Aurelius Augustine, bishop of Hippo (354–430), used the allegorical method of interpreting scriptures to reconcile the Bible with many of the insights of Neoplatonism. The allegorical method recognizes the historical, or literal, meaning of scriptures and also seeks their symbolic, or spiritual, meaning. Platonism held that through reason and choice, humans can overcome the evil world and ascend to the realm of pure ideas. But St. Augustine knew that in his youth his decision to forsake his love of sex for the love of wisdom had not borne fruit. For many years he earnestly sought a pure life but lived one he found corrupt. After his conversion to Christianity, he believed the grace of God, not his own will, had saved him from sin and damnation.

His classic book *The Confessions* reveals that Platonist philosophy helped him convert to Christianity. Through the excellent sermons of St. Ambrose, bishop of Milan, and through reading some Platonist books, Augustine discovered Christianity as a fulfillment of Plato's dream for a society governed by philosophy.[8] Humans are not evil; through their free will they can choose to move toward God or away from him. The good life is to know God. A person can turn away from the transitory world of senses and passions of flesh and find tranquility of soul in the presence of God. This idea is set forth in the beginning of *The Confessions,* in a prayer to God:

> For Thou madest us for Thyself, and our heart is restless, until it repose in Thee.[9]

St. John Chrysostom (347–407), of the Orthodox Church, differs with St. Augustine.[10] John Chrysostom's position is more representative of the Greek Orthodox view—human beings, although born sinners, after baptism can be good, can be trusted, and can achieve god-manhood. The grace of God is essential for salvation, but it is freely given and readily available. When a person turns toward God, God's grace assists his or her becoming more godlike.

Jews have found St. Augustine and St. Chrysostom particularly harsh. These church fathers thought Jews should have become Christians. Both fathers supported Christians placing harsh burdens on Jews to induce their repentance of Judaism and acceptance of Christianity. The fathers disliked the Jewish religion; Jewish people who converted to Christianity, however, were fully acceptable.[11]

Trinity [TRIN-i-tee]
The Christian belief that three persons in union, Father, Son, and Holy Spirit, are one God.

Monasticism

While Christianity was seeking legal status in the Roman Empire and defining official theological positions, spiritual developments were taking place as well. For example, Christianity attracted men and women who wanted to deny the passions of the flesh and the comforts of the world to devote time to strengthening the spirit and praying for the kingdom of God. Some embraced poverty, celibacy, and obedience to the teachings of Christ. Some lived alone in caves or in wilderness areas and denied their bodies food, clothing, water, and ease from pain; some wanted to share the sufferings of Christ. Others sought a vision of Christ; some wanted to have the marks (stigmata) of the nails hammered through his hands appear in theirs, as a sign of identity with him. Yet others were better satisfied to live together in groups, encouraging each other and learning how to live a more productive and rewarding life of the spirit. Some women pledged themselves to virginity and to dedicating all their lives to the service of Christ, fasting and praying.

From these expressions of personal preferences, Christianity developed rules, or ways of life, for monks and nuns. A person could deny the gross excesses of the sinful world and yet affirm a love for human beings. St. Ambrose of Milan (339–397) praised and established houses for women and men who maintained virginity. St. Augustine, also, supported orders for Christian men and women in North Africa.

© Scala/Art Resource, NY

St. Francis of Assisi. In a popular tradition, this painting from the school of Giunta Pisana surrounds the saint with scenes of events in his life.

Perhaps the most famous order was that developed by St. Benedict of Nursia (480–547) and instituted in Monte Cassino in Italy. Benedict's model was a garrison of Christ's soldiers.[12] The rule provided for periods of study and prayer alternating with periods of work necessary to maintain the life of the monastery. St. Benedict's Rule (way of life) attracted many men to monastic life.[13]

The famous Franciscan order had a fascinating founder, Francis, whose baptismal name was Giovanni Bernadone of Assisi (1182–1226).[14] His father, a businessman, disapproved of the wild, playboy life Francis enjoyed with his friends. He served in the military and spent time as a prisoner of war. Later, illness changed his attitude toward life. He spent his time meditating at a local grotto, encountered a leper, and experienced God's invitation to repair the abandoned chapel of San Damiano. Studying Matthew 10, he dedicated himself to imitating Christ and the kingdom of God. By 1208 other men had joined him, seeking to share his life in a brotherhood. In 1212, a noblewoman, Clare, put on religious clothing and began to share the monastic life at San Damiano. Soon other women joined her.

In all his activities and teachings, Francis was aware of the triune God. In 1215, the Fourth Lateran Council promulgated reforms he had advocated in his preaching. For his own companions, he emphasized using only what is needed, owning nothing, and engaging in fraternal service. In every way, including poverty, he sought to imitate Christ. The famous Franciscans, or Gray Friars, minister to the poor and ill of society.

About the same time, St. Dominic (1170–1221) formed the Dominican order, or Black Friars, who devoted their lives to preaching Christian doctrine and studying so they could maintain the purity of teachings of the Catholic Church. Missionaries had to deny themselves and live in the kind of poverty the apostles had practiced. They had to beg for their daily food.

Besides men such as St. Augustine and St. Francis, whose lives included some dimensions of mysticism among their other practical interests and works, some men and women devoted most of their lives to contemplation, seeking direct communication with Christ. For example, Catherine of Siena (1347–1380) received her first vision of Christ when she was six years old. Pledging her virginity, she was devoted only to Christ, whom she often saw in visions. Her solitude was balanced by activities in the political world. She advocated that Popes Gregory XI and Urban VI unite Christendom in holy war to oversee Palestine as a Christian trust. At the invitation of Pope Urban VI, she attempted to mediate his dispute with the anti-Pope, Clement VII. Catherine believed that knowledge of God in oneself and oneself in God is the foundation of all spiritual life.

The Roman Catholic and Greek Orthodox Traditions

Governance in the early church developed several different forms. The apostles were authorities from the beginning. Peter, mentioned often with James and John, was a conspicuous leader. James, the brother of Jesus, was a leader of the Christian church in Jerusalem. Paul was an authority for the churches he founded. A distinction was gradually made between the churches of the Latin tradition and those of the Greek tradition. In both groups, the leader of a metropolitan district was an overseer of the priests who served the churches in the

© Scala/Art Resource, NY

Saints Boris and Gleb on Horseback. Russian icon, second half of fourteenth century. The Cathedral of the Dormition, Moscow.

area. Deacons, presbyters, and bishops were established offices. Elders were mentioned too, as were widows. The churches of a metropolitan area were usually autocephalic; that is, they stood alone. When a council of the church, such as that at Nicaea in 325, reached agreement on matters of required belief, most churches conformed.

Over a long period, ecclesiastical power was concentrated in cities important to secular government. The center of the Latin power was in Rome; the center of Greek power, Constantinople (earlier called Byzantium, and later, Istanbul). The Orthodox, or Greek, Church remained autocephalic, self-governing, but the patriarch of Constantinople had the status of first among equals. He was a symbol and a spokesman for the Greek Christian tradition. The Latin, or Roman Catholic, Church frequently looked to the bishop of Rome as its symbol of power. Initially, he was first among equals, but later popes claimed to be first without equal. As the civil government became weak and then abandoned Rome for Constantinople, the pope assumed more civil power in order to meet the great needs of Christians in the area. Gradually, the doctrine was affirmed that Jesus had appointed Peter his vicar for the church (Matthew 16:18) and that Peter, as the first bishop of Rome, appointed his successors to enter that office.[15] Only priests who had received the laying on of hands from Peter or those in his succession were regarded as clergy who could forgive sins or celebrate the Mass.

The Greek Orthodox and Roman Catholic traditions formalized their split in the year 1054. A controversy over doctrine and practice led a legate of Pope Leo IX to **excommunicate** Patriarch Cerularius. The patriarch with his council in turn excommunicated the legate. Agreement on doctrine in the two traditions ended after the seventh ecumenical council; they went their separate ways. Some attempt at cooperation was made during the Muslim threat to Constantinople, but the crusaders—mostly Catholic—did more damage to the Orthodox center in 1204 than did the Muslims. The sack of Constantinople left Christendom with two separate traditions.

Even though the Latin and the Greek churches had agreed on the creeds of the first seven ecumenical councils, they had a different view of humans and, thus, a different view of governance and some different expressions of devotion. The Roman Catholic priests were in full view of the congregation throughout the service; the Orthodox priests were sometimes hidden behind an **iconostasis,** a screen composed of sacred pictures, or icons, that divided the laity from the most holy part of the church. Catholics had three-dimensional statues and two-dimensional paintings that reminded them of holy persons; Orthodox worship featured two-dimensional paintings of holy persons, or icons.

Both Orthodox and Roman Catholic traditions engaged in missionary outreach. Pope Gregory I (the Great) became interested in England, perhaps because of some English slaves he saw in Rome. In 596, seeking to convert the English, he sent Augustine (not of Hippo) from Rome to the kingdom of Kent, where he baptized the king and thousands of his subjects. In Arles, Augustine was consecrated as Archbishop of Canterbury.

Europe and Scandinavia became Christian in the Roman tradition. The patriarch of Constantinople, supported by the pope, sent Cyril and Methodius, in the ninth century, to convert the Slavs. The story has circulated that Jews, Christians, and Muslims, in turn, asked Prince Vladimir of Kiev to convert to their religions. All were part of his domain or his neighbors. After his delegates reported the splendor of worship in the Cathedral of Saint Sophia in Constantinople he chose Christianity. In 988, Vladimir turned Christian and had most of his subjects baptized.

excommunicate
[ex-ku-MYUU-ni-caat]
The forced exclusion of a person from a religious organization, such as a church. People who continued, after warning, to practice errors, often were excommunicated from the church.

iconostasis
[ii-con-NOS-ta-sis]
A screen at the front of an Orthodox church that displays many precious icons.

© Giraudon/Art Resource, NY

Hagia Sophia (Saint Sophia). This Christian church was started in 532 C.E. in Constantinople by the emperor Justinian. Muslim conquerors from Turkey turned it into a mosque. The building was secularized in 1934.

In the sixteenth century, Moscow became one of six patriarchates, large territories governed by priests of the rank of patriarch in the **Eastern Orthodox Church.**

The missionary outreach of Christianity has continued in every century since its inception. This growth of new congregations has been balanced, periodically, with consolidations of theological beliefs, the worldview of Christians.

St. Thomas Aquinas

St. Thomas Aquinas (1225–1274), a Dominican friar who had studied at the University of Paris with Albert the Great (Albertus Magnus), accomplished another reconciliation of philosophy and theology.[16] He was a follower of **Scholasticism,** a type of education that had taken hold in the schools of France in the eleventh century. It applied logic to theological questions and endeavored to draw logical implications from religious faith. St. Thomas used his knowledge of new Latin translations of the works of Aristotle (384–322 B.C.E.) to reinforce the position of St. Augustine of Hippo and St. Anselm (1033–1109) of Canterbury that faith and reason support each other. In *Summa Theologica,* his most famous work, he reiterated that both faith and reason lead to truth. Nevertheless, revealed truths cannot be discovered by reason alone. However, once revealed, they are perfectly reasonable.

St. Thomas thought the existence of God could be proved by reason, apart from revelation. He wrote,

> *I answer that,* The existence of God can be proved in five ways.
>
> The first and more manifest way is the argument from motion. It is certain, and evident to our senses, that in the world some things are in motion. Now whatever is

Eastern Orthodox Church
[OR-tha-dox]
The Christian church of the Orthodox tradition. The churches of the eastern Mediterranean countries retained a more democratic form of governance.

Scholasticism
[sku-LAS-ti-siz-um]
A medieval movement of education in which Christian schools taught particular methods of philosophy and theology.

moved is moved by another, for nothing can be moved except it is in potentiality to that towards which it is moved; whereas a thing moves inasmuch as it is in act. For motion is nothing else than the reduction of something from potentiality to actuality. But nothing can be reduced from potentiality to actuality, except by something in a state of actuality. Thus that which is actually hot, as fire, makes wood, which is potentially hot, to be actually hot, and thereby moves and changes it. Now it is not possible that the same thing should be at once in actuality and potentiality in the same respect, but only in different respects. For what is actually hot cannot simultaneously be potentially hot; but it is simultaneously potentially cold. It is therefore impossible that in the same respect and in the same way a thing should be both mover and moved, i.e., that it should move itself. Therefore, whatever is moved must be moved by another. If that by which it is moved be itself moved, then this also must needs be moved by another, and that by another again. But this cannot go on to infinity, because then there would be no first mover, and, consequently, no other mover, seeing that subsequent movers move only inasmuch as they are moved by the first mover; as the staff moves only because it is moved by the hand. Therefore it is necessary to arrive at a first mover, moved by no other; and this everyone understands to be God.[17]

In subsequent paragraphs, St. Thomas described proofs from the nature of efficient cause, from possibility and necessity, from the gradation found in objects, and from governance of the world.

The goal of theological inquiry for St. Thomas was to know God and the nature and destiny of humans. The scriptures, interpreted in the light of the church fathers and the councils, yield final authority. God is the highest substance and supreme good. God does only what is right. Humans make free choices, but only within the providence of God. Sin in the world often leads to virtues. Humans can return to God only through the grace he gives them. That grace became available through Christ, who accomplished what humans could not do for themselves.

With St. Thomas, Christian theology shifted from Platonism to Aristotelianism. Later, Protestant theologians as well as Catholics found inspiration in St. Augustine. But Thomism dominated Roman Catholic theology into the twentieth century, as the teachings of St. Thomas were a required part of every priest's education.

The Crusades

Jews, Christians, and Muslims revered the Holy Land, Palestine, and the city of Jerusalem. Abraham had taken his son there as an offering to God. It was the site of the Temple. Jesus suffered and died there. The Dome of the Rock mosque was there. Thus peoples of three faiths sought to protect and control access to their holy places. Since the seventh century when Muslims occupied Jerusalem, they had controlled the area. In the eleventh century Muslim forces threatened trade in Byzantine territories and the city of Constantinople. For political, economic, and religious reasons, Christians sought a Holy War against Muslims.

Conflicts between Christians and Muslims deepened during crusades organized by Christians to free the Holy Land, particularly Jerusalem, from Muslim domination. The object of the crusaders was to place the Holy Land with its sacred places under Christian control so that pilgrims could freely visit them and carry out Christian devotions. Pope Urban II proclaimed the first crusade at a synod, an assembly of church officials, in Clermont in 1095. Several crusades were led by nobles of Europe. Jerusalem was conquered and, for a short while, controlled by Christians. Christian slaughter of Muslims in Jerusalem in July 1099 was extremely bloody, even for those times. Battles between Muslims and Christians during the crusades built a deep hatred on each side. Moreover, on their way to the Holy Land crusaders attacked Jewish quarters and persecuted Jews, claiming they had murdered Christ.[18] In the fourth crusade, Christians from the Latin church turned on the populace of Constantinople in 1204 and plundered the city, using much of the loot, including Christian treasures, to pay their Venetian allies for use of their transport ships. Nicetas, a secretary to Isaac of Cyprus, who recorded the events of the crusades, accused the Latin Christians of numerous crimes in Constantinople:

> You have taken up the Cross, and have sworn on it and on the holy Gospels to us that you would pass over the territory of Christians without shedding blood and without turning to the right hand or to the left. You told us that you had taken up arms against the Saracens only, and that you would steep them in their blood alone. You promised to keep yourselves chaste while you bore the Cross, as became soldiers enrolled under the banner of Christ. Instead of defending His tomb, you have outraged the faithful who are members of Him. You have used Christians worse than the Arabs used the Latins, for they at least respected women.[19]

The crusaders generated many tales of heroism that circulated in Western Christendom, but in the process, they deepened divisions among Christians, Muslims, and Jews.

Martin Luther. Luther's protest was based on his serious studies of the scriptures.

Protestant and Reformed Churches

A third major division in Christianity, the Protestant, became distinct in the sixteenth century. The rift occurred in Germany, France, and Switzerland; soon most countries of Europe had participants. England and Scotland were deeply involved.

Numerous interests and forces converged to inspire Christian Reformation. Many people were sick, angry, and fearful over corruption in the priesthood, waste of revenue from local parishes, and conflicts between princes of the world and princes of the church. The conflict of authorities was between the papacy and all others; the authority of the papacy was also disputed. Many reformers sought to revive earlier forms of holy life, inner piety expressed in good deeds. A few reformers challenged the basic authority of the medieval church, preferring scripture over tradition. Seeing a religious solution to secular problems, many secular princes supported the reformers. As historian C. Scott Dixon has written, "In the sixteenth century religion was central to all aspects of daily experience."[20]

Martin Luther

On October 31, 1517, in Wittenberg, Germany, Professor Martin Luther (1483–1546) of the local university announced a meeting to discuss openly some urgent questions of **theology.** He posted on the door of the castle church his Ninety-Five Theses for academic debate. The theses pertained to the ecclesiastical practice of **indulgences,** which had not been dogmatically defined. In the Roman Catholic Church, an indulgence remitted temporal punishment after the sin had been forgiven. The debate was introduced as a probing inquiry. At the same time, Luther cited a number of popular grievances against the Roman church.

theology [THEE-ol-e-jee] The discipline that describes and explains God and his relationship to the world. Theology is a formal, reasoned explanation of the beliefs of the faithful people of a religion.

indulgences [in-DUL-jenses] Remissions of temporal punishment for sins that have already been pardoned. Indulgences became a subject of debate for Martin Luther.

© Archive Iconografico, S.A./CORBIS

John Calvin. Leader of the Reformation in Switzerland.

Luther was not prepared for the situation that developed. The list of issues for a quiet, academic debate in Wittenberg was copied, using the latest technology—printing presses—and distributed over much of Europe. Horrified by the issues, Tetzel—a promoter of the sale of indulgences—and others sent copies to Pope Leo X, Giovanni d'Medici. The pope recognized at once that Luther raised the question of authority. In Roman Catholicism, authority for doctrine rested on the Bible and its interpretation by the fathers of the church, the ecumenical councils, and popes. As Luther argued about the legitimacy of the church's sale of indulgences, the proceeds being used to finance the building of St. Peter's Basilica in Rome, he advanced the idea that the Bible is the main source of authority for a Christian. Moreover, as he was threatened by the church, he argued that each layperson is free to read the Bible without aid from a priest. To reinforce his views, Luther translated the Bible into everyday German. Luther, his creative genius stimulated by opposition, published many small books, amply illustrated with cartoons, attacking the pope and sundry other people he thought sinful. Luther's emphasis on scripture led him to declare that a Christian is free, for being justified by faith before God, he is no longer subjected to the law of works. He is in a new personal relationship with God, free to serve both God and his neighbor.

The pope excommunicated Luther and placed him under ban of empire; anyone finding him was to arrest him. The German princes were divided in their support for the pope and Luther, so the pope was never able to punish Luther. In the Peace of Augsburg in 1555, Germans were assigned to Protestant or Catholic churches according to the faith of their prince.

The Roman Catholic Church did not compromise its principles. In the Council of Trent, the church affirmed several positions opposed to Protestant doctrine. The council held that the Bible is only one source of authority among others for Christians. The fathers, the councils, and the popes cannot simply be dismissed as worthless. Moreover, the Vulgate, a Latin Bible, was the only official scripture. It was to be interpreted by the church and not by any untrained layperson. The Roman Catholic Church retained seven sacraments: baptism, eucharist, confirmation, marriage, holy orders, penance, and anointing of the sick. Luther recognized, on the basis of scriptures, only two sacraments: baptism and the Lord's Supper. Luther and his followers were still considered heretics. They were also denounced by Rome because some monks and nuns who followed Luther renounced their vows of chastity. Luther and many of his followers married and raised families, establishing a precedent among Protestant clergy.

John Calvin

humanist
A person who believes the values of humans are the highest in the universe. Humans are "on their own" in the universe. A Christian humanist, such as Erasmus, believed in God.

The reform movement gained strength in Switzerland. John Calvin (1509–1564) differed from Luther in temperament. Luther had abandoned his intent to study law; Calvin was well trained in law. In 1533, Calvin, until then a **humanist,** experienced God speaking to him through the scriptures. King Francis of France attacked Lutheranism, a reformed ideology Calvin had expressed. Later, the king charged French Protestants with anarchy. Safe in Basel, Calvin began work on his *Institutes of the Christian Religion.* It was a systematic presentation of Protestant theology, revised several times before its final edition in 1559. Calvin sent a cover letter to King Francis, pointing out that his early edition would show that the charges the king was making were baseless. Calvin was immediately recognized as the leader of the French Protestants. One of Calvin's milder criticisms of the papacy reads,

> Now, if any one will closely observe and strictly examine this whole form of ecclesiastical government, which exists at the present day under the Papacy, he will find it a nest of the most lawless and ferocious banditti in the world. Every thing in it is clearly so dissimilar and repugnant to the institution of Christ, so degenerated from the ancient regulations and usages of the Church, so at variance with nature and reason, that no greater injury can be done to Christ, than by pleading his name in defence of such a disorderly government.[21]

Calvin's leadership came to fruition in Geneva, Switzerland. Responding to an invitation, he helped establish a theocracy governed by the scriptures. Calvin, as did Luther, emphasized that human sinners cannot save themselves through good deeds but must rely on the grace of God, who gives faith to those whom he has predestined to be among the elect.[22] Calvin's position was based on the letter of St. Paul to the Romans. Calvinists denounced the whole system of indulgences and penance of the Roman church. Under Calvin and John Knox of Scotland, Presbyterian churches developed. In them, a republican form of government replaced the episcopal form, which is based on monarchy.

King Henry VIII

Henry VIII (1491–1547), of England, forged yet another kind of Protestantism. The king, outraged when the pope declined to grant him a divorce from Catherine of Aragon so he could marry Anne Boleyn, separated the Church of England from the authority of the pope. Henceforth, the monarch of England would be head of the church. Services of worship had a Catholic form, and the episcopal structure remained in place. The services were conducted in English. Nobility, at least, could read the English Bible. The church published a Book of Common Prayer to be used in all services and a confession of faith.

Although the reformers agreed on a break with the authority of the pope, they did not agree on the expression of Christian faith. Luther, a hearty participant in family and community life, enjoyed good food and drink, conversation, and singing. He relied on support from the state. Calvin, a systematic scholar with legal training, was more guarded against the pleasures of the world, such as dancing and alcohol. Calvinists preferred a theocracy under the leadership of reformed clergy and laity. Henry VIII was a dedicated Catholic who had no serious doctrinal dispute with Catholicism—he wanted to retain Catholic beliefs and practices. He insisted only on his political and economic control of the church; his allowing scriptures to be read by nobles was not an invitation to the doctrinal and political reforms found in Switzerland and Germany. Other reformers appeared before the Reformation reached full flower.

These main divisions from Rome—the Lutheran, the Presbyterian, and the Church of England—stimulated smaller divisions. When laypeople could read the Bible and develop doctrine as the Holy Spirit might lead them, dozens of groups formed in England, Scotland, France, Belgium, Holland, and Germany. Although unity among Christians weakened, most Protestants thought the principle of individual interpretation of God's revelation was fully justified. Congregational form of government, a kind of town-meeting democracy, permitted small groups of members to organize and appoint their own leaders.

The Catholic Reformation

Forces that produced the Protestant and Reformed churches also inspired reform within the Catholic Church. Because the Catholic Reformation was contemporaneous with the Protestant Reformation, it is less often discussed. The Roman Catholic Church, however, reformed as it responded to challenges from individuals with exemplary holy lives. Both women and men became role models for higher Christian spirituality and morality.

The Society of Jesus, which began in Spain, expressed the work of two men who helped change Catholic education and missions. Ignatius of Loyola (c. 1491–1556) and Francis Xavier (1506–1552) met while they studied theology in Paris. Their zeal, however, exceeded that of most academics.

St. Ignatius was a man of deep spiritual devotion and superb administrative abilities. Born in 1491 in Azpeitia, Spain, he served in a military force until wounded in battle with the French army. While he was convalescing, he read the *Life of Christ* and the *Lives of the Saints.* Subsequently, he had a vision of the Virgin Mary with the child Jesus. Breaking away from his former sins, he devoted himself to prayer and to writing about Christ and Our Lady. Besides an account of his life, St. Ignatius wrote the *Spiritual Exercises,* a guide to a disciplined spiritual life under command of God, and the *Constitutions,* an outline for administering the Company of Jesus (later known as the Society of Jesus, or Jesuits).[23] Pope Julius III recognized the group in 1550. The Jesuits played a major role in church reform and missionary activities. The Society members were scholarly, well-disciplined students in the spiritual life. Their goal was missionary outreach rather than military conquest.

Francis Xavier, of the Society of Jesus, introduced Christianity to Japan in 1549. By the end of the century, the number of churches had reached about 200, and membership was about 150,000. The harsh treatment of Christians under the Emperor Hideyoshi reversed the liberal policy of Lord Oda Nobunaga, a cycle often repeated in Japan. Throughout these periods, "hidden Christians" operated underground to keep faith alive.

In 1873, when Japanese feudalism gave way to industrialization, proscriptions against Christianity were removed. Catholic, Orthodox, and Protestant missionaries became active. As Japan came into conflict and wars with Russia, China, European countries, and eventually America, the Japanese weakened ties with outside churches and developed their own finances and leadership. Although Japanese churches were small, they were free of imperialistic encroachments from other nations.

When the Jesuits arrived in China under the leadership of men such as Alessandro Valignano and Matteo Ricci, they sought to adapt Christianity to Chinese culture. Nestorian Christians had been in China since the eighth century. But now an orthodox Christianity was introduced along with Western academic knowledge. To make Christianity acceptable to Chinese scholars, Jesuits combined it with studies of Chinese classics. Successful with the Chinese, the Jesuits were opposed by Dominicans and Franciscans for giving too much honor to Chinese religions.

Mystics, also, set examples of Christian piety. Teresa of Ávila (1515–1582), an aristocrat, lived as a Carmelite nun and suffered paralysis. Eventually she experienced visions, voices, and revelations that culminated in an image of the wounded Christ. In her renewed piety, she developed a stricter life for nuns of her order. Her devotion reformed religious lives for both women and men; she founded thirty-two reformed houses of devotion.[24]

© Stock, Montage

John of the Cross. With St. Teresa, he founded the Decalced Carmelites. He was renowned for his poetry in mystical theology.

John of the Cross (1542–1591) was inspired by Teresa, his elder example. While imprisoned by monks who opposed his efforts at reform, John experienced visions. Escaping from his imprisonment, he reformed monasteries and founded houses for exemplary religious life.

Popes, also, sought reforms in Rome. Catholic leaders were painfully aware that some popes had been too worldly. New popes had opportunities to set examples of pious living. Pius V (1566–1572), a Dominican, lived as an ascetic in the Vatican. He and his court rejected the more fragrant abuses that had marred the Vatican, in favor of exemplary spiritual and moral lives.

Although the lines between Protestants and Catholics were drawn and reinforced, Christianity had undergone a renewal of faith and morals. Members of the divided churches debated vigorously who was the real church and who had departed from it.

Religious Diversity in North America

The earliest missionaries in North America were Roman Catholics, who had organized several missions for Indian converts before Protestants reached Virginia and New England. Protestants, having multiplied rapidly since Luther's debate in Wittenberg in 1517, were represented in a variety of denominations. They found the new colonies in North America attractive for economic reasons as well as for liberty to develop, without threat of persecution, the full implications of doctrines they had fashioned from fresh studies of the Bible. The new colonies, states, and territories in North America permitted even more fragmentation of the Christian churches and doctrines than had been possible since the earliest centuries of Christianity.

Anglicans, descending from the Church of England under Henry VIII, settled in Jamestown, Virginia, in 1606. They were the forerunners of the Protestant Episcopal Church. **Puritans** and **Separatists** departed farther from Roman Catholic practices than Anglicans cared to go. These English people settled in Massachusetts. **Anne Hutchinson** (1591–1643), dissenting from these groups, settled with her children in Rhode Island.[25] **Baptists** emphasized a gathered community of believers who had been baptized by immersion. In Pennsylvania, **Quakers** were given a safe haven under William Penn, as were Catholics and Jews. **Presbyterians** from Scotland and Switzerland, adherents to Calvin's views, settled along the coast of several colonies, one being North Carolina. **John Wesley** (1703–1791), who inspired **methodists** to ride circuits on the frontier. **Lutherans** from Germanic states and Scandinavian countries, Lutherans, brought Lutheran churches based on the Augsburg Confession of 1530. These Protestant groups blazed a trail for hundreds of other forms of Protestant Christianity that developed in the next century.

In Canada the first Anglican Church met in Halifax, Nova Scotia, in 1750. In 1832 the Anglican Church became the established church of Canada. The Anglican Church, the Roman Catholic Church, and the United Church of Canada comprise two-thirds of religious memberships in Canada. Jews, Greek Orthodox Christians, and Protestant groups comprise the remainder.

Although the first Greek colony in the New World was in New Smyrna, Florida, in 1786, it did not endure. The first Orthodox community that lasted began in Alaska with Russian explorers. The Russian Imperial Missionary Society helped support the Eastern Orthodox Church in Alaska and adjoining islands. In the next century, Orthodox centers appeared in San Francisco and in New York City.

Anglicans [ANG-gli-cuns] Members of the Church of England. Their church government is episcopal; the clergy is directed by bishops.

Puritans [PYOOR-i-tuns] Former members who sought to purify the Church of England. They settled in Massachusetts and sought to establish a theocracy, a government under rule of God.

Separatists [SEP-ar-a-tists] Former members of the Church of England who believed it beyond reform and separated to form a new church. They settled in Massachusetts and sought a theocracy.

Anne Hutchinson A dissenter banished in 1637 from Massachusetts Bay Colony. She found more freedom in Rhode Island.

Baptists [BAP-tists] Members of the Baptist tradition. Adherents are baptized when they are old enough to choose Christ as their savior. Immersion is the preferred, often required, form. Government is by members of each congregation.

Quakers [KWAY-kurs] Members of the Society of Friends; established in England by George Fox. Quakers are led by the Inner Light, through democracy.

Presbyterians [PREZ-bit-tir-ee-uns] In the tradition of John Calvin, Presbyterians base their beliefs primarily on the Bible. Governance of the church is through the Presbytery and other elected representatives.

An Orthodox Service on Good Friday. In New York City members of this major branch of Christianity observe the traditional rituals recalling Jesus' crucifixion.

Peoples in what became the United States have always exhibited religious diversity. The early settlers brought different religions. Protestants, Catholics, and Jews have always practiced their own faiths. In spite of sporadic episodes of discrimination and intolerance, no widespread religious wars have been fought. The Constitution of the United States, in the First Amendment, has prevented governmental establishment of any religion. The principle of separation of church and state has encouraged religious liberty. Although Christianity has been the religion of the majority, diversity of religion continues to multiply.

New Forms of Protestant Christianity

The environment of religious freedom in America, helped major denominations of Protestant Christianity produce many other denominations. Leaders who could find followers were free to break away from parent bodies and form new denominations. Some sought to be known simply as Christian. Others emphasized the second advent of Christ, holiness of life, or being disciples of Christ. All were free to form new organizations, beliefs, practices, and missions.

Africans brought to the United States as slaves had their own religions, but they could relate to the story of Moses and the Exodus of Hebrew slaves from Egypt and to the belief that suffering in this life can be rewarded in the next. Some African Americans developed denominations of their own, such as the African Methodist Episcopal (A.M.E.) Church; others, especially after the abolition of slavery, joined traditional Protestant denominations. The church is a center of community life for many African Americans, and it helps shape community ideals and achievements. Clergy model the belief that inner piety expresses itself in good works, and some—such as Ralph Abernathy, Jesse Jackson, **Martin Luther King Jr.,** and Andrew Young—are nationally known leaders of social and political reform.

Another example of the freedom of establishing new churches is the work of **Mary Baker Eddy** (1821–1910), founder of Christian Science. Appealing to the new interest in science, Mary Baker Eddy sought to combine insights of science with the gospel. In particular, she was concerned with alleviating suffering and promoting healing. She established the practice of healing through reading the Bible, interpreting it through her principles in *Science and Health with Key to the Scriptures.* Although the Church of Christ, Scientist, has local congregations, Eddy wanted all Christian Scientists to belong to the mother church in Boston. Since her death, the church has continued as a highly respected institution.

John Wesley
An Anglican priest who formed the Methodist Church. Methodist circuit riders ministered to frontier families in America.

Methodist [METH-u-dist]
A member of the church that follows the "method" of John Wesley, former Anglican clergyman. Governance is episcopal, that is, through bishops.

© Katrina Thomas/City Lore

The Church of Jesus Christ of Latter-Day Saints

In the nineteenth century **Joseph Smith** (1805–1844) formed the Church of Jesus Christ of Latter-Day Saints. Smith was born in Vermont and raised in New York during a time of religious fervor. At age 14 he claimed that God and Jesus Christ appeared to him in answer to a prayer and instructed him not to join any of the churches. He was told he would be used as an instrument to organize a new church. Four years later he published the **Book of Mormon.** Believers accept this as a book of scripture that records God's dealings with the ancient inhabitants of the Americas. It details the origins and history of the American Indians and the visit of Christ to the Americas shortly after his death and resurrection in Jerusalem.

In 1830 Smith organized the Church of Jesus Christ of Latter-Day Saints, known popularly as the Mormon Church. Believers consider themselves Christians, members of the restored, historic Kingdom of God on earth. Smith led members of the new church from New York to Ohio and finally to Nauvoo, Illinois, where they became a very large and influential group. The movement aroused suspicion and unrest in neighboring towns. Some of the practices, such as polygamy, caused additional friction. A local group of citizens killed Smith and his brother while they were being held in jail. In 1847–1848 **Brigham Young,** the successor to Smith, led the main body of the church on the arduous journey from Illinois to its current headquarters in Salt Lake City, Utah. The church officially abandoned the practice of polygamy in 1890.

Mary Morse Baker Eddy. Marble, 1889. The founder of Christian Science. Smithsonian Institution, Washington, D.C.

Lutherans [LOO-ther-ans] Members of the Protestant denomination based on the teachings of Martin Luther. Their beliefs are based on the Bible rather than on teachings of the church fathers, ecumenical councils, or the pope.

Martin Luther King Jr. (1929–1968) Baptist minister who was a leader of the U.S. civil rights movement. He adopted Gandhi's methods of nonviolence to awaken public conscience to racial injustice.

Mary Baker Eddy Founder of the Church of Christ, Scientist. She was the author of *Science and Health with Key to the Scriptures.*

Joseph Smith Founder of the Church of Jesus Christ of Latter-Day Saints.

Book of Mormon A book of scripture revealed to Joseph Smith.

Brigham Young Joseph Smith's successor, who led Mormons to Salt Lake City, Utah.

The Mormon Temple, Salt Lake City, Utah. The Temple is a sacred center for members of the Church of Jesus Christ of Latter-Day Saints.

Mormonism presents a distinct form of Christianity with many theological differences such as the belief that God and Christ are separate beings, both with physical bodies, and the belief that Jehovah of the Old Testament is the premortal Christ. These doctrines are developed in a canon of scripture that includes the Bible, the Book of Mormon, and additional revelations received by church leaders. The Church of Jesus Christ of Latter-Day Saints has always been active in worldwide missions and has grown significantly. The church is also known for adhering to a strict moral and health code and fostering a strong sense of family and community. The unique brand of Christianity of the Mormon Church is gaining acceptance and regard among the larger social and religious community.[26]

Major Roman Catholic Reforms

Two Vatican Councils have had major impact on contemporary Roman Catholicism. Concerned about the church's role in the world, popes called councils at the Vatican. The first Vatican Council (1869–1870) developed a syllabus of errors and the dogma of papal infallibility. Catholicism's vitality as a rapidly expanding church stimulated lively discussions among clergy and laypeople in new countries. Among the issues raised for serious discussion were ecumenism, Eastern churches, religious life, missions, Christian education, the relationship of the church to non-Christian religions, and religious freedom. In response to these discussions, Pope John XXIII issued a call for the Second Vatican Council (1963–1965) to let in "a little fresh air."[27] The major achievement of the Second Vatican Council was its emphasis that the church is the light of Christ in the world rather than an institution existing for itself. Some of the changes that ensued from the council

© AP Photo/Pier Paolo Cito

St. Peter's Basilica, Rome: Main Altar. Pope John Paul II celebrates Mass.

were permission to have translations of the Bible other than the Latin Vulgate, to say Mass in the language of the country where it was celebrated, to have priests participate in Christian services of worship with other Christians in Protestant churches on occasion, and to have nuns wear street clothes other than the uniform habits of their orders. The Index of Prohibited Books was abolished. Protestants were acknowledged as Christians, as were members of the Eastern Orthodox Church. Jews were no longer held to be the murderers of Christ.[28] Yet Roman Catholics are still divided on many points of authority and doctrine, especially in the United States. These include issues of marriage and the family as well as of the proper role of women in the church. At the beginning of the twenty-first century, celibacy of clergy in the Roman Catholic Church has become an issue of discussion both within the Church and in the larger community. Also, Pope John Paul II reconfirmed excommunication of women priests. Pope Benedict XVI, a theologian, succeeded him in 2005.

Christianity and Liberation

Jesus's teachings emphasized that piety is an inner spirit that motivates good deeds, and many people who have read his words have sought to change the world. When Christians read the New Testament with a focus on the life of Christ, ordinary values reversed. Jesus began his Sermon on the Mount with Beatitudes, a list of people who will be happy in the kingdom of God (Matthew 5:1–12). The people who will be happy are those whom society has considered too low to be of value: the poor in spirit, those who mourn, the meek, those who hunger and thirst for righteousness, the merciful, the pure in heart, the peacemakers, and those persecuted for righteousness' sake. In Nazareth, Jesus identified his mission with these people when he quoted from the prophet Isaiah:

> The Spirit of the Lord is upon me, because he has anointed me to preach good news to the poor. He has sent me to proclaim release to the captives and recovering of sight to the blind, to set at liberty those who are oppressed, to proclaim the acceptable year of the Lord. (Luke 4:18–19)

Readers who identify themselves as the people in these words—whether they are in Latin America, South Africa, or the United States—rejoice that Christ established a better place for them among humans.

The development of Christianity resembles the growth of a gigantic tree, extending its welcome shade against a harsh sun. Its roots extend deep into the fertile soul of Judaism, drawing nourishment from rich experiences of Jewish people. Its solid trunk is dedicated to the life and teachings of Jesus, who unites believers into one body. The main branches of the tree are the traditions of Greek, Roman, Protestant, and other churches. These branches multiply the historical forms of authority, flourishing most recently in the women's movements and in churches of peoples in the Third World.

Worldview: Christianity

At the beginning of the twenty-first century, Christianity's worldview, although different from New Testament, medieval, or modern times, still shares basic beliefs with earlier Christians. Sources of religious authority divide adherents, but all agree the ultimate head of the church is Jesus Christ. This section outlines only a few of the widely shared views of Christians.

The Absolute

Christians believe in one God. God has no partners or rivals; idolatry is strictly prohibited. Nevertheless, the most complete revelation of God has been through God the Son, who was incarnate in Jesus of Nazareth. He is coeternal with God the Father and was born in human form through the Virgin Mary. He is both God and man. He is God in respect to revealing God; he is man in bearing all human afflictions except sin. God also reveals himself as the Holy Spirit, who bestows on human beings power, comfort, peace, and love. Although God appears in three persons, Christians insist that there is only one God. On the doctrine of the Trinity, then, Christians have an understanding of God that is rejected by Jews and Muslims.

The role of Jesus of Nazareth is subject to various interpretations among Christians. All agree on the importance of his teachings through words, examples, and the excellence of his life. Jesus's sermons, parables, and miracles set him above all other men and women. In every way, he reveals the power and love of God. The majority of Christians have always gone beyond this understanding of the role of Jesus. The New Testament emphasizes that Jesus was crucified in order to demonstrate the depth of God's love for humans. Even as the blood of lambs sacrificed to God removed sin for Jews, so the blood of Christ has removed sin from those who believe in him. Christians believe that Jesus died on the cross and was buried. On the third day he rose again to life, and he ascended, after forty days, to heaven, where he lives with God the Father.

The gospels give several views of how Jesus was the Son of God. In Matthew, he is shown to be born of the virgin, Mary. He is the fulfillment of the expected Messiah in the Jewish scriptures. In Mark, at the baptism of Jesus, God announces that Jesus is his Son. In Luke, Jesus is born of the virgin, Mary, and angels announce his coming to shepherds in the field. In the Gospel of John is the idea of a preexistent Christ who came to the earth to live among humans as the **incarnation** of God:

> In the beginning was the Word, and the Word was with God, and the Word was God. He was in the beginning with God; all things were made through him, and without him was not anything made that was made. In him was life, and the life was the light of men. The light shines in the darkness, and the darkness has not overcome it. (John 1:1–5)

> And the Word became flesh and dwelt among us, full of grace and truth; we have beheld his glory, glory as of the only Son from the Father. . . . And from his fullness have we all received, grace upon grace. For the law was given through Moses; grace and truth came through Jesus Christ. No one has ever seen God; the only Son, who is in the bosom of the Father, he has made him known. (John 1:14, 16–18)

incarnation
[in-cahr-NA-shun]
To invest God in human flesh. Christians consider the Christ as God in human form.

Writers in the New Testament describe several ways that Christ has meaning for Christians. The Gospel of John provides a favorite quotation for many Christians in 3:16:

> For God so loved the world that he gave his only son, that whoever believes in him should not perish but have eternal life.

Paul has another description that emphasizes the importance of Jesus's death and resurrection. One form of expression is given in I Corinthians 15:19–20:

> If in this life we who are in Christ have only hope, we are of all men most to be pitied. But in fact Christ has been raised from the dead, the first fruits of those who have fallen asleep.

Although liberation theologies draw inspiration from examples in the life of Jesus, most Christians have turned away from the quest for the historical Jesus that occupied earlier writers, such as Albert Schweitzer. Karl Barth and Emil Brunner, called *neo-orthodox* theologians because they returned to views of Christ held by theologians of earlier centuries, minimized the need for trying to reconstruct a detailed biography of Jesus.

The World

Christians draw on the Genesis account and the Psalms for their view of the world in its original form. God created a good universe and good humans. But many Christians find that nature and humans have gone awry since the rebellion of Adam and Eve. St. Paul speaks of the whole universe groaning in pain (Romans 8:22). Influences from Platonist and Manichaean (Persian dualism) thought reinforced Christian ideas that the human body is not good and that the soul should, as far as possible, deny the desires of the body. From early days, there was a theme in Christianity that the world, with its life in the human body, is an environment of suffering to be escaped or overcome with spiritual discipline. For many Christians, heaven is their home; they are only pilgrims passing through the desolation of earthly existence. St. Francis sometimes minimized the importance of physical pleasures, but he rejoiced in the world of nature. Some Christians rejoice in the goodness of nature and humans, but the majority think humans and nature have become alienated from God and require his assistance in effecting reconciliation.

Christians have accepted the insights of Copernicus, who wrote that Earth travels around the Sun; of Galileo, who found that contrary to Aristotle's beliefs, the Moon only reflects the light of the Sun; and of Newton, who found that celestial bodies are attracted to each other by universal gravitational force. Many Christians are still divided over Darwin's theory of evolution, some accepting it as absolutely essential, even if the views of Genesis must be dismissed as myth. Others insist on the verbal inspiration of God's word in Genesis and reject any scientific theory that seems to question it. Christians who seek to accommodate scriptures and science are called *liberals*. They regard scriptures as largely human products recording spiritual insights, many of which have been subsequently outmoded. Christians who insist that all scriptures are the revealed word of God, and that any theory that seems to conflict with them must be dismissed as erroneous, are known as *fundamentalists*.

Humans

Christians believe humans are created "in the image of God." Differing on details of the concept, they agree humans differ from all other animals in that they have responsibility to God. Humans are accountable for how they live their lives.

Two traditions have influenced Christian views of humans. One tradition teaches that since the time of Adam and Eve, humans have been influenced by sin so pervasive only God can overcome it. That sin is present in every infant, and deliverance from it can be accomplished only by baptism. The other tradition is that humans have a capacity for both good and evil; through family nurture and individual devotion to God, humans can live with God's approval. Although both traditions emphasize that God's grace is essential, the second view assigns a greater responsibility to each person. Grace is the power of God affecting human lives. Present in all human situations, it is especially available in the sacraments and rites of the church.

The Problem and the Solution for Humans

Christians believe God has replaced his old covenant expressed in the Torah with a new covenant based on faith in Christ. The new covenant is necessary since humans, because of the sin of Adam, cannot by their efforts alone fulfill the law. Only by God's effective action in human lives can the results of Adam's sins be overcome. As Paul has shown in his letter to Christians in Rome, salvation is through the grace of God, who bestows faith on those he would save. Christians believe they are saved by grace through faith in Christ. Good deeds alone cannot save sinful humans. Good deeds, the evidence of repentance, are possible only after a person has been saved through faith in Christ. A person who has been saved will live an exemplary life in love to God and fellow humans. Christians believe that those who have been saved by grace through faith in Christ will seek fellowship with those who are called to be saints, in the church, which is the body of Christ.

The doctrines of the Trinity, the Incarnation, Resurrection of the dead, and the Atonement provide Christianity with ideas that are, in their full depths, mysteries. They can be understood sufficiently by humans for the purpose of salvation, but they cannot be completely understood by human reason. Human reason is good and leads to truth, said St. Augustine, just as surely as does the authority of the scriptures. Nevertheless, scriptures and faith are more reliable guides than reason, which is more or less limited in humans. Individuals can read and interpret scriptures and reason from their contents to individual conclusions. However, individual reason and interpretation serve Christians better when they balance their interpretations with the teachings of the traditional church.

Most Christians believe evil is real. Unnecessary suffering of humans and other animals is evil. The world of nature is good, a gift of God that should be received with gratitude and used with care. Humans should avoid doing harm to others; Jesus said, "And as you wish that men would do to you, do so to them" (Luke 6:31). It may be necessary, under some circumstances, for Christians to endure suffering rather than escape it. Theodicy is an attempt to explain how a good God can allow unnecessary suffering. Why should innocent people suffer? Christianity has taught that through the suffering of some innocent people other people have been saved. Jesus Christ accepted torture and death on the cross to save humankind. Church martyrs have suffered to bear witness to the value of the Christian faith. Other human suffering may be the result of punishment for the sin of Adam, taught St. Augustine.[29] St. Irenaeus taught that suffering helps humans learn how to live as children of God.[30]

Community and Ethics

A person becomes part of the Christian community through baptism—it is a matter of choice rather than of birth. The Christian community is a gathered community of those who believe that Jesus is the Christ and that they have salvation in his name. It is open to men and women of any age, race, or nationality. A Christian is normally affiliated with a particular parish or congregation that is under the care of a particular clergyperson. A believer is usually accepted as a Christian by all Christians everywhere; however, there may be some additional requirements to meet if a person transfers to a church of a different tradition.

Rev. Martin Luther King Jr. In the United States and abroad peoples of all races honor this leader of the civil rights movement.

Giving money and goods needed by others has long been a part of Christian living. Some Christians *tithe,* donating 10 percent of their income to support the work of the church, which includes charitable services to those in need. Other Christians give smaller amounts of their income to the church but contribute either directly to those in need or to organizations that serve human beings or other animals.

Although some Christians believe the world will continue to become more evil until Christ returns to earth, many others think they are obliged to improve the world. Christian service to God means, to them, not only providing charity to meet current needs but also altering institutions and structures of society to alleviate poverty, illness, and injustices. For some Christians, the social implications of the gospel are religious. John Woolman visited slaveholders in the United States to persuade them to free their slaves. Henry Ward Beecher openly supported a campaign to free all slaves. Walter Rauschenbusch labored to improve living and working conditions for poor people in cities. Albert Schweitzer brought modern medicine to peoples in Africa. Martin Luther King Jr. used the nonviolent resistance methods pioneered by Mohandas K. Gandhi to win recognition of civil rights for African Americans. Mother Teresa worked to save abandoned children in Calcutta. These few examples give some idea of the variety of activities Christians have fostered to improve the living conditions of their fellow humans.

Divisions in Christianity express differences in sources and channels of authority. Other than God—Father, Son, and Holy Spirit—Christians recognize value in both scriptures and tradition. The scriptural foundation is the Bible, writings of the Old and the New Testaments. Tradition supplies three other foundations. A second foundation is the teaching of church fathers. A third foundation is the record of decisions by ecumenical councils. A fourth foundation is the pope. Although Roman Catholics use four foundations, the Orthodox Church omits the fourth, the pope. The Anglican Church omits the fourth foundation, substituting the monarch of England. Many Protestant churches often recognize as binding authority only the Bible. The Society of Friends gives primacy to guidance of the Inner Light, some Protestant churches follow only the teachings of Jesus, Unitarians emphasize God as authority, omitting the Son and the Holy Spirit, and Mormons recognize authority restored directly from God and continuing in modern-day prophets.

Another way to classify authority is by channels through which it flows. Episcopal organization depends on authority flowing from the top, God, down through Peter, his successors, and various orders of clergy who have been or-dained by the laying on of hands from the time of Peter, the first bishop of Rome. In the Roman Catholic Church, the pope is an essential successor of Peter, head-ing the hierarchy to the present day. In the Orthodox Church, patriarchs of major groups of churches provide leadership; there is no pope. Presbyterial organiza-tions channel authority from church members through elected representatives of the congregation, a number of congregations—the Presbytery—and a larger body of churches, the Synod. Congregationally organized churches, such as Bap-tists, recognize the congregation of members as highest authority; however, con-gregations may delegate authority to organizations that represent larger numbers of churches, such as a Convention. In congregational and presbyterial forms of government, the Holy Spirit, acting continuously, as in the Bible, is credited with guiding decisions of official meetings. Protestant churches generally emphasize the Bible and the Holy Spirit above ecumenical councils and church fathers. They are skeptical of assigning spiritual authority to a pope.

In the twenty-first century, Christians are reconsidering issues of marriage and family. The Jewish views of the proper roles of men and women in society and their roles in marriage carried over into first-century Christianity. As Christianity moved into cities of the Roman and Greek empires, converts needed guidance on these subjects, because Judaism had not been well established in them. A new value appeared in Paul's celibacy and in two gospels of the New Testament that proclaimed the virginity of Mary, the mother of Jesus. Marriage was valued, but celibacy was more valued.

Medieval Christianity emphasized marriage, but celibacy in men and women was presented as a higher calling. The Church expected those who married to cre-ate children without artificial birth control or abortions. Families that had more children than they could support could offer some to the Church to be raised by holy orders.[31] Could Christians be allowed to partake in worship and sacraments if they engaged in sex without possibility of procreation or if they chose to termi-nate a pregnancy? No. Moreover, clergy were celibate men; nuns could serve the church, but no woman could be clergy. Orthodox priests could marry before ordination, but they could not become bishops.

Luther and Calvin came to a different conclusion in their reading of the Bible. They married, and clergy in the Protestant Reformation usually married. Although sex is for procreation, as in Judaism it could bring pleasure to husband and wife. However, virtually all Christians agree that pedophilia is not permitted by either church or secular law. Those who have failed to heed that fact have paid a heavy price.

Some issues of marriage and family are still hotly contested in national and state capitols. At what age can a woman legally decide for herself whether to prac-tice birth control or to have an abortion? Aside from the question of marriage be-ing a Catholic sacrament, can states permit marriage contracts between same-sex partners? Can stem cells from human embryos be collected, stored, and studied to find solutions for illness? In the first part of the twenty-first century, Christians are likely to be occupied with these human issues. Their decisions will help define Christian worldviews.

An Interpretation of History

Christians believe all history, from the creation of the world to its end, is sub-ject to the Christ. The Son was present with the Father and the Holy Spirit at the creation of the world. The teachings of Moses and the teachings of the prophets prepared the way for the Father to send the Son into the world. The coming of the Christ was the apex of history, separating all time into before and after the incarnation of the Christ. Since the ascension of the Son to join the Father in heaven, people who are reconciled to God actively participate in the earthly body of Christ, which is the church. Those who reject salvation through the Christ bring judgment on themselves. Although people good and bad live in the same world, at the time of the last judgment they will be separated. Good people will enter heaven and evil people will enter hell. At the end of history, God will defeat all evil.

Rituals and Symbols

Coming to be identified as a Christian is to choose a fellowship with over a billion people of all nations and races who believe that Jesus is the Christ, the Son of God, and the Savior from sin for inclusion in God's kingdom. With baptism, a person joins the church, a fellowship of believers organized to continue learning about Christian living, to support each other in living a Christian life, to worship God, and to serve him in the name of Christ by acts of love to fellow human beings, both Christian and non-Christian.

After affirming their identity in the social group, Christians can choose a number of different lifestyles. Working in commerce or in professions or serving in politics is encouraged. A person can be a good Christian in any of these pursuits. A Christian may marry and raise a family in a stable relationship for a lifetime, similar to the Jewish model, or choose a life of celibacy, living as a single person in the secular world. Some may choose to live a life of celibacy, poverty, and obedience within one of the many orders for men or women within churches. Catholics, Orthodox, and some Protestant groups make provisions for monastic living for those who desire it. Christians may become scholars or mystics whether they are in an order or in the secular world. In most Protestant groups, both men and women may aspire to become clergy. Currently in Catholicism and Orthodoxy, only men can become clergy. Other roles are open to women in all these churches.

Christians are urged to participate in congregational worship every Sunday and on several weekdays. Christian worship services have similarities in their themes, but there are differences in their emphases. Roman Catholic services have as their central ritual the Mass, the Holy Eucharist, in which the sacrifice of Christ on the cross is recalled in the bread and wine. Orthodox churches focus on the divine liturgy, a cooperation of priests and laity in the praise of God. Protestant services, on the whole, give greater emphasis to reading and interpreting the Bible in a sermon. Charismatic groups depart from these formal structures and focus on the gift of the Holy Spirit, evidenced in healings, testimonials, and speaking in tongues. All these forms have developed over many centuries and are shared across national boundaries.

The Christian year has several occasions that all Christians celebrate and many others that are celebrated by the Orthodox, Catholic, or Episcopal churches. Most Christians celebrate Palm Sunday, the occasion when Jesus entered Jerusalem in triumph. Many Christians also observe Maundy Thursday, the last supper Jesus shared with his disciples, and Good Friday, the day of Jesus' crucifixion. Easter is the most important day of celebration in the Christian year, for it expresses joy that God has raised Jesus from the dead; and it renews the

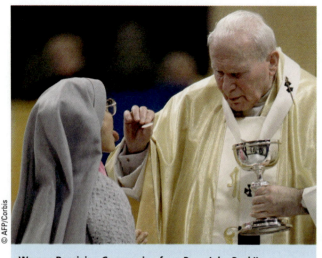

© AFP/Corbis

Woman Receiving Communion from Pope John Paul II.

Christian hope that God will also raise from the dead followers of Christ. The meaning of Easter is the same in western and eastern churches, but the days of the year on which it is celebrated are different. The same is true of Christmas, which commemorates the birthday of Jesus of Nazareth. Pentecost comes after Easter and marks the day when the Holy Spirit descended on the apostles in Jerusalem and when, through inspired preaching, they added about three thousand members to the church.

Points of passage in a Christian's life are marked by sacraments. A sacrament is a sign Christ instituted so that believers might receive God's grace for their salvation. Baptism is a sacrament a Christian shares with Jesus, who was baptized. For the believers, it is a symbol of dying to the old life of sin and of being resurrected to a new life in Christ. If a person receives baptism as an infant, it is followed by Confirmation, when, at the age of discretion, he or she freely chooses to identify with the Christian church. First Communion may follow—the participation of the believer in the last supper of Jesus and his disciples.

Believers who marry in the church promise before God and the congregation to remain married until their spouse dies. Only on the death of a spouse is a person free to remarry. In the Catholic Church, marriage is a sacrament, but in the Protestant churches it is not. Although the Catholic Church has recently broadened grounds that may lead to annulment of marriage, its stand against divorce has remained firm. People who divorce in secular courts and who remarry are not welcome to receive the sacraments of the Catholic Church. The Catholic Church does not remarry divorced people. Protestant churches generally recognize divorce, although they discourage it. Many Protestant churches now permit Christian marriage of divorced people, although particulars differ according to various denominations.

Holy Orders is a sacrament in the Catholic Church. Ordination in Protestant churches is a sacred occasion, but it is not a sacrament.

Christians are expected to visit the sick and those in prison. Prayers are said for healing the sick, and in Catholic and Orthodox churches the ancient rite of anointing the sick with holy oil may be practiced. Christians near the point of death are encouraged to make a final confession of sins and to receive forgiveness so they can enter death with a clear conscience. Christians are taught that death is a part of God's plan for human life, and that beyond death, those who have lived a Christian life have hope of living from age to age in the presence of God. Heaven is a state of bliss, free from suffering and death. Many Christians believe the unrighteous will suffer in hell, which is commonly thought to be a place of flames and extreme pain.

Christianity, then, provides for every major transition in human life. It takes care of personal anxieties and gives support and guidance. It gives people ways to live beyond themselves and also to contribute to the welfare of social groups.

It balances self-interest at every stage of life with a larger social interest that builds up other individuals and groups. Christians view world peace and world welfare as being in their own best interest and therefore worth working for throughout their lives.

Life after Death

Christianity teaches that those who believe in Christ as their savior will be resurrected from death. They will become a unity of soul and spiritual body that can recognize and be recognized by other resurrected people. Most Christians believe that those who have lived righteous lives will live happily in the presence of God in heaven; those who are wicked will endure hell. The kingdom of God will not be completed before Christ comes again to earth.

There are also some minority views on life after death. Immortality of the soul, the soul's living on without need of any physical manifestations, is a belief from Greek thought that many Christians have shared. Some early Christian writers entertained possibilities that the soul might be reincarnated in another human body. These ideas are overshadowed by the belief in the resurrection of the body, held by a majority of Christians.

Christianity and Other Religions

Christian views have emphasized that all people should be considered children of God who ought to become Christians. As a missionary religion, Christianity has sought converts among all peoples. Missionaries have studied thousands of dialects, reduced them to writing, and translated the Bible into them. People who have not had a chance to decide for Christ are the responsibility of Christians; those who have declined to convert bear responsibility for their decisions. In *Nostra Aetate,* the Second Vatican Council addressed relationships with other world religions. Speaking for tolerance and against persecution, the document advocates brotherly attitudes toward all people. At the same time,

> as the Church has always held and continues to hold, Christ in his boundless love freely underwent His passion and death because of the sins of all men, so that all might attain salvation. It is therefore the duty of the Church's preaching to proclaim the cross of Christ as the sign of God's all-embracing love and as the fountain from which every grace flows.[32]

Given their belief that a new revelation was given in Jesus Christ, Christians see all history in terms of before and after Christ, *anno Domini,* "in the year of the Lord." His appearance has interpreted all faith before his time and has influenced all faith since his time. God continues to reveal himself through the Holy Spirit who leads to truth, but Christians believe the more complete revelation will not contradict the revelation through Jesus Christ but will bring to light and understanding what has been given through him. As Scott Dixon has written of the Reformation in Germany, "any fundamental reform of the basic principles of the faith would naturally and necessarily have broader implications for the culture and society of the age. A reformation of religion would, in time, lead to a reformation of both the secular and the spiritual world."[33]

Which is the Christian century? Christianity counts time not from creation of the world but from the birth of Jesus, about 6 B.C.E. The 2 billion Christians worldwide have different preferences for traditions and teachings from different centuries. One U.S. periodical publishing during the last half of the twentieth century, titled itself *Christian Century*.

Many Christians prefer the first century, focusing on the life and teachings of Jesus, the gospels, the letters of the New Testament, and Revelation. Relationships between men and women, they think, should imitate those of the early church, when men were leaders and women kept silent. These Christians are not interested in the reasons for those customs; they only insist that they remain as they were in the primitive church.

Other Christians prefer later centuries. The fourth century saw the development of the Nicene Creed. The fifth century saw the *City of God* of St. Augustine, a champion of celibacy in Christian men and women. Some Catholics like the time when the pope controlled secular authorities; other Christians like the time when the pope was controlled by secular authorities. Protestants who think all believers should have a copy of the Bible and interpret it for themselves like the fifteenth and sixteenth centuries. Anglicans prefer the era of Henry VIII of England, when their church was established independent of Rome.

Some Christians think that all churches should be one. The Orthodox church and the Roman church should heal their split of 1054 C.E. Protestants and Anglicans should return to the Catholic church. Jesus prayed that all should be one as the Father and he were one. The passage in the gospel of John (17:11) is often cited, but experience has shown that uniting Christians across church boundaries is extremely difficult. Perhaps the best practices of each past century of Christianity will come together in a future century.[34]

CONSIDER THIS
Timeless Christianity

VOCABULARY

adoptionist [a-DOPT-shun-ist]
Anglicans [ANG-gli-cuns]
Anne Hutchinson
apocalypse [u-POCK-u-lips]
apocalyptic literature
[u-POCK-u-LIP-tic]
apostle [a-POS-ul]
Baptists [BAP-tists]
Book of Mormon
Brigham Young
Christian canon [CAN-on]
catechumen [KAT-i-KYOO-mum]
Christ [KRIIST]
church [CHURCH]
Eastern Orthodox Church
[OR-tha-dox]
ecumenical [ek-yu-MEN-i-kul]

epistles [i-PIS-els]
excommunicate
[ex-ku-MYUU-ni-caat]
gospels [GOS-puls]
heresies [HER-i-sies]
heretics [HER-i-tiks]
humanist
iconostasis [ii-con-NOS-ta-sis]
incarnation [in-cahr-NA-shun]
indulgences [in-DUL-jenses]
John Wesley
Joseph Smith
Judaizers [JOO-day-iiz-ers]
kerygma [ke-RIG-ma]
Lutherans [LOO-ther-ans]
Martin Luther King Jr.
Mary Baker Eddy

Methodist [METH-u-dist]
miracle [MIR-a-kul]
monophysite [mu-NOF-u-SITE]
mystery religions
pantheon [PAN-the-on]
parable [PARE-u-bul]
Pentecost [PEN-ti-cost]
Presbyterians [PREZ-bit-tir-ee-uns]
Puritans [PYOOR-i-tuns]
Quakers [KWAY-kurs]
resurrection [RES-u-REC-shun]
sacraments [SAK-ra-mints]
Scholasticism [sku-LAS-ti-siz-um]
Separatists [SEP-ar-a-tists]
theology [THEE-ol-e-jee]
Trinity [TRIN-i-tee]

QUESTIONS FOR REVIEW

1. Tell the story of the life of Jesus.
2. Tell the story of the growth of the early churches.
3. How did Roman and Orthodox churches begin? How do they differ?
4. How did Roman government influence early Christianity?
5. What is important in medieval Christianity?
6. What splits and reforms occurred in Christian churches in the fifteenth through nineteenth centuries?

7. In the twentieth century, what did Christians contribute to social change?
8. Is Christianity a missionary religion? Support your answer with examples.
9. If Christians are exhorted to live by faith, why do they get involved in charitable works?
10. What issues do you see on the national and international scene that will require decisive action by Christians?

QUESTIONS FOR DISCUSSION

1. In the twenty-first century, what are the most important issues the churches must face?
2. What is the future of Christianity in Asia?
3. What are the major differences between Judaism and Christianity?

4. How may relationships of Catholics, Protestants, and Orthodox churches change in the next half century?
5. Must one become a socialist to practice Christianity?

NOTES

1. This quotation and others in this chapter are from the Revised Standard Version of the Bible (New York: Thomas Nelson, Old Testament Section, 1952; New Testament Section, 1946).
2. James L. Price, *The New Testament: Its History and Theology* (New York: Macmillan, 1987), pp. 283–287.
3. Passio Perpetua, as quoted in *Adam, Eve, and the Serpent: Changing Patterns of Sexual Morality,* by Elaine Pagels (New York: Random House, 1988), p. 35.
4. Raymond E. Brown, *The Community of the Beloved Disciple* (New York: Paulist Press, 1979), p. 59.
5. Price, pp. 309–397.
6. Charles Bigg, *The Christian Platonists of Alexandria* (Oxford, UK: Clarendon Press, 1886).
7. Henry Bettenson, ed., *Documents of the Christian Church* (New York: Oxford University Press, 1947), p. 37.
8. Peter Brown, *Augustine of Hippo* (Berkeley: University of California Press, 1967).
9. Augustine, *The Confessions of St. Augustine,* trans. E. B. Pusey (New York: Dutton, 1951), p. 1.
10. Elaine Pagels, *Adam, Eve, and the Serpent: Changing Patterns of Sexual Morality* (New York: Random House, 1988).

11. Rosemary Radford Ruether, *Faith and Fratricide: The Theological Roots of Anti-Semitism* (New York: Seabury Press, 1974), pp. 173–174.
12. Williston Walker, *A History of the Christian Church* (New York: Scribner's, 1952), p. 139.
13. John Chapman, *Saint Benedict and the Sixth Century* (Westport, CT: Gatewood Press, 1971).
14. Omer Englebert, *St. Francis of Assisi,* trans. E. M. Cooper (Chicago: Franciscan Herald Press, 1965).
15. J. T. Shotwell and J. R. Loomis, eds., *The See of Peter* (New York: Octagon Books, 1965).
16. Josef Pieper, *Guide to Thomas Aquinas,* trans. R. Winston and C. Winston (New York: New American Library of World Literature, 1962).
17. St. Thomas Aquinas, *Summa Theologica,* part I, question 2, art. 3, as quoted in Anton C. Pegis, *Basic Writings of St. Thomas Aquinas* (New York: Random House, 1945), p. 22; this translation is based on the English Dominican translation begun in 1911, which was the work of Father Laurence Shapcote, O.P.
18. H. H. Ben-Sasson, ed., *A History of the Jewish People* (Cambridge, MA: Harvard University Press, 1976), pp. 413–414.

19. As quoted in Edwin Pears, *The Fall of Constantinople* (New York: Cooper Square Publishers, 1975), p. 346.

20. C. Scott Dixon, *The Reformation in Germany* (Oxford, UK: Blackwell, 2002), p. 140.

21. John Calvin, *Institutes of Christian Religion,* trans. John Allen, 7th ed. (Philadelphia: Presbyterian Board of Christian Education), pp. 360–361.

22. Ibid.

23. Ignatius Loyola, *St. Ignatius' Own Story,* trans. Young (Chicago: Loyola University Press, 1956); James Broderick, *The Origin of the Jesuits* (Westport, CT: Greenwood Press, 1971).

24. Kenneth Scott Latourette, *A History of Christianity* (New York: Harper, 1953), p. 851.

25. Gaius Glenn Atkins and Frederick L. Fagley, *History of American Congregationalism* (Boston: Pilgrim Press, 1942), p. 89.

26. My sincere thanks to Steve Wainwright for his contribution to this section on the Church of Jesus Christ of Latter-Day Saints.

27. Walter M. Abbot, S. J., ed., *The Documents of Vatican II* (New York: Herder and Herder), 1966, Contents.

28. Ibid.

29. St. Augustine, "The City of God, XIII, 14." *A select History of the Nicene and Post Nicene Fathers of the Christian Church,* vol. 2, ed. Philip Schaff (Grand Rapids, MI: Eerdmans, 1983), p. 251.

30. St. Irenaeus, *Against Heresis,* 4, 37–38. *The Anti-Nicene Fathers,* vol. 1, ed. Alexander Roberts and James Donaldson (Grand Rapids, MI: Eerdmans, 1980), pp. 518–522.

31. Christine E. Gudorf, "Contraception and Abortion in Roman Catholicism," in *Sacred Rights,* ed. Daniel C. Maguire (Oxford: Oxford University Press, 2003), p. 55.

32. Abbott, p. 667.

33. Scott Dixon, p. 141.

34. Martin E. Marty, "Revising the Map of American Religion," in *Americans and Religion in the Twenty-First Century,* ed. Wade Clark Roof (Thousand Oaks, CA: Sage, 1998).

READINGS

Dixon, C. Scott. *The Reformation in Germany.* Oxford, UK: Blackwell, 2002.

Ehrman, Bart D. *The New Testament.* New York: Oxford University Press, 1997.

Frankel, Sandra S. *Christianity.* Hagerstown, MD: Torch, 1985.

Kee, Howard Clark, et al. *Christianity: A Social and Cultural History.* New York: Macmillan, 1991.

Maxwell, David. *Christians and Chiefs in Zimbabwe.* Westport, CT: Praeger, 1999.

Price, James L. *The New Testament.* New York: Macmillan, 1987.

Roof, Wade Clark, ed. *Americans and Religions in the Twenty-First Century.* The Annals of the American Academy of Political and Social Science 558. Thousand Oaks, CA: Sage, 1998.

Spivey, Robert A., and D. Moody Smith. *The Anatomy of the New Testament.* Englewood Cliffs, NJ: Prentice Hall, 1995.

Walker, Williston. *A History of the Christian Church,* rev. Cyril C. Richardson, Wilhelm Pauck, and Robert T. Handy. New York: Scribner's, 1985.

Weaver, Mary Jo. *Introduction to Christianity.* Belmont, CA: Wadsworth, 1991.

BASIC TENETS OF CHRISTIANITY

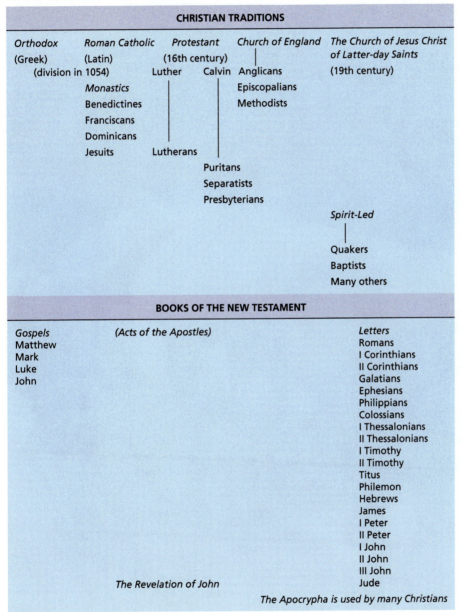

CHRISTIAN TRADITIONS

Orthodox
(Greek)
(division in 1054)

Roman Catholic
(Latin)
Monastics
Benedictines
Franciscans
Dominicans
Jesuits

Protestant
(16th century)
Luther   Calvin
Lutherans

Church of England
Anglicans
Episcopalians
Methodists

The Church of Jesus Christ of Latter-day Saints
(19th century)

Puritans
Separatists
Presbyterians

Spirit-Led

Quakers
Baptists
Many others

BOOKS OF THE NEW TESTAMENT

Gospels
Matthew
Mark
Luke
John

(Acts of the Apostles)

Letters
Romans
I Corinthians
II Corinthians
Galatians
Ephesians
Philippians
Colossians
I Thessalonians
II Thessalonians
I Timothy
II Timothy
Titus
Philemon
Hebrews
James
I Peter
II Peter
I John
II John
III John
Jude

The Revelation of John

The Apocrypha is used by many Christians

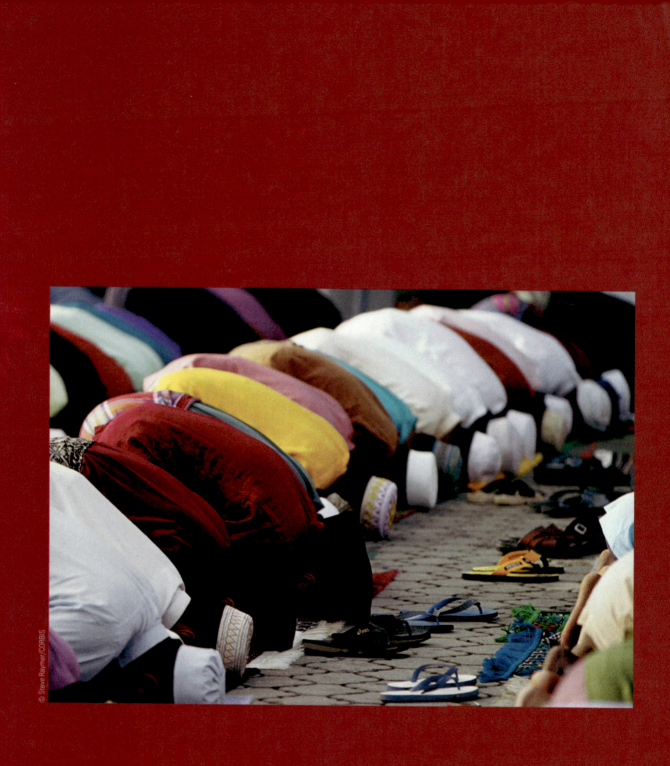

CHAPTER 10

Islam

OVERVIEW AND THEMES

"In the Name of God, the Merciful, the Compassionate

Praise belongs to God, the Lord of all Being,

the All-merciful, the All-compassionate, the Master of the Day of Doom.

Thee only we serve; to Thee alone we pray for succour.

Guide us in the straight path

The path of those whom Thou has blessed, not of those against whom Thou art wrathful, nor of those who are astray."

— *Qur'an 1:1–7* *

IMPORTANT MUSLIM TEACHINGS

Follow the Five Pillars of Islam.

There is no God but Allah, and Muhammad is his Prophet.

Pray toward Mecca five times a day.

Give alms, and contribute a portion of wealth to the welfare of the community.

Make a pilgrimage to Mecca at least once in a lifetime if possible.

AREAS OF MUSLIM CONCENTRATION

Africa: 344,920,000

Asia: 869,880,000

Europe: 32,117,000

Latin America: 1,752,000

Northern America: 4,828,000 (Of which 4,132,000 are in the United States. There are also 1,650,000 Black Muslims in the United States.)

Oceania: 725,000

World 1,254,222,000

*From *The Koran Interpreted,* trans. Arthur J. Arberry; copyright 1955, by George Allen & Unwin, Ltd.

When Muhammad, the Messenger of God, appeared in Arabia in the seventh century of the Common Era, Judaism had already completed the Bible and the Babylonian Talmud. The Christians, now leaders of the official religion of the Roman Empire, had long ago agreed on the collection of their New Testament. Although Rome had fallen to the Visigoths, Constantinople thrived as the center of the Byzantine empire. Muhammad's recitations of God's word to him set in motion dynamic religious and political fervor that threatened or toppled Jewish and Christian strongholds around the Mediterranean Sea.

Inspired by God, Muhammad combined religious, military, and administrative genius to unify the tribes of Arabia into one people, Muslims. God's revelation to him affirmed the tradition of Abraham and Ishmael as builders of the Ka'bah in Mecca (Makkah). Prophets to Israel were also honored in Islam; John the Baptist and Jesus were accepted as true prophets of God. Muhammad's recitations, uttered after inspiration by God, were piously written down by his followers, later to be combined into the Holy **Qur'an,** who accepted it as the final, flawless revelation of God's will for humankind.

Always known as a reverent, admirable person, Muhammad endured attacks from some factions within his city of Mecca and from polytheists of the countrysides. Persevering despite an assassination attempt on his life, he established a rival holy city in Medina that eventually reaffirmed Mecca as the preeminent center of Islam. When Muhammad died, Arabs were unified in one faith and prepared to promote their religion in the Byzantine empire.

Muhammad's closest family and associates included influential women as well as the men who would become his successors. Khadijah, his

Muslims praying in Malaysia.

sympathetic and supportive older wife; 'A'ishah, his younger wife, married after the death of Khadijah; and his four daughters undoubtedly influenced his reforms initiated on behalf of all women in Islam. Although his marriages evoked criticism from Jews and Christians, Muslims interpreted them as evidence of his compassion for women, particularly for the widows of his fallen comrades.

Among the youngest of the world's major religions, Islam, the third sibling among the children of Abraham, spread from Arabia into the Middle East, Asia, North Africa, and Europe.

Islam's record of expansion is filled with impressive accomplishments. Like any record, however, it is open to interpretation by those who preserve it and those who read and apply it. Within the first century, two sharply different ways of telling the story appeared.

Although Islam is largely unified in its own view of its historical development, Jews, Christians, and secular historians see things differently. Focusing on God's revelation to Muhammad, Muslims believe that the central fact of Islam is the **Qur'an.** Aware that divine and human forces are at work in the dynamics of their faith, they deny their Prophet adapted social influences from Jews and Christians. Peoples of those religions, however, were skeptical of the "revelation" that set aside their own scriptures as erroneous and antiquated. Ever ready to denigrate Muhammad, they often pointed out his social experiences in his travels that led to his "erroneous" revelation about their beliefs and practices. Secular historians, although more tolerant of Muhammad's religious experiences and sociological practices, have tried to explain his religious teachings as a result of social, historical, and political influences.

The ensuing account tries to present the facts of history with respect for the Muslim views that Muhammad's actions, words, and teachings were inspired by his own religious experiences. Nevertheless, other forces interacted with his recitations of the Qur'an and his actions based on them. In the history of this religion, as I have with others, I try to present a sympathetic, understanding account of the religion's beliefs about its origin and development.

Historical Development: The Background of Islam

Qur'an [KUR-an]
The sacred scripture of the Muslims, regarded as the word of God dictated to Muhammad by God through the archangel Gabriel. The Prophet received and recited the messages over approximately twenty years.

Islam emerged in Arabia, specifically in the city of Mecca, in the seventh century C.E.[1] A peninsula that had some fertile land on the coasts and some scattered oases of excellent agriculture, Arabia also had vast stretches of barren hills and valleys and an immense area of desert sands. There were some well-established cities, such as Mecca, but the inhabitants of the open spaces were the bedouin, who moved their tents and flocks as necessary to find food and water. In both situations, the key organization was the tribe, and within the tribe, the clan. The tribal identities superseded any loyalty to geographic area or city. Survival depended on water and vegetation, to be sure, but just as surely it depended on the strength of the tribe. An isolated individual or even family had little chance of survival in a natural and human environment that was usually hostile.

© AP Photo/Anne Emric

The Grand Mosque, Mecca. The holy Ka'bah.

Economically, there was some interdependence among the desert tribes and the city tribes. The bedouin were largely independent, but they could trade their sheep, goat, and camel wool to peoples of oases for products of their trees and fields. Farmers could gain through trading dates and wheat for the wool used in making clothes, carpets, and tapestries. Then there were peoples such as the Meccans, who produced little but made a business of buying and selling and providing markets where the various tribes could come together and exchange goods. Mecca also had individuals who could organize large caravans and trade with other population centers, among which were Damascus, in Syria; South Arabia; and Ethiopia. Although poor in natural resources themselves, the Meccans managed to maintain a level of commercial activity that brought them economic and political importance.

The Meccans had something even more important than most oases had. The famous **Ka'bah** was located there. The cubic building possessed the Black Stone in its southeast corner, which was a symbol of divine power. The building contained some 360 idols, many of them representing forces of nature and celestial beings. Every Arab tribe could find its deities there, and religious pilgrimages could be combined with caravans organized for trade within the city limits. Mecca also had an established tradition of truce for pilgrimages during part of the year; tribes that were normally at war with each other could enter an area of safety and carry on trade for a period of time without being in constant fear of a surprise raid on their persons and possessions.

The keepers of the Ka'bah were members of the Quraysh tribe. They had considerable status among Arabs due to their stewardship of this most sacred precinct. It is obvious that they also had considerable economic advantage from the pilgrims and traders who came to their city to conduct religious rituals and business activities. They were also aware that theirs was not a monopoly, for

Ka'bah [KUH-bah]
The cube-shaped building of stone in the open court of the Grand Mosque of Mecca. In Islamic tradition, the first Ka'bah was built by Abraham and Ishmael.

there were other centers where goods could be exchanged. So the Quraysh were always alert to anyone or anything that could undermine their social position or livelihood.

The Life of Muhammad

The child Muhammad, born to a powerful but impoverished clan, was not to inherit wealth. His father, Abdullah, died in Yathrib before Muhammad was born to Aminah, his mother. Any inheritance Abdullah might have received would have passed to brothers, not to his son. Pious Muslims tell stories of the holy birth of Muhammad. God willed his truth to a fixed abode, transferring the Purified One to Aminah. She had become pregnant with one of the Lights of Essence. All nature informed the Quraysh of his being expected. At his birth many strange and miraculous signs proclaimed heaven's triumph over satanic spirits.[2]

Following the custom of the time, Muhammad was sent to the country to live with a wet nurse and her family until he was six years old. Because Halimah, a member of the tribe of Banu-Asad, was married to a shepherd, Muhammad enjoyed his earliest childhood roaming the countryside with this family that spent most of its days looking for sustenance for themselves and their flocks. After Halimah returned Muhammad to his mother, she took him on a journey to see her family in Yathrib, the city where his father had died on a trading mission when he was only twenty-five years old. Unfortunately, his mother did not survive the return journey, and Muhammad was an orphan when he reached Mecca again. Now he was entirely dependent on his grandfather and, after his grandfather's death, on his uncle Abu Talib.

The time between Muhammad's birth in 570 C.E. and his marriage to Khadijah at the age of twenty-five is only sketched in outline, except for some stories circulated by some of the pious that are by no means accepted by the majority of Muslims. At some point, Muhammad had accepted employment from the well-to-do widow Khadijah and had led some caravans for her. Tradition reports that she was about forty years old when Muhammad married her. The marriage was successful; Muhammad did not have another wife as long as Khadijah lived. In the twenty-five years they lived together, they had at least two sons, who died in infancy, and four daughters, Zaynab, Ruqayyah, Umm-Khulthum, and Fatima, all of them except Fatima dying before their father. Khadijah was a counselor and companion to her husband, and her wealth enabled him to spend some of his time in religious meditation. Always a moral person, he sought now to deepen his spiritual life. He sometimes wandered outside the city to meditate among the hills.

Muhammad's spiritual quest led to results that were absolutely startling for him. While he was meditating in a cave on Mt. Hira about 610, the angel Gabriel confronted him and delivered a message from Allah (Arabic for "the God"). Gabriel challenged Muhammad to read or recite the message of God.

> In the Name of God, the Merciful, the Compassionate
> Recite: In the Name of thy Lord who created,
>   created Man of a blood-clot.
> Recite: And thy Lord is the Most Generous,
>   who taught by the Pen,
>   taught Man that he knew not. (Qur'an 96:1–5)[3]

Far from ecstatic, Muhammad was anxious as he described his experience to Khadijah. Was he becoming possessed? Khadijah consulted a cousin of hers, a

hanif (worshiper of one God), Waraqa Ibn Nawfal, who had become a Christian; he assured her the experience of Muhammad was in line with the experience of other prophets recognized by Jews and Christians. He was not possessed by **jinn.** Khadijah supported him from the beginning of his revelations until the time of her death.

Once Muhammad was sure God was really speaking through him, he did his duty and recited the messages exactly as he received them. That took exceptional courage, for the message God gave him to recite was one of social and religious reform. At its heart was emphasis on God as the only deity and the absolute requirement that all idols of the Arabs be destroyed. Muhammad was to recite these words of God to the people of Mecca, including the tribe of Quraysh. There was not much resistance to the idea that Muhammad was a prophet; there was, however, immediate resistance to the message that all idols had to be destroyed. The Quraysh did not take long to see that following the message could jeopardize their traditional means of livelihood. They could not very well assail God, but they could ridicule Muhammad so that no one socially acceptable to the Meccans would take him seriously, let alone identify with his beliefs. A tradition reporting that Muhammad received certain "satanic verses" is regarded by many Muslims as untrue.[4] The account states that two verses he received, permitting Arabs to worship three traditional goddesses, were rejected as inspired by the "satan." Sura 53 of the Qur'an now describes these goddesses as only imaginary, deserving no worship.

The first converts came from his own household. Besides Khadijah and Muhammad's cousin 'Ali, son of Abu Talib, Zayd Ibn Horithah, his adopted son, accepted him. The first convert outside his household was Abu Bakr, who, although a little younger than Muhammad, was a man of some wealth and influence in Mecca. Two other converts, Khalid Ibn Said and 'Uthman Ibn Affan, came from the rival branch of the Quraysh, the Ummayads. These first converts were to figure significantly in the development of the organization of the new religion. Eventually Muhammad gave daughters in marriage to 'Ali and 'Uthman. After the death of Khadijah, Muhammad married Abu Bakr's daughter Aishah. Early Islam was maintained with strong family ties.

Other converts came slowly from ranks of young people and slaves. Tremendous pressure was placed on the converts to renounce their new faith and return to traditional Arab polytheism. Yet they persisted and were even successful in making converts of some of the persecutors, for example, 'Umar. Eventually, several Muslim families had to emigrate to Ethiopia to seek safety; even there the enemies of Muhammad sought their deportation. To bring further pressure, leaders of the Quraysh placed a boycott on the house of Hashim, Muhammad's clan. Abu Talib did not give in to their threats, nor did he ask Muhammad to compromise the message of God. With the deaths of Abu Talib and Khadijah within a period of a year, Muhammad became even more desolate.

In the year 620, Muhammad had contact with representatives from Yathrib who were seeking someone to arbitrate conflicts there and serve as an impartial leader. Muhammad accepted the challenge on condition the Medinans embrace Islam. Some of them returned and agreed to practice a rigid monotheism. Muhammad sent a teacher with them when they returned to Yathrib and helped them prepare a body of Muslims in their own city. Later, Muhammad chose twelve leaders from the Khazraj and the Aws, tribes of Yathrib, and set them apart to become the leaders of his religious community in Yathrib. Muhammad counseled his adherents in Mecca to get their affairs in order and leave the city to make a new life in Yathrib. Muhammad's enemies in Mecca looked on this development

hanif [HA-neef]
In Arabia, prior to Muhammad's recitations, a person who worshiped one God. Waraqa Ibn Nawfal, a kinsman of Khadijah, was a hanif.

jinn [JIN]
In Arabia, a race of beings created from fire, distinguished from humans, who were created from clay. Some jinn are good; others are bad.

Islam in History

570 Muhammad born

610 Muhammad receives first revelation

622 The Hijrah; Muhammad moves from Mecca to Yathrib

630 Muhammad controls Mecca

632 Muhammad dies at Medina; Abu Bakr succeeds him

634 'Umar succeeds Abu Bakr

635 Muslims take Damascus

638 Muslims take Jerusalem

641 Muslims take Egypt

644 'Uthman succeeds 'Umar

656 'Uthman assassinated

661 'Ali assassinated

697 Arabs destroy Carthage

716 Arab empire extends to China

732 Charles Martel turns back Muslims near Tours

935 Al-Ash'ari dies

1055 Seljuk Turks conquer Baghdad

1099 Crusaders conquer Jerusalem

1111 Al-Ghazali dies

1183 Genghis Khan invades Russia

1244 Muslims gain control of Jerusalem after crusades

1251 Kublai Khan governs China

1258 Mongols sack Baghdad, ending Abbasid caliphate

1798 Napoleon extends French rule to Egypt

1347 Black Death (bubonic plague) begins to afflict Europe

1453 Constantinople falls to Turks

1492 Spain expels all Muslims

1703 Ibn Abd al-Wahhab born

1833 Slavery abolished in British Empire

1838 Jamal al-Din al-Afghani born

1849 Muhammad Abduh born

1947 Pakistan independent from India and Great Britain

1949 Indonesia independent of Netherlands

1966 Arab–Israeli war

1973 October War between Egypt and Israel

1979 Ayatollah Khomeini returns to Iran

1993 Israel and Palestine Liberation Organization sign peace accord

1995 Vatican forms joint committee for better understanding between Christianity and Islam

2001 Al-Qaeda attacks World Trade Center and Pentagon

as a new threat. They wanted him and his converts where they could keep an eye on them and, if possible, control them.

Forty men, representing several different clans in Mecca, excluded the house of Hashim from a secret meeting called to discuss the fate of Muhammad. Because the forty would act as one person to kill Muhammad, the Hashimites could not afford to attack all the various clans in blood revenge. The forty men guarded Abu Bakr's house, where Muhammad was supposed to be staying. However, 'Ali took the place of the Prophet in bed, and Muhammad and Abu Bakr slipped out of the city and hid in a cave to the south of Mecca. The enemies conducted a rigorous search, but eventually Muhammad and Abu Bakr escaped and made their way north to Yathrib. 'Ali escaped as well. Yathrib became the new home of the Prophet. The **Hijrah**, the migration, was in 622, which became the beginning year of the Muslim calendar.

Muhammad's move to Yathrib added a new dimension to the story of Islam. Until that point, the life of the Prophet was parallel to the calling of several different leaders of world religions, including Jesus and Gautama. But Muhammad had to add, almost at once, an administrative element to his leadership without diminishing at all his spiritual leadership; indeed, the two had to be inseparable if the new religion was to survive. An element of that administrative leadership that has been widely misunderstood outside Islam was the necessity in Arabia of military leadership. The tribes of Arabia lived by honor and retaliation; individuals who were also tribe members were expected to defend not only themselves and their property but also their honor and other members of their tribe. To identify with Muhammad in Islam was, in a sense, to give allegiance to a new type of tribe. Thrust upon Muhammad were the responsibilities of a sheik to lead, defend, and avenge the members of his tribe. To fail in that responsibility would have made him unworthy of respect in the eyes of Arabs. Muhammad from this point may seem very different from Jesus; they lived in very different societies. Muhammad's course, however, would not be unheard of for those who have studied the history of Judaism, for there are several precedents for leaders who combined administrative, military, and spiritual leadership roles. The Sikh gurus had to take a similar stance to survive among Muslims and Hindus.

When Yathrib became Medina, the city of the Prophet, not all inhabitants shared with equal enthusiasm Muhammad's leadership. The **ansar** (helpers), who had helped him come to the city of Medina, welcomed him, and the **muhajirun** (companions), who came from Mecca to make their new homes with Muhammad, welcomed a chance to live without persecution for their new faith. But a third group, which included many Jews, was composed of those who did not honor Muhammad as a prophet and who wished that he and his followers would get out of their lives and stay out. Tensions were present from the beginning of his stay, and they grew as it became necessary for Muhammad to make new rules for the lives of the faithful. As Muhammad built his house and the main mosque and as his supporters acquired places to live and took such jobs as were available, frictions developed that added to the smoldering resentments that carried over from earlier conflicts among the various tribes and clans. The startling revelations of the Qur'an continued to stir the Prophet. An illiterate man, Muhammad received the messages during periods of withdrawal from his surroundings. His periods of reception were filled with awe. Later, he would recite the message he had received. He then applied the messages to developing law and practices.

> It belongs not to any mortal that
> God should speak to him, except

Hijrah [HEJ-rah]
Muhammad's migration from Mecca to Yathrib (Medina) in 622. He and Abu Bakr made the journey in less than the normal eleven days.

ansar [AN-sahr]
Helpers; Medinans who helped Muhammad relocate from Mecca to Medina. They were joined by Muhammad and his companions after the Hijrah.

muhajirun
[mu-HAJ-i-roon]
The emigrants from Mecca who joined Muhammad in Medina. These early converts to Islam lost their property and income when they followed Muhammad.

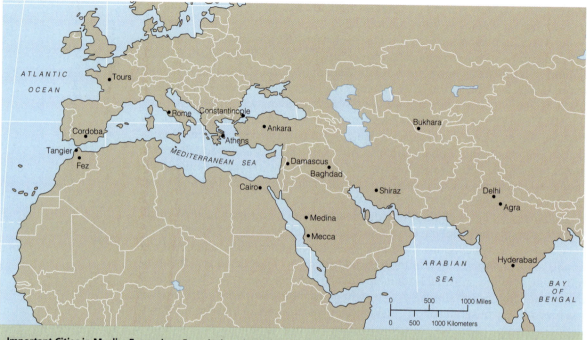

Important Cities in Muslim Expansion. From its base in Arabia, Islam spread rapidly through the Middle East, North Africa, Europe, and Asia.

by revelation, or from behind a veil,
or that He should send a messenger
and he reveal whatsoever He will,
by his leave; surely He is All-high, All-wise.
Even so We have revealed to thee a
Spirit of Our bidding. Thou knewest
not what the Book was, nor belief;
but We made it a light, whereby We
guide whom We will of Our servants. And thou,
surely thou shalt guide unto a straight path—
the path of God, to whom belongs whatsoever is in
the heavens, and whatsoever is in the earth.
Surely unto God all things come home.
    (Qur'an 42:50–53)

Muhammad's role was, indeed, an awesome responsibility, as Fazlur Rahman has written:

> Muhammad, like all other prophets, is a "warner and giver of good tidings" and his mission is to preach—constantly and unflinchingly. Since this message is from God and is direly needed by men for survival and success, it has to be accepted by man and implemented. His preaching, therefore, is no conventional speech-making but has to "bring home" the crucial message.[5]

The Meccans were not satisfied with having Muhammad free in Medina building a rival faith. Abu al-Hakam, the chief of Muhammad's main enemies, and others sought ways to cause difficulties for the Muslims beyond confiscating their properties. The Muslims were sending out armed parties to various territories; sometimes these were led by Muhammad, but often they were led by lesser persons. Many times these expeditions were well received in peace, and Muhammad's cause gained friends, if not military allies. Eventually, a Muslim raid on a Meccan caravan south of Mecca incited a retaliatory raid from the Meccans that took place at Badr in 624. To their surprise, the Meccans were soundly defeated, and the Muslims gained not only more wealth but also more respect among the sheiks whose alliance they sought. Abu Sufyan of the Meccan Ummayads raised money for an army to avenge the defeat that they had suffered at Badr. Things were reversed at Uhud in 625, and the Meccans defeated the Muslims, even wounding Muhammad. The Meccans failed to finish the war, however, and the Muslims were able to recoup their losses and make preparations for the next encounter. The next attack was on Medina itself by a superior force of Meccans led by Abu Sufyan, including numerous other tribes they enlisted along the way. Medina survived for two reasons: Muslims had gathered in provisions from the fields that the Meccan force would have needed to sustain a siege, and they borrowed a Persian expedient of digging a trench on the north or open side of the city, the other sides being protected by hills. These unexpected developments and unseasonably cold and stormy weather eventually led Abu Sufyan to lift the siege and return to Mecca.

In March 628, Muhammad took sixteen hundred men and set out for Mecca, intending to make a religious pilgrimage. The Meccans were upset, and some of them under Khalid Ibn al-Walid, the budding military genius, set about to block Muhammad's progress. Taking a different route, the Prophet arrived at al-Hudaybiyyah, a few miles from Mecca. Both sides were divided over whether to fight. The truce Muhammad negotiated with the Quraysh gave ten years of peace and let the Muslims return the next year to make a pilgrimage to the Ka'bah. The truce worked to the advantage of Muhammad: As Muslims and Meccans intermingled in peace, some of the brightest and most able Meccans, Khalid Ibn al-Walid among them, decided to become Muslims.

Muhammad continued to seek converts among Arab tribes, Christians, Jews, and foreign leaders. Sometimes he was successful and sometimes not. The Jews of Khaybar to the north of Medina were relentless in their opposition to Muhammad, so he marched on the city to defeat it. The Jews who continued to live there had to give half of their produce each year to the Muslims. In revenge for the loss of her husband at Khaybar, a Jewish captive, Zaynab Bint al-Harith, gave Muhammad some poisoned meat to eat. Although the poison killed a companion of Muhammad, he detected it in time to escape death. Muhammad and Jews had reached a parting of the ways; even earlier in Medina the Prophet had changed the direction Muslims faced in prayer from Jerusalem to Mecca. His approaches to Arab tribes asking them to join him in Islam were successful, and the Meccans were losing support month after month.

The next year brought the Muslims some success and a notable failure. The success was in a long-delayed pilgrimage to Mecca. The Muslims had three days to perform their religious duties at the Ka'bah, something they had not been allowed to do for about ten years. The failure was an expedition under Khalid sent into the Christian territory to the north of Medina. The Byzantine army was too strong for the Muslim force, and after losing some very important men, the Muslims were fortunate to escape with their lives. The humiliation hurt, but Muhammad did not abandon his hopes of making inroads to the north.

The year 630 was the year of triumph for the Muslims. Their eight-year exile from Mecca ended when Muhammad judged that the Meccans had broken their truce by fighting a tribe in alliance with the Muslims. Ten thousand men marched with Muhammad as he approached the holy city. When Abu Sufyan saw the force, he tried to negotiate as much safety as possible for the inhabitants. Muhammad granted amnesty to those who did not resist his invasion.

The only military opposition seems to have been in the southern quarters, advanced on by Khalid. The real destruction Muhammad carried out was on the idols of the Ka'bah. The polytheism he had denounced for nearly twenty years was crushed for all time from the sacred city of the Arabs. Seven persons were executed. Within a month, he moved to crush two remaining tribes who opposed him, the Hawazin and the Thaquf.

Although Muhammad had control of Mecca, he continued to make Medina the place of his residence. There, during the remaining years of his life, he received the stream of delegations seeking alliance with him. He made his farewell pilgrimage to Mecca in the spring of 632, and he delivered a final sermon there during his ten-day sojourn. He returned to Medina and continued his leadership in administration and religion despite health problems. Tradition reports that he went to the mosque on the morning of the day he died in 632.

An orphan without property, a prophet denounced by many leaders of his own tribe, Muhammad persevered through faith in God until most of the tribes of Arabia joined him in Islam and made Mecca the center of pure monotheism. For the first time, someone had succeeded in unifying the peoples of Arabia into a powerful nation. As yet, Arabia was untried against the other nations of the world, but Muhammad had sown the seeds, and expeditions to spread the faith were already planned. Muhammad died the revered prophet of a new religion that embraced nearly all Arabs and was ready to make converts in all parts of the world.

The Pillars of Islam

What was the teaching of the Prophet, as Muhammad became known, who moved so many proud men to join him in service to God? If his teachings were so different that they were rejected by a majority of his own tribe, how could they be embraced by people who would be persecuted for their allegiance? The profundity of Muhammad's message and the intricate implications of his revelations were carried out in acts that could be performed by the simple shepherd or his wife, warriors, merchants, scholars, and saints. Five requirements are made of all Muslims: First, they must declare in the **Shahada**, witness, that there is no god but Allah and that Muhammad is his **rasul,** or messenger. Second, they must participate in **salat,** five periods of prayer each day. Third, they must pay an obligatory tax, called **zakat,** to the needy. Fourth, they must fast during the daylight hours in the month of Ramadan, known as **sawm.** Fifth, if they are able, they should make a pilgrimage to Mecca, a **Hajj,** once during their lifetime. These are acts even the simplest person can understand and practice; they are the **Five Pillars of Islam.** That is not to say, however, that the full understanding of the beliefs behind the practices is easy or that keeping all of the practices is always convenient.

There is only one God, without partners or descendants (**Tawhid**). Angels, as well as Shaytan, and adversaries to God and tempters of humans, are all clearly lesser beings than God, for they do not share his essence. The Christian belief in a Trinity or in a Son of God is clearly denounced in Islam. Muhammad is the spokesman of God, a prophet in the tradition of the Jewish prophets but in no way a divine being. The Qur'an is the revealed word of God and as such is not a

Shahada [sheh-HAH-da] Means "witnessing." The Muslim profession of faith. There is but one God and Muhammad is his rasul or messenger.

rasul [ra-SOOL] "Messenger." One who recites for God. Muhammad was the rasul of God.

salat [sa-LAHT] Obligatory prayer five times daily.

zakat [za-KAHT] In Islam, the payment of a due to support the community. It is an act of purification through giving.

sawm [SOM] Fast during daylight hours of Ramadan.

Hajj [HAHJ] The pilgrimage to Mecca, expected of all Muslims who are able.

Five Pillars of Islam In Islam, the five requirements made of all Muslims.

Tawhid [TAHW-heed] The Muslim doctrine of the unity of God. Islam denies any partners to God such as Christians are believed to have in their Trinity.

creation of humans, even Muhammad. God is merciful and compassionate to those who repent and submit to him. But he is just in his law and requires justice in social relations. At the end of time, God will judge every person and every deed. Rewards will be given to the righteous and punishments will fall on the liars and hypocrites. There will be a resurrection of the dead and a final judgment. Paradise and hell are places of physical reward and punishment. These are just a few of the beliefs outlined in the Qur'an and related to the Shahada.

Prayer is encouraged and can be volunteered at any time. At a bare minimum, every Muslim is required to participate in prescribed prayer five times a day. Although these prayers can be said alone or with groups, there seems to be special benefit in reciting them in groups. Noon on Friday is the time of community prayer in the mosque. Dawn, noon, midafternoon, nightfall, and evening are the five times of prayers that consist of prescribed **rak'as,** or postures and recitations. The faithful in the community are called to prayer by a **muezzin,** and there is a sense of community in prayer at one time even though individuals are not gathered into a physical congregation for prayer. One of the prayers repeated more than a dozen times a day is the opening *surah* (section) of the Qur'an.

> In the Name of God, the Merciful, the Compassionate
> Praise belongs to God, the Lord of all Being,
> the All-merciful, the All-compassionate, the Master of the Day of Doom.
> Thee only we serve; to Thee alone we pray for succour.
>   Guide us in the straight path,
> the path of those whom Thou has blessed,
> not of those against whom Thou art wrathful, nor of those who are astray.
>   (Qur'an 1:1–7)

Giving alms may take the form of a direct gift of compassion from one believer to another. This is called "charity" (**sadaqa**), and should be given frequently. But there is a more organized concept of giving (*zakat*) to a common treasury from which the needs of the community can be met. In a sense, alms are to be voluntary, but in another sense they are obligatory, like a tax. In any case, alms are different from the *jizyah* exacted from the non-Muslims and used for administration and military expenses. Alms are related to the nature of God, who is merciful and requires mercy in his worshipers toward each other. Compassion toward weak and defenseless persons of the community is a reflection of the compassion of God. Widows, orphans, and females in general are of particular concern in the words of Muhammad, and believers are exhorted to be compassionate to them in administering their trusts or permitting them to live through infancy, particularly unwanted females.

The month of Ramadan is set aside to recall the month in which God began to reveal the Qur'an to Muhammad. Although Islam does not despise the human body or advocate a rigid asceticism, it does recognize the value of fasting for clearing a person's spiritual perception. The fast, then, is enjoined on able-bodied believers for one month each year, but only during the daylight hours. After sunset, nourishment can be taken; believers can even celebrate with friends while taking much food and nonalcoholic drink.

rak'a [RAK-ah]
Each complete cycle of ritual movements that is part of Muslim prayer. During prayer Muslims stand, bow, kneel, and touch their foreheads to the ground.

muezzin [mu-EZ-in]
One who calls Muslims to prayer. Muhammad preferred the human voice to the Christian use of bells.

sadaqa [sah-DAH-ka]
Informal charity between Muslims.

© CORBIS

The Qur'an. Cairo Koran created for the Sultan of Morocco in the 18th century. The Maghribi Script is a cursive particular to North African countries.

Muhammad set the precedent for pilgrimages to Mecca while he was at Medina. All Muslims should make a pilgrimage to Mecca at least once in a lifetime if they can afford it and health permits. The journey is to be made in the period of the Hajj, and pilgrims are to remain in the state of *ihram,* or purity, for the two-week period of activities that center around Mecca but also involve Arafat and Mina. The most sacred place, of course, is the Ka'bah, which includes the Black Stone. Muslim tradition ties the Ka'bah to Abraham, who built the first building.

Muhammad's formation of Islam involved two sources, the Qur'an and the **Sunna.** The first, and most important, was the Qur'an. This revelation from God came to the prophet over many years and was given in suras, or chapters, applicable to specific situations in the life of the prophet and the community. The lines came in the poetic form of the Arabs, so beautiful that Muhammad challenged any poets to try to duplicate it. Indeed, the Qur'an is the one miracle in Islam; it is not at all the product of Muhammad's efforts or prior experiences. As Sheik Muhammad Abduh wrote,

> The mighty Book was vindicated as being speech *par excellence,* and the judgments superior to all others. Is not the appearance of such a Book, from the lips of an illiterate man, the greatest miracle and clearest evidence that it is not of human origin? Is it not rather the light that emanates from the sun of divine knowledge, the heavenly wisdom coming forth from the Lord upon the illiterate Prophet?[6]

Muslims have the Qur'an in Arabic; they believe it cannot be translated into other languages. According to tradition, the book Muslims have today was transcribed by Zayd Ibn Thabit, secretary to Muhammad, who collected the scraps on which followers had written oral messages. Muhammad did not write the messages he received. Nor did he seek the revelations; on the contrary, they came to him sometimes during periods of extreme physical ordeal, in which he broke out in a sweat and heard a loud ringing like a bell in his head.

The second source of guidance was Muhammad's word and practice. During his long period of political and religious leadership, the prophet was called on hundreds of times to make decisions and take actions that were not at the time clearly covered by revelation from God. His personality was so charismatic that his followers honored his words and examples, regarding them as binding on themselves. Given a chance to mingle with his followers and to observe and hear him, even his worst enemies sometimes joined his religion. These **hadiths,** or traditions of the prophet, once collected and evaluated as to their authenticity, became guides to the practice of Islam along with the Qur'an and comprise the literary form of the Sunna. The Qur'an and the Sunna, or custom of Muhammad, together form the guidelines for the beliefs and practices of the Muslim community.

The Beginnings of Sunni and Shi'a

Muhammad died without announcing to the whole community of Muslims his choice of successor. The disagreement over what principle should be employed in naming a successor threatened to divide the community at once; within a short time, it led to the major division that continues until the present time with little signs of healing. The person first chosen as successor, or **caliph** (*khalifah*), of the Prophet was Abu Bakr, one of his oldest companions. Although he was the father of Muhammad's wife Aishah, he was not of his immediate family as was 'Ali, his cousin, the son of his uncle Abu Talib. When Abu Bakr died after two years, the

Sunna [SUN-na]
The custom or tradition of Muhammad. It supplements the Qur'an as a source for the Shari'a.

hadiths [had-EETHS]
Reports of what Muhammad said or did; examples for faithful Muslims to follow. The *Sunna* are the traditions of the prophet in the literary form of *hadiths*—reports.

caliph [KAA-lif]
A successor of the prophet Muhammad. The first caliph was Abu Bakr. The ideal of Islam is that religion and state are not separated.

next successor was 'Umar. Under 'Umar, Islam expanded rapidly into other countries. After 'Umar's murder, 'Uthman, a son-in-law of the Prophet, succeeded him and ruled for about ten years. 'Uthman was from the rival faction of Mecca, and the original supporters of Muhammad regarded him as a usurper. He was murdered in Medina.[7] The old division culminated with the choice of the fourth caliph. 'Ali was the choice of the community at Medina, but Mu'awiyah, governor of Syria, refused to acknowledge him and held out to be the caliph himself. To the old guard at Medina, this suggestion was impossible, for Mu'awiyah was from the Ummayad branch of the Quraysh, the clan that had opposed Muhammad in his early years and made the Hijrah necessary, who refused him entrance to Mecca for a pilgrimage until he had the military strength to crush the Meccans. Now a descendant of that infamous clan was claiming to be the successor of the Prophet. The assassination of 'Uthman and the problem of choosing a successor weighed heavily on the community.

The details of the story vary somewhat between the accounts of the **Shi'a,** the partisans of 'Ali, and the **Sunni,** the traditionalists who accept the outcome that left Mu'awiyah the next leader. 'Ali agreed to submit the dispute between himself and Mu'awiyah to arbitration. A group, the Kharijites, seceded from 'Ali. These puritans thought that the community had a right to select any morally pure Muslim as caliph and that any true successor would let God settle the issue through battle. 'Ali was assassinated in 661, and Mu'awiyah retained power. 'Ali's son Hasan served briefly in Iraq, but he renounced his claim and returned to Medina. 'Ali's son Husayn attempted to establish a caliphate in 680, but he was intercepted on his way to Iraq near the town of Karbala. The Ummayad troops killed and beheaded him and sent his head to Damascus. This deed is regarded as an act of martyrdom by Shi'tes who fervently recall it in a passion play each year during the month of Muharram.

The Shi'tes hold to the institution of *imam,* the spiritual leader of the community, and regard 'Ali as the first imam. Although 'Ali had the ideal of temporal power as well as spiritual, other imams have had only spiritual power. For the Shi'a, 'Ali and those who succeeded him—not Mu'awiyah and his successors—are true imams.

The Expansion of Islam

The phenomenal spread of Islam beyond Arabia is one of the most rapid expansions of a religion in the history of the world. From the dates alone, it would appear this marching of Muslim armies was an idea of the first caliphs that developed after the death of Muhammad. Other sources, however, indicate Muhammad had already contemplated expeditions to the north, such as the first encounter with the Byzantine armies that led to Muslim reverses, salvaged only by the abilities of Khalid Ibn al-Walid. Apparently Muhammad had already mapped out another campaign and appointed a leader, Usamah, the son of Zayd. Abu Bakr simply carried out the plans of the Prophet when he sent Usamah out into Byzantine domains. This first expedition after the death of the Prophet was not a disaster, but it was not followed up immediately. Some tribes of Arabia considered that their alliance was with Muhammad and that it ended with his death. Only with force could the caliphs maintain the unity of the Arabs until they realized they were part of a new community of Islam, committed to the Muslim way and not just to the man Muhammad.

Shi'a [SHE-a]
Members of the "party" of 'Ali, who believed that he should have been the next leader after 'Uthman.

Sunni [SOON-e]
The traditional, majority, Muslims who accepted Mu'awiyah as the next leader after 'Uthman.

Dome of the Rock, Jerusalem, Israel. This mosque was built over a stone believed to have had a significant place in the life of Abraham.

Under 'Umar, the second caliph from 634 to 644, the Arab armies moved in a series of rapid thrusts that captured most of the Middle East. Popular religious author Karen Armstrong has written, "There was nothing religious about these campaigns, and 'Umar did not believe that he had a divine mandate to conquer the world. The objective of 'Umar and his warriors was entirely pragmatic: they wanted plunder and a common activity that would preserve the unity of the *ummah*."[8] However, most scholars of the past have written that there was a religious motivation.

Damascus, the capital of Syria, fell after a siege of six months in the year 635. Khalid offered the inhabitants security of person, property, and churches so long as they did not resist and paid the required tax. The Byzantines lost battle after battle to the horse- and camel-mounted warriors of the Arabs. The population of Syria welcomed the overthrow of the harsh Byzantine rulers by Semitic forces more similar to themselves. Jerusalem was a religious prize that fell into Muslim hands in 638. Its importance to Muslim religion came only after Mecca and Medina, for many of the events of the Hebrew Bible were shared in the accounts of the Qur'an. In the beginning of Muhammad's prophecy, he had enjoined Muslims to face Jerusalem in prayer. Egypt fell in 641, and soon the other North African countries to the west fell. Religious zeal motivated the soldiers: Converting idolaters (which did not include Christians and Jews) to Islam was an act of merit that aided others as well as themselves. Worshipers of one God could be tolerated, but believers waged war on all idolaters. Fighting that cost believers their lives could lead them directly to paradise, another religious motive. Wealth that could be shared by the warriors and sent back to the treasury of Islam to help the needy of the community also was a motive.

ummah [UM-mah]
The Muslim community.

After the time of 'Umar, the expansion continued rapidly until about 750. Muslim forces moved into Spain and even into France until turned back by Charles Martel in 732. To the east, Muslim forces entered Persia, eventually making it a center for Islam. Other campaigns moved Muslims to Turkestan and Mongolia and even into India. The Mogul Empire was established by descendants of Mongols, the most enlightened of whom was Akbar, the grandson of Babur. Constantinople survived many threats before it fell to the Muslim Turks in 1453. The success of Muslims in gaining territory limited Christians in their travels for trade and religious pilgrimages.

Muslim victory did not mean, however, that everyone in a territory became a Muslim. It is true that people without a book of religion were sometimes given a choice of conversion or death. Nevertheless, Jews and Christians could retain their faith by paying a tax. They were offered the status of **dhimmi,** or a person protected by Muslims, so long as they abided by agreements with their conquerors, remaining submissive as second-class citizens. The relations between these "People of the Book" and Muslims varied greatly from time to time and place to place. Occasionally they lived together in creative cooperation, as in medieval Spain. More often, there were conflicts and oppressions, with Jews and Christians managing to survive but not able to live very well. Where Muslims ruled, there was great incentive for converting to Islam.

The Shari'a in Muslim Lands

As Muslims expanded their rule to other countries, they had to extend their administrative and legal structure. The law that would govern the life of Muslims in all countries was the **Shari'a.** It included the revealed law of the Qur'an, of course, but it was more than that. The Sunna had to be considered. Also, the consensus of the community, **ijmā,** had to be assessed; in practice, this consensus contained the considered judgments of the scholars of jurisprudence. To a lesser extent, and somewhat more controversial, the fourth dimension was the employment of **qiyas,** or analogy. When a circumstance arose that was not clearly covered in the other three sources, reasoning from known cases could be applied to the new situation, and people could determine how the case would have been handled if Muhammad had considered it. Eventually, four different Sunni schools of interpretation of the Shari'a emerged. The Hanifite school is somewhat liberal in that it also employed **ra'y,** or personal opinion, in some decisions, which could lead to forsaking even the commands of the Qur'an in some applications. The law was formulated primarily for Iraq and is still employed there and in Turkey, Pakistan, and India. The Malikite school developed in Medina and relied heavily on ijmā, or consensus, of the Medina community. It is still followed in eastern Arabia; West, Central, and North Africa; and parts of Egypt. The Shafi'ite school rejected all forms of opinion and tended to elevate hadiths even above the Qur'an. This school tends to prevail in Cairo and in the southern areas of Arabia and in Malaysia and Indonesia. The Hanbalite school is the most conservative of all. Founded in Baghdad by a student of al-Shafi, Hanbal rejected opinion and gave primary emphasis to the Qur'an with secondary place to hadiths. This school is prevalent in Saudi Arabia. Where Muslim governments control countries, the Shari'a can still carry weight. In countries that have secular governments in spite of large Muslim populations, it is still influential in the lives of the faithful.

dhimmi [THIM-mi]
A client of the Muslims. In exchange for protection, non-Muslims agreed to certain conditions of subservience to Muslims. Jews and Christians were often dhimmis of Muslim rulers.

Shari'a [SHA-ree-a]
The duties that God has placed on the Muslim community. It is sometimes translated as "law."

ijmā [IJ-mah]
The consensus of Muslim religious leaders on matters of practice.

qiyas [KEE-yas]
In Islam, analogies used in applying the Qur'an and the Sunna to other practical situations.

ra'y [RAA-ee]
In Muslim law, the considered opinion of Muslim leaders acting for public good.

Muslim Spiritual Experiences

Islam is more than institutions; for Muhammad and his early converts there were religious experiences of God. To experience the presence of God was always an aim of Muslim worshipers, although to submit to God was even higher in priority. The majesty of God comes through clearly in the earliest experiences of the Muslim community. He is not only compassionate to repenting sinners and those in need, but God is also just and requires justice in believers' conduct toward himself and fellows. Both awe and fascination are characteristic of the worship experience of Muhammad and his close companions.

The importance of worship was never lost in Islam. The very rapid influx of converts during the period of military expansion challenged Muslims to maintain consistently deep spiritual lives in spite of worldly success. Some gentle souls wanted to move away from the constant strife of the world and focus on a closer walk with God. Although Islam developed its own models in time, looking to Muhammad who could live simply even when wealth was pouring into the community treasury, some Muslims also found help among the Christians and even among the Buddhists. Asceticism was not a rule for Muslims or Jews, but some of them, as well as early Christians, gave it an important place in expressing their faith. Muslims in northern Arabia encountered Christian monks and sometimes shared their asceticism as an approach to the holy life. Others realized that denial of the body was not the main goal of the holy life but an experience of the reality of God and being in his presence. The practice of devotion involved ritual, but it also led to speculation about the nature of God, the Qur'an, Truth, Being, and the nature of destiny and freedom. Although some theology was devoted in Islam to apology and legalism, other theology developed to explain the devotional life of the mystics.

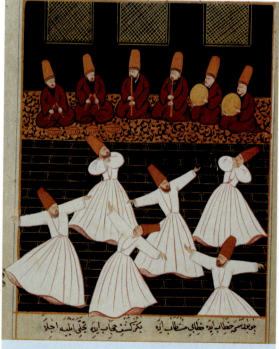

Dancing Dervishes. A sixteenth-century painting of dervishes who whirl to reach a state of mystical ecstasy.

Sufis

The Sufis are associated with Muslim mysticism.[9] They took their name from the clothing they wore—rough woolen garments.[10] Their organizations sometimes paralleled those of Christian mystics, and their theology shared insights with Neoplatonism and Gnosticism.[11] Their goals varied somewhat, but their direction was toward experiencing in this life the union of the soul with God. Through various leaders, such as Ibn Arabi (1165–1240), a body of knowledge developed that outlined steps toward union with God. Perhaps their turning from the world was regarded by some Muslims as selfishness, for to the more worldly believers, Sufis seemed to look only to their own experience and not to the well-being of the larger Muslim community. Indeed, their concentration on meditation and the mystical experience led them away from rigid concentration on everyday ritual and legalism.

Was mysticism selfishness? After reading the works of Rabia, a woman mystic of Basra who died in 802, it is hard to come to that conclusion. Her words do focus on the individual's relationship to God, but they deny seeking any rewards other than knowing God:

> O God! If I worship Thee in fear of Hell, burn me in Hell; and if I worship Thee in hope of Paradise, exclude me from Paradise; but if I worship Thee for Thine own sake, withhold not Thine Everlasting Beauty.[12]

Many other mystics wrote in the same spirit, thirsting to know and worship God, but asking nothing beyond that experience itself. The Persian poet Jalal al-Din Rumi (1207–1273) used the analogy of lover and beloved.[13]

> Lovers, lovers, whoever sees His face, his reason becomes distraught, his habit confounded.
> He becomes a seeker of the Beloved, his shop is ruined, he runs headlong like water in his river.[14]

But what of those who experienced union with God? How could that loss of self and the ascendancy of God in human life be expressed? That problem became acute for mystics and ordinary orthodox believers alike. Three centuries after the Hijrah, a Persian Sufi, Hosayn ibn Mansur al-Hallaj (d. 922), cried out that he was the True (ana al-Haqq). Misunderstanding him, thinking that he had claimed to be God, orthodox Muslims tortured and then crucified him for his blasphemy. Other mystics understood the message the orthodox community had sent and decided to find other ways of expressing the experience of the soul and God being in union. Sufis had a bad reputation with the orthodox, and legalism made mysticism seem heretical.

The larger Muslim community has always balanced the Law and the Way, the Shari'a and the Tariqah (spiritual path). Seyyed Hossein Nasr has employed the symbol of the walnut to illustrate their relationship. The Shari'a is the shell that protects and permits growth. The kernel is the Tariqah, which gives it end and purpose. Both are necessary for the walnut to subsist and manifest itself.[15]

Al-Ghazali

The person who helped most to overcome the division between orthordox practices of Islam and the mystics was Abu Hamid al-Ghazali, who died in 1111. A brilliant young student of jurisprudence, he was invited to become a professor at the Nizamiyah, a new university in Baghdad, where he attracted some three hundred students. From his twentieth year, he tells his readers, he had pursued every kind of dogma or belief so as to understand as many as possible. Ascetics, Sufis, theologians, and philosophers all attracted him as much as jurisprudence. He was well-established as a professor with acclaim and income. However, he became dissatisfied in his work and was deeply concerned to prepare his soul for the final judgment. He was more concerned to be right with God than to have the approval of humanity. He had already read thoroughly the theoretical works on mysticism and therefore had gone as far as he could progress without actually leaving the university and his ties to the world to practice the disciplined life of a mystic. Eventually, he found the courage to leave his teaching post, and for eleven years he made an in-depth practice of the mystical life. He did respond favorably to the request of his sultan and returned to teaching for a few years, combining intellectual disciplines with his practices of the mystical life.

Al-Ghazali did not become anti-intellectual in his total outlook, but he did see the limitations of human intellectual activity in the light of the importance of the mystical experience of God. Theology, he concluded, was directed toward preserving the creed of orthodoxy against heretical ideas. In philosophy, he found that the materialists (those who believe only in atoms and space), the naturalists (those who believe that nature is the highest reality), and the theists (those who believe in a supreme God), including Plato and Aristotle, were all affected with unbelief. They believed the world is eternal and that God knows only universals, and they denied the resurrection of the body.[16] He also lumped with them in their unbelief their Muslim followers Ibn Sina and al-Farabi as well as others who employed a Neoplatonic framework in understanding the world. Works in mathematics, logic, and natural sciences in general he found outside any religious controversy; they were sciences that Muslims could accept as readily as they could medicine. He did insist that the material world is created by God and does not exist of itself alone. In the end, he rejected those ideas from any secular knowledge that contradicted the revelation of the Qur'an and generally accepted knowledge that was not superstitious or did not threaten the essential revelation of God. To submit to God and his revelation was to be placed first beyond all human knowledge and practices, no matter what rewards might be attached to them.

Sufism gained considerable respectability after al-Ghazali; it was not automatically regarded as heretical or anti-orthodox. However, the established orders of Sufis did not escape the kind of decline that seems to manifest itself in all such groups, regardless of the religion. The high ideals and practices of the founders were relaxed in subsequent generations to provide a more comfortable and rewarding livelihood for members. The kinds of doctrines and practices that win enthusiasm from the masses who despise intellectual rigor and prefer credulity were adopted by various holy men and orders. Here and there, however, individual saints and groups continue to practice the presence of God in human life and to keep doctrines and practices that are intellectually respectable.

Islam and Other Religions: The Middle Ages

From the beginning, Islam's relationship with other religions has been somewhat ambiguous. Muslims have no doubts about Islam's being the final revelation of God through Muhammad. Nor is there any doubt that polytheism is to be stamped out and Islam substituted for it, as when Muhammad took control of Mecca. The problem is complicated in Islam's relationship to Judaism and Christianity. The Qur'an makes favorable references to the prophets of Judaism and the personalities of the New Testament. There is also the idea that peoples of the Book are to be treated with more respect than pagans, those without a sacred literature. Jews and Christians were not forced to convert to Islam but were allowed to keep their religions as long as they paid a tax. But Muhammad obviously changed in his relationship to Jews in Arabia when they opposed theocracy in Medina. The Muslim clashes with Byzantine forces, who were nominally Christian, added the conflicts of military enemies to some problems of theology. Muslims had problems with the Christian doctrine of the Trinity, which seemed to add partners to God. This was also a problem with the Christian doctrine of the Incarnation, holding that Jesus was truly God. Islam could regard Jesus as a true prophet, but it had to denounce the idea that Jesus was the Son of God or God. Add to these problems the more complete and final revelation from God, and these religions shared the makings of tense relationships in spite of their sharing certain stories, personalities, and beliefs from ancient times.

Territories occupied by Muslims tended to become predominantly Muslim. The Jews and the Christians who remained firm in their faith had to make considerable sacrifices. How severe these sacrifices were depended on the time and place and the wishes of the ruler. The pattern was sometimes based on the old Arab concept of a client people; that is, Jews or Christians had to place themselves under the protective custody of a strong Muslim who could guarantee them certain privileges of survival and practice in exchange for compensation. Although the tradeoffs might make sense in terms of making the best of a bad situation, usually a measure of humiliation was involved for the client peoples.

The Crusades

The patriarch of Constantinople was always concerned about the Muslim threat on his doorstep. When Muslims in control of Jerusalem and other Christian holy places became particularly harsh to Christian pilgrims during medieval times, there was an additional reason for Roman Catholic Christians to be concerned about the Muslim occupation of so much land at the eastern end of the Mediterranean Sea. Statements of concern from Constantinople and tales of horror from Jerusalem pilgrims began to add up, and eventually sentiments in Europe favored doing something to alter the situation. A pope took leadership in calling for crusades of Christian soldiers to journey to the Holy Land and free the Christian places of worship from the so-called Muslim infidels. A variety of motives—including, perhaps, both piety and economic gain—moved monarchs in Britain and Europe to respond to the call and raise armies to assault Jerusalem and other places of importance to pilgrims.

Pope Urban II responded to the appeal for help from Alexius I by calling for a crusade at a synod in Clermont in 1095. Any Christians falling in battle would be forgiven their sins and win immediate entrance into eternal life. The response was enthusiastic, if sometimes misdirected against Jews and others living along the way. The nobility of Europe, however, eventually captured Jerusalem on July 15, 1099. When the Muslims were united under Saladin in the twelfth century, he defeated the Latin army at Hattin and soon recovered the city of Jerusalem and other territory for the Muslims. A fifth crusade under Holy Roman Emperor Frederick II gave Jerusalem, Bethlehem, and Nazareth to Christians for a while, together with access to the coast, beginning in 1229. But the area was lost to the Muslims again in 1244.

There are stories of chivalry and horror on both sides of the struggle. For example, T. A. Archer, in his account of the crusade of Richard I, the Lion-Hearted, gives both a Christian account and a Muslim account of Christians killing Muslim hostages. A Christian account says that Saladin, the Muslim

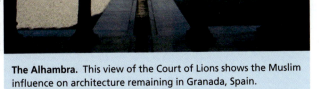

The Alhambra. This view of the Court of Lions shows the Muslim influence on architecture remaining in Granada, Spain.

leader, waited past the deadline for redeeming Turkish hostages. Besides, according to Roger of Howden, Saladin had, two days earlier, already beheaded all his Christian prisoners; thus King Richard was completely justified in having 2,700 Turks led outside the city of Acre and beheaded.[17] A Muslim account by Behaed-Din (Bohadin) reports that Saladin had arranged a payment in three parts over a month's time to redeem Muslim hostages. King Richard had promised the Muslims that on surrender they could go free with their families if Saladin redeemed them; otherwise they would become slaves. Those were the conditions they accepted in surrender. Seeing Saladin's delays, King Richard did what he planned to do if he had received payment: He had the Franks kill the Muslim hostages. Behaed-Din concludes,

> The motives of this massacre are differently told; according to some, the captives were slain by way of reprisal for the death of those Christians whom the Musulmans had slain. Others again say that the king of England, on deciding to attempt the conquest of Ascalon, thought it unwise to leave so many prisoners in the town after his departure. God alone knows what the real reason was.[18]

The Christian massacre of Jews and Muslims and eventually even their sack of their own city of Constantinople cannot be pointed to as the finest examples of Christian behavior. Considerable bitterness built up on all sides among the three religions, with stories told to justify behavior and condemn the cause of the enemy. These examples have circulated through the centuries and have done their parts to nourish suspicion and mistrust among the three religions.

Cooperation

These horror stories can be balanced, however, with instances of cooperation. It was not unheard of for a Jewish physician to serve a Muslim monarch; Maimonides so served Saladin in Cairo. Muslims also provided services to Christians—one example is their discovery of Aristotle and the translations and commentaries they shared with Christians. Muslim intellectual influence was very strong in Spain, particularly Cordoba. A Christian, Alvaro, wrote in 854,

> My fellow-Christians delight in the poems and romances of the Arabs; they study the works of Mohammedan theologians and philosophers, not in order to refute them, but to acquire a correct and elegant Arabic style. Where today can a layman be found who reads the Latin commentaries on Holy Scriptures? Who is there that studies the Gospels, the Prophets, the Apostles? Alas! the young Christians who are most conspicuous for their talents have no knowledge of any literature or language save the Arabic; they read and study with avidity Arabian books; they amass whole libraries of them at a vast cost, and they everywhere sing the praises of Arabian lore. On the other hand, at the mention of Christian books they disdainfully protest that such works are unworthy of their notice. The pity of it! Christians have forgotten their own tongue.[19]

Islam in India

Islam reached India through three different sources—conquest, immigration, and conversion.[20] Conquest started in 712 with the Arab takeover of Sindh. Arabs and Turks continued their conquest through the centuries. But these invading armies were relatively small, and they customarily built garrison cities outside the cities of the local population. The invading warriors were not numerous enough to win sweeping allegiance to a religion. Muslim ideas and customs were borrowed by Hindus, but complete abandonment of Hinduism was not typical. Nevertheless, Muslims from central and western Asia, seeking new opportunities, arrived to settle in the new land.

In South India, the earliest Muslims were Arab traders and settlers who arrived in the seventh century.[21] These Muslims settled among Hindus and practiced the faith of Islam. In this region some Hindus embraced Islam, but others adapted Islam to their Hindu heritage. In many situations Islam and Hinduism lived together in harmony.

Other Hindus were converted to Islam by missionaries who lived exemplary spiritual lives. By the eleventh century, Ismaili missionaries from Yemen arrived in Gujarat. In the fifteenth and sixteenth centuries, many conversions came through the influence of Muslim mystics. Lower castes of Hindus and outcastes found that Islam's emphasis on the unity of all Muslims opened new opportunities for them. Although force sometimes played a role in conversions, many conversions came about voluntarily. Some Hindus were attracted to the high spiritual teachings and examples of Islam.

Through the Moguls and other groups, Islam made a lasting impression on India. The most famous building in India for outsiders, the Taj Mahal (see p. 342), is a monument to the wife of Shah Jahan, a Muslim ruler. The Moguls related to Hindus in several ways, ranging from tolerance, to appreciation, to persecution for their polytheism. Sikhism, which sought to harmonize Islam and Hinduism, was largely rejected by Hindus and Muslims, and Sikh gurus were sometimes severely tortured by Moguls in an attempt to return them to orthodox Islam.

Muslim Responses to Modernism

Islam could not escape the waves of modernism any more than could Judaism or Christianity. The new ways of looking at the universe that developed after Copernicus and the new ways of looking at human beings after the writings of Darwin could not be avoided, for Islam was often thrown against its will into contact with European colonial powers. Young Muslim scholars who encountered ideas from European university faculties had to make some sort of accommodation between their secular, scientific views and the theology and practices of the Prophet, his companions, and medieval institutions.

The educational problems brought to Islam by the pure and social sciences were serious. Although young Muslims could learn technology and engineering without challenging the Qur'an studies and theologies that prevailed in their societies and their *madrassahs* (religious schools), other branches of learning were not easily assimilated. Studies of order in the universe in themselves did not attack order in creation established by God. Order in society, the philosophy of the Europeans, ethics, and law were difficult to study in the languages of Europe. More serious than the limited resources in textbooks was their secular orientation, which seemed to undermine the **'ulama'** (clerical scholars) in each country. In countries where the 'ulama' were excluded from the formal educational system, secularism threatened to bring the social problems familiar to Muslims observing the immoralities of the West. Where the 'ulama' had a good working relationship with the state they were able, to a great extent, to limit the development of any scholarship that challenged their very conservative traditions.

'ulama' [UL-ah-mah] Muslim clerical scholars.

The Taj Mahal. The Muslim mausoleum in Agra, India, is not only an example of Muslim architecture but is also widely regarded as one of the most beautiful buildings in the world.

© Scala/Art Resource NY

Islam offered a variety of responses to modernism. One response, the **Wahhab,** rejected not only Western innovations but also many of the popular practices of medieval Islam. Muhammad Ibn 'Abd al-Wahhab (1703–1792) was a purist for his faith. He wanted a faith based on only the Qur'an and the Sunna of the Prophet. This radical fundamentalism attacked Sufism, philosophies of monism and pantheism, worship at tombs of saints, beliefs that Muslim saints could pray for sinners, and schools of law other than the Hanbalite. Despite resistance by the 'ulama', Wahhabism had widespread political, economic, and religious impact. It gained political support from the Saudi royal family, which continues at this time as protector of the Wahhabis and enforcer of the puritan movement. Through a Syrian disciple of 'Abd al-Wahhab, Rashid Rida, the Salafiya movement spread to Africa, India, and Indonesia and is identified by many in the twenty-first century as the inspiration for radical Islam.

Jamal al-Din al-Afghani (1838–1897) agitated throughout the Muslim world for a Pan-Islam movement that would stand against Western colonialism. He supported Abd al-Hamid II of the Ottoman Empire, who claimed to be the true caliph

Wahhab [WAH-hab]
One of the 99 names of Allah. 'Abd al-Wahhab means "The Servant of the Bestower."

of Islam. Weak governments and minority Muslim communities were inspired by the theme of strength through unity.

A disciple of al-Afghani, Muhammad Abduh (1849–1905), with British support became chief legal consultant of Islam in Egypt and an administrator of al-Azhar, the famous Islamic school in Cairo. He argued that the advance of modern sciences and scholarship is in keeping with the Qur'an. Long before Christians did, Muslims who understood the Qur'an led the way in sciences and medicine. Abduh urged that animosity to rationalism, freedom, and scientific studies be changed and that Islam regain its leadership in education.

Muslims, as do other peoples, want the benefits of scientific studies without the moral corruption of the societies that first developed them. Whether the spirit of free inquiry that promotes creative sciences can be joined to traditional Qur'an and hadith interpretations is still an open question for Muslim educators such as Fazlur Rahman.[22] If tradition does not permit free inquiry in Muslim countries and stifles students who have studied in universities of the West, Islam will have a majority of adherents who are isolated from the fruitful educational achievements of the most advanced countries in science, technology, manufacturing, and trade. Much of the ferment in Muslim countries arises from the conflicting views on educational ideals to be supported in the next century.

Comparison of Shi'ites and Sunnis in the Twenty-First Century

A chart at the end of this chapter lists the caliphs of the Sunnis and the imams of the Shi'ites. However, the differences in their beliefs that led to separate leaders are more important, in some cases, than the names on a chart.

Think of Shi'ites as the minority, the 10–15 percent of Muslims who regard themselves as the most pious, holy, and God-inspired members of the Prophet Muhammad's family. They think of themselves as guardians and examples of the Prophet's revelations of the word of Allah, and as preservers of the Prophet's application of those words. In their highest forms, they are theologians and mystics; Sufis are an example. They believe that they have been unjustly excluded from the leadership of Islam, which the Prophet intended for them. In fact, they think of themselves as persecuted martyrs.[23] One object of their hatred is Mu'awiyah of the Umayyad branch of Hashimites; another is Yazid, Mu'awiyah's son and successor.

The Shi'ites believe that the Prophet intended 'Ali, his cousin, to be *imam* (religious leader) after him because God alone chooses his imam, not human votes. 'Ali had preserved in writing both the Qur'an and the Hadiths. Muhammad's grandson Husayn is the one through whom the imamate should have continued. Martyred, he is hidden away now, but he will return at the time of the last judgment as **Mahdi** to set the record straight. His martyrdom is remembered each year in the month of Muharram. During the first ten days, the gates of paradise stand open for those who meet their deaths. Self-flagellation is the way that groups of Shi'ite men commemorate Husayn's martyrdom.

Sunnis, the majority of Muslims, do not believe the Shi'ite claims. After the Prophet Muhammad's death in Medina in 632 B.C.E., his companions, other than 'Ali, chose Abu Bakr as their first caliph. He had been a close companion of the Prophet and accompanied him on the Hijrah. He was also the father of Aishah, the Prophet's only virgin bride—thus he was also family. Sunnis believe that it was proper to have an election to choose a spiritual and civil leader. They also differed

Mahdi [MAH-di]
In Islam, the expected one. Twelvers believe that an imam is in occultation and will return as a messianic figure.

from the Shi'ites because they left the Qur'an in oral form for a while and resisted reducing the Hadiths to writing.

The Sunnis had nothing against the Umayyad branch of the Hashimites, for when the Prophet Muhammad entered Mecca in 630 C.E. he had presented gifts to Abu Sufyan and welcomed his branch of the family into Islam. To the Sunnis, Abu Sufyan, Mu'awiyah, and Yazid were all approved by the Prophet. Only the Shi'ites disagreed. Eventually, a line of caliphs descended from Abbas, an uncle of the Prophet Muhammad, replaced the Umayyads. The Abbasid caliphate ended in Egypt in 1215 C.E.

The Shi'ites see the role of imam as spiritual; he is a moral, theological, and even mystical leader. Sunnis have been more pragmatic and regard leadership in Islam as a matter of majority rule, power, and practicality. The Qur'an reveals the word of God, and the Shari'a applies it to daily life. The caliph is the head of a religious institution that encompasses all life, including government. These are sufficient guides for leaders. The Sunnis find no need for a "hidden" imam who will one day appear as the Mahdi. For Shi'ites, that imam rules today through a representative. For Sunnis, an imam is simply one who leads services in a mosque. They accept the history of Islam as what Allah willed; regret is not a notable characteristic of Sunnis.

Islam in the United States

Only recently have many Americans become aware that Islam is a significant religion in the United States. Islam is represented by two major groups. One group is immigrants who voluntarily came to the United States seeking a better life. Although Syrian and Lebanese immigrants were the first Muslims, now large groups have come from Pakistan, Iran, Afghanistan, Turkey, and eastern Europe.[24] The other major group is African Americans who sought a religion more congenial to their experience than the Christianity of most whites. There are approximately six hundred mosques and Islamic centers in the United States. Estimates of membership vary widely; some Muslim groups avoid letting outsiders know statistics of their organization. The various groups have associations of mosques and Islamic centers. The oldest is the Federation of Islamic Associations, headquartered in Detroit, Michigan. More recently, the Muslim World League, of Mecca, has a Council of Masajid at the United Nations which helps fund the building of mosques and distribution of Qur'ans. There is a Muslim Student Association with members on many campuses. The Islamic Society of North America (ISNA) is the largest Muslim "umbrella" organization.

Muslims in the Midwest

The Muslims of the U.S. Midwest are primarily Arabs, most from Syrian and Lebanese descent, from families that have been in the United States for many years. These immigrants from the Middle East, coming from areas controlled by the Ottoman Empire, began arriving in the late nineteenth century and continued, in waves, until World War II. They brought their Islamic observances with them, but over time they have modified their practices until they have some parallels with the practices of Christians and some Jews. For example, mosques are more than places of worship. They are also social and educational centers. Their imams do more than lead worship. They are counselors to members of the congregation,

Minister Louis Farrakhan. The leader of the Nation of Islam, in his Chicago office, c. 1985.

conductors of funerals and weddings, and general administrators of Islamic laws and principles. They perform functions that in other countries would be conducted by other people in Muslim communities.

Muslims of the Midwest have become part of the American scene. They participate fully in social, economic, and civil religion activities of their communities. Criticism of their Islam comes from members of other faiths and from newly arrived Muslims from countries that practice a more conservative Islam. Many Muslims from Pakistan now live near Chicago.

Muslims on the East Coast

Many Muslims on the East Coast have arrived more recently. They comprise highly educated professionals and semiprofessionals who have entered the United States to pursue higher education, economic opportunities, and a better life for their families. Coming from Pakistan, Iran, Saudi Arabia, and other countries where conservative Islam is the rule, they prefer a more rigorous practice of traditions than their fellow Muslims in the Midwest. For example, they are more likely to reserve the mosque for worship only. Their dress and economic and social activities are limited by their Muslim heritage. They reject jobs associated with serving alcohol or taking interest on money. They are more likely to have imams who insist on practices that prevail in the "old country."

Although Muslim men are permitted to marry women of other faiths, Muslim women are supposed to avoid marrying anyone other than a Muslim. The goal is that children of Muslims should be raised as Muslims. These positions lead many Muslims to keep their children from practicing the American custom of dating. Unmarried men and women should socialize, if at all, only when it may lead to marriage. Arranged marriages are considered preferable to those entered into by the choice of the couple alone.

Black Muslims

Black Muslims have their own history. **Timothy Drew** (1886–1929), who called himself Noble Drew Ali, the Prophet, taught in New Jersey, in 1913, that blacks were really Asiatics, or Muslims. His teachings were only remotely Islamic, and his Qur'an bore little resemblance to the Muslim Qur'an. Another prophet, W. D. Fard, began a temple in Detroit. His movement linked Islam with antiwhite activities. After his disappearance, leadership of the temple was taken by **Elijah (Poole) Muhammad** (1897–1975). He formed the **Nation of Islam,** which was antiwhite and anti-Christian. Part of the story of the Black Muslim movement centered around an account that a superior black race once ruled the world. Mr. Yakub, an evil scientist, created an inferior white race through genetic engineering. The whites were devils, and their religion was Christianity. The religion of original black people was Islam. Through trickery, the whites gained power over the black race. In their view of last things, Black Muslims expected to see the extermination of "white devils" and the black race's proper restoration to dominance.

Malcolm X (**Malcolm Little;** 1925–1965), who was converted to the Nation of Islam in prison, rose to leadership of a Harlem temple. Malcolm X broke with the movement in 1964 after a pilgrimage to Mecca. He converted to Sunni Islam, which rejected racial discrimination. Malcolm X was assassinated in 1965.

The successor of Elijah Muhammad, Wallace Deen Muhammad, espoused traditional Islam. To signify the new position, he named the group the

Timothy Drew
In 1913, in New Jersey, he taught that blacks are Asiatics, or Muslims. He was a contributor to the Black Muslim movement in the United States.

Elijah (Poole) Muhammad
Founder of the Black Muslim movement, the Nation of Islam. Dissatisfied with Christianity, which appeared to be a white religion, Poole organized a religion for blacks.

Nation of Islam
The branch of Black Muslims that struggles with Christianity and whites. It is not accepted by orthodox Muslims as Islam, which welcomes all races.

Malcolm X (Malcolm Little)
Formerly of the Nation of Islam, he formed his own group in 1964 in the tradition of Sunni Islam. A major change in his teaching was that all people are brothers and sisters, whites as well as blacks.

American Muslim Mission. A dissenting group, led by Louis Farrakhan retained the title Nation of Islam and the antiwhite position of Elijah Muhammad. Thus there are two main Muslim groups among African Americans. One group continues the tradition of rejecting the white race and the Christian religion, whereas the other participates in worldwide Islam, which is inclusive of all races and considers Christians and Jews as people of the Book.

Worldview

In the worldview of Muslims, symbols, rituals, and actions are important. But confessing the proper beliefs is the foundation on which a life of exemplary action is built. In the Pillars of Islam, action overshadows belief. Reflection shows, however, that actions are based on a few fundamental beliefs. The most important belief is the nature of God; the second is the nature of everything created by God.

The Absolute

Islam is a firm monotheism. The Shahada recited by every Muslim emphasizes that there is no god but God. God is great; God is merciful (Qur'an 1:1). Muslims attribute ninety-nine most beautiful names to God, but he is beyond human ability to comprehend. God has been pleased to reveal through his prophet Muhammad that he is a just God, requiring each person to live according to his will and to act justly toward other members of the community. He will require every person to stand before him for a final judgment.

God communicates with humanity through the Qur'an, through prophets, through prayers of individuals, and through direction of individual lives. All Muslims agree on the sovereignty of God over human life; the question is only how much choice individuals have in directing their own affairs. Some Muslims hold to a rigid predestination of human lives. Others believe that God allows humans to exercise great freedom. The middle position is most widespread— God plans human lives, and individuals become responsible for their deeds by assenting to participate in them.

The absolute singleness of God leads Islam to denounce every form of idolatry. Muslims retain, however, a belief in angels as messengers of God. Gabriel delivered the words of the Qur'an to Muhammad. The Prophet spoke by the Spirit of God. But the Qur'an denounced any references to a son of God. Muslims also believe in Iblis, the personification of evil. There are other beings, such as jinn. According to Muslims, none compromise the absolute unity of God.

> He who created the heavens and earth, and sent down for you out of
> heaven water;
> and We caused to grow therewith gardens full of loveliness whose trees you
> could never grow.
> Is there a god with God?
> Nay, but they are a people who assign to Him equals! (Qur'an 27:60)[25]

American Muslim Mission
A Muslim group formed for African Americans by Wallace Deen Muhammad. World Islam accepts these adherents as Muslims.

The World

Muslims think God created a good world. Having been created, it is not eternal. It was made by God, but it is not God. It is sustained by the will of God, but God is not coursing through it as sap through a vine. Orthodox Islam has rejected the pantheism of philosophers who influenced certain Sufis. Al-Ghazali rejected Neoplatonist influences on Muslim philosophers. However, study of mathematics, astronomy, and all sciences of the natural world should be pursued in the spirit of appreciating God's great handiwork.

The world is made for humans to enjoy. Food is good. Drink, other than alcohol, is generally good. Comfortable clothing and shelter are good. Marriage is expected. Sex and procreation are good. Having property and wealth is good, so long as believers remember to share with those in need. The world is a wonderful place, a kind of preview of conditions that can be found in even purer form in the next life.

It is proper for Muslims to reflect in their fine arts the beauties of God's creation. Themes of nature can be expressed in carpets and mosaics. Manuscripts can show the beauty of forms. Architecture and landscaping can help humans appreciate natural beauty. Muslims generally avoid, however, pictorial representation of human and animal forms in a religious context, such as in a copy of the Qur'an or a mosque. Islam never encouraged its adherents to turn their backs on the world to pursue some supposed spiritual reality.

© Art Resource, NY

The Ascent of Muhammed to Heaven on Buraq. He is guided by Gabriel and escorted by angels. Made for Tahmasp, Safavid dynasty, 1539–43. British Library, London.

Humans

Islam has a story of Adam and Eve, the first humans created by God. Humans are above all other creatures in the order of nature, for they have the moral responsibility to live according to the commandments of God.

> And recite to them the tiding of him to whom
> We gave Our signs, but he cast them off,
> and Satan followed after him, and he became one of the perverts.
> And had We willed, We would have raised him up
> thereby; but he inclined towards the earth
> and followed his lust. So the likeness of him
> is as the likeness of a dog; if thou attackest it
> it lolls its tongue out, or if thou leavest it
> it lolls its tongue out. That is that people's likeness
> who cried lies to Our signs. So relate the story; haply they will reflect.
>   (Qur'an 7:174, 175)

When possible, humans are to live at peace with each other, recognizing that all humans of any race or location are called to submit to God. All who submit to God are brothers and sisters and part of one community.

Islam brought considerable improvement in the status of females. Eve was created by God to be a helper and companion for Adam. Islam does not permit infanticide or abuse of women. Wives should be properly treated. Women are able to inherit and own property, but they are dependent on men. Their roles are not separate from men's roles but supportive of them. Once the supportive relationship is understood, life for both men and women becomes more pleasant and rewarding.

> Mankind, fear your Lord, who created you
> of a single soul, and from it created
> its mate, and from the pair of them scattered
> abroad many men and women; and fear God
> by whom you demand one of another
> and the wombs; surely God ever watches over you.
> Give the orphans their property, and do not
> exchange the corrupt for the good; and devour
> not their property with your property; surely that is a great crime.
> If you fear that you will not act justly
> towards the orphans, marry such women
> as seem good to you, two, three, four;
> but if you fear you will not be equitable,
> then only one, or what your right hands own;
> so it is likelier you will not be partial.
> And give the women their dowries as a gift
> spontaneous; but if they are pleased
> to offer you any of it, consume it with wholesome appetite.
> But do not give to fools their property
> that God has assigned to you to manage;
> provide for them and clothe them out of it,
> and speak to them honourable words.
> Test well the orphans, until they reach
> the age of marrying; then, if you perceive
> in them right judgment, deliver to them
> their property; consume it not wastefully and hastily
> ere they are grown. If any man is rich,
> let him be abstinent; if poor, let him consume in reason.
> And when you deliver to them their property,
> take witnesses over them; God suffices for a reckoner.
> To the men a share of what parents and kinsmen
> leave, and to the women a share of what
> parents and kinsmen leave, whether it be
> little or much, a share apportioned;
> and when the division is attended by
> kinsmen and orphans and the poor,
> make provision for them out of it,
> and speak to them honourable words. (Qur'an 4:1–9)

In Islamic beliefs, body and soul are strongly united. Except in Sufism, the soul is not emphasized apart from the body. The whole person communicates with God and answers to him for conduct. The person carries out the duties of the Pillars of Islam. The practice of mortifying the flesh to release the spirit has not been well-received in Islam. Responsibilities of benevolence, defense, and witnessing for the faith require whole persons, not spirits.

The Problem for Humans

Islam acknowledges the sin of Adam and Eve, but it does not see the effects as extending to all other humans.

> And when thy Lord took from the Children of Adam,
> from their loins, their seed, and made them testify
> touching themselves, "Am I not your Lord?"
> They said, "Yes, we testify—lest you should say
> on the Day of Resurrection, 'As for us, we were heedless of this,'
> or lest you say, 'Our fathers were idolaters
> aforetime, and we were seed after them.'
> What, wilt Thou then destroy us for the deeds of the vain-doers?"
> (Qur'an 7:172, 173)

Sin is refusal to submit to the will of God revealed through his prophets, especially his final one, Muhammad.

The Solution for Humans

Salvation comes in acknowledging that there is no god but God and that Muhammad is his prophet. When a person can recite the Shahada without reservation and live according to the direction of the Qur'an, he or she has success. Offering prayers five times each day, giving alms to the poor, keeping the fast of Ramadan, and making a pilgrimage to Mecca if circumstances permit, as well as reciting the Shahada comprise Muslims' obligations. When Muslims have fulfilled these religious duties and refrained from prohibited actions, they can trust God will find them acceptable in the day of judgment. Most students of world religions find Islam's teachings of alienation and reconciliation the easiest of all religions to understand.

Community and Ethics

The term for a Muslim community is *ummah*. Although Islam attacked many tribes from the deserts, its beginnings were in cities. Muslim cities are built around a mosque, a symbol for a community centered on God. An individual apart from family and community is an anomaly in Islam. The unity of Muslims, regardless of race, economic status, or location, has long been the ideal.

> It is not piety, that you turn your faces
>   to the East and to the West.
>   True piety is this:
> to believe in God, and the Last Day,
> the angels, the Book, and the Prophets,
> to give of one's substance, however cherished,
>   to kinsmen, and orphans,
> the needy, the traveller, beggars,
>   and to ransom the slave,
> to perform the prayer, to pay the alms.
> And they who fulfill their covenant

Muslim Teacher and Students. A Muslim madrassah school in Jakarta, Indonesia.

> when they have engaged in a covenant,
>   and endure with fortitude
>   misfortune, hardship and peril,
> these are they who are true in their faith,
>   these are the truly godfearing. (Qur'an 2:172)

Alms include an individual's giving not only to a beggar but also to a common treasury used to support the welfare of all in the community—even slaves and strangers—who have need. Individuals may offer prayers anywhere, but special value is given to praying with other Muslims in a mosque, especially on Friday at noon.

Personal ethics of Islam require that believers avoid certain prohibited things. Among them are gambling, drinking alcohol, lying, and stealing. For religious reasons, believers must not eat pork. The Qur'an teaches against being an aggressor; however, when an injustice has been done, fighting to avenge it is required. Aggression is to be met with force until the enemy ceases to resist. Usury is prohibited, but Muslims may be compensated by sharing profits if risk is entailed.

Although marriage is usually between one man and one woman, the Prophet Muhammad relied on his wives to help support his religion and Islam permits up to four wives if a man can support them adequately and treat them equally.[26] For many reasons, one being economic, polygamy has declined. Marriage is contractual rather than a sacrament.

Extramarital sex and offspring are prohibited. In order to avoid sex outside marriage, Shi'ites instituted the practice of *mut'ah,* or temporary marriage. They believe that the Prophet Muhammad considers it legitimate marriage rather than a form of adultery. Family planning is permitted. Abortion, if required for a women's health, is permitted prior to the 120th day, when the soul joins the fetus.

Islam considers homosexual acts sinful. Nevertheless, there seems to have been uneven enforcement of punishments for homosexual acts.

Muslim women have status because they can own property, and if divorced, they may keep their dowries. They are, however, to dress modestly and originally could be spoken to only from behind a curtain. Eventually this "curtain" became a veil.

Rituals and Symbols

Muslim tradition has rites of passage for individuals and annual holidays for the community. Beliefs of Islam support well-established acts or rituals.

Islam welcomes children as signs of God's blessing. Male infants are usually circumcised, a practice of Semitic peoples prior to Muhammad. Many children, especially boys, memorize the Qur'an, which means they memorize in Arabic. A few young people continue their studies until they have memorized every surah, but most know selective stories, characters, and teachings.

Marriages are usually arranged by parents or guardians. A young woman must freely give consent before she is married. Divorce can be initiated by men, but the husband may take the wife again up to a third marriage. After a third divorce, he cannot marry her again until she has been married to another man.

Funerals provide opportunities for mourning and burial of the body. Muslims believe the person will be resurrected and live after death in either paradise or hell.

In the daily prayers, there are prescribed cycles of kneeling, touching the forehead to the ground, and standing while reciting appropriate formulas. Men use the mosques more than women do. Women in the mosque must be kept out of the sight of men. A mosque is a place of prayer, although there are provisions for pulpits so that an imam may address the adherents. In each mosque is a **mihrab,** or niche, indicating the direction of Mecca, which the congregation faces in prayer.

Some of the annual observations are Ramadan, followed by Id al-Fitr (the festival of breaking the fast), and the birthday of the Prophet. The month of Ramadan recalls the appearance of Gabriel to Muhammad to give him the Qur'an. During the daylight hours, able-bodied Muslims are to refrain from food, drink, sex, and acts that take their attention from God. In the hours of darkness, they may enjoy what He has denied them by day. Deep suffering is avoided, but when the fast falls in a hot season it is especially trying. Muslims claim benefits from identifying with the needs of the poor and suffering of humanity. The feast of rejoicing after Ramadan lasts for three days.

Charity may be extended in alms at any time. But Muslims are expected to give annually approximately 2.5 percent of their wealth to the needs of the community. It is sinful for some Muslims to have so much and others to suffer for lack of necessities. Distributing gifts to the poor acknowledges God's mercy and the unity of Islam.

The holy city that all Muslims face in prayer five times a day is Mecca. Every Muslim who is financially and physically able is expected to make a pilgrimage to Mecca. Only a small percentage of Muslims can attend in a given year. But the gathering of more than a million faithful assembled from all over the world is an impressive display of the universal appeal of the prophet Muhammad and his call to worship Allah, or God. Dressed in clothes that show their unity, the pilgrims wear two seamless pieces of white cloth sewn together, emphasizing that before

mihrab [MIH-rahb]
The niche in a mosque that signifies the direction of Mecca. Muslims face Mecca when they pray.

God all believers are equal. For the duration of the pilgrimage, no Muslims (women and children can also participate) cut their hair or nails or engage in sex.

Pilgrims participate in rituals that recall the faithful acts of their father Abraham. In the Haram Mosque of Mecca, Muslims walk around the Ka'bah seven times. The cubic stone building, usually covered by a **kiswah,** a black cloth, is a replacement of one that Muslims believe was built by Abraham, whose footprint remains nearby. Muslims begin by kissing the sacred Black Stone they believe was given to Abraham by the angel Gabriel. They then run between two low hills, imitating Abraham's concubine Hagar, who frantically searched for water in the desert to save their child, Ishmael, after Sarah had excluded them from her camp. At noon on the ninth day, the pilgrim stands on the Mount of Mercy facing Mecca, fourteen miles distant. Here, on the Plain of Arafat, Muhammad recited verses on his last pilgrimage indicating that God had completed the Islamic religion.

> Today I have perfected your religion
> for you, and I have completed My blessing
> upon you, and I have approved Islam for your religion. (Qur'an 5:5)

On the tenth day, during a stop at Mina, the pilgrim joins others in throwing stones at three stone pillars representing devils that tried to persuade Abraham to disobey God and refuse to sacrifice his son Isaac. In the 'Id al Adha, any pilgrims who can afford it sacrifice animals and share the meat with the poor, recalling that God allowed Abraham to sacrifice a ram instead of his son. Only after returning to Mecca and circumambulating the Ka'bah are pilgrims allowed to cut hair and nails, ending the state of purity, **ihram.** Pilgrims who can, continue north to Medina to visit the tomb of the prophet Muhammad, the greatest and last of all God's prophets. Having completed the Hajj, the pilgrim is a changed person, remembering his or her experience and bearing the title *hajji* (for men) or *hajjiyah* (for women).

Life after Death

Islam believes in life after death. Each person will be resurrected to appear before God and judged according to his or her deeds on earth (Qur'an 56). God will decide who will be rewarded in paradise or punished in hell:

> And those who believe, and do deeds
> of righteousness—We charge not any
> soul, save according to its capacity;
> those are the inhabitants of Paradise, therein dwelling forever;
> We shall strip away all rancour that is in their breasts;
> and underneath them rivers flowing and they will say,
> "Praise belongs to God, who guided
> us unto this; had God not guided
> us, we had surely never been guided.
> Indeed, our Lord's Messengers came with the truth."
> And it will be proclaimed: "This
> is your Paradise; you have been
> given it as your inheritance for what you did."
> The inhabitants of Paradise will call
> to the inhabitants of the Fire:
> "We have found that which our Lord
> promised us true; have you found

kiswah [KIS-wa]
The robe, or covering, usually placed over the Ka'bah in Mecca.

ihram [IH-rahm]
The consecrated state in which Muslims perform the Hajj. Muslims abstain from sex, perfume, hunting, and other things during the pilgrimage to Mecca.

what your Lord promised you true?"
    "Yes," they will say.
And then a herald shall proclaim
between them: "God's curse is on the evildoers
who bar from God's way, desiring
to make it crooked, disbelieving in the world to come." (Qur'an 7:40–44)

Paradise is a pleasant oasis where a man's every desire, according to popular tradition, is satisfied either by his wife or by beautiful houris, or virgins. Hell is a place of burning and heat where excruciating pains are perpetual (Qur'an 104).

Islam and Other Religions

Because God has sent his prophet and revealed the Qur'an, all humans should become Muslims. Polytheists and idolaters have never had a proper knowledge of God and should convert at once. Jews and Christians have received through the prophets, including Jesus, a proper, although incomplete, knowledge of God. Muslims cite the errors of Jews in worshiping Elijah and Christians in worshiping a Trinity and in claiming that Jesus is God's son. Jesus gave many wonderful signs that he was a great prophet, born of the virgin Mary. He will come again before the last judgment. But Jesus is not in any way divine. Muhammad has recited God's word that corrects the erroneous beliefs of Jews, Christians, and all other religions. Although they can be tolerated as people of the Book, Jews and Christians should convert. The Qur'an requires that Muslims denounce all idolaters. It directs Muslims not to choose friends among Christians and Jews rather than Muslims (Qur'an 3:25ff).

Considering the Qur'an and the traditions of Islam, what view of Jesus do Muslims have today? Kenneth Cragg, a Christian who is a scholar of Islam, wrote,

> Through all we have reviewed there runs a great tenderness for Jesus, yet a sharp dissociation from his Christian dimensions. Islam registers a profound attraction but condemns its Christian interpretation. Jesus is the theme at once of acknowledgement and disavowal. Islam finds his nativity miraculous but his Incarnation impossible. His teaching entails suffering but the one is not perfected in the other. He is highly exalted, but by rescue rather than victory. He is vindicated but not by resurrection. His servanthood is understood to disclaim the sonship which is its secret. His word is scripturised into the incidence of the Qur'an fragmentarily. He does not pass as personality into a literature possessing him communally. Islam has for him a recognition moving within a non-recognition, a rejectionism on behalf of a deep and reverent esteem.[27]

From time to time, Muslims have cooperated with Jews, Christians, and even Hindus. In many countries they have learned to live with other religions—India is one example. In some former republics of the Soviet Union, Muslims often predominate over Orthodox Christians. Granted religious as well as political freedom, these Muslims have recently participated fully in the community of world Islam. Cooperation with other religions, although sometimes practiced by Muslims, is not as high a priority as making converts to Islam. It is a missionary religion that seeks adherents among all peoples.

Whether Islam is a militant religion of aggression or a peaceful religion where struggle is a matter of the soul overcoming evil within seems to depend on one's point of view and wishes. Two passages of the Qur'an seem to emphasize a peaceful approach:

> And fight in the way of God with those
> who fight with you, but aggress not: God loves not aggressors. (Qur'an 2:187)

> No compulsion is there in religion.
> Rectitude has become clear from error.
> So whosoever disbelieves in idols
> and believes in God, has laid hold of
> the most firm handle, unbreaking; God is All-hearing, All-knowing. (Qur'an 2:256)

In other passages, however, instructions seem more activist:

> Then, when the sacred months are drawn away,
> slay the idolaters wherever you find them,
> And take them, and confine them, and lie in wait
> For them at every place of ambush. But if they
> Repent, and perform the prayer, and pay the alms, then
> Let them go their way;
> God is All-forgiving, All-compassionate. (Qur'an 9:5–6)

> Fight those who believe not in God and the Last Day
> and do not forbid what God and His Messenger have forbidden—such men as
>   practice not the religion of truth, being those who have been given
> the Book—until they pay the tribute out of hand
>   and have been humbled. (Qur'an 9:29)

Other passages in the Qur'an can be considered on this subject (such as Qur'an 47), but enough has been printed here to provide samples for discussion.

According to Asma Gull Hasan in *American Muslims: The New Generation,* the term *jihad* is used differently in various cultures. In the Middle East, leaders use *jihad* as meaning struggle against Western countries' influence and power in the world, particularly America, which is perceived as bent on destroying the Arab way of life. Hasan writes, "In America, Muslims understand *jihad* for what it really means: struggle." Here *jihad* does not mean a holy war against America.[28]

Islam and the Future

The Islamic state is a primary issue, not only for outsiders but also for Muslims. Are Muslims to establish rules under religious leaders, return to the Shari'a, and seek to live under customs similar to those at Mecca and Medina during the time of Muhammad? Or are they to take the course of some liberal reformers of the late nineteenth and early twentieth century? Will Muslims participate fully in the new global community, keeping only the essential religious and moral principles of their faith?

Ismail R. al-Faruqi states the problem this way:

> Islam is not opposed to Judaism but regards it as the religion of God. . . . Rather, Islam is opposed to Zionism, to Zionist politics and conduct. . . . For its crimes against the individual Palestinian men and women, against the corporate existence of the Palestinians, against the individual Arabs of the surrounding countries as well as the *ummah,* Islam condemns Zionism. Islam demands that every atom's weight of injustice perpetrated against the innocent be undone. Hence, it imposes upon all Muslims the world over to rise like one man to put an end to injustice and

to reinstate its sufferers in their lands, homes, and properties. . . . Therefore, the Islamic position leaves no chance for the Zionist state but to be dismantled and destroyed, and its wealth confiscated to pay off its liabilities.[29]

Some states that are predominantly Muslim have accepted the United Nations resolutions granting Israel the right to exist. Some Palestinian groups are adamantly opposed to anyone who accepts those conditions.

Islam in the twenty-first century has a wealth of tradition to draw on. Which parts of the tradition will be emphasized, and at what pace, will help determine Islam's role in the world economy and world culture. Islam once enjoyed widespread prosperity and supreme intellectual leadership. Whether it will seek to return to the days of the Prophet or to apply the ideals of the Prophet to the ways of the twenty-first century depends on whose leadership is supported by Muslims in the worldwide community.

With Islam, the introduction to the major world religions has been completed. Minor religions around the world now are no less interesting. In the Conclusion are brief introductions to some religions that show how major religions are transformed in new times and places.

Because Islam dates from Muhammad's journey from Mecca to Medina in 622 C.E., 2008 C.E. will be the Muslim year 1429 A.H. Their history records many achievements. Umayyads in Spain, Abbasids in Baghdad, Seljuk Turks, the Ottoman Empire, and the Sultanate of Delhi were all built on a dynamic Islam. Countering those expansions have been the British Empire, the Union of Soviet Socialist Republics, and various colonial powers in Africa. The ideal during the time of the Hijrah was no separation between worship and state. Shi'ites regard a theocracy as the ideal form of Muslim society.

For Muslims the question of the best period is, in some ways, similar to that for Jews and Christians. Which period of history is the ideal by which to shape their future? Are the practices of Medina and Mecca in Islam's first century the best for Muslims today? Should Muslims seek a pan-Islamic culture from the United States to Indonesia? Can a country with a secular government, such as Turkey, be considered an Islamic country? What about the United States, which welcomes freedom of religion but forbids establishment of any particular religion? Defining the ideal to seek in the twenty-first century is a timely quest for Islam.

CONSIDER THIS
Timeless Islam

VOCABULARY

American Muslim Mission
ansar [AN-sahr]
caliph [KAA-lif]
dhimmi [THIM-mi]
Elijah (Poole) Muhammad
Five Pillars of Islam
hadiths [had-EETHS]
Hajj [HAHJ]
hanif [HA-neef]
Hijrah [HEJ-rah]
ihram [IH-rahm]
ijmā [IJ-mah]
jinn [JIN]
Ka'bah [KUH-bah]

kiswah [KIS-wa]
Mahdi [MAH-di]
Malcolm X (Malcolm Little)
mihrab [MIH-rahb]
muezzin [mu-EZ-in]
muhajirun [mu-HAJ-i-roon]
Nation of Islam
qiyas [KEE-yas]
Qur'an [KUR-an]
rak'a [RAK-ah]
rasul [ra-SOOL]
ra'y [RAA-ee]
sadaqa [sah-DAH-ka]

salat [sa-LAHT]
sawm [som]
Shahada [sheh-HAH-da]
Shari'a [SHA-ree-a]
Shi'a [SHE'a]
Sunna [SUN-na]
Sunni [SOON-e]
Tawhid [TAHW-heed]
Timothy Drew
'ulama' [UL-ah-mah]
ummah [UM-mah]
Wahhab [WAH-hab]
zakat [za-KAHT]

QUESTIONS FOR REVIEW

1. Tell the story of Mecca and the competing tribes of Arabia.
2. Describe Muhammad's religious experiences outside Mecca, and his recitations in the city.
3. What experiences of Muhammad in his home led him to protect women, widows, and orphans?
4. Relate the struggles of Muhammad and the Muslims against the Ummayads.
5. Who were the earliest caliphs? How were they chosen?
6. Describe the expansion of Islam from Arabia that began in the seventh century.
7. Who are the Shi'ites? How do they differ from Sunnis?
8. Are most Muslims Arabs? Which country has the most Muslims?
9. What is the status of women in Islam?
10. How effective is the Shari'a in today's world?

QUESTIONS FOR DISCUSSION

1. What is "modernism"? What serious issues does it raise among Muslims?
2. What evidence supports Islam as a religion of peace? As a religion of violence?
3. How do Muslims, Jews, and Christians differ on the person and role of Jesus?
4. What difference is there between Shi'ite views of "Imam" and the Sunni view of Caliph?
5. If Jews, Christians, and Muslims are descended from Abraham, and each claims to worship one God, what are their differences?

NOTES

1. Montgomery Watt, *Muhammad at Mecca* (Oxford, UK: Clarendon Press, 1953).
2. Andrew Rippen and Jan Knappert, *Textual Sources for the Study of Islam* (Chicago: University of Chicago Press, 1990), pp. 66–67.
3. Reprinted in the U.S. with the permission of Simon & Schuster from *The Koran Interpreted*, trans. Arthur J. Arberry. Copyright © 1955 by George Allen & Unwin, Ltd. Reprinted by permission of Harper-Collins Ltd. All quotations from the Qur'an in this chapter are taken from this source.
4. Karen Armstrong, *Muhammad: A Biography of the Prophet* (New York: HarperCollins, 1992), p. 111.
5. Fazlur Rahman, *Major Themes of the Qur'an* (Minneapolis: Bibliotheca Islamica, 1980), p. 83.
6. Muhammad Abduh, *The Theology of Unity,* trans. Kenneth Cragg (London: Allen & Unwin, 1965), pp. 118–122, as quoted in Kenneth Cragg and R. Marston Speight, *Islam from Within* (Belmont, CA: Wadsworth, 1980), pp. 19–20.
7. Alfred Guillaume, *Islam* (Harmondsworth, Middlesex, UK: Penguin Books, 1954), pp. 80, 81.
8. Karen Armstrong, *Islam: A Short History* (New York: Modern Library, 2002), pp. 29–30.
9. Annemarie Schimmel, *Mystical Dimensions of Islam* (Chapel Hill: University of North Carolina Press, 1975), p. 3.
10. Idries Shah, *The Way of the Sufi* (London: Octagon Press, 1980), pp. 13–14.
11. Fazlur Rahman, *Islam* (Chicago: University of Chicago Press, 1979), p. 131; his view is that Sufism began and developed in Islam, following the example of the Prophet.
12. Arthur J. Arberry, *Sufism* (London: Unwin Paperbacks, 1979), pp. 42–43; copyright © 1979 by Unwin Hyman, an Imprint of HarperCollins Publishers Limited; reprinted by Permission.
13. Jalal al-Din Rumi, *"Divan-e Shams,"* in *Mystical Poems of Rumi*, trans. Arthur J. Arberry (Boulder, CO: Westview Press, 1979).
14. *Mystical Poems of Rumi*, trans. Arthur J. Arberry (Boulder, CO: Westview Press, 1979), p. 53, no. 268.
15. Seyyed Hossein Nasr, *Ideals and Realties of Islam* (London: Unwin Hyman, 1988), p. 124.
16. Fakhry, *A History of Islamic Philosophy* (New York: Columbia University Press, 1970), p. 250.
17. T. A. Archer, *The Crusade of Richard I, 1189–92* (New York: Putnam's, 1889), p. 126.
18. Ibid., pp. 130–131.
19. Gustave E. Von Grunebaum, *Medieval Islam* (Chicago: University of Chicago Press, 1953), pp. 54–58.
20. M. Mujeeb, *The Indian Muslims* (London: Allen & Unwin, 1967), p. 20.

21. Peter Hardy, "Islam in South Asia," in *The Encyclopedia of Religion*, vol. 7, ed. Mircea Eliade (New York: Macmillan, 1987), pp. 390–404.
22. Fazlur Rahman, *Islam and Modernity* (Chicago: University of Chicago Press, 1982), pp. 145–162.
23. 'Allāmah Sayyed Muhammad Husayn Tabatba'i. trans. Seyyed Hossein Nasr. *Shi'ite Islam.* (New York: State University of New York, 1975), p. 228.
24. Yvonne Yazbeck Haddad and Adaire T. Lummis, *Islamic Values in the United States* (New York: Oxford University Press, 1987), p. 3.
25. Suggestions for passages from the Qur'an in the "Worldview" given in Rahman *Major Themes.*
26. Hammudah Abdalati, *Islam in Focus* (Indianapolis: American Trust Publications, 1975), p. 117.
27. Kenneth Cragg, *Jesus and the Muslim* (London: Allen & Unwin, 1985), pp. 278–279.
28. Asma Gull Hasan, *American Muslims: The New Generation* (New York: Continuum, 1999), p. 49.
29. Ismail R. al Faruqi, "Islam and Zionism," in *Voices of Resurgent Islam*, ed. John L. Esposito (New York: Oxford University Press, 1983), pp. 261–262.

READINGS

Ahmed, Akbar S. *Postmodernism and Islam.* London: Routledge, 2004.

Armstrong, Karen. *Islam: A Short History.* New York: Modern Library, 2002.

_____. *Muhammad: A Biography of the Prophet.* New York: HarperCollins, 1992.

Barlas, Asama. *Believing Women in Islam: Unreading Patriarchal Interpretation of the Qur'an.* Austin: University of Texas, 2002.

Bodman, Herbert L., and Nayereh Tohidi, eds. *Women in Muslim Societies.* Boulder, CO: Lynne Reinner, 1998.

Browers, Michaelle, and Charles Kurzman, eds. *An Islamic Reformation?* Lanham, MD: Lexington Books, 2004.

Cragg, Kenneth. *The House of Islam.* Belmont, CA: Dickinson, 1969.

Cragg, Kenneth, and Marston Speight. *Islam from Within.* Belmont, CA: Wadsworth, 1950.

de Corancez, Louis Alexandre. *The History of the Wahabis from Their Origin until the End of 1809.* Trans. Eric Tabet. Reading, UK: Garnet, 1995.

Denny, Frederick Mathewson. *An Introduction to Islam.* New York: Macmillan, 1993.

_____. *Islam.* San Francisco: Harper & Row, 1987.

Ernst, Carl W. *Following Muhammad.* Chapel Hill: University of North Carolina Press, 2003.

Esposito, John L. *Islam, The Straight Path.* New York: Oxford University Press, 1988.

_____, ed. *Voices of Resurgent Islam.* New York: Oxford University Press, 1983.

Esposito, John L., and John O. Voll. *Makers of Contemporary Islam.* Oxford, UK: Oxford University Press, 2001.

Guillaume, Alfred. *Islam.* Harmondsworth, Middlesex, UK: Penguin, 1954.

Halm, Heinz. *Shi'ism.* New York: Columbia University Press, 2004.

Hasan, Asma Gull. *American Muslims: The New Generation.* New York: Continuum, 1999.

Lewis, Bernard. *What Went Wrong?* Oxford, UK: Oxford University Press, 2002.

Nasr, Seyyed Hossein. *Ideals and Realities of Islam.* London: Unwin Hyman, 1988.

Pipes, Daniel. *Militant Islam Reaches America.* New York: Norton, 2002.

Rahman, Fazlur. *Islam.* Chicago: University of Chicago Press, 1979.

_____. *Major Themes of Qur'an.* Minneapolis: Bibliotheca Islamica, 1980.

_____. *Revival and Reform in Islam: A Study of Islamic Fundamentalism.* Oxford, UK: One World Publications, 2000.

Rippin, Andrew, and Jan Knappert, eds. *Textual Sources for the Study of Islam.* Chicago: University of Chicago Press, 1990.

Rodinson, Maxime. *Mohammed.* Trans. Anne Carter. New York: Pantheon, 1971.

Sheehi, Stephen. *Foundations of Modern Arab Identity.* Gainesville: University Press of Florida, 2004.

Thompson, Michael J., ed. *Islam and the West.* Lanham, MD: Rowman & Littlefield, 2003.

Tabātabā'i, 'Allāmah Sayyid Muhammad Husayn. Trans. Seyyed Hossein Nasr. *Shi'ite Islam.* Albany: State University of New York Press, 1977.

Watt, W. Montgomery. *Mohammed at Mecca.* Oxford, UK: Clarendon Press, 1953.

_____. *Muhammed at Medina.* Oxford, UK: Clarendon Press, 1956.

BASIC TENETS OF ISLAM

SCRIPTURE		
The Qur'an		
ISLAMIC GROUPS		
Sunnis *(Caliphs)*	*Shi'ites* *(Imams)*	

Sunnis (Caliphs)	Shi'ites (Imams)		
The Prophet Muhammed		The Prophet Muhammed	
Abu Bakr		'Ali	
'Umar			
'Uthman			
'Ali			
Mu'awiyah	Zaidis_____	'Ali al-Husayn	
		Jafir al-Sadiq	
	Ithna Ashari (Twelvers)		Ismaili
	Musa al-Kazim		Ismail
	(6th) Muhammed al-Mahdi (873)		Mustansirbillah (1094)
	Nizari Ismailis *Continues*		Mustali Ismailis (*ends* 1130)

Conclusion

A taste of the major religions increases one's appetite for examples of more of the world's religions. Many exist beyond those usually covered in world religions courses. Presented here are a variety of religions that have attracted adherents and interested the public. As were the major world religions, the history and worldview of these religions are presented empathetically, although without the details of the first ten chapters.

Baha'i [buh-HI]
A religion formed in 1844 on the prophetic work of Baha'u'llah.

Baha'i

Baha'i is an independent religion that promotes worldwide unity. Contrary to the assumption of some outside the religion, Baha'i is neither Shi'ite nor even Muslim.[1] Baha'is consider Haifa, Israel, their center, particularly the shrine to the Bab (Arabic for "gateway"), Sayyid Ali Muhammad of Shiraz, Iran (1819–1850). He experienced religious visions, including one of the martyred Imam Husayn, descendant of Muhammad. The Babi movement gained enough support to be considered a threat by the Muslim clergy and the government of Iran. He was imprisoned and executed in Tabriz in July 1850.

The great prophet Baha'u'llah (1817–1892) succeeded the Bab. Before long, he too was imprisoned and then exiled. From exile, he wrote *Katab'i'qan, The Book of Certitude*, an inspired writing. In 1863, he proclaimed he was the new messenger of God whom the Bab had predicted. In 1873 he completed the *Kitab'i'-Aqdas, The Book of Laws*, which established customs and morality for Baha'is. He died at age 75 in Acre, Israel, and was succeeded by his son, Abdul-Baha.

The fourth Baha'i leader was Shoghi Effendi Rabbani (1897–1957), the grandson of Abdul-Baha. He appointed the First International Baha'i Council and the Hands of the Cause of God. In 1963 in Haifa, delegates elected the first Universal House of Justice, the global governing body of Baha'i.

The Baha'i religion has continuously changed since the mid-nineteenth century. Bahai'is believe that God has sent a series of prophets to humanity—Adam, Abraham, Moses, Krishna, Zoroaster, Buddha, Jesus, Mohammed—and that the two most recent are the Bab

© AP Photo/Lefteris Pitarakis

A Bahai believer from Thailand, wearing her region's traditional costume, poses during ceremonies marking the inauguration of eighteen terraces of gardens, waterfalls, and marble staircases leading to the Bahai Shrine of the Bab, one of the religion's founders, in the northern coastal Israeli town of Haifa.

and Baha'u'llah. Its inclusiveness, however, does not extend beyond its base, for Baha'is cannot be members of any other religion. Baha'is believe that Baha'u'llah brought the latest word of God, correcting mistakes and inadequate teachings of other religions.

Bahai'is believe that all humans are basically good, but they do not know the highest and best teachings of God. Baha'u'llah envisioned one world at peace. Divisions of nation, race, and gender must disappear and the earth become as one country. In the age of the United Nations and a global economy, the Baha'is' belief in the oneness of God and of all humanity is an alluring vision.

Baha'i is open to anyone who accepts Baha'u'llah as the final prophet of God. The religion now claims some 5 million members in 234 countries and territories. Baha'i has no sacraments, but meditation and service are practiced as well as prayers of praise and petition; prayer three times a day is advised. Witnessing and voluntary contributions are expected. No work is permitted on the nine holy days. The Baha'i year has nineteen months of nineteen days each; the number 19 represents Bahai's initial disciples. Baha'i has no clergy, and worshipers meet in homes. Of Bahai's seven Houses of Worship around the world, Wilmette, Illinois, is the site of the one in the United States.

Baha'u'llah wrote to world leaders (including Queen Victoria, or "O Queen in London") promoting peace and human welfare; Baha'is prize these letters as "Tablets to Kings." He instructed his followers to also work to exert a positive influence on the world. To that end, their Universal House of Justice periodically sends open statements to the United Nations and other international bodies. In 2002 the Baha'is ruling body posted a six page letter to the world's religious leaders calling for an end to religious prejudice. It concluded with these words from Baha'u'llah: "The well-being of mankind, its peace and security, are unattainable unless and until its unity is firmly established."

Church of Satan

First of all, the Church of Satan, founded by Anton Szandor LaVey (born Howard Stanton Levey; 1930–1997), does not worship the devil. Devil worship is attributed to witches and heretics and regarded as rebellion against God and Christ. In glorifying a personality of evil, devil worship is dependent on Christianity in popular folklore; it focuses on the black mass, a deliberately corrupted form of the Mass of Christ.

In contrast, the Church of Satan is a public, open-membership group of law-abiding citizens in a New Age expression of paganism. The **Satan** it worships is the Self. Self and selfishness are the highest source of power. The doctrine focuses on seeking one's selfish desires amid the demands of society. Basically, according to these Satanists, humans are not spiritual but carnal—so rejoice. There is no reason to feel guilt about being what one is and always has been. Among the "Nine Satanic Sins" are stupidity, self-deceit, herd conformity, forgetfulness of past orthodoxies, and lack of aesthetics.

LaVey formed the first "magic circle," which turned into the Church of Satan, in San Francisco on April 30, 1966. He conducted a Satanic wedding, a funeral, and a baptism. Each week he led courses and rituals, building a membership interested in the occult. The Church of Satan has been termed an "elitist counter-culture,"[2] because one's aim is to become an authentic self rather than a social antinomian.

Satan [SAY-tun]
In Anton LaVey's Church of Satan, the Self or selfishness. Elsewhere, an evil being opposed to God.

Philosophies of self over society are not new. They have had a place in ritual Tantrism, in the philosophy of Friedrich Nietzsche (e.g., *Beyond Good and Evil* and *Genealogy of Morals*—master morality versus slave morality), and in the novels of Ayn Rand (e.g., *Atlas Shrugged*—selfishness). LaVey's *Satanic Bible* (1969) was a publishing success; *The Compleat Witch* (1970) and *Satanic Rituals* (1972) also disseminated his teachings. The symbols of the Church of Satan prominently include a pentagram, but nothing else particularly sinister, even though the church considers itself among the religions of "the Left-Hand Way."

One sign that the Church of Satan is a dynamic, growing religion is that it has spun off another group: the Temple of Set. In 1975, Michael Aquino and other members left over philosophic and administrative disagreements.

The Satanic emphasis of the Church of Satan and the Temple of Set stimulated a backlash. Church of Satan leaders were deeply concerned that teenagers involved in antisocial crime would claim to be performing Satanic rituals and bring down persecution and prosecution upon the church.[3] LaVey deplored drug use and aberrant behavior that could endanger the Church of Satan. The Church of Satan moved its headquarters, or Central Grotto, to New York City after LaVey's death; the High Priest and Priestess are now Peter H. Gilmore and Peggy Nadramia. *The Cloven Hoof,* the official bulletin of the church, is edited by Magistra Blanche Barton, LaVey's common-law wife.

Druids

Druids are an example of a neopagan movement. Curiosity has always surrounded the practices of the Druids, but they were highly respected among the ancient **Celts** (a people in the British Isles who originated from Indo-European

Druids [DREW-ids]
Among Celts, the three orders were Bards, Ovates, and Druids, who were advisors to kings.

Celts [KELTS]
An ancient people of Europe and the British Isles.

© Adam Woolfitt/Corbis

Druid Ceremony at Stonehenge. Druids gather for a summer solstice ceremony within the ring of trilithons at the ancient site of Stonehenge, in Wiltshire, England.

and local megalithic cultures). Their rituals and lore have been revived (in part) by people who want to explore religious practices that were overrun and overruled by Christianity. There are Christians who deplore neopaganism, but generally Druids are accepted as just another group of people reenacting the past.

Druids did not write their teachings but instead relied on an oral tradition that took about twenty years for a practitioner to master. Consequently, exactly who the Druids were and what they did has remained a matter of conjecture. According to even Julius Caesar's contemporary account in the sixth book of *Gallic War* (ca. 52 B.C.E.), there is more to be curious about than to know with confidence. Some scholars torture a few more references to Druids out of the historical records, but the results are sparse. Another approach is to examine oral traditions from other Celtic cultures.[4] Texts from Ireland in the eighth century C.E. give information on Druids, and the Welsh tradition of Druids comes from about the thirteenth century. Scottish tradition is later still, late nineteenth century C.E., but it confirms the pre-Christian sources as well as those of Ireland and Wales.

Modern Druids proceed with what they have. Philip Carr-Gomm, Chief of the Order of Bards, Ovates, and Druids, one of the oldest and largest modern Druid groups, learned basic traditions from Chief Druid Philip Ross Nichols (1902–1990). Starting at the age of 15, he participated in Druid rituals and became involved in their studies.[5]

Three orders of Druids seem to have been widespread. Bards kept tradition of their tribe and the sacred word. Ovates understood the mysteries of death and rebirth, divining the future, and conversing with ancestors. They were knowledgeable about trees, herbs, and healing. The Druids were advisors to kings and rulers. They were teachers, judges, and authorities on worship and ceremonies. Quite a few reports agree that Druids were philosophers, perhaps of the Pythagorean school.

The Druids' severest punishment was ostracism.[6] In Carr-Gomm's account it was the Gauls, not the Druids, who offered live sacrifices of criminals and other humans.

The **eight-fold calendar** of Druids and Wicca (which will be described in a later section) attracts people to the rituals of these groups. The names are different (see the calendar chart at the end of the chapter), but the quarterly solar and lunar holidays are essentially the same, and many are celebrated in great circles. Solar energy is male, and lunar energy is female. The solar calendar has to do with soil and agriculture; the lunar calendar has to do with farm animals. Solar events celebrated are winter solstice, spring equinox, summer solstice, and fall equinox. The lunar calendar celebrated the times when lambs are born, when animals are cleansed, when food for humans and animals is gathered, and when surplus animals that cannot be fed over the winter are slaughtered. The great circular monuments, such as Stonehenge, are places where these calendar rituals were celebrated.[7]

Isaac Bonewits, Archdruid Emeritus of Ár nDraíocht Féin: A Druid Fellowship tells what neopagan Druids believe. They are polytheistic, believing in male and female deities. Nature is divine in her own right. As an organic religion, neopaganism is always growing and changing. It believes in religious tolerance and living life to the fullest. Druids connect to the universe through rites of intensification, solstices, equinoxes, and phases of the moon. They believe in life after death, probably with rest before reincarnation. They believe in community service. Druids seek to cooperate with faiths that share most of their beliefs. They resist members of religions that seek to persecute them or suppress their human rights. Neopagan Druids seem to do little of the philosophy, teaching, and advising of kings of Druids past.

eight-fold calendar
Four solar holidays and four lunar holidays observed in great circles by Druids and witches.

Orishas in the New World: Candomblé, Santería, and Vodun

It is estimated that more than 2 million Yoruba were taken from West Africa to be slaves in the New World between 1650 and 1850. Although they were mixed with slaves from other countries, the Yoruba (see Chapter 2) successfully maintained their home culture. Their language survived imposition of the language of their owners, and the religion of the **orishas** survived their conversion to the religion of their owners—Catholicism. They modified their beliefs in orishas as their new homes required. Similarities are strong; differences are weak. The names of the beliefs now are Candomblé in Brazil, Santería in Cuba, and Vodun (or Voodoo) in Haiti.

Candomblé, centered in the state of Bahia, is the most important and most African of the Macumba (Afro-Brazilian) sects. African elements include outdoor ceremonies, sacrifice of animals (such as cocks), and spirit offerings (such as candles and flowers). Nature worship is part of the spirit world, and spirit possession leads some devotees to impersonate deities as they dance to sounds of drums. Candomblé is a syncretization of African and Roman Catholic practices, such as use of the cross and worship of saints, who are given African names. Until 1970, practitioners of Candomblé were targeted in an attempt to suppress minority groups. African ethnic pride reasserted itself then, and Candomblé was recognized for its contributions to the culture of Brazil.[8]

Santería of Cuba is known as *la Regla de Ocha* (Spanish for "the rule of the orishas," or in Cuba, *orichas*).[9] As in Nigeria, the babalawos (priests) are diviners who use kola nuts. In Cuba as in Africa, orichas' identities are fluid. The Cuban orichas combine different characteristics. They may be old women or old men, such as Olofi, the Creator. Another oricha may be a warrior. Catholic saints are also identified with

orishas [or-E-shas]
Yoruba spirits whose names are used in conjunction with Catholic saints in the New World.

Candomblé
[can-dome-BLAY]
Yoruba-based religion found among Christians of Brazil.

Santería [san-ta-REE-a]
Yoruba-based religion of Cuba.

A sacrificial goat is used in a Voodoo ritual.

© Caroline Penn/Corbis

orichas. For example, Ogun is identified with Saint Peter, who holds an iron key. After the Cuban Revolution of 1959, many adherents of Santería moved to other countries. Thus the Yoruba religion was planted in new regions and with new forms.

Vodun originated as a religion of the Watchi people of Togo, near Benin, where about half the population retains its indigenous beliefs. (The rest are about 20 percent Muslim and 30 percent Christian.) Although some Vodun live in the countryside, others, both male and female, live in special shelters within communities. Individual Watchi are selective about which Vodun they interact with at any given time. Their attitude seems to be that my own Vodun will protect me, but another one could cause me misery. Cult leaders, either male or female, help influence which Vodun are considered powerful.[10]

The Yoruba slaves sent from Nigeria through Benin were often shipped to serve French plantation owners in Haiti. The owners urged their slaves to become Catholics. In time the slaves also spoke French. Beneath this layer of accommodation, slaves retained their connections with Yoruba culture, and in particular with Vodun. Yoruba deities came to dominate the culture of Africans in Haiti. Ogun is lord of the fire, and Ezile is the water goddess of love.[11] Oshun is another goddess of the Nigerian Yoruba prominent in Haitian Vodun.

In Haiti an Ongun is a mediator between a Vodun and a congregation. A **Loa** is a Vodun spirit that can be called down on a person. The person whom the spirit descends on may seem to be controlled by the spirit; that control expresses itself through almost uninhibited behavior.

In Haiti Vodun is associated with zombies. A **zombie** is supposedly a disembodied soul or a corpse raised from the dead to serve as an automaton. In reality, it is likely that a Vodun priest rubs poison on the skin of a victim, who becomes paralyzed for a considerable length of time. This belief is found in other African religions and seems to be a particular fear that crossed the Atlantic with slaves.

Haitians long shared their hidden culture for tourists. Now that more Haitians are immigrating to the United States, Vodun can be found in many cities.

Church of Scientology

A period of physical recuperation seems to generate spiritual insight. In Chapter 9 we saw that St. Ignatius Loyola's spiritual visions led to creation of a religious order recognized by Pope Julius III in 1550. L. Ron Hubbard's recovery from war-related ailments at Oak Knoll Naval Hospital after World War II led to his Original Thesis in 1948 and, later, to *Dianetics.* These works along with his other published and unpublished writings constitute the scriptures of the Church of Scientology.[12]

L. Ron Hubbard's (1911–1986) early life in middle America, Nebraska and Montana, and on the West Coast was in a substantial family of a teacher mother and a naval officer father. Along the way, he became friends with an elderly Blackfoot medicine man as a very young Eagle Scout. Then he served in naval intelligence in Australia and on vessels off the coast of the United States.

Perhaps his most helpful experience was working as a writer in the 1930s. Writing fiction, including science fiction, prepared him well to express his views of the world to New Age youth. The worldview of Scientology is regarded as inspired. Less gifted students may have wandered through Hinduism, Gnosticism, Manichaeism, and electricity in medicine, but Hubbard was the first to arrive at such a worldview.

Vodun [voh-DUN]
Sometimes called "Voodoo." Yoruba religion among Christians in Haiti.

Loa [lwa]
an invisible supernatural being in Vodun.

zombie [ZOM-bee]
A spirit or a corpse enslaved by a priest of Vodun.

Dianetics [dye-uh-NET-ics]
A book by Scientology founder L. Ron Hubbard. Of eight principles, the first is survival.

In Hubbard's worldview, **Thetans**, the souls of humans, appear near the earliest time of creation. Matter, Energy, Space, and Time (MEST) made the empirical universe. Unfortunately, Thetans fell into the MEST and came to Earth. To be restored, a Thetan must be assisted to survive and then to include family, groups, and all species. Scientology added four more dynamics of survival: life forms, physical universe, spirits, and Infinity or God. Defining God is up to the individual who reaches that level of experience, but Hubbard insisted on the existence of a Supreme Being.[13]

The central religious practice of Scientology is "auditing," or listening, a precise form of spiritual counseling between a Scientology minister and a parishioner. The goal is to help the parishioner improve his ability to be what he is where he is.[14] The Auditor may use a special electrophsychometer, or biofeedback device, to help the parishioner identify experiences that lie at the root of spiritual troubles. These "engrams" can be removed. The goal is to reach the state of "**Clear**."

The Church owns impressive real estate. For example, the Scientology Church in Washington, DC, instructs, ministers to human needs, and works on community problems, such as drug rehabilitation. The highest level of auditing available to parishioners is aboard a 440-foot vessel, *Freewinds*, home of the Scientology Flagship Service Organization. New churches are franchises that are tightly linked (for quality control) to Scientology. Hubbard was a religious and organizational "genius" who emphasized a positive outlook on life and the future. The Church of Scientology is successful and prosperous.

Theosophical Society

Theosophy, or "divine wisdom," took organized form as the Theosophical Society of Chittenden, Vermont, in 1875. The organizers were H. P. Blavatsky, a Russian émigré with a strong interest in the occult; Colonel Henry Steele Olcott, one of the first prominent Westerners to convert to Buddhism; and a young lawyer, William Quan Judge.[15]

Madame Blavatsky's insights were developed in her travels, she reported, which included stays in Tibet and in Egypt. All the great Masters had arrived at the unified Ancient Wisdom. Her task was to teach the Truth known to the Masters. She taught that in each person there is something divine, and uniting with it brings wisdom. Blavatsky's *Isis Unveiled* appeared in 1878, and *Secret Doctrine* appeared in 1888. In 1889 she published *The Voice of Silence*. A critic, W. E. Coleman, charged plagiarism from dozens of books. However, she argued, since the teachings were universal knowledge given her by the Adepts, why would it not have appeared elsewhere also? These early charges that she had made it all up from published books seemed to fall on deaf ears.

The story of Theosophy grew in intensity as Madame Blavatsky and Colonel Olcott made their way to Bombay in 1879. With the help of A. P. Sinnett and A. O. Hume, they introduced Theosophy to Hindus, who received it enthusiastically. Blavatsky and Theosophy were warmly received by educated Buddhists of Sri Lanka.

A former worker with Theosophy, however, charged Blavatsky of fraudulently presenting works from the Masters. In poor health, she returned to India, then to London. In 1891 she died, leaving a power vacuum.

The most interesting leader to emerge was an English woman, Annie Besant. Theosophy entered a new phase. Mrs. Besant was convinced that a new World

Thetans [THE-tans]
The souls of human beings.

Clear
In Scientology a Thetan whose engrams have been removed.

Theosophy [the-OS-uh-fee]
"Divine Wisdom"; a religion organized in 1875 by H. P. Blavatsky.

Teacher would appear. With the help of her associate, Charles Leadbeater, she identified a young Brahman Hindu boy, B. F. Krishnamurti as that teacher. According to Besant, Krishnamurti, like Jesus, was a form of Christ. She sponsored Krishnamurti through the Order of the Star of the East. In 1930, however, he renounced the title and began to lecture and teach his own doctrines of self discovery.[16]

The faction of the Theosophical Society led by Besant and Olcott lists its international headquarters as Adyar, Chennin (Madras), India. Its branch the Theosophical Society in America is located in Wheaton, Illinois. Humans have been given bodies, although they are sparks of the divine. The ego is alienated from higher order of spirit, but through reincarnation and education humans can reach their spiritual destinies. Theosophy tries to reconcile the one truth of all religions and philosophies.

The Unification Church/Family Federation for World Peace and Unification

Reverend Sun Myung Moon is always the central symbol for Unification, whether church or family federation. His wife, Hak Ja Han, is also essential but not so visible. Born in North Korea in 1920, Moon learned Christian doctrine, and on Easter Sunday of his sixteenth year he had a vision of Christ. He received revelation that he would complete the interrupted salvation of the world. The Japanese occupation of Korea, Communist warfare, and confinement as a political prisoner prevented him from launching the unification movement until 1954.

© JUNG YEON-JE/AFP/Getty Images

Some 3,600 couples attend a Unification Church ceremony at a gymnasium in Cheonan, 80 Kilometers south of Seoul, in The Republic of Korea. The ceremony is part of what the church called the International Blessing of 400 million couples to wrap up a week-long World Culture and Sports Festival sponsored by the church.

Reverend Moon's essential message, *Divine Principle*, translated by Young Oon Kim in 1973, is an exposition of the Christian Bible. God intended that Adam and Eve become true parents of a child who would form the family under God. God, father, mother, and child is the essential form to be multiplied in the world. Adam and Eve did not get the relationship God had intended, so they failed their mission to be the true parents of humans.

In *Divine Principle* Moon explains that God prepared and sent another person, Jesus, to become a True Parent and save the world. Since John the Baptist failed to prepare the way for Jesus, he was rejected and killed by his people before he could marry, father a child, and save humans. So the world needed to wait for the coming of Jesus the Messiah a second time. Moon taught that a new Messiah would appear near the end of the century in Korea. This person would fill the failed mission of Adam and Jesus.

Moon's introduction of the Unification Church in the United States attracted widespread attention, and it infuriated many Americans, including Christians. He utilized hundreds of young volunteers to raise money for Unification, and then he invested the money in businesses operated by the movement so that the seed money would earn more money for his mission. Some people alleged that "Moonies" kidnapped and brainwashed young people. Eventually, the group overcame that serious criticism. Moon's conflict with tax collectors in the 1980s led to a term in prison. Some important friends reportedly thought that he was more persecuted than prosecuted. He bounced back on the scene and seemed to be more successful than ever, even establishing a daily newspaper in Washington, DC, *The Washington Times*.

According to Moon's Founder's Address in Seoul, Korea, in January 2004, he and his wife had ended the Unification Church in 1996 and had given it a new beginning as the Family Federation for World Peace and Unification. He announced that he and his wife are the **True Parents.** He said that Jesus is the Messiah who will return again, marry, and have a child as God planned. But until that time, Moon and his wife are the True Parents for those who have no parents.

The mass weddings in public places are important witness to Reverend Moon's essential teachings. As True Parents, he and his wife select couples to be married. In the past, men and women who were to be married remained celibate for three years. Then the couples paired by the Moons were married quickly. It was hoped that each couple would produce children.

Unification has stirred waves and received a full share of criticism in the United States. Nevertheless, it has continued its work to become a family for young people who are without parents. The church has also come to be regarded as a way for intercultural families to worship God. Its mission seems larger and more focused on promoting world peace.

Wicca

Wicca is a revival of parts of an old religion. It is sometimes identified as neopaganism.[17] Some practitioners refer to themselves as **witches,** and some do not. Many witches emphasize Diana, the Roman goddess, and most of them emphasize the moon, which is also feminine. Some witches worship a triune goddess, but others call on multiple gods or spirits and consider all things in nature divine. Covens of 10 to 15 members perform their rituals in a nine-foot circle. Some

True Parents
A title for Reverend Sun Myung Moon and his wife, reflecting the belief that God, Father, Mother, and Child are the building blocks of the world.

Wicca [WICK-uh]
A modern form of witches organized by Gerald B. Gardner in 1954.

witches
A term that Wiccans, male or female, may apply to themselves.

Time Line

BCE					
▲ 2000					
▲ 1500					
▲ 1000					
▲ 500					
0	**52 B.C.E.** Julius Caesar. Druids in *Gallic War*				

CE					
0					
500 ▼			**8th century C.E.** Ireland. Druid traditions found		
1000 ▼				**13th century C.E.** Wales. Druid traditions found	**19th century C.E.** Scotland. Druid traditions found
	1817–1892 Baha'u'llah	**1819–1850** The Bab	**1831–1891** H. P. Blavatsky	**1844** Baha'i is formed	**1875** Theosophy formed
	1884–1864 Gerald B. Gardner (Wicca)	**1911–1986** L. Ron Hubbard (Scientology)	**1920** Sun Myung Moon born in Korea	**1930–1997** Anton Szandor LaVey (Church of Satan)	**1951** Witchcraft laws of Britain repealed
	1954 Unification Church organized	**1954** Scientology Church formed	**1966** Church of Satan formed		
2000 ▼					

witches, in the tradition of founder Gerald B. Gardner (1884–1964), perform the rituals nude. Other witches wear robes. Witches pass through two degrees of learning rituals, and the third degree is for those in the priesthood. All of them believe that they share beliefs and rituals from ancient times.

As do the Druids, they particularly value rituals associated with the summer and winter solstices and spring and fall equinoxes. Their calendar is essentially like the Druid calendar, with some differing names (see the chart at the end of the chapter). As do the Druids, witches perform rituals and ceremonies in a circle.

Witchcraft is more associated with traditional witches than with Wicca. The crafts of witches included Magick, astrology, necromancy (calling forth the dead), numerology, palmistry, tarot cards, and spiritualism (calling the dead to appear). Wicca generally renounces casting spells and curses.[18]

In any part of the world, people known as "witches," regardless of language or translation, receive a kind of "status." They are acknowledged to have unusual powers, and no one wants to cross them and risk experiencing their anger. Sometimes people seek out one witch to provide protection from another witch. When societies fear an outbreak of witchcraft, they mobilize religious, legal, or mob power to overcome the witch threat.[19]

Western tradition has been severe in condemning witches, (mediums, sorceresses, or other translations). The King James Version of the Bible reads, "Thou shalt not suffer a witch to live" (Exodus 22:18). That was a clear mandate should a witch be identified. It is regrettable that Jews of Europe, especially students of the Kabbalah, were sometimes condemned for witchcraft. After repeal of witchcraft laws in Britain in 1951, public practices of rituals were more acceptable to the general population there.

Wicca and witches are not usually worshipers of Satan. Nevertheless, in earlier centuries, many poor, elderly women, especially those without husbands, were accused of consorting with Satan and practicing unspeakable sins at witches' Sabbat (reputed to have been a vile corruption of the Mass of Christ), manipulated into confessing, and then burned.

Most Christians still oppose Satan, but they seem to have cooled their fear of witches. Recently, a few Christians have become anxious about possible effects on their children of tales of black magic in the novels of J. K. Rowling. Other Christians think their children know a good story when they read one, understanding that it is not real.

Wicca is a revival of traditions as old as human societies. New Age religions values Asian and American Indian insights. Neopaganism revives Celtic beliefs and rituals that preceded the Romans who overran their culture.

The author hopes that the reader's interest in world religions will grow and that the rewards of studying them will increase. For the moment, however, this text must end.

VOCABULARY

Baha'i [buh-HI]
Candomblé [can-dome-BLAY]
Celts [KELTS]
Clear
Dianetics [dye-uh-NET-ics]
Druids [DREW-ids]

eight-fold calendar
orishas [or-E-shas]
Santería [san-ta-REE-a]
Satan [SAY-tun]
Theosophy [the-OS-uh-fee]
Thetans [THE-tans]

True Parents
Vodun [voh-DUN]
Wicca [WICK-uh]
witches
zombie [ZOM-bee]

QUESTIONS FOR REVIEW

1. Where did H. P. Blavatsky obtain her knowledge?
2. What is the emphasis of Baha'is?
3. What is Satan according to the Church of Satan?
4. Are Druids the same everywhere?
5. What three countries on the New World did Yoruba religion influence?
6. What is the primary Dianetic of Scientology?
7. Outline the lifetime of Reverend Sun Myung Moon.
8. Describe Wicca.

QUESTIONS FOR DISCUSSION

1. Do religious teachers of world religions agree on one ultimate Truth?
2. How would you respond to earlier writers who regarded Baha'is as Shi'ites?
3. In your estimation, is Selfishness equivalent to Satan?
4. What do you think Druids of today are interested in?
5. Will the influence of orishas in the New World increase or fade away?
6. Will Scientology continue to grow, or will it fail to connect with new generations?
7. How would you classify the Unification movement? Can it outlast Reverend Moon?
8. What does observance of the eight-fold calendar imply about Druids and Wicca?

NOTES

1. Allamah Sayyid Muhammad Husayn Tabatabna i, *Shi'ite Islam*, trans. Sayed Hasen Nasr (New York: State University Press, 1977), p. 76.
2. Jesper Aagaard Petersen, "Modern Satanism: Dark Doctrines and Black Flame" in *Controversial New Religions*, eds. James R. Lewis and Jesper Aagaard Petersen (Oxford: Oxford University Press, 2005), pp. 423–457.
3. Gareth J. Medway, *Lure of the Sinister* (New York: New York University Press, 2001), p. 22.
4. Philip Carr-Gomm, *The Elements of Druid Tradition* (Longmead, Shaftesbury, Dorset, UK: Elements Books, 1991), p. ix.
5. Ibid, p. 14.
6. Ibid, p. 57.
7. Ibid, p. 69ff.
8. Luis Nicolau Pares, "The Nagoization Process in Bahain Candoble" in *The Yoruba Diaspora in the Atlantic World*, trans. Toyin Falola and Matt D. Childs, eds. (Bloomington: Indiana University Press, 2004), pp. 185–208.
9. Christine Ayorinde, "Santería of Cuba: Tradition and Transformation" in *The Yoruba Diaspora in the Atlantic World*, pp. 209–230.
10. Nadia Lovell, *Cord of Blood* (London: Pluto Press, 2002).
11. Kevin Roberts, "The Influential Yoruba Past in Haiti" in *The Yoruba Diaspora in the Atlantic World*, pp. 177–204.
12. Dorthe R. Christensen, "Inventing L. Ron Hubbard," *Controversial New Religions*, James R. Lewis and Jesper Aagaard Petersen, eds. (Oxford: Oxford University Press, 2005), pp. 227–258.
13. L. Ron Hubbard, *Dianetics* (Los Angeles, CA: Bridge Publications, 1992).
14. *Scientology, A Reference Book Presented by the Church of Scientology International* (Los Angeles: Bridge Publications, 1998), pp. 22–25.
15. Charles J. Ryan, *H. P. Blavatsky and the Theosophical Movement*, Grace T. Knoch, ed. (Pasadena, CA: Theosophical University Press, 1975), p. 61.
16. J. Krishnamurti, *The First and Last Freedom* (Wheaton, IL: Theosophical Publishing House, 1954), p. 156.
17. Sarah M. Pike, *New Age and Neopagan Religions in America* (New York: Columbia University Press, 2004).
18. Craig S. Hawkins, *Witchcraft: Exploring the World of Wicca* (Grand Rapids, MI: Baker Books, 1996).
19. Jim Sharpe, "Women, Witchcraft, and the Legal Process," in *The Witchcraft Reader*, Daren Oldridge, ed. (London: Routledge, 2002), pp. 289–302.

READINGS

Baha'u'llah. *Katab-i-Iqan*. Wilmette, IL: Baha'i Publishing Trust, 1983.

Baha'u' llah, *Gleanings from the Writings of Baha'u'llah*. Trans. Shoghi Effendi. Wilmette, IL: Baha'i Publishing Trust, 1976.

Berger, Helen A., ed. *Witchcraft and Magic*. Philadelphia, PA: University of Pennsylvania Press, 2005.

Blavatsky, H. P. *The Abridgment of the Secret Doctrine*. Eds. Elizabeth Preston and Christmas Humphries. London: Theosophical Publishing House, 1966.

————. *The Key to Theosophy*. Covina, CA: Theosophical University Press, 1946.

Carr-Gomm, Philip. *The Druid Tradition*. Longmead, Shaftesbury, Dorset, Great Britain: Element Books Limited, 1991.

Chadwick, Nora K. *The Druids*. Cardiff: University of Wales Press, 1997.

Cole, Juan I. *Modernity and the Millennium*. New York: Columbia University Press, 1998.

Ellis, Bill. *Lucifer Ascending*. Lexington, KY: University Press of Kentucky, 2004.

Toyin, Falola, and Matt D. Childs, eds. *The Yoruba Diaspora in the Atlantic World*. Bloomington: Indiana University Press, 2004.

Hawkins, Craig S. *Witch Craft*. Grand Rapids, MI: Baker Books, 1996.

Heelas, Paul. *The New Age Movement*. Cambridge, MA: Blackwell Publishers, Inc., 1996.

Hexam, Irving, and Karla Poewe, *New Religions as Global Cultures*. Boulder, CO: Westview Press, 1997.

Hubbard, L. Ron. *Dianetics*. Los Angeles, CA: Bridge Publications, 1992.

Kim, Young Oon. *Unification Theology*. New York: Holy Spirit Association for the Unification of World Christianity, 1980.

Lewis, James R., and Jesper Aagaard Petersen, eds. *Controversial New Religions*. Oxford: Oxford University Press, 2005.

Lonigan, Paul R. *The Druids*. Westport, CT: Greenwood Press, 1996.

Lovell, Nadia. *Cord of Blood*. London: Pluto Press, 2002.

Medway, Gareth J. *Lure of the Sinister: The Unnatural History of Satanism*. New York: New York University Press, 2001.

Moon, Sun Myung. *Divine Principle*. Trans. Young Oon Kim. New York: The Holy Spirit Association for the Unification of Christianity, 1973.

Oldridge, Darren. *The Witchcraft Reader*. London: Routledge, 2002.

Pike, Sarah M. *New Age and Neopagan Religions in America*. New York: Columbia University Press, 2004.

Scientology. Church of Scientology International. Los Angeles: Bridge Publications, 1998.

CALENDAR OF DRUIDS AND WICCA

Solar Calendar: Crops in Agriculture		Druids	Wicca
December 21	Winter Solstice	Alban Arthuan	Yule
March 21	Spring Equinox	Alban Eiler	Ostara
June 21	Summer Solstice	Alban Heruin	Litha
September 21	Fall Equinox	Alban Elued	Mabon
Lunar Calendar: Animals in Agriculture			
February 2	New Moon	Imbol	Candlemas
May 1	Full Moon	Beltane	Walpurgis Night
August 1	Old Moon	Lughnasadh	Lammas Eve
Oct. 31–Nov 2	Dark Moon	Samhuinn	Samhain

Philip Carr-Gomm, *The Druid Tradition*
Craig S. Hawkins, *WitchCraft: Exploring the World of Wicca*

Glossary

abathakati [u-bah-TAH-kah-ti] In Zulu society, a person who uses spiritual forces for evil ends. A witch or wizard.

Adi Granth [AH-di-grunth] The scripture of the Sikhs. Hymns by the Sikh gurus are recorded in the Adi Granth.

adoptionist [a-DOPT-shun-ist] A person who believes that at the baptism of the man Jesus, God adopted him as his Son.

Agamas [AH-ga-mas] (Hinduism) Scriptures from tradition that divide according to deity.

Agamas [AH-ga-mas] (Jainism) Collection of Jain scriptures subdivided into three categories: *Purva, Anga,* and *Angabahya.*

Aggadah [ug-GAHD-u] The nonlegal, story aspect of rabbinic literature. It is distinguished from Halakhah, the legal side of Judaism.

Agni [AG-ni] Fire used in sacrifice. The Vedic god of fire.

ahimsa [u-HIM-su] The Sanskrit word that is translated "nonviolence." In Jainism, it is a reverence for all living things.

Ahone [A-hone] The beneficent diety of the Powhatans, whose powers were of less concern than those of the malevolent Okeus.

Ahura Mazda [u-HOOR-u MAZ-du] The Zoroastrian god of light; the Wise Lord who is the highest deity.

ajiva or nonjiva [AH-JEE-va] Category of existence that is insentient; lacking soul.

akh or **ikhu** [AHK] A part of the soul; the ghost that goes to the land of the blessed.

Amaterasu [AH-MAH-te-RAH-su] In Shinto, the goddess of the sun, created by purification of Izanagi. She is sister to Susanoo, the god of storms.

American Muslim Mission A Muslim group formed for African Americans by Wallace Deen Muhammad. World Islam accepts these adherents as Muslims.

Amesha Spentas [u-MEE-shu SPIN-tas] In Zoroastrianism, the higher spirits directly under Ahura Mazda. They are modes of divine being that bear names of ethical virtues, such as "Good Thought."

Amitabha (Amida) [a-mee-TAH-ba] The Buddha who presides over Western Paradise. Hozo Bosatsu is the Japanese name for a legendary monk who long ago took a vow to become a Buddha if his merits could be used to help others. After fulfilling 48 vows, he became Amitabha.

Amon-Re [AH-mun-ray] A sun god of Egypt. His symbol was the obelisk, a ray of the sun. Amon, originally the god of Thebes, became highest god in 2000 B.C.E. when Thebes dominated all Egypt.

Anahita [anna-HEE-tu] In later Zoroastrianism, a mother goddess who was worshiped with fertility rites.

anatta [a-NAT-ta] The Pali word for no soul, or Sanskrit for no Atman.

Anglicans [ANG-gli-cuns] Members of the Church of England. Their church government is episcopal; the clergy is directed by bishops.

Angra Mainyu [ANG-gra MIN-yu] In Zoroastrianism, the evil spirit who opposes Ahura Mazda.

anicca [a-NICH-cha] Impermanence. The Buddhist doctrine that there are no permanent entities. All phenomena continuously change.

ankh [angk] In Egypt, the circle-topped cross representing life. Some forms incorporate a cat on top of the circle.

Anne Hutchinson A dissenter banished in 1637 from Massachusetts Bay Colony. She found more freedom in Rhode Island.

ansar [AN-sahr] Helpers; Medinans who helped Muhammad relocate from Mecca to Medina. They were joined by Muhammad and his companions after the Hijrah.

antyesti [un-TYES-ti] Funerals. Last rites.

apocalypse [u-POCK-u-lips] A revelation. A prophetic vision of the destruction of evil and salvation of righteous people.

apocalyptic literature [u-POCK-u-LIP-tic] Writings describing the last days, or the end of time. This literature inspires the faithful to stand firm in spite of the severe hardships of their time.

apostle [a-POS-ul] A person who was a disciple of Jesus sent out to proclaim the coming of the kingdom of God. Traditionally, Jesus chose twelve apostles.

Aranyakas [ah-RAN-yu-kuz] Shruti ritual of the Vedas for ascetics living in the forest.

arhat [UR-hut] An enlightened, holy person.

Ark of the Covenant A box containing the Ten Commandments. Priests carried it in processions and then housed it in the tabernacle.

Aryans [AHR-yuns] Indo-Europeans who entered the Indus Valley prior to 1000 B.C.E. They expressed their evolving religion in the hymns of the Rig-Veda.

Asanga [a-SANG-a] Made famous in the fourth century C.E., the Yogacara school of Buddhist philosophy that was founded by Maitreyanatha.

ase [AH-se] Spiritual forces of the Yoruba; divine energy.

asha [ASH-u] In Zoroastrianism, spiritual truth. Some scholars equate asha with the Hindu Rita.

Asherah [ash-u-RAH] A goddess of Canaan and a counterpart to the male god, Baal. She was another example of the Mediterranean mother goddess.

Ashkenazim [ahsh-ku-NAH-zim] A Yiddish-speaking group of Jews who settled in central and northern Europe. The term in Hebrew referred to Germany.

Ashoka [a-SHOW-ka] This king, who reigned in India 273–232 B.C.E., sponsored Buddhist missionary activities.

Atman [AHT-man] The essence of Brahman that is present in individuals. The universal self.

Aton [AHT-un] In Egypt, this god's symbol was a disk, representing the sun. After Akhenaton established his throne in Akhetaton, Aton was the only god worshiped.

avidya [a-VID-ya] In Hinduism, the term means "ignorance," or not seeing things as they are.

awon iya wa [u-WON I-YAH wa] Yoruba term for "the mothers."

aworo [a-WOH-roh] A priest of the Yoruba.

ba [BAH] In Egypt, a kind of human consciousness. Sometimes described as the soul.

Baal [BAA-ul] A god or gods of Canaan. Baals were landlords or keepers of the land. Canaanites worshipped them to make crops grow.

Baha'i [buh-HIGH] A religion formed in 1844 on the prophetic work of Baha'u'llah.

Baptists [BAP-tists] Members of the Baptist tradition. Adherents are baptized when they are old enough to choose Christ as their savior. Immersion is the preferred, often required, form of baptism. Government is by members of each congregation.

Bar Mitzvah [bar-MITS-VU] The ceremony that recognizes a thirteen-year-old Jewish boy as a son of the commandment. He is considered an adult responsible for religious duties.

Bat Mitzvah [bat-MITS-VU] In Reform and Conservative Judaism, the ceremony that recognizes a daughter of the commandment, a Jewish female between twelve and fourteen years of age. She is considered an adult responsible for her religious duties.

bhais [BA-iz] The brothers of a Sikh gurdwara who assist in worship. It is also the title used for a Sikh priest.

bhakti yoga [BAKH-ti] Personal devotion to deity. In Hinduism, a path that leads to salvation.

Bodhgaya [BOWD-GAH-ya] A temple that commemorates the grove where the Buddha found enlightenment.

Bodhidharma [BOW-dee-DAHR-ma] The monk who brought meditative Buddhism to China. His example inspired Chan (Zen) Buddhism.

bodhisattvas [bow-dhee-SAT-tvas] In Buddhism, people who have qualified to enter Nirvana, but who, out of compassion for others, remain available to help others.

Bon [PAIN] The ancient animistic religion of Tibet.

Book of Mormon
A book of scripture revealed to Joseph Smith.

Brahma [bram-HAH] Ultimate reality; the creator.

Brahman [bram-MUN] In Hinduism, the name of the highest deity, the Absolute.

Brahmanas [BRAH-muh-nuhs] Commentaries and manuals instructing priests in rites associated with Vedas.

Brahmin [BRAH-men] In Hinduism, the name of the highest, priestly caste. After the Aryans were settled in India, the priests became more important than the warriors of the Kshatriya caste.

Brigham Young Joseph Smith's successor, who led Mormons to Salt Lake City, Utah.

bushido [bu-shi-DOOH] A code of honor for Japanese warriors. It incorporated both Daoist and Zen Buddhist concepts and governed the samurai, the feudal military class.

butsudan [Bu-tsu-DAH-NAH] A Buddhist altar. Tablets commemorating ancestors are kept on it.

caliph [KAA-lif] A successor of the prophet Muhammad. The first caliph was Abu Bakr. The ideal of Islam is that religion and state are not separated.

Canaanites [kay-nu-NIGHTS] The people among whom the Israelites settled on their return from slavery in Egypt. Canaan comprised the area bordered by the Sea of Galilee, the Jordan River, and the Dead Sea.

Candomblé [can-dome-BLAY] Yoruba-based religion found among Christians of Brazil.

caste [CAST] In Hinduism, the permanent social group into which a person is born and which determines one's social and religious obligations.

catechumen [KAT-i-KYOO-mun] A convert to Christianity who received instruction in preparation for baptism.

Celts [KELTS] An ancient people of Europe and the British Isles.

Chan (Ch'an) [CHAHN] The Chinese Buddhist school of meditation founded by Bodhidharma.

Chiang K'ai Shek [CHUNG-kai-SHEK] The leader of Nationalist China who established a government in Taiwan. He was driven from mainland China by Mao Zedong.

Chinvat Bridge [CHIN-vaht] In Zoroastrianism, the bridge of judgment that a soul must walk over after death.

Christ [kriist] The Greek word meaning "the anointed one." The Hebrew word for the concept was *messiah*. Christians believe that Jesus was the long-awaited Messiah.

Christian canon [can-on] The list of books accepted as scripture by Christians.

church [church] A congregation of Christians. All Christians considered together as the mystical body of Christ.

Clear In Scientology a Thetan whose engrams have been removed.

Confucius [kun-FYOO-shus] **Kongfuzi,** The Chinese founder of Confucianism. Primarily a teacher, he sought to develop good government through a responsible ruler and ethical people.

covenant [CUV-u-nunt] The binding agreement between God and his chosen people. The covenant was repeatedly renewed. Unlike a contract, the covenant had no date of expiration.

dakhma [DAHK-ma] A Zoroastrian Tower of Silence used for disposal of corpses of the faithful. It is believed to be necessary because a corpse cannot be allowed to contaminate either soil or fire.

Dao (Tao) [DOW] In China or in Daoism (Taoism), the path, course, or way of the universe. Although its influence is in nature, the eternal Dao is believed to be hidden from empirical experience.

Dao De Jing (Tao Te Ching) [dow-du-JING] *The Way and Its Power.* A book attributed to Laozi, founder of Daoism.

Daoists (Taoists) [DOW-ists] Followers of a philosophy or religion expressed in the *Dao De Jing,* attributed to Laozi, a sage of ancient China.

Days of Awe In Judaism, ten days in the fall of the year when Jews observe their new year and a period of prayer and self-examination, ending with Yom Kippur. Also known as the High Holy Days.

dharma [DAR-ma] In Buddhism, law. It can be the law of the universe or the law or tradition taught by the Buddha.

dhimmi [THIM-mi] A client of the Muslims. In exchange for protection, non-Muslims agreed to certain conditions of subservience to Muslims. Jews and Christians were often dhimmis of Muslim rulers.

Dhyana [DYAH-na] In Buddhism, mental concentration. It is the term for Buddhist meditation.

Dianetics [dye-uh-NET-ics] A book by Scientology founder L. Ron Hubbard. Of eight principles, the first is survival.

diaspora [di-AHS-pe-ra] A Greek word for the dispersion of Jews. These were the Jews who lived outside the Holy Land.

Digambaras [di-GAHM-ba-ras] The Jains who believe that a true monk is "sky clad." These monks think women cannot become liberated until they are reborn as men.

diviners [di-VII-nurs] Women who are spirit possessed and know how to discover people's destinies.

Dravidians [drah-VID-e-uns] Dark-skinned inhabitants of India. They differed from the light-skinned Aryans who entered from the Northwest.

Druids [DREW-ids] Among Celts, the three orders were Bards, Ovates, and Druids, who were advisors to kings.

dukkha [DUK-kah] The Buddhist term for the suffering of humans and other sentient beings.

Dumuzi [DUM-u-zi] (Tammuz) The Mesopotamian god of fertility, who gave life to vegetation and children to women.

Ea [eah] A water god. He was sometimes known as Enlil.

Eastern Orthodox Church [OR-tha-dox] The Christian church of the orthodox tradition. The churches of the eastern Mediterranean countries retained a more democratic form of governance.

ecumenical [ek-yu-MEN-i-kul] Refers to the whole household of faith. It is in contrast to matters of local or special interest.

Efile Mukulu [e-fu-le mu-KOO-loo] Among the Congolese Basongye, the chief god of good. His counterpart is the evil god, Kafilefile.

eight-fold calendar Four solar holidays and four lunar holidays observed in great circles by Druids and witches.

Eightfold Path The fourth Noble Truth, the path of deliverance in Buddhism.

Elijah (Poole) Muhammad Founder of the Black Muslim movement, the Nation of Islam. Dissatisfied with

Christianity, which appeared to be a white religion, Poole organized a religion for blacks.

Enkidu [IN-ki-du] In Mesopotamian tradition, a wild man befriended by Gilgamesh. He was killed by Enlil for slaying the monster Huwawa.

epistles [i-PIS-els] Letters, particularly those that have become part of the New Testament scriptures. Many epistles of the New Testament were attributed to Paul and to the apostles who walked with Jesus.

Essenes [ES-eens] A group of pious Jews of the first century C.E. who lived in separate communities and practiced ritual washing and other acts for purity. Some scholars think that the inhabitants of the Qumran community, near the Dead Sea, were Essenes.

Esu [e's-zoo] A Yoruba god who is amoral; he is a trickster deity and a messenger.

excommunicate [ex-ku-MYUU-ni-caat] The forced exclusion of a person from a religious organization, such as a church. People who continued, after warning, to practice errors, often were excommunicated from the church.

Fajia (Fa-Chia) or **(Legalists)** [fah-JEE-a] In China, the Legalist school of philosophy that taught governance by reward and punishment. An example of a Fajia philosopher is Han Feizi.

Five Pillars of Islam In Islam, the five requirements made of all Muslims.

Five Relationships In Confucianism, ruler–subject, husband–wife, father–son, older brother–younger brother, and elder friend–younger friend.

Gelugpa [ge-LUG-pa] The Buddhists of Tibet known as Yellow Hats. They reformed the practices of the Nyingmapa, or Red Hat Buddhists.

Gemarah [ge-MAHR-u] The "learning" of the rabbis. It was combined with the Mishnah to form the Talmud.

Genku (Honen Shonin) [GEN-koo] Twelfth-century C.E. founder of the Jodo Buddhist sect in Japan. As the monk Genku, he was trained at Tendai monasteries on Mt. Hiei.

Gilgamesh [GIL-gu-mesh] A Mesopotamian king of Uruk about 2600 B.C.E. He searched for immortality, found the plant that was its source, and lost it to a serpent.

gospels [GOS-puls] Messages of good news. The four stories of the life of Christ found in the New Testament.

Guanyin (Kwan-yin) [GUAHN-YIN] Guanyin, bodhisattva of mercy, is also known as Avalokiteshvara. In Pure Land Buddhism, he is placed beside Amitabha as his attendant.

gurdwara [GUR-dwah-ra] A place of Sikh worship, fellowship, and hospitality. It is a temple, the dwelling of the guru.

guru [GU-RU] or [GOO-ROO] A Hindu teacher of religious duties. For a student, the guru represents the divine in human form.

Guru [GU-ru] OR [GOO-ROO] In Sikhism, one of ten early spiritual leaders. God is the one, true Guru.

hadiths [had-EETHS] Reports of what Muhammad said or did; examples for faithful Muslims to follow. The *Sunna* are the traditions of the prophet in the literary form of *hadith*-reports.

Haggadah [hah-gah-DAH] The story used at the Seder during the Jewish holiday of Passover. This term is distinguished from *aggadah*, nonlegal stories of rabbinic Judaism.

Hajj [HAHJ] The pilgrimage to Mecca, expected of all Muslims who are able.

Halakhah [ha-la-KAH] The legal part of Jewish religion that was developed in rabbinic writings.

Han Feizi (Han Fei Tzu) A representative of the Fajia, or Legalist, school of philosophy in China. He taught that people were governed best by a ruler who harshly enforced rigid laws.

hanif [HA-neef] In Arabia, prior to Muhammad's recitations, a person who worshiped one God. Waraqa Ibn Nawfal, a kinsman of Khadijah, was a hanif.

Hanukkah [khan-nu-ka] The eight-day celebration near the end of the solar year. It commemorates the lights in the rededicated Temple, 164 B.C.E. after Syrians had desecrated it during the Maccabean revolt.

Haoma [HOE-mu] In late Zoroastrianism, the divinity of the sacred elixir prepared during Zoroastrian ritual.

hara-kiri [HAH-RAH-kee-ree] In Japan, a ritual suicide to preserve or to restore a person's honor. It is considered an act of bravery rather than cowardice.

Hathor [HAH-thor] The Egyptian goddess who created the world. Her symbol was a woman's body with the head of a cow.

henotheism [HEN-uh-thee-IS-um] A belief that one deity is supreme over other deities.

herbalist [UR-ba-list] (*izinyanga zemithi*) One who specializes in the use of herbs, especially medicinal herbs.

heresies [HER-i-sies] Beliefs contrary to the accepted teachings of the religious organization.

heretics [HER-i-tiks] People who have been judged by the church to teach doctrine dangerously contrary to the teachings of the church.

Hijrah [HEJ-rah] Muhammad's migration from Mecca to Yathrib (Medina) in 622. He and Abu Bakr made the journey in less than the normal eleven days.

Hillel [hil-EL] A prominent Jewish teacher and founder of the Hillel school of rabbis in the first century. He was considered more liberal in his views than the conservative Shammai.

Holocaust [HOL-u-cost] An offering brought to a deity and completely burnt. The term now refers to the Nazi extermination of Jews in occupied countries during World War II.

Horus [HOH-us] In Egypt, the son of Isis and Osiris who opposed his uncle, Seth. Horus was also the sun, symbolized by a falcon.

Hozo Bosatsu [ho-zo bo-SAHT-soo] In Shinran Buddhism, a meritorious person who became Amida Buddha.

Hua-Yen [HWAH-YEN] The Chinese Buddhist sect whose primary Buddha is Vairocana. The school had a holistic view of Buddha nature and the universe.

huacas [WAH-cas] In Inca religion, natural phenomena that provide unusual manifestations of the holy. Unusual rocks, for example, could symbolize the presence of the holy.

Huitzilopochtli [HWEET-zi-low-POK-tli] The chief god of the Aztecs. He was god of the sun who led his people, the Aztecs, to their home in Tenochtitlán.

humanist A person who believes the values of humans are the highest in the universe. Humans are "on their own" in the universe. A Christian humanist, such as Erasmus, believed in God.

iconostasis [ii-con-NOS-ta-sis] A screen at the front of an Orthodox church that displays many precious icons.

Ife [IF-fe] The most sacred city of the Yoruba peoples of Nigeria.

ihlambo [ih-LAHM-boh] The ceremony of washing spears after mourning the death of a Zulu chief.

ihram [IH-rahm] The consecrated state in which Muslims perform the Hajj. Muslims abstain from sex, perfume, hunting, and other things during the pilgrimage to Mecca.

ijma' [IJ-mah] The consensus of Muslim religious leaders on matters of practice.

Inanna [in-AHN-nu] In Mesopotamia, the goddess who was wife of Dumuzi (Tammuz). She descended into the underworld to seek her husband's release.

incarnation [in-cahr-NA-shun] To invest God in human flesh. Christians consider the Christ as God in human form.

Indra [IN-dra] A god of the Rig-Veda. The creator and ruler of the universe.

indulgences [in-DUL-jenses] Remissions of temporal punishment for sin that has already been pardoned. Indulgences became a subject of debate for Martin Luther.

Inkosazana [in-KOH-sa-zAH-na] The Zulu Princess of Heaven who assists women and girls.

Inkosi Yezulu [in-KOH-si ye-ZOO-loo] In Zulu religion, one name for the god of the sky.

Inti [IN-ti] An early god of the Incas, probably symbolized by a hummingbird. Inti was a creator god who was later combined with Viracocha.

isangoma [i-san-GO-ma] A Zulu woman diviner.

ishatpragbhara [ee-shut-PRAHG-bu-ru] The Jain state beyond life and death.

Ishtar [ISH-tar] In Babylonia, a mother goddess who descended into the underworld. She was also known as Inanna.

Isis [ii-sis] In Egypt, the wife of Osiris, god of the dead, and the mother of their son, Horus. She was the giver of life.

Islam [is-LAHM] Like other religions of the family of Abraham, it emphasizes worship of one God. It believes that Muhammad is the last and most important of the prophets of God.

Itihasa-Purana [iti-HAHT-sah poo-RAH-na] Ancient mythological texts, including Mahabharata, Ramayana, and 18 *puranas* honoring Brahma, Shiva, and Vishnu.

Izanagi [ee-zah-NAH-gee] In Shinto, the male-who-invites. Cocreator, with Izanami, of Japan.

Izanami [ee-zah-NAH-mee] In Shinto, the female-who-invites. Cocreator, with Izanagi, of Japan.

izinyanga zezulu [iz-in-YAN-ga ze-ZOO-loo] The deity in Zulu religion who herds weather or sky as boys herd cattle.

Jade Emperor A mythical emperor of ancient China. In 1012 C.E., the emperor (Chen Tsung) claimed to have received revelation from Huang Di (Yu Huang), the Jade Emperor.

janëu [JAN-ëu] The sacred thread worn by the three upper castes.

Japji [JAP-ji] A Sikh hymn recited in devotions every morning. A guide for Sikh conduct.

Jatakas [JAH-ta-kas] Stories of the previous lives of the Buddha, which were collected and used in the teachings of Theravadin monks.

jhana [JHAH-na] Buddhist meditation, or the states reached in Buddhist meditation.

Jimmu [jee-moo] In Shinto, the first human emperor, a descendant of the gods. As part of the Shinto religion, the emperor of Japan has been revered.

Jina [JI-na] In Jainism, a person who has conquered rebirth. Mahavira was a Jina.

Jingtu (Ching-t'u) [JING-too] Pure Land, or Western Paradise, Buddhism. It believes in Sukhavati, which is ruled by Amitabha Buddha. [In Japan the sect is Jodo.]

jinn [JIN] In Arabia, a race of beings created from fire, distinguished from humans, who were created from clay. Some jinn are good; others are bad.

jiva [JEE-va] In Jainism, the soul. The opposite is *ajiva*, body.

jnana yoga [JYNAH-na] *Jnana* means knowledge or wisdom. Jnana yoga, the Hindu path of release based on intellectual knowledge, appeals to people who emphasize rational understanding of religious beliefs.

Jodo [JO-DO] The Japanese Buddhist sect of the Pure Land. Founded in twelfth century C.E. by the monk Genku. Salvation comes by grace, through faith.

John Wesley An Anglican priest who formed the Methodist Church. Methodist circuit riders ministered to frontier families in America.

Joseph Smith Founder of the Church of Jesus Christ of Latter-day Saints.

Judaizers [JOO-day-iiz-ers] Persons who advocated the practice of Jewish observances for all Christians. They opposed Paul's emphasis on freedom from the law.

junzi (chun-tzu) [JUN-dzi] In Confucianism, the gentleman or superior man. He was a role model for the conduct of the Chinese people.

Ka'bah [KUH-bah] The cube-shaped building of stone in the open court of the Grand Mosque of Mecca. In Islamic tradition, the first Ka'bah was built by Abraham and Ishmael.

ka [ka] In Egypt, divine breath that supported life. Sometimes referred to as the soul.

kachinas [ka-CHI-nas] Among the Hopi, masked, costumed dancers that represent gods, ancestors, or spirits.

Kaddish [KAY-dish] In Judaism, a prayer. Recited also by mourners, it begins with words of Ezekiel and asks that God's name be blessed forever.

Kafilefile [kah-FI-le-FI-le] Among the Congolese Basongye, the god of evil. His counterpart is the good god, Efile Mukulu.

Kalachakra [kah-lah-CHAK-ra] The space–time doctrine in Tibet. The whole universe is related in its flow to the vital currents of the human body.

kalpa [KAL-pa] In Hinduism, a long period of the created world. When one period ends, a new one begins with another creation.

kami [KAH-mee] Natural and supernatural persons and powers worshiped in Shinto. Kami are present everywhere, in nature and in people.

kami-dana [KAH-mee-DAH-NAH] In Japanese homes, a center of symbols honoring the kami. Sometimes the center is a shelf.

karma [KAHR-ma] The law that a person's thoughts and deeds are followed eventually by deserved pleasure or pain. In Hinduism, it is an explanation for caste. In Buddhism, karma is primarily psychological; in Jainism, it is understood in primarily physical terms.

karma yoga Doing one's caste duties without expecting a reward; selfless action.

kashruth [KASH-root] Jewish dietary regulations.

kerygma [ke-RIG-ma] The message or proclamation of the early Christians. Peter gave a proclamation on the day of the Pentecost.

kikudu [ki-KOO-doo] The soul of a human being that may live after the death of the body.

kiswah [KIS-wa] The robe, or covering, usually placed over the Ka'bah in Mecca.

kivas [KEE-vas] Underground chambers that the Hopi used for religious ceremonies.

koan [KO-an] A problem used by Zen Buddhists to reduce dependence on ordinary ways of thinking about self and the universe.

kosher [KO-sher] In Judaism, meat that has been properly prepared for eating. One requirement is that most of the blood be removed from the meat.

Krishna [KRISH-na] An incarnation of Vishnu, who is also the chariot driver of the warrior Arjuna of the Bhagavad Gita.

Kshatriya [KSHA-tri-ya] A Hindu caste of warriors and administrators. Originally, this caste was the highest, but it was later subordinated to the Brahmins.

Kukai (Kobo Daishi) [KOO-KAI] The ninth-century C.E. founder of the Japanese Buddhist Shingon sect. All Buddhas are emanations of the great sun, Vairocana or, in Japan, Dainichi.

kusti [KOOS-ti] A sacred thread worn to indicate initiation into a religion. Hindus and Zoroastrians use the symbol.

lama [LAH-mah] The term means "supreme being," comparable to the term *guru* in Indian Buddhism. A priest in Tibetan Buddhism.

Laozi (Lao Tzu) [LAHOW-dzi] The sage of China once believed to have been the author of the *Dao De Jing (Tao Te Ching)*. He is regarded as the founder of Daoism.

law of karma [KAHR-ma] The principle in Hinduism that a person's thoughts and deeds are followed eventually by deserved pleasure or pain.

Laws of Manu [MAH-noo] A Hindu code of conduct compiled about 200 B.C.E to 200 C.E.

Li Ji (Li Chi) [LEE-jee] The Chinese classic on rites supposedly edited by Confucius. Although it is one of five Confucian classics, it is now regarded as coming from a period later than Confucius.

Li [LEE] The Confucian principle of righteousness or propriety. Li can refer to ritual and correct conduct in society.

Loa [LOW-ah] In Vodun, a spirit that can be called down upon a person.

loka [LOW-ka] The universe where categories of sentient beings are reborn.

Lutherans [LOO-ther-ans] Members of the Protestant denomination based on the teachings of Martin Luther (1483–1546). Their beliefs are based primarily on the Bible rather than on teachings of the church fathers, ecumenical councils, or the pope.

Madhyamika [ma-DYAM-ee-ka] The Buddhist philosophy that the phenomenal objects one experiences are not ultimately real. Nagarjuna found the Madhyamika school.

Magi [MAY-jii] Among the ancient Persians, priests. Their doctrine reduced Ahura Mazda from a transcendent principle to a good spirit, opposed by an evil spirit.

Mahabharata [ma-HAH-BAH-ra-ta] Epic poem featuring activities of the god Krishna.

Mahayanists [ma-HAH-YAH-nists] Those of the great vehicle, who emphasized universal Buddhist enlightenment.

Mahdi [MAH-di] In Islam, the expected one. Twelvers believe that an imam is in occultation and will return as a messianic figure.

Maitreya [mi-TRAY-ya] In the tradition of East Asia, the next Buddha to appear on earth.

Malcolm X, or **(Malcolm Little)** Formerly of the Nation of Islam, he formed his own group in 1964 in the tradition of Sunni Islam. A major change in his teaching was that all people are brothers and sisters, whites as well as blacks.

mamanatowick [ma-ma-na-TOW-wick] The supreme king or chief of the Algonquian-speaking peoples of eastern Virgina. Powhatan was the first mamanatowick that the English settlers dealt with at Jamestown.

mandala [MAN-da-la] A geometric pattern used in worship.

Mani [MAH-nee] A Persian teacher of religious dualism; he considered himself the Holy Spirit.

mankishi [man-KI-shi] Among the Congolese Basongye, a small carved figure used to represent a child desired by a couple. The figure can also be used to bring success in fishing and to protect homes and people from bad magic.

mantra [MAN-tra] A special formula of words recited in worship.

Mantu [MAHN-too] Among the Naskapi, the soul of nature, animals, and humans. The soul of a person is referred to as the "Great Man."

Manu [MAH-noo] In Hinduism, the first man.

Mao Zedong (Mao Tse-tung) [MAOW-tse-DONG] The Marxist leader of China who overthrew the Nationalist government of Chiang K'ai Shek in 1949. He established the People's Republic of China.

Mara [MAH-rah] The evil one who tempted the Buddha at Bodhgaya.

Marduk [MAHR-dook] The Babylonian god of creation. To create the world, he defeated the goddess of chaos, Tiamat.

Martin Luther King Jr. (1929–1968) Baptist minister who was a leader of the U.S. civil rights movement. He adopted Gandhi's methods of nonviolence to awaken public conscience to racial injustice.

Mary Baker Eddy Founder of the Church of Christ, Scientist. She was the author of *Science and Health with Key to the Scriptures.*

matzah [MUT-za] (pl. *matzot*) Unleavened bread eaten by Jews during the Passover. During Passover, no leaven should be present in a Jewish home.

Maya (queen) [MAH-ya] The mother of Siddhartha Gautama, the Buddha.

Maya [MAH-ya] For Hindus, appearance or illusion; power of creation.

Mayet [MU-yut] (Maat) The Egyptian goddess of order and truth, who prompted the deceased at the time of judgment.

Mengzi (Mencius) [MENG-dzi] A later disciple of Confucius who emphasized an inborn goodness of humans. He differed from Xunzi (Hsun Tzu), who argued that men are born evil.

Messiah [mi-SIGH-u] The one whom the Jews expected to come and deliver Israel from oppression and establish a kingdom of righteousness. It can refer to a historical person or to a supernatural being.

Methodist [METH-u-dist] A member of the church that follows the "method" of John Wesley, former Anglican clergyman. The church's government is episcopal, that is, through bishops.

Midrash [MID-rash] (pl. *Midrashim*) Rabbinic exposition explaining the meaning of the scriptures. The root meaning is "to search out."

mihrab [MIH-rahb] The niche in a mosque that signifies the direction of Mecca. Muslims face Mecca when they pray.

Miki Nakayama [MI-ki NAH-KAH-YAH-MAH] In Japan, founder of the new religion, Tenrikyo. She experienced divine healing through the kami of Divine Reason.

mikishi [mi-KI-shi] Among the Congolese Basongye, human spirits bent on doing harm. Sorcerers can control them.

miracle [MIR-a-kul] An event judged to be brought about by divine intervention in the ordinary events of history.

Mishnah [MISH-na] Teachings of the rabbis compiled about 200 C.E. The Mishnah records discussions of rabbis on how best to live according to the Torah.

Mista'peo [mis-TAH-pe-oh] Among the Naskapi, the Great Man—an individual's soul that lives in the heart; it is a person's essential self. It reveals itself in dreams.

Mithra [MITH-ra] The god of light in Zoroastrianism.

Mitra [MI-tra] A deity of the Vedas. A god of faithfulness and keeping promises.

Mitzvoth [MITZ-VOTH] (sing. mitz-va) In Judaism, responses to obedience to God according to the covenant. How to live in covenant relationship; with God is a central teaching of Judaism.

modernism [mod-ur-NIZ-um] In religion, emphasis on reason in philosophy and science instead of traditional beliefs.

Mohists [MOW-hists] Followers of Mozi (Mo Tzu). They advocated curing the ills of society by practicing mutual love among people. Confucians objected to Mohist universal love because it did not allow for special feelings for kin.

moksha [MOWK-sha] In Hinduism, the release of the soul from a cycle of rebirths; one of the four goals of life for Hindus.

monophysite [mu-NOF-u-SITE] Someone who believes that Christ had only one nature: divine.

monotheism [MAH-nuh-thee-IS-um] A belief that there is only one deity.

Mosaic Law The ancient law of Hebrews contained in the Pentateuch. The Law of Moses.

Mozi (Mo Tzu) [MOW-dzi] Founder of the Mohist philosophy, which advocated brotherly love. Brotherhood meant sharing equally the essentials of food, clothing, and shelter.

mudras [MUD-ras] Special positions of hands used in worship.

muezzin [mu-EZ-in] One who calls Muslims to prayer. Muhammad preferred the human voice to the Christian use of bells.

muhajirun [mu-HAJ-i-roon] The emigrants from Mecca who joined Muhammad in Medina. These early converts

to Islam lost their property and income when they followed Muhammad.

Muslim [MUS-lim] One who surrenders to God. A follower of the prophet Muhammad.

Mut [mut] In Egypt, a goddess whose symbol was the cat.

mystery religions Greek religions that practiced secret rites guaranteeing initiates immortality.

myth [MITH] A story of gods acting in a different time. Creation myths are stories of how the gods acted before humans were created, how they created humans, and how they communicate with humans. The word *myth* in religious studies does not mean untrue.

Nagarjuna [NAH-GAHR-ju-NAH] The Buddhist philosopher of the second century C.E. who established the Madhyamika school of philosophy.

Naozot [NAY-ow-zot] Zoroastrian vesting of a child with a sacred shirt.

Nation of Islam The branch of Black Muslims that struggles with Christianity and whites. It is not accepted by orthodox Muslims as Islam, which welcomes all races.

Nichiren [NEE-chee-REN] A monk in Japan who established a school based on the Lotus Sutra.

nihangs [NI-hangs] The Sikhs with military skills who are always ready to fight for the community.

nirguna Brahman [NIR-goo-na] In Hinduism, Brahman as he is in himself, beyond attributes.

Nirvana [ner-VAH-na] In Buddhism, the state of being free of egocentrism and the suffering that it causes. Positively, it is joy and peace.

Nubians [NOO-bee-ans] People of the southern Nile valley; neighbors of the ancient Egyptians. Their leaders formed the twenty-fifth dynasty of Egyptian pharaohs.

Nyingmapa [ning-MAH-pa] The Red Hat Buddhists of Tibet. Their Buddhism retained an element of pre-Buddhist beliefs and practices.

oba [OH-ba] A chief or king of the Yoruba.

Obatala [oh-bah-TUH-lu] Creator of earth, according to the Yoruba, who brought to it sixteen people created by Olorun.

Odudwa [oh-DOO-doo-wah] A Yoruba creation god associated with the city of Ife.

Okeus [OH-kee-us] Among the Powhatans, a god, or group of gods, that caused suffering. His counterpart is the beneficent deity, Ahone.

Olodumare [oh-LOH-du-MA-ree] In Yoruba religion, the supreme deity of the sky. Also called Olorun.

Olorun [OH-lu-roon] Supreme deity of the sky in Yoruba religion.

orishas [or-E-shas] Yoruba spirits. In the New World, their names are used in conjunction with Catholic saints in syncretized religions.

Orisha-nla [oh-REE-sha-nla] A Yoruba creation god.

Orun [oh-roon] In Yoruba religion, the supreme king; the sky. Also known as Olodumare.

Oshun [OH-shun] Yoruba mother goddess.

Osiris [oh-SI-ris] In Egyptian myth, a king who became lord of the underworld. With his wife, Isis, he fathered Horus, the king of Egypt.

pantheon [PAN-the-on] All the gods or a temple dedicated to them.

parable [PARE-u-bul] A simple story told to illustrate a religious truth or lesson.

Passover [PASS-o-ver] A Jewish holiday in the spring. It celebrates God's deliverance of the Hebrews from slavery in Egypt during the time of Moses.

Pentecost [PEN-ti-cost] A festival coming fifty days after Easter. The time when the Holy Spirit descended on the early Christian church. A Christian name for Feast of Weeks in Judaism.

Pharisees [PHAR-i-sees] A group of Jews who represented the piety of the common people in the centuries immediately after the Maccabean War.

prakriti [pra-KRI-ti] In Hinduism, matter, as opposed to *purusha*, spirit.

pratitya-samutpada [pra-TEET-ya sam-ut-PAH-da] The Buddhist doctrine of dependent origination. It explains the experienced universe without resorting either to chance or a first cause.

Presbyterians [PREZ-bit-tir-ee-uns] In the tradition of John Calvin, Presbyterians base their beliefs primarily on the Bible. Governance of the church is through the Presbytery and other elected bodies.

prophet [PROF-it] A person inspired by God to speak in his name. In Hebrew history, prophets in groups gave way to the messages of individual prophets such as Isaiah, Jeremiah, and Ezekiel.

puja [POO-ja] Hindu worship of household deities. Brahmins often performed rituals desired by householders. The ritual worship of India.

puranas [pu-RAHN-as] "Ancient lore" treatises or the deities of popular Hinduism.

Puritans [PYOOR-i-tuns] Former members of the Church of England who sought to purify it. They settled in Massachusetts and sought to establish a theocracy, a government under rule of God.

Purusha [PU-roo-sha] Primal spirit, or soul of an individual.

qiyas [KEE-yas] In Islam, analogies used in applying the Qur'an and the Sunna to other practical situations.

Quakers [KWAY-kurs] Members of the Society of Friends; established in England by George Fox. Quakers are led by the Inner Light, through democracy.

Quetzalcoatl [KET-zal-coatl] The Aztec god known as the Plumed Serpent. He was god of civilization, teacher of the arts and priestcraft.

Qur'an [KUR-an] The sacred scripture of the Muslims, regarded as the word of God dictated to Muhammad by God through the archangel Gabriel. The Prophet received and recited the messages over approximately twenty years.

ra'y [RAA-ee] In Muslim law, the considered opinion of Muslim leaders acting for public good.

rabbi [RAB-eye] In Judaism, a teacher. After 70 C.E., rabbis were ordained interpreters and leaders of Judaism.

raja yoga [RAH-jah] Path to salvation by disciplining the mind and body.

rak'a [RAK-ah] Each complete cycle of ritual movements that is part of Muslim prayer. During prayer Muslims stand, bow, kneel, and touch their foreheads to the ground.

Ramayana [rah-MAH-ya-na] An epic of the ideal man, Rama, and Sita, the ideal woman.

rasul [ra-SOOL] "Messenger." One who recites for God. Muhammad was the rasul of God.

reincarnation [REE-in-cahr-NAY-shun] A belief, widely shared among world religions, that a soul that has left a body can, after a period of time, return in the body of a newborn child. Although bodies are replaced, the soul remains essentially the same.

ren (jen) [RUN] In Confucianism, the humane principle, based on fellow-feeling. Deep empathy or compassion for other humans.

resurrection [res-u-REC-shun] A belief that a person who has been dead will be restored as a whole, living person.

Rita [RI-ta] The Hindu god of order and principles.

Rosh Hashanah [rosh hah-SHA-nah] In Judaism, the first of the Days of Awe, Tishri 1 and 2. Celebrates God's creation of the world. Fall of the year period of prayer and self-examination.

Ryonin [RYO-neen] In the early twelfth century C.E., founder of Amida worship in Japan.

sacraments [sak-ra-mints] Rites instituted by Jesus as recorded in the New Testament to bestow a grace of God.

sadaqa [sah-DAH-ka] Informal charity between Muslims.

Sadducees [SAD-u-sees] Jewish leaders who claimed allegiance to the priestly descendants of Zadok, a priest in the days of King David. These wealthier Jews followed only the Torah.

saguna Brahman [SA-goo-na] In Hinduism, Brahman as he is known with his attributes; this form has personlike qualities.

Saicho (Dengyo Daishi) [SAI-CHOH] The monk who introduced Tendai (T'ien-T'ai) Buddhism in Japan. He helped the emperor Kwammu establish a new capital at Kyoto, diminishing the power of Buddhists at Nara.

salat [sa-LAHT] Obligatory prayer five times daily.

sallekhana [sal-lek-HAN-na] In Jainism, a holy death achieved by fasting.

samadhi [sa-MAH-di] Concentration that unifies; absorption.

samsara [sam-SAH-ra] The Hindu concept of the wheel of rebirth that turns forever. Souls are reborn until they reach perfection.

Samskaras [sam-SKAHR-as] The sacraments or rites by which a Hindu is fully integrated into the community.

Sangha [SANG-ha] The Buddhist monastic order. Buddhism accepted both monks and nuns. The term can also include laity.

Sanhedrin [san-HEED-rin] In times of the temple, the supreme judicial body of the Jews.

sannyasin [san-NYAH-sin] One in the last stage of renunciation or detachment.

Santería [san-ta-REE-a] Yoruba-based religion of Cuba.

Satan [SAY-tun] In Anton LaVey's Church of Satan, the Self or selfishness. Elsewhere, an evil being opposed to God.

satori [SAH-TOH-ree] The Japanese term for the Zen Buddhist experience of enlightenment.

sawm [SOM] Fast during daylight hours of Ramadan.

Scholasticism [sku-LAS-ti-siz-um] A medieval movement of education in which Christian schools taught particular methods of philosophy and theology.

scribe [scriib] From the centuries after the Babylonian captivity of the Jews, a scribe was a trained scholar, particularly in Torah studies.

Seder [SAY-der] The meal of unleavened bread eaten after sundown at the beginning of Passover.

Separatists [SEP-ar-a-tists] Former members of the Church of England who believed it beyond reform and separated to form a new church. They settled in Massachusetts and sought a theocracy.

Sephardim [se-fahr-DIM] Jews who lived in medieval Spain until expelled in 1492. Those who refused to become Christians moved to North Africa, Italy, and especially Turkey, where Sultan Bayzid II admitted them gladly.

Seth [seth] In Egyptian myths, the wicked brother of Osiris. He stole the third eye from Osiris. Horus, the son of Osiris, fought Seth and recovered the third eye, symbol of kingship in Egypt.

Shahada [sheh-HAH-da] Means "witnessing." The Muslim profession of faith. There is but one God and Muhammad is his rasul or messenger.

Shakyamuni [SHAH-kya-MOO-nee] The sage of the Shakya clan, Siddhartha Gautama, the Buddha. The term is widely used in China and Japan.

shaman [SHAH-man] A Siberian term for people who have been initiated in rituals that enable them to control spirits. Shamanlike men were found among Indians of North America. In Asia, some shamans were women. Today, the term is applied to persons of many cultures.

Shang Di [shang-DI] In China, the lord of heaven. Ancestors are believed to be obedient to Shang Di as living persons are to the emperor.

Shari'a [SHA-ree-a] The duties that God has placed on the Muslim community. It is sometimes translated as "law."

Shavuot [sha-voo-OT] In Judaism, marks the early harvest and commemorates God's giving of the Ten Commandments.

Shehitah [she-HEE-tah] The Jewish method of slaughtering permitted animals or birds for food. The method is to kill the living thing as swiftly and as painlessly as possible with one swift cut across the throat.

Shema [SHEE-ma] Hear. The beginning word of Deuteronomy 6:4, "Hear, O Israel!" A declaration of God's unity, it is recited twice daily.

Shi'a [SHE-a] Members of the "party" of 'Ali, who believed that he should have been the next leader after 'Uthman.

Shingon [SHIN-GOHN] Japanese for the Chinese Chen Yen school of Buddhism. It taught that matter and other Buddhas emanate from Vairocana.

Shinran [SHIN-RAN] Genku's disciple, who established the Jodo-Shin sect of Buddhism in Japan.

Shinto [SHIN-TOOH] The Japanese religion of *kami no michi*, the way of the gods. Japanese people participate in Shinto, a combination of religion and patriotism.

Shiva [SHEE-va] The Auspicious. Ultimate Lord; the destroyer.

Shivah [shi-vah] In Judaism, the seven days of mourning that Jews observe for loss of members of their family.

shogun [SHOW-GUN] In Japan, a military ruler serving, ostensibly, under the emperor.

shohet [SHOW-het] A Jewish slaughterer of animals, who kills according to ritually correct methods.

Shotoku (Shotuku Taishi) [SHOOH-TOH-ku] The Japanese prince who supported the establishment of Buddhism in his country.

shouyi (shou-i) [shoo-yi] In Daoism, to preserve the One or to meditate on the One. It includes methods of meditation on the One.

shraddha [SHRAD-dha] Last rites. The prescribed rituals for the deceased.

shruti [SHROO-ti] Hindu sacred writings, such as the Vedas, based on "heard," or revealed, knowledge.

shu [SHOO] In Confucianism, reciprocity; individuals treating others as they would like to be treated. They do not do to others what they would not want done to themselves.

Shudras [SHOO-dras] In Hinduism, those of the fourth caste, the caste of laborers. Shudras were not permitted even to hear the reading of the Vedas.

Shvetambaras [SHVAY-TAHM-ba-ras] The Jains who follow the tradition that allows monks to wear clothes. Shvetambaras believe women can obtain release from life without being reborn as men.

Singh [sing] A "lion" of the Sikhs. The term was initiated by Guru Gobind, the tenth guru, in 1699 C.E.

skandhas [SKAN-dhas] Five strands, similar to strands in a skein of yarn, that constitute the self.

smriti [SMRI-ti] Writings based on what human authors "remembered" of revelations to Hindus; less authoritative than revealed scriptures.

Soma [sow-ma] The Hindu deity of a plant that is intoxicating. In the Vedas, soma was used in worship.

Sthanakvasis [STAHN-AK-va-sees] A group of Jains that separated from the Shvetambaras over use of idols in worship.

Suddhodana [SUD-DHOH-da-na] The king who was father of Siddhartha Gautama. He is said to have tried to keep Siddhartha ignorant of human suffering.

sudreh [SHOOD-reh] The sacred shirt used in vesting a Zoroastrian child.

Sun Yat-sen The first leader of the republic in China after the fall of the Manchus. He reasserted Confucian virtues.

Sunna [SUN-na] The custom or tradition of Muhammad. It supplements the Qur'an as a source for the Shari'a.

Sunni [SOON-e] The traditional, majority, Muslims who accepted Mu'awiyah as the next leader after 'Uthman.

Susanoo [su-SAH-NOOH] In Shinto, the storm god, who was brother of Amaterasu, the sun goddess.

Taiji (Tai Chi) [tie-JEE] The Great Ultimate in Zhuxi's (Chu Hsi's) Neo-Confucian philosophy. It is the rational law, or li, that works within everything.

taixi (t'ai-hsi) [tai-SHEE] In Daoism, the art of embryonic breathing, a method of holding one's breath in contemplation.

Talmud [tal-mud] The collection of rabbinic teachings. It had deep influence over the lives of Jews from the beginning of the medieval period. The Mishnah and the Gemara were incorporated in the Talmud.

Tammuz [TAM-muz] The Babylonian version of Dumuzi, the Mesopotamian god of springtime. He was a god of fertility.

Tanakh [ta-NAK] The complete Jewish Bible, comprising three parts: Torah, the five books of Moses; Nevi'im, the prophets; and Kethuvim, the writings. The first letters of the three terms yield Tanakh.

tanha [TAN-ha] In Buddhism, the thirst or craving that leads to suffering. In the second Noble Truth, it is identified as the cause of suffering.

tantras [TUN-trus] Religious treatises for developing latent powers in persons. Dialogues between Shiva and Shakti.

Tara [TAH-rah] The popular mother goddess of Tibet, associated with Avalokiteshvara, the Lord Who Looks Down.

Tathagata [ta-TAH-ga-ta] A title of the Buddha, meaning one who has thus gone.

Tawhid [TAHW-heed] The Muslim doctrine of the unity of God. Islam denies any partners to God such as Christians are believed to have in their Trinity.

Tenochtitlán [TEN-ok-tit-LAN] The Aztec island city on Lake Texcoco. It was the site of the major temple to the Aztec god Huitzilopochtli.

Tenrikyo [TEN-ree-kyo] A religion of Japan based on the teachings of Miki Nakayama. It reveres the kami of Divine Reason.

Tezcatlipoca [tez-CAT-li-POH-ca] The Aztec lord of the night sky.

theodicy [THEE-od-i-se] A justification, in the presence of evil, of God's goodness, justice, and knowledge. How can an all-good, all-powerful, and all-knowing God allow evil?

theology [THEE-ol-e-jee] The discipline that describes and explains God and his relationship to the world. Theology is a formal, reasoned explanation of the beliefs of the faithful people of a religion.

Theosophy [the-os-uh-fee] "Divine Wisdom"; a religion organized in 1875 by H. P. Blavatsky.

Theravadins [ter-a-VAH-dins] The elders, monks who imitated the Buddha's ascetic life to attain enlightenment.

Thetans [THE-tans]. The souls of human beings.

Three Purities In China, three deities of Daoism: Ling Bao, the Jade Emperor, and Laozi.

Tiamat [TYU-mut] The Babylonian goddess of chaos. She was defeated by the god Marduk, who created the world.

Tian Tai [TYIAN-TAI] The Mahayana Buddhist sect of China (and Japan) that is based on the Lotus Sutra. All beings can actualize their Buddha nature and become Buddhas.

tianming (t'ien-ming) [TYIAN-MING] In Confucianism, the mandate of heaven. Zhou and Han emperors claimed to rule successfully because they followed the mandate of heaven.

Timothy Drew In 1913, in New Jersey, he taught that blacks are Asians, or Muslims. He was a contributor to the Black Muslim movement in the United States.

Tirthankara [ter-TAN-ka-ra] In Jainism, a spiritual leader who has found the crossing, or ford, to the farther shore.

Tlaloc [TLAH-loc] The Aztec god of earth and rain.

Tonatiuh [TOE-na-TI-uh] An Aztec sun god.

Torah [TOR-ah] Teachings that comprise the first five books of the Bible: Genesis, Exodus, Leviticus, Numbers, and Deuteronomy.

torii [TOH-RE-EE] In Shinto, a formal gate to a shrine. It marks the entrance to sacred space.

totem [TOW-tem] An animal, plant, or object serving as the symbol of a traditional people's clan or tribe.

trickster [TRIK-stur] A male character found in stories of Native North Americans as well as most other cultures. Although the trickster was not the creator, he audaciously performed deeds that altered creation. He represents the canniness admired by nonliterate peoples.

Trikaya [tre-KAH-ya] According to Buddhist doctrine, the three bodies of Buddha. The first body was indescribable, the second body is the almost divine body in which the Buddha appeared to the Mahayana faithful, and the third body was his appearance as a human being.

triloka [tri-LOW-ka] The areas of the universe considered together: upper, middle, and lower.

Trinity [TRIN-i-tee] The Christian belief that three persons in union, Father, Son, and Holy Spirit, are one God.

Tripitaka [TREE-PI-ta-ka] The "three baskets" collection of Buddhist scriptures. It is comprised of the "Vinaya Pitaka" (monastic rules), the "Sutta Pitaka" (discourses), and the "Abhidhamma Pitaka" (supplement to the doctrines).

True Parents A title for Reverend Sun Myung Moon and his wife, reflecting the belief that God, father, mother, and child are the building blocks of the world.

Tsaka'bec [tsah-KAH-bec] Among the Naskapi, a hero figure. He was a trickster who altered the natural world. He exhibited a craftiness admired by the Naskapi.

Tsukiyomi [tsoo-ki-yoh-mi] In Shinto, the moon god. He is related to Amaterasu and Susanoo.

u mueling angi [oo MWE-ling AHN-gi] In the creation story of Zulus, the first "comer out," followed by humans, animals, and nature.

ubuthongo [oo-boo-THON-go] Zulu term for deep sleep in which ancestors can appear.

ukubuyisa idlozi rite [oo-KOO-boo-YI-sa id-LOH-si] The Zulu ritual of bringing home the ancestor after a period of mourning.

'ulama' [UL-ah-mah] Muslim clerical scholars.

ummah [UM-mah] The Muslim community.

umnayama [oom-nay-YAH-ma] Zulu term for a weakened state that makes a person vulnerable to environmental influences.

umnumzane [oom-nam-ZAH-ni] The head of the kraal in Zulu society.

umsamo [oom-SAH-mo] In Zulu religion, the place where people communicate with ancestors.

untouchables In Hinduism, people, often Shudras, who are considered by upper castes to be too impure to allow physical contact. Untouchability has been abolished.

upanayana [oo-PA-na-YAH-na] The initiation rite indicating that a boy is a twice-born person.

Upanishads [oo-PA-ne-shads] "Sitting close to a teacher"; the last of the Vedas.

Utnapishtim [OOT-nu-PISH-tim] In Mesopotamia, a religious man whom the gods saved from the world flood and to whom they gave immortality. He informed Gilgamesh where he could find the plant of immortality.

Vairocana [vai-ROH-cha-na] In Japanese Buddhism, the Sun, who is also the Buddha. It is also Dainichi and Amaterasu.

Vaishya [VAI-shya] The third Hindu caste, that of merchants and artisans. Its members participate in the Vedic practices of religion.

varna [VAR-na] Color once associated with caste.

Varuna [VA-roo-na] The Rig-Veda god of the high-arched sky.

Vedanta [ve-DAHN-ta] The "end of the Vedas." Schools of philosophy founded on teachings of the Upanishads.

Vedas [VAY-daz] Knowledge or wisdom. Scriptures of the Hindus.

Viracocha [VI-rah-COH-cha] A creator god of the Incas. He symbolized the sun.

Vishnu [VISH-noo] The Supreme Lord; the preserver.

vivaha [vi-VA-ha] Marriage. The rite of entry into the second stage or ashram, that of householder.

Vodun [voh-DUN] Sometimes called "Voodoo." Yoruba religion among Christians in Haiti.

Vohu Manah [VOH-hoo-MAH-nu] In Zoroastrianism, Good Thought, one of the Amesha Spentas.

Wahhab [WAH-hab] One of the 99 names of Allah. 'Abd al-Wahhab means "The Servant of the Bestower."

Weroances [WEH-row-ances] The subchiefs, or commanders, of the Powhatan empire. Female commanders were known as weroansquas.

Western Wall In Jerusalem; the platform of the former Temple, destroyed by the Romans in 70 C.E.

Wicca [WICK-uh] A modern form of witches organized by Gerald B. Gardner in 1954.

wisakon [WI-sa-kon] The Powhatan term for medicine and substances tasting like medicine. The priests controlled all medicines of significance.

witches A term that Wiccans, male or female, may apply to themselves.

wuwei [WOO-WAY] The Daoist principle of accomplishing tasks without assertion. Individuals in harmony with the flow of the Dao can accomplish more than individuals who assert themselves.

Xunzi (Hsun Tsu) [SHUN-dzi] A Confucian who argued that humans are evil by nature and must be taught good rather than evil. He differed from Mengzi (Mencius), who believed that humans are born good.

Yahrzeit [YAHR-zeit] Based on German for year-time, it is an anniversary of the death of a parent. Children leave a stone at the grave to recall the custom of adding a stone to maintain a grave.

Yang [YAHNG] In China, the male side of the Dao. It is exemplified in bright, warm, and dry conditions. Its opposite is Yin, the female side of the Dao.

Yashodhara [ya-SHOW-dha-ra] The wife of Siddhartha Gautama and mother of Rahula. She is said to have been a neighboring princess chosen for Prince Siddhartha.

yi [YEE] In Confucianism, internalized li, or righteousness; li as it has become a part of an individual's conduct.

Yijing (I Ching) [YEE-jing] An ancient book of China that assists people in deciding how to plan their lives in accord with the forces of the universe. The *Yijing* influenced both Daoism and Confucianism.

Yin [YIN] In China, the female side of the Dao. It is exemplified in dark, cool, and moist conditions. Its opposite is Yang, the male side of the Dao.

Yogacara [YOH-ga-CHAH-ra] The Buddhist school of philosophy that teaches that neither the phenomenal world nor the mind is real. Founded by Maitreyanatha in the third century C.E., it was made famous in the fourth by Asanga.

Yom Kippur [yom-kip-PUR] The tenth day of the Days of Awe. A twenty-four-hour period of fasting when Jews stand or kneel in prayer much of the time in the synagogue.

zakat [za-KAHT] In Islam, the payment of a due to support the community. It is an act of purification through giving.

Zaoshen (Tsao Shen) [ZOW-SHEN] In Daoism, the god of the stove. The stove was essential in family life and in work of the Daoist alchemists.

Zealots [zel-uts] A party of Jews actively opposed to Roman occupation of Judea. They were active in the first century C.E., especially in the revolt that began in 66.

Zen [ZEN] The Japanese Buddhist meditation sect (in China, Chan) that was based on the practices of the Indian Buddhist, Bodhidharma.

Zhiyi (Chi-kai or Chi-i) [ZHIR-YEE] The monk who founded the Tian Tai sect of Buddhism in China.

Zhuangzi (Chuang Tzu) [JYAHNG-dzi] A later Daoist. Zhuangzi wrote, in part, to distinguish Daoism from Confucianism.

Zhuxi (Chu Hsi) [JYOO-SHEE] The leader of the Neo-Confucian revival in the twelfth century.

ziggurats [ZIG-gu-rats] In Mesopotamia, pyramid-like structures used in worship. The brick- or stone-covered mounds were topped by a house that represented the court of the deity.

Zionism [zii-e-NIS-em] A movement led by Jews to provide a home country for themselves. Theodor Herzl was a leader at the end of the nineteenth century.

zombie [ZOM-bee] A spirit or a corpse enslaved by a priest of Vodun.

Zulu [zoo-loo] A member of the Bantu peoples of southeast Africa. Inhabitants of South Africa.

Zurvan [ZUR-van] Among a minority of Zoroastrians, boundless time. It embraces both Ahura Mazda and Angra Mainyu.

Index

Page numbers in bold refer to terms defined in the margin.

Credits

Introduction: Pg. 3, 35, timeline: © Francois DuCasse/Photo Researchers, Inc.; pg. 4: Neg. #336871, Courtesy of the Department of Library Services/American Museum of Natural History; pg. 5, top: © Penny Tweedie/Corbis; pg. 5, bott: The University Museum, University of Pennsylvania (neg. #S4-78542); pg. 6: The University Museum, University of Pennsylvania (neg. #S8-55887); pg. 7: © Bojan Brecelj/Corbis; pg. 8: © Chris Bland/Eye Ubiquitous/Corbis; pg. 9: © Bob Mahoney/The Image Works; pg. 10: © Noboru Komine/Photo Researchers, Inc.

Chapter 1: pg. 14: © Dave G. Houser/Corbis; pg. 20: Library of Congress; pg. 22: Library of Congress/Corbis; pg. 24: © Chris Marona/Photo Researchers, Inc.; pg. 25, 35, timeline: © James Chisholm/Anthro-Photo; pg. 31, 35, timeline: © Richard A. Cooke/Corbis; pg. 34: United Nations Photo/neg. #154655/A. Minaev.

Chapter 2: pg. 40, 45, timeline: © Lila Abulughod/Anthro-Photo; pg. 43: © The William MacQuitty International Collection; pg. 46, 45, timeline, pg. 48: © Brian Brake/Photo Researchers, Inc; pg. 50: © Irven DeVore/Anthro-Photo; pg. 52, 45, timeline: © Ed Kashi/Corbis; pg. 53: © Lindsay Hebberd/Corbis; pg. 56: © Davis Factor/Corbis; pg. 64: © John Miller/Robert Harding Picture Library.

Chapter 3: pg. 75, 86, timeline: © Werner Forman Archive/Art Resource, NY; pg. 78: United Nations Photo/neg. #125261/J. Isaac; pg. 81: © Michael Holford; pg. 83, 86, timeline: © Corbis-Bettman; pg. 89, 86, timeline: Nelson-Atkins Museum of Art, Kansas City, Missouri. (Purchase: Nelson Trust) 50-20: Photographer Robert Newcombe; pg. 92: © Craig Lovell/Corbis; pg. 93: © Bruce Gordon/Photo Researchers, Inc.; pg. 95: © Katrina Thomas.

Chapter 4: pg. 100: © Thomas Liard/Peter Arnold, Inc.; pg. 105: © Allison Wright/Robert Harding Picture Library; pg. 107, 127, timeline: © Ann & Bury Peerless—Slide Resources and Picture Library; pg. 110: © Mary Altier; pg. 125: © Fujifotos/The Image Works; pg. 126, 127, timeline: © Allison Wright/Corbis; pg. 128: © Gary Conner/PhotoEdit Inc.; pg. 134: © Mike Greenlar/The Image Works; pg. 135: © David Samuel Robbins/Corbis.

Chapter 5: pg. 142, 156, timeline: © Jeremy Bright/Robert Harding Picture Library; pg. 144: © Mary Altier; pg. 150: Ann & Bury Peerless—Slide Resources and Picture Library; pg. 154, 156, timeline: © Christine Osborne/Corbis; pg. 159: © The William MacQuitty International Collection.

Chapter 6: pg. 168: © David Samuel Robbins/Corbis; pg. 173: © Reunion des Musees Nationaux/Art Resource, NY; pg. 180, 202, timeline: © Snark/Art Resource, NY; pg. 190: © Ewing Galloway; pg. 193: © Victoria & Albert Museum, London/Art Resource, NY; pg. 198: © The William MacQuitty International Collection.